SIMPLER SYNTAX

SIMPLER SYNTAX

Peter W. Culicover
Ray Jackendoff

OXFORD
UNIVERSITY PRESS

OXFORD
UNIVERSITY PRESS

Great Clarendon Street, Oxford OX2 6DP

Oxford University Press is a department of the University of Oxford.
If furthers the University's objective of excellence in research, scholarship,
and education by publishing worldwide in

Oxford New York

Auckland Cape Town Dar es Salaam Hong Kong Karachi
Kuala Lumpur Madrid Melbourne Mexico City Nairobi
New Delhi Shanghai Taipei Toronto

With offices in

Argentina Austria Brazil Chile Czech Republic France Greece
Guatemala Hungary Italy Japan Poland Portugal Singapore
South Korea Switzerland Thailand Turkey Ukraine Vietnam

Oxford is a registered trade mark of Oxford University Press
in the UK and in certain other countries

Published in the United States
by Oxford University Press Inc., New York

© Peter W. Culicover and Ray Jackendoff 2005

The moral rights of the authors have been asserted
Database right Oxford University Press (maker)

First published 2005

British Library Cataloguing in Publication Data
Data available

Library of Congress Cataloging in Publication Data
Data available

Typeset by SPI Publisher Services, Pondicherry, India
Printed in Great Britain on acid-free paper by
Biddles Ltd., King's Lynn

ISBN 0-19-927108-9   978-0-19-927108-5
ISBN 0-19-927109-7 (Pbk.)   978-0-19-927109-2 (Pbk.)

1 3 5 7 9 10 8 6 4 2

We shall not cease from exploration
And the end of all our exploring
Will be to arrive where we started
And know the place for the first time.

T. S. Eliot, *Little Gidding*

I'm not here to tell you the news,
I'm here to tell you the truth.

Morris Halle

Contents

PART II THE SYNTAX–SEMANTICS INTERFACE

PART III BINDING AND CONTROL

PART IV CONNECTIONS BETWEEN CLAUSES

Preface

The overall questions addressed by this book are: What is the role of syntax in the grammar vis-à-vis semantics, and what are the consequences for syntactic structure? In the late 1960s, when we were graduate students at MIT together, these questions were being hotly debated in the "Linguistic Wars" between Generative Semantics and Interpretive Semantics. Both of us wrote our dissertations on aspects of these questions, naturally taking the Interpretive side, as befit our position as Chomsky's students. At the time, it looked to us as though the Interpretive position was leading generative grammar toward a leaner syntax with less complex derivations, and that a great deal of the work of predicting grammatical distribution would be pushed into the lexicon, into semantics, and into what were then called "projection rules" and are now called "correspondence rules" or "interface rules", i.e. the rules that mediate between syntax and meaning. Somehow this didn't come to pass: instead mainstream generative syntax became steadily more abstract, derivations more complex.

One of the reasons the Interpretive Semantics position could not be implemented adequately at the time was that the field lacked a theory of semantics sufficiently robust to help explain syntactic phenomena. Thirty-five years later, although the issues are still the same, the field has explored a lot more syntactic, semantic, and psychological phenomena, and the range of theoretical options is broader. So we think it's worth trying again.

An important part of our work here involves picking through the history and philosophy of generative syntax to identify the reasons for the way it developed as it did. Part I (Chapters 1–4) is devoted to these issues. Beginning at the end of Chapter 4 and continuing through Part II (Chapters 5–9), we engage in developing many details of what might be thought of as a contemporary version of Interpretive Semantics: the theory of Simpler Syntax. Parts III and IV (Chapters 10–14) discuss further phenomena that provide evidence for Simpler Syntax: a far leaner syntax coupled with a somewhat richer syntax–semantics interface. More broadly, Simpler Syntax leads to a vision of the language faculty that better facilitates the integration of linguistic theory with concerns of processing, acquisition, and biological evolution.

Our discussion is mainly focused on English. This happens to be the style of investigation with which we feel most comfortable, and besides, we think there are still lots of interesting things about English that the lore has not recognized.

This does not mean that we think linguistics can be studied in the context of English alone, only that we think others can do other languages better.

This book grows out of a friendship that goes back to our graduate student days, when we lived three doors apart on Inman Street in Cambridge. All these years we've gotten a big kick out of thinking together about linguistics—for us it's "playing syntax"—and we've gone out of our way to find opportunities to do so. Around 1990 we began working seriously on some joint projects, and, despite millions of other things going on in our lives, we managed to scrape together a number of published papers, working together catch-as-catch-can when we happened to meet at conferences or when we passed through each other's towns on the way to someplace else.

When it became clear by the late 1990s that this habit of ours was not a fluke, we began to envision collecting the papers together into a volume, with a short introduction that tied them together. However, the plot began to thicken as we independently found ourselves developing critiques of and alternatives to larger developments in the field, culminating in Culicover's *Syntactic Nuts* and *Dynamical Grammar* (the latter jointly with Andrzej Nowak) and in Jackendoff's *Architecture of the Language Faculty* and *Foundations of Language*. As we started to plan our joint book, we realized that we needed to offer a more concrete overview of what we think syntax is like, and that our joint papers in fact provided an important source of corroborating evidence. The result is the present volume, in which Parts I and II and Chapter 15 offer new material and Parts III and IV offer reworked versions of previous papers.

We consider ourselves fortunate indeed to be able to take on this assignment, thanks to our friendship, our collaboration, and the influence of many friends and colleagues over the years. We have been lucky to have experienced so much of the history and to have participated in many of the theoretical developments. Given our long involvement in cognitive science, we have been able to view the situation from a broader perspective than syntax alone. In particular, Culicover's work on learnability and Jackendoff's work on psychological foundations of semantics provide important boundary conditions—and opportunities—for exploring the interfaces between syntax and the rest of the mind.

One of our closest friends back in graduate school was Adrian Akmajian, who lived a few blocks away on Dana Street in Cambridge. Adrian went on to write two of the most influential textbooks in linguistics and was a founding editor of the journal *Natural Language and Linguistic Theory*. Both of us published in collaboration with him at one time or another, and much of his work—both in its substance and its spirit—has had a lasting influence on us. Had he not died in 1983, much too early, after a decade of intermittent illness, he might well have collaborated on this book with us. We would like to dedicate this book to his memory.

Acknowledgements

Peter Culicover did a substantial portion of his part of this work while he was a visitor during 2002 at the University of Groningen, Department of Alfa-Informatica, with the assistance of a Besoekerbeurs from the NWO. He gratefully acknowledges the assistance provided by the NWO, the hospitality of the University of Groningen, the Department of Alfa-Informatica, and John Nerbonne, and the contributions of the participants in the Groningen Syntax Seminar, especially Jan Koster, Jan-Wouter Zwart, and Mark de Vries. In the earlier years of the research that ultimately led to this book, Culicover received critical support, both financial and moral, from Edward F. Hayes, Vice President for Research at the Ohio State University. Regrettably, Ed passed away in 1998, much too soon.

Ray Jackendoff did much of his part of the work while he was a visitor in the Psychology Department at Harvard University in 2002–3. He is especially grateful to Marc Hauser for providing facilities and such a congenial group of colleagues during the year. Some earlier conceptualization of the work took place while he was a Fellow of the Wissenschaftskolleg zu Berlin in 1999–2000, for which he is also supremely thankful.

We had the opportunity to present parts of this work in our courses at the 2003 LSA summer Linguistic Institute at Michigan State University, and we wish to thank our students in those courses. Many colleagues offered comments and discussion on earlier versions, including Fritz Newmeyer, Tom Wasow, Ida Toivonen, Jason Merchant, Andrew Spencer, Paul Postal, Barbara Citko, Jim Blevins, Vera Gribanov, Bob Borsley, Idan Landau, Shalom Lappin, Klaus-Uwe Panther, Jan-Wouter Zwart, Jan Koster, Mark deVries, Carl Pollard, Robert Levine, Joan Maling, Ivan Sag, Kara Hawthrone, Shanna Hollich, and students in Stan Dubinsky's seminar at University of South Carolina. Our editor, John Davey, gently pushed us and pulled us through the project, with good humor and good taste. Any deficiencies are of course our responsibility. In particular, we apologize in advance to anyone whose work we have failed to cite or to cite sufficiently despite its relevance. We hope readers will be relatively indulgent in light of the scope of this work: it is a full-time occupation to keep up with the literature in any single one of the many areas we have tried to cover here.

Chapters 10–14 are reworked versions of the following previously published papers of ours, and are reprinted with the kind permission of the publishers:

Chapter 10: 'Mme. Tussaud Meets the Binding Theory', *Natural Language and Linguistic Theory* 10 (1992), 1–31 (Kluwer Academic Publishers).

Chapter 11: '*Something else* for the Binding Theory', *Linguistic Inquiry* 26 (1995), 249–75 (MIT Press).

Chapter 12: 'The Semantic Basis of Control in English', *Language* 79 (2003), 517–56 (Linguistic Society of America) and 'Control is Not Movement', *Linguistic Inquiry* 32 (2001), 493–512.

Chapter 13: 'Semantic Subordination Despite Syntactic Coordination', *Linguistic Inquiry* 28 (1997), 195–217.

Chapter 14: 'The View from the Periphery: The English Comparative Correlative', *Linguistic Inquiry* 30 (1999), 543–71.

Each of these chapters contains the acknowledgements from the original version.

Financial support for this research came in part from NEH Grant DC 03660. Work on Chapters 10–14 was supported in part by NSF Grants IRI 88–08286, IRI 90–46528, and IRI 92–13849 to Brandeis University, by a John Simon Guggenheim Fellowship to Ray Jackendoff, and by a grant from the James S. McDonnell Foundation to the Ohio State University.

Finally, we are grateful to our families for their tolerance of this continuing obsession throughout the many years of our collaboration.

PART I

Cutting Syntax Down to Size

CHAPTER 1

Why Simpler Syntax?

1.1 Different notions of simplicity

Within the tradition of generative grammar, the most prominent focus of linguistic research has been the syntactic component, the part of language concerned with the grammatical organization of words and phrases. The present study will develop and defend a view of the syntactic component that is on one hand thoroughly within the generative tradition but on the other markedly at odds with views of syntax that have developed in mainstream generative grammar (MGG).[1] Our approach concurs in many respects with many alternative theories of generative syntax, most notably Head-Driven Phrase Structure Grammar (Pollard and Sag 1987; 1994), Lexical-Functional Grammar (Bresnan 1982a; 2001), and Construction Grammar (Fillmore 1988; Fillmore and Kay 1993; Zwicky 1994; Goldberg 1995; to appear); it also shares commonalities with others such as Autolexical Syntax (Sadock 1991; 2003) and Role and Reference Grammar (Van Valin and LaPolla 1997). We will refer to this collection on occasion as "the alternative generative theories."

The differences between our approach and the mainstream can be divided roughly into two major aspects, which it is important to distinguish. The first aspect is technological: what formal devices does the theory adopt for its description of language? The second, deeper and more difficult to characterize

---

[1] Throughout this study we will use the term "mainstream generative grammar" (or MGG) to refer to the line of research most closely associated with Noam Chomsky, including *Syntactic Structures* (1957), the Standard Theory (*Aspects of the Theory of Syntax*, 1965), the Extended Standard Theory (*Studies on Semantics in Generative Grammar*, 1972b), the Revised Extended Standard Theory (*Reflections on Language*, 1975c), Principles and Parameters Theory (*Lectures on Government and Binding*, 1981), and the Minimalist Program (1993; 1995). Readers who feel it is a mistake to call this line the "mainstream" should feel free to substitute their own favorite term.

precisely, is the theory's vision of what language is "like". Insofar as possible, we will attempt to sort out what in our approach to syntax is technological and what is conceptual, and in which of these respects we concur with and differ from both MGG and the alternative theories.

There is of course interplay between technology and conceptualization. On one hand, a formal theory is chosen in part to reflect one's vision of the phenomena. On the other hand, the scientific success of a formal theory is measured in part by its ability to generalize or "scale up" to an ever broader range of data. Although the same initial vision may be served equally by two or more alternative technologies (they are superficially "notational variants"), different choices of formal apparatus often lend themselves to different potential extensions. In turn, some extensions may lead to fundamental changes in one's vision of the phenomena, including how the theory integrates with neighboring fields, one important criterion for theoretical success.

Another important criterion for theoretical success, of course, is Occam's Razor: "Do not multiply (theoretical) entities beyond necessity." The problem in describing language is: Which entities should not be multiplied? What counts as simple? We can see four criteria, which, though they often overlap, turn out to lead in different directions:

(1)   a. Minimize the distinct components of grammar.
      b. Minimize the class of possible grammars.
      c. Minimize the distinct principles of grammar.
      d. Minimize the amount of structure generated by the grammar.

Position (1a) is advocated in Paul Postal's paper "The Best Theory" (1972a). He argues that Generative Semantics, which derives surface structure directly from semantic structure by transformations interspersed with lexical insertion, is inherently superior to the (Extended) Standard Theory (Chomsky 1972b; Jackendoff 1972), which has separate components for generating surface structure from deep structure, for relating deep structure to some aspects of semantics, and for relating surface structure to other aspects of semantics. Chomsky's (1972b) reply is that the goal should really be to minimize the class of possible grammars (1b), and that a better way to achieve this goal is to have more components, each of limited scope. He justifies this goal on grounds of learnability, an issue to which we will return shortly.

One way to achieve a more limited class of possible grammars is to have fewer principles of grammar that languages can choose from. This goal (1c) is taken as primary in Principles and Parameters Theory (Chomsky 1981), part of whose vision is that crosslinguistic syntactic variation is tightly constrained. In the Minimalist Program (Chomsky 1993; 1995) this goal is carried further, attempting to minimize not only the principles responsible for crosslinguistic variation but the entire set of principles necessary to characterize syntactic structure. In part, these goals are just good science: one always tries to characterize natural phenomena in maximally general and explanatory terms. But in recent years, the agenda has gone further, attempting to characterize language as in some sense a "perfect" system for relating sound and meaning, with a "Galilean" vision of an extremely simple Grand Unified Theory that accounts for all relevant phenomena.

Although the principles that characterize syntactic structure in mainstream research are relatively general, the actual syntactic structures ascribed to sentences have turned out to be not at all simple. The derivation of sentences is regarded as justifiably complex and abstract, and even surface structures are full of complexity that does not show in the phonological output. Chapter 2 will show how this position has developed over the fifty-year history of MGG.

The present work explores a different priority:

Simpler Syntax Hypothesis (SSH)
The most explanatory syntactic theory is one that imputes the minimum structure necessary to mediate between phonology and meaning.

The simplification of structure comes with a price: the characterization of syntactic structure requires a multitude of principles, of varying degrees of regularity. This is a radical break from the spirit of mainstream generative grammar. Our overall vision of language conforms not to the majestic Galilean perspective but rather to a view, attributed to François Jacob, of biology as a "tinkerer". The language faculty, developed over evolutionary time, provides human communities with a toolkit of possibilities for cobbling together languages over historical time. Each language, in turn, "chooses" a different selection and customization of these tools to construct a mapping between sound and meaning. We will call this the Toolkit Hypothesis.

As there are decades of tradition behind mainstream generative grammar, and a vast literature, our brief for the Simpler Syntax Hypothesis and the Toolkit Hypothesis necessarily spends considerable time being predominantly critical. The form of our argument will be that, given some phenomenon that has provided putative evidence for elaborate syntactic structure, there nevertheless exist numerous examples which demonstrably involve semantic or pragmatic factors, and in which such factors are either impossible to code uniformly into a reasonable syntactic level or impossible to convert into surface structure by suitably general syntactic derivation. Generality thus suggests that, given a suitable account of the syntax–semantics interface, all cases of the phenomenon in question are accounted for in terms of the relevant properties of semantics/pragmatics;

hence no complications are necessary in syntax. We spend much of the present study chipping away at one grammatical phenomenon after another, some well-known and some less so, showing in each case the virtues of the Simpler Syntax Hypothesis (and often drawing on previously published arguments). However, we are also constructive: we take it upon ourselves to develop an overview of what the syntax–semantics interface looks like under the new regime.

1.2 A sample argument: Bare Argument Ellipsis

To convey the spirit of our enterprise, we begin with a brief look at the phenomenon of Bare Argument Ellipsis (BAE, also known as "Stripping": Ross 1969a), which we take up in more detail in Chapter 7. BAE appears in the nonsentential responses in examples like these:

(2) a. A: I hear Harriet's been drinking again.
        B: i. Yeah, scotch.
            ii. Yeah, every morning.
            iii. Scotch?
            iv. Not scotch, I hope!
     b. A: Has Harriet been drinking scotch again?
        B: i. No, bourbon.
            ii. Yeah, bourbon too.
     c. A: What has Harriet been drinking?
        B: Scotch.

B's responses are interpreted as though B were saying something like (3).

(3) a.   i. Yeah, Harriet's been drinking scotch.
         ii. Yeah, Harriet's been drinking every morning.
        iii. Has Harriet been drinking scotch?
         iv. I hope Harriet hasn't been drinking scotch.
     b.   i. No, Harriet's been drinking bourbon.
         ii. Yeah, Harriet's been drinking bourbon too.
     c. Harriet has been drinking scotch.

MGG's approach to this phenomenon is based on an assumption that we will call Interface Uniformity:

Interface Uniformity (IU)
The syntax–semantics interface is maximally simple, in that meaning maps transparently into syntactic structure; and it is maximally uniform, so that the same meaning always maps onto the same syntactic structure.

Since, on the surface, Interface Uniformity is patently false, it is necessary for MGG to introduce a "hidden" or "underlying" level of syntax (Deep Structure in the Standard Theory, Logical Form in subsequent versions) that maps directly onto semantics and is related derivationally to surface form.[2] Under these assumptions, B's responses in (2) must have underlying syntactic structures along the lines of (3), and all parts repeated from A's sentence have been deleted (or are encoded as empty nodes) in the course of deriving phonological form. For example, (2a.i) has the derivation shown in (4).

(4)   Harriet's been drinking scotch $\Rightarrow$ scotch

  or $[_{NP}$ e$][_T$ e$][_{VP}$ e scotch$]] \Rightarrow$ scotch

The Simpler Syntax alternative claims instead that the responses in (2) have no syntactic structure beyond that present at the surface. The syntax–semantics interface, which does not observe Interface Uniformity, supplies the rest of the details of interpretation, relying on the semantic/pragmatic structure of A's sentences.

An IU-based account like (4) is attractive in part because there exist responses that contain apparent sentential modifiers.

(5)   A: i. I hear Harriet's been drinking again.
   ii. Has Harriet been drinking again?
  B: i. Yeah, but not scotch.
   ii. Yeah, scotch, probably.
   iii. Yeah, I think scotch.
   iv. Yeah, scotch this time.

The argument is that the pieces of the response, e.g. *scotch* and *probably*, can be treated as syntactically well-formed only if there is an underlying sentential structure to which both are connected. This argument depends on a methodological principle we will call Structural Uniformity:

Structural Uniformity
An apparently defective or misordered structure is regular in underlying structure and becomes distorted in the course of derivation.

An SSH account, by contrast, requires the theory to countenance syntactically ill-formed utterances along the lines of (6), in violation of Structural Uniformity.[3]

---

[2] In Generative Semantics, which originated as an offshoot of the Standard Theory, the hidden level was taken to be *identical* to meaning—while retaining its syntactic character; the derivation from the hidden level to surface structure was still taken to be in terms of syntactic operations such as movement and deletion. See section 3.3.

[3] The SSH account as sketched here does not account for facts such as that in case-marking languages, BAE shows case-marking appropriate to its understood role in the antecedent. This is often taken to be evidence for Structural Uniformity. We will deal with this issue in Ch. 7.

(6)

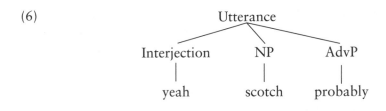

The two approaches may seem at some level equivalent; and from the mindset of MGG, an IU-based account like (4) is far more elegant. However, let us dig a little deeper into the evidence. The IU-based account claims that the deletions in (4) are licensed on the basis of identity with the syntactic form and lexical content of relevant parts of the antecedent sentence. But in fact the correspondence between antecedent and response is less than perfect. For instance, B's response (2a.i) does not mean "I hear Harriet's been drinking scotch again", with a literal copy of the antecedent. Rather, *I* uttered by B refers to B, not to A; B's response would have to say *you*. Moreover, even with this substitution, "Yeah, you hear Harriet's been drinking scotch again" is not the correct interpretation. Rather, B's response confirms what A has heard and adds information that A has *not* heard. Consider also B's responses in (2b,c). Again it is impossible to directly copy the syntactic form of A's sentence, which is a question; it must be adjusted to a declarative.

Of course the SSH account must provide for such adjustments as well. However, when we look at the basis for the adjustments, we find that they all involve semantic/pragmatic factors rather than syntactic ones. For instance, the *I/you* switch comes from maintaining constant reference in the antecedent and the response. Thus the SSH account, which derives the interpretation of the response from the *meaning* of the preceding sentence rather than from its *syntax*, does not need to say anything at all in order to get the pronoun switch for free. Similarly, the switch from question to statement is a natural part of any semantic/pragmatic treatment of discourse.

Semantics/pragmatics is still more deeply implicated in cases of BAE where the syntactic relation between the antecedent and response is more remote:

(7) a. A: Why don't you fix me a drink?
        B: In a minute, ok?
        [cf. infelicity of *Why don't I fix you a drink in a minute?* as response: response is understood as *I'll fix you a drink in a minute*]
     b. A: Would you like a drink?
        B: i. Yeah, how about scotch?
           ii. No, but how about some lunch?

[cf. *How about I would like scotch/some lunch? as well as other improbable variants]

  c. A: Let's get a pizza.
     B: OK—pepperoni?
    [cf. *Let's get pepperoni pizza?: response is understood as something like OK, should we get pepperoni pizza?]

  d. A: I hear there's been some serious drinking going on here.
     B: i. Not Sam, I hope.
        ii. Not my favorite bottle of scotch, I hope.

Such examples show that the plausibility of a putative syntactic reconstruction depends primarily on its semantic/pragmatic plausibility as a response; its degree of syntactic parallelism to the antecedent is a negotiable secondary factor. What this means is that a syntactic account needs, in addition to its syntactic machinery, all the machinery of the semantic account. In short, an account of BAE that assumes Interface Uniformity and Structural Uniformity ends up increasing rather than decreasing the overall complexity of the grammar. Once this is acknowledged, there is no justification for proposing all the extra hidden syntactic structure of (4); hence the overall complexity of syntactic structure can be reduced, while still accounting for the interpretation.

The argument can go further. Once we develop formal machinery that accounts for the interpretation of BAE in terms of the SSH, we can ask what other phenomena naturally fall under the same machinery, and whether they present similar difficulties to an IU-based theory. To the extent that a consistent story emerges across a range of phenomena, the overall choice is vindicated. This will be our tack in Chapters 7 and 8, where we extend the SSH approach not only to BAE but to a range of ellipsis constructions, including Gapping, Sluicing, and VP ellipsis, by use of a formal mechanism we call Indirect Licensing.

This brief discussion of BAE is just a sketch; it is intended to set out a bit of empirical context in terms of which we can lay out our overall goals and hypotheses for a theory of language, the task to which we now turn.

1.3 The goals of linguistic theory

We begin a more thorough examination of the situation by reviewing the first principles of generative grammar, articulated in detail by Noam Chomsky in *Aspects of the Theory of Syntax* (1965) and many subsequent works. With only minor modulation and reinterpretation, these principles have stood the test of time and have received further confirmation through the flood of research in cognitive science in the past forty years. Here we will be brief; a more extended reappraisal appears in Jackendoff (2002a).

Generative grammar is grounded in the stance that the object of study is the instantiation of language in the context of the human mind/brain, rather than an abstract phenomenon that exists "in the community" (as posited e.g. by Saussure), in a collection of texts, or in some sort of Platonic space (Katz 1981; Langendoen and Postal 1984). The fundamental linguistic phenomenon is a speaker producing an utterance that is understood by a hearer, and the fundamental question is what is present in the speaker's and hearer's mind/brain that enables this interchange to take place. A language "exists in the community" insofar as there is a community of speakers able to participate equivalently as speakers or hearers in an appropriate range of such interactions. In other words, generative grammar seeks a mentalistic account of language.

Unlike vocal communication systems in other primates, human language is not limited to a relatively small number of isolated signals. Rather, a speaker of a human language can create and understand an unlimited number of different utterances, concerning an unlimited number of different topics. This entails that a language user with a finite brain must have a productive system for constructing new utterances online (in both production and perception) from a finite basis stored in memory. The finite basis is standardly called the *lexicon* and the productive system is standardly called the *grammar*; we will re-evaluate this division in section 1.5. Crucially, the productive system is not consciously accessible to the speaker: it is like the principles by which the visual system constructs a perception of the physical world, not like one's knowledge of the rules of games or traffic laws.

It has been customary since Chomsky (1965) to make a distinction between linguistic *competence*—the language user's knowledge of his or her language, and linguistic *performance*—the processing strategies by which this knowledge is put to use. At bottom, this is a distinction of convenience: a linguist investigating the grammatical details of a linguistic pattern finds it useful to idealize away from how these details are actually achieved in real time in a language user's brain. However, an idealization always implies a promissory note: in principle, the theory of competence should be embedded in a theory of performance—including a theory of the neural realization of linguistic memory and processing. One of the criteria for an explanatory theory of competence is how gracefully it can be so embedded, to the extent that we can determine within our current understanding of processing and neural instantiation of *any* cognitive process.

From this mentalistic view of language, the question arises of how speakers acquire their lexicon and grammar. In particular, since the grammar is unconscious, parents cannot impart the rules to their children by instruction. Rather, the process of language acquisition must be understood in terms of the child unconsciously constructing the grammar on the basis of linguistic and contextual input. However, this raises two further questions. What sorts of inputs does the child use and, most crucially, what are the internal resources that the child brings to bear on the construction of a grammar based on the input? Surely, part of what the child must be able to do is to extract statistical regularities in the input; but since the work of Miller and Chomsky (1963), the generative tradition has stressed that there must be more than this to the child's ability (see Culicover and Nowak 2003 for a current assessment). The complexity of the achieved grammar, as discovered by investigation in linguistic theory, demands that the child be provided in advance with some guidelines along which to pursue generalization—a pre-narrowing of the class of possible analyses of the input.

The generative tradition has taken as its most important goal the characterization of these guidelines, calling them *Universal Grammar* (UG) or *the language capacity*. The nature of UG has been investigated by examining large-scale patterns of similarity across the grammars of languages (spoken and signed), language acquisition by children and adults, patterns of language loss and impairment, and historical change due to drift and language contact, as well as through mathematical/computational modeling of all these phenomena.

The goal of accounting for language acquisition gives empirical teeth to the desire to minimize the crosslinguistically variable principles of grammar. For this reason Chomsky says (1965: 46):

[T]he most crucial problem for linguistic theory seems to be to abstract statements and generalizations from particular descriptively adequate grammars and, wherever possible, to attribute them to the general theory of linguistic structure, thus enriching this theory and imposing more structure on the schema for grammatical description.

The intent is to reduce the amount of the adult grammar that the child must learn, by attributing as much of it as possible to UG. If there is less to learn, it is easier to understand how the child becomes grammatically competent so rapidly and effortlessly. This aspect of minimization reaches its zenith in Principles and Parameters Theory, where all the child has to acquire is a rather small number of parameter settings, and the rest of the grammar follows from UG. (Optimality Theory takes a similar tack; see e.g. Tesar 1995.)

We agree that this is an important explanatory move. But we think Chomsky overstates the case when he says (1965: 35), "Real progress in linguistics consists in the discovery that certain features of given languages can be reduced to universal properties of language, and explained in terms of these deeper aspects of linguistic form." Such a discovery is indeed progress, but a theory of language also stands a better chance of being learnable if its syntax can be shown to have less abstract machinery such as extra nodes, hidden elements, and covert movements—all of which require the learner to be prompted by UG. Hence, it is also real progress in linguistics to show on independent empirical grounds—as well as on general grounds of parsimony—that one can dispense with all this machinery, so that there is less to acquire, period. This is the direction in which the Simpler Syntax Hypothesis points us in the case of BAE above.

Another kind of real progress consists in the discovery of how certain features of given languages, for which there is no UG input, can nevertheless be learned by the child from the input. Such features include of course voluminous facts of vocabulary, for instance that the noise /dɔg/ happens to mean "dog". This is just a matter of historical contingency, and the child has no choice but to learn it as such. And there is a vast amount of such material in any language. Hence a theory of language acquisition must be robustly equipped to cope with the task of learning it.[4] In seeking an explanatory theory of language, then, the theorist is often forced to judge when deeper explanation is called for, and when to give up and settle for a description in terms of learning. Section 1.5 discusses some phenomena that show how difficult a choice this is; the theme is continued throughout the book.

Next the theorist must face the question of where the child's internal resources for learning language come from. The answer must be that they are innate, for they precede and enable learning. One can further ask what parts of these internal resources are specific to language learning, and what parts are shared with other components of other human—or primate—capacities. To the extent that some parts *are* specific to language, we are led to the claim that the capacity to acquire and use human language is a human cognitive specialization, a claim that has been central to generative grammar since the 1960s. We might distinguish the child's full internal resources for language acquisition, which include *inter alia* various social skills and the capacity for imitation, from the language-specific resources, calling the latter "Narrow UG" and the rest "Broad UG". Then an eventual goal of linguistic theory is to sort out Narrow UG from Broad UG. Doing so, of course, may require a comparable account of the other aspects of human cognition subserved by elements of Broad UG, an account at present far beyond the horizon (cf. Pinker and Jackendoff 2005).

---

[4] Fodor's (1975) proposal that word meanings are all innate, even if it were independently plausible (see Jackendoff 1990a), does not help. The child still faces the problem of deciding which innate meaning goes with which noise: does *chien* match up with the innate monad DOG, or ANIMAL, or POODLE, or PET? and how does the child figure it out? That is, there is still a severe learning problem here. See Bloom (2000) for a review of this and related issues.

Finally, if Narrow UG is innate, it must be coded genetically, just like any specialized cognitive capacity in any animal, such as bat sonar. And to the extent that natural selection is responsible for the evolution of other complex cognitive capacities, we might expect the same to be true of the language capacity. Thus a plausible longterm goal for linguistic theory is to delineate the evolutionary origins of human language, to the extent permitted given the near absence of evidence. In the short term, this goal can be anticipated by asking of a theory of UG whether it lends itself to the logical possibility of incremental development over evolutionary time (cf. Jackendoff 2002a: ch. 8).

This goal often comes into conflict with the previous goal of pushing the complexity of language into UG, since the result of the latter is that UG itself becomes overloaded with complexity. Critics of generative grammar (e.g. Tomasello 1995) are justified in being suspicious of a learning theory that depends on the child having an innate language capacity that contains, say, an intricately crafted definition of government (Chomsky 1981; 1986a). This is more than a quibble about scientific elegance. In order for such intricacy to be present in the prelinguistic child, it must be constructed in the brain (somehow) from the human genetic code. In turn, the genetic code ultimately has to be a product of genetic variation and natural selection in prelinguistic hominids (or perhaps earlier, if it serves some purpose more general than language). Granted, we know virtually nothing about how any innate cognitive capacity is installed in a brain by a genetic code, much less the dimensions of variation possible in such codes. But that doesn't absolve us from at least keeping this problem in mind, and therefore trying to minimize the complexity of UG in an effort to set the stage for eventual explanation.

Speaking to this concern, the Minimalist Program attempts to minimize the machinery in UG, while still explaining the acquisition of grammar on the basis of a finite set of parameters. It offers an overall vision of language as a "perfect" or "optimal" system, reducible to a few very general principles such as Merge and Economy. Within this context, Hauser et al. (2002) suggest that the only feature of language that had to evolve specifically for Narrow UG is recursion, so that natural selection may have had little to do with the emergence of language. *A priori* this is a welcome result—but only if the Minimalist Program is empirically adequate on independent grounds (see section 3.2 and Pinker and Jackendoff 2005).

Again, these goals have been present in linguistic theorizing since the middle 1960s; and introductions like this one appear frequently in works on generative grammar. In the present study, we are trying our best to take all these goals—mentalism, relation of competence to performance, acquisition, and the innateness of Narrow UG—absolutely seriously. We will not mention processing and acquisition and evolution very often here, but we are relying on grounding provided by our previous work (Jackendoff 2002a; Culicover and Nowak 2003), to which the reader is referred for justification.

1.4 The architecture of the grammar

By "the architecture of the grammar", we mean the articulation of the grammar into rule types: a specification of what phenomena each type is responsible for and how the various types interact with each other. Each rule type will be responsible for characterizing aspects of particular levels of representation. Thus a theory of the architecture of grammar will also delimit the significant levels of linguistic representation. Are there multiple levels of syntax such as D-structure, S-structure, and Logical Form, or is there only one? Which of these levels interacts directly with the lexicon? Which level interacts with semantic interpretation? And so on. The issue of architecture is supremely important in linguistic theory, for it has to be assumed that the language learner does not have to discover the architecture. In other words, the architecture is a fundamental part of Narrow UG, and therefore languages will not differ significantly in this respect, if at all.

All linguistic theories posit—at least implicitly—three essential levels of representation: phonological (sound) structure, syntactic (grammatical) structure, and semantic (meaning) structure. They differ widely in whether there are further levels (such as morphology or functional structure or pragmatics or phonetics), in how each level is further articulated, in how they interact, and indeed in how much emphasis is placed on them (many theories of syntax/semantics ignore phonology almost entirely).

We wish to call attention to four important architectural hypotheses on which we differ from mainstream generative grammar. Although MGG has gone through many different architectures since 1957, these four aspects of its conception have remained constant:

- The formal technology is derivational.
- There are "hidden levels" of syntax.
- Syntax is the source of all combinatorial complexity; phonology and semantics are "interpretive".
- Lexicon is separate from grammar.

We replace these with the following architectural hypotheses, which we share in various degrees with the alternative generative theories:

- The formal technology is constraint-based.
- There are no "hidden levels" built of syntactic units.
- Combinatorial complexity arises independently in phonology, syntax, and semantics.
- There is a continuum of grammatical phenomena from idiosyncratic (including words) to general rules of grammar.

The last of these calls for extensive discussion and is treated in the next section. This section takes up the first three plus two further issues:

- Semantics is served by a richly structured representation that is to a great degree independent of language.
- The combinatorial principles of syntax and semantics are independent; there is no "rule-to-rule" homomorphism.

1.4.1 *Constraints rather than derivations*

In MGG, the technology of the competence grammar is formulated in terms of *derivations*: linguistic structures are constructed by applying a sequence of rules, each applying to the output of the previous step.[5] Hence there is an inherent directionality in the logic of sentence construction: certain rules and rule components necessarily apply "after" others. This conception of rules of grammar is shared by approaches such as Categorial Grammar (Montague 1974; Steedman 2000) and Tree-Adjoining Grammar (Joshi 1987; Frank and Kroch 1995).

By contrast, we, along with the alternative theories (LFG, HPSG, Construction Grammar, etc.), formulate the competence grammar in terms of the technology of *constraints*.[6] Each constraint determines or licenses a small piece of linguistic structure or a relation between two small pieces. A linguistic structure is acceptable overall if it conforms to all applicable constraints. There is no logical ordering among constraints, so one can use constraints to license or construct linguistic structures starting at any point in the sentence: top-down, bottom-up, left-to-right, or any combination thereof. Thus a constraint-based grammar readily lends itself to interpretations in terms of performance (see Jackendoff 2002a: ch. 7).

---

[5] This style of grammar has also been called "procedural", "automata-theoretic", and "proof-theoretic".

[6] This treatment of rules of grammar was suggested as early as McCawley (1968a), who referred to "node admissibility conditions"; other terms for this formulation are "declarative", "representational", and "model-theoretic".

1.4.2 *No "hidden levels" of syntax*

The most striking technological innovation of early generative grammar, of course, was the transformation, an operation on syntactic structure that added, deleted, or reordered material. Transformations are perfectly natural extensions of a derivational construal of phrase structure rules: like phrase structure rules, they are a way to rewrite a string based on its structure. This leads to the possibility of "hidden levels" of syntactic structure that do not bear a direct relation to the phonological string. For example, Deep Structure in the Standard Theory is the level after phrase structure rules and lexical insertion have applied and before all transformations; Logical Form in GB is the level derived from S-structure by "covert movement". Crucially, because transformations can only move, insert, or delete constituents, these levels are necessarily made of the same "stuff" as overt syntax: they are tree structures whose nodes are syntactic categories such as N, V, AP, and PP. The "hidden levels" are a fundamental part of the vision of MGG. In particular, as we have seen in section 1.2, they are what make it possible to impose Interface and Structural Uniformity, thus bringing syntactic structure very close to meaning and permitting more crosslinguistic homogeneity in syntax than is evident from the surface.

The alternative theories, by contrast, are "monostratal": they have no hidden levels of syntax related to overt syntax by movement, insertion, and deletion. They therefore are forced to conceive of the relation between syntax and semantics as more flexible. Needless to say, the absence of "hidden levels" is an important hypothesis of Simpler Syntax. LFG does posit a second level of syntax called "functional structure", but it is built of different "stuff" than overt syntactic structure and it is related to syntactic structure by constraints, not by operations that distort syntactic structure. In Chapter 6 we will motivate a similar level, the "Grammatical Function tier", that proves necessary to implement the mapping between syntax and semantics.[7]

Looking back for a moment at the goals for the theory laid out in section 1.3: the choice of a monostratal theory has implications for acquisition. It was early recognized that one of the most difficult problems for the learnability of syntax was discovering the proper conditions for the application of transformations (Chomsky 1964a). During the 1970s, a great deal of effort went into discovering general conditions limiting the application of transformations, in order to

---

[7] The possibility of a generative theory without transformations and without "hidden levels" was envisioned as early as Harman (1963), Shopen (1972), Brame (1978), and Bresnan (1978), each of these independently of the others. The technological innovation of traces of movement in MGG made it possible to translate (most of) a multi-stratal MGG-style theory into monostratal constraint-based terms; such approaches have been explored by Koster (1978) and Brody (1995).

reduce or even eliminate idiosyncratic conditions of application that would have to be learned. Wexler and Culicover (1980) in particular linked this undertaking to issues of learnability (see also Baker and McCarthy 1981). By abandoning movement rules altogether, this particular issue of learnability is sidestepped; different and potentially more tractable problems for acquisition come to the fore (Culicover and Nowak 2003; Tomasello 2003). We return to this issue in section 1.6 and at many subsequent points throughout the book.

1.4.3 *Multiple sources of combinatoriality*

In MGG, all the combinatorial richness of language stems from the rules of the syntactic component; the combinatorial properties of phonology and semantics are characterized entirely in terms of the way they are derived from syntactic structure. The basic characteristic of language—that it is a mapping between meanings and phonetically encoded sounds—follows from the way a meaning and a phonetic encoding are derived from a common syntactic structure.

Our architecture contrasts with this "syntactocentric" view, both as a matter of technology and as a matter of conceptualization. In the early days of generative grammar, a syntactocentric architecture seemed altogether plausible, though Chomsky (1965: 16–17, 75, 136, 198) makes clear that it is only an assumption. Phonological rules appeared to be low-level rules that adjusted the pronunciation of words after they were ordered by the syntactic component. And there was no serious theory of meaning to speak of, so it made most sense to think of meaning as "read off" from syntactic structure. These considerations, combined with the brilliant success of early transformational syntax, made syntactocentrism virtually unquestionable.

The development of a multitiered phonology in the 1970s offered (in principle but not in practice) a significant challenge to the idea that syntax is the sole generative component in language, in that phonological structure was recognized to require its own autonomous generative grammar, parceled into tiers that must be related by association rules. Association rules, because they relate structures made of different sorts of "stuff", must be stated as constraints rather than as transformations. Furthermore, the relation between syntax and phonology can no longer be stated in terms of syntactic transformations, because phonological constituency is constructed out of prosodic/intonational units rather than NPs and VPs. Thus, a constraint-based component relating the two is inevitable.

Similarly, during the 1970s and 1980s, many different theories of semantics developed, all of which took for granted that semantics has its own independent combinatorial structure, not entirely dependent on syntax. Hence again it is impossible to *derive* semantic combinatoriality from syntax by movement and deletion; rather, a constraint-based component is necessary to coordinate the two structures. On both the phonological and semantic fronts, therefore, the conditions that led to the plausibility of syntactocentrism were severely undermined. Nevertheless, syntactocentrism has continued for the subsequent twenty-five years as the reigning architectural hypothesis in mainstream generative grammar and many other frameworks. (For much more discussion, see Jackendoff (2002a).)

The architecture we are supposing here therefore abandons syntactocentrism and acknowledges the independent combinatorial character of phonology and semantics. It can be diagrammed roughly as in Figure 1.1. The grammar consists of parallel generative components, stated in constraint-based form, each of which creates its own type of combinatorial complexity. At the very least, these include independent components for phonology, syntax, and semantics, with the possibility of further division into subcomponents or "tiers". The grammar also includes sets of constraints that determine how the parallel components are related to each other; these are called "interface components". Language thus provides a mapping between sound and meaning by (a) independently characterizing sound, syntax, and meaning and (b) using the interface components to map between them. A sentence is well-formed if each part of each structure is licensed and each connection between parts of the parallel structures is licensed by an interface constraint. In particular, syntax plays the role of a mediator between the linearly ordered phonological string of words and the highly hierarchical but linearly unordered structure of meanings.

Next we must address the role of the lexicon. In every theory, a word is conceived of as a long-term memory association of a piece of phonological structure, a piece of syntactic structure, and a piece of meaning. In MGG, words are inserted (or Merged) into syntactic structure, and their phonological and

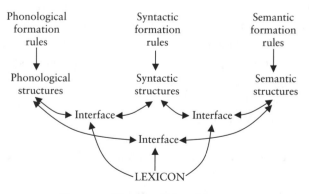

Fig. 1.1. The parallel architecture

semantic features are read off in the appropriate "interpretive" components. In the parallel architecture, a word is instead conceived of as a piece of the interfaces between phonological, syntactic, and semantic structures. Thus instead of lexical insertion or Merge introducing lexical items into syntax, we can think of lexical items as being inserted simultaneously into the three structures and establishing a connection between them. Or we can simply think of lexical items as licensing a connection between fragments of the three structures. In either sense, as interface constraints, they play an active role in the construction of sentences.

We should also make brief mention of morphology here (unfortunately so brief as to ignore and/or prejudge many important issues that we cannot address here). We take morphology to be the extension of the parallel architecture below the word level. Morphophonology deals with the construction of the phonological structure of words from stems and affixes: roughly, how the sounds of stems and affixes influence each other. Morphosyntax deals with syntactic structure inside words, for instance the syntactic category that an affix applies to and the syntactic category of the resultant, the feature structure of morphological paradigms, and the morphosyntactic templates involved in multiple affixation. Morphology also has a semantic component, delimiting the range of meanings that can be expressed morphologically (Talmy 1985 is an example of such work). Many productive affixes, for instance the English regular plural, can be treated as lexical items that, like words, provide an interface between pieces of (morpho)phonology, (morpho)syntax, and semantics. (See Jackendoff (1997a; 2002a) for some discussion of the interaction between productive, semiproductive, and irregular morphology in this architecture.)

This architecture has enough flexibility that it can be used to compare different frameworks. For instance, the syntactocentrism of mainstream generative grammar can be modeled by eliminating the contribution of the formation rules for phonology and conceptual structure: these levels then receive all their structure through the interfaces from syntax. Cognitive Grammar (Langacker 1987) can be modeled by minimizing the syntactic formation rules: here syntax is mostly derivative from semantics (and as far as we know little is said about phonology at all). LFG can be modeled by interposing the level of functional structure between syntax and semantics, and connecting it with similar interfaces.

Thus the traditional division of linguistics into phonology, morphology, syntax, semantics, and lexicon is not accepted here. Rather, the parallel architecture involves the three-way division into generative components of phonology, syntax, and semantics, plus a crosscutting division into phrasal and morphological departments, plus interface principles between various components. And the lexicon cuts across all of these.

1.4.4 Conceptual Structure

A key assumption of our position concerns the status of meaning, represented formally as the level of Conceptual Structure (CS). We take it that Conceptual Structure is one aspect of human cognitive representations in terms of which thought takes place. By contrast with aspects of thought that are probably geometric (or quasi-topological) and analog, such as the organization of visual space, Conceptual Structure is an algebraic structure composed of discrete elements.[8] It encodes such distinctions as the type–token distinction, the categories in terms of which the world is understood, and the relations among various individuals and categories. It is one of the mental frameworks in terms of which current experience, episodic memory, and plans for future action are stored and related to one another. And it is the formal basis for processes of reasoning, both logical and heuristic.

In other words, Conceptual Structure is a central system of the mind. It is not a part of language per se; rather it is the mental structure which language encodes into communicable form. Language per se (the "Narrow Faculty of Language") includes (a) syntactic and phonological structure, (b) the interface that correlates syntax and phonology with each other, and (c) the interfaces that connect syntax and phonology with Conceptual Structure (the "Conceptual–Intentional Interface") and with perceptual input and motor output (the "Sensorimotor Interface", actually one interface with audition and one with motor control).

We take it that the richness of Conceptual Structure is justified not simply on the basis of its adequacy to support linguistic semantics, but also on its adequacy to support inference and on its adequacy to support the connection to nonlinguistic perception and action. In principle, then, we should find evidence of some type of Conceptual Structure in nonlinguistic organisms such as babies and higher primates—a type of mental representation used for thinking but not for communication. Indeed, virtually all research in language acquisition presumes that the learner surmises the intended meaning of an utterance on the

---

[8] A terminological point: Algebraic combinatorial systems are commonly said to "have a syntax". In this sense, music has a syntax, computer languages have a syntax, phonology has a syntax, and so does Conceptual Structure. However, within linguistics, "syntax" is also used to denote the organization of sentences in terms of categories such as NP, VP, and the like. These categories are not present in any of the above combinatorial systems, so they are not "syntax" in this narrower sense. Throughout this book, we use "syntax" exclusively in the narrow sense.

basis of context, and uses it as an essential part in the process of internally constructing the lexical and grammatical structure of the utterance.[9] And an account of the extraordinarily complex behavior of primates, especially apes and especially in the social domain (e.g. Hauser 2000; Byrne and Whiten 1988), leads inexorably to the conclusion that they are genuinely *thinking* thoughts of rich combinatorial structure—not as rich as human thought, to be sure, but still combinatorial in the appropriate sense. In short, Conceptual Structure is epistemologically prior to linguistic structure, both in the language learner and in evolution.

The richness and epistemological priority of Conceptual Structure plays an important role in our argument for Simpler Syntax. In a syntactocentric theory, particularly under the assumption of Interface Uniformity, every combinatorial aspect of semantics must be ultimately derived from syntactic combinatoriality. In other words, syntax must be at least as complex as semantics. On the other hand, if Conceptual Structure is an autonomous component, there is no need for every aspect of it to be mirrored in syntax—only enough to map it properly into phonology. This presents the theorist with a different set of options. For example, consider again bare argument ellipsis. In a syntactocentric theory, the interpretation could come from no place other than the syntax, so an account in terms of deletion or empty structure is unavoidable. A parallel architecture presents the option of accounting for the interpretation in terms of semantic principles, leaving the syntax with minimal structure. Because of syntactocentrism and Interface Uniformity, mainstream practice has virtually always favored accounts in terms of syntax, leading to elaboration of principles and structures in the syntactic component. However, if it can be shown that the generalization in question can be stated at least as perspicuously in terms of the meanings of sentences, regardless of their syntactic form (as we sketched for BAE), then good scientific practice demands an account in terms of semantics. A semantic account is particularly supported if the posited elements of meaning are independently necessary to support inference.

In turn, if independently motivated distinctions in Conceptual Structure are sufficient to account for a linguistic phenomenon, Occam's Razor suggests that there is no reason to duplicate them in syntactic structure. In such cases, syntactic structure will be constrained, not by internal conditions, but rather by the necessity to interface properly with meaning—what Chomsky (1995)

---

[9] We note, however, that there is a strand of research on language acquisition in the generative tradition that presumes that the learner's strictly syntactic experience triggers the setting of parametric values of grammatical principles or structures; for discussion and criticism, see Fodor (1998; 2001), Culicover (1999), and many others.

calls "Bare Output Conditions". In other words, if the desired constraint on syntax can be achieved without saying anything within syntax itself, the extra syntactic structure should be slashed away by Occam's Razor.

Should *all* syntactic structure be slashed away? Our goal, a theory of syntax with the minimal structure necessary to map between phonology and meaning, leaves open the possibility that there is *no* syntax at all: that it is possible to map directly from phonological structure (including prosody) to meaning. Although some people might rejoice at such an outcome, we think it is unlikely. Perhaps this represents a certain conservatism on our part, and someone more daring will be able to bring it off. But at minimum, we believe that *syntactic categories* such as noun and verb are not definable in purely semantic terms—and that fundamental syntactic phenomena such as agreement and case-marking are based on these categories. And we believe that there are *syntactic constituents* whose categories are determined (for the most part) by the categories of their heads, i.e. that there is something like X-bar phrase structure. We think it is not a matter of phonology or semantics that English verbs go after the subject, Japanese verbs go at the end of the clause, and German inflected verbs go in second position in main clauses but at the end in subordinate clauses. We think it is not a matter of phonology or semantics that English sentences require an overt subject but Italian sentences do not; that English has ditransitive verb phrases but Italian does not; that English has *do*-support but Italian does not (but see Benincà and Poletto 2004 for a northern Italian dialect that does have *do*-support); that Italian has object clitics before the verb but English does not. That is, we are going to take it for granted that there is some substantial body of phenomena that require an account in terms of syntactic structure. It is just that we think this body is not as substantial as mainstream generative grammar has come to assume. This is why we call our hypothesis "Simpler Syntax" rather than just plain "Simple Syntax".

1.4.5 *Combinatorial autonomy of syntax and semantics*

A recurring line of thought in syntactic theory takes it that, even if syntax has some properties autonomous from semantics, its basic principles of combination are in some sense homomorphic with those of semantics. Thus every syntactic rule has a semantic counterpart that says: "When syntactic constituents X and Y are combined into constituent Z, the meanings of X and Y are combined in such-and-such a fashion." This hypothesis has appeared in venues as different as Katz and Fodor's (1963) early proposal for a semantic component in generative grammar and versions of syntax–semantics based on Categorial Grammar such as Montague (1974) and Steedman (2000). In Cognitive

Grammar (Langacker 1987) and some versions of Construction Grammar (Goldberg 1995; to appear) this hypothesis follows from the central claim that all syntactic structure is inherently meaningful. It also is implicit in the formalism of HPSG, where the fundamental unit of combinatoriality is a "sign", a complex of phonological, syntactic, and semantic features; when units are combined syntactically, they must be simultaneously combined phonologically and semantically as well. Finally, it is the intuition behind the Uniform Theta-Assignment Hypothesis (UTAH, Baker 1988) in MGG, which we discuss in Chapter 3.

We take issue with this intuition, or at least we would like to keep our options open. The parallel architecture allows the possibility that syntactic and semantic structures are to some degree independent in organization. For instance, the last subsection mentioned some factors in syntax that we think have little to do with meaning, such as verb position, agreement, requirement for an overt subject, and so on. These define the *forms* that are available for expressing meaning. To be sure, some of these choices will have semantic correlates. For example, if a language has a ditransitive construction, it will most probably be used with verbs of giving, because these are the stereotypical three-argument verbs. But this does not tell us what *other* three-argument verbs will make use of the same syntactic structure, and languages vary. Similarly, the syntactic structure *NP's N* can be used to express a possessor (8a), an agent (8b), or a time (8c), among other things; and each of these semantic relations can be expressed in other ways as well (9).

(8)   a. the professor's hat
      b. the teacher's examination of the students
      c. Monday's meeting
(9)   a. the hat of the professor
      b. the examination of the students by the teacher
      c. the meeting on Monday

To say that *NP's N* is the outcome of several distinct rules, each paired with different semantics, misses the point that this simply is an available syntactic structure in English. It makes more sense to us to say that the mapping between syntactic and semantic combinatoriality is many-to-many.

Another example dates back to the Generative Semantics/Interpretive Semantics dispute of the late 1960s. It turns out that the relative scope of negation and a quantifier such as *many* is to a great extent determined by their linear order in the clause, no matter how they achieve their position (Jackendoff 1969a; 1972):[10]

---

[10] Focal or topical stress and intonation on *many* can alter the scope in some of these examples (Jackendoff 1972). This only complicates the problem further, of course.

(10)   Negation is to the left of and takes scope over *many*:
       a. Not many arrows hit the target.
       b. We didn't shoot many arrows at the target.
       c. We didn't shoot at the target with many arrows.
       d. The target wasn't hit by many arrows.
       e. Never did many arrows hit the target.
       f. Never did we shoot many arrows at the target.
       g. Never was the target hit by many arrows.
       h. I told nobody's secrets to many spies.
       i. Only then didn't many of the arrows hit the target.
       j. Only then wasn't the target hit by many arrows.
       k. Only then was the target not hit by many arrows.

(11)   *Many* is to the left of and takes scope over negation (on primary reading):
       a. Many arrows didn't hit the target.
       b. Many arrows never hit the target.
       c. Many targets weren't hit by the arrows.
       d. Many arrows, the target wasn't hit by.
       e. We shot many arrows at no targets.
       f. I told many spies nobody's secrets.
       g. Only then did many arrows not hit the target.

These examples show that the principle relating quantifier scope to syntax is oblivious to which other principles happen to be involved in establishing linear order—including the active/passive alternation ((10d) vs. (11a)), the dative alternation ((10h) vs. (11f)), adverb fronting ((10e) vs. (11b)), and topicalization ((10d) vs. (11d)). Even the choice of negative contraction combined with subject–aux inversion can make a difference ((10i) vs. (11g)), but only if the consequence is reordering of negation and the quantifier (compare (10i)/(11g) to (10j)/(10k)). To say that each of these principles contains a condition involving scope misses the generalization among them all. On the other hand, if the principles of quantifier scope apply as independent constraints, dependent on linear order in the clause but not on how that linear order is established, then there is no longer a rule-to-rule match between the principles of syntactic composition that build the phrase structures of (10)–(11) and the principles of semantic composition responsible for surface phrase structure and quantifier scope. Both HPSG (Pollard and Sag 1994) and formal semantics (e.g. Cooper 1983) develop technology to deal with this problem, but they are forced to resort to such complexity because of their commitment to rule-to-rule isomorphism. Similarly, in order to preserve Interface Uniformity in light of such facts, MGG introduces the level of Logical Form and the covert movement rule of quantifier raising. We prefer a more direct and intuitive account which allows interface rules for different aspects of semantics to attend to different (but inseparably entangled) aspects of syntactic structure, and which preserves Simpler Syntax.

1.5 The continuum from words to rules; "syntactic nuts" and the core/periphery distinction

Mainstream generative grammar makes two divisions among linguistic phenomena, with the goal of identifying those aspects of language where deep generality and rich abstract deductive structure are to be expected. The first is the traditional division between grammar—the rules of the language—and the lexicon, which mainstream generative tradition takes to be the locus of all irregularity. In *Aspects* (p. 214), Chomsky cites approvingly Bloomfield's (1933: 274) characterization: "The lexicon is really an appendix of the grammar, a list of basic irregularities." The second division, introduced around the time of *Lectures on Government and Binding* (Chomsky 1981), distinguishes between two parts of the grammar itself, the "core" and the "periphery". The core rules represent the deep regularities of language, those that are governed by parameter settings. The periphery represents "marked exceptions" such as irregular verbs, for which there are no deep regularities. The research program idealizes the study of the language faculty to the study of the core:

A reasonable approach would be to focus attention on the core system, putting aside phenomena that result from historical accident, dialect mixture, personal idiosyncrasies, and the like. As in any other empirical inquiry, theory-internal considerations enter into the effort to pursue this course, and we expect further distinctions to be necessary. (Chomsky and Lasnik 1993, reprinted in Chomsky (1995: 20))

Such an idealization is indeed "reasonable" but, as always, an idealization carries with it an implicit promissory note to make good on the phenomena it has omitted. And "periphery" tends to become a tempting dumping ground for any irregularity one's theory cannot at the moment explain.

We have found ourselves taking a different tack, being attracted over and over again to "peripheral" phenomena. There turn out to be substantial numbers of them in English (several of which we treat in detail in Chapters 7, 10, 11, 13, and 14; see also Culicover (1999) and Culicover (2004)); we presume the same is true of other languages. We find over and over again that "peripheral" phenomena can lead to judgments as sharp and unexpected as the "core" phenomena, and, recalling our basic goals, we are led to ask how the language learner could possibly acquire these "syntactic nuts". That is, the periphery presents at least as much a problem for acquisition as does the core.

In addition, we must bear in mind the problem of lexical acquisition. Children acquire thousands of words in a relatively short time, and each word presents severe problems, particularly in the semantic domain; a vast and subtle experimental and theoretical tradition has grown up around this problem (see Bloom 2000 for a survey). In other words, even if we were to solve the acquisition problem for "core" grammar, it would still leave mysterious the acquisition of the rest of the language—which, including the lexicon, constitutes *most* of the language.

Conversely, it might turn out that a learning theory adequate for the lexicon and the "peripheral" rules would, with only moderate adjustment or amplification, be able to learn the "core" as well. This is the hypothesis we are going to pursue here, leading in a direction quite different from the mainstream program. To motivate this approach, this section will briefly sample some "peripheral" phenomena of English, some well known, some less so. Aside from their shock value, they are presented with three morals in mind:

• "Peripheral" phenomena are inextricably interwoven with the "core".

• The empirically most adequate analyses of the peripheral phenomena conform to the Simple Syntax Hypothesis.

• There is a continuum of phenomena between words and rules and between periphery and core.

We will draw two important conclusions:

• An idealization to the "core", while a priori reasonable, has proven in practice to be systematically misleading.

• The traditional distinction between lexicon and grammar is mistaken.

The latter conclusion, also reached by HPSG and Construction Grammar, is in a sense our most radical break with both MGG and traditional grammar. It also points up the importance of choice of technology: only through using a constraint-based rather than a derivational technology has it been possible to arrive at this important change in our vision of what language is like.

1.5.1 *Words that go in the wrong place*

Enough is a degree word that modifies adjectives and adverbs, alternating with *so*, *too*, and *as*. However, unlike these others, it follows its head.

(12)   so/too/as/sufficiently/*enough big
       big enough

As a nominal modifier, where it functions like a sort of quantifier, it can go either before or after its head.

(13)   much/more/sufficient/enough pudding
       pudding enough

The quantifiers *galore* and *aplenty* also go after the head rather than before it—obligatorily:

(14)   many/numerous/*galore/*aplenty balloons
       balloons galore/aplenty

Responsible, unlike other adjectives, can occur either before or after its head.

(15)   a. the responsible/guilty parties
       b. the parties responsible/*guilty

The word *notwithstanding* parallels other prepositions such as *despite*, *in spite of*, and *regardless of* in its semantics, but it can go on either side of its complement NP (fuller discussion in Culicover 1999; see also Huddleston and Pullum 2002). The related word *aside* goes on the right of its complement, though *aside from* goes on the left:

(16)   a. Notwithstanding/Despite/In spite of/Regardless of your preferences,
           we're going ahead.
       b. Your preferences notwithstanding/*despite/*in spite of/*regardless
           of, we're going ahead.
       c. Your preferences aside, what kind of syntax is left to do?
       d. Aside from your preferences, what kind of syntax is left to do?

Hence and *ago* are either prepositions which occur on the wrong side of their complement (a) or intransitive prepositions which, uncharacteristically, require a specifier (b).

(17)   a. He's leaving three years hence = He's leaving **in** three years.
           He left three years ago = *German* Er ist **vor drei Jahren** weggefahren.
       b. He's leaving three years hence = He's leaving three years **from now**.
           *He is leaving hence.
           He left three years ago = He left three years **before now**.
           *He left ago.

How are these exceptional words to be characterized? In the old days we could formulate a rule of "*enough*-shift" that applied to a single word (cf. Jackendoff 1977); perhaps other, similar rules would apply to the others. Or we might introduce a feature [+wrongheaded] on all of them and have a general movement rule that applied to words containing this feature. However, such a rule simply presumes Structural Uniformity, the insistence that in underlying form these words must be regular. The feature and the movement rule localize the irregularity at a point in the grammar that preserves the underlying regularity in the language.

What does this story entail for acquisition? It entails that children hear *enough* in the "wrong" place, and, knowing that it's in the "wrong" place, they "correct the error" and construct a grammar in which it is in the "right" place in underlying structure. Then, in order to create the right output, children construct a rule of "wrongheaded-shift" and tag the relevant words with the feature that this rule detects.

A more direct alternative would be that children hear these words in these positions, so that's where they put them, in violation of the general phrase structure rules of English. That is, these words are learned with their position explicitly marked. In order to accept such a story, of course, we have to accept that the phrase structure order of a language is not totally rigid, but is rather just the unmarked default. We might then consider the stipulated positioning of *enough* et al. as rather like morphological blocking, where, for example, the explicitly stored irregular form *drank* blocks the form **drinked* that the regular rules would produce. This solution is of course more in tune with SSH, in that it posits no additional hidden syntactic structure.

These two solutions are not notational variants. The feature+movement solution sees underlying form as altogether regular, and deviations from it are the result of movement. The consequence is that the learner must construct considerable abstract machinery to correctly produce and understand these forms.[11] The direct solution dispenses with movement and abstract features that trigger movement, at the price of reducing the exceptionless regularity of underlying phrase order and of having some lexical items that specify their own position. The word contains (or *is*) a rule for its syntax.

A bit of evidence for the latter approach emerges from a *very* minor system in English that concerns names of geographical features. There are four classes of words, each of which dictates a different form for the names built from them:

---

[11] Alternatively, one might say the underlying regularity of *enough* is a fact of competence and not of performance, in which case competence is being ignored by the processing systems, a very strange position indeed.

(18) a. the Atlantic/Pacific/Arctic **Ocean**
        the Mediterranean/Black/Caspian/Aegean **Sea**
        the Mississippi/Hudson/Danube **River**
    b. the **Bay** of Fundy/Biscay
        the **Gulf** of Mexico/Aqaba
        the **Isle** of Man
    c. Beaver/Wissahickon **Creek**
        Loon/Arrowhead **Lake**
        Biscayne/Hudson/Buzzard's **Bay**
        Vancouver/Mackinaw **Island**
        Spot/Claypit/College **Pond**
        Laurel/Sideling **Hill**
        Loon/Sugarloaf **Mountain**
    d. **Lake** Michigan/Superior/Geneva
        Mount Everest/Washington/Monadnock

These words are productive, so they apply to fictional place names as well, e.g. *the Bojoric Sea*, not **Sea Bojoric*, and *Gloggle Mountain* but *Mount Gloggle*. (It so happens that *lake* and *bay* go in two classes—though a different two—so one has to learn each lake's and each bay's name individually.) Now this is no fancy recursive system, but it illustrates that a word can carry in its lexical entry a specific grammatical frame into which it fits. (It's certainly not the case that a rule dictates that *Mount* moves around the name preceding it in underlying structure, and that *Lake* moves around just some of the names preceding it in underlying structure!) This is just what we're proposing for *enough* et al. If the grammar/lexicon needs this for the *really* peripheral system illustrated in (18), why not use it as well for exceptional deviations from core phrase order?

1.5.2 Sluice-stranding

(19a) is clearly understood as meaning the same as (19b).

(19) a. John went to NY with someone, but I couldn't find out who with.
    b. John went to NY with someone, but I couldn't find out who John
        went to NY with.

(19a) is a case of what Ross (1969a) calls "sluicing", where an isolated *wh*-phrase stands in the place of an understood indirect question. It is especially interesting because it contains not only the *wh*-phrase but also a preposition from whose complement the *wh*-phrase has apparently been moved. Culicover (1999) (where there is more detailed discussion) calls this case "sluice-stranding". The issue for syntax, of course, is the source of the syntactic fragment *who with*. As usual, the strategy in MGG, following Interface and Structural Uniformity, is to derive it from an underlying regular structure, in fact from the underlying structure responsible for (19b). The issue is how *who with* gets there.

The literature offers two main possibilities. Both assume what we will call Derivational Uniformity: since sluice-stranding is understood like a *wh*-question, it must undergo *wh*-movement. The first analysis, represented by Ross himself, assumes an underlying form of the usual sort; then *who* moves to the front in the usual fashion. The omitted part then deletes (alternatively it could be empty to start with), leaving just the fragment *with*. The other analysis, of which Lobeck (1995) is representative, first fronts the entire PP. Then—on the condition of the rest of the sentence being empty, either by deletion or by base generation—*who* is moved around the preposition.

(20)   a.   *Ross's derivation*
             ... but I couldn't find out [CP John went to NY with who] ⇒
                                          [who John went to NY with t] ⇒ [who with]
       b.   *Lobeck's derivation*
             ... but I couldn't find out [CP with who(m) John went to NY t] ⇒
                                          [CP with who(m)] ⇒ [CP who with]

The difficulty is that sluice-stranding is both more productive and more restricted than these accounts would suggest. As for productivity: Ross notes that sluicing is possible where the purported extraction site normally forbids extraction. (21a) illustrates for ordinary sluicing of a PP; (21b) illustrates for sluice-stranding.

(21)   I saw a fabulous ad for a Civil War book, but I can't remember
       a.   by whom.
       b.   who by.
       c.   *by whom I saw a fabulous ad for a Civil War book.
       d.   *who I saw a fabulous ad for a Civil War book by.

As for restrictiveness: sluice-stranding severely constrains what combinations of *wh*-word and preposition are acceptable. (22) shows a range of possibilities with normal sluicing of a PP, all of which are acceptable. (23) shows that only a curiously restricted range of these are grammatical with sluice-stranding. In particular, different *wh*-words are felicitous with different lists of prepositions, e.g. *what about* but *who about*.

(22)   *Normal pied-piped preposition*
       ... but I couldn't figure out
       a.   with/to/from/for/next to/about/beside whom

b. with/for/from/of/on/in/about/at/before/into/near beside what

c. for/by/with how much

d. to/from/near where

e. with/to/from/next to/about/beside which (book)

(23) *Sluice-stranding*

... but I couldn't figure out

a. who with/to/from/for/*next to/*about/*beside

b. what with/for/from/of/on/in/about/at/

c. how much for/*by/*with

d. where to/from/*near

e. * which (book) with/to/from/next to/about/beside

The upshot is that under standard assumptions, sentences with sluice-stranding have perfectly regular underlying structure; but (a) they are derived by applications of *wh*-movement that sometimes violate the regular constraints on movement, and (b) the acceptable combinations of *wh*-word+preposition nevertheless must be learned pretty much one by one (though there are sub-regularities that have the flavor of those in semiproductive morphology). What does this imply about acquisition? Since UG is supposed to take care of the constraints on movement, it must contain a rider that abrogates the constraints when movement takes place across deleted (or empty) structure—this is Ross's proposal. How do we feel about this, aside from the fact that it makes the analysis work? Is it an *explanation*? Moreover, once this is accounted for, there is the fact that the learner can make no secure generalizations about which instances of sluice-stranding are possible.

Suppose instead that the learner acquires the possible forms of sluice-stranding directly, without reconstructing a derivation from a regular sentential underlying structure. There is after all only a finite number of such forms, perhaps fifteen or twenty. This implies that the interpretation of (19a) as synonymous with (19b) is not a matter of common underlying syntax: like BAE, it is a matter of the syntax–semantics interface. And the bizarre syntax of the construction is not a matter of derivation from a fully regular form; rather, like BAE, it just is a fact of English that such forms are possible. This would be the conclusion urged by the Simpler Syntax Hypothesis, as by now should begin to sound familiar.

This case presents two complications beyond those of *enough* et al. The first is that the peculiarity of sluice-stranding cannot be localized in particular words. It is not *who, what, how much*, and *where* per se that are exceptional, nor is it particular prepositions. Thus no distribution of features on individual words can account for the exceptionality. Rather, what is exceptional is the syntactic structure itself. Sluice-stranding extends the normal sluicing structure to a *wh*-phrase plus a stranded preposition. It is sufficiently special that its individual cases must be learned one by one. But these cases are not marked on individual words: it is the combination of words that is idiosyncratic.

The other new thing here is that sluice-stranding, because it involves *wh*-phrases, superficially looks like a case of *wh*-movement, one of the "core" rules of grammar. But if the *wh*-phrase in sluice-stranding is interpreted without movement from a canonical underlying form, what does this say about normal sluicing, not to mention *wh*-movement itself? Is movement the right analysis? We put these questions off until Chapters 7 and 9. Our purpose for the moment is to show how consideration of the "periphery" leads to questions about the basic assumptions surrounding analyses of the "core". If the analysis of clause-initial *wh*-phrases in terms of movement must be taken for granted (as is the case in MGG), there is no way to achieve a smooth transition from normal "core" indirect questions, through the marked case of sluicing, to the truly exceptional sluice-stranding.

1.5.3 *Constructional idioms in the VP*

Our last example in this section concerns the principles by which a verb's semantic arguments are realized in syntax, surely a supreme instance of a core system. The core principle is that the verb licenses everything in the VP adjacent to it, in particular direct objects. Adjuncts, which are not selected by the verb, are out to the right.

But now consider cases like (24a–c). These are syntactically congruent with verb–particle constructions like (24d,e), in which the verb licenses its complements in the usual way.

(24)   a. Pat sang/drank/sewed his heart out. [also *his guts*]
       b. Terry yelled/wrote/programmed her head off. [also *her butt, her tush,* etc.]
       c. Leslie talked/cooked/composed up a storm.[12]
       Normal verb–particle constructions
       d. Pat threw the trash out.
       e. Leslie picked up the garbage.

The difficulty is that in (24a–c) the verb does not license the complements. Rather, *X's heart out*, *X's head off*, and *up a storm* are idiomatic combinations,

---

[12] Unlike normal verb–particle constructions, these have fixed order with respect to the object—and different orders to boot. We take it that this is just a brute fact about these cases.

all of which mean approximately 'intensely and/or excessively'—that is, semantically they function like adverbials. Yet at the same time, they apparently "use up" the direct object position, since the verb is not allowed to license its own object:

(25) a. * Pat sang the Marseillaise his heart out.
 b. * Terry yelled insults her head off.
 c. * Leslie cooked eggs up a storm.

There are two possible treatments of this that preserve the regularity of argument selection, in accordance with Structural Uniformity. One is to suppose that in underlying structure the NP+particle combination is not part of the verb's VP but is rather in another clause or an adjunct position. It is of course never superficially visible in this putative other position—*but the child hearing this construction knows it belongs there!* It is then necessary to invent a rule that moves the NP+particle to its surface position and somehow guarantees that the verb has no other arguments. Such a solution is little more than a counsel of desperation.

The other possibility is to propose a "lexical rule" that freely converts intransitive verbs into idioms of the form V+*your heart out*, so that by the time argument selection takes place we have a unit that does not select any further arguments. This works. But notice that this claims that the lexicon as well as the syntax can accomplish free phrasal combination. *Drink your heart out* is not an not idiosyncratic phrasal combination like *kick the bucket*: *X's heart out* combines freely with verbs, within semantically defined limits. Such free combination "in the lexicon" is exactly what syntax is supposed to be for. So, according to this solution, the rock-bottom basic function of syntax has been abandoned for the sake of maintaining the assumption that the verb licenses all the elements of VP, an assumption that we assume ought to have lower priority in the theory.[13] Something is amiss.

The solution we favor is to preserve phrasal syntax as a locus of free combination, but to relax the absolute requirement that the verb license its syntactic complements. To be sure, the default (or "core") way to license constituents of VP is via the verb, but this is not the only way. Another way is for the constituents of VP to license themselves. Here is what we mean: (Pretty much) everyone treats *kick the bucket* as a lexical VP, where *bucket* is licensed by the idiom as a whole, not by *kick*. Likewise, we propose that [V *X's heart out*] is a lexical VP,

---

[13] We don't think such a solution in terms of lexical rules has been proposed for this construction. But it has been for several of the other constructions to be mentioned below (Simpson 1983; Levin and Rappaport Hovav 1995; Toivonen 2002), and the same objection obtains.

where *V* is a freely chosen verb and *X* is a pronoun bound to the subject; all of its constituents are licensed by the idiom, not by the verb. The idiom is combined with the verb in syntax, where free phrasal combination properly belongs. In addition, because this idiom prescribes the form of the VP, there is no room left in the VP for arguments licensed by the verb. The price for this solution is (a) a richer treatment of the syntax–semantics interface, in particular a new kind of principle for licensing syntactic complements of the verb, and (b) a new sort of lexical item consisting of a VP with a free choice of verb. If these adjustments were required for just this case, they might not be worth it.

But this is not an isolated case. English harbors several more of these VP constructional idioms, of which (26) illustrates four.

(26)   a. *Way-construction* (Jackendoff 1990a; Goldberg 1995)
           Elmer hobbled/laughed/joked his way to the bank.
           (≈ 'Elmer went/made his way to the bank hobbling/laughing/joking')
       b. *Time-away construction* (Jackendoff 1997b)
           Hermione slept/drank/sewed/programmed three whole evenings away.
           (≈ 'Hermione spent three whole evenings sleeping/drinking/sewing/
           programming')
       c. *Sound+motion construction* (Levin and Rappaport Hovav 1995)
           The car whizzed/rumbled/squealed past Harry.
           (≈ 'the car went past Harry, making whizzing/rumbling/squealing
           noises')
       d. *(One case of) Resultative construction* (above references plus Simp-
           son 1983b, Goldberg and Jackendoff 2004)
           The chef cooked the pot black.
           (≈ 'the chef made the pot black by cooking in/with it')

Again these constructions preclude the verb selecting its own object:

(27)   a. * Elmer told jokes his way to the bank.
       b. * Hermione drank scotch three whole evenings away.
       c. * The car made loud squeaks past Harry.
       d. * The chef cooked the beans the pot black.

There is no way to predict the meanings of (26a–d) from the words (for the remarkable subtleties, see the cited sources[14]). Yet in each case the choice of

---

[14] One might think the meaning of the sound+motion case is obvious from the words. But the words alone do not predict an important part of the construction's meaning: the sound must be interpreted as caused by the motion. This is demonstrated, for instance, by the contrast between

verb is free within semantic limits—as long as it is intransitive. Hence it doesn't make sense to list the full VPs as idioms like *kick the bucket*. What are the alternatives?

As in *X's heart out*, it proves syntactically and semantically difficult to derive these from underlying structures in which the verb licenses all the complements of VP (see references cited in ex. (26)). And a derivation by "lexical rule" subverts the fundamental role of syntax in forming free phrasal combinations. Moreover, since some verbs can appear in several of these constructions, the "lexical" solution is forced to say, for instance, that the lexicon contains not only the verb *laugh* but also the productively derived "idioms" *laugh X's head off*, *laugh X's heart out*, *laugh X's way*, *laugh NP[time] away*, and *laugh Xself into a stupor*.

The approach urged by Goldberg (1995), Jackendoff (1997b), and Goldberg and Jackendoff (2004) is to view the constructions in (26), like (24a–c), as lexical VP idioms with open verb positions. Unlike (24a–c), these idioms also select other arguments—within VP to be sure, but not selected by the verb:

(28) a. [$_{\text{VP}}$ *V X's way PP*], 'go PP, while/by V-ing'
      b. [$_{\text{VP}}$ *V NP away*], 'spend [NP amount of time] V-ing'
      c. [$_{\text{VP}}$ *V PP*], 'go PP, making V-ing noise as a result of motion'
      d. [$_{\text{VP}}$ *V NP AP/PP*], 'make NP become AP/PP, by V-ing'

Because the idiom dictates the form of the VP, there is no room for the verb to have its own arguments there; this is why the verb must be intransitive.

The sound+motion and resultative cases are especially interesting because they have no special morpheme such as *heart out, way*, or *away* that overtly marks them. All there is to mark the sound+motion case is the semantic clash of a sound emission verb against a path complement; to mark the resultative, the presence of an object and a PP that the verb would not normally license. That means that there can be no *word* in the lexicon marked for these special interpretations. But where then do the rules of interpretation encoded roughly as (28c,d) belong in the grammar? Well, if *kick the bucket* is in the lexicon, and *V X's heart out* is in the lexicon, and *V X's way PP* is in the lexicon, then the logical place for sound+motion and the resultative is in the lexicon as well. That is, the lexicon must contain, besides words and idioms, pieces of

---

The bullet whistled down the hall, where the whistling is caused by the bullet's motion, and **The boy whistled down the hall*, where whistling is an independent action. The intended sense of the latter might be conveyed by *The boy whistled his way down the hall* or *The boy went whistling down the hall* (for which, see n. 15 below).

meaning-bearing structure without phonological content. Thus we are dealing here with pure "constructional meaning".[15]

There is no question that the constructions in (24a–c) and (26) are "peripheral". Every language has to have a way for verbs to license arguments, but not every language has to have this other way to license arguments in VP. And certainly these particular constructions in English are peculiar and must be learned. But it is precisely in this that their interest lies:

• On the one hand, as with the other "syntactic nuts" discussed in this section, they are sufficiently idiosyncratic that they cannot possibly fall under a finite parameterization of the language faculty of the sort desired for MGG's "core grammar". On the other hand, they interact richly with the core system of argument selection—one might say they are "parasitic" on it, in much the same way as sluice-stranding is parasitic on core *wh*-constructions.

• Not only do they challenge the strict distinction between core and periphery, they challenge the even more traditional distinction between lexicon and rules of grammar, by offering a smooth continuum from clearly lexical idioms such as *kick the bucket* to "rules of constructional meaning" such as the sound+motion construction.

• They radically change our view of argument selection. An examination of the "core" shows us only cases in which the verb selects the contents of VP. These constructions show us other strategies at work which, because they exclude transitive verbs, must be in competition with those of the core.

---

[15] Another VP construction in English, unlike (24a–c) and (26), results in a violation of normal phrase structure.

(i) The cop came/went/ran whistling/smiling down the hall.

The verb in *-ing* form, semantically an adjunct, intervenes between the main verb and the PP expressing path of motion, which is a complement of the main verb. We know something special is going on because only certain main verbs license this construction, as seen in (iia). On the other hand, if the *-ing* verb is parenthetical (iib) rather than just jammed between the main verb and the PP, other verbs sound somewhat better. However, the parentheticals permit complements (iiia) while the nonparentheticals do not (iiib), showing there is an essential difference between them.

(ii) a. * The cop hopped/jumped/crawled/squirmed whistling/smiling down the hall.
      b. ? The cop hopped/jumped/crawled/squirmed, whistling/smiling, down the hall.
(iii) a. The cop crawled/went, whistling under his breath, down the hall.
      b. * The cop went whistling under his breath down the hall.

Our intuition (although this requires further investigation) is that this is a sort of serial verb construction, licensed by a small class of motion verbs such as *come*, *go*, and *run*. In this construction, a bare verb in *-ing* form is licensed in what would normally be a position for an adverb, and it is interpreted as an action accompanying the motion.

• We take it that these strategies, like those of the core, are not entirely wild; there must be a typology of them that explains the range of possibilities into which (24a–c) and (26) fit. That is, "peripheral" phenomena must be constrained by UG as well, and an idealization to the "core" leads us to miss whole ranges of phenomena crucial to the characterization of UG.

Finally, if this account of VP constructions is correct on empirical grounds (and we refer the reader to the references above for justification), they support the Simpler Syntax Hypothesis, in that, although the items contributing to syntactic structure are unusual, the syntactic structure itself has nothing special about it—no extra nodes, no hidden elements, no movements or deletions. Section 6.5.2 shows how these VP constructions are integrated into syntactic structure.

We note also that this "constructional" approach lends itself to other phenomena discussed earlier in this section. The "wrongheaded" elements such as *enough* and the geographical words such as *ocean* are like *X's heart out*, in that they carry with them a syntactic frame that dictates how they are integrated with the phrase in which they occur. Sluice-stranding is defined by an unusual syntactic structure [$_{CP}$ wh-word P], of which the possible instances are listed. It thus parallels the family of NP+particle idioms *X's heart out*, *X's head off*, *X's butt off*, etc., which have a common pattern made of known words but which have to be learned one by one. This suggests that at bottom all peripheral constructions can be treated as special sorts of lexical item.

We should add that we are aware of no attempts to analyze any of these phenomena (aside from the resultative and sluice-stranding) in recent mainstream generative grammar. Moreover, any attempt to do so will have to encode their idiosyncratic properties in some way; simply using the very powerful formal vocabulary of MGG to capture these properties does not alter the fact that they are idiosyncratic, nor does it count as an explanation any more than does the Simpler Syntax approach.

1.6 Core grammar and its relation to UG

We hear some mainstream readers objecting: "This may be all well and good for the periphery. But that has no bearing on the core, which has quite different properties altogether. The periphery may be learned by brute force, like words, but the core isn't. We know the core is very complex and abstract, so it requires a different sort of learning theory." We might start our reply by observing that word learning is far from brute force—it involves very sophisticated use of environmental input and Conceptual Structure. But let's put that aside and concentrate on the core.

Chapters 2–4 will be devoted to showing that a large proportion of the complex abstract structure claimed by mainstream generative grammar has been motivated by flawed chains of argumentation. Over and over, alternative hypotheses have been ignored, and foundational assumptions have not been re-evaluated in the light of new evidence. We will show that much of the complexity and abstraction has resulted from efforts to patch over earlier mistakes instead of going back and starting over—compounded by the effects of dogmatically accepting Interface and Structural Uniformity. We will further show that, once one recognizes these mistakes, it becomes possible for syntax to mediate between sound and meaning with far less structure than mainstream generative grammar has been accustomed to, even in the core, and with at least as much explanatory power.

Still, it might be that "core grammar", even if less abstract than usually claimed, is quite different in character from the periphery and therefore calls for a different learning theory. Here is the reason why we think this is not the case.

Consider again the constructional idiom [*V X's heart out*], surely a part of the periphery. This has to be stored in the lexicon, so that it is available for free combination with verbs. However, it is also a "parasitic" specialization of the more general principle of English that permits VPs containing a particle after the direct object. The standard old-time way to write this rule was as a phrase structure rule like (29a). But it could just as well be stated as the structural constraint (29b), a form totally parallel to the idiom.

(29)   a. VP → V NP Prt
       b. [$_{VP}$ *V NP Prt*]

Now (29) is not a "core" rule: the precise behavior of English particles is far from well attested in the languages of the world. And cousins of English such as German, Dutch, and Swedish have variants on this construction with slightly different behaviors (Dehé et al. 2002). We find it unlikely that these variants are realizations of different abstract parameter settings, where the parameters are of sufficient generality to belong in an innate language capacity (and to be coded on the genome and selected for by evolution!). So let us suppose that (29) is a peripheral rule of English. Still, it is more general in its application than [*V X's heart out*], because it has more variables in it and therefore allows more dimensions of variation in its realization. At the same time, if the sound+motion construction (28c) is in the lexicon, generality bids us put (29) in the lexicon too. (In a moment we will ask whether (29), like (28c), has a meaning component.)

But in turn, (29) is a specialization of a still more general rule of English, the one that says the VP begins with the verb. Written as a phrase structure rule, this is (30a); as a structural constraint, it is (30b).

(30) a. VP → V...
      b. [$_{VP}$ V...]

This is beginning to look like a "core" rule: in fact it is the setting of the "head parameter" for the English VP. Going still further, (30) is a specialization of an even more general rule (31): phrases have heads, and the category of the phrase is determined by the category of its head.

(31) a. XP →...X...
      b. [$_{XP}$...X...]

This is of course (part of) X-bar theory, a basic component of UG—at last a believable candidate for a component of an innate language capacity.

There are other rules of English that are not specializations of these principles, at various levels. The "wrongheaded" words of section 1.5.1 carry with them structures that violate normal head position for the phrases they are embedded in; that is, they are violations of rules like (30b). As is well known, gerundive complements such as *John's habitually drinking scotch* occur in all the syntactic positions appropriate for NPs; but they are headed by a V, so they violate (31). An even worse violation of (31) is the minor construction exemplified by *head to head, side by side, dollar for dollar*, and so on (Williams 1994a; Jackendoff 1997a; to appear b). These expressions occur in adverbial positions, have no obvious head, and permit no complementation and only extremely limited modification (e.g. *day by miserable day*). But they too are expressible in a constructional format.

This analysis leads us to believe that there is a smooth continuum of linguistic material in the lexicon, ranging from words through idioms through truly idiosyncratic constructions through more general but still specialized constructions to the most general core-like principles. There is no principled distinction between core and periphery, only a gradation of generality. This is in fact how the grammar is treated in HPSG and Construction Grammar. What are its implications for learning?

Our vision of learning (Culicover 1999; Culicover and Nowak 2003; Jackendoff 2002a; Tomasello 2003; Croft and Cruse 2004) is that the learner stores current analyses of novel heard utterances in the lexicon. The learning procedure then attempts to construct new and more general lexical entries, in which common parts of existing lexical entries are retained and differing parts are replaced by a variable. This makes the new lexical entry function as a schema or rule that encompasses existing entries and permits construction of new utterances. In turn, this schema along with others may be further abstracted into a still more general schema by replacing further dimensions of variation with variables. The result is a hierarchy of lexical entries, in which each layer consists of generalizations of items in the more specific layers below (the term used in HPSG and Construction Grammar is "inheritance hierarchy").

What does UG have to do with this? We conceive of UG as pre-specifying the highest, most general layer of the hierarchy. The gradual creation of lower, more specialized levels from idiosyncratic input is guided by the criterion that, if at all possible, lower levels should be specializations of the highest layer, so that the hierarchy is maximally coherent. Thus UG guides but does not determine the course of language acquisition. If the input contains curiosities such as *day by day* and *who with*, the child can learn them by the usual procedures, even if they do not fall entirely under UG. It is just that these constructions fail to generalize any further with anything else, and hence remain *sui generis* excrescences on the language. On the other hand, relatively "core" phenomena such as (30) are quite direct specializations of UG, and represent degrees of abstraction and generality that probably could not be achieved without the principles of UG as "goals" or "attractors" for the process of generalization. In short, with the addition of these "attractors", a theory adequate for acquisition of the lexicon and the periphery will also be adequate for the core.

What sorts of things would one want in UG, on this picture? Here are some pieces of the toolkit that UG offers for syntax, for a first approximation:

(32) *Structural principles*
    a. Basic principles of phrase structure
       i. X-bar theory: phrases of category XP, headed by lexical category X
      ii. Some of the most common alternatives such as the conjunction schema
    b. Basic principles of agreement and case-marking (where we mean morphological case rather than abstract case)
    c. Principles of long-distance dependencies, whereby an element at the front of a clause is identified with a gap somewhere within that clause, potentially deeply embedded (cf. Chapter 9)

(33) *Principles of the syntax–semantics interface* (cf. Chapters 5–6)
    a. Basic principles of mapping: syntactic heads map to semantic functions; syntactic arguments (subjects and complements) map to semantic arguments; syntactic adjuncts map to semantic modifiers

    b. Supplements to basic principles of mapping
        i. Some version of a thematic hierarchy, specifying how various con-
           figurations of thematic roles map into configurations of syntactic
           roles, specified in terms of position and/or case-marking
       ii. More elaborate marked options for argument mapping, including
          passive, and principles for "argument sharing" among heads (these
          include the prototypes of raising and control and also of light verb
          and serial verb constructions)
    c. Basic options for mapping information structure (topic/focus) into
       syntactic structure
    d. Basic options for mapping coreference and quantification into syntactic
       structure

In addition, there may be some more primitive "protolinguistic" principles that
appear as fallbacks when (32)–(33) do not apply:

(34) *More primitive "protolinguistic" principles*
    a. Structural principles: parataxis (jamming constituents together in
       some linear order)
    b. Interface principles: pragmatic construal in context (e.g. BAE).

And there are probably further "functional" principles that help shape formal
grammar in the interests of more effective processing, of which (35) presents
some samples (cf. Bates and MacWhinney 1982; Newmeyer 1998; Hawkins
1994; 2004). Because these have the effect of favoring simpler processing, they
may simply emerge as a consequence of historical change and may not need to
be an explicit part of UG, coded on the genome.

(35) *"Functional" principles*
    a. Structural principles: prefer putting all heads on same side of their
       complements.
    b. Interface principles
       i. Syntax to information structure
          Topic/given information early; focus/new information late
       ii. Syntax to prosody
          Short constituents early; long constituents late (motivating e.g.
          rules of extraposition)

(32)–(35) are concerned purely with the construction and interpretation of
syntactic phrases. Phonology and morphology of course have their own indi-
genous principles of UG. Conceptual Structure—the system which all of this
expresses—is defined by its own principles of well-formedness.

We have taken care to divide (32)–(35) into principles that specify autonomous syntactic structure and those that connect syntactic structure to meaning (and prosody). This accords with our view (section 1.4.5) that syntactic and semantic structure are to some extent de-linked—that there is no "rule-to-rule" homomorphism. The English verb–particle construction [VP V NP Prt], which played a role in the discussion of section 1.5.3, provides another example. This syntactic configuration is used for at least five different semantic purposes (Jackendoff 2002b):

(36)   a. *Prt serves as an argument of the verb, substituting for a directional PP*
          Dana tossed the eggs in/over/around.
          [cf. Dana tossed the eggs into the pan/over the counter/around the room.]
       b. *Prt is an aspectual modifier (i.e. not an argument of the verb), specifying completion*
          Gus ate the eggs up; Gus packed his suitcase up; Gus read the article through.
       c. *Prt and verb form an idiomatic unit*
          Pat looked the information up; Pat turned the light off.
       d. *Prt and NP form an idiomatic unit* (cf. (24))
          Terry sang her heart out; Terry studied her tush off.
       e. *Prt marks a VP construction whose argument is the NP* (cf. (26b))
          Leslie knitted the afternoon away.

We see no semantic commonality among all these uses (though there are some pairwise commonalities), so a common vague meaning seems out of the question. One could certainly call the construction polysemous. But to us, such a conclusion would miss the point that English has this structure available and, say, French does not. Perhaps historically the structure arose from one of the meanings in (36). But once there in English structure, it was available for other meanings to be poured into it as well—that is, it took on an autonomous syntactic life of its own.

We take this generally to be the situation; it is what it means for a linguistic phenomenon to become "grammaticized". For instance, it is argued by some functionalists that subject position is a "grammaticization" of topic and/or agent. Our point is that although subject position often plays this role (and stereotypically so), there are many other uses for subject position, including even filling it with a meaningless expletive. And in fact, in response to the grammaticization of subject position, English has grown another topic position, ahead of the subject, which is used exclusively for highlighting information structure.

We do not take the list in (32)–(35) to be complete or necessarily correct. And one of the most important goals of linguistic theory ought to be to establish the proper balance between purely structural principles, interface principles, and functional principles. Mainstream generative grammar, of course, has emphasized the first of these at the expense of the other two. We are attempting to some degree to right the balance.

This conception of the rules of grammar leads to a different take on the notion of what the child is capable of learning. As we have said earlier, a boundary condition on language acquisition is that, whatever the nature of the *grammar*, the child must also learn thousands upon thousands of *words*. It is clear that there is some innate basis behind this, but the quantity of information acquired on the basis of input has to be vast. The child also learns thousands of idioms—there are probably as many idioms in English as there are adjectives. Here we have offered the possibility of treating rules of grammar as "bleached-out" idioms: they are more or less idiomatic syntactic structures, sometimes with learned interpretations. Thus whatever mechanism is appropriate for learning words and idioms ought to be capable of learning rules as well, with some guidance from principles like (32)–(35). To be sure, rules may be more difficult to learn than individual words, because they depend on combinations of words and have open argument places—that is, they are further from the direct input than simple words. That might lead us to believe there are fewer of them than there are words. But how many fewer? If English has, say, 8,000 idioms, 500 constructions doesn't seem unreasonable to us. But of course it's silly to prejudge it; we await the empirical results.

There remains the issue of the complexity of UG. The sketch of UG in (32)–(35) is perhaps less complex than the UG of Government-Binding Theory (Chomsky 1981), but more complex than the aspirations of the Minimalist Program. Possibly it can be reduced further, and if so, that would be desirable. At this point, however, we leave the question open, and adopt (32)–(35) as a plausible working hypothesis.

Returning to the issues from the beginning of the chapter: The upshot is that minimizing the rules of grammar, either in terms of number or in terms of how much they can be absorbed into UG, is only a secondary goal. To be sure, one wants one's theory to be elegant, beautiful, optimal. But the actual "size" of a grammar is an empirical question. We think the primary goal of explanation is how the child acquires a grammar with a minimum of UG. We think we have shown how the Simpler Syntax Hypothesis is a legitimate route to explore toward that goal.

CHAPTER 2

How Did We Get Here?
Principles and Early
History of Mainstream
Syntax

Before undertaking a reconstruction of syntactic theory along the lines of the Simpler Syntax Hypothesis, it is useful to engage in some reflection, and ask why one should want to give up an approach as apparently successful as MGG. The next three chapters take on this burden. This chapter and the next undertake a survey of the historical and conceptual development of mainstream generative grammar. Our major concern is to understand where in the development of the successive versions of mainstream theory there were clear empirical motivations for innovation, and to what extent various aspects of these theories were motivated instead on the basis of general methodological principles that were perhaps not even well articulated. One of the most important of these principles is what we will call Uniformity, three cases of which were introduced in Chapter 1. We will discuss it further in section 2.1.2.

It might appear at first blush that empirical and conceptual factors should be paramount in the development of MGG. However, a close examination of the history shows that the nature of scientific practice is at least as central to an understanding of how the field has developed. Section 2.1.3 will outline some practical factors in the conception of "theoretical elegance" that have contributed to the style of syntactic argumentation. We assign them special prominence not only because of their importance but also because of the fact that as far as we know their proper role in the development of the theory has never been fully articulated.

Section 2.2 summarizes the key considerations that underlie all subsequent development of MGG: briefly, that the English active and passive constructions are related in a way that can *only* be captured in transformational terms. We show how Uniformity has been used to produce first the Standard Theory (*Syntactic Structures* (Chomsky 1957) through *Aspects* (Chomsky 1965)), and then key components of various versions of the Extended Standard Theory (especially the *Conditions* framework (Chomsky 1973) and the *Barriers* framework (Chomsky 1986a)).

Section 3.1 explores the consequences of a particular instantiation of Uniformity, called UTAH (Uniform Theta-role Assignment Hypothesis). Repeated application of UTAH drives the development of MGG from Government/Binding Theory to later Principles and Parameters Theory. Section 3.2 considers the Minimalist Program in light of this development, and highlights what aspects of MP are shared with earlier theories. In section 3.3 we show how the application of Uniformity in the development of MGG has produced the consequence that the Minimalist Program is indistinguishable in its essential architecture from Generative Semantics, long discredited. Strikingly, many of the key arguments raised against Generative Semantics (see especially Chomsky 1971) are directly applicable to the Minimalist Program.

Finally, section 3.4 outlines the architecture of a theory that incorporates alternatives to the formal devices in MGG which are motivated principally by Uniformity rather than empirical considerations, and which moreover introduce an arguably unacceptable cost in terms of theoretical complexity elsewhere in the grammar. The theory of Simpler Syntax, to be developed in the rest of this study, is designed along the lines of this new architecture.

2.1 Principles of argumentation in mainstream syntax

2.1.1 *General considerations*

Theoretical development in science is not always driven by the need to revise current theories in the light of empirical discoveries. Much development is driven by judgments that a particular theory can be revised in the direction of greater naturalness, generality, or simplicity without significant loss of empirical coverage. Sometimes, such theory revision actually leads to broader empirical coverage, which suggests that the general methodological approach is a valid one. Such is the case in physics, in particular, where the results of imposing a very demanding criterion of mathematical elegance and simplicity have been impressive and numerous.

However, language is a biological, cognitive, and psychological phenomenon. Its properties are not quantifiable, for the most part, and thus the kind of mathematics suited to physics is not applicable to linguistics. In particular, the fact that language must be learned imposes different constraints on the adequacy of a linguistic theory. As discussed in Chapter 1, various criteria for simplicity can be applied to linguistic theory, based on (a) theoretical elegance, (b) the need for the grammar to be learnable, and (c) the need for UG, the innate component of language, to be genetically codable and amenable to incremental evolution by natural selection. As stressed in Chapter 1, simplicity and economy must be weighed against empirical adequacy.

We wish to suggest here that arguments for simplicity in the criteria of mainstream syntactic theory have often been justified by a basic aesthetic principle that Chapter 1 called Uniformity.

2.1.2 Uniformity

The basic idea behind Uniformity is that whenever it is possible to analyze two disparate phenomena as instances of a single uniform phenomenon, the theory must lead us to do so. Occam's Razor says you should not multiply entities needlessly. The reasoning in syntactic argumentation is that if we assume Uniformity, we should strive always to use an existing device or structure or relation or rule in analyzing a new phenomenon.

Let us elaborate on the three different instantiations of Uniformity presented in Chapter 1:

Structural Uniformity
An apparently defective or misordered structure is actually a distorted regular form.

We saw this in the previous chapter, in the proposal that *enough* is inserted in a regular position for a degree word, then moved around its head. We also saw it in the proposal that bare argument ellipsis actually has the syntactic structure of a sentence. A more central case would be the proposal that infinitivals and gerunds always have syntactic subjects, either trace or PRO, so that they are structurally assimilated to garden-variety tensed clauses. This last proposal also leads to the conclusion that languages like Spanish and Italian are "pro-drop" languages—that is, that all sentences in these languages have syntactic subjects, some of which are deleted or otherwise rendered phonetically null in the course of the derivation. Yet another application of Structural Uniformity is the proposal (Kayne 1994) that underlying syntactic structure is uniformly binary and right branching, which we take up in Chapter 4.

Interface Uniformity (IU)

The syntax–semantics interface is maximally simple, in that meaning maps transparently onto syntactic structure; and it is maximally uniform, so that the same meaning always maps onto the same syntactic structure.

As a consequence, if two sentences with apparently different syntactic structures paraphrase or semantically parallel each other, they must be related by derivation to a common or parallel syntactic structure at the level of syntax that interfaces with semantics (e.g. Deep Structure in the Standard Theory, LF in PPT). Interface Uniformity applies in bare argument ellipsis, in that the interpretation parallels that of a full sentence. And it also applies in the case of absent subjects, since infinitives and gerunds are interpreted "as if" they had subjects.

A stronger version of Interface Uniformity proposes in addition the converse: if a sentence is ambiguous but none of its words are, it must be related by derivation to two distinct syntactic structures at the interface level. For example, Strong Interface Uniformity motivates proposals that quantifier scope ambiguities are due to syntactic ambiguity at the interface level (Deep Structure in 1960s "abstract syntax" (Lakoff 1965/70), LF in PPT).

Derivational Uniformity

Where possible, the derivations of sentences are maximally uniform.

This form of uniformity lies behind proposals, for instance, that languages with *wh*-in-situ actually undergo *wh*-movement, but in a "covert" component mapping from "overt" syntax to LF; that sluice-stranding is derived by *wh*-movement plus deletion; and that languages without overt case have "abstract case" which participates in case-checking just like overt case.

In practice, though, Uniformity is not simply the application of Occam's Razor, for it typically comes with a cost: in the course of eliminating entities in one domain, one often has to multiply entities in another domain. Consider for the sake of illustration Kayne's (1994) proposal that underlying syntactic structure is uniformly binary and right branching. The empirical motivation for this proposal is that languages show numerous left–right asymmetries; for example, languages have *wh*-movement to the left, but never to the right (Baker 1970: 207–8; Bresnan 1972). The advantage is a reduction in the number of branching possibilities for [A B C] and more complex structures: the only possibility is [A [B C]]. The cost is the burden of explaining, first, why some constructions appear to be left-branching, and second, if all left-branching is derived by movement, why such movement should occur, other than to help the theoretician avoid the consequences of the superficially counterfactual assumption that all branching is to the right. The mechanisms for ensuring that the correct superficial orders are derived (e.g. in head-final languages like Japanese) are non-trivial, and not required in accounts that do not assume uniform right branching. We return to this issue in Chapter 4.

Uniformity has been used from the very earliest work in generative grammar. Chomsky (1957) argues that the close semantic similarity between the active and the passive (as reflected in selectional restrictions on active and passive verbs) can be captured if the two share the same underlying structure—i.e. he is arguing from Interface Uniformity. The cost of underlying uniformity is a transformation that derives the passive order from the active. At the time, such a multiplication of entities was seen, in linguistics at least, not as a violation of Occam's Razor but as a welcome revelation regarding the nature of language and thus of important aspects of the architecture of the human mind. (We discuss Chomsky's arguments in more detail below.)

An early formal articulation of Uniformity as a methodological principle appears in Katz and Postal (1964: 157):

Throughout the discussion of apparent counterexamples we have tacitly made use of a principle whose explicit formulation should have heuristic value for those engaged in investigating syntactic structure. This principle, it should be stressed, is not a statement in the linguistic description of a language, nor is it a statement in linguistic theory, but rather it is a rule of thumb based on the general character of linguistic descriptions. The principle can be stated as follows: Given a sentence for which a syntactic derivation is needed; look for simple paraphrases of the sentence which are not paraphrases by virtue of synonymous expressions; on finding them, construct grammatical rules that relate the original sentence and its paraphrases in such a way that each of these sentences has the same sequence of underlying P-markers. Of course, having constructed such rules, it is still necessary to find independent syntactic justification for them.

This rule of thumb is essentially Interface Uniformity as stated above.[1]

Chomsky (1977: 86) proposes a form of Derivational Uniformity: when two phenomena obey similar constraints, they have similar derivations.

The rule of *wh*-movement has the following general characteristics:
(49) a. it leaves a gap
      b. where there is a bridge, there is an apparent violation of subjacency, PIC, and SSC
      c. it observes CNPC
      d. it observes *wh*-island constraints

---

[1] Jackendoff (1972) observes that although Katz and Postal defended the weaker form of Interface Uniformity, the field nearly universally interpreted them as having demonstrated the stronger form. Interestingly, Chomsky (1965: 224) finds the Katz–Postal Hypothesis "somewhat too strong", citing arguments from quantification and from temporal and iconic features of discourse, the latter due to Grice and Jakobson.

The properties (49) follow, on the theory outlined, from the assumption that *wh*-movement moves a phrase (implying (a)), observes SSC, PIC, and subjacency (implying (c) and (d)) [footnote omitted] and is permitted from COMP-to-COMP under "bridge" conditions (implying (b))....

Now I want to turn to the main question of this paper, namely, (50):

(50) Where we find the configuration (49) in some system of data, can we explain it on the assumption that the configuration results from *wh*-movement?

In other words, does the configuration (49) serve as a kind of "diagnostic" for *wh*-movement.... The following remarks, then, have a narrower and a broader aim. The narrower aim is to provide evidence that certain examples with the configuration (49) may in fact plausibly be understood as cases of *wh*-movement. The stronger aim is to suggest that this may be true in general. By the logic of the question, the stronger proposal cannot be demonstrated but only suggested.

Chomsky goes on to argue that a wide range of constructions, including comparatives, relative clauses, clefts, and topicalization, actually involve *wh*-movement, even when there is no apparent *wh*- to move. The benefit of Uniformity in this case is that it is not necessary to entertain a number of different rules, each of which could have different properties. But the cost is that it must now be assumed that there are invisible *wh*-phrases with rather idiosyncratic distributions.[2] In Chapter 9 we will discuss an alternative explanation of the generalizations pointed out by Chomsky, according to which a "displaced" *wh*-phrase is a symptom of two more general phenomena, neither of which alone involve movement.

Structural Uniformity is also found in X'-theory of the 1970s: no matter what the category of the head, the structure of a phrase conforms to a fixed schema, with Specifiers, Complements, and a particular number of bar-levels. It was found to be possible to make all phrases headed by lexical categories conform to this schema, though often at the price of many independently unmotivated nonbranching nodes (see Jackendoff 1977). Starting with Chomsky (1986a), the Structural Uniformity of X' theory was extended to functional categories: first I and C, then a continually broader range of categories over the next decade, and to all categories in all languages.[3] The cost of Uniformity, in this case, was a proliferation of empirically unmotivated structures and rampant

---

[2] See Chomsky and Lasnik (1977) for one attempt to deal with the consequences. The need to develop an auxiliary theory of "filters" to deal with the overgeneration that results from a uniform account of syntactically diverse constructions such as *wh*-questions and topicalization illustrates our general point that use of Occam's Razor in one domain has consequences in another. For us the important question is whether the cost of a theory of filters is more acceptable than the cost of specific statements about the individual constructions.

[3] For discussion of the historical antecedents of this feature of the theory, see Zwart (1994).

structural ambiguity, as simple strings could be assigned any number of equivalent syntactic analyses.[4]

These few examples, which could be multiplied endlessly, should suffice to demonstrate the point that Uniformity in general is not equivalent to Occam's Razor. In syntactic theory, in order to simplify a theoretical account by making two superficially distinct objects the same, one must typically create some additional syntactic mechanism, syntactic structure, or syntactic representation in order to account for their differences. These additional mechanisms, structures, or representations are in general not independently motivated by empirical considerations, although it may be possible to reuse them for other analyses.

As suggested in Chapter 1, there is often an alternative: that the independently motivated Conceptual Structure representation, along with the independently required rules of the syntax–semantics interface, can account for the common features among the constructions, while their differences may remain the province of the syntactic component and the lexicon. Such an analysis (e.g. the semantics-based analyses for Bare Argument Ellipsis) may well violate Uniformity, but its overall cost may be easier to bear. If we have any general methodological message in this book, it is to urge honest accounting.

2.1.3 A consequence of Occam's Razor applied locally: VP-shells

As a more concrete illustration of the points above, we will go through an extended example, the development of "Larsonian VP-shells". Our intention is to show how simplification in one domain does not necessarily lead to overall simplicity.

Larson (1988) begins with evidence such as the following, concerning binding in the double object construction.

(1) *Reflexives*
    a.   I showed Mary$_i$ herself$_i$.
    b. * I showed herself$_i$ Mary$_i$.
(2) *Variable binding*
    a.   I gave every worker$_i$ his$_i$ paycheck.
    b. * I gave its$_i$ owner every paycheck$_i$.

---

[4] For some discussion of the strict application of X'-theory to adverbs, see Ernst (2001). There have been many articles demonstrating that aspects of X'-theory are not applicable to particular languages; see e.g. Gao (1994) for Chinese. The argument in each case is that there is simply no evidence from these languages to support the full X'-structure, and that to impose such a structure would entail otherwise unmotivated analyses and syntactic derivations. Many of these sentiments have been echoed in OT approaches to syntax, e.g. Grimshaw (1997).

[plus four other phenomena: Weak Crossover, Superiority, *each…the other*, negative polarity]

As can be seen, a reflexive must be to the right of an antecedent that binds it in VP, and a bound variable pronoun must be to the right of a quantifier phrase that binds it in VP. In sum, extending observations of Barss and Lasnik (1986), Larson demonstrates that binding in VP goes from left to right.

How is this generalization to be captured? Larson (1988: 388) considers two basic alternatives. We could make linear precedence part of the theory of binding, as it was in traditional approaches going back to Langacker (1969), and as Barss and Lasnik suggested. Alternatively, we could maintain that these facts are due instead to a purely structural c-command relation, thereby simplifying binding theory, so that it refers *only* to structural relations and not to linear order. However, traditional analyses of the VP, as in (3) (to be discussed in Chapter 4), do not display the relevant c-command relations and therefore are an obstacle to this approach, whatever its elegance and simplicity.[5] In particular, the direct object does not c-command what is to the right of it.

(3)

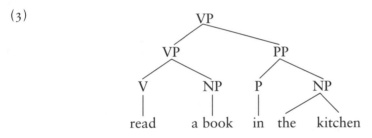

Larson proposes to favor elegance in the binding theory—a form of Structural Uniformity: all instances of reflexives should be licensed by the very same structural condition. It should not be the case that some are licensed by c-command, some by linear order, and some by both. He shows that it is possible to express the linear precedence facts in terms of c-command if it is assumed that the verb originates in a deeply embedded VP and raises up through empty verb positions (each of which heads a "VP-shell"), assigning thematic roles as its goes. (4) illustrates.[6]

---

[5] In this example and throughout we use the term NP to refer generically to noun phrases, and the more theoretically contentful term DP to refer to the specific analysis of NPs in which the head is the determiner D whose complement is a phrase headed by N.

[6] This derivation bears a certain resemblance to a proposal in Chomsky 1957 (76), where it is proposed that *Everyone in the lab considers John incompetent* is derived from an underlying form *Everyone in the lab [considers incompetent] John*. We are grateful to Jim Blevins for pointing out this precedent.

(4)

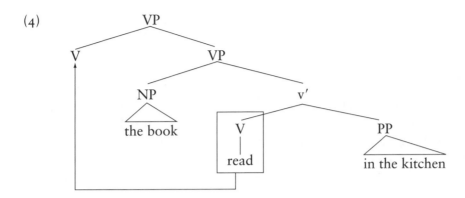

The verb *read* assigns objective Case to the NP *the book* after moving into a position where it c-commands and governs it. And in this structure, the direct object c-commands, and thus may bind, what is to the right of it.

As noted by Jackendoff (1990b: 427), Larson opts for this second, "more elegant" alternative without even attempting to rule out the first. Given the epistemological priority of linear order—it is immediately available to the learner in a way that structure is not—it seems to us that the natural approach would be to see how much explanatory mileage one can get out of linear order, before resorting to a radical reformulation of syntactic structure. But in Larson's response (1990: 590), he takes the opposite tack: "Jackendoff's conclusion [that it is simpler to accept linear order] is not justified . . . and indeed cannot be reached by simple inspection. This is because there is another possible explanation for the facts"—one that Larson takes to be simpler. The problem is that Larson is applying Occam's Razor strictly locally, to binding theory alone, and he takes as secondary the consequence that there is considerable new complexity elsewhere in the grammar.

We take Larson's conclusion to manifest three errors. First, as emphasized in the previous section, Occam's Razor applies to a theory globally: one must measure all the costs as well as all the benefits of a theoretical change. Second, more specifically, a theory of UG should always favor analyses that make learning simpler without adding innate knowledge. This consideration always favors linear precedence over structure when there is no compelling evidence for structure (Culicover and Nowak 2003).

Third, Larson omits mention of a further possibility: that binding theory also contains conditions pertaining to semantics, as had already been explored by Jackendoff (1972) and Kuno (1987), among many others (see Chapters 10 and 11). Of course, Structural Uniformity (all reflexives should be licensed in the same way), as well as Occam's Razor, disfavors this option.

Nevertheless, we should be prepared to consider it if the facts drive us in that direction.[7]

One important and influential application of the VP-shell hypothesis is due to Hale and Keyser (1991; 1993; 2002).[8] They claim that lexical argument structure is syntactic; and in order to make their proposal work, they assume that each thematic property associated with a verb is actually associated in syntax with a distinct 'light' verb. On their view, lexical word formation, e.g. derivational morphology, is syntactic, and obeys the same principles as non-lexical syntax.

On the Hale and Keyser account, everything about the meaning of a sentence is explicitly encoded as syntactic structure. For example, a sentence like *she shelved the books* has the syntactic structure shown in (5). The verb *shelve* originates as the noun *shelf* which adjoins to an empty verbal position; the resulting complex then moves through successive VP-shells to its eventual surface position. (We omit some details for simplicity of exposition.)

(5)

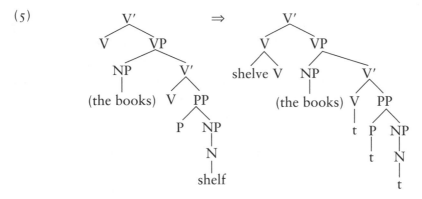

The property of being the theme is associated with the Specifier position of the lower (empty!) verb; this semantic property is derived from the overall interpretation associated with the structural configuration. Other alternations such as causatives and de-adjectival verbs also express thematic structure through syntactic structure.

---

[7] In addition to Jackendoff's (1990b) critique of Larson, which exposes myriad empirical difficulties in the proposal, critiques have been offered by, among others, Kiparsky (1997), Kuno and Takami (1993), Newmeyer (2001), and Wasow (2002). Nevertheless, on the whole it appears that researchers outside MGG found Larson's analysis too outrageous to merit discussion. Meanwhile, within MGG many researchers adopted it enthusiastically and set out to find ways to apply it further.

[8] There are important differences between Larson's specific proposals and the Hale/Keyser proposals, especially with respect to the assignment of θ-roles and the character of the 'light' verbs. These differences are not central to our concerns here, and both Larson and Hale/Keyser are credited in the literature with the VP-shell hypothesis.

The evident virtue of this approach is that it explains semantic parallelism by virtue of syntactic identity in underlying structure—i.e. it observes Interface Uniformity. Moreover, it purports to show why certain possible types of denominal verbs don't exist: independently necessary syntactic constraints rule out their derivations. In particular, nominal heads cannot lower to a light verb position,[9] and raising of a nominal head to a light verb position is constrained by locality (in particular, Baker's (1988) interpretation of the ECP).[10]

Hale and Keyser (1993) are not deterred by the price they have to pay for these virtues, namely a considerable increase in the complexity of syntactic derivations. Moreover, they relegate crucial empirical difficulties to footnotes. Their footnote 3 (p. 104) addresses the fact that the verb in (5) is pronounced *shelve* rather than *shelf*: "We do not attempt to account here for the morpho-phonological developments (final voicing in this instance) that characterize certain denominal verbs."

This minimizes a serious problem. Voicing is not the only issue. Another case is *wide* → *widen*, where the de-adjectival verb acquires a suffix. Even worse, some denominal verbs of removal such as *unmask*, *declaw*, and *defang* require a negative prefix, while others such as *skin* and *weed* have no prefix. Such alternations are not only not predicted by the Hale/Keyser analysis, they are technically difficult to implement. In the absence of concrete proposals, we will not engage in knocking down straw men.

Hale and Keyser's footnote 7 (1993: 105) addresses the even more vexing problem of the semantics of denominal verbs:

In assuming complex VP structures as the basis of denominal location (e.g., *shelve*) and locatum (e.g., *saddle*) verbs, we do not intend to imply that a conflation like *shelve* "means" the same thing as its analytic paraphrase *put on a shelf* (cf., *put the sand on a shelf* [cannot be expressed as] *shelve the sand*). We maintain simply that they share the same LRS [Lexical Relational Structure] (a claim that could also be wrong, to be sure). We will not address here the very real linguistic problem of accounting for the fact that conflations typically do not, in the full sense, mean the same things as the expressions usually put forth as their analytic paraphrases.

---

[9] One of these purportedly nonexistent cases is Agent incorporation, since an Agent would have to move *down* to its verb in order to incorporate. However, we have identified three verbs that are apparent counterexamples: to *chair* a meeting is to act as the *chair* whose agentive action guides the course of the meeting; to *father* a child is to act as the paternal agent bringing about the child's birth; and to *waitress* is to perform the duties of a waitress.

[10] A possible counterexample to this generalization is *mother*, as in *He mothers his students*. *Mother* is arguably in an adjunct (cf. the inexact paraphrase "He treats his students in the manner of a mother/like a mother"). ECP should block extraction of the head of the adjunct to the higher light verb position (Chomsky 1986a).

This "very real linguistic problem" involves at least three factors:

• Which particular nouns can become verbs? Those in (6a) do, those in (6b) do not.

(6) a. chair, table, fan, bed, panel, wall, carpet, mat, couch, ...
     b. desk, sofa, settee, rug, bathmat, ...

• Given a particular noun, which of many possible derivations into a denominal verb is possible? For instance, why does (7) mean (7a) and not (7b–d), all of which have parallels in other denominal verbs?

(7) Mary carpeted her van.
     a. Mary covered (the floor of) her van with carpet.
     b. Mary threw carpet at her van. (cf. The crowd stoned the President.)
     c. Mary put her van on (the) carpet. (cf. The wave beached the whale.)
     d. Mary put her van in the carpet. (cf. Mary garaged her van.)

Notice also the radical semantic difference between the verbs *father* and *mother* (see nn. 9 and 10), not at all predictable from the difference in meaning between the nouns.

(8) a. John fathered several children.
     b. Mary mothered her children.

• Given a particular structural realization of a denominal verb, how does the syntactic derivation encode all of the idiosyncratic information that can be expressed in a lexical entry, but that does not follow systematically from a syntactic alternation? For example, going back to the list of nouns in (6a), we observe that there is something special about each case. To *table* something does not literally mean to put something on the table, it means to postpone something, while to *carpet* a room means to lay carpet on the floor of the room. But these verbs are clearly derived from nouns. They cannot be derived through the syntactic mechanisms offered by Hale and Keyser, at least not without including an entire encyclopedic entry in the syntactic representation.[11] So there must be a process in the lexicon for deriving (or otherwise encoding) such verbs that takes into account their nominal sources, and the regular and idiosyncratic aspects of their meanings. Given such a process for metaphorical or idiomatic cases, there is no reason why more regular cases cannot be derived in similar fashion.[12]

---

[11] The need to include such information in syntax was the primary weakness of Generative Semantics, and led to its downfall (with the help of a big push by Chomsky (1970; 1971; 1972a)). We make a more detailed comparison of MGG and Generative Semantics in section 3.3.

[12] These arguments and others appear in Jackendoff (1997a: 231–2), Kiparsky (1997), Farrell (1998), and Fodor and Lepore (1999). For a response to the last of these, see Hale and Keyser (1999).

Although Hale and Keyser notice these severe phonological and semantic problems, they simply forge ahead with the more manageable technical problems presented by the syntactic machinery. They do not return to these issues in Hale and Keyser (1993), and treat them only in the most tentative and (by their own admission) clumsy fashion in Hale and Keyser (2002).

Why, if there are such serious empirical difficulties with the Hale/Keyser approach, is it nevertheless so generally accepted within MGG? There are at least two plausible reasons.[13] First, it assumes and extends the use of Larsonian VP-shells. Second, it purports to explain semantic parallelism without having actually to invoke a structured theory of semantics, a preferred technique in MGG throughout its history. The use of VP-shells and the syntacticization of semantics thus count as virtues of the approach.

2.2 *Syntactic Structures* through early PPT: transformational passive and its consequences

Having laid out our overall themes, we now undertake a review of the history of modern mainstream syntactic theory. We show that most of the machinery of mainstream generative grammar—classical transformational grammar, GB Theory, Principles and Parameters Theory, and the Minimalist Program—is a consequence of four fundamental axioms.

• The assumption of syntactocentrism, discussed in section 1.4: syntax is the sole generative component in language, and phonology and semantics are interpretive.

• This in turn encourages the second assumption, Interface Uniformity: in particular, lexical items always project their arguments into phrase structure the same way.

• Passive is transformationally related to the active by movement.

• Binding can be accounted for entirely in terms of syntactic configuration.

The edifice that is built on these four principles is complex and impressive. Some of it has been jettisoned in the recent move to minimalist theories, but much has been retained. Our overall argument in this book is that a careful re-examination of these assumptions and their consequences points clearly to a

---

[13] We are well aware of the difficulty of imputing motivations to a research community, and speculation cannot substitute for evidence. However, given the consistent invocation of uniformity considerations in the literature over many years as motivation for formulating a range of phenomena in terms of phrase structure and movement, we believe that our speculations here are reasonably well founded.

radical rethinking of the form of a syntactic theory and its role in a theory of language.

2.2.1 Uniform lexical projection and passive

A fundamental intuition of transformational theory is that the lexicon projects uniformly onto phrase structure, an assumption that falls under Interface Uniformity. Without this assumption of Uniformity, phrase structure is simply the organization of a string of words into phrases, or what the Structuralists referred to as Immediate Constituent Structure (see e.g. Harris 1951; Wells 1947).

The strict imposition of Uniformity entails that two strings containing the same lexical items and with the same meaning have in some sense the "same" syntactic structure, even though the strings may be distinct, as for instance in active/passive pairs. Since two distinct strings cannot have exactly the same superficial structure (in the sense of Immediate Constituent Structure), there must be another, "hidden" structure, distinct from the superficial structure, which the two strings share. Interface Uniformity dictates that this shared structure must be a syntactic structure. (Without Interface Uniformity, the possibility arises that the two strings mean the same because there are two different interface principles that map the same meaning to different strings.)

For convenience of exposition, we refer to the distinct superficial structures as S-structures and the shared structure as D-structure, although these are relatively recent terms. It does not follow from Uniformity that the D-structure of any given string is necessarily distinct from its S-structure, although the possibility exists that it is. If two distinct strings share a single D-structure, then for at least one of them the D-structure and the S-structure must be distinct. Hence there is some relation, call it T, that relates D- and S-structure.[14]

This reasoning is familiar to anyone who has been exposed to transformational grammar. It constitutes the basic motivation for syntactic derivations. From a completely naive perspective, however, it is reasonable to ask what the

---

[14] Current minimalist approaches such as Chomsky's (1995) Minimalist Program do not assume that there are levels of representation (D-structure and S-structure) that have independently identified properties (e.g. D-structure is the level at which θ-roles are assigned, while S-structure is the level that determines binding relations). However, there is an analogy in the MP to D-structure and S-structure. The analogy to D-structure is the primitive structure produced by the operation Merge applied to all primitives in the enumeration, while the analogy to S-structure is the output of all operations of Move, Delete, and Copy prior to Spell Out. Since in the MP all of these operations are interleaved, there is no single representation corresponding to the output of all Merges. Such a representation could be constructed for purposes of comparison, of course, and so we will not explicitly distinguish the MP from other derivational theories that assume Uniformity in subsequent discussion.

motivation is for associating a string of words and morphemes with two, and perhaps more, distinct syntactic structures, an overt one and a "hidden" one. Chomsky (1957) addresses this question in a chapter entitled "Limitations of Phrase Structure Descriptions", in which he discusses coordination, the English auxiliary system, and the passive construction, and argues that they must be transformationally derived.

Seen in the light of contemporary syntactic theory, Chomsky's arguments for transformations are no longer so compelling. For example, he argues that coordination cannot be accounted for by a phrase structure grammar. However, it *can* be accounted for (see Sag et al. 1985) if phrase structure grammar is enhanced by elaborating the syntactic categories with features. Such enrichment of phrase structure grammar was of course not available in 1957 (though experimental proposals were being developed as early as Harman (1963)).

Chomsky next notes that a verbal inflection such as *-ing* is selected by the auxiliary *be*. The problem, viewed strictly from the perspective of a string of morphemes, is that *be* and *-ing* are never adjacent, so their cooccurrence cannot be expressed in terms of the appearance and configuration of a single constituent [*be+ing*], which can be expressed in terms of a context free phrase structure rule. Such a constituent can be used to capture this co-occurrence, however, if there is a transformation (Affix Hopping) that maps the string [*be+ -ing*] *V* into *be V+ -ing*.

But again Chomsky's argument is no longer conclusive. If we treat inflectional morphology as the expression of a syntactic feature on the verb, then *be* can select a VP complement with the feature [+ *-ing*]. On the plausible assumption that the phrase and the head share such features, the head of the phrase will have the feature [+ *-ing*], from which it will follow that the verb that is inserted into the structure will have the progressive form. Of course, features such as [+ *-ing*] and the device of feature sharing among nodes were not available in 1957 either.

It is the argument from passive, however, that is most fundamental to the subsequent development of mainstream theory. Chomsky (pp. 42 f.) notes that the passive shares many properties with the active, and many other properties make reference to the active. Specifically,

(9)   a. *be+en* occurs only with a transitive verb
      b. V in the passive cannot be followed by a direct object.[15]
      c. An agentive *by*-phrase can occur only if the sentence is passive.

---

[15] With caveats for examples like *Sheila was sent flowers*.

    d. The selectional restrictions on subject and object of the active are reflected in the selectional restrictions on the *by*-phrase and subject of the passive, respectively.

Chomsky concludes (p. 43), "This inelegant duplication, as well as the special restrictions involving the element *be+en*, can be avoided only if we deliberately exclude passives from the grammar of phrase structure, and reintroduce them by a rule such as [description of passive transformation follows—PWC/RJ]." The elimination of "inelegant duplication" of semantic and syntactic restrictions is of course a variety of Uniformity—a combination of Structural and Interface Uniformity.

    Note the crucial rhetorical device "only if". What turns on this "only if" is the conclusion that there *must* be a transformation that refers to the constituent structure of one string in order to derive the constituent structure of another string. In other words, in this framework there is no other conceivable way of accounting for the facts. In the absence of a theory of semantics for natural language, this conclusion was a reasonable one.

    However, as was known early on, the properties (8a–d) do not always cooccur in passive constructions (10e–g) are from Emonds (2003); more such evidence appears in Postal (2004: ch. 8).

- It is possible to have a passive without overt *be*.

(10)   a. Robin got arrested by the police immediately after the rally began.
       b. We had Robin arrested at the rally.
       c. The first person arrested by the police was Robin.
       d. Arrested last night by the cops, Robin missed class today.
       e. The players heard insults shouted at them by the fans.
       f. Many customers wanted their samples handed to them by our employees.
       g. You may see/need your receipts processed by the file clerk.

- It is possible to have a passive of an intransitive (e.g. in German).

(11)   Es wurde   getanzt.
       it became   dance-Pst.Prt
       'There was dancing.'

- There are apparently transitive verbs that don't undergo passive.

(12)   a.   Everyone expected/wanted Robin to win the race.
       b.   Robin was expected/*wanted to win the race.
(13)   a.   This book weighs ten pounds/costs ten dollars.
       b.   *Ten pounds are weighed/*Ten dollars are cost by this book.

• As recognized as early as Lakoff (1965/70), there are also verbs that occur *only* in the passive, so on the transformational analysis they have to be derived by obligatory movement.

(14) a. Leslie was believed/said to be a dead ringer for Gertrude Stein.
       b. Everyone believed/*said Leslie to be a dead ringer for Gertrude Stein.

(15) a. It was known/rumored that Robin had won the race.
       b. Everyone knew/*rumored that Robin had won the race.

• There are many verbs that allow passive on a prepositional object (so-called pseudo-passives), as in (16); but there are also many verb+preposition combinations which do not permit this. The distinction appears to be in part semantic (see Chapter 6), so it should be invisible to the (purely syntactic) passive transformation.

(16) a. Leslie was being looked at by everyone.
       b. The bed has been slept in by my little brother.
       c. Robin's book was being talked about by the right-wing press.

(17) a. *This address was lived at by Einstein.
       b. *The bed was eaten in by Harry.
       c. *The bed was slept under by Harry.
       d. *The telescope was looked inside by the technician.

• *By*-phrases in nominals have to be agentive or instrumental—unlike in the verbal passive, where the *by*-phrase gets whatever θ-role the underlying subject had.

(18) a. The present was received by my mother-in-law.
       b. the receipt of the present (*by my mother-in-law)

(19) a. The damage was seen at once by the investigators.
       b. the sight (*by the investigators) of the damage

As observed by Bresnan (1982c), facts such as these undermine the original simple analysis of the passive construction, or require substantial complication (the introduction of dummy NPs, exception features, etc.). Subsequent work has shown that a semantic theory and a theory of argument structure can provide a basis for a non-transformational account of the passive (and other phenomena); cf. Bresnan (1978; 1982c), Brame (1978), Hudson (1984), Gazdar et al. (1985), Pollard and Sag (1994) and many others (see also section 6.3). These alternatives, like Chomsky's analysis, capture the commonalities between related constructions in terms of a common level of representation, but the common level is semantics or argument structure, not a syntactic level of D-structure. The distinction between active and passive is captured in the interface between syntax and these other levels, rather than in terms of the syntax itself. Crucially, these are not notational variants of the transformational approach, because the primitives of the level at which Uniformity is imposed are not those of syntax: they are semantic or lexical. In addition, these argument structure/lexical approaches potentially allow for a greater range of phenomena, because of the fact that some lexical relations may be deficient, disallowing either the active or the passive variant.

Despite the development of arguments against it and alternatives to it, the movement analysis of passive (specifically the movement of object to subject) has remained a bulwark of mainstream generative grammar. All of the substantive details are familiar to those working in syntactic theory, so we will concern ourselves with the details only to the extent that they help us reveal the logical structure of the theory, which we diagram below. To begin, as already noted, one consequence of Uniformity is that for some strings, at least, there are two (or more) syntactic structures, related transformationally. Specifically, the passive is derived through movement. We illustrate the connections in (20). (Here and throughout, we mark assumptions or stipulations in CAPITALS and empirical observations in **boldface**.)

(20)

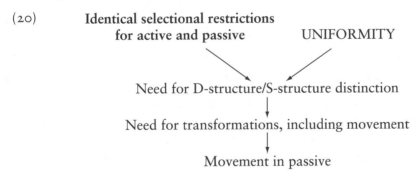

The conclusion that passive is movement does not follow directly from the hypothesis that movement is possible. However, under the circumstances this conclusion is unavoidable, since it was the passive construction that motivated the postulation of transformations in the first place.

2.2.2 *The Structure-Preserving Hypothesis*

An important theoretical development arises from the observation that the subject of the passive (a) is the object of the active and (b) is in a position independently required by the phrase structure. From (a) it is concluded that there is "movement" from the object position in D-structure to the subject in S-structure, as we have noted. From (b), as well as from evidence involving other constructions, it is hypothesized that, with a stipulated class of exceptions, all movements are "structure-preserving", in the sense that they replicate independently required phrase structures (see Emonds (1970; 1976)). Notice that this Structure-Preserving Hypothesis (SPH), if applied rigorously, removes from transformations any structural function. The only function of a transformation, given the SPH, is to capture the distinctness of S-structure from D-structure, in order to preserve Interface Uniformity.

Of course, it is also possible to conclude from this evidence that (possibly aside from the stipulated exceptions) there is *no* movement, and that selection and subcategorization are only indirectly, albeit systematically, related to syntactic configuration. This requires relaxing Interface Uniformity. On this view, subcategorization is an outcome of the principles for realizing semantic arguments through the interface. As suggested above, this can be accomplished through the manipulation either of lexical entries prior to lexical insertion or of an independent level of argument structure. Such strategies, which were not available in 1957, are fundamental to non-mainstream approaches to generative grammar such as Relational Grammar, HPSG, LFG, Role and Reference Grammar, and Construction Grammar. Chapters 5 and 6 will develop a version of this approach.

2.2.3 *Raising to subject*

Another important consequence of Uniformity occurs in the context of raising. There are two cases of raising, illustrated in (21)–(22).

(21)   a. It seems that **linguistics** is an interesting subject.
        b. **Linguistics** seems to be an interesting subject.   [Raising to subject]
(22)   a. I expected that **linguistics** would be a lot more fun.
        b. I expected **linguistics** to be a lot more fun.   [Raising to object]

As in the case of the passive, the parallelism of selectional restrictions (23) suggests that *linguistics* in the infinitival constructions is the subject of the infinitival predicate, even though it does not bear the same structural relationship to the predicate as it does in the finite case.

(23)   a. *Linguistics seems to have bought a side of beef.
        b. *I expected linguistics to have bought a side of beef.
            [Cf. *Linguistics has bought a side of beef.]

The argument is a familiar one and we will not elaborate it here.

From Structural and Interface Uniformity it follows that (21b) is derived from a structure in which *linguistics* is the subject of *to be an interesting subject*. This derivation involves a structure-preserving movement.

Raising to subject can apply to its own output, as seen in (24a). It can also apply to the output of passive, as in (24b). Hence transformations on inner sentences can feed transformations on higher sentences.

(24)   a. John seems to tend to play video games after work.
       b. Linguistics seems to have been abandoned by many universities.

Another classic example of application of rules in a feeding relationship involves the interaction between passive and the rule of raising to object (Rosenbaum 1967; Postal 1974). The latter rule makes the subject of an infinitive into the object of the upper verb (22b). One piece of evidence for this rule is that passive can apply to its output (25b).

(25)   a. Everyone expects the dam to break.
       b. The dam is expected (by everyone) to break.

Then the passive subject can become the object of a higher verb (26b), and passivize again (26c).

(26)   a. Robin believes everyone to expect the dam to break.
       b. Robin believes the dam to be expected by everyone to break.
       c. The dam is believed by Robin to be expected by everyone to break.

Hence there is evidence that raising precedes passive, but also that passive precedes raising, an ordering paradox. The paradox is resolved by assuming the Transformational Cycle (proposed by Fillmore (1963)): rules apply in a particular order first to the lowest embedded S, then to the next one, and so on, in the order (i) raising to object, (ii) passive. (This latter evidence for the cycle disappears when it is assumed that there is no raising to object per se, a point to which we turn in section 2.2.4.) The logic of the theory so far is shown in (27).

(27)   Identical selectional restrictions

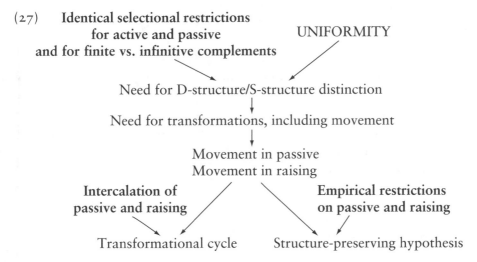

for active and passive   UNIFORMITY
and for finite vs. infinitive complements

Need for D-structure/S-structure distinction

Need for transformations, including movement

Movement in passive
Movement in raising

Intercalation of   Empirical restrictions
passive and raising   on passive and raising

Transformational cycle   Structure-preserving hypothesis

An important sub-area of research then arises from the conclusion that there is movement: why should particular movements occur or fail to? In the case of raising, for example, there is the question of why the subject of the infinitive cannot remain *in situ* in S-structure.

(28)   *It seems Linguistics to be an interesting subject.

One possibility, proposed by Lakoff (1965/1970), was that verbs such as *seem* have a lexical exception feature that requires raising with an infinitival complement. But lexical exception features for movement were never adopted in MGG. Another possibility, explored in the nontransformational theories, is that there is no movement, and that *seem* subcategorizes for exactly the forms in (21). Thus the semantic relations between (21a) and (21b) are again captured in lexical or argument structure relations instead of syntax. That is, again Interface Uniformity is relaxed.

Within MGG, though, the strategy adopted after the early 1980s (e.g. Chomsky (1980), following a suggestion of Vergnaud) was to posit a theory of Abstract Case: (a) every NP has to have case assigned to it, and (b) this case is abstract when it is not overtly manifested in a language such as English (and even when it is, as in Russian[16]). Then, crucially, nothing in the infinitival assigns this abstract case (or, Case) to the subject of the infinitival. As a consequence the subject is forced to move to a position that does receive Case in order for the sentence to be well-formed.

With respect to the cycle, the question arises as to whether other orderings of operations are possible, and if some are not possible, why. The solution in this instance was to assume that movement leaves behind a trace, and to encode the cycle as a set of conditions on the distribution of traces (see Freidin (1978; 1999)). We return to Case and traces in sections 2.2.5 and 2.2.6.

2.2.4 *(No) Raising to object*

A crucial formal property of transformations as Chomsky conceived of them in his early work is that the structural condition for their application is based on string-adjacency of constituents, not on hierarchical structure. For example, the postverbal NP to be moved by the passive transformation was identified in terms of the sequence . . . V–NP. . . rather than the configuration [$_{VP}$ V NP]; there was no requirement that the NP be a sister of V. In fact, in Chomsky (1975a) (written in 1955) and in Chomsky (1957), the tree was not the object of relevance in defining grammatical operations; the parsing of the string into

---

[16] See Zaenen et al. (1990) for some of the difficulties this raises.

constituents was. (See Lasnik 2000 and Blevins 1994 for discussion.) In part, this approach to transformations is a legacy of Harris's structuralism. But in addition, the formulation of transformations in terms of strings of categories requires a less expressive formal vocabulary than the formulation of transformations in terms of hierarchical structures. There are many fewer transformations that can be formulated in the less expressive vocabulary (assuming that reference to linear order is possible in either case) and so, other things being equal, it is the preferred option.

An important consequence of this lack of expressiveness, to which we now turn, is that the passive transformation can in principle apply to a postverbal NP that is *not* the object of the verb, and in fact it *must* be able to do so.[17] One such NP is the subject of an infinitive, on the assumption that an infinitive is an S. Structural Uniformity suggests that an infinitive is an S, because it expresses the same propositional content as a tensed S, with the same assignment of thematic relations, etc.

(29)   a. Robin expects that the river will flood the village.
       b. Robin expects the river to flood the village.

By Uniformity, these sentences would have (essentially) the same structure, that in (30).

(30)

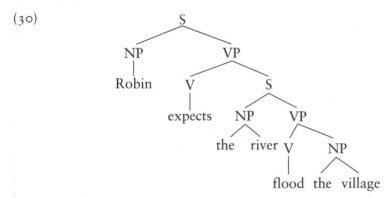

It follows from the less expressive formulation of the rule of passive that it can apply to the subject of the infinitive, even though the subject of the infinitive is not the direct object of the verb in the (narrow) structural sense: it is not the sister of the verb, and does not need to become the sister of the

---

[17] We are not sure if the absence of structural information in the structural condition was originally intended to have this consequence, but it does appear that Chomsky was able to take advantage of it in later work (e.g. 'Conditions on Transformations', 1973) with fruitful results.

verb.[18] The simplest assumption under the circumstances is that there is no raising of this NP to object position. We will refer to this assumption as No Raising to Object, or NRO.

Empirical arguments have been raised against the assumption there is no movement from subject of the infinitive to object of the matrix verb (Postal 1974; Postal and Pullum 1988; Ruwet 1991; Postal 2004). Some typical cases appear in (31); in each case something arguably from the upper clause, marked by boldface, intervenes between the putative subject of the infinitive and the infinitive itself.

(31)   Prevent-*type verbs*
       a. Robin prevented there **from** being trouble.
       Verb–particle combinations
       b. I figured it **out** to be impossible to square most circles.
       c. I made there **out** to be over 5 million termites in his floor.
       Intervening adverbs
       d. I believed her **with great conviction** to be a spy.
       e. They proved it **very easily** to be hot on Mars.

In (31a), *there* is the subject of *being trouble*; as an expletive, it cannot be a thematic object of *prevent*. Yet it is on the wrong side of *from* to be within the gerundive clause, where it belongs. Rather, it looks as though it is in the position of the direct object of *prevent*. Similar considerations pertain to the other cases in (31). Some of these cases can undergo passive but others cannot:

(32)   a.   *There was prevented from being trouble.
           (but *The demonstration was prevented from getting out of hand.*)
       b.   It was figured out to be impossible to square most circles.
       c.   There were made out to be over five million termites in his floor.
       d.   ?She was believed with great conviction to be a spy.
       e.   It was proven very easily to be hot on Mars.

In addition, one class of verbs pointed out in Postal (1974) appears to raise the subject of an infinitive complement to the object of a preposition:[19]

---

[18] We understand 'sister' here to refer to the situation in which two constituents are immediately dominated by the same node. This is the 'narrow' definition of the term. It is possible to redefine 'sister' differently, or to define 'direct object' so that *the river* is a sister of *expects* and/or the direct object of *expects*. Such terminological obfuscation does not affect the main point that we are making here.

[19] Postal (2004: ch. 2) points out that this case of raising is explicitly excluded by GB (McCloskey (1984), building on assertions of Chomsky (1981)), LFG (Bresnan 1982a: 348), and HPSG (Pollard and Sag 1987: 20).

(33)   a. You can count on there to be a great outcry when this data comes up.
       b. You can bank/depend/rely on it to be hot in Houston.

However, such evidence has not led to NRO being abandoned by its proponents (although a form of raising to object is reintroduced by Lasnik (2001)).

We omit here discussion of the development of the move from construction-specific transformations such as passive to simpler rules such as Move NP, Move *wh*, and, later, Move α. As discussed in section 2.1, this shift arose out of a desire to reduce as much as possible the expressive power of transformations, putting the burden of grammatical description on the interaction of general principles (Derivational Uniformity). The intended consequence of such a shift would be that the transformations would not describe the language—rather the principles would explain the language. We return to some of these issues in Chapter 9 in connection with long-distance dependencies.

(34)

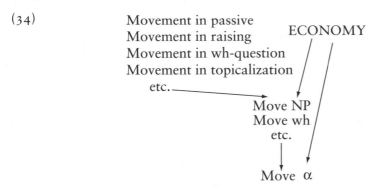

2.2.5 Government and binding

The consequences of NRO prove to be considerable. First, although movement in the case of passive must be able to apply to the subject of an infinitive (35a), it cannot apply to the subject of a tensed complement (35b).

(35)   a. Linguistics was expected [_____ to be ignored by the university]
       b. *Linguistics was expected [(that) _____ would be ignored by the university].

A potential solution is suggested by the fact that the subject of a tensed S cannot be moved into the subject position of the higher S by raising to subject, either.

(36)   *Linguistics seemed [(that) _____ was exciting].

The generalization between these two cases led first to the Tensed S Condition of the Conditions framework (Chomsky 1973), then the Propositional Island

Condition and the Nominative Island Condition (NIC) (Chomsky 1980). The first was a simple stipulation about the syntactic context blocking extraction, the second characterized the island in terms of binding of the trace of the extracted subject, and the third characterized it in terms of the Case assigned to the subject position. In none of these manifestations of the constraint is there a deep explanation, but at least the restrictions on the rule of Move NP were general principles rather than an idiosyncratic property of the rule itself.

In passing, let us consider the alternative possibility that there *is* raising to object from the subject of infinitives, or that, as in the nontransformational approaches, the NP in *expect NP to VP* is selected as the object of *expect*. In this case the problem illustrated in (35), which led to these developments, does not arise, and the constraints treated at length in MGG are unnecessary. The lexical account of raising to object 'explains' the same data as does the Tensed S Condition. If it can be argued that the lexical apparatus is independently required, then by Occam's Razor we would be justified in choosing a nontransformational account of these data.

A second consequence of NRO is that we must explain why the subject of an infinitive is marked with the objective case.

(37)   I expected [him/*he to complain].
         *Him/he complained.

On the assumption that the subject of the infinitive does not raise to become a structural direct object of the higher verb, it must be marked with objective case under *government* by the verb, which is not sensitive to the presence of the sentence node of the infinitive—where government is a new structural relation that must be introduced into the theory (Chomsky 1981).

Government is a relation defined on syntactic structures; it does not have a unique phonological or morphological realization; hence it is an abstract relation for which there is no direct empirical evidence. Note that while the passive transformation was not sensitive to hierarchical structure, government is stated over tree structures, either in terms of the classical c-command or the later m-command.[20]

If the subject of an infinitive cannot raise to object, it is necessary to explain what causes an NP to undergo raising to subject. The answer proposed in the

---

[20] α c-commands β iff the first branching node that dominates α dominates β. α m-commands β iff the first cyclic node (S or NP) that dominates α dominates β. It would be of some interest to compare the overall expressive power of a theory that incorporates such structural notions to that of a theory that only makes use of linear precedence relations, but to do so here would take us too far afield. The question is a complex one, since the linear precedence theory uses lexical relations that serve some of the functions that government plays in the structure-based approach.

Barriers framework (Chomsky 1986a) is that a verb fails to govern an NP and assign abstract Case to it if there are barriers to government of the NP by the verb. In raising to subject, among other cases, the NP will fail to get Case in its underlying position and therefore has to move to another position to get Case assigned to it. Thus the logic of the theoretical development proceeds along the following lines:[21]

(38)   NRO $\Rightarrow$ Conditions
       NRO $\Rightarrow$ Government + Case Theory $\Rightarrow$ Barriers

Again, either if there is raising to object, or if the surface object of *expect* is generated as such, this theoretical development is not needed.

But this is not all that follows from NRO. It is also central to the development of binding theory. The crucial fact is that the subject of an infinitive can be a reflexive or reciprocal bound by constituents of the higher clause.

(39)   The students$_i$ believed themselves$_i$ / each other$_i$ to have been singled out for special treatment.

In a syntactic theory of binding, the possibility that a reflexive can be bound by something that is not in the same clause (i.e. not a 'clause mate') requires that there be locality conditions stated in terms of syntactic configurations. These conditions are expressed in terms of government in GB theory: the subject of the infinitive is local with respect to the higher clause because it (but nothing else in the infinitive) is governed by the higher verb. The logic of the theory is summed up in (41).

(40)   NRO + Government $\Rightarrow$ binding theory

(41)   ECONOMY

Limited expressive power of structural descriptions of transformations

Morphological case

Overt binding (e.g. reflexives)

No Raising to Object ← Government

ASSUMPTION : BINDING IS SYNTACTIC

Conditions   Barriers

CASE theory

Binding theory

---

[21] Here and throughout we use the connector $\Rightarrow$ to mean 'leads to' without an implication that the relationship is one of logical entailment.

Although there certainly appear to be syntactic conditions on binding, the assumption that binding theory belongs entirely to syntax is not a necessary consequence of any assumptions other than syntactocentrism and Structural Uniformity; as mentioned in section 2.1.3, there have been arguments that semantics is also involved (see also Chapters 10–14).

Note again that either if there is raising to object or if, as in the nontransformational theories, the NP following *believe* in (39) is generated as its object, there is no need to make these further moves. Rather, the anaphor, being an object, is bound by the subject of its clause, just like any other object.[22]

2.2.6 *Trace theory and quantifier movement*

Syntactic binding theory leads to the postulation of traces (see Wasow 1972).

(42)   Binding theory + A'-movement ⇒ TRACES

The original motivation for traces was Postal (1971)'s observation that a moved *wh*-phrase behaves with respect to binding as though it was in its underlying position, in two respects. First, although a fronted *wh*-phrase c-commands the subject, it cannot bind a constituent of the subject.

(43)   *Who$_i$ did his$_i$ mother love?

Second, a fronted *wh*-phrase cannot be coreferential with a subject pronoun (44a), parallel to the situation when it has not moved (44b); the latter is normally ruled out by what has come to be called Condition C of the binding theory.

(44)   a. *Which man$_i$ does he$_i$ think that Robin saw?
        b. *He$_i$ thinks that Robin saw John$_i$.

However, if movement leaves a trace, then the configuration that rules out binding in (44b) will also appear in (44a): the subject pronoun c-commands the trace.[23]

---

[22] Since the superficial object functions at least semantically as the subject of the lower clause, it may bind a lower object, as in (i).

(i) I believe Mary to have behaved herself.

If we maintain Structural Uniformity, (i) is not a problem but (ii) is.

(ii) Mary believes herself to be the winner.

If we do not maintain Structural Uniformity, the situation is reversed. The resolution of this problem depends on one's theory of binding. For our treatment, see section 6.4.

[23] In the MP the trace is a phonetically empty copy of the moved constituent, which makes the Condition C violation more transparent and 'reconstruction' unnecessary.

(45)   which man$_i$ does he$_i$ think that Robin saw t$_i$.

Such phenomena fall under the rubric of 'crossover' and 'reconstruction': a *wh*-phrase in some respects behaves as though it is in both its position at the front and its "original" position. We discuss these phenomena in some detail in sections 7.5, 7.6, and 9.4.

Constraints on movement may then be reformulated in terms of the distribution of traces, leading to components of the Barriers theory, including the ECP.[24]

(46)   TRACES ⇒ Barriers

A trace, in turn, should not be introduced by a specific movement but should be a general consequence of movement, a conclusion that arises out of Derivational Uniformity. In order to make this follow, Chomsky (1981) introduces the Projection Principle, which generalizes Uniform Lexical Projection to all structures in a derivation: it requires that all syntactic relations hold at all levels of syntactic representation, which entails that all movements leave behind copies.

(47)   TRACES + Uniform Lexical Projection ⇒ Projection Principle

Assuming the strongest form of Interface Uniformity also forces a syntactic account of quantifier scope variation. It is a fact that (in English) the scope of quantifiers cannot unambiguously be read directly off the linear order of the quantifiers in S-structure. The following sentences, for example, are both ambiguous, and in the same way.

(48)   a. Every student read a book.
       b. A book was read by every student.
       a'. $\forall x$ (x a student) $\exists y$ (y a book) [x read y]
       b'. $\exists y$ (y a book) $\forall x$ (x a student)[x read y]

By Interface Uniformity, there must be a syntactic representation in which quantifier scope is explicitly represented. In Lakoff (1970) this representation was Deep Structure; in GB this level is Logical Form (LF). The Projection Principle and a generalized view of movement entails that there will be traces at LF. Therefore there must be a theory of movement that constrains unobservable LF movement as well as observable movement.

Empirical evidence from languages such as Japanese and Chinese, in which there is no overt *wh*-movement, originally suggested that the *wh*-phrases in

---

[24] A trace must be *properly governed*, which is a stronger condition than simply *governed*. For various formulations, see Kayne (1981), Chomsky (1981; 1986a), and Rizzi (1990).

these languages move covertly, to occupy the same position in LF as they do in English (see Huang 1982a). This argument was motivated by the claim that the distribution of such in situ *wh*-phrases is constrained by the same principles as overt movement. Although Huang's argument for LF based on in situ *wh*-phrases is still widely cited (e.g. Lasnik's (2002) tutorial on the Minimalist Program), evidence appeared quite early on (even in Huang (1982a), as well as Watanabe (1992)) that the constraints on *wh* in situ are indeed not identical to those on extracted *wh*, undermining the force of the empirical arguments for LF considerably. This led to a range of elaborations and modifications to produce this result.[25]

The logic of the theory at this point is shown in part in (49), to which other aspects shown in (27) and (41) should be appended. It is evident that many of the theoretical innovations are interdependent and mutually confirmatory. This gives the theory a rich and abstract deductive structure, which has been taken by many to be a desideratum of theoretical investigation, moving linguistics in the direction of the "hard sciences".

(49)

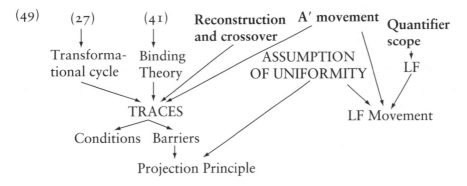

---

[25] Although the evidence used to motivate LF in the mid-1970s was largely what led Lakoff (1965/70) to propose that quantifiers are higher verbs in Deep Structure, to our knowledge the advocates of LF did not revisit and answer the intricate critiques of Lakoff's position such as Chomsky (1971) and Jackendoff (1969a; 1972).

CHAPTER 3

Later History of Mainstream Syntax

3.1 Late PPT: UTAH, Head Movement, and beyond

3.1.1 UTAH and its consequences

We pick up the narrative in the late 1980s, when important developments in MGG were driven by a major technological innovation, the operation of Head Movement. This innovation was motivated by a major extension (or perhaps simply a major reassertion) of Interface Uniformity, the Uniform Theta Assignment Hypothesis (UTAH) (Baker 1988: 46).

(1) **Uniform Theta Assignment Hypothesis**
     Identical thematic relationships between items are represented by identical
     structural relationships between those items at the level of D-structure.

This is a special case of the original Strong Katz–Postal Hypothesis, which implies that two constituents that fulfill the same semantic function with respect to a given head must occupy the same underlying position in the syntax with respect to the head. UTAH is a more precise formulation of Strong Interface Uniformity; in particular, it rules out the possibility of cases in which thematic function is the same but grammatical structure is different.

Baker (1997: 73) justifies UTAH on the following grounds:

Generative theory then as now aspired to achieve explanatory adequacy by having a very tightly constrained view of what syntax could do. However, in practice the result of this approach was often not deeper analyses of interesting phenomena, but rather a banishing of those phenomena from the domain of syntax—typically into the realm of the lexicon. Within the terms of the theory, this seemed regrettable: *if one is going to have a nontrivial syntax at all, then that syntax should be required to pull its own weight.* The UTAH, then, was an attempt to identify a domain in which the answer to analytic questions *must be a syntactic one* [our italics—PWC/RJ].

Baker's rationale for syntacticizing relations that were amenable to a lexical treatment is given in the following remarkable passage.

Outside of Chomsky's Principles and Parameters (P&P) framework, the most popular way to constrain the linking problem is ... to say that there is essentially no difference between the initial grammatical representation and the surface grammatical representation. This choice leads to the various "monostratal" theories of grammar, including Lexical Functional Grammar, the various Phrase Structure Grammars, Role and Reference Grammar, and others. Since the syntax proper is so tightly constrained, these approaches tend to take on a rather asyntactic flavor, with much of the explanatory burden being carried by the lexicon and/or the semantics rather than syntax. As such, they shade into functionalist approaches, which downplay the existence of syntax as something distinct from semantics, discourse, pragmatics, and diachrony.

At play here is a judgment to the effect that constraining syntax had better not lead to eviscerating it. Baker offers no *argument* against the monostratal approaches, whose syntactic components are, as he admits, highly constrained. He simply believes that there *has* to be more to syntax than this, and lays out a program in which this view is central. He is asserting not only architectural syntactocentrism, which is a legitimate theoretical position, but also a more dogmatic, perhaps even imperialistic, syntactocentrism.

The core empirical phenomenon that UTAH was designed to address is noun incorporation in languages such as Onondaga, whereby a noun complement of a verb can be expressed either as a normal complement (2a) or as a morpheme adjoined to (or "incorporated" into) the verb (2b) (Baker 1988: 76–7).

(2)   a.   Pet waʔ -ha-   htu-ʔt-   aʔ neʔ o- hwist- aʔ
            Pat past-3mS/3n-lose-caus-asp the   pre-money- suf
            'Pat lost the money.'

      b.   Pet waʔ -ha-   hwist- ahtu-ʔt-   aʔ
            Pat pst-   3mS-money-lose-caus-asp
            'Pat lost money'

Baker proposes to capture the identical selectional properties of these two constructions by having the head noun of the object in (2a) adjoin to the verb. The argument is of course exactly like Chomsky's (1957) argument for the passive, and in fact a proposal for Mohawk similar to Baker's appears in Postal (1964) and is defended on similar grounds.

What is novel, then, in Baker's proposal? Postal's work on Mohawk took place during a period where transformations were relatively unconstrained. After the Lexicalist Hypothesis of Chomsky (1970), which gave rise to X′ theory, transformations in MGG ceased to be used to produce derivational morphology, and in practice virtually all movement came to be movement of full phrases to positions where full phrases were licensed. Baker's innovation, then, is movement of a head, without the rest of its phrase, into a position where only a head, not a phrase, is possible. UTAH is proposed in service of justifying such movement. As we will see, head-to-head movement lies behind many of the subsequent changes in MGG. For instance, the VP-shells discussed in section 2.1.3 would be impossible without it.

But before looking for conceptual reasons to impose UTAH, so that head-to-head movement is forced by the theory, it would be important to ask whether such movement is empirically justified. At least one argument has appeared in the literature that suggests it is not. Rosen (1989) argues against Baker's strictly syntactic approach, on the basis of evidence that crosslinguistically there are in fact two different kinds of noun incorporation. In one of these, Classifier NI, the incorporated noun is not an argument of the verb, while in the other, Compound NI, the incorporated noun is an argument of the verb. Clearly, only the second type is compatible with a syntactic derivation. Given that both types of incorporation occur, Rosen argues that the more general approach is a lexical one. Anderson (2000) arrives at the same conclusion on the basis of comparable evidence. As far as we know the concerns they raise have not been addressed by MGG. In addition, Baker's (1988) theory crucially forbids incorporation out of adjuncts, as ECP violations, and takes the absence of such incorporation as evidence for the UTAH/Head-Raising approach. Yet one of the languages Baker (1996) cites as "polysynthetic", Chukchi, allows just such incorporations, as shown by Spencer (1995).[1]

We note also that an empirical verification of UTAH depends on an independent characterization of θ-roles, which so far as we know has not been undertaken in MGG. In particular, UTAH entails that in all argument structure alternations, either there is a difference in θ-roles or one form is derived from the other. (3) illustrates a typical paradigm in which θ-roles are apparently preserved despite surface syntactic differences. Many more such examples appear in section 5.6.4.[2]

---

[1] We are grateful to Andrew Spencer for pointing out this last argument. See also Van Valin (1992) for important empirical and theoretical critiques of UTAH/Head-Raising.

[2] Larson's (1988) application of the VP-shell hypothesis to the dative alternation only scratches the surface of argument structure alternations and in fact derives the dative alternation from two different underlying structures, in violation of UTAH.

(3) a. John gave the class [*recipient*] software [*theme*].
     b. John provided the class [*recipient*] with software [*theme*]
     c. John supplied/gave software [*theme*] to the class [*recipient*].
     d. The class [*recipient*] got/received software [*theme*].

For the most part MGG did not seriously address these difficulties with UTAH. Rather it pursued other consequences deemed to be of greater theoretical interest. For example, UTAH entails that every NP that bears the subject θ-role with respect to some predicate must be the syntactic subject of that predicate in the D-structure representation. This leads to a number of consequences. First consider (4)–(5). In the (a) examples, with the verb *found*, the NP *the man* bears the same thematic relationship to the predicate following it as does the subject of a finite or nonfinite clause, as evidenced by selectional restrictions (4b,c) and also binding (5b,c). Therefore *the man* must be a subject in the (a) sentences as well. But since there is no verb, it is necessary to invoke a new category "small clause" of which *the man* can be subject (as first proposed by Williams (1975)).

(4) a. I found the man /*the book asleep. (i.e. I found [$_{SC}$ the man asleep])
     b. The man /*the book is asleep.
     c. I believe the man /*the book to be asleep

(5) a. I found the man pleased with himself/*myself.
        (i.e. I found [$_{SC}$ the man pleased with himself])
     b. The man was pleased with himself.
     c. I believe the man to be pleased with himself/*myself.

Thus,

(6) UTAH ⇒ There are small clauses that have subject / predicate structure.

(For discussion of what the head of the small clause might be, see Stowell (1983).) In Chapter 4, we will give evidence that there are indeed such things as small clauses, but their distribution is far more limited than UTAH requires.

Second, control structures such as (7a) have the same thematic properties as tensed clauses (7b), again as evidenced by selectional restrictions and binding.

(7) a. The woman expects to surpass herself.
     b. The woman expects that she will surpass herself.

And in (7a) the reflexive must have a local antecedent, which cannot be the subject of *expects* if *to surpass herself* is a distinct sentential domain. Thus

(8) UTAH ⇒ PRO in control structures

Of course, PRO is a consequence of earlier assumptions such as Structural Uniformity as well.

Third, in a 'pro-drop' language such as Italian, what corresponds to the pronominal subject in English is typically not overtly expressed.

(9) Non parla   bene italiano
     NEG speak-3.sg. well Italian
     'S/he doesn't speak Italian well.'

By UTAH (as well as Structural Uniformity) there must be an empty pronoun in such sentences, corresponding to the subject θ-role. Similar and more thoroughgoing conclusions hold for languages like Japanese and Korean, where pronominal *non*-subjects may also be tacit (see Jaeggli and Safir (1989)). Thus

(10) UTAH ⇒ null pronominal arguments

Given the existence of small clauses, a more radical consequence of UTAH concerns the superficial lack of structural parallelism between small clauses and full clauses.

(11) *Small clauses*
         a. I consider [$_{SC}$ linguistics fun]
         b. I consider [$_{SC}$ Bill a genius]
         c. I consider [$_{SC}$ Bill off his rocker]
      Full clauses
         d. I consider [$_{CP}$ linguistics to be fun]
         e. I consider [$_{CP}$ Bill to speak French well]
         f. I consider [$_{CP}$ that linguistics is fun]

UTAH implies that the small clauses (11a–c), like any other complement, must be constituents. Since the subject of a predicate bears the same thematic role with respect to the predicate regardless of its precise location in S-structure, UTAH dictates that the subject must originate in the same D-structure position in all the configurations in (11). This position must be the minimal possible position, that is, within the phrase [*NP Predicate*]; and it must be independent of the inflection, since it appears regardless of what the inflection is, or whether there is any overt inflection at all.

By Structural Uniformity, then, the subject is always the underlying sister of a predicate, whether or not there is an inflection, and regardless of whether the predicate is headed by V, A, P or N. It follows that even in tensed sentences, the subject is the underlying sister of the predicate, i.e. V′ (the phrase headed by V), and in a tensed clause the subject raises to IP. This is, in effect, the VP

Internal Subject Hypothesis (VPISH), illustrated in (12) for a predicate headed by V.

(12)

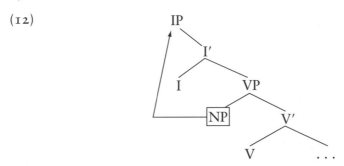

By Uniformity/UTAH, a nominal will have the same structure, since θ-roles are assigned in nominals as they are in sentences, and the subject grammatical role must have the same structural representation in the NP as it does in the VP. This conclusion gives rise to the DP analysis of Abney (1987), where there is a functional head D° corresponding to the I° of the sentence.

(13)   UTAH ⇒ VP Internal Subject Hypothesis
       UTAH ⇒ DP analysis

Thus, we find that UTAH leads to a uniform X′ structure for all projections of lexical heads, and unifies a number of previously independent applications of uniformity.

(14)   UTAH

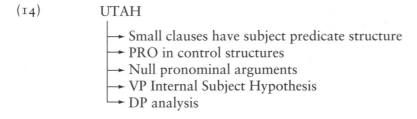

Another thread arising from Uniformity/UTAH concerns raising to object. There is no question that raising to subject involves movement (given the usual assumptions), because it produces a string that is distinct from that associated with the D-structure configuration. In particular, the surface subject is not the underlying subject. But in the standard cases, raising to object is string-vacuous (though see (31)–(33) in Chapter 2 for instances where it is not). Thus, as we noted earlier, in the framework of early transformational grammar, raising to object is not required in order for passive to take place. In fact a derivation involving raising to object is taken to be more complex than simply having passive directly move the subject of an embedded clause.

In later theory, a variant of the notion that less complex takes precedence over more complex is that movements do not occur unless they are required in order to satisfy some grammatical principle. Such an assumption can be made to follow from a more general intuition of "economy of derivation", i.e. that the derivations that occur are the maximally simple ones in some independently defined comparison set.

(15)   UTAH + ECONOMY ⇒ No Raising to Object (NRO)

This notion of economy of derivation is carried through to the Minimalist Program of Chomsky (1995), to which we will return in section 3.2. Thus the picture shown in (16) emerges.

(16)   **Selectional restrictions**

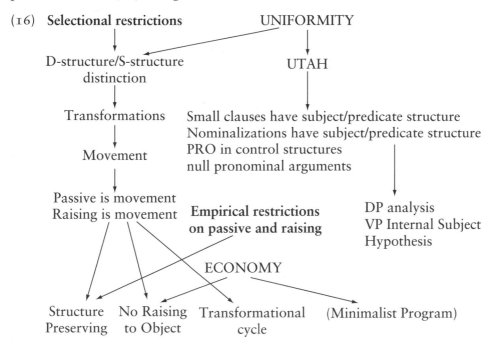

3.1.2 *Further consequences of Head Movement*

Another consequence of Structural Uniformity concerns phrase structure. Generalizing from the structure of NP and S to all categories, we arrive at the notion that every individual word in a string is the head of some maximal projection. This is a strong version of X′ theory, already anticipated in the DP analysis and the VP-Internal Subject Hypothesis. An even stronger version of Structural Uniformity suggests that, in addition to the lexical heads, inflectional morphemes and other functional categories must also head full phrases (these were treated as explicit exceptions in the early X′ theory of Jackendoff (1977)). The first such "functional heads", I and C, are rather casually introduced by Chomsky (1986a: 160–1), based on earlier proposals that AUX is the head of S and C is the head of S′(= CP).[3] The basic empirical motivation in this case is that subject-aux inversion in English interacts with *wh*-movement to produce the sentence-initial sequence XP[+wh]-V[+AUX]..., which resembles the order NP-V[+AUX]...in the declarative S. Moreover, only one *wh*-phrase may appear in initial position, which appears to generalize with the fact that there is only one NP in the subject position. Finally, and importantly, the inflected verb in languages like French, Dutch, and German undergoes inversion in questions, which can be formulated as movement to the head position denoted by C in the CP structure (see e.g. Den Besten 1986).

The full elaboration of this structure also interacts with the VP Internal Subject Hypothesis, the Structure-Preserving Hypothesis, and Economy. By Structural Uniformity, the subject originates in VP, under the assumption that the head V assigns all θ-roles to its arguments within its maximal projection. But the subject must move to a licensed (i.e. Case-marked) position in languages like English (a special case of the Structure-Preserving Hypothesis). It is economical to assume uniformly that such a licensed position is the specifier of a functional head, on the grounds that licensing between head and specifier is the only possibility. The specifier agrees with the head in the same way that the subject agrees with the inflectional head of the sentence.

(17)   Uniformity ⇒ X′-theory

(18)   X′-theory + VP-Internal Subject + Structure-Preserving Hypothesis + Economy ⇒ functional heads

Given that some of the functional heads are bound morphemes, there must be movement of heads to other heads in order to combine them in their S-structure arrangement.[4]

(19)   functional heads ⇒ head movement

Head movement produces the need for the extension of constraints on movement so that the heads, like phrases, will only move locally (Baker 1988). But this generalization is a welcome consequence of the analysis.

---

[3] Antecedents are found in Bresnan (1972), Stowell (1981), and Pesetsky (1982). For discussion, see Zwart (1994).

[4] Of course, use of the syntax to produce surface morphology runs into problems when the semantic complexities of derivational morphology are involved, as in the case of the Hale/Keyser proposal discussed in 2.1.3.

(20) head movement ⇒ Extended ECP

(21)

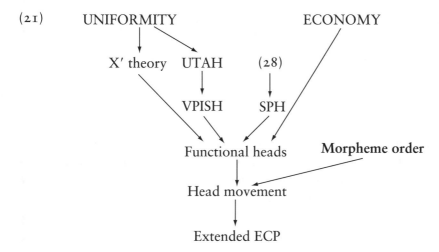

This "exploded" structure of the clause allowed for the analyses of Larson (1988) and Hale and Keyser (1993), as discussed in 2.1.3. It also formed the foundation for the influential analysis of Pollock (1989). Pollock argued that there is a basic difference between languages like French and English, evidenced by the fact that in French, the inflected verb appears to the left of negation and undergoes inversion, while in English the auxiliary bears these functions.

(22) a. Je ne parle pas français
          I NE speak not French
      b. *I speak not French.
      c. I do not speak French.
(23) a. Parlez-vous français?
          speak-you French?
      b. *Speak you French?
      c. Do you speak French?

Thus in French, the inflected verb appears to function as the head of the clause, and in English, the inflected auxiliary does. Pollock proposes to account for this difference by saying that in French the main verb raises from VP and adjoins to Infl, the head of the clause. Of course, this account is only available because the theory now contains the possibility of head movement.

(24)   *(French)*

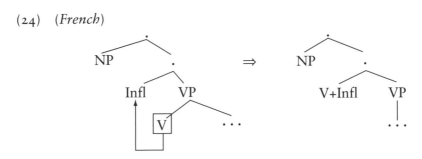

The question that arises in the case of such an analysis is why languages differ in this way. It is of course possible to stipulate that French has and English lacks V-raising. Pollock sought to situate the difference in the 'strength' of the inflectional morphology, a notion that was taken over in late PPT/MP. On this account, if a feature is 'strong', movement must occur before the syntactic structure is mapped into phonology. Lasnik (1999b) shows that this simple picture cannot be maintained, and that overt V-raising cannot constitute the only difference between French and English. English must have some form of Affix Hopping, where the inflectional affix lowers onto the verb. (Lasnik also points out a number of technical difficulties in making the Pollock analysis compatible with recent versions of MP.)

3.1.3 Branching

Uniformity and economy also suggest that all branching is binary. Much branching is indeed binary, e.g. where there is a head and a single complement or specifier. So it is natural under Structural Uniformity to stipulate further that *all* branching is binary (Kayne 1994).

(25)   Uniformity + Economy ⇒ Uniform Binary Branching

As will be shown in Chapter 4, the binding facts suggest generally that an antecedent can only bind a variable to its right, within the minimal clause that contains both of them.[5] As discussed in section 2.1.3, the "most elegant" version of syntactic binding theory is formulated in terms of c-command, which is a strictly configurational notion. So the binding facts, binding theory and the binary branching assumption together support the hypothesis that branching in the English VP is downward and to the right, as proposed by Larson (1988). If branching is to the right, linear order correlates with c-command.

---

[5] An important class of counterexamples involve fronting of the bound element to the left of its antecedent, as in Reinhart's *In his$_i$ room every student$_i$ keeps a dog*. Cases such as these constitute an important argument for traces and antecedent/trace chains. See sections 7.4, 9.4.5.

(26) Binding theory + Uniform binary branching ⇒ Uniform rightward branching

In Chapter 4 we discuss in detail the interactions between the binary branching hypothesis and the analysis of binding as syntactic. Chapters 6, 9, 10, and 11 present arguments that most of the syntactic contribution to binding is linear order, and the structural contribution is largely provided by CS.

As already noted, Structural Uniformity within X' theory suggests that the structure of VP is a cascade of VP-shells, where each constituent of the VP is introduced into the structure as the specifier of some verb.

(27) Uniform rightward branching + Uniformity ⇒ VP-shells

From VP-shells it follows that there must be phonetically empty v-heads and raising of the verb to the left, as in the Larson/Hale/Keyser analysis.

(28) VP-shells ⇒ empty v-heads
VP-shells ⇒ head movement (verb)

Finally, the empirical evidence regarding branching shows that there are asymmetries; in particular, certain head-final languages lack overt *wh*-movement, and no language has rightward *wh*-movement. Kayne (1994) argues that these facts and many others can be accommodated by assuming that all branching is to the right. For example, a head-final language that lacks *wh*-fronting would be one in which the IP comes to occupy Spec,CP, as illustrated in (29); thus Spec,CP is not available for a *wh*-phrase.

(29)

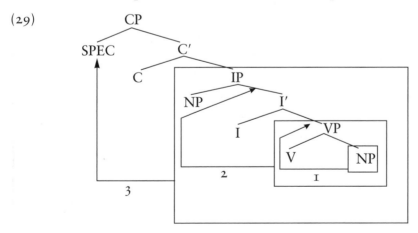

Presumably some languages (e.g. German and Dutch) would have only movement 1 or perhaps movements 1 and 2 (see Zwart 1997). Whether other combinations of movements are possible remains an open question. (See Cinque

(1996) for discussion of this issue with respect to the derivation of orders within NP.)

A further generalization brings us to Antisymmetry, the notion that only rightward binary branching structure can be mapped into a linear ordering of constituents, effectively ruling out any other branching possibilities.

(30)   VP-shells ⇒ ANTISYMMETRY

In summary, we have (31).

(31)

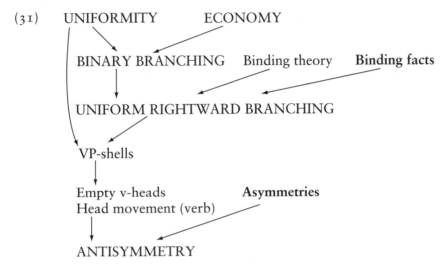

We now note how little of the theoretical development is motivated on the basis of the facts. To be sure, there are empirical phenomena, such as the asymmetry of branching and movement in natural language, and they must be accounted for in any theory. But by this point, much of the theoretical apparatus is motivated not by the goal of accounting for the facts but by other considerations, particularly Uniformity and Economy.

3.1.4 Agreement through movement

As we have noted at several places in the discussion, one of the concerns that arises out of Economy is the question of why movements take place. In the earliest work, it was sufficient to stipulate that a particular movement transformation was an option in a language. But the logic of Economy puts a particular premium on explaining why certain transformations occur while others do not. For instance, it is possible to simply stipulate that a language can have a rule of *wh*-fronting that moves a *wh*-phrase to initial position, but that no language can have a rule that moves a *wh*-phrase to a position between the determiner and the head noun of the subject NP. But doing so gives no sense of what is natural and possible in human language, and what is unnatural or impossible.

One major step in the desirable direction of making it impossible or very difficult for the theory to describe nonexistent grammatical phenomena was the Structure-Preserving Hypothesis. The idea that the phrase structure of the language also constrains the possible outputs of all grammatical operations is a natural one. Of course, as we have noted, the structure-preserving quality of many such movement operations also raises the question of whether movement is in fact the correct way to account for the phenomena, given that the structures are independently required. Interface Uniformity/UTAH eliminates this question by forcing analyses in the direction of movement, since otherwise it should be possible to directly capture the fact that different structures have the same meaning in terms of the rules of interpretation, as Baker (1997) points out in the quote earlier.

Even assuming the Structure-Preserving Hypothesis, there is a question of why certain structures occur. This question is particularly pertinent in cases where Interface Uniformity forces some shared underlying structure for two very different sentences. Given that the two sentences share some structure, why are they different at the surface? For example, in the case of raising to subject, why is the tensed complement untransformed, while the subject of the infinitival complement must raise to the higher subject position? As noted in our discussion of raising to subject, the answer to this question was that some principle is violated if the infinitival subject is not raised. Logically, either the subject has an illicit feature that it loses if it raises, or it lacks a required feature that it acquires if it raises. The answer given in successive accounts within MGG is essentially the latter: the subject of the infinitive is in a non-Case position and the higher subject is a Case position, and the subject must have Case. It is not necessary to go through the various technical mechanisms for representing the difference among various formulations. Let us adopt here the most recent version: the subject of the infinitive has a Case feature that is checked or 'licensed' by a higher functional head.

This approach to the problem generalizes a property that was originally assumed for inflectional functional heads in Pollock's early proposal, which is that in many languages a subject agrees morphologically with the inflected verb. Generalizing according to Derivational Uniformity, it was proposed that all surface inflectional morphology is a reflection of agreement between some specifier and some functional head.

(32) functional heads ⇒ generalized specifier–head agreement

Agreement is therefore the mechanism by which features are licensed.

Now, if all inflectional morphology is a reflection of specifier–head agreement, then all NPs must move to the specifier of some functional head. Assuming uniform rightward binary branching, the idea of movement to satisfy Case requirements generalizes to the idea that all linear order can be characterized in terms of movements to license features.

(33)   generalized specifier–head agreement ⇒ movement for licensing

At this point, the primitives of the theory can be reduced to the following. First, there is a set of functional categories and a set of lexical categories. Each category has its particular features, and the feature values of a given element are specified in the lexicon. Movement occurs when a feature is not licensed in a particular position.[6] The feature (or the constituent that bears it) moves, subject to some constraints, until it reaches a position in which it is licensed. Linear order results from the movement of various constituents to positions where their features are licensed. Languages differ in their lexicons; the syntax is universal and uniform (see Borer (1984)).

Uniformity and Economy now bring us perilously close to the false proposition that there is only one language, i.e. that there is no variation. Consider two languages, one of which is SOV and one of which is SVO. On the assumption of uniform rightward branching, both should be SVO. If SOV is derived by movement of O to have some feature licensed, it is unclear why this movement should not occur in the SVO language—which would of course predict that there are no SVO languages.

The answer, anticipated by Pollock and developed in MP, is that languages differ in whether particular features have to be licensed before the point in the derivation where the hierarchical arrangement of elements is mapped into the linear order of phonetics. This difference has been characterized in terms of the property of "strength". If [+F] is strong, it must be licensed before phonetic interpretation, if it is weak, it need not be.

The example of SOV/SVO variation shows that if a feature is weak, it cannot be licensed at a point in the derivation that serves as input to phonetics, since otherwise SVO languages would also be SOV. Since by Uniformity *all* features must be licensed at some point in a derivation, licensing without apparent movement is therefore done through LF movement, often referred to as "covert" movement; hence the logic in (34).

---

[6] The actual situation is more complex, since a constituent may have a number of features, only one of which is required by a higher head for licensing purposes.

(34)

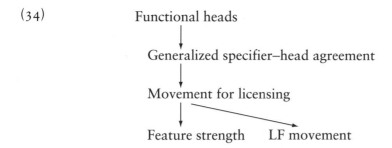

Functional heads

Generalized specifier–head agreement

Movement for licensing

Feature strength   LF movement

It is interesting that there actually is very little empirical content to this whole line of particular development of the theory; it is driven almost exclusively by Uniformity. If we assume uniform binary branching and a crosslinguistically uniform interface with semantics,[7] it follows that linear order must be derived entirely through movement, and various formal devices must then be invoked to require or prevent movement of a given phrase in a given language. In the case of apparent optionality of movement, it must be presumed that the given device is optionally present (e.g. the feature can be optionally "strong" or "weak"). Empirical considerations enter only into the question of what the features are and at what point in the derivation they must be licensed.

Cinque (1999) carries the idea of deriving linear order from hierarchical structure to its logical conclusion. He demonstrates how linear order can be correlated with hierarchical structure to a high degree of precision, if for every element that appears in the linear order there is a functional head in the tree. To illustrate, we let x = α, β, ... be morphemes, words or phrases. Assume that each x is the specifier of some functional head, $\mathscr{F}(x)$. Assuming that linear order is correlated with relative height in the tree (Kayne 1994), α precedes β iff $\mathscr{F}(\alpha)$ c-commands $\mathscr{F}(\beta)$.

(35)

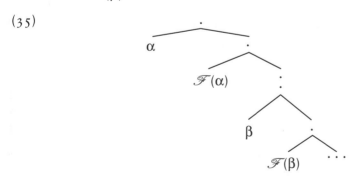

---

[7] The latter assumption revives the "universal base hypothesis" discussed occasionally in the late 1960s (e.g. Fillmore 1968: 1; Bach 1968: 91).

Cinque shows that there are word order universals of adverbs that can be characterized in terms of a fixed hierarchy of functional heads, given these assumptions.

3.2 The Minimalist Program

The Minimalist Program of Chomsky (1995) assumes that the structures and derivations of Principles and Parameters Theory are essentially correct. The objective of MP is to explain why PPT works the way it does on the basis of first principles, especially those of Economy. In its overt philosophy MP is indeed minimalist. But in practice, it is a variant of PPT.

A strictly minimalist syntactic theory would begin by eliminating all theoretical devices except for what is known to exist: sounds paired with meanings. It would then seek to find the minimal assumptions that would explain how a learner acquires the mapping between these, in order to account for the learner's capacity to identify relationships and generalizations. The theory would not assume any formal operations that were not required, and it would assume that the learner came to the task equipped only with knowledge that s/he could not extract from the primary linguistic data of sound/meaning pairs. That is, the theory would be Simpler Syntax in our sense.

There are several respects in which MP does not meet these general conditions for an adequate minimalist theory. First, it does not take the task of the learner to be central; rather, it develops out of a conception of human language as a "perfect" system. Second, it assumes without argument that the correct characterization of linguistic knowledge takes the form of a derivation (section 1.4.1). Third, it imposes certain notions of economy on its formulations that appear to have little if any empirical motivation. And fourth, it relies heavily on the Uniformity methodology of much earlier work. We will develop each of these points as we survey the Minimalist Program.

3.2.1 Perfection

Chomsky (n.d.) characterizes the search for perfection in language in the following way:

We are now asking how well language is designed. How closely does language resemble what a superbly competent engineer might have constructed, given certain design specifications. . . . I suggested that the answer to the question might turn out to be that language is very well designed, perhaps close to "perfect" in satisfying external conditions.

If there is any truth to this conclusion, it is rather surprising, for several reasons. First, languages have often been assumed to be such complex and defective objects as to be hardly worth studying from a stern theoretical perspective.... Second, one might not expect to find such design properties in biological systems, which evolve over long periods through incremental changes under complicated and accidental circumstances, making the best of difficult and murky contingencies.

Suppose nonetheless that we turn aside initial skepticism and try to formulate some reasonably clear questions about optimality of language design. The "minimalist program", as it has come to be called, is an effort to examine such questions.

So, to put it somewhat differently, there is little if any empirical evidence to suggest that language is a perfect system. The fact that it is a biological system also weighs against this view. Therefore, the Minimalist Program has been launched as an attempt to discover a way in which language can be construed as a perfect system, in spite of the prior indications that it is not. The notion of perfection is imposed upon the Principles and Parameters framework, requiring that it be re-evaluated in light of this demanding criterion.

The notion of perfection goes beyond the standard scientific criterion of simplicity and generality that might be demanded by Occam's Razor, i.e. what might be called "methodological minimalism". Methodological minimalism requires that our descriptions be maximally simple, general, and elegant, given empirical observations. The MP imposes the further criterion of "substantive minimalism" (the term used by Atkinson (2001)): that language is maximally simple, general, and elegant—independent of empirical observations.

Thus, the goal of the MP is to design a computational system for human language (C_{HL}) that aspires to "perfection". Since language does not obviously appear to be such a "perfect" system, there are three choices when encountering recalcitrant facts. (i) We can complicate the computational system, departing from maximal economy in order to accommodate the facts, concluding that language deviates (minimally) from perfection. It may even be possible to explain why this deviation occurs. (ii) We can make the facts the responsibility of systems other than the computational system itself (e.g. PF and LF). (iii) We can set aside the facts if we don't see how to do this.

Let us consider, then, what the minimal requirements are for a computational system that can "do" language. Chomsky (1995) reasons as follows: C_{HL} must be able to combine words into phrases. Therefore a derivation begins with a set N (the "numeration") of primitive elements of the language, taken from the lexicon.[8] The primitive operation Merge recursively combines elements of N and eliminates them from N. The minimal domain of Merge would be two elements of N. Therefore, it is concluded, Merge *always* applies to two elements, producing uniform binary branching structures. Since language is produced in real time, the interface level PF must interpret the output of Merge as an ordered string of these two elements. This interpretation process is called Spell Out. Spell Out occurs throughout the derivation (or, in subsequent work, in cyclic "phases"—Chomsky 1999); hence in the MP there is no level of S-structure that interfaces with PF.

Since expressions have meaning, the result of Merge must also be mapped into the interface level LF. This interpretive operation occurs throughout the derivation (again, possibly in cyclic phases); hence in the MP there is no level of D-structure that interfaces with LF.

Given this, the minimal conception of a computational system that forms strings is the following:

Given N, C_{HL} computes until it converges (if it does) at PF and LF with the pair (π, λ). In a "perfect language" any structure Σ formed by the computation—hence π and λ—is constituted of elements already present in the lexical elements selected for N; no new objects are added in the course of computation (in particular, no indices, bar-levels... etc). (Chomsky 1995: 393)

---

[8] Postal (2004: ch. 6) disputes even this apparently obvious move. He observes that there exist sentences of English with constituents that are not English expressions, and in some cases not expressions of any language.

(i)   a.   The Martian said, "Klaatu barrada nikto".
       b.   A cow doesn't go "foog", it goes "moo".
       c.   The sign @ was invented in 1541.
       d.   [Teenspeak:] And then I was all, like, [gesture of annoyance].

Such examples include all manner of metalinguistic talk used in linguistic theory:

(ii)   a.   *Ishkabibble* doesn't rhyme with *sklerf*.
       b.   The ungrammaticality of a string like *eat the* must be a consequence of its failure to map to LF.
       c.   In forming the passive of (7), *-en* hops over *forget*.

Postal discusses three possible moves, all of which have unfortunate consequences. (1) Such non-English constituents are not part of the English lexicon. Consequence: a numeration is not restricted to the lexicon as assumed, but can be totally wild. (2) These constituents *are* part of the lexicon. Consequence: the English lexicon goes way beyond knowledge of English. (3) The sentences in (i)–(ii) are not grammatical sentences of English. Consequence: there is no explanation of how they receive truth-values (nor of how linguists manage to talk to one another). Postal suggests that the problem is a fundamental one: the derivational character of MP requires sentences to be built up from a fixed lexical basis. He observes that a constraint-based approach (he uses the term "model-theoretic") does not suffer from this problem: some contexts simply do not constrain their contents to expressions of the language, but rather allow "leakage".

For convenience of exposition, we will call C_{HL} in the MP "syntax". From what we have said so far, it would appear that the responsibility of syntax in MP is significantly more limited than it is in GB/PPT. Syntax in MP is not responsible for linear order; that belongs to PF. Syntax in MP is not responsible for binding; that belongs to LF (where the indexing can be done). Subcategorization does not belong to syntax in MP, since Merge can pair any two elements in N. Hence the ungrammaticality of a string like *eat the must be a consequence of its failure to map into a well-formed object at LF. It appears that word order variation, of the sort encountered in extraposition, is not the province of syntax in MP, but of PF. And so on. On the maximally minimalist view, syntax does nothing but put things together, pairwise.

There is a problem with the view just arrived at, though: fifty years of syntactic research have made it abundantly clear that the facts of language cannot be accounted for simply in these terms. In particular, linguistic relations are structure-dependent, but whatever structure is constructed in the syntax is lost in the mapping to PF. So PF does not have sufficient information actually to carry out the operations that are being required of it.[9]

The fact that languages have word order variation is important evidence that language is not a perfect system in this sense. Introducing mechanisms to address this empirical fact appears to be a tolerable complication of the system, since it is a fact that is hard to ignore. Hence, reasons Chomsky, we introduce into the concept of C_{HL} an additional operation that takes part of an already constructed string σ, copies it, and attaches the copy to σ. This operation is called Move (or in more recent formulations, Internal Merge). The intuition of MP is that copying is the minimal operation that will change the arrangement of elements. Literal movement involves not only copying but erasure.[10] Given that there are two copies, call them "original" and "new", either copy or both (or neither) can be mapped onto PF. If only the original copy is mapped onto PF, we derive the effect of "LF movement", where the moved constituent functions as though it is adjoined high in the structure but appears in situ (as in the case of *wh*-movement in Japanese).

(36) PF: ~~New~~ [.... Original]
      LF: New$_i$[.... Original$_i$]

---

[9] Chomsky (1999) proposes that certain movements take place in PF, which presumes that enough syntactic information remains in PF to permit movements to be formulated there. Of course, making PF into a syntactic component is a perfectly reasonable way to actually construct a grammar. On the other hand, such a move is patently a way to evade the strong assumptions of MP.

[10] These primitive operations were originally identified in Chomsky (1975a/1955).

If only the new copy is mapped into PF, we derive the appearance of overt movement.

(37)   PF: New [.... ~~Original~~]
        LF: New$_i$ [.... Original$_i$]

Given that actual copying is not often found in natural language in place of movement, some additional complication of the theory will be required, perhaps some notion of functional economy.

The question now arises as to what licenses the result of Move. MP borrows the PPT view of movement as licensed by feature checking (see section 3.1.4). Crucially, there is limited independent empirical evidence to suggest that the features assumed by PPT that are implicated in movement actually exist, let alone that they are "strong" or "weak", and there is no such evidence in languages that lack a robust inflectional morphology. But putting this aside, MP can adopt the PPT devices more or less without alteration: Move derives the hierarchical structure, and PF expresses this structure in linear terms.

3.2.2 Derivational economy

With the introduction of Move comes the question of whether all combinations of Merge and Move yield grammatical sentences in a language, assuming that the results satisfy the requirements of the PF and LF interfaces. The answer is "no". As is well known, many logically possible movements produce ungrammaticality in natural language. Constraints on movement have been treated as irreducible properties of syntactic theory. A natural goal of MP is to explain them in terms of the overall criterion of computational simplicity.

Again there must be a complication of the theory beyond what is minimally required, in order to accommodate the empirical facts. MP assumes that the critical property of a derivation, i.e. a sequence of Merges and Moves, is whether it is the computationally simplest one against some comparison set. PPT assumes that all features must be licensed, and furthermore that some features must be licensed prior to the mapping to PF. Given these two assumptions, research has been devoted to investigating whether there is a cogent characterization of computational economy in terms of the number of Moves, and the length of each Move. Questions also arise regarding the definition of the comparison set for any given derivation; see Johnson and Lappin (1999) for discussion, and Collins (1997) for a mechanism to limit the comparison set. We will not go into these technical matters here, except to note that at this point in the theory, considerations of inherent computational simplicity of the system have been supplanted by questions of whether there is evidence for one concept of computational simplicity over another.

Moreover, there does not appear to be any strong empirical motivation for any constraint on derivations in terms of the number of moves or the length of moves, with one exception. It appears that in many cases, when there are two candidates for a move to a particular location, the closer one is the one that moves, as illustrated in (38). This result follows from the requirement that the shortest move is more economical than the longer move.

(38)

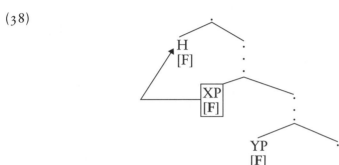

Empirical evidence that is generally consistent with this result involves Superiority, where a lower *wh*-phrase cannot move to a position above a higher *wh*-phrase:

(39) a.   Who saw what.
      b. *What did who see?

(40) a.   Robin forgot where Leslie saw what.
      b. *What did Robin forget where Leslie saw.
      c. *Where did Robin forget what Leslie saw.
      d.   What did Robin see where?
           Where did Robin see what?

It is possible to analyze cases such as these as demonstrating the preference for moving the closest *wh*-phrase to agree with the interrogative complementizer.

What is striking at this point is that relatively little of PPT has been reconstructed in terms of the MP. As Koopman (2000: 2) writes,

The MP has had led to a much improved and cleaner theory. However, compared to the GB framework, the Minimalist Program led to relatively few new insights in our understanding of phenomena in the first half of the nineties. This is probably because it did not generate new analytical tools, and thus failed to generate novel ways of looking at well-known paradigms or expand and solve old problems, an essential ingredient for progress to be made at this point.

We agree with this sentiment except for the word "improved", which is difficult to substantiate in the face of the empirical limitations that Koopman notes. The MP lacks an account of most of the phenomena handled by GB/PPT and other syntactic theories. In some cases we consider this to be a welcome result, consistent with our own minimalist principles. For example, the absence of syntactic indices forces binding theory out of syntax into semantic structure, although we would argue that the proper representation is Conceptual Structure and not LF. But it is not clear how the MP can incorporate the relevant syntactic relations of linear precedence into its account of Binding, since in MP linear order is not in syntax, but in PF. Other descriptive limitations of MP are its inability to express constraints on movement in terms of inherent computational economy; its inability to account in a natural way for true optionality of syntactic structure, or for syntactic alternatives that are linked not to LF but to information structure (in the sense of Roberts (1998) and other work in Discourse Representation Theory); and its disavowal of responsibility for the "periphery" of language, which is a nontrivial aspect of linguistic knowledge (see Chapter 1 and Culicover 1999). By now there are numerous critiques of the philosophy behind the MP, the adequacy of its technical machinery, and its empirical results, varying considerably in politeness but remarkably similar in substance (e.g. Pullum 1996; Johnson and Lappin 1999; Lappin et al. 2000; Newmeyer 2003; Postal 2004; Seuren 2004; and Pinker and Jackendoff 2005).

3.3 Uniformity entails Generative Semantics

3.3.1 MP meets GS

While MP diverges from earlier mainstream syntactic theories in regard to empirical coverage, it does share many important architectural features with earlier work. In MP, branching is binary and uniform, as in PPT. MP, like previous mainstream theories, insists on Uniformity and on the centrality of derivation. These latter two are inextricably linked, since without derivations (and in particular, movement) it is impossible to map a single underlying structure into distinct surface strings.

As we have discussed, UTAH ensures a uniform assignment of θ-roles on the basis of syntactic configuration. The consequence of applying UTAH rigorously is that all derivational as well as inflectional morphology is syntacticized in MP, as foreshadowed by Baker (1988).

Many researchers have observed that the rigorous application of UTAH produces analyses that are hauntingly reminiscent of Generative Semantics of the late 1960s and early 1970s. We reproduce here a representative passage from Bach and Harms (1968: viii).

The main point that we would like to mention is the development of "deeper" and more abstract underlying structures than are to be found, say, in Chomsky's *Aspects of the Theory of Syntax*. We cite one example: the surface sentence *Floyd broke the glass* is composed of no less than eight sentences [which we discuss below—PWC/RJ].... Each can be justified on syntactic grounds. It is but a step, then, to the position represented in McCawley's "Postscript" where these "deep structures" are taken to be identical with the semantic representations of sentences.

It is fundamental to an understanding of the history of syntactic theory to recognize that Generative Semantics was based on a literal and uniform application of the Katz–Postal Hypothesis, a precursor of UTAH. Its major innovation was to say that lexical insertion is scattered through the derivation. Moreover, GS carried out all inflectional and derivational morphology derivationally in the syntax. The similarity between MP and GS is noted by Hale and Keyser (1991):

When we claim that the English verb *saddle* has underlying it a syntactic representation of the form ... [[v saddle$_i$ v t$_i$ p *the horse*]—PWC & RJ], it is clear that we are accepting—to some extent, at least—a viewpoint represented in the Generative Semantics framework, as in the work of Lakoff (1971), McCawley (1971), and others. The Generative Semantics program was motivated, in part, by a vision of the nature of lexical items which is essentially the same as ours. This is the idea that the notion "possible lexical item" (in relation to the view that syntax is projected from the lexicon), is defined, or constrained, by certain principles of grammar which also determine the well-formedness of syntactic structures.

Given this convergence, it will be important to reconsider the original arguments raised against the GS program, and see whether or not they are relevant to the MP.

3.3.2 *Classic cases*

Let us consider some classic cases from GS.

i. Syntactic derivation of agentive nouns. Lakoff (1965/70) observed that an agentive noun, such as *builder*, is subject to the same selectional restrictions as the verb *build*. So, if *builder of* X violates a selectional restriction, *build* X violates the same selection restriction, and in the same way. For instance:

(41) a. Robin is building a house/?similarity.
      b. Robin is the builder of a house/?similarity.

Similarly, the subject of *build* and the subject of *is the builder of* are subject to the same restrictions.

(42) a. Robin/?Sincerity built a house.
      b. Robin/?Sincerity is the builder of this house.

Applying the Katz–Postal Hypothesis, Lakoff argues that *builder* must be derived from *build* in a derivation along the following lines.

(43) Robin is [$_{NP}$ (one) [who build ...]] ⇒
      Robin is [$_{NP}$ build +er ...]

The relative lack of syntactic precision of the early analysis can be ameliorated by imposing reasonable constraints on the derivation, such as the requirement that heads move to head positions, which would make it look a lot like Baker, Hale/Keyser, and Larsonian head-movement/VP-shell derivations. The other central aspect of Lakoff's derivation is the substitution of +*er* for the underlying *(one) who*, a step that can be aligned with Spell Out in the MP.

ii. Causative alternation (head-to-head). Lakoff (1965/70) and McCawley (1968b) argued that verbs of causation have an underlying structure in which there is a predicate that conveys the relation CAUSE. The derivation of *John opened the door* along these lines, in a version due to McCawley (1968b), is summarized by Shibatani (1976) as shown in (44). The parallels with the more recent treatments of V-raising are striking. At the same time, there are significant differences. The choice of primitives, e.g. NOT CLOSED instead of OPEN, has a distinctly arbitrary quality. And, as has often been noted, there were no constraints in GS on the types of operations that could be involved in the derivation of complex structures that correspond to lexical items.

In fact, Lakoff and Ross (1967/73) wrote a note entitled "Is Deep Structure Necessary?" in which they argue, in many ways anticipating Chomsky (1995), that there is no need to stipulate a level of Deep Structure distinct from semantic representation. Deep Structure is taken to have the properties in (45).

(44) a.

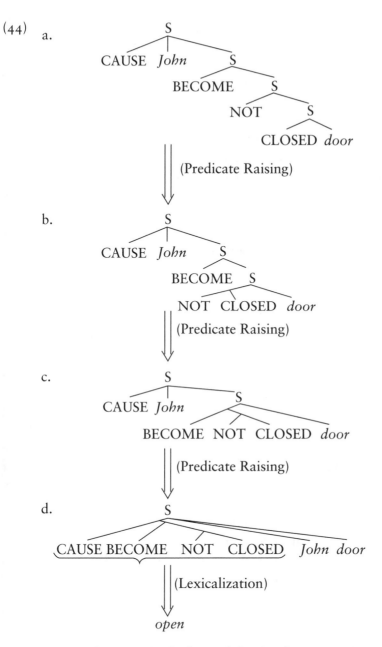

(45) a. Deep Structure is the base of the simplest syntactic component.
      b. Deep Structure is where cooccurrence and selection restrictions are
         defined.
      c. Deep Structure is where basic grammatical relations are defined.
      d. Deep Structure is where lexical items are inserted from the lexicon.

Lakoff and Ross argue that none of these properties have to be associated with a particular level of representation: they can be associated with steps in a derivation where the appropriate conditions are met.

Similar arguments are made in MP. Merge and Move derive sequences of structures that conform to the conditions associated with (45), but there is no single representation that meets these conditions. In MP, as in GS, cooccurrence and selection are defined by the lexical entries and can be checked at any point in the derivation where they are applicable. In GS, the grammatical relations subject and object are not relevant for semantic interpretation, and they are not relevant notions in the MP either. And in MP, as in GS, "lexical items are inserted at many points of a derivation" (Chomsky 1995: 160). In MP, lexical insertion is taken to be Spell Out, where a morpheme or combination of morphemes receives a phonetic interpretation. This is more or less equivalent to the way that lexical insertion was conceived of in GS, as well.

iii. Association of temporal and aspectual morphology with independent heads.   The flavor of a GS analysis is given by the structure for *Floyd broke the glass* in (46).[11] There are a number of important points of similarity between this tree and what we would expect to find in a MP representation. First, as noted already, each temporal and aspectual component of the meaning is represented by a distinct head (PAST, HAPPEN, DO, INCHOATIVE). In GS this head is called V (since GS lacked functional categories), and every maximal projection is called S. It is a small step to reinterpret this tree using contemporary categories, particularly since the category of the heads and of the projections lack independent syntactic justification.[12] Second, the subject *Floyd* appears twice, as the subject of CAUSE and as the subject of DO. Again, this is eerily prescient, since one contemporary derivation proposed within the MP (Hornstein 1999) would move *Floyd* up to the subject position of higher verbs in order for it to get assigned the proper θ-roles, leaving behind a copy in each lower position. Third, as in Larson's proposals, the direct object of *broke* is the underlying subject of the intransitive *broken,* denoting the property of the glass. Transitivity in both approaches is a property of an abstract verb.

---

[11] We reconstruct this tree from memory, including memory of a mobile of it constructed by Susan Fischer and Steve Anderson that hung in Ross's office at MIT in the late 1960s. The representation given here is somewhat richer than that cited by Bach and Harms in the passage given earlier and, we believe, somewhat more accurate. A version of the tree is also cited in Newmeyer (1986), based on a handout from a lecture by Ross and Lakoff.

[12] Which is not to say that independent justification is irrelevant. For example, Ross (1969b) argued that English auxiliaries are verbs, and Ross (1970) and R. Lakoff (1968) provided arguments that performative heads are verbs. It is not clear whether such arguments would be valid in the MP.

(46)

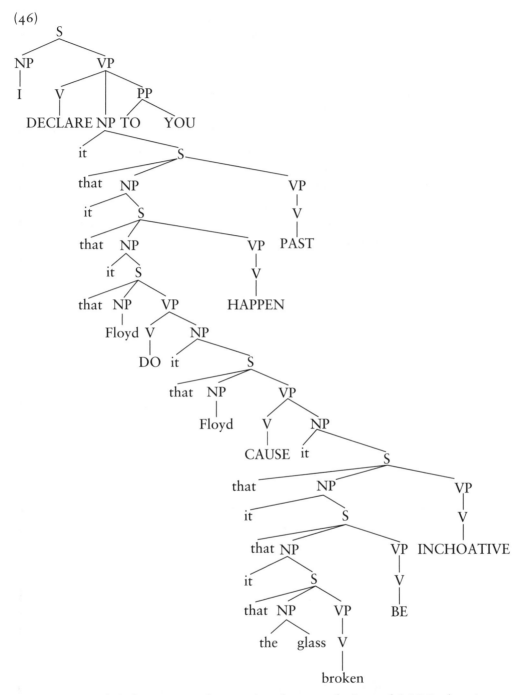

iv. VP Internal Subject Hypothesis. Another conclusion of MGG that is anticipated in GS is McCawley's (1970) proposal that English is a VSO language. Viewed from the present perspective, McCawley's main (though perhaps unintended) contribution in this paper is the demonstration that without a principled account of movement, any initial configuration can be manipulated so as to produce the observed word order and constituent structure.[13] As we noted earlier, current approaches to the core structure of a sentence assume that it arises from a verb that Merges with one argument or adjunct, yielding an interpretation that is equivalent to the assignment of a θ-role; then the verb raises to the next verbal head and repeats the operation on the next argument or adjunct. The NPs raise up in order to have their Case feature checked (e.g. the direct object moves to the AgrO position), or to satisfy other grammatical requirements (e.g. a sentence in English must have a subject, a requirement known as the EPP and satisfied by a feature sometimes called 'EPP'). In English, the verb raises so that it ends up to the left of the VP arguments and adjuncts.

(47)

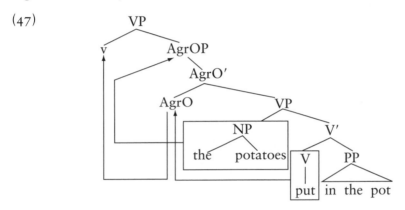

On McCawley's account, the V originates to the left of the rest of VP. Subsequent movement moves the subject NP to the left of V. Since modals and tense are also verbs, the derivation from this point is strikingly similar to that of MP, where the subject continues to move up until it is in initial position.

3.3.3 How is this possible?

Taking a larger view, the fact that the machinery of GS is so similar to that of PPT/MP appears inevitable, given their common assumption of Strong Interface Uniformity. Two questions naturally arise. First, why was GS so roundly criticized and ultimately discredited, given that the major critic, Chomsky, and his contemporary colleagues are now pursuing what appears to be essentially the same line of research? And second, do the criticisms that held then hold now?

---

[13] Such a criticism has been directed against derivations in Kayne's Antisymmetry theory; cf. e.g. Rochemont and Culicover (1997).

The answer to the first question appears to be largely tied to the sociology of the field. For extensive discussion of sociological questions concerning the widespread adoption of the MP, see Lappin et al. (2000) and the subsequent exchange. And indeed, many of the sociological forces that are active today also held sway in the late 1960s during the dispute over GS (see Newmeyer (1986), Harris (1993), Huck and Goldsmith (1995)). At the same time, there were substantive problems with the GS program which rendered it intractable as an account of syntactic structure per se. Perhaps most significantly, as GS developed, it came not to distinguish between literal meaning and non-literal meaning (or pragmatics), and proposed to incorporate into the syntax/semantics representation—in syntactic format—everything that a native speaker might need to know about the world to properly interpret any particular sentence. Moreover, there were serious criticisms of the part of the program that concerned lexical semantics.

Turning to the second question, let us consider the specific criticisms of GS in the literature. A fundamental criticism comes from Chomsky (1970: 14ff.). Chomsky considers the analysis of sentences like *John felt sad*. If the underlying structure were *John felt [John be sad]*, then we would expect that *John felt sad* could mean the same as *John felt that he was sad*. However, Chomsky writes, "if we are correct in assuming that it is the grammatical relations of the deep structure that determine the semantic interpretation," *John felt sad* must have a different Deep Structure representation from *John felt that he was sad*—which it doesn't, according to the analysis of Lakoff (1965/70: appendix A). So *feel* would subcategorize both an S complement and an AP complement. This conclusion is, of course, in violation of Structural Uniformity, as it posits that *feel* permits more than one type of complement structure.[14] If this conclusion is accepted, it undermines the GS program, as Chomsky intended. Chomsky goes on to make the same kind of argument for nominalizations, showing that the semantic interpretation of a nominal, while related in argument structure to its corresponding verb, is nevertheless distinct. This is the 'lexicalist' view of grammar.

Similarly, Chomsky (1972b: 80–84), following Bresnan (1969), offers an argument against the GS/MP approach to argument structure articulated originally by Lakoff (1968) and subsequently by Baker/Hale/Keyser. Lakoff proposes that the two sentences in (48) have the same Deep Structure.

---

[14] In contemporary terms, these sentences would be represented as *John felt [$_{sc}$PRO sad]* and *John felt [$_{CP}$that he was sad]*. The lack of uniformity still exists, although it takes a different form. At the same time, the fact that "I am sad" is not a feeling attributed to John in the case of the small clause could be attributed to the fact that *PRO* is not referential and therefore not within the scope of John's belief. See Zwart (1999).

(48)   a. Seymour cut the salami with a knife.
       b. Seymour used a knife to cut the salami.

Lakoff concludes that the instrumental role associated with *with* in Surface Structure is actually expressed by an argument of the verb *use*. Chomsky's arguments against this view are, first, that *use* can cooccur with *with* (49a), and second, that *use* cannot always be paraphrased by *with* (49b).

(49)   a. Seymour used a knife to cut the salami with.
       b. Seymour used this car to escape.
          ≠ Seymour escaped with this car.
          (cf. *Seymour used this car to escape in.*)

Examples parallel to (49a) arise in the Hale–Keyser hypothesis: in (50) the position allegedly vacated by the noun that incorporates into the verb is actually occupied by something else.

(50)   a. Joe buttered the toast with rancid margarine.
       b. Fred bottled the wine in cheap flasks.

So the fact that certain examples appear to be paraphrases of one another in terms of Argument Structure does not in itself support the conclusion that they share the same underlying syntactic representation, contrary to the Baker/Hale/Keyser view.[15]

The issue then devolves upon the status of non-argument structure aspects of interpretation in the grammar, such as internal details of lexical meaning. Chomsky (1972), Jackendoff (1972; 1975; 1983; 2002a), Pustejovsky (1995), and Fodor and Lepore (1999) argue that non-argument structure information is an essential part of the content of a lexical item. The Baker/Hale/Keyser approach, on the other hand, abandons lexicalism in favor of a theory in which the argument structure aspects of interpretation are encoded in uniform syntactic structures, while (presumably) the non-argument structure aspects of interpretation are still associated with individual lexical items. The argument structure part of the account is intended to explain certain facts about 'possible lexical item' in terms of movement and conflation of complex underlying structures, along the lines of GS. However, as we showed in section 2.1.3, arguments parallel to Chomsky's can be mounted against these accounts, based on

----

[15] Another line of argument mounted by Chomsky against GS is not pertinent to MP, namely that at least some semantic interpretation is determined only at S-structure (later at LF). With the introduction of traces, all semantic interpretation can be determined at S-structure, and with linear ordering relegated to PF, D-structure has no role beyond constraining the combinatorial relationships among words and phrases.

differences in non-argument structure aspects of word meaning; Hale and Keyser are aware of such arguments but declare that they will not address them. Since the non-argument structure information must be associated with individual lexical items in any case, the move to a syntactic account of argument structure relations between lexical items can only be motivated by a demonstration that a lexical account cannot correctly account for them. To our knowledge no such demonstration has ever been made, or even attempted; and there has been no reply from the derivational camp to the various lexicalist accounts in the literature such as Jackendoff (1972; 1976; 1983; 2002a), Pinker (1989), Pustejovsky (1995), Talmy (1988), Kiparsky (1997), and Farrell (1998).[16]

3.4 The alternative

Our survey of the history of mainstream generative grammar has shown how at every stage of development, innovations have been motivated by Uniformity, particularly Interface Uniformity. As we went through the earlier stages, we mentioned some alternative positions that have arisen in the literature. On the other hand, the development of the later stages of MGG, from UTAH on, has been driven more on theory-internal grounds, and there have been virtually no points of substantive contact with other syntactic frameworks. At this point, however, it is useful to step back and see what syntactic theory might look like if the MGG train of argument were not adopted.

As mentioned in section 2.2, the empirical drawbacks of the transformational account of the passive were addressed by the middle 1970s (e.g. Shopen 1972; Bresnan 1978; Brame 1978). Ten years later there were at least two major

---

[16] This is not to say, however, that a syntactic account is impossible in principle. Marantz (1997) argues that the properties of lexical items are not uniformly represented in the lexicon, but parceled out among various components of the grammar in such a way that the combinatorial devices that derive new lexical items are just those of phrasal syntax, while the core meanings and idiosyncratic properties are stored in various "lists" that interface with syntactic representations in different ways.

On this view, the core lexicon contains primitive roots, and thematic properties such as Agent are associated with primitive light verbs. The alternation between *destroy* and *destruction* discussed by Chomsky (1970) is expressed not as a lexical one but as a syntactic one, with the special meanings associated with the Nominalizations represented in a distinct list. Let v-1 represent the verb that assigns agent, and D the nominalizing morpheme.

(i)   a. v-1 $+\sqrt{}$ DESTROY $\Rightarrow$ destroy
     b. D $+\sqrt{}$ DESTROY $\Rightarrow$ destruction

Hence there must be a list that specifies the form of D $+\sqrt{}$ DESTROY and another (or the same one) that specifies any idiosyncratic semantic properties of *destruction*.

frameworks, LFG (Bresnan 1982a) and GPSG (Gazdar et al. 1985), in which the active–passive relation was captured not through syntactic movement, but rather through relations in argument structure in the lexicon. This implies relaxing Interface Uniformity.

(51)   No passive movement ⇒ Weaker Interface Uniformity

If the passive is done through argument structure, then so is raising to subject; similar mechanisms of argument structure can account for the interpretation. The alternation between a tensed complement of *seem* and an infinitival with a "raised" subject is a matter of lexical subcategorization by *seem* plus an extra principle of interpretation.

(52)   No passive movement ⇒ No raising to subject movement

Furthermore, consider the NPs originally analyzed as undergoing raising to object, then by NRO treated as complement subjects governed by the matrix verb. The reason they had to be subjects of the complement is to satisfy Interface Uniformity. If "raised" subjects are generated in situ, then "raised" objects can be as well, using a parallel principle of interpretation.

(53)   No raising to subject movement ⇒ "Raised" objects in situ

   Next recall that NRO was used to motivate conditions on movement such as NIC, plus the notions of government and abstract Case. If "raised" objects are generated in situ, these additions to UG are unnecessary.

(54)   "Raised" objects in situ ⇒ No need for Nominative Island Constraint, government, or abstract Case

   A weakened criterion of Interface Uniformity also has consequences for quantifier scope. Should we accept the price of LF and covert movement in UG in order to assure that different quantifier scopes correspond to different syntactic structures? Or, given that Interface Uniformity is weakened anyway, should we forgo these additions to syntactic theory and substitute a richer syntax–semantics interface, as urged in Chomsky (1972a) and Jackendoff (1972)? Chapters 11, 13, and 14 of the present study will show that this latter course is empirically preferable.

(55)   Weaker Interface Uniformity ⇒ No level of LF, no covert movement

   The enrichment of the lexicon required by nontransformational passive and raising makes it easy to formulate lexicalist alternatives to Baker's account of noun incorporation. As pointed out above, the empirical basis of Baker's move was in any event challenged by Rosen (1989). Noun incorporation, in turn, was the principal motivation for head movement. In addition, since movement in the passive has been eliminated, head movement is independently less plausible.

(56)   No passive movement + Weaker Interface Uniformity ⇒ richer lexical relations ⇒ no head movement

If there is no head movement, there can be no VP-shells (with their attendant empirical difficulty). In turn there can be no Hale–Keyser-style derivational morphology (with its attendant empirical difficulties), and no Pollock-style functional heads.

(57)   No head movement ⇒ No VP shells ⇒ No syntactic derivation of denominal verbs ⇒ No functional heads to which verbs move

And the absence of head movement makes it impossible to implement strictly binary branching and agreement through movement.

(58)   No head movement ⇒ No strictly binary branching
                          ⇒ No agreement through movement

At this point we also see that, with so much movement eliminated, it is hardly such a central concern in linguistic theory to outlaw all kinds of exuberant movement through constraints on movement or derivational economy.

(59)   Little if any movement ⇒ Many fewer constraints
                                ⇒ No need for derivational economy

In this chapter and the previous one we have examined primarily theoretical developments surrounding argument structure alternations and their formulation in terms of A′-movement and head movement. We have not said much about long-distance dependencies, formulated in MGG as A′-movement. However, similar arguments could be made there (an important and virtually neglected critique of the MGG approach to A′-movement is Bresnan 1977). We return to these issues in Chapter 9.

The upshot is that adopting a nontransformational account of passive forces us to adopt a theory of UG in which many of the theoretical and empirical problems of MGG do not arise. As mentioned in Chapter 1, most of the non-mainstream frameworks of generative grammar have gone the route of non-movement, constraint-based description (an exception is Tree-Adjoining Grammar, which is derivational). That does not mean that the goals of explanation, of constraining the grammar, of learnability, and of innateness go away. From our point of view, the issue for these non-mainstream frameworks is how lexical relations, argument structure relations, and the syntax–semantics interface—as well as the syntactic component—can be constrained appropriately so as to achieve these goals.

CHAPTER 4

Flat Structure

4.1 Introduction

The position advocated by the Simpler Syntax Hypothesis is that syntactic structure should be the minimum necessary to map between phonological and semantic structure. Syntactic structure has always been seen as the basis for semantic interpretation. However, as we noted in Chapters 2 and 3, at several points in the history of MGG this position has mutated into the stronger position that there is a covert syntactic structure that is virtually equivalent to semantic interpretation. We showed that such a position inevitably has a high price in the complexity of the resulting theory of syntactic structure. We wish here to explore a different approach: to abandon Interface Uniformity, to adopt the SSH, and to investigate whether the resulting theory has less overall complexity in syntax and the syntax–semantics interface combined. Chapters 5–9 develop a treatment of the interface; the present chapter deals with syntactic structure proper, in particular its branching structure. We will arrive at a conception of syntax approximately consistent with that of LFG, HPSG, and the *Cambridge Grammar of the English Language* (Huddleston and Pullum 2002), and more or less in accordance with the view of syntax generally adopted in psycholinguistic research.

Much of the early research on syntactic structure was devoted to considerations about the specifics of branching structure in various types of phrases. The earliest explicit overall theory of branching structure was Chomsky's (1970) X′ syntax, based on work of Zellig Harris, which posited a uniform schematic structure for all types of phrases in terms of their heads, complements, specifiers, and adjuncts. Reviewing proposals made up to its time, Jackendoff (1977) works out a comprehensive and relatively uniform account.

More recently, the question of branching structure has ceased to be an entirely empirical issue. As mentioned in Chapters 1 and 3, Kayne (1994) has argued on the grounds of simplicity that all underlying structure is uniformly binary branching to the right, and the MP adopts a similar uniform approach to structure, through application of Merge and Move. We will argue here that both the earlier highly articulated syntactic structures and the current uniform branching structures are in error, and that the correct structure is the minimal structure sufficient to account for the regularities of word and morpheme order and for the correspondence between strings and meanings.

This does not mean that there is no structure at all. For instance, the classical argument for constituents of the type NP is that strings consisting of the same linearly ordered categories, namely *(Det)-(AP)-N-(PP)-(Relative clause)*, can appear in several configurations within a sentence: before the auxiliary, after the verb, after a preposition, and conjoined with another string of the same organization. Moreover, such strings usually function as a semantic unit; for instance, an adjective preceding a noun is generally understood as a modifier of that noun and not of some other noun in the sentence. It is from such evidence that we can argue that strings are organized into headed phrases. We do not want so little structure that we have to find another account of such facts. But there can also be too much structure, i.e. structure that plays no role in determining either word order or interpretation. Such structure, we argue, is an artifact of the theoretical apparatus adopted within the syntactic theory, and not empirically motivated.

Thus the Simpler Syntax Hypothesis is by necessity a matter of degree. This chapter argues that the appropriate complexity for syntax is relatively flat: headed phrases that are linearly ordered and that correspond to constituents in Conceptual Structure, but not more. Should it prove possible to make do with even less structure, we would consider that an improvement.

4.2 Overview of syntactic structure

We take syntactic structure to be a linearized hierarchical tree structure whose nodes consist of syntactic features. One important difference between our treatment of syntactic structure and common practice, including that of MGG, is that we explicitly do not take the terminal nodes in the tree to be full lexical items, complete with phonological and semantic features. Rather, following the parallel architecture laid out in Chapter 1, syntax contains only the purely syntactic features of lexical items, such as grammatical category, grammatical number, and grammatical gender (the so-called "formal features" of MGG). The phonological and semantic features of words appear only in phonological and semantic structure respectively; the function of the lexical item in the grammar is to establish part of the correspondence between the three structures. Thus, when we write a syntactic tree in conventional notation (1a), the line connecting N to *dog* has a different meaning from the line that connects N to NP. The latter means 'is a constituent of', in the usual fashion. But the former means 'is linked to corresponding phonological and semantic structures', and a form like (1b) with indices or (1c) with association lines is formally more appropriate.

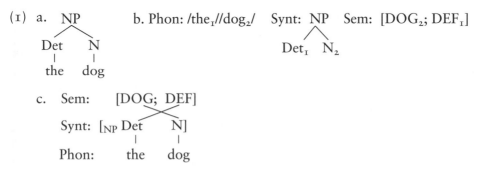

For convenience we will persist in using the standard notation, with the understanding that its meaning is as in (1b,c).

Here are some concrete examples of the syntactic structures we are aiming for. The structure of *the long story about Bill* might be as minimal as (2a), and that of *give Harry a book on Tuesday* might be (2b), corresponding approximately to the typical analyses of introductory linguistics courses. (2c) is a larger illustration.

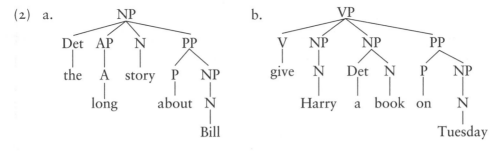

c.

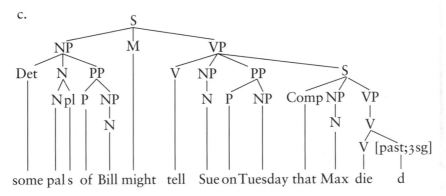

A number of characteristics mark these structures as "flat" in our sense: (a) there is no hierarchical distinction in the NPs in (2a) and (2c) between the attachment of the Determiner and the other complements and adjuncts; (b) the adjunct *on Tuesday* in (2b) is likewise a sister of the verb and the argument NP; and (c) the lower clause in (2c) has no special Infl or CP nodes.

Turning to a more formal statement of our assumptions: The terminal nodes of syntactic structure are chosen from the set of X° (or *lexical*) categories N, V, A, P, Q, Adv, Det, M, and so forth, plus various affixal categories that consist of complexes of grammatical features, such as plurality, case, grammatical gender (or noun class), agreement, and tense. Some of the lexical categories—the *major* categories N, V, A, P, and Adv—are characteristically dominated by a phrasal category XP whose label is featurally related to that of X; the X° category is the *head* of the XP. For instance, we can think of N° as [N, −phrasal] and NP as [N, +phrasal]. The other lexical categories—*minor* categories such as Det and Modal—do not (generally) have associated phrasal nodes.[1]

We retain the core insight of X′ theory: a phrasal node typically has a unique lexical node as its head; all its other dependents are either phrasal or minor categories.[2] There is no phrasal adjunction (XP dominating XP plus an adjunct); we will assume that inflectional affixes are adjoined at the X° level, as shown in (2c).[3] Thus, with one exception, the phrasal schema is only one layer deep. The exception, in violation of Structural Uniformity, is the projection of V,

---

[1] Our position here departs from a widely accepted view in MGG in which every element heads a phrase (a "maximal projection"). We will not be able to discuss this particular aspect of MGG in detail because of space limitations. Suffice it to say here that many of the details are motivated not by empirical considerations but by Structural Uniformity (Chapters 2 and 3).

[2] There are various ways one could treat nonbranching phrasal nodes such as NPs that consist of just a proper name and APs that consist only of a single unmodified adjective. The best would be a notation that allows [X, +phrasal] and [X, −phrasal] to collapse into a single node if the former does not branch. We finesse this technical detail here; we will often abbreviate such constituents as simply a phrasal node dominating a lexical item.

[3] The English possessive might be an exception, being attached to NP as a whole.

where in English there seems justification for an additional layer of structure: V dominated by VP dominated by S. (On the other hand, S may be a projection of AUX=Tense/Modal—or, following the practice of LFG, V and Tense/Modal are "coheads" of S.) We leave open whether a further layer is needed for complementizers, appositives, and parentheticals; for the moment we assume there is not. Finally, for present purposes we set aside word-internal structure such as derivational morphosyntax, though not for lack of interest.

An important exception to this canonical phrase structure schema is the conjunction schema, in which a phrasal node has two or more phrasal nodes as dependents, usually of the same category, with a conjunction as an additional dependent.[4] English also contains various language-specific idiosyncratic configurations such as the small clauses to be discussed in section 4.5.3 (*him drunk*), the nonsentential utterance frames to be discussed in section 7.2 (e.g. *Into the room with you!*), the paratactic correlative comparative to be discussed in Chapter 14 (*The more I read, the less I understand*), and exotica such as the N-P-N construction exemplified by *day by day* (Williams 1994a; Jackendoff, to appear b). Thus Structural Uniformity is taken to be only a default, not a rigid condition on syntactic structure.

Our conception of syntactic structure also differs from MGG in that we give up entirely the notion of movement in syntax, and with it the notion of any "hidden levels" of syntactic structure. Eliminating movement has ample precedent in the history of generative syntactic theory, as witness Harman (1963), Brame (1978), LFG (Bresnan 1982a), GPSG (Gazdar et al. 1985), HPSG (Pollard and Sag 1987; 1994), Construction Grammar (Goldberg 1995; to appear), and RRG (Van Valin and LaPolla 1997), among others. In many instances, what MGG has treated as syntactic movement of a constituent from position X to position Y will be replaced by a principle in the interface that says that a constituent bearing such-and-such a semantic role may appear in either position X or position Y, depending on various conditions. On the face of it this might appear to be simply a strange notational variant of movement. In each case we will show that such a formulation of positional alternations is simpler overall, and does not just replace the syntactic complexity of MGG with exactly parallel complexity or worse in the interface. The discussions of Bare Argument Ellipsis, "wrong-headed" modifiers, and sluice-stranding in Chapter 1 give a foretaste of such arguments; we will take them up in detail in Chapters 5–9.

---

[4] Sameness of syntactic category turns out to be less critical than sameness of semantic category; see Sag et al. (1985).

4.3 In-principle arguments for binary branching

The question of flat vs. ramified structure is relevant only when there are more than two constituents A, B, and C that can form a single phrase: they could be organized as [A-B-C], [[A-B]-C], or [A-[B-C]]. Otherwise, flat structure and binary branching are indistinguishable. In this section we begin the argument for flat structure with a review of the in principle motivations for binary branching. We then turn to the empirical evidence in sections 4.4–6.

4.3.1 Learnability

The impetus for the move to uniform binary branching appears to be located largely in the proposals of Kayne (1983), to whose arguments we return in a moment. However, the great appeal of binary branching seems to be due largely to arguments of Haegeman (1992b), who has suggested that binary branching is to be preferred over other branching possibilities on the grounds of simplicity and learnability. Haegeman's argument is that, given a constituent [A-B-C], uniform binary branching in a uniform direction limits the possible parses that a learner can hypothesize to just one, namely:

(3)   [A [B C]]

—and therefore facilitates the learning process. This is certainly true, but the superficial facts of language are not all consistent with uniform right-branching structure. Therefore the learner has to figure out the derivation that yields the actual surface structure from the uniform underlying structure—and in much current work, the triggering conditions that require the derivation. This task is arguably at least as complex from the perspective of learning as is the task of identifying the correct branching structure. (See Wexler and Hamburger (1973) for relevant discussion.)

In fact, as Culicover (1997) points out, learnability issues arise only when there is a choice of branching possibilities. For example, for a sequence X°-A-B there are in principle three branching configurations:

(4)   a. [X° A B]
       b. [[X° A] B]
       c. [X° [A B]]

But if the theory stipulates a specific type of branching, then the task for the learner is significantly simplified. The single type of branching could be a particular type of binary branching, or it could be flat branching as in (4a). None of these stipulations requires more of the learner than any of the others.

4.3.2 Binary branching as a desideratum of minimalism

Collins (1997) argues for binary branching on the grounds that it follows from minimalist principles applied to the application of Merge in the Minimalist Program of Chomsky (1995). The simplest form of Merge is purely binary. But as Johnson and Lappin (1999) point out, any operation of any sort, including but not limited to Merge or even to linguistic operations, is minimally binary. Furthermore, as shown by Curry (1961), any complex operation can be reformulated as a set of binary operations (and Categorial Grammar takes advantage of this possibility profusely). Showing that this is the case does not lead to the conclusion that non-binary branching does not exist.[5]

One might wish to argue that binary branching is maximally simple on grounds of Structural Uniformity. The argument would be that, first, there are many relations that are binary, and second, we would gain maximum generality by assuming that *all* relations are binary. However, since everywhere in the universe as well as everywhere in language there will be binary relations, it would follow from this reasoning that only binary relations exist everywhere. It is difficult to see the value of such reasoning, unless it were to turn out that there were positive empirical consequences of generalizing binary relations uniformly, and doing so required no additional complications of the theory. To our knowledge this has not been demonstrated for language, let alone in general.

In fact, given the interaction between branching and the number of nodes in a tree, it seems that there is no uniform minimalist position. Simplifying the branching possibilities requires the tree to have more nodes, and reducing the number of nodes requires more branching possibilities. It seems that in the absence of an independently justified measure of complexity on the basis of which we can take a particular minimalist position, the most that we can say is that the question is an empirical one.

There is evidence from outside language that human cognition includes grouping operations more general than binary Merge. Consider the visual array shown in Fig. 4.1 (next page).

The principle behind the construction and perception of this array is clearly recursive: it is built out of discrete elements which combine to form larger discrete constituents: rows of five *x*s or five *o*s, columns of three such rows, rows of three such columns, and so on. One could further combine nine of these arrays into a still larger 3 × 3 array, and continue the process indefinitely. So, to use Chomsky's term, we have here a domain of "discrete infinity"; its

---

[5] Thanks to John Nerbonne and Shalom Lappin for helpful discussion on this point.

XXXXX OOOOO XXXXX   XXXXX OOOOO XXXXX   XXXXX OOOOO XXXXX
OOOOO XXXXX OOOOO   OOOOO XXXXX OOOOO   OOOOO XXXXX OOOOO
XXXXX OOOOO XXXXX   XXXXX OOOOO XXXXX   XXXXX OOOOO XXXXX

XXXXX OOOOO XXXXX   XXXXX OOOOO XXXXX   XXXXX OOOOO XXXXX
OOOOO XXXXX OOOOO   OOOOO XXXXX OOOOO   OOOOO XXXXX OOOOO
XXXXX OOOOO XXXXX   XXXXX OOOOO XXXXX   XXXXX OOOOO XXXXX

XXXXX OOOOO XXXXX   XXXXX OOOOO XXXXX   XXXXX OOOOO XXXXX
OOOOO XXXXX OOOOO   OOOOO XXXXX OOOOO   OOOOO XXXXX OOOOO
XXXXX OOOOO XXXXX   XXXXX OOOOO XXXXX   XXXXX OOOOO XXXXX

Fig. 4.1. A visual array built on recursive principles

organization is governed by the classic gestalt principles explored by Werthei-mer (1923). As far as we know, there is no justification for saying that it is built up by binary Merge. For instance, the first row of five xs does not have an internal structure $[x[x[x[x[x]]]]]$ or any other internal organization: it is just a collection of five xs grouped into a constituent. Moreover, because the array extends in two dimensions, the spatial relation between adjacent elements must be stipulated: are the elements related horizontally or vertically? Thus the basic principle cannot just be "Merge two elements" or even "Merge n elements"; rather it has to be "combine n elements in such-and-such a spatial configuration".

Musical grouping is a one-dimensional case of the same thing. Consider the tune to *Happy Birthday*, which is grouped as shown below (each syllable of the text corresponds to a note of the tune):

(5) [[[Happy Birthday to you] [Happy Birthday to you]] [[Happy Birthday
                     dear Daniel] [Happy Birthday to you]]]

The first phrase consists of six concatenated notes, corresponding to the six syllables of text. There is absolutely no musical justification for any smaller grouping, particularly that required by rightward binary branching:

(6) *[Hap [py [Birth [day [to [you]]]]]]

Thus again the operative recursive principle has to be "combine n elements into a group" where n can be two or more.

If such n-ary recursive combinatorial principles exist outside of language, it is no great innovation to introduce them into the language capacity as well. We are therefore skeptical of the claim by Hauser et al. (2002) that binary Merge may be the major cognitive innovation in humans that makes language possible. Binary Merge is nothing but a degenerate one-dimensional version of n-ary grouping. We see no reason why the language capacity could not have borrowed the full n-ary operation from the start. An early argument to this effect comes from Chomsky (1965: 196), who argues that neither uniform left-branching nor uniform right-branching analyses can be justified for the concatenated adjectives in phrases like *a tall, young, handsome, intelligent man*. He says that flat structure is the "weakest assumption".

Nevertheless, phrase structure in language cannot be reduced to the principles governing visual and musical grouping. Two formal properties distinguish linguistic grouping:

Headedness. One member of the group has a distinguished status, such that the other members are considered dependent on it. This property, which is not a minimal property of binary branching, is incorporated into the formulation of the Minimalist Program's Merge. (It is, however, not a property of conjoined phrases.)

Category. All basic elements and all groups have a syntactic category label, and, following X-bar theory, the category of a group is (usually) related canonically to the category of its head. This too is not a necessary property of binary branching.

Either of these properties can be incorporated just as well into a formulation of linguistic phrase structure that permits *n*-ary branching. It is an open question whether they are widely shared in cognitive representations elsewhere in the mind/brain. The categories of syntax, of course, are *sui generis* to syntax.

4.3.3 C-command and unambiguous paths

Kayne (1983) explores the question of why c-command should be implicated in the identification of an antecedent for an anaphor. He suggests that if branching is binary, and α c-commands β, then the path through the tree from β to α does not lead to anywhere other than α when it goes down from the node dominating both α and β. Kayne calls this an "unambiguous path". If unambiguous path is substituted for c-command in the definition of such relations as government and binding, then in order for there to be binding, there must be binary branching. While *n*-ary branching is not ruled out in principle, Kayne's hypothesis suggests that the constituents in such a structure cannot be governed, which severely limits the utility of such a structure in natural language (though it might still be possible in the case of the concatenated adjectives mentioned above).

The data that Kayne (1983) adduces in support of uniform binary branching are consistent with binary branching, but do not require it. Kayne argues that if there is binary branching in NP, the structure (7a) will produce ungrammaticality in examples like (7b,c) because $N°$ does not govern across the boundary. Therefore the subject of the infinitive is prevented by the branching structure from getting case assigned to it by the head noun.

(7) a. [_NP_N°[NP YP]]
     b. *John's belief [(of) Mary to be a genius]
     c. *their obligation of John to join the army   [Kayne 1983, (84)]

However, the ungrammaticality of (7b) seems to be due not to deep properties
of government but to relatively superficial subcategorization: *belief* does not
allow *of*-NP complements at all, although it does allow other sorts of complements corresponding to those of the verb *believe*.

(8) a. I believe your story.
     b. *my belief of your story
     c. I believe in your story.
     d. my belief in your story
     e. I believe that your story is true.
     f. my belief that your story is true

And (7c) is a nominalized form of *they obliged John to join the army*, which is a
control structure. Other syntactically and semantically similar cases are well-
formed. (Thanks to Robert Levine for (11b).)

(9)   a. I relied on Otto to guard the entrance.
      b. my reliance on Otto to guard the entrance

(10) a. The committee approved (of) Sharon to invest the money.
      b. the committee's approval of Sharon to invest the money

(11) a. We accepted John to be the next king of Columbus.
      b. our acceptance of John to be the next king of Columbus

While there is often something problematic about [N° *of* NP *to* VP], simply
blocking this structure by appeal to case-marking does not appear to get to the
bottom of the difficulty.

    As far as we can determine, there has been no other extended discussion
of binary branching on principled or factual grounds in the literature. The
uniform assumption of binary branching in derivational approaches to syntax
has made it possible for theorists to hold this issue constant and focus on
other issues. However, in the context of current minimalist perspectives,
it seems clear that any set of assumptions that entails more structure than
is required on empirical grounds should be subjected to closer scrutiny.
On our view, the minimalist approach should be carried out unselectively,
attending to the empirical requirements and not trying to hold onto
earlier theoretical positions that themselves have only limited empirical motivation.

4.4 Empirical arguments for right-branching

We now turn to the canonical arguments about branching in the VP. There is a fundamental conflict: classical generative grammar argued that the English VP is predominantly left-branching; but in the late 1980s arguments were offered that the English VP is exclusively right-branching. This section discusses the arguments for right-branching; the next section discusses the older arguments for left-branching, plus the response by the advocates of right-branching. Given the tension between these two views, we argue that English actually has flat structure; we do so in part by defusing both sets of previous arguments. Section 4.6 goes through some parallel arguments concerning the structure of NP.

4.4.1 *The structure of the evidence*

All the arguments for right-branching have to do with the fact that the antecedent of a variable or other dependent element E must be to the left of E. It should be recalled that the earliest proposals about binding (e.g. Langacker 1969; Ross 1967) invoked a combination of linear order and command (the latter a predecessor of c-command). However, it was argued by Reinhart (1983) and Larson (1988) (see section 2.1.3) that the theory of binding would be simplified if dependence on linear order could be excluded, leaving c-command as the only relevant relationship. The operative assumption is then that binding can take place only if the antecedent c-commands the dependent element. In particular, binding is impossible if the antecedent is more deeply embedded than the variable, as shown schematically in (12a), and more concretely in (12b).

(12) a. [... Antecedent$_i$ ...] ... Variable$_i$ ...
      b. *The fact [that everyone$_i$ owed taxes] didn't bother him$_i$.

There is a price for this simplification of binding conditions: in order to account for the asymmetry in (13), one is forced to say that the VP is binary right-branching, since linear order no longer plays a role.

(13) a. The picture showed John$_i$ himself$_i$ as a young man.
      b. *The picture showed himself$_i$ John$_i$ as a young man.[6]

As we have mentioned earlier, there is a question as to whether this price is appropriate. After all, linear order is present in the string whether or not there is further structure. Adding extra structure, in order to simplify binding, entails

---

[6] The reflexive must be read as noncontrastive in this and all succeeding examples. Contrastive reflexives *do* permit binding under otherwise impossible conditions.

a cost either in learning or in UG (which will have to stipulate that linear order always corresponds to right-branching structure).

However, we will now show that c-command is neither a necessary nor a sufficient condition to determine binding possibilities. And if in turn right-branching in the VP is motivated primarily by c-command, the case for right-branching is consequently undermined as well.

What proves necessary in place of c-command are linear order plus two constraints that correlate with syntactic c-command under most but not all circumstances. One is a constraint defined over conceptual structure that we will call the 'CS-command condition'. Because in most cases syntactic and semantic embedding are parallel, many cases of c-command simulate the CS-command condition. However, as Chapter 10 will show, there are cases in which c-command and CS-command make different predictions, and the CS-command condition is more adequate. The second constraint is defined over a structure to be introduced in Chapter 6 as part of the syntax–semantics interface, the Grammatical Function tier, which plays much the same role as f-structure in LFG and the structures of Relational Grammar. Relative prominence in the GF-tier proves to constrain binding alongside the CS-command condition. These three constraints—linear order, CS-command, and GF-prominence—appear to account for many of the binding facts more comprehensively than does c-command. This is not a minimal system, nor is it nonredundant, but it appears empirically necessary, as has been argued by many researchers outside the MGG tradition such as Kuno (1987) and Golde (1999), and as we will suggest immediately below.

4.4.2 Binding of anaphors

Let us look at the binding facts in somewhat more detail. As mentioned above, if the VP is flat, c-command makes the wrong predictions for the binding of reflexives (Condition A) in double object constructions, since each NP c-commands the other; see Barss and Lasnik (1986). If the relevant condition is that the antecedent c-commands the reflexive, both (14a) and (14b) should be good; if the condition is that the antecedent *asymmetrically* c-commands the reflexive, both should be bad.

(14) a. Mary showed John$_i$ himself$_i$.
      b. *Mary showed himself$_i$ John$_i$.

Thus if c-command is taken as the proper condition for binding, we are forced to the conclusion that the structure is the right-branching [*showed* [*John* [*himself*]]], or a more complex structure, in which c-command is asymmetric.

Alternatively, we might assume that the structure is flat and that the linear order plays a crucial role in determining the antecedent of the reflexive. In fact we see that this must be correct when we consider examples involving heavy shift in the VP.

(15) *Canonical order*
    a. *John showed herself$_i$ as a young girl to Mary$_i$.[7]
    b. *The surprising outcome revealed herself$_i$ as a monster to Mary$_i$.
    c. *John discussed herself$_i$ as a presidential candidate with Mary$_i$ during the dinner party.
    d. *John presented herself$_i$ as a presidential candidate to Mary$_i$ during the dinner party.
    e. *I talked herself$_i$ as a young child over with Mary$_i$.

(16) *Heavy shift*
    a. John showed to Mary$_i$ herself$_i$ as a young girl.
    b. The surprising outcome revealed to Mary$_i$ herself$_i$ as a monster.
    c. John discussed with Mary$_i$ during the dinner party herself$_i$ as a presidential candidate.
    d. John presented to Mary$_i$ during the dinner party herself$_i$ as a presidential candidate.
    e. I talked over with Mary$_i$ herself$_i$ as a young child.

What seems to be crucial here is (a) that *Mary* is an argument of the verb, (b) that *Mary* is in the same clause as the constituent that contains the reflexive, and (c) that *Mary* is to the left of the reflexive. The presence of an intervening VP-adjunct in some of these examples strengthens the claim that the crucial syntactic relation is that of linear order within VP. It also provides evidence that flat structure includes not only the head and its arguments but also adjuncts. We turn to a closer examination of adjuncts in section 4.5.

---

[7] Examples such as (i) are not entirely ungrammatical.

(i) ?John showed a beautiful picture of herself$_i$ to Mary$_i$.

Following the analysis to be proposed in section 6.4, the reason for this is that a reflexive within a NP (a "picture-noun reflexive") does not fall under the binding constraints of the GF-tier, and therefore functions more like a type of pronominal. For discussion of such "exempt anaphors", see Pollard and Sag (1992) (and Culicover and Wilkins (1984) for an earlier and less well-developed proposal).

    Complications and refinements in the behavior of anaphors have been documented by Kuno (1987), Sells (1987), Reinhart and Reuland (1993), and many others. Golde (1999) argues that there are syntactic, semantic and discourse constraints that govern the distribution of such anaphors.

The relation of c-command interpreted strictly as a relation on syntactic structure does not play any role at all in (15)–(16), since *Mary*, as the object of a preposition, does not c-command *herself* in (16). One might try to rescue c-command by proposing that *to* and other prepositions are simply case-markers that do not affect c-command relations, or, as suggested by Kuno (1987) and Pesetsky (1995), that the proper definition of c-command ignores PP nodes.

Nevertheless, such analysis is still subject to problems. No derivation of heavy shift involving movement avoids the consequence that the antecedent fails to c-command the reflexive in configurations like (16). Consider (16c). On a classical rightward movement analysis, the NP *herself as a presidential candidate* is adjoined to the right of and outside of the VP, ruling out a c-command relation. On a Larsonian analysis, the V' *discussed with Mary* undergoes movement to the left, producing a structure along the lines of (17).

(17)

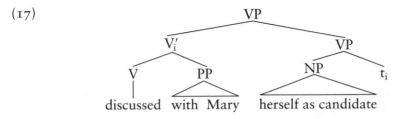

It is possible to imagine other derivations in which the antecedent is not as deeply embedded, but minimally the preposition will block the antecedent from c-commanding the reflexive. For instance, we might suppose that the verb and the PP move independently to the left, as in (18). (We leave some details unspecified in order to illustrate the basic trajectories of the movements.)

(18)

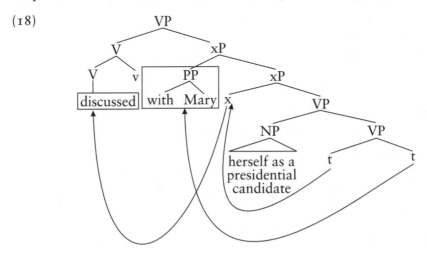

But even if *Mary* can be made to c-command *herself* by ignoring the preposition, it is not clear how to arrange matters so that such a derivation must take place.

This "simple" solution, even if it can be made to work by adopting a carefully crafted definition of c-command and accepting complex movement in the course of derivations, is still inadequate, for c-command is not a sufficient condition for the binding of reflexives. In an important set of cases, first pointed out by Postal (1971), the reflexive is c-commanded by its antecedent—and is to its right, but binding still is not possible. Note that these involve the same verbs as (15–16c,d,e), with the syntactic roles of *Mary* and *herself* exchanged.

(19)   a. *I mentioned Mary to herself.
       b. *I discussed Mary with herself.
       c. *I talked Mary over with herself.

In these examples, heavy shift only makes matters worse:

(20)   a. *I mentioned to herself Mary as a presidential candidate.
       b. *I discussed with herself Mary as a presidential candidate.
       c. *I talked over with herself Mary as a young child.

Thus the full picture is that only one of the four possibilities in (15), (16), (19), and (20) is acceptable.

Postal's account of (19) was that the ungrammaticality is a consequence of moving an anaphoric expression over its antecedent (the so-called Crossover Condition). Jackendoff (1972) suggested instead that the binding relation must satisfy thematic (i.e. CS) as well as syntactic conditions. In particular, in these examples, a recipient of information may bind a topic of information, but not the reverse. This condition is satisfied in (15) and (16), because *Mary* is the recipient of information whose topic is *herself*. However, only (16) is grammatical, because (15) violates the independent condition involving linear order. (19) and (20) both violate the thematic condition, because *herself* is the recipient of information whose topic is *Mary*. Hence even having the NPs in the proper linear order, as in (19), does not produce grammaticality. We develop this suggestion further in section 10.8.2, showing how it falls under the more general CS-command constraint.

C-command is also not sufficient because of the following well-known type of example.

(21)   a. Mary pushed the food away from her(??self).
       b. Mary saw/found/heard a leopard near her(*self).
       c. Mary has a blanket under her(*self).
       d. My pocket has a hole in it(*self).

In these examples the appropriate anaphoric element is an ordinary pronoun rather than a reflexive. Yet it is certainly c-commanded by its antecedent under usual assumptions, given that the PP containing the pronoun is a standard argument. Chapter 6 will show where the difference lies between these cases and standard clause-mate reflexives: in these cases the anaphoric element is not assigned a role on the Grammatical Function tier, which is necessary for binding clause-mate reflexives.

To sum up, syntactic c-command is not appropriate as the exclusive condition to determine binding. To the extent that other factors are involved as well, binding cannot be used as a diagnostic for c-command. Therefore there is no motivation for attempting to reduce c-command to unambiguous paths, and therefore binding does not provide evidence for binary rightward branching.

4.4.3 C-command and quantifier binding

Let us consider whether asymmetrical c-command determines the binding domain of a quantifier. This looks plausible based on examples such as these:[8]

(22) *Quantified NP c-commands* him
    a. Mary questioned [every policeman on the force]$_i$ about his$_i$ political attitudes.
    b. Mary questioned [every policeman on the force]$_i$ after he$_i$ retired.
    c. Mary$_j$ questioned [every policeman on the force]$_i$ without PRO$_j$ offending him$_i$.

    Quantified NP does not c-command him
    d. *Mary talked to [every policeman on the force]$_i$ and wrote about his$_i$ attitudes in her thesis.
    e. *Mary$_j$ said that I had planned to talk to [every policeman on the force]$_i$ without PRO$_j$ expressing herself$_j$ clearly to him$_i$.

However, if we claim that a QP must c-command a pronoun that it binds, this also entails that the object of a preposition c-commands various things to its right:

(23) a. *Object of a preposition c-commands into an argument*
       Mary talked to [every/no policeman on the force]$_i$ about his$_i$ political attitudes.

---

[8] Examples can be complicated further by putting the quantifier into the specifier position of the NP, e.g.

(i) Mary talked to every policeman$_i$'s wife about his$_i$ political attitude.

We do not have an account of why the quantifier can take scope out of this position.

b. *Object of a preposition c-commands into a temporal adjunct*
Mary talked to [every/no policeman on the force]$_i$ after he$_i$ retired.

c. *Object of a preposition c-commands into an adjunct that is controlled by the subject*
Mary$_j$ talked to [every/no policeman on the force]$_i$ in order to convince him$_i$ to take the captain's exam.

Again, a wide range of prepositions produces the same patterns.

(24) a. Mary talked with [every policeman on the force]$_i$ about his$_i$ political attitudes.

b. Mary dumps a bucket of water on top of [every policeman on the force]$_i$ when he$_i$ retires.

c. Mary$_j$ stole from [every policeman on the force]$_i$ without PRO$_j$ offending him$_i$.

Thus, it is necessary at least to adopt something like Kuno's and Pesetsky's "everything but PP" version of c-command, as well as a right-branching account of sentential adjuncts such as the *in order to* clause in (23c).

Furthermore, consider examples that parallel our examples of Heavy Shift with reflexives:

(25) a. Mary showed [every cop]$_i$ the contract being offered him$_i$.

b. *Mary showed the contract being offered him$_i$ to [every cop on the force]$_i$.

c. Mary showed to [every cop]$_i$ the contract being offered him$_i$.

(26) a. Mary discussed [every cop]$_i$ with his$_i$ wife.

b. *Mary discussed his$_i$ wife with [every cop]$_i$.

c. Mary discussed with [every cop]$_i$ his$_i$ wife and her relatives.

If the c-command restriction is to be maintained, such examples again call for derivations of heavy shift along the lines of (17) or (18). One might take this as further evidence that (17)–(18) are correct.

However, there is a simpler approach: what all the acceptable cases have in common is that the bound pronoun is within the clause immediately containing the quantifier (i.e. it is *commanded*, not c-commanded, by the quantifier), and it is to the *right* of the quantifier. Admitting linear order into the conditions for quantifier scope appears necessary in any event (recall the evidence in section 1.4.5), and it results in great savings in abstract structure and complexity of derivation. It is moreover plausible that the command relation is a reflection of a dominance relation in conceptual structure (see Chapters 5 and 6).

We conclude overall that the case for binding being determined solely by c-command, with linear order playing no role, is weak on both theoretical and empirical grounds. Since it is this hypothesis that forms the link between the empirical evidence and the conclusion that the VP is uniformly right-branching, we can abandon the right-branching hypothesis without hesitation.

4.5 Arguments for left-branching

4.5.1 Basic arguments from VP anaphora

The main argument for left-branching in VP is the classical observation that VP anaphora constructions such as *do so* replace the verb and its complement, leaving behind adjuncts. (We will call the left-behind adjunct the *remnant*.)[9]

(27)   a. Robin smokes a pipe after dinner, and Leslie does so during break-fast.   [*does so* = smokes a pipe]

         b. Robin will work in Chicago, and Leslie will do so in Milwau-kee.   [*do so* = work]

         c. Robin cooked the hamburgers on the grill, and Leslie did so on the stove.   [*do so* = cook the hamburgers]

         d. Robin flipped the hamburgers with a spatula, and Leslie did so with a chef's knife.   [*did so* = flipped the hamburgers]

(28)   Mary will cook the potatoes for fifteen minutes in the morning, and Susan

         a. will do so for twenty minutes in the evening.

                                   [*do so* = cook the potatoes]

         b. will do so in the evening.

                   [*do so* = cook the potatoes for fifteen minutes]

         c. will do so too.

         [*do so* = cook the potatoes for fifteen minutes in the morning]

The basic assumption behind the argument is that the antecedent of *do so* is a constituent. It leads to the conclusion that the maximal VP consists of nested VP's, along the lines of (29).

---

[9] We use VP anaphora rather than VP ellipsis because of the decidedly marginal status of the latter when there is a remnant (e.g. ?*Robin will work in Chicago, and Leslie will in Milwaukee*). As discussed in Ch. 8, such cases of ellipsis appear to fall together with pseudo-gapping, which is also a highly marked construction.

(29)

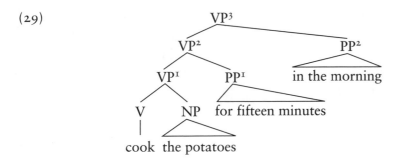

Such evidence in fact constitutes a variant of the standard textbook argument for the structure of VP.[10]

Another standard argument involves VP-topicalization. Here, a part of the VP, consisting of the V and one or more consecutive complements or adjuncts, undergoes movement to sentence-initial position.

(30) a. They said that John would cook the potatoes, and cook the potatoes he did.
b. They said that John would cook the potatoes, and cook the potatoes he did for fifteen minutes in the morning.
c. …and cook the potatoes for fifteen minutes he did in the morning.
d. …and cook the potatoes in the morning he did for fifteen minutes.

It appears that in this case, the sub-VPs *cook the potatoes*, *cook the potatoes for fifteen minutes*, and *cook the potatoes in the morning* can be moved, leaving behind the rest of the VP.

Although these facts have customarily been taken as evidence for left branching, a closer look undermines the argument. The reason is that the antecedent of *do so* is not necessary a continuous portion of another sentence. Consider the following examples. The crucial one is (31c), which readers may find more felicitous if *twelve* in the first clause receives contrastive stress.

(31) a. Robin slept for twelve hours in the bunkbed, and Leslie slept for eight hours on the futon.
b. Robin slept for twelve hours in the bunkbed, and Leslie did so on the futon. 　　　　　　　　　[*do so* = sleep for twelve hours]
c. Robin slept for twelve hours in the bunkbed, and Leslie did so for eight hours. 　　　　　　　　[*do so* = sleep … on the bunkbed]

Since the verb can be ellipted along with either or both of its adjuncts, the target of ellipsis apparently cannot be a fixed constituent. That is, it must be possible

---

[10] The standard argument in fact involves ellipsis, not VP anaphora; see n. 9 above.

for either *sleep for twelve hours* or *sleep in the bunkbed* to be a constituent. In order for there to be a stage of derivation where *sleep in the bunkbed* is a constituent, the analysis will have to make certain ad hoc assumptions regarding movement, perhaps along the lines of (32) (we will refer to this sort of derivation, which turns up repeatedly, as "Iterated Raising"[11]).

(32)
Merge: [sleep [in the bunkbed]]
[*do so* anaphora licensed at this point]
Merge: [[for 12 hours][sleep [in the bunkbed]]]
Raise *sleep*:   [sleep$_i$ [[for 12 hours][e$_i$ [in the bunkbed]]]]
Raise *in the bunkbed*: [[in the bunkbed]$_j$ [sleep$_i$ [[for 12 hours][e$_i$ e$_j$]]]]
Raise *sleep for 12 hours*:
                    [[sleep$_i$ [[for 12 hours][e$_i$ e$_j$]]]$_k$ [[in the bunkbed] e$_k$]]

Thus although the first clause of (31) has a single surface order and is unambiguous, it must have multiple derivations that produce different constituent structures, each of which can feed a different case of *do so* anaphora. When the number of arguments and adjuncts is greater than two, the complexity of the analysis is correspondingly greater.

The notion that anaphora involves syntactic identity with an antecedent misses an obvious point, reminiscent of our discussion of bare argument ellipsis in Chapter 1. The remnant of ellipsis is typically a focus, which contrasts with the focus in the antecedent VP. (This is why contrastive stress in (31) aids interpretation.) The missing material in the *do so* clause is understood to match all of the meaning of the VP except for the contrasting foci. Flat structure is sufficient for this purpose, since a richer structure does not provide any information that ellipsis can use. We return to the formulation of such computation in Chapter 8.

Other pro-VPs like *do it* and *do the same thing* also appear to stand in for a subpart of a VP—including the verb itself and non-contiguous portions of the VP (33c,d).

(33) a. Robin ate the cake and Mary did {it, too/the same/the same thing/
         likewise/the opposite/something else}.
      b. Robin broke the window and Mary did {it/the same/the same thing/
         likewise/the opposite/something else} to the table top.

---

[11] See Rochemont and Culicover (1997) for an argument that the power of Iterated Raising renders the binary branching hypothesis vacuous.

   c. Robin broke the window with a hammer, and Mary did {it/the same/ etc.} to the table top.

   d. Robin proved to George that Mary would win the race, and Bill did {it/the same/etc.} regarding Susan.

Example (33a) shows that it is possible to use expressions like *do the same, do the same thing*, to refer to an event already expressed in the discourse. Example (33b) shows that the same expressions can pick out part of an event expressed by a VP. As in *do so* ellipsis, the remnant is a contrastive focus. Example (33c) shows that, as in *do so* ellipsis, the interpretation can correspond to a discontinuous part of a VP, here *break . . . with a hammer*. And example (33d) shows that the antecedent may even involve arguments and adjuncts of more than one V.

As pointed out by Chomsky (1971), forms such as (33b–d) also show that the anaphora cannot be derived by reference to a literal VP that is a copy of the antecedent, because the remnant cannot serve as a well-formed piece of such a VP:

(34) b. . . . *and Mary broke to the table top.

      c. . . . *and Mary broke to the table top with a hammer.

      d. . . . *and Bill proved to George that regarding Susan would win the race.

Moreover, as observed by Hankamer and Sag (1976), pro-VPs can also be constructed in response to situations in which there is no linguistic antecedent at all:[12]

(35) a. I bet you can't do **this**!   [performing a handstand]

      b. I bet you can't do this to the table top!

                      [breaking a brick with one hand]

      c. I bet you can't do this with a fork!

                      [breaking a brick with a hammer]

Thus the basic assumption leading to the left-branching hypothesis of VP structure fails: there is no way a pro-VP can be consistently interpreted as related to a constituent of an antecedent sentence, with the remnant outside this constituent. We will return to some of the problems raised by such constructions in Chapter 8.

---

[12] To be sure, this is not true of all pro-VPs: **I bet you can't do so (to the table top)*. But the behavior of adjunct remnants is the same, so we have reason to think the same syntactic factors are operative.

4.5.2 *Arguments/adjuncts in VP*

Another classic observation involving *do so* anaphora is that arguments in VP are closer to the verb than adjuncts. Consider the following examples.

(36) a. Robin read the book on the train, while Leslie was doing so on the bus. [do so = reading the book; on the bus = adjunct]

    b. *Robin put a book on the couch, while Leslie was doing so on the table. [do so = putting a book; on the table = argument]

On the standard assumption that *do so* replaces a VP, the difference between (36a) and (36b) is evidence that the direct object and the locative PP are both sisters of V when the PP is an argument, so the two cannot be grouped separately; but the PP adjunct is higher up.[13] The two structures would be

(37) a. [$_{VP}$ put NP PP]

    b. [$_{VP}$ [$_{VP}$ read NP] PP]

This structural difference also correctly predicts the behavior of pro-VPs like *do it*, *do the same thing*, etc. in these contexts.

(38) a. Robin read the book on the train, and Leslie did it/the same thing on the bus.

    b. *Robin put the book on the table, and Leslie did it/the same thing on the floor.

Similar evidence comes from descriptive predication and resultatives.

(39) *Predicate applies to direct object*

    a. *Mary eats her vegetables raw, and Bill does so/does it/does the same thing cooked.

    b. *Mary pounded the cabbage to shreds, and Bill did so/did it/did the same thing to pieces.

    c. *Mary sang herself hoarse, and Bill did so/did it/did the same thing to sleep.

    d. *Mary hammered the metal flat, but Bill did so/did it/did the same thing very flat.

---

[13] There was a famous unpublished (and possibly unwritten) paper by Ross and Lakoff in the 1960s called "Why You Can't *Do So into the Sink*", the reason being that PPs with *into* can serve only as arguments, not as adjuncts, and arguments cannot serve as remnants for *do so* anaphora. Jackendoff (1977) treated this distinction by attaching arguments to V′ and adjuncts to VP.

(40) *Predicate applies to subject*

    a. Mary ate her vegetables nude, but Groucho did so/did it/did the same thing in his pajamas.

    b. Mary pounded the cabbage vigorously, but Bill did so/did it/did the same thing gently.

    c. Mary left the lecture a true believer, but Bill did so/did it/?did the same thing a skeptic.

    d. Mary read the article tired, but Bill did so/did it/did the same thing wide awake.

Here, a predicate whose antecedent is the subject appears to be outside of the VP, while one whose antecedent is the direct object appears to be inside of the VP, as in (41).

(41) a. (39a) = Mary$_i$ [$_{VP}$ eat vegetables$_j$ raw$_j$]

    b. (40a) = Mary$_i$ [$_{VP}$ [$_{VP}$ eat vegetables$_j$] nude$_i$]

Thus the classical evidence is consistent with flat structure, to the extent that in (41a) it allows two constituents of VP both to be sisters of the verb.

Of course, binary branching can be preserved in these cases by stipulating that when there appear to be two sisters of VP, as in the case of *eat vegetables raw*, there is actually branching structure; but the pro-VP must take the maximal structure as its antecedent, and not the inner VP. On such an approach, we might say when the predicate applies external to the VP, as in *eat vegetables nude*, the string *eat vegetables* is a VP and *nude* is adjoined to some higher non-VP projection. So the structures would be the following, with binary branching preserved.[14]

(42) a. Mary$_i$ [$_{VP}$ [$_{VP}$ eat vegetables$_j$] raw$_j$]

    b. Mary$_i$ [$_{XP}$ [$_{VP}$ eat vegetables$_j$] nude$_i$]

However, the stipulation that the antecedent of a pro-VP must be the highest VP appears to be nothing more than a way to maintain branching structure when there is no evidence for it. It also fails to account for the fact that VP-topicalization treats the subject-oriented predicate (i.e. *nude*) as part of the VP:

---

[14] We are simplifying for convenience. Assuming a uniform binary branching structure, this difference would play out in such a way that *raw* would be within the VP while *nude* would be outside, e.g.

(i) a. [$_{VP}$ v[$_{VP}$ vegetables$_i$[$_{V'}$ eat raw$_i$]]]

    b. [$_{XP}$ nude$_j$ ... [$_{VP}$v [$_{VP}$vegetables[$_{VP}$eat]]]]

Somehow *eat vegetables* will have to be raised to the left of *nude* in the sentence corresponding to (i.b).

(43)   They said that she would eat the vegetables nude/in her pajamas/raw, and eat the vegetables nude/in her pajamas/raw she did.

Further evidence along similar lines is that, although adjunct PPs are quite freely ordered (44a–c), an argument PP is uncomfortable to the right of an adjunct PP in VP (44d,e).

(44)   *PP adjuncts reorder freely*
    a.   Robin slept for ten hours with her cat on the couch on Thursday.
    b.   Robin slept with her cat on Thursday for ten hours on the couch.
    c.   Robin slept on the couch for ten hours on Thursday with her cat.
    PP argument plus PP adjunct do not reorder freely
    d.   Robin put the books on the table on Thursday.
    e.   ?*Robin put the books on Thursday on the table.

Again, it could be that argument PPs are inside of VP, while some adjuncts are adjoined to VP. But an argument can be placed after an adjunct by heavy shift, as seen in the following examples.

(45)   a. Robin will put the books next Tuesday on the table to the right of the front door.
    b. Robin walked quickly into the room.
    c. Robin muttered under his breath about the decision.
    d. Robin will lecture on Thursday in the Grand Ballroom about the decision.
    e. Robin alluded on many occasions to the fact that the primary evidence for this theory had never been verified experimentally.

An alternative account of (44) appeals simply to linear order: arguments preferably precede adjuncts in VP, but this preference is defeasible. It can be mitigated by factors such as length (heaviness) and focus, which bias a constituent towards being positioned at the end of a phrase. Under this account, which we will work out further in section 5.5, there is no need for further articulation within the VP. This still leaves open the question of how arguments and adjuncts are distinguished in VP anaphora; we return to this question in section 8.1.

A critic might find this solution contrived. In the prevailing aesthetic of the field, it seems less elegant to distinguish arguments and adjuncts by linear order than by structural attachment. In response, we wish to point out that in information-theoretic terms, the structural solution is actually redundant. The distinction between arguments and adjuncts is a semantic one, depending on the meaning of the verb (Koenig et al. 2003). The syntax–semantics interface might map this onto a syntactic distinction or it might not. If it does, linear order is as good as structure, in fact better because it is available in the phonology. To be sure, the structural solution *explains* the linear order, but it does so by stipulating that the argument/adjunct distinction maps into structure—which doesn't come for free. In information-theoretic terms, this stipulation actually costs just as much as stipulating a direct mapping onto linear order. So why invoke a middleman?

In short, the evidence from the argument/adjunct distinction and from subject- versus object-oriented predication is inconclusive in establishing a left-branching structure in the VP. Moreover, in order to make this evidence consistent with uniform binary right branching along the lines suggested in section 4.4, one must work out a derivation in which the verb plus its complements and adjuncts form a constituent at some point where the anaphora conditions can be met. The Iterated Raising derivation in (32) above gives an idea of the sort of artificiality that seems necessary. Moreover, the possible configurations should be constrained in some principled way; if the tests suggest that all combinations of V+argument and V+adjunct are constituents, then the assumption that there is uniform branching structure does not explain anything about the data (although it can surely be made consistent with it). We take this to be an indication that there is no internal structure to the VP.

4.5.3 *Small clauses*

Let us turn to small clauses. We argued above that for depictive and resultative predicatives in VP, the structure of VP is V-NP-Pred, regardless of the orientation of the predicate. This conclusion conflicts with the assumption of Strong Interface Uniformity, which requires every predicate to form a "small clause" constituent with the NP of which it is predicated (section 3.1.1). The actual situation is more interesting: a fuller look at the syntactic evidence shows that some NP-Pred combinations do form small clauses, and others do not. This is important, because it shows that it is possible to motivate richer structure on empirical grounds as well as to argue *against* it on empirical grounds—each case must be considered on its own merits. If there is evidence to support small clauses, then where this evidence is not found, the structure *must* be flat (in the absence of some other explanation).[15]

True small clauses are found as the complements of *imagine* and some related verbs, as the complement of *without*, and as event subjects of predicates like *would be a scandal, would surprise me*, etc. Here we summarize the

---

[15] This evidence and its implications were first noted by Pollard and Sag (1994).

evidence that these are actually small clauses, that is, constituents of the form NP-Pred.

i. Pseudo-clefts suggest that NP-Pred is a constituent when the verb is of the *imagine* class, but not of the closely related class including *consider.*

(46) a.   What I imagined / visualized / conceived of was Robin drunk.
      b.   *What I considered / judged was Robin drunk.
                  [*considered* in the sense of 'believed', not 'thought about']

That is, the structure of *imagine Robin drunk* is (47a), and that of *consider Robin drunk* is (47b).

(47) a.   [$_{VP}$ imagine [$_{SC}$ NP AP]]
      b.   [$_{VP}$ consider NP AP]

The impossibility of (46b) might be attributed to the fact that it is difficult to focus pseudo-clefts with clausal complements using these verbs.

(48) a.   I considered/judged your proposal.
      b.   I considered/judged that you were on the right track.

(49) a.   What I considered/judged was your proposal.
      b.   *What I considered/judged was that you were on the right track.

Hence if the small clause is clausal, it could be excluded in (46b) simply on these grounds. But as Hukari and Levine (1991) argue, the same argument cannot be made for *find*, which disallows the pseudo-cleft with putative small clauses but allows it with full clause complements.

(50) a.   I found Robin stupid.
      b.   I found that Robin was stupid
      c.   *What I found was Robin stupid.
      d.   What I found was that Robin was stupid.

ii. Adverbs cannot precede direct objects, but they can precede argument clauses, perhaps as a consequence of heavy shift. The *imagine* class permits such adjuncts before the NP-Pred string, suggesting they form a type of clause. By contrast, the *consider* class does not, suggesting that the NP is a direct object of the verb, as in structure (47b) above.

(51) a.   I could visualize clearly/only with great effort Robin drunk.
      b.   *I could judge clearly/without difficulty Robin drunk.

iii. A possible small clause configuration is one in which the Pred is a gerundive, e.g. *falling on the ice* as in:

(52) Robin falling on the ice would be a disaster.

The putative true small clause contexts allow gerundives, while the false ones do not.

(53) a. I imagined Robin falling on the ice.
      b. We got all the way home without Robin falling on the ice.
      c. *I considered/judged Robin falling on the ice.
                           [*considered* in the sense of 'believed']
      d. *I found Robin having fallen on the ice.

iv. As Guéron and May (1984) show, *that*-resultatives are ambiguous when the antecedent *so* is in an embedded clause, because *so* can be interpreted with either low scope or high scope, e.g.

(54) Bill said that so many people got drunk that the police had to be called.
                                                              [ambiguous]

The ambiguity occurs because *so* can be interpreted low, with the *that*-clause adjoined inside the embedded clause, or *so* can be interpreted high, with the *that*-clause adjoined to the main clause. When there is only one clause, only the high adjunction site for the *that*-clause is possible, and there is no ambiguity.

(55) a. The police arrested so many people that we were outraged.
      b. So many people were rude that the police had to be called.

In an NP-Pred sequence with the *imagine* class, there is an ambiguity; with the *consider* class, there is no ambiguity.

(56) a. I imagined so many people drunk that I had to call {the police/my
          psychiatrist}.   [ambiguous]
      b. We gave a party without so many people getting drunk {that the police
          had to be called/that we won a citation from the Chamber of Com-
          merce}.   [ambiguous]
      c. I considered so many people drunk {that I needed to call the police/
          *that we won a citation}.   [unambiguous]

Example (56a) can be taken to mean that in my imagination, there were so many drunk people that I called the police, or it can mean that the number of people that I imagined to be drunk was so great that I (actually) called my psychiatrist. (Who I might or did call varies in these interpretations to make them more plausible.) Similarly, example (56b) can be taken to mean either that there were so few people drunk at the party that we won a citation, or that we gave a party where the number of drunk people was small enough that the police did not have to be called. Example (56c) can only mean that the number of people that I considered drunk was sufficiently large that I called the police. It does not mean that I had the belief that the number of people drunk would require calling the police or win us a citation. The pattern of interpretations here is consistent with the hypothesis that there is a clausal structure in (56a,b) but not in (56c).

v. An NP–Pred sequence in subject position is a good candidate to be a constituent, as there is no other way to create the string. It has a clausal interpretation, as shown by the possibility of its including a *so that*-resultative.

(57)   a. [sc So many people drunk] would really ruin my party.
       b. [sc So many people drunk that the police have to be called] would really ruin my party.

In this case, *so* cannot have scope over the entire sentence.

(58)   *So many people (getting) drunk annoyed me that I had to call the cops.

An alternative possible structure for (57a) would have *people* as head of a normal NP and the AP *drunk* as a postnominal modifier, as in *the book yellow with age*. However, we can reject this possibility. There is a constraint against interpreting *so* within a clausal subject as having wide scope, as illustrated in (59a). (57a) follows this pattern. In contrast, with a normal NP where *so* is a specifier of the head noun, wide scope is possible, as seen in (59b). And if the predicate in (57a) is changed to *drunk with power*, thus truly paralleling *yellow with age*, again wide scope is possible (59c).

(59)   a. *For so many people to be drunk annoyed me that I called the cops.
       b. So many people who were drunk came to my party that I called the cops.
       c. So many people drunk with power annoyed me that I called the cops.

We conclude that in (57a) *people* is not a normal head noun, but indeed the subject of a small clause.

   Given these tests, we have an empirical basis for determining whether an NP–Pred sequence is a true small clause or not. In the absence of such evidence, it is reasonable to conclude that an NP–Pred sequence is not a small clause. In most cases, especially with V–NP–Pred, it is safe to conclude that if the pseudo-cleft is not possible, NP–Pred is not a small clause, e.g.

(60) a. We hammered the metal flat.
           *What we hammered was the metal flat.
      b. We sang ourselves hoarse.
           *What/who we sang was ourselves hoarse.
      c. We hung the flag high.
           *What we hung was the flag high.
      d. Robin gave Leslie the book.
           *What Robin gave was Leslie the book.

Putting the matter simply, it is safe to say that most putative small clauses are not small clauses. But if they are not small clauses, then the structure of the VP that contains them is either [$_{VP}$ [$_{VP}$ V NP] Pred] or [$_{VP}$ V NP Pred]. Since we have already ruled out the left-branching analysis, the remaining possibility is that of flat structure.

4.6 NP structure

The evidence regarding the structure of VPs can be adapted straightforwardly to the structure of NPs. There are two basic views of branching in NP, one more traditional and one emerging from the move to encode inflection in the form of functional heads.

On the more traditional view of NP structure, the N is the head, the complements and modifying phrases are adjoined to the right, and the prenominal material is adjoined to the left. A typical structure is given in (61).

(61)

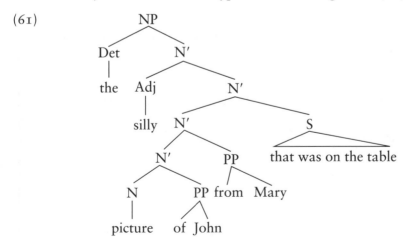

On the more current view, the structure is more like (62).

(62)

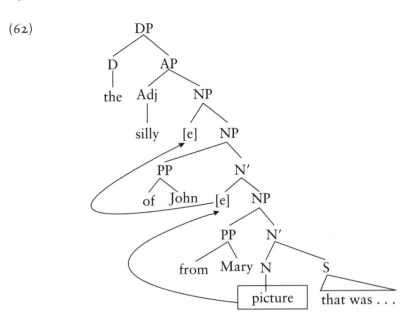

This is almost certainly just an approximate structure, since it leaves out functional heads such as NUM and AGR, but it will suffice to illustrate the point.

We will first take up the structure of NP complements, then turn to the specifiers. In each case we will argue that the evidence actually supports less structural differentiation than is generally accepted, on either of the views above.

4.6.1 NP complements

The primary evidence for (61), the left-branching structure of NP, like the evidence for left-branching in VP, involves anaphora and ellipsis. The data in (63) is typical.

(63) I put that silly picture of Robin from Mary that was on the table next to
    a. this artful one of Susan from Gretel that was on the shelf.

[one = picture]

    b. this one of Susan from Gretel that was on the shelf.

[one = (silly) picture]

    c. this one from Gretel that was on the shelf.

[one = (silly) picture (of Susan)]

    d. this one that was on the shelf.

[one = (silly) picture (of Susan) (from Gretel)]

    e. this one.

[one = (silly) picture (of Robin) (from Mary) (that was on the table)]

In the interpretations following the examples, the parentheses around the modifiers indicate that while *one* may be interpreted as the full NP in the preceding conjunct, minus the contrastive material, it need not be.

The structure in (61) is clearly consistent with these data, since *one* seems to correspond to an N′. It is not entirely clear how to account for these data in terms of the structure in (62), but there is little doubt that the movement machinery is sufficiently powerful to produce intermediate structures that correspond to the N′ constituents in (61) for the purpose of these constructions.

In any case, the issue is moot, because the test involving *one(s)* can pick out nonconstituents, just like the parallel cases of *do so* anaphora.

(64)   that silly picture of Robin from Mary that is on the table, and
       a. this artful one from Susan
                          [one = picture (of Robin)(that is on the table)]
       b. this one from Susan
                          [one = (silly) picture (of Robin)(that is on the table)]

Since *(silly) picture of Robin that is on the table* is not a constituent of the first NP, it is not clear how it could be a syntactic antecedent of *one* in the second NP. Of course, we could always assume that there is a stage in the derivation of the NP where the required constituent exists, and that it is then broken up. Such an approach might be most natural if we assumed something like the structure in (62), since there could be hidden movements that create this constituent in the course of an "Iterated Raising" style of derivation, along the lines of (65), paralleling (32) for VP.

(65)   Merge: [picture [that is on the table]]
       Merge: [of Robin] [picture that is on the table]
       [*one* anaphora licensed at this point]
       Raise *picture*:   [[picture$_i$] [[of Robin] [e$_i$ that is on the table]]]
       Merge: [from Mary] [[picture$_i$] [[of Robin]
                                    [e$_i$ that is on the table]]]
       Raise *of Robin*: [of Robin]$_j$ [[from Mary] [[picture$_i$]
                                    [e$_j$ [e$_i$ that is on the table]]]]
       Raise *picture*:   [picture$_i$] [[of Robin]$_j$
                      [[from Mary] [[e$_i$] [e$_j$ [e$_i$ that is on the table]]]]]

As suggested in our discussion of VP structure, if such movements are permitted simply for the purpose of getting the correct intermediate structures, then there is no principled basis for arguing for or against any structure.

But it is possible to construct a factual as well as a conceptual argument against such a general approach. In the following examples, there are fixed orders for the modifiers (similar examples appear in Jackendoff (1977: ch. 7).

(66)   a.   an article about Ohio State that describes the various research programs
       b   *an article that describes the various research programs about Ohio State
       c.   an article about Ohio State that describes the various research programs, and one about Michigan
                    [one = article (that describes the various research programs)]

(67)   a.   a picture of Robin showing his famous smile
       b.   *a picture showing his famous smile of Robin
       c.   a picture of Robin showing his famous smile, and one of Mary   [one = picture (showing her famous smile)]

(68)   a.   the man arrested in the park who was carrying a rifle
       b.   *the man who was carrying a rifle arrested in the park
       c.   the man arrested in the park who was carrying a rifle and the one found hiding in the gazebo [one = man (who was carrying a rifle)]

In each case the antecedent cannot be a constituent of the preceding NP. While it is mechanically possible to arrange a derivation that creates such an antecedent temporarily for the purpose of anaphora, the fact that such constituents cannot exist on the surface casts serious doubt on any such mechanism. What seems to be going on, rather, is that the constraints on surface ordering do not interfere in the construction of an interpretation for *one*: it is simply the interpretation of the antecedent NP less the material in contrast. Given that there is no syntactic constituency involved here, there is no reason to pick a particular branching structure for the NP on the basis of *one*. It is in fact sufficient to take the post-nominal constituents to be sisters of one another and the head noun. Each plays a particular role in the interpretation of the NP, either as a complement or a modifier, and this function must be correctly represented at CS.

This analysis of *one*-anaphora in NPs has an interesting consequence for learnability. Lidz et al. (2003) show that 18-month-old children already appreciate the possible interpretations of *one*-anaphora expressions such as those in (63). They conclude that these children must already have in place the recursive N′ structure that the standard approach claims is necessary for such interpretations. This is taken as evidence that the N′ structure is provided by UG. On our view, UG need not be so elaborate: what the children appreciate is that the remnant of an ellipsis construction has to be understood as fitting into the interpretation of its antecedent—much like bare argument ellipsis, which very young children also handle nicely. There is no need for further syntactic elaboration in order for the interpretation of *one* to be successful.

4.6.2 NP specifiers

There are some well-known puzzles regarding the structure of specifiers in NP. For instance, Partee (1975) argues that, on grounds of interpretation, a relative clause must be within the scope of a quantifier.

(69)   every woman that showed up at the party

In (69) the quantifier appears to take scope over the set denoted by *woman*, restricted by the modifier *that showed up at the party*. The syntactic structure in which *every woman* is a constituent does not directly reflect the scope of the quantifier. So given this line of argument, the structure should be (70a) and not (70b).

(70)   a. [every [woman that showed up at the party]]
       b. [[every woman][that showed up at the party]]

This conclusion is further confirmed by examples such as the following, where the interpretation suggests that the relative clause is a sister of the head, while the adjective is not, parallel to (70a).

(71)   the last guy who showed up   (= [the last [guy who showed up]])

   On the other hand, this conclusion is contradicted by cases of conjoined NPs with a shared relative clause.

(72)   a. every woman and every man who showed up at the party (looked drunk)
       b. the men and the women who were married to one another (looked very similar)

In these cases, because of the distinct determiners and especially the symmetrical predicate in (72b), it appears that the structure must be that of (70b). Note also that it is possible, perhaps in a somewhat archaic style, to have a relative clause on a pronoun, which is itself a full NP, again arguing for (70b) as the structure.

(73)   a. He who hesitates is lost.
       b. We who are about to take the exam salute you.

Hence it appears that both right- and left-branching structures are possible, a situation that we found in the case of VP structure as well.

Our solution is to abandon the claim that the syntactic structure is fixed and dependent on the CS representation. Rather, the structure is flat. The apparent requirement that certain constituents must be grouped together semantically is a consequence of the scope of the quantifier and the modifiers at CS. To be specific, in the case of (69) the structure is (74a); and (71) is (74b).

(74)   a.

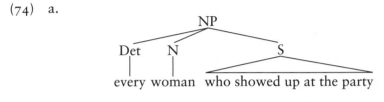

b.

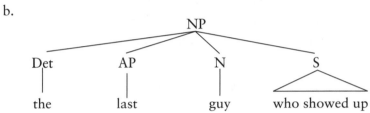

This structure conforms, of course, to more recent views about the logical form of quantified expressions (e.g. Heim 1982).

(75)   [Every x, x a woman, s.t. x showed up at the party]

On the other hand, as Chomsky (1975b) argues, the syntactic structure can always be translated into some logical form, and so there is no requirement that it be isomorphic to the logical form in all respects.

Similar problems arise in conjoined structures.[16] In (76), the predicate in the relative clause is not symmetrical, and the relative clause may be interpreted as distributed over the two antecedent NPs.

(76)   a. [[[every woman] and [every man]] [who showed up at the party]]
       b. [every x, x a woman, s.t. x showed up at the party] and [every y, y a man, s.t. y showed up at the party]

The quantifiers seem to behave normally with respect to their capacity to take wide or narrow scope and to bind pronouns, in spite of the structure.

---

[16] It may be of interest for historical purposes that we worked extensively on the material in the next few paragraphs while furiously playing ping pong during the summer of 1975. Some of the examples appeared in Jackendoff (1977).

(77) a. Every woman and every man who showed up at the party met someone interesting.
b. Every woman and every man who showed up at the party met his or
her spouse before the evening was over.

However, when the predicate in the relative clause is symmetrical, it imposes a
different interpretation on the antecedents.

(78) a. [[[the men] and [the women]] [who were married to one another]]
b. [[[every man] and [every woman]][who were married to one an-
other]]

Here *the men and the women* and *every man and every woman* denote man–
woman pairs that satisfy the condition imposed by the relative clause.

Similar distinctions arise with PP adjuncts (79a,b) and even PP complements
(79c,d):

(79) a. the men and the women with big ears
[= the men with big ears and the women with big ears—distributive]
b. the boy and the girl with {the same birthday/a common background/
matching shirts/different-colored eyes}   [≠the boy with the same
birthday and the girl with the same birthday—collective]
c. three students and two teachers of French   [distributive]
three members and two vice-chairmen of the committee
d. three students and two teachers of the same language   [collective]
three members and two vice-chairmen of interlocking committees

Moreover, if a relative clause is separated from its NP host, the antecedent of
the relative pronoun does not need to be a constituent (as pointed out by
Perlmutter and Ross (1970)):

(80) a. A man came in and a woman left who turned out to be married to one
another.
b. I met a man yesterday and a woman last week who turned out to be
married to one another.

These examples show that the syntax must be sufficiently unstructured to
allow for all of the possibilities that arise from the semantic properties of the
determiners and the modifiers. That is, the structure is flat and the relative
clause is paratactically attached to the sentence in (80); the choice between
distributive and collective interpretation is a function of the semantics of the
modifier and has nothing to do with syntax:

(81) [a man$_i$ came in] and [a woman$_j$ left] [who$_{i+j}$ turned out ...]

Let us now consider in a little more detail the structure to the left of the head noun. In English there is a fixed order, described in the very early studies in generative grammar (see Hall 1965 and Jackendoff 1977, among others). A partial version is given in (82). All constituents are optional.

(82) a. Det Num/Quan Adj* N
      b. the three/many big fat horses

In the earliest work it was suggested that the prenominal sequence is a constituent (e.g. Hall 1965; Jackendoff 1969b). In fact there is evidence to support this view, as illustrated by the following.

(83)   the three big and the three small horses

On the view that what is conjoined is a constituent, it would follow that *the three big* is a constituent. Of course, this view is somewhat controversial, and there are alternative ways to account for constructions such as (83) without accepting this conclusion. For example, we could take the head of *the three big* to be an empty N. More radical approaches to coordination would take the head *horses* to be shared by the two conjuncts (e.g. Goodall 1984), as in (84).

(84)

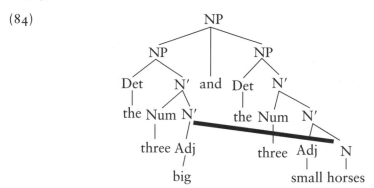

The point of assuming that there is an empty head or a shared head is to preserve the right-branching structure of the prenominal sequence in the absence of a nominal head in the left conjunct. But there is yet another possibility: what is conjoined is the prenominal sequence, and there is right node raising of the head. In this case the structure would be the unintuitive (85).

(85)   [[[the three big] and [the three small]] horses]

As in the case of RNR in VPs and Ss, the condition on the well-formedness of such constructions is that they be interpretable using the standard rules of interpretation for dealing with non-coordinate right-branching structures.

If we say that the interpretation of *the three big* is a lambda expression with a variable in place of the head, then interpretation of the conjoined phrase is straightforward without resorting to empty Ns or discontinuous constituency.

(86) λx [[the [three [big x]] and [the [three [small x]](horses)

The idea that what we are dealing with here is RNR and not an empty N or discontinuous constituency is confirmed by the fact that the construction exemplified in (83) is possible only when there is nothing to the right of the "head" in the left conjunct. If both conjuncts were full NPs then we would expect (87a,b) to be grammatical, but they are not.

(87) a. *the three big that Robin owns and the three small horses that Mary owns

     b. *the three long about Mary and the three short stories about Susan   [cf. *the three long and the three short stories about Susan*]

To sum up, what we see in the case of conjoined NPs is that the semantic demands on the syntactic structure are variable. The syntactic structure is licensed by the possible correspondence to a well-formed CS, and any particular configuration is well-formed just in case this correspondence can be established. The *hierarchical* structure associated with an NP is the structure of its corresponding CS, which is the level where binding and scope relations are defined. The syntactic structure per se of NP is invariant over different correspondences: it is flat structure, to some degree linearly ordered. Again, we suggest that the linear order represented in the flat structure is the fundamental asymmetry in syntactic structure that is epistemologically indisputable; on intuitive grounds it should certainly be available for defining the interface rules, as well as for defining semantic relations such as binding and scope. And, as we have also argued, this is the only syntactic information that is available for such purposes.

4.7 A sketch of English phrase structure

We conclude this chapter with a sketch of the rules of phrase structure for English. In Chapter 1 we laid out our overall position that the principles of phrase structure are to be thought of as constraints on possible structures rather than as rewriting rules; they are stated in terms of permissible pieces of structure. Some of these will be specializations of very general frames provided by Universal Grammar, but some will be special constructions peculiar to English.

It proves of interest to divide the phrase structure rules into principles of constituency and principles of linear order. This enables us to arrange constituents in different ways without affecting hierarchical structure, an advantage in dealing with some kinds of free word order phenomena. Such a division was first pioneered in generative grammar by GPSG and has become a staple of the constraint-based frameworks.[17] It is harder to make such a division in a conception of phrase structure rules as rewriting rules, which establish a basic constituency and order simultaneously; free word order phenomena are typically attributed to a movement operation called Scrambling, which is often formally rather vague in character (see the brief discussion in section 9.6.2).

There is another reason for dividing phrase structure rules into constraints on constituency and constraints on linear order. There are some autonomous syntactic principles that determine order—for example, the fact that the English verb comes at the beginning of VP and the Japanese verb comes at the end, the fact that English has particles that can appear on either side of the direct object, and the fact that relative clauses follow nouns. However, there are also some facts about order that depend on semantics—for example that phrases expressing focus tend to be later in the sentence crosslinguistically, that in English argument PPs normally precede adjunct PPs in the VP, and that subject–auxiliary inversion is always connected to a variety of semantic effects. Such effects are due to phrasal interface rules that are sensitive to word or phrase order. This section will concentrate on the autonomous syntactic principles; Chapters 5 through 9 will take up the interface rules in detail.

With this preparation, we can begin to look at the phrase structure rules of English. Given the flat structures motivated in the rest of this chapter, we can get away with something like (88) for some basic structures of English. In (88), "[XP" means XP is at the left edge; "X > Y" means X precedes Y; "X $>_{\text{default}}$ Y" means that X preferably precedes Y, i.e. this is the default order.

---

[17] This distinction has an ample tradition—see Curry (1961), who distinguishes between "tectogrammar" (the structure) and "phenogrammar" (the surface realization), GPSG (Gazdar et al. 1985), recent work in the Prague School (e.g. Sgall 1992), work in categorial grammar such as Dowty (1996), work in HPSG such as Kathol (2000), and work in Dependency Grammar (e.g. Petkevic 1987). Chomsky (1965: 124–7) alludes to such proposals by Curry (1961) and Šaumjan and Soboleva (1963), rejecting them summarily on the grounds that they are not sufficiently worked out. He observes that unordered constituency would be useful for describing free word order languages, but then claims that "there is no known language that remotely resembles this description" (p. 126). (Warlpiri attracted attention only later.) He then speaks of free word order in terms of "rules of stylistic inversion" and suggests these are "not so much rules of grammar as rules of performance. . . . " He continues: "In any event, though this is surely an interesting phenomenon, it is one that has no apparent bearing, for the moment, on the theory of grammatical structure" (p. 127). However, once a grammar is stated in terms of constraints (as in GPSG and practically all other non-mainstream forms of generative grammar) rather than sequential derivation, it becomes much more feasible to separate constituency and linear order.

(88)   *Autonomous phrase structure rules*

Constituency	Order
a. $\{_S(XP/C)\ NP\ T\ (PP/AdvP)\ (VP)\}$	$[XP/C;\ NP >_{\text{default}} T >_{\text{default}} VP$
b. $\{_{VP}(V)\ (Prt)\ (XP)^*\}$	$[V;\ NP >_{\text{default}} XP;$
	$Prt > PP >_{\text{default}} CP$
c. $\{_{NP}N\ (Det/[NP+poss])\ (AP/PP/CP^*)\}$	$[Det/NP+poss;$
	$AP >_{\text{default}} N;\ N > PP >_{\text{default}} CP$
d. $\{_{PP}P\ (QP)\ (NP/AP)\ (PP/CP)\}$	$[QP > P > NP/AP > PP/CP$
e. $\{_{NP}(NP(+poss))\ ing+VP\}$	$NP > ing + VP$
f. $\{_{SC}\ NP\ AP/PP/ing+VP\}$	$NP > AP/PP/ing+VP$

Working through these: In the rule for S (88a), XP is the topic position, the target position for long-distance dependencies; it is always at the left edge if present. It alternates with a complementizer (which, the reader will recall, we are regarding as a daughter rather than a sister of S). The VP is optional to allow for VP ellipsis and tag questions (see Chapter 8). The order of subject and tense is only default because we want subject–auxiliary inversion to be able to license the opposite order. The order of tense and VP is likewise the default here because we want VP-topicalization (...*and eat a banana he did*) to license the opposite order. Sentence adverbials are freely ordered among the constituents of S, so they have no ordering constraints. (We have not accounted for negation, auxiliaries, or the special properties of *be* used as a main verb.)

In the rule for VP (88b), the verb is optional, to allow for the main verb *be* being attached to tense and being inverted. The verb, when present, is always at the left edge (this is the Head Parameter); we have not taken account of preverbal adverbs. The rest of the verb phrase is a collection of phrasal constituents of any type, plus a particle (or bare preposition) (we take CP as an abbreviation for the special form required for Ss serving as subordinate clauses). The ordering of the parts is as shown. In particular, the particle is not ordered with respect to the NPs, allowing for either *look the answer up* or *look up the answer* as alternative linearizations of the VP.[18] The NPs and PPs are ordered only by default with respect to other constituents, in order to allow for the possibility of heavy shift, which we discuss briefly in a moment.[19]

In NP (rule (88c)), the main novelty is the absence of NP as a possible complement, so that, for instance, *a picture Bill* is ungrammatical. We have omitted all the detail of quantifier and numeral phrases. The ordering of APs

---

[18] There are lots of other accounts of particle placement; see Dehé et al. (2002), Toivonen (2003) for some recent discussion.

[19] This ordering of constituents in VP is similar to that worked out by Ross (1967), Sadock (1999), Wasow (2002), among others.

with respect to the head is the default order. In addition there has to be a specific rule that requires APs and gerundives containing a complement to follow the noun, in order to yield *a man proud of his children* and *a dog sleeping in the alley* instead of **a proud of his children man* and **a sleeping in the alley dog*. The rule might be (89).

(89)   N > [$_{XP}$X YP]

The rule for PP (88d) as stated allows for combinations like *way down the road from my house*; more baroque combinations are possible as well.[20]

The last two rules in (88) are special rules that go beyond the standard X-bar schema. (88e) says that an NP can consist of a gerundive complement, as in the underlined part of *(Ozzie('s)) leaving now would disturb Harriet*. As is well known, gerundive complements have the distribution of NPs, despite the fact that they are apparently headed by a verb. We take it that this is a special fact about English which doesn't follow from much in UG. Similarly, section 4.5.3 showed that English has a class of "small clauses", such as the underlined part of *I imagined Ozzie drunk/in the kitchen/drinking beer.* This constituent type has a very special distribution as the complement of a small class of verbs and prepositions. Rule (88f) licenses it as a possibility in English.

Let's return briefly to heavy shift. In our approach, heavy shift is not a movement rule, but rather an alternative linearization that makes the prosodic tier of phonology happier. The operative principle is something like (90), a phonological rule stated in terms of Intonational Phrases rather than syntactic units.

(90)   *Heavy Late*
       [$_{IntP}$ X] >$_{default}$ [$_{IntP}$Y]   if Y is heavier than X

In a case such as reordering PPs, nothing more need be said. Consider examples such as (91).

(91)   a.   Robin talked with Dana about the cockroach that ate Cincinnati.
       b.   ?Robin talked about the cockroach that ate Cincinnati with Dana.

---

[20] Some of these constraints can be generalized away from particular rules. For instance, in *any* phrase, NP complements (if they exist) precede AP complements (if they exist), which precede PP complements and modifiers, which precede clausal complements and modifiers. By stating the constraints pairwise rather than in an overall phrase structure rule, it becomes more feasible to state the generalizations. One of the problems faced in Jackendoff's (1977) attempt to generalize the phrase structure rules of English in terms of X-bar theory was that the then-current standard phrase structure rule format required full rules rather than piecewise constraints on constituency and order.

    c. Robin talked about Leslie with the former vice-chairman of the sociopathy department.

    d. ?Robin talked with the former vice-chairman of the sociopathy department about Leslie.

The standard principles for connecting syntax to intonation will result in (91a,c) observing Heavy Late and (91b,d) violating it. Since syntax does not stipulate the ordering of PPs, this consideration alone should be sufficient. In addition, one might advert to processing considerations, along the lines of Hawkins (1994): in order to parse a sentence, it helps to close off constituents after the verb as soon as possible. Thus processing is optimized if long constituents are saved for last. Furthermore, long constituents are often new information, i.e. Focus, and there is a syntax–semantics interface rule that favors final focus (see section 5.5). Thus the positioning of heavy phrases at the end is preferred on a number of independent and often redundant grounds. (We essentially concur with Hawkins and with Wasow (2002) on this point.)

The question then arises as to whether any syntactic principles are needed for the case in which an NP is reordered with respect to PPs or a PP with respect to a CP, as in (92). These are violations of the default ordering constraints in (88b).

(92)   a. Fred discussed with the class [the strong constraints on long-distance *wh*-movement].

       b. Janet mentioned that Rick was sick [to everyone she ran into at the faculty club].

The most favorable solution would be that these follow from the same principles as (91), except that perhaps more heaviness is needed to overcome the default ordering constraints. Alternatively, it might be necessary to add a syntax–prosody interface rule that more directly overrides the syntactic default. We leave the issue open. (See further discussion of consequences of Heavy Late in section 6.4.)

We might add that in a free phrase order language, the autonomous linear order rules are either absent or default. In such a language, any strong constraints on linear ordering are provided by phrasal interface rules, especially those concerned with information structure, which we discuss in section 5.5.

This sketch gives only a preliminary flavor of the phrase structure of English. More details will develop in the course of subsequent chapters. In particular, we wish to remind the reader that, unlike MGG, we do not expect all the quirks of English syntax to disappear into general conditions. Sooner or later a description of the speaker's knowledge of English has to encompass warts and all, and we would just as soon confront them sooner. As stressed in Chapter 1, the principles are constraints rather than rewriting rules. As a consequence they can be stated in the same format as lexical items and they represent generalizations over patterns in which lexical items appear. If one can learn tens of thousands of lexical items, a few dozen or even a few hundred idiosyncratic syntactic patterns would not seem to be such a problem.

PART II

The Syntax–Semantics Interface

CHAPTER 5

Basic Clause Structure

5.1 Looking ahead

The preceding three chapters have demonstrated that much of the elaborate and complex syntactic structure that has served as the primary subject matter of mainstream generative grammar is far less highly motivated than usually thought. It is now time to show how a far simpler syntax still permits an insightful account of the relation between sound and meaning. The major step that makes possible this simplification of syntax is the abandonment of Interface Uniformity in favor of a more flexible theory of the syntax–semantics interface, the component that establishes the correspondences between syntactic and semantic/conceptual structures.

Our program of simplification in syntax has two central components. One is to significantly flatten syntactic structure, along the lines proposed at the end of Chapter 4. The other is to give up entirely the notion of movement in syntax, which we focus on in this and the next four chapters. We account for the effects attributed to movement in terms of flexibility in the interface, showing in each case that our approach is superior on independent grounds. In many cases our approach has antecedents in one or more of the alternative generative frameworks.

Consider again the relation between theories of competence and theories of language processing, discussed briefly in section 1.3. Language perception has to create semantics on the basis of syntax; language production has to go in the opposite direction. Thus a competence theory of the syntax–semantics interface is ideally bidirectional, so that it can suit the needs of both language production and language perception. For convenience, we describe the interface here primarily in terms of how semantics is mapped to syntax. Thus the problem to be addressed is: Given a conceptual structure CS to be expressed linguistically, how do the interface and the autonomous principles of syntax construct a syntactic structure SS in correspondence with CS? The opposite direction, mapping from syntax to semantics, will be shown to follow unproblematically from our eventual formulation of the principles.

To outline what is to follow, here are the factors involved in establishing a connection between a conceptual structure and a syntactic structure.

• Carving CS into corresponding words, morphemes, and constructions, so that there is a collection of associated syntactic categories to be connected into a tree (section 5.3). This has to take into account what parts of CS will be unexpressed because of ellipsis constructions in syntax (Chapters 7 and 8), and which parts will remain unexpressed through coercion (section 6.5.3).
• Arranging the hierarchical structure of syntax in accordance with (a) default principles of head/argument/adjunct mapping (section 5.4), (b) the idiosyncratic syntactic demands of individual words, in particular subcategorization (section 5.6), (c) the demands of constructions (section 6.5).
• Linearizing the syntax in accordance with (a) the demands of autonomous phrase structure such as head position (section 5.5), (b) the demands of the syntax–prosody interface such as heaviness (section 5.5), (c) the demands of Information Structure (section 5.5), (d) the demands of argument prominence hierarchies (section 5.7), and (e) the demands of constructions such as inversion (section 5.5) and long-distance dependency (Chapter 9).

In addition to all this, there is a further complication. We had originally explored the feasibility of a direct single-step mapping from meaning to surface syntax (see Culicover and Nowak 2003: ch. 4). In the end, we have concluded that the mapping actually requires a small but indispensable component, formulated in terms of grammatical functions (e.g. subject and object), which does the work of certain traditional transformations such as passive and raising. This component shows up in one form or another in every theory of syntax (although it is disguised in MGG). Here, we formulate it in a fashion consistent with our theory, in part taking our cue from LFG and especially Relational Grammar: it is a small rule system that explicitly manipulates the expression of certain semantic arguments in terms of a hierarchy of grammatical functions. This system does not really constitute a full level of grammar, since it only applies to a small subsystem within the organization of sentences, namely the syntactic NP arguments. Thus instead of a purely monostratal syntax we will end with a "sesquistratal" approach. We discuss this component of "GF structure" in Chapter 6.

In these proposals, the reader will recognize aspects of syntactic theories that have been at issue for many years. We do not wish to suggest that what we are proposing is entirely novel. However, we must take care not to get carried away with the particular formal devices proposed within other frameworks. For example, MGG has taken syntactic configurations and not grammatical relations as primitive. From this standpoint, formal devices such as movement appear to be necessary to account for language. MGG has explored to what extent these devices are sufficient, and in many cases, we think, it has gone well beyond the explanatory advantages afforded by these devices. (This is true as well for feature checking, for functional heads, for grammatical relations, etc.)

With a larger overview provided by hindsight, we wish to develop a more accurate picture of the architecture of the grammar, by delimiting as needed the scope of the various formal devices that have been hit upon in earlier theories. In a real sense, every theory has been right, but every one has gone too far in some respect. Our goal here is to let the phenomena, and the requirement of simplicity, dictate which devices are most appropriate.

The overall theory of the syntax–semantics interface will be that it consists of a collection of mechanisms, each of limited power—the "Toolkit Hypothesis" of Chapter 1. This contrasts with most grammatical frameworks, which favor formal devices of maximal generality.

5.2 Overview of CS

In order to work out the interface between syntax and CS, we need to know what sorts of structures the interface is connecting. The principles of autonomous syntax were outlined in Chapter 4. This section offers a brief introduction to the form of CS, attending particularly to the aspects relevant to the syntax–semantics interface.[1] Like syntactic structure, CS is a hierarchical combinatorial structure. All its constituents belong to one of the *major ontological types* such as Archi-Object, Situation, Property, Location, Time, or Amount. There are potentially five parts to the internal structure of each constituent:

• A set of *aspectual features* which, in the case of Situations, distinguish between states, processes, and completive events, and which in the case of Archi-Objects, distinguish between count (Object), mass (Substance), and aggregate (including Plural). We will not have much to say about these here; see Jackendoff (1991b; 1996) for some details.

---

[1] Much more detail on word and phrase meaning appears in Jackendoff (1983; 1990a; 2002a: chs. 9–12. Readers should feel free to substitute their own formalism, as long as it makes the same distinctions we make here.

- A set of *referential features* such as the type/token distinction and (in)definiteness.
- A *function* of zero to (probably) three arguments. Typical common nouns such as *dog* express zero-argument functions; *friend* expresses a one-argument function; the verb *give* expresses three arguments.
- The *arguments* of the function, which are themselves typed constituents.
- Modifiers of the constituent such as those expressed by prenominal adjectives and by place, time, and manner adverbials. These too are typed constituents.

The formalism can be sketched as (1a). A sample CS would then look like (1b).[2] It can be seen that this is basically an enriched predicate calculus-like formalism.

(1) a. $[\text{FUNCTION (ARG}_1, \ldots \text{ARG}_i); \text{MOD}_1, \ldots \text{MOD}_m; \text{FEATURE}_1, \ldots,$
$\text{FEATURE}_n]$

b. Pat might eat some green apples on Thursday.
$[_{\text{Situation}} \text{MIGHT}([_{\text{Situation}} \text{EAT}([_{\text{Object}}\text{PAT}], [_{\text{Object}} \text{APPLE};$
$[_{\text{Property}}\text{GREEN}];\text{INDEF PLUR}); [_{\text{Time}}\text{THURSDAY}]]$

Just as in syntax, tree structures are easier to read than labeled bracketings. The tree notation in (2a) is an alternative notation for (1a), yielding the tree in (2b) for (1b).[3] The different roles within the constituent are designated by different types of line attaching them: a double line for the function, a single line for arguments, dashed lines for properties and features.

(2) a.

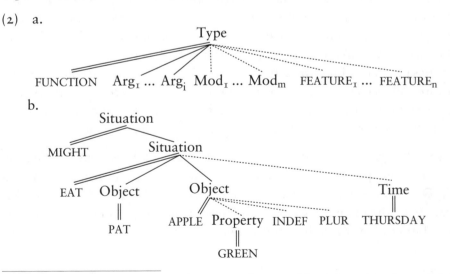

b.

---

    [2] We adopt the usual convention of using capitals to stand for the meaning of a word. In fact word meanings are themselves elaborately composite (Jackendoff 1983; 1990a).
    [3] This notation is introduced in Jackendoff (2002a) as novel, but it is apparently an unconscious adaptation of a nearly identical notation appearing in Levelt (1989), which differs only in lacking the double lines for functions.

We need two more formal devices. First, in order to encode the semantics of relative clauses, we need something rather like lambda-extraction. (3a) shows the general schema; (3b) shows the CS associated with *the boy who you met* in tree format, where the relative clause expresses a Property of *the boy*. (We will modify this notation in section 9.2.)

(3) a. $[_{Type} \lambda x [F ... [_{Type} x] ...]]$
     b. the boy who you met

```
              Object
          /‾‾‾\············
    BOY  Property        DEF
          /‾\
       λx  Situation
          /‾‾‾\
      PAST  Situation
          /‾‾‾‾\‾‾‾‾‾‾
     MEET  Object  Object
            ‖        ‖
           YOU       x
```

The second device involves breaking CS into two semi-independent *tiers*, along the lines of the segmental/syllabic, metrical, and intonational tiers in phonology. Let us call what we have proposed so far in CS the "propositional structure". It has become common in the literature to set apart from this a tier called "information structure",[4] the breakdown of the utterance in terms of new and old information, or in terms of Topic, Focus, and Ground.[5]

To see the independence of propositional and information structure, consider an example like *The bear chased the lion*, which describes an event of chasing in which the bear is the chaser and the lion is "chasee". The propositional structure (simplifying out all but the basic functions) is [CHASE (BEAR, LION)]. We can leave these roles intact but change the information structure by using stress (4a–c) or various focusing and topicalizing constructions (4d–g):

(4) a. The **bear** chased the lion.   [Focus = the bear]
     b. The bear chased the **lion**.   [Focus = the lion *or* chased the lion]
     c. The bear **chased** the lion.   [Focus = chased]
     d. It was the bear that chased the lion.   [Focus = the bear]

---

[4] See e.g. Erteschik-Shir (1997), who uses the term 'focus structure', Roberts (1998), Kadmon (2001), and work cited there.

[5] In addition, Jackendoff (2002a) suggests that propositional structure can be further divided into the "descriptive tier", which encodes functional information such as thematic roles and modification, and the "referential tier", which encodes the sentence's referential commitments such as specificity and quantifier binding. We will not deal with this further division here in any detail; however it is crucial for a full statement of quantifier scope.

e. What chased the lion was the bear.
    [Topic = something chased the lion; Focus = the bear]
f. What the bear did was chase the lion.
    [Topic = the bear did something; Focus = chase the lion]
g. What happened to the lion was the bear chased it.
    [Topic = something happened to the lion; Focus = the bear chased it]

Thus the choice of Topic and Focus is orthogonal to the relations among the characters referred to in the sentence.

One could encode this multidimensionality in Conceptual Structure with an iota operator (Russell's definite description operator), along the lines of (5) (or some other formal variant such as lambda-extraction):

(5) a. $\iota x(\text{CHASE } (x, \text{LION})) = \text{BEAR}$
     b. $\iota x(\text{CHASE } (\text{BEAR}, x)) = \text{LION}$

(5) conveniently parallels the syntactic form of the pseudo-cleft construction in (4e), a syntactic focus construction (Rochemont and Culicover 1990). However, it is not so convenient for explaining why the simplex forms (4a,b) happen to lack syntactic correlates of the iota operator and bound variable. Moreover, a form like (5) is not so easy to set up when the focus is *chase*, as in (4c), or *chase the lion*, as in (4f). (It can be done, but at a cost!) Section 7.3 goes through the evidence that, even if this were the correct CS, it could not be encoded as such in syntax: too many things can be focused through intonation that cannot be focused syntactically.

Rather than follow this line any further, we will treat information structure as an independent tier, rather like the metrical grid in phonology. For present purposes, this tier is very simple. It requires a Focus (roughly, new information): every utterance must be informative, or at least purport to be. In addition there may be further "figural" constituents. The second one is usually called Topic, as in (4f,g) and (6a), but it is sometimes treated as a second Focus. In addition there may be a third figural constituent, as in (6b,c). Here it is unclear whether we should speak of three correlated foci, a topic plus two foci, or two topics plus a focus; for present purposes it is not a crucial matter. (It is hard to construct examples with more figural constituents, presumably for performance reasons.)

(6) a. **Fred** ate the **beans**, and **Sue** ate the **clams**.
     b. On **Monday**, I bought **books** in **Cambridge**; on **Tuesday**, I bought **clothes** in **Newton**.
     c. On **Monday**, **Bill bought** clams; on **Tuesday**, **Fran cooked** them.

Just as with the tiers of phonology, the constituents of the information structure tier have to be associated with the propositional structure of the sentence. For present purposes, this can be accomplished by associating the features FOCUS and TOPIC with constituents of propositional structure.[6] However, the fact that there is at least one focus and possibly one or two other figural constituents—which may be in many different locations in propositional structure—is governed by the well-formedness conditions on information structure, and cannot be stated locally over propositional structure. (7) shows how this formalism might be implemented in various examples.

(7) a.   The **bear** chased the lion.

          CS: [CHASE (BEAR, LION)]
                         |
                       FOCUS

     b.   Bill ate a **big** pizza.

          CS: [ATE (BILL, [PIZZA; [BIG]])]
                              |
                            FOCUS

     c.   **Johnson** died!   [whole sentence is focus]

          CS: [DIE (JOHNSON)]
                |_____|
                        |
                     FOCUS

     d.   On **Monday**, I bought **books** in **Cambridge**.

          CS: [BUY (I, BOOKS); [IN (CAMBRIDGE)]; [MONDAY]]
                        | | |
                      FIG_3 FOCUS   TOPIC

It should be clear from the discussion above how these analyses work. (The pseudo-clefts in (4e–g) are a bit more complex and we set their analysis aside.)

Within this analysis, it is possible to coindex constituents of the information structure tier directly with phonological structure, producing the characteristic stress and intonation patterns that mark focus and topic. This means that it is not necessary to posit any difference whatsoever in syntactic structure among (4a,b,c)—explaining why there is in fact no syntactic difference among them (Culicover and Rochemont 1983). Even when there is a syntactic construction that marks information structure, as in (4d–g), the characteristic stress and intonation are present, suggesting that the prosodic correlates of information structure are independent of the syntactic correlates.[7]

---

[6] For simplicity we set aside metalinguistic focus such as in *I say to-MAY-to, you say to-MAH-to.*

[7] Mainstream generative grammar, because of its syntactocentric character, does not lend itself to such an account: it is necessary to put dummy placeholders for topic and focus in syntax that can be read independently by phonology and semantics but which are syntactically inert. This was

It is important to see that Conceptual Structure is not just a kind of (narrow) syntax with semantic features as its terminal symbols, as was proposed by Generative Semantics, for instance. The categories are different in syntax and CS: nouns and verbs vs. Objects and Situations. The kinds of branching are different: syntax has only a single kind of daughterhood, while CS has (at least) three kinds: for heads, arguments, and modifiers. CS has in addition a multidimensionality afforded by the existence of a number of tiers (of which we have discussed here only two). Thus there is no direct one-to-one relation between the syntactic and the conceptual hierarchies. We will see more in the way of mismatch as we go on.

5.3 Carving out the words and morphemes

To review the position laid out in Chapter 1: a typical lexically stored word is a long term memory association of a piece of phonology, a piece of syntax, and a piece of semantics. In mainstream generative grammar, words are inserted as a whole into syntactic structures and moved around passively in accordance with their features and those of their context, until their pronunciations are read off at Spell Out and their meanings are read off at Logical Form. In the parallel architecture adopted here, words play a more active role: a word is a small-scale idiosyncratic interface rule. Its components serve to link parts of the parallel phonological, syntactic, and conceptual structures. (On a larger scale, the structures are linked by phrasal interface rules, to which we will turn in the remaining sections of the chapter.)

The general format for a lexical item, then, is a coindexed triple of structures in the three domains. We can think of "lexical insertion" as simultaneously inserting the three parts of a lexical item into the three structures, along with the indices or association lines that establish the connections among them. Syntactic structure contains only the syntactic features of lexical items (the "formal features" in the sense of Principles and Parameters Theory) plus their links to phonological and conceptual structure. Alternatively, we can think of lexical items as constraints on well-formed associations of phonological, syntactic, and conceptual structures, along the lines of HPSG. This is the way we will treat the role of lexical items here. What is important in the end is the resulting structure, not the mechanical procedure by which the structure is put together.

---

the account in e.g. Jackendoff 1972. Under the parallel architecture and the Simpler Syntax Hypothesis, such placeholders should be shunned: we should think of the correlation of prosody and information structure as a direct mapping between a tier of sound and a tier of meaning, requiring no syntactic support.

In addition to a lexical item's overt content, it may have contextual features in any of the three domains. These stipulate what must appear in the item's environment. In the CS domain, these are selectional restrictions; in syntax, they are subcategorization features; in phonology, they are the phonological environment.

The lexicon is not exclusively populated by words. Idioms such as *kick the bucket* and *take NP for granted* are stored as lexical VPs, as are the VP constructions such as *V pro's way PP* discussed in Chapter 1. In addition, regular affixes such as the English regular past tense can be considered lexical items on their own. For instance, the regular past is a long-term memory association of a piece of phonology, a piece of syntax, and a piece of semantics that combines freely with structures that satisfy its contextual variables. On the other hand, items with irregular morphology such as *sank* and *thought* are stored in the lexicon as whole units, parallel to idioms (see Jackendoff 1997a; 2002a for some details).

As suggested in section 5.1, we will approach the syntax–semantics interface by proceeding in the direction from semantics to syntax; we will then show that the machinery we develop can also be used in the direction from syntax to semantics. So the basic problem is how a thought comes to be expressed linguistically. We take it that a thought to be expressed, i.e. a CS not yet linked to syntax and phonology, does not come exhaustively carved into words. The psycholinguistic literature (e.g. Levelt 1989; 1999) amply documents the complex processing involved in finding the right words to express a thought (often in the context of naming pictures or in the production of speech errors). Formally, the word-finding problem might be stated like this:

- Given a CS to be expressed, every segment of it must be licensed by exactly one lexical item.[8]
- For a lexical item *Lex* to license a segment *Seg* of CS,
  - (a) *Seg* must be included in the range of possibilities encompassed by *Lex*.[9]
  - (b) The contextual variables (selectional restrictions) of *Lex* must be satisfied by the relevant segments of CS. However, these segments are not licensed by *Lex*; they must be licensed by other lexical items.

---

[8] An immediate apparent counterexample is the light verb construction (e.g. *give/make NP a promise*), where the verb and the nominal appear to share semantic information. We will deal with this case in section 6.5.1.

[9] A more realistic account might say instead "The range of possibilities encompassed by the CS of *Lex* is acceptably close to *Seg*", where "acceptably close" might be "as close as the lexicon of my language lets me get", or "as close as I need to be for present communicative circumstances", or perhaps other pragmatically influenced possibilities. We abstract away from this very profound problem, which has a strong bearing on e.g. problems of translation.

• Since *Lex* also licenses segments of syntactic structure and phonological structure, these are thereby linked to *Seg*.

The lexicon may contain more than one item that licenses the same segment of CS. For example, in the authors' dialect the lexical items pronounced *cellar* and *basement* license identical segments of CS (i.e. these words are synonymous); they link the same CS to different phonological structures—though the same syntactic structure. For another example, there is a range of CSs that fall equally into the range encompassed by the verb *die*, the verb-particle idiom *pass away*, and the transitive VP idiom *kick the bucket*; here not only the phonological structure but also the syntactic structure linked to CS differs.

For a simple example: the CS of *Bill crossed the street*, the upper line in (8), can be carved into lexical items as shown. Each lexical item is notated as a separate line of (8), and its CS is lined up with the parts of the whole CS that it matches. The contextual features are shown in italics. Each lexical item also has coindexed pieces of syntactic and phonological structure—this is what makes it an interface rule.[10] (The choice of numbers for indices is a purely arbitrary fact of notation. The important point is that indices are distinct from each other. A formally better notation would be association lines, and we will use this notation from time to time, but in general it risks making a sentence structure look like a plate of spaghetti.) Thus we end up with a list of lexical items that will appear in the sentence being constructed.[11]

(8) Conceptual structure   Syntax   Phonology
     [PAST ([GO ([BILL], [ACROSS ([STREET; DEF])])])]
  i.   [PAST (*SITUATION*$_x$)]$_1$ V_x-T_1 $Word_x$-d_1
  ii.   [GO (X,   [ACROSS (Y   )])]$_2$ V_2 cross$_2$
  iii.   [BILL]$_3$ N_3 Bill$_3$
  iv.   [STREET   ]$_4$ N_4 street$_4$
  v.   DEF$_5$ Det$_5$ the$_5$

---

[10] Notice that the Tense has syntactic and phonological contextual features that are coindexed with the contextual feature in CS. The syntactic and phonological contextual features are what make Tense turn up as an affix; we return to them in section 5.4.

[11] This unstructured list of syntactic and phonological items bears some resemblance to the "numeration" in the Minimalist Program, a syntactically unstructured list of the lexical items to be built into a sentence. It differs from a numeration, though, in that we presume the list is selected by virtue of its relation to a full conceptual structure that the sentence is intended to express. Hence the syntactic and phonological structures containing these items are not assembled randomly, using something like Merge. Rather, interaction of the conceptual structure, the phrasal interface rules, and the autonomous constraints of syntax and phonology determine how these structures are put together, as will be seen in succeeding sections. The way that we characterize how a sentence is put together, with its meaning, syntactic structure, and associated sound, offers the potential for tying the theory of linguistic competence to the theory of linguistic performance, while the Minimalist Program does not. See the end of this section.

Although each of the lexical items licenses a piece of syntax and phonology, so far the pieces are totally disconnected. Assembling the words into syntactic and phonological structures which reflect the relations among them in CS is the task of the phrasal interface rules, which we take up shortly.

A CS may be carved up into lexical items in more than one way. For a simple case, the sentences *Bill crossed the street* and *Bill went across the street* are realizations of a common CS. In the former case the lexical verb pronounced *cross* licenses the segment of CS shown in (8.ii); in the latter case the same part of CS is divided into two segments, licensed by *go* and *across*, as in (9).

(9)   Conceptual structure   Syntax   Phonology
       [GO (BILL, [ACROSS (STREET)])]
       i. [GO (X, Y)]$_6$ V_6 go$_6$
       ii.   [ACROSS (Z)   )]$_7$ P_7 across$_7$

Similarly, (10) shows two different ways to carve up the same CS, in case (a) as *Bill died*, and in case (b) as *Bill kicked the bucket*.

(10)   Conceptual structure   Syntax   Phonology
       CS: [PAST ([DIE ([BILL])])]
a.   i. [PAST (*SITUATION$_x$*)]$_1$ V_x-T_1 *Word$_x$*-d$_1$
       ii.   [DIE (X)]$_8$ V_8 die$_8$
       iii.   [BILL]$_3$ N_3 Bill$_3$
b.   i. [PAST (*SITUATION$_x$*)]$_1$ V_x-T_1 *Word$_x$*-d$_1$
       ii.   [DIE (X)]$_9$ [$_{VP}$V$_{10}$[$_{NP}$Det$_{11}$N$_{12}$]]$_9$ kick$_{10}$ the$_{11}$ bucket$_{12}$
       iii.   [BILL]$_3$ N_3 Bill$_3$

In (10b.ii), the CS *DIE* corresponds to a lexical VP, each of whose X° nodes is indexed to a separate piece of phonology. Thus the pieces of phonology do not correspond in a one-to-one way with meaning; this is precisely what makes *kick the bucket* an idiom.[12] Section 6.5.2 will show how this procedure extends to VP constructions such as *V one's way PP*, such that *Bill belched his way out of the restaurant* is an alternative realization of the CS expressed by *Bill went out of the restaurant, belching.*

This description of lexical licensing has been couched in terms of mapping from a given CS to syntax and phonology. Let us see how it works in the other direction. Given a syntactic structure alone, it is impossible to map to Conceptual Structure, because syntactic structure does not make enough distinctions.

---

[12] McCawley (1981) discusses a number of cases in which it is clear that the interpretation of an idiom cannot be easily situated in one of the words that are contained in it. The problem of representing idioms in HPSG has been addressed by Riehemann and Bender (1999) and Erbach and Krenn (1994), among others.

Recall that the only parts of a lexical item that appear in syntactic structure are its syntactic features, such as syntactic category, gender/class, number, and subcategorization. Thus *street* and *carburetor* are identical as far as syntax is concerned (both singular count nouns), as are *cross* and *approach* (both optionally transitive verbs), *across* and *along*, *four* and *nine*, and *big* and *tall*. Each of these pairs of words is differentiated only by semantics and phonology.

Consequently, the proper way to think about using the syntax–semantics interface in the other direction is in terms of a language perceiver, whose input is phonology. We can think of an incoming phonological string as being licensed by lexical items in exactly the same way as a CS to be expressed is licensed: the string must be exhaustively carved up into segments, each of which corresponds to the phonological structure of a lexical item.[13] And it is the phonology of a lexical item that cues the listener to the corresponding conceptual structure. (11) is the counterpart of (8), only viewed from the perspective of language perception.

(11) | Phonology | Syntax | Conceptual structure |
|---|---|---|
| Ph.S: Bilkrɔstðəstriyt | | |
| i.   Bill$_3$ | N$_3$ | [BILL]$_3$ |
| ii.   cross$_2$ | V$_2$ | [GO (X, ACROSS (Y))]$_2$ |
| iii.   Word- t$_1$ | V-af$_1$ | [PAST (*EVENT*)]$_1$ |
| iv.   the$_5$ | Det$_5$ | [DEF]$_5$ |
| v.   street$_4$ | N$_4$ | [STREET]$_4$ |

Here it is the syntax and CS that are initially unstructured, and the phrasal interface rules have to determine how the pieces are put together (i.e. the classical parsing problem).

This way of characterizing the mapping between form and meaning might suggest that we are thinking of the grammar in terms of processing, not in terms of pure competence as is more traditional in generative grammar. This is correct. We take the proper characterization of the correspondence between form and meaning to be the *idealized* mapping between sound and conceptual

---

[13] For a first approximation only! We are not correcting for the effects of systematic phonological adjustments such as conditioned variation in voicing, tensing, height, and so forth, not to mention more radical effects such as reduplication. We are also not correcting for systematic phonetic differences due e.g. to accent. We might view these adjustments as counterparts of the semantic accommodations mentioned in n. 9 above: the form in which the lexical item is stored has to accommodate to the combinatorial form in the input phonological structure. One codification of such a view has been developed by Wiese (2000), who proposes that lexical semantics is to fully fleshed out CS as lexical phonology is to phonetics. See Jackendoff (2002a: ch. 7), for how this position on the interfaces brings out a strong parallel with the psycholinguistic literature on lexical access in production and perception.

structure. The correspondence is idealized in the sense that it is not subject to the constraints that apply to actual processing by humans in real time. But the logic of the relationship between sound and meaning is the same. It is for this reason that we say that the theory of performance is intertwined with the theory of competence. The competence grammar encodes the knowledge involved in the correspondences between phonology, syntax, and semantics, and it is the establishment of these correspondences in real time that constitutes the computations that speakers and hearers perform in the course of using language.

5.4 Default principles for determining syntactic embedding

Two very strong default principles link the hierarchical structures in semantics and syntax. For the moment, they can be stated informally as follows:

Head Rule
A semantic function F canonically maps to the head H of a syntactic phrase HP.

Argument/Modifier Rule
The arguments and modifiers of F canonically map to syntactic constituents of HP.[14]
These principles are independent of the linear order of the constituents of HP. For example, a noun's modifiers typically appear as constituents of the NP that the noun heads, and a verb's complements and adjuncts typically appear in the VP that the verb heads. On the other hand, as mentioned in Chapter 1, cross-linguistic differences in word order that are not contrastive within the language itself make no difference to the meaning of sentences. It is of no interest to the semantics whether the verb goes consistently at the beginning or end of VP, whether the language is prepositional or postpositional, on which side of the noun its modifying adjectives go, whether pronominal objects follow the verb or, as in Romance, cliticize to the left of the verb—or whether, for that matter, the language has free word order. Section 4.7 bifurcated the rules of syntax into principles that determine the embedding of constituents and principles that determine the order of constituents, so that these different effects can be factored out.

The principles of the syntax–semantics interface also bifurcate into those that concern embedding and those that concern syntactic linear order. The latter include subject–auxiliary inversion, the tendency for focus to fall toward the

---

[14] Interestingly, precisely this assumption is made in the computational theory of language acquisition described in Culicover and Nowak (2003); it appears that without it, it is impossible to determine the correspondences from raw input, although it remains to prove this formally.

end of the sentence, and principles of binding and quantifier scope.[15] The Head and Argument/Modifier Rules deal with embedding; we get to linear order in the next section and continue with it through to section 6.3.

Here is a somewhat more precise formulation of these rules. In (12), material in italics is context; syntactic constituents are enclosed in curly brackets to indicate that they are unordered. The ⇔ indicates that a correspondence is licensed; the subscript *default* indicates that this correspondence is the preferred (or "unmarked") case but can be violated.

(12)   <u>Conceptual structure</u>   <u>Syntax</u>

Head Rule $[F(Arg_1, \ldots, Arg_n); Mod_1, \ldots, Mod_m]_j$ ⇔$_{default}$ $\{_{HP} \ldots, H_j, \ldots\}_j$

Argument/Modifier Rule $[F \ldots X_i \ldots]_j$ ⇔$_{default}$ $\{\ldots, YP_i, \ldots\}_j$

First consider the Head Rule. The schematic Conceptual structure is a function F with n arguments and m modifiers. As notated by the co-subscripting, the corresponding syntactic structure is an HP, with H as its head. A couple of technical points bear explanation. First, we assume that both VP and S count as the phrasal category associated with V; we'll see how this works out as we proceed. (Huddleston and Pullum (2002) take this position as well.) Second, for technical reasons it proves convenient to coindex the CS to both the head and the whole phrase. HPSG has a corresponding principle, the Head Feature Principle (Pollard and Sag 1987: 58), which makes the head share features with the phrase it heads. In a sense this coindexing also expresses the intuition behind Chomsky's (1995) theory of Bare Phrase Structure to the effect that the head and the phrase that it heads are "the same item". In the simplest case, such as the proper noun *Bill*, the semantics maps directly into both the N and the NP, and they need not be distinct syntactic nodes (although *Bill* counts both as an N and an NP in terms of syntactic category). In the case of a more complex phrase such as *the fat old dog*, both the head

---

[15] The relative ordering of constituents with respect to a head often reflects their relative scope. It is not an accident that the constituents of NP typically reveal the following orders, and a few others, but not all possible permutations.

(i) Det Num Adj N
   N Det Adj Num
   N Adj Num Det

Verbal modifiers also appear to line up canonically as a reflection of their relative scope; see Jackendoff (1972) and Cinque (1999) for a plethora of evidence (Cinque offers a somewhat different interpretation than we suggest here). As shown in chapters 1 and 4, scope is to a certain extent independent of head–modifier configurations.

N and the whole NP will both be coindexed with the CS [DOG]. However, the correspondence to phonology proceeds via the index on the head.

The Head Rule is marked as a default correspondence because it has violations. An important type is exemplified by the *way*-construction, as in *Bill belched his way out of the restaurant*; this is understood as a paraphrase of 'Bill went out of the restaurant belching' (and in many languages it can only be expressed that way). The verb *belch* functions semantically as a manner or means modifier, not as the main semantic function of the sentence, which is GO. So there is not a one-to-one mapping between syntactic heads and semantic functions. We return to this case in section 6.5.2; other violations of the Head Rule come up below.

Next consider the Argument/Modifier Rule. This says that if conceptual constituent X is embedded in another constituent indexed *j*, the syntactic YP coindexed with X is embedded in the syntactic constituent coindexed *j*. However, it does not stipulate how deeply either X or YP is embedded in the corresponding constituent. This indeterminacy is important, for often the syntax requires deeper embedding than the semantics, as in (13a), or vice versa, as in (13b). We notate the CS in (13b) as a tree for somewhat greater clarity. (We have not yet justified all the syntactic structure in (13a) or the linear order in either example; see succeeding sections. For convenience, the phonology associated with syntactic categories is notated here by association lines; coindexing could be used equally.)

(13) a. $[\text{PICTURE } ([\text{BILL}]_2)]_1 \quad \Leftrightarrow \quad [_{\text{NP}} N_1 [_{\text{PP}} P [_{\text{NP}} N_2]_2]]_1$
$$\text{picture} \quad \text{of} \quad \text{Bill}$$

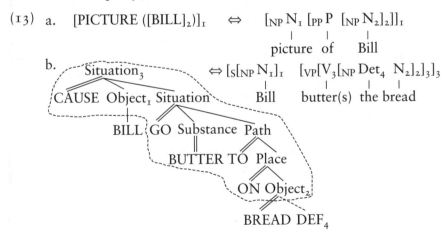

b.

(13a) has a PP constituent in syntax headed by the dummy *of*, which does not map into semantics. But the correspondence of *BILL* in semantics to N_2 in syntax still obeys the Argument/Modifier Rule. Similarly, (13b) has a whole collection of semantic constituents that are all bundled up in the verb *butter* (as indicated by the dashed line surrounding them), and that do not correspond to any syntactic embedding. This is shown by the dashed line around the part of the CS tree that corresponds to *butter*. Hence, BREAD, deeply embedded in semantics, still corresponds properly to BREAD, which is rather shallowly embedded in syntax.[16]

However, if there is an intervening constituent that *is* coindexed between syntax and semantics, the Argument/Modifier Rule requires it to be respected. Consider (14).

(14)

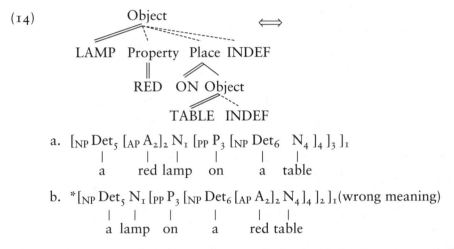

a. $[_{NP} Det_5 [_{AP} A_2]_2 N_1 [_{PP} P_3 [_{NP} Det_6 \quad N_4]_4]_3]_1$
       a   red lamp on   a   table

b. *$[_{NP} Det_5 N_1 [_{PP} P_3 [_{NP} Det_6 [_{AP} A_2]_2 N_4]_4]_2]_1$ (wrong meaning)
       a lamp on   a   red table

The modifiers in syntactic structure (14a) correspond to the CS in a fashion that satisfies the Argument/Modifier Rule. But consider (14b). *Red* satisfies the Argument/Modifier Rule with respect to the outer NP headed by *lamp*: it is within the constituent indexed *1* in both syntax and semantics. However, it does not satisfy the rule with respect to the inner NP, headed by *table*: it is outside the constituent labeled *4* in semantics but inside it in syntax. So the Argument/Modifier Rule correctly says this is an improper correspondence. (Of course, (14b) correctly expresses a CS in which RED modifies TABLE.)

The Argument/Modifier Rule, like the Head Rule, is only a default mapping. Prominent violations include "raising to subject" (section 6.2) and long-distance dependencies (Chapter 9).[17] For the moment, to see how violations can be licensed, we deal with one simple violation of this rule, so-called Extraposition from NP:

---

[16] See Jackendoff (1983; 1990a; 2002a) for defense of this semantic decomposition of *butter*. The insight goes back at least to Gruber (1965); similar ideas appear in Talmy (1985). See Ch. 2 for our reasons for rejecting an approach (e.g. Hale and Keyser 1993) that copies all this elaborate structure into syntax, and our reasons for thinking that our approach is not a notational variant.

[17] Quantifier scope is a different matter, not to be dealt with here. Jackendoff (2002a: section 12.4) uses the referential tier to express these dependencies.

(15) a. **Three people** came to the meeting *who had the same birthday.*
  b. **A story** came out in the Globe last week *about a newly discovered novel by Tolstoy.*
  c. I got **that book** from Harry the other day *that everyone's been raving about.*

The italicized constituents are in the "wrong place": semantically they are modifiers of the boldfaced NPs, yet they appear at the end of the verb phrase. Presumably this displacement is motivated by heaviness—it is a way to get long subconstituents to the end of the VP (Hawkins 1994; Wasow 1997). We can make this option available in the syntax–semantics interface by adding the following rule:

(16) **Extraposition from NP**

$$[F(\ldots[G(\ldots);\ldots X_i \ldots]_j \ldots)]_k \Leftrightarrow [_{S/VP} \ldots NP_j \ldots YP_i]_k$$

This is *not* a movement rule.[18] Rather, going from semantics to syntax, it says that a semantic modifier X of a constituent *j* can be realized outside of the syntactic realization of *j*, just in case *j* is an NP and the larger constituent is an S (actually this may also occur inside of NPs—Akmajian (1975)). Going from syntax to semantics, it says that one may interpret a phrase at the end of a clause as a modifier of one of the NPs in the clause.

Extraposition from NP is not the default option, so it is dispreferred, all else being equal. But because it permits a postnominal modifier to be realized not only adjacent to the noun but also further to the right of the noun, it enables the syntax–*phonology* interface to achieve better prosodic balance, which is a strongly preferred option (the principle Heavy Late of section 4.7). Thus the typical situation where one uses Extraposition from NP pits an optimal syntax–semantics connection (normal modifier position) but non-optimal prosody against a non-optimal syntax–semantics connection (extraposition) but more optimal prosody. The heavier the extraposed modifier and the lighter the rest of the sentence, the better the extraposed version sounds (Wasow (1997; 2002); also Ross (1967)—and for ease of processing, Hawkins (1994)). Extraposition

---

[18] There have been substantial arguments in the literature that extraposition cannot be movement (see e.g. section 4.6.2 and Culicover and Rochemont 1990), along with a general recognition that such movement is problematic from a theoretical perspective, because the trace within NP is not properly c-commanded by the extraposed constituent. Within the antisymmetry framework (Kayne 1994), a way to deal with the c-command problem is to posit that the head noun and its prenominal material moves higher and to the left of the postnominal modifiers, perhaps in a leapfrogging manner (or Iterated Raising, in the sense of Chapter 4). Such a derivation is of course not possible if we do not posit movement, and, we argue, not necessary in order to account for the facts.

from NP also permits a focused NP modifier to appear at the end, a factor we will incorporate below.[19]

Another nonoptimal mapping is the tense marker. In (8) it is treated as the outermost operator in the propositional structure of the sentence ('the event of Bill crossing the street was in the past').[20] This analysis lies behind the common theoretical intuition that the tense is the syntactic head of the clause, in accordance with Interface Uniformity. Under a Uniformity analysis, the syntactic component has to either move the tense marker down to the verb or move the verb up to the tense marker. In the present analysis, the tense morpheme is an interface rule, and it can stipulate where it turns up in surface syntax and phonology, in violation of the Head Rule—namely as an affix which generally ends up on the verb (we defer treatment of *do*-support). This is how it is encoded in (8.i). When we work out the coindexation, both Tense and the verb end up coindexed with the whole sentence. The verb is the syntactic head of the sentence, while the Tense is the semantic head, with the verb as the next function down in the semantic embedding. So in a sense the tense and verb are co-heads of the sentence.[21] (The modals *will*, *may*, etc. can be treated as tenses that have more normal mappings to syntax instead of affixing to verbs.)[22]

At this point let's see how far we can get with mapping three example CSs into syntax. (Unordered syntactic and phonological constituents are enclosed in { }.)

---

[19] Another well-known violation of the Argument/Modifier Rule goes in the other direction: a modifier is embedded more deeply than it should be:

(i)   a. I enjoy an **occasional** drink. [≈ I occasionally enjoy a drink.]
      b. Every day ten **new** people contract AIDS. [≈ Every day ten people newly...]

Within the framework of Ross (1967), who has an early discussion, this construction was amenable to treatment in terms of downward movement of the modifier. We know of no discussion of this construction in post-1975 MGG frameworks, which all disallow lowering.

[20] An alternative would be to consider it a time modifier.

[21] The notion that a phrase has only one head is standard in MGG (see Kayne 1994). In contrast, Bresnan (2001) introduces the notion of "co-head" in LFG, where two f-structure nodes map into the same c-structure.

[22] A construction that violates *both* the Head Rule and the Argument/Modifier Rule is illustrated in (i).

(i)   a monster of a book
      that travesty of a marriage

These mean roughly 'a book that is a monster', 'that marriage, which is a travesty', i.e. the syntactically subordinate noun functions as the semantic head, and the syntactic head noun functions as a modifier. This construction also supports idiomatic cases such as *a hell of a N*. For evidence that this is the correct analysis, see Asaka (2002) and Booij (2002) and references therein; the latter briefly discusses a cognate construction in Dutch.

(17) a.

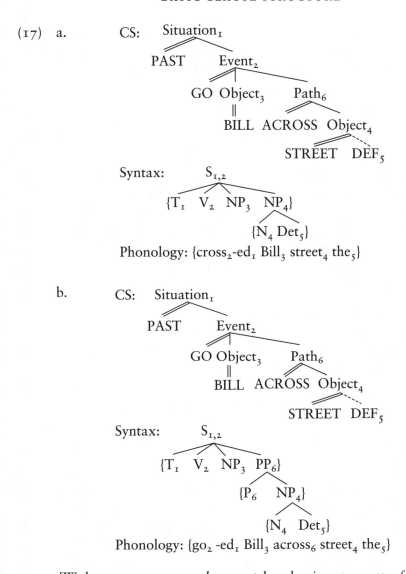

[We have to correct *go-ed* to *went*, but that is not a matter for the syntax–semantics interface]

This is an improvement on the situation at the end of the last section, since the morphemes are now not merely a list but rather a hierarchical structure, an unordered labeled bracketing. Next we have to impose order.

5.5 Constraining (most of) linear order

The constraints on linear order come in two varieties. The first variety corresponds to traditional phrase structure rules: these are the autonomous syntactic principles discussed in section 4.7. The second variety consists of semantic constraints on word/phrase order; these are phrasal interface rules.

We repeat from section 4.7 the phrase structures relevant to the discussion in this section. They are divided into principles of constituency and principles of linear order. (In (18), "[XP" means XP is at the left edge; "X > Y" means X precedes Y; "X >$_{default}$ Y" means the default order is that X precedes Y but other orders are possible.)

(18) **Autonomous phrase structure rules**

<u>Constituency</u>   <u>Order</u>

a. $\{_S$ (XP/C) NP T (PP/AdvP) (VP) $\}$ [XP/C; NP >$_{default}$ T >$_{default}$ VP

b. $\{_{VP}$ (V) (Prt) (XP)* $\}$ [V; NP >$_{default}$ XP;

                                      Prt > PP >$_{default}$ CP

c. $\{_{NP}$ N (Det/[NP+poss]) (AP/PP/CP*) $\}$ [Det/NP+poss; AP >$_{default}$ N;

                                     N > PP >$_{default}$ CP

d. $\{_{PP}$ P (NP/AP) (PP/CP) $\}$ [P; NP/AP > PP/CP

When we apply the constraints in (18) to the examples in (17), matters improve: they constrain the order of noun and determiner in NP, they put the verb inside a VP, they make the PPs follow the verb in VP, and they make a preposition precede its object. There are several things these constraints don't do. First, they don't determine whether the NP arguments go in subject or in object position. For example, given (19a) (= (17a)), which conforms to the Head and Argument/Modifier Rules, the constraints of this section are consistent with either of the realizations (19b) or (19c).

(19) a. CS: [PAST [GO ([BILL]$_3$,

                             [ACROSS ([STREET; DEF$_5$]$_4$)])]$_2$]$_1$

       Syntax: $\{_{S/VP}$ NP$_3$ T$_1$V$_2$ $\{_{NP}$ N$_4$ Det$_5\}_4\}_{1,2}$

       Phonology: $\{$cross$_2$-ed$_1$ Bill$_3$ street$_4$ the$_4\}$

    b. Syntax: $[_S$ NP$_3$ T$_1$ $[_{VP}$ cross$_2$ $[_{NP}$ Det$_5$ N$_4]_4$]$_{1,2}$

       Phonology: Bill$_2$ cross$_3$-ed$_1$ the$_4$ street$_5$

    c. Syntax: $[_S[_{NP}$ Det$_5$ N$_4]_4$ T$_1$ $[_{VP}$ cross$_2$ NP$_3]_{1,2}$

       Phonology: the$_5$ street$_4$ cross$_2$-ed$_1$ Bill$_3$

We set this crucial problem aside until sections 5.7–6.3.

The second problem is illustrated in (17c) (= (20a)): because an NP cannot have an NP complement, the NP *Bill* cannot be incorporated into the structure. However, the dummy *of* in (20b), which lacks CS features, enables the constraints to be satisfied as in (20c).

(20) a. CS: $[PICTURE ([BILL]_2); INDEF_3]_1$
         Syntax: $\{_{NP} N_1 \{_{NP} N_2\}_2 Det_3\}_1$
         Phonology: $\{picture_1 Bill_2 a_3\}$
      b. CS: n/a
         Syntax: P_4
         Phonology: of_4
      c. Syntax: $[_{NP} Det_3 N_1 [_{PP} P_4 [_{NP} N_2]_2]]_1$
         Phonology: $a_3 picture_1 of_4 Bill_2$

Notice that the PP in (20c) is licensed only in syntax, and does not correspond to a constituent in semantics.

A third thing the rules in (18) do not account for is word order possibilities that are tied to particular lexical items. For instance, section 1.5.1 observed that the order N-Adj is possible in English with the adjective *responsible*. In Romance languages some adjectives are prenominal, some are postnominal, and some appear in either position with a difference in meaning (e.g. Italian *uomo povero* 'man (who is) poor (indigent)', vs. *pover' uomo* 'poor (pitiable) man'). Such lexical ordering relations, to the extent that they are not fully predictable from general rules, must be stipulated in the correspondences associated with the particular lexical items.

This gives the flavor of the contribution of autonomous syntactic rules to the mapping between syntax and syntax. We next add in a sample of the true interface rules that connect linear phrase order to semantics. One important rule involves order of constituents in VP: it is preferred that semantic arguments precede semantic modifiers. Note that rule (18b) does not know whether a constituent of VP is an argument or a modifier, since the difference is not overtly marked in syntax. This issue is most acute with multiple PPs following the verb, since PPs may be either arguments or modifiers, and the same preposition may serve as the head of either type.

(21) a. John gave the books to Mary [*arg*] on Thursday [*mod*].
                                                    [unmarked order]
         John gave the books on Thursday to Mary.   [marked order]

b. John decorated the table with flowers [*arg*] for Mary [*mod*].

[unmarked order]

John decorated the table for Mary with flowers.   [marked order]

c. John lowered the books to the table [*arg*] with a shovel/flourish [*mod*].   [unmarked order]

John lowered the books with a shovel/flourish to the table.

[marked order]

In each marked case, making the argument PP heavier or stressing it to mark it as focus improves the prosodic acceptability of the VP, e.g. *John gave the books on Thursday to the woman who had asked for them.* On the other hand, if there are two PP arguments or two PP modifiers, the order is free, although (as noted in section 4.7) a difference in heaviness or focus still plays a role:[23]

(22)   a. Bill talked with Mary [*arg*] about chess [*arg*].
Bill talked about chess with Mary.

b. Bill left Boston with Mary [*mod*] on Thursday [*mod*]
Bill left Boston on Thursday with Mary.

The preference for argument-modifier order can be stated as (23).

(23)   **Arguments before modifiers**

Conceptual structure   Syntax

$[F(\ldots X_i \ldots); \ldots Y_j \ldots]_k \iff_{\text{default}} \{XP_i > YP_j\}_k$

Another important interface principle links linear order to information structure:

(24)   **Focus Last** $[\ldots X_i \ldots]_k \iff_{\text{default}} \{YP > XP_i\}_k$
$|$
Focus$_i$

This principle appears to be operative even in the most rudimentary forms of language such as pidgins (Bickerton 1981) and the "Basic Variety" acquired by beginning second language learners (Klein and Perdue 1997). As mentioned in section 4.7, it is often redundant with the prosodic rule Heavy Late, since foci are typically new information and therefore longer. But a contrastive focus can be short and still be pushed to the end, as in *He mentioned to the boys only me*.[24]

---

[23] An exception is the two arguments in *think of NP as NP/AP*, whose order cannot be reversed.

[24] In free phrase order languages, rules like Focus Last that involve information structure typically play a more prominent role in determining phrase order. For instance, the German VP is more or less freely ordered aside from the position of the verb and the separable particle; the focus is typically the phrase immediately preceding the final verb. Samek-Lodivici (2003) argues that in Italian, the strict phonological requirement for main stress (which correlates with focus) to come last can override canonical word order, e.g. *Ha riso GIANNI*, 'JOHN has laughed'. He couches the conflict between the principles in an OT format.

Subject–auxiliary inversion might be stated something like (25) (leaving many aspects to the imagination):

(25) **Inversion**

(variety of semantic environments[25]) $\iff$ {$_S$T > NP}

To sum up so far: we now have all the adjuncts and PP arguments in their proper places. (Or, mapping from syntax to semantics, we know that phrases in particular places can count as modifiers and as certain kinds of argument in semantics.) But argument structure is not yet complete. Section 5.6 is concerned with how the semantic arguments of the verb are realized as syntactic categories, and shows how argument structure alternations are realized. Sections 5.7–6.3 deal with the position of NP arguments: which one gets mapped into subject position, which into postverbal position(s), and which into "raised" positions outside the verb's clause.

5.6 What a verb can say about its arguments

We next turn to the argument structure of verbs (and other heads). Recall that within the present framework, a verb is an interface rule that licenses a correspondence between the syntactic structure V, a piece of CS, and a piece of phonology. It also specifies a set of contextual features or structures within which the correspondence is licensed. The contextual features in CS are standardly called selectional restrictions; those in syntax are called subcategorization. The verb's argument structure is the most important part of these contextual features or structures. The issues involved in argument structure include the following:

• As part of its meaning, a verb specifies a certain number of semantic arguments—entities intrinsically involved in the situation that the verb denotes. Which are semantically obligatory, and which are semantically optional? (i.e. in order for the verb to be selected to express the intended message, is the semantic argument required or not?)

• If an argument is semantically present, is it expressed in syntax *obligatorily* or only *optionally*? (i.e. is the argument required in the syntactic context in order for the verb to license the correspondence?)

• If a semantic argument is expressed syntactically, does the verb have to stipulate anything about its syntactic category (i.e. subcategorization or s-selection), and if so, what?

---

[25] Inversion does not occur in English questions when the interrogative is the subject: *Who called?*, *Who did t call?* A number of ways of accounting for this restriction come to mind. A natural possibility is that the constraint requiring the *wh*-phrase to be at the left edge of the phrase overrides the ordering stipulated by inversion. Such a solution has an Optimality-Theoretic flavor, perhaps along lines suggested by Grimshaw (1997).

• If a semantic argument is expressed syntactically, does the verb have to stipulate anything about its position and/or morphological form (e.g. case)? If so, how?

• How much of this machinery generalizes to arguments of other syntactic categories: nouns, adjectives, and prepositions?

In 5.6.1 we highlight the fact that an argument may be optional in two senses: it may be semantically optional, or it may be semantically obligatory but syntactically omissible. In 5.6.2 we find that while the syntactic category of an argument is for the most part predictable from its semantic category, it is not entirely predictable, and provision must be made for individual verbs to specify the categories of their arguments. In 5.6.3 we distinguish between two sorts of NP argument: those that are expressed *directly*, as NPs and those that are expressed *obliquely*, as objects of PPs. The choice proves often to be a property of individual verbs and is not entirely predictable from semantic role, although there are some very general patterns. Section 5.6.4 shows that some verbs select arguments that may be realized syntactically in more than one way. In such cases, the linearization of the arguments is sensitive to the syntactic category of the arguments, not their semantic properties. As mentioned above, the linearization of direct NP arguments proves to be a matter of some complexity and theoretical significance, and we take it up in sections 5.7–6.3.

5.6.1 *Obligatory vs. optional semantic arguments*

First, it is important to distinguish truly optional semantic arguments from obligatory semantic arguments that are optionally expressed in syntax. A good example is *swallow* vs. *eat*.

(26)   a.   He swallowed/ate (the food).
       b.   He swallowed, but he didn't swallow anything.
       c.   *He ate, but he didn't eat anything.

Both verbs have an optional object (26a). However, if the object is omitted from *swallow*, there need be no implied entity being swallowed (26b). If the object is omitted from *eat*, the implication remains that there is some eaten entity (26c). The way to understand this difference is that the entity swallowed is an optional semantic argument; but the entity eaten is an obligatory semantic argument that is optionally expressed in syntax.

Another example is *kick* vs. *throw*.

(27) a. He kicked/threw the pumpkin (down the stairs).
      b. He kicked the pumpkin, but it didn't move at all.
      c. *He threw the pumpkin, but it didn't move at all.

Both verbs allow an optional expression of the direct object's path of motion (27a). If such a path is not expressed with *kick*, the direct object need not have undergone any motion; thus a path of motion undergone by the direct object is an optional semantic argument of *kick*. However, throwing something inherently causes it to move; so even if the path expression is omitted, some path is still implicit.

We learn from these examples that the term "optional argument" is ambiguous, and the theory must make a distinction between semantically optional arguments and obligatory semantic arguments that are optionally expressed syntactically. Only in the latter case can we speak of an "implicit argument", i.e. one that is unexpressed.

An important case of optional semantic arguments is the causative alternation, for example (28a,b).

(28) a. John opened the door.   [causative]
      b. The door opened.   [noncausative]
      c. The door suddenly opened—but nothing opened it (it just spontan-
          eously opened).   [noncausative]
      d. The door was suddenly opened—*but nothing opened it.
                                                [passive of causative]

It is sometimes said that the noncausative (28b) has an implicit agent, so that *open* is always semantically causative. However, the pattern in (28c,d), shows this is incorrect. Parallel to (26/27b,c), the noncausative does not imply an external causer, whereas the passive of the causative does. This intuition is confirmed by the fact that the noncausative does not allow for an adjunct controlled by an implicit agent, while the passive does.

(29) a. *The door opened in order to let in the fresh air.
      b. The door was opened in order to let in the fresh air.

Similarly, the noncausative but not the passive is incompatible with adverbs that implicate agency.

(30) a. *The door deliberately opened.
      b. The door was deliberately opened.

We conclude that a verb that undergoes the causative alternation has an optional *semantic* argument, the agent. As far as the verb per se is concerned, when the agent is present, it must be expressed; but the passive can render this argument implicit. (See Jackendoff 1990a: ch. 4 for a formalization of this alternation in terms of CS.)

A further distinction must be made among implicit arguments. In (26c) and (27c), the implicit arguments are indefinite, i.e. he ate *something*, he threw the pumpkin *somewhere*. On the other hand, *He knows* and *He forgot* have a definite implicit argument, i.e. 'he knows/forgot *it*', for some previously specified entity. Consider also *That's frightening*. Something can't be frightening without someone whom it frightens. But *that's frightening* doesn't mean it's frightening to *someone* or to some specific person. Rather, it seems to mean roughly *that frightens people* or *that's frightening to people*, i.e. it has a generic implicit argument. Finally, the verbs *wash*, *dress*, and *shave*, when used intransitively, paraphrase *wash oneself*, *dress oneself*, and *shave oneself*, i.e. they have a reflexive implicit argument. Verbs can have two implicit arguments of different types. Asking, for example, requires as semantic arguments an asker, an addressee, and a question, and *I'll ask* implies a definite question and either a definite or indefinite addressee.

The semantic types of arguments are stipulated as contextual restrictions on the corresponding variables. So, for example, the fact that *drink* stipulates one of its arguments as a liquid accounts at once for the interpretation of *something/it/whatever he wanted* as a liquid in (31a), for the understood liquidity of the implicit argument in (31b), for the anomaly of (31c), which has an expressed argument, and for the anomaly of (31d), where the implicit argument is identified by a pointing gesture (Jackendoff 1990a: section 2.3).

(31) a. He drank something/it/whatever he wanted.
      b. He drank.
      c. *He drank the telephone.
      d. #Please drink! [*pointing at a telephone*]

In addition, *drink* must stipulate under certain conditions that its implicit argument is an alcoholic beverage, as in *I hear Harriet's been drinking again*. Is this another lexical item or a different meaning of the same lexical item? However the difference is couched, we are verging into areas where the syntax–semantics interface becomes lexically idiosyncratic, and we drop this part of the issue here.

5.6.2 *Category of syntactic arguments*

To a great extent, the syntactic category used to express a semantic argument can be predicted from the argument's ontological type. Archi-objects (including objects, substances, and aggregates) are invariably expressed as NPs. Places and Paths are almost invariably expressed as PPs. Properties are expressed as APs, predicate nominal NPs, and the occasional idiomatic PP (*in luck*, *out of sorts*). Situations (including Events) and Propositions are expressed as Ss or NPs (*earthquake*, *concert*). Thus when a verb takes a semantic argument of a particular ontological type, the category of the corresponding syntactic argument is fairly restricted on general grounds.

However, it is not quite restricted enough. It appears that verbs can in addition impose *syntactic* restrictions on the category of their arguments, further restricting the possibilities. For example, the verbs grouped in (32) and (33) are semantically quite close but permit different syntactic realizations of their arguments.

(32) a. John was angry/a raving maniac/out of luck.
      b. John seemed angry/*a raving maniac/out of luck.
      c. John became angry/a raving maniac/*out of luck.
      d. John got angry/*a raving maniac/*out of luck.

(33) a. John mentioned his feelings of guilt/that he felt guilty.
      b. John expressed/described his feelings of guilt/*that he felt guilty
      c. John objected that he felt guilty/*his feelings of guilt.

When an argument is expressed as a clause, a verb can stipulate the choice of complement type.

(34) a. John mentioned growing older/that he was growing older.
      b. John discussed growing older/*that he was growing older.

(35) a. John claims that he is smart/to be smart/*himself smart.
      b. John imagines that he is smart/*to be smart/himself smart.

We take this to be an irreducible stipulation in the lexical entry of a verb, part of its syntactic contextual features. Such a stipulation is not problematic, because it is learnable on the basis of the evidence the learner experiences. We therefore include the possibility of strict subcategorization in the syntactic contextual features of a verb.

We must also mention verbs that take pleonastic reflexive arguments, either optionally or obligatorily.

(36) a. Paula behaved (herself).
        *Paula behaved Sam.
      b. Paula perjured/composed herself.
        *Paula perjured/composed (Sam).

    c. Albert availed himself of the facilities.
       *Albert availed (Sam) of the facilities.
    d. Tammy took it upon herself/*Sam to clean the toilet.
    e. This poem lends itself to translation.
    f. Beulah is beside herself.
    g. Kim concerns/preoccupies himself with syntax.

These verbs have a syntactic argument whose form is stipulated as reflexive, but the syntactic argument does not express a distinct semantic argument. For a first approximation, we might think of these as rather like the idiom *kick the bucket*, which also stipulates a syntactic NP object that does not express a semantic argument. In section 6.4 we will come back to how the reflexive is bound.

    We conclude that although much of the syntactic argument structure of a verb is predictable on semantic grounds, the verb still has some freedom in how it chooses to constrain the syntactic realization of its arguments. This theme continues through succeeding sections.

5.6.3 *Direct vs. oblique NP arguments*

We next draw attention to an important mismatch in English between semantic arguments and their syntactic realizations. If a semantic argument denotes a physical object (including a person), its standard realization is as an NP in syntax. If a semantic argument denotes a location or path, its standard realization is as a PP in syntax, where the preposition is freely chosen from semantically relevant alternatives:

(37) a. Amy sat in the room/outside the house/next to the bed/between the lamps/etc.
      b. Beth ran into the room/down the hall/along the street/under the bridge/etc.

Here the semantic relation is between the verb and the PP as a whole; the object of the preposition serves to specify a reference object for the location or path in question. But in addition there is a third case, in which a semantic argument that denotes a person or physical object is expressed as a PP in syntax, and the choice of preposition is fixed:

(38) a. Sue covered/decorated the table **with** flowers.
      b. She presented/rewarded/provided Phil **with** a prize. Sue showered us **with** gifts.
      c. She gave/awarded/presented a prize **to** Phil.
      d. She seems/looks/appears sad **to** me.

e. She bought/sold the book **for** $5. She traded/exchanged the book **for** a cat. She paid $5 **for** a cat.

f. She talked/chatted/yelled **about** the war.

g. She treated Bill **as** a pariah.

h. She was looking **at** the newspaper.

i. She relied **on** us **for** information/to tell the truth.

Let's call these cases *oblique NP arguments*, in contrast with "direct NP arguments". In some languages they would be expressed by case-marked NPs (say, dative or instrumental) instead of PPs.

The choice of preposition for an oblique NP argument is often consonant with the NP's semantic role. For instance, *with* is frequently used for themes: e.g. in (38a) the flowers move so as to end up on the table, and in (38b) the prize and gifts change possession. *To* is often used for recipients (38c)[26] and also for experiencers (38d); *for* is often used for items that change possession in exchange for something else (38e); *about* is often used for topics of thoughts and speech acts (38f); *as* is often used for predicate NPs (38g). In other cases the preposition is idiosyncratic, e.g. *think of NP, believe/trust in NP, count/depend/ rely on NP.* Whatever the choice of preposition, the argument in question is a syntactic PP. Hence rule (18b) requires it to follow an NP or AP argument, as can be seen in (38a–e,g).

Verbs with similar meanings can differ as to whether a particular semantic argument is realized as a direct or oblique NP. For instance, *mention* and *discuss* fall into the same semantic class as the verbs in (38f), but the topic of the speech act is a direct object: *She mentioned/discussed (*about) the war.* Similarly, one sense of *strike* falls into the same semantic class as the verbs in (38d), but the experiencer is a direct object and the predicate AP is oblique: *She strikes me as sad.*

Oblique arguments, despite being semantic arguments of the verb, are syntactic complements of prepositions. For instance, the syntactic structure of *look at NP* is V-PP. This is apparent from the fact that the PP is separable from the verb.

(39) a. She looked intently at me.

b. the people at whom she was looking

There is no more reason to claim that *look at* is a member of the category V than there is to say that *trade . . . for* is a V in (38e). This evident discontinuity is a

---

[26] RJ has always treated *to* as contentful before (e.g. Jackendoff 1990a), so this is a departure from previous practice. The present approach clears up various matters, in ways too picky to discuss in the present context.

problem for traditional MGG accounts of lexical insertion and Merge, which require a lexical item to occupy a single terminal node. But it presents no difficulty in a constraint-based approach. Treating them as truly discontinuous is the correct account, since there are numerous VP idioms like *take NP for granted* and *take NP to task*, which are similarly discontinuous and submit to traditional lexical insertion under a V° node only with the greatest artificiality.

5.6.4 *Syntactic argument structure alternations*

We next address argument structure alternations in which the number of semantic arguments remains constant but the syntactic expression varies. A good starting case is the verb *mention*. This has three semantic arguments: the mentioner, the thing mentioned, and the addressee (who is optionally expressed in syntax). The point of interest is that, as seen in (33a) above, the thing mentioned can be expressed as either an NP or a tensed clause. When it is an NP, it precedes the addressee; when it is a clause, it follows the addressee.

(40)   a. Bill mentioned the race to John.
       b. Bill mentioned to John that the race took place.

The position of this argument follows automatically from its syntactic realization: rule (18b), the phrase structure rule for VP, stipulates that NP arguments precede PPs and clausal arguments follow PPs. So the verb need not stipulate anything about where the argument is positioned, only that it can be expressed by either of these syntactic categories.

A similar situation obtains with the sense of the verb *look* shown in (41): the subject's appearance can be expressed either as an AP, a PP, or a *like*-clause.

(41)   a.   i.   Bill looks sad and lonely to Harriet.
            ii.   ?*Bill looks to Harriet sad and lonely.
       b.   i.   Bill looks out of sorts to Harriet.
            ii.   ?Bill looks to Harriet out of sorts.
            iii. Bill looks to Harriet [a little bit out of sorts].
       c.   i.   Bill looks to Harriet like he's having a hard time.
            ii.   ?*Bill looks like he's having a hard time to Harriet.
            iii. Bill looks like he's having a hard time to most of his dearest friends.

The position of the "appearance" argument is predicted by (18b). When it is expressed as AP, it is happiest preceding the experiencer argument, which is expressed as a PP. When it is expressed as PP, it is ordered more or less freely with the experiencer. Here heaviness plays a role, as seen in (41b.ii) vs. (41b.iii).

This contrasts with (41a), where the AP, even though heavier, preferably precedes the PP. Finally, when the "appearance" argument is expressed as a clause, it must follow the experiencer (41c.i). However, this ordering can again be mitigated by heaviness or focus, as seen in (41c.ii,iii).

This machinery also applies to some aspects of more well-known argument structure alternations. The idea is that the same verb can allow alternate syntactic realizations in which arguments differ in obliqueness:

(42) a. She presented a new car to her son.

[direct theme, oblique recipient]

    b. She presented her son with a new car.

[direct recipient, oblique theme]

    c. Water slowly filled the tank.   [direct theme]

    d. The tank slowly filled with water.   [oblique theme]

Such alternations are idiosyncratic to the verb in question. For instance, *reward* is semantically very close to *present* but has only the form with oblique theme (*She rewarded a prize to her son*); *cover* is very close to *fill* but has only the form with direct theme (*The yard slowly covered with snow*). The order of arguments in (42a,b,d) is predicted by the fact that one is direct and one is oblique, so all the verb has to do is say which one of its arguments is oblique. The order in (42c), however, is not yet predicted, because both arguments are direct.

A further case of this sort is the dative alternation, where the verb leaves open whether the recipient is direct or oblique:

(43) a. She gave/awarded them the prize.   [direct recipient]

    b. She gave/awarded the prize to them.   [oblique recipient]

This is exactly the same as the alternation in (42a,b), with semantically similar verbs, except that the theme does not covary in obliqueness. The fact that the oblique recipient in (43b) comes at the end follows from the rules of phrase order. However, we have not yet accounted for the order of the NP arguments in (43a).

In a further class of alternations, one alternant has a direct theme argument and a free path PP (44a). The other alternant has an oblique theme argument and a direct NP argument that serves as reference object for the path; the path-function is semantically fixed by the verb (44b). Again, the PP follows the NP, whichever of the two semantic arguments it expresses.

(44) a. We sprayed water on the wall/into the bucket/through the window.

    b. We sprayed the window with water.

[water goes **on** the window only]

We conclude that in an interesting range of cases, the order of syntactic arguments follows from their syntactic category, without any notion of syntactic movement being invoked. In order to make this work, a verb must stipulate whether a particular NP argument is expressed directly or obliquely, and sometimes whether a particular argument can be expressed as an NP as well as a PP or CP; but the verb does not have to further stipulate the order of arguments.[27]

5.7 Hierarchical linking of direct NP arguments

We turn now to the direct NP arguments, namely the Subject, Direct Object, and Indirect Object. In a language like English, the direct arguments differ from the oblique arguments by the fact that the semantic role of the latter can often be identified by the preposition, while the direct arguments have no distinguishing characteristics—they are just NPs. We will see that it is the absence of distinguishing characteristics of the direct arguments that gives rise to the special way in which they are treated in the grammar.

An intuition that keeps resurfacing in the literature is that the position of syntactic arguments is connected with their thematic roles. The strongest version of this view is UTAH (Baker 1988), which connects thematic roles uniquely with syntactic positions. On this view, the mapping of a thematic role to a particular grammatical function is rigid. Chapter 3 discussed some of the reasons why we think such a view is too strong. Basically, the UTAH approach entails movement, since semantic roles cannot be uniquely linked to surface grammatical function. By abandoning UTAH, we allow for the possibility that a given semantic argument can be realized in more than one syntactic position. Such possibilities give the illusion of movement only if one is committed to Interface Uniformity.

Many researchers (e.g. Anderson 1977; Carter 1976; Grimshaw 1990; Bresnan and Kanerva 1989; Dowty 1991; Pollard and Sag 1987; Van Valin and LaPolla 1997; Jackendoff 1990a) have proposed the weaker position that thematic roles and syntactic positions are matched by means of a hierarchy, such that the highest-ranked thematic role, whatever it may be, occupies the highest-ranked syntactic position, namely the subject; and one works one's way down the two hierarchies in parallel until one runs out of arguments.

---

[27] The literature on argument structure alternations is too extensive for us to be able to compare our approach to all the others here. For an important empirical study, see Levin (1993). We think our approach is somewhat novel in its attention to precisely how the verb codes for the alternation.

The hierarchical approach immediately yields a nice account of the causative alternation (28). When the semantics includes both agent and patient arguments, the agent outranks the patient and thus occupies subject position; the patient therefore must settle for the next best syntactic slot, the direct object. On the other hand, when the agent argument is absent, the patient is the highest-ranked argument and therefore becomes subject. Under this account, then, the verb only needs to say that the agent is an optional semantic argument, and everything else follows from the linking theory.[28]

Of course there are also alternations where arguments do not shift around, for example the alternation with *swallow* (26). The reason is that the swallower is always agent and therefore is always of highest rank. The optional argument, the stuff swallowed, is patient. If it is present, the linking rules assign it to the second-ranked syntactic position; if it is absent, the linking rules run out of arguments after taking care of the subject. So again the verb only has to specify that the second argument is optional, and everything else about the position of direct arguments follows.

There is substantial agreement in the literature about the disposition of these two particular examples. The key issues are whether a consistent thematic hierarchy can be developed that accounts for *all* linking, and what the hierarchy is. Before giving our current version of the hierarchy, we want to add two specifics to the hypothesis that seem to make it work more adequately, for English at least.

(a) We limit hierarchical linking to direct NP arguments. Thus we do not have to find thematic differences correlated with argument structure alternations such as the dative alternation and the alternations with *present* and *fill* in (42). As far as thematic structure is concerned (though perhaps not information structure), *present X to Y* and *X fill Y* are synonymous with *present Y with X* and *Y fill with X* respectively. In these cases, the fact that the PP follows the NP has nothing to do with thematic role but is simply an issue of phrase structure, as we have already outlined. Similarly, the order in *Y fill with X* (42d) is explained not by its thematic role, but by the fact that the theme argument is oblique. The hierarchy is used only to explain why the recipient NP precedes the theme NP with *give* (43a), and why the ordering comes out as it does in *X fill Y*.

---

[28] In particular, there is no need for "unaccusative movement" of the sort argued for by Burzio (1986) and many others. See Levin (1989) and Levin and Rappaport Hovav (1995) for discussion of the linking account. It is nevertheless necessary to note the difference between unaccusative and unergative verbs (i.e. intransitives that do not show unaccusative properties).

(b) We are inclined to think that the hierarchy does not apply to all combinations of thematic roles. In particular, the dyad Stimulus–Experiencer shows up in either order:

(45)   a. *Experiencer subject; Stimulus object*
          John fears sincerity.
          John finds/regards sincerity repulsive.
       b. *Stimulus subject; Experiencer object*
          Sincerity frightens John.
          Sincerity strikes John as repulsive.

There have been attempts to demonstrate a consistent semantic difference associated with these configurations (e.g. Grimshaw 1990; Pesetsky 1995), but we find them unpersuasive when one considers the full range of predicates in each configuration (Jackendoff, to appear a). To be sure, some of the Stimulus subjects do partake (optionally) of agentive properties ('sincerity makes John frightened') but others do not (*'sincerity makes John be struck as repulsive'). In general it may be necessary for these verbs individually to stipulate the ranking of their arguments, rather than doing it by general principles.

We find this an acceptable result. The point of the hierarchical linking theory is not just that it predicts where the arguments of existing verbs go: it also predicts where the arguments of new verbs *must* go. For instance, Carter (1976) argues that it is no accident that there is no verb in English like the hypothetical *benter*, which means the same as *enter* except that the arguments are reversed in syntax:

(46)   John entered the room = *The room bentered John

Rather, any verb that involves a theme moving with respect to a reference object will have the syntactic pattern of *enter*, with the theme in subject position and the reference object in object position, because theme outranks reference object on the hierarchy. By contrast, (45a,b) presents pairs parallel to (46), where both verbs *are* real verbs—but with a different pair of thematic roles. We conclude that this pair does not fall under the thematic hierarchy. Still, such verbs are learnable, since learners are presented with primary linguistic evidence that shows them where the arguments belong. The special argument properties of these verbs play a role in their behavior with respect to passive (section 6.3.5) and binding (sections 6.4 and 10.8.2).

With these two caveats in mind, here is our current version of the thematic hierarchy:

(47)   **Thematic hierarchy**
       Actor/Agent > Patient/Undergoer/Beneficiary > non-Patient theme > other[29]

This hierarchy pertains specifically to the correspondence between semantic roles and direct NP arguments. (48) gives some common patterns that illustrate the hierarchy. (Jackendoff (1990a) justifies these thematic roles in terms of structural positions in CS, rather than arbitrary labels or features; note that an argument can have multiple thematic roles.)

(48)   a. John opened the window.
          agent   patient+theme
       b. John   entered the room.
          actor+theme   reference object (=other)
       c. Water   slowly filled the tank.
          undergoer+theme   reference object (=other)
       d. John helped Harry.
          agent   beneficiary
       e. John   received a letter.
          beneficiary   non-patient theme
       f. John gave Bill   the letter
             agent   beneficiary   non-patient theme
       g. John sprayed the wall   with paint.
          agent   patient+reference object   (oblique)
       h. John sprayed paint   on the wall.
          agent   patient+theme (PP)
       i. The road   parallels the river.
          non-patient theme   reference object (other)

---

[29] Actor/agent can be identified by the standard test *What X did was...* (example i); patient and undergoer are alternative names for the role identified by the test *What happened to X was...* (ii); beneficiary is identified (in some cases) as X in the test *What Y did for X was...*" (iii).

(i) What John did was kiss Bill/run away/*be tall/?*bleed to death.   [*John* = actor/agent]
(ii) What happened to John was Bill hit him/he bled to death/he underwent surgery/*he was tall/
     *he kissed Bill.   [*John* = patient/undergoer]
(iii) What Sue did for John was give him a kiss/fix him a drink/help him/*hit him.
                                                                          [*John* = beneficiary]

Theme designates an entity in motion, being located, or changing possession or other properties. An example of a non-patient theme is that in a change of possession. Compare *What happened to the money is John dropped it/? John gave it to Fred.* The latter requires some contextual support. See Jackendoff (1990a).

    j. Bill named   the baby   Fred.
       agent   (patient+)theme other
    k. The book   weighs three pounds.
       non-patient theme   other
    l. He   made me   a milkshake.
       agent   beneficiary   non-patient theme
  m. He   made me   a linguist.
       agent   patient/beneficiary+theme   other

(48) does not cover all possible cases, particularly those whose thematic roles we do not understand adequately (e.g. *I envy you your reputation*, *the meal cost him $75*, *smoke means fire*). But our reading of the literature indicates a consensus that there is some form of hierarchical linking, and our emendations eliminate many of the historically more troublesome cases.

CHAPTER 6

The Grammatical Function Tier

6.1 The need for grammatical functions

The machinery surveyed in Chapter 5 enables us to map pretty well from CS to single declarative active clauses. We now must incorporate some of the standard constructions that motivated transformational grammar in the first place, the most notable of which are passive and raising (more generally, "argument movements" or "A-movements"). Chapter 2 presented some of the reasons why we do not wish to treat passive as movement of NPs; from this it follows that raising cannot be treated as movement either.[1] In addition to the evidence from English given in Chapter 2, there is the crosslinguistic evidence that motivated Relational Grammar (Perlmutter and Postal 1983), LFG (Bresnan 1982a), and Role and Reference Grammar (Van Valin and LaPolla 1997) to abandon the notion of passive as syntactic movement: many languages have functional equivalents of passive that involve not change of position but rather change in case-marking. The basic insight in these approaches is that the passive is a way of promoting a lower-ranked syntactic argument to a higher rank—however syntactic rank happens to be determined in the language in question.

A popular alternative to passive as movement, found in essence in both LFG and HPSG, treats passive as a "lexical rule" that manipulates the argument structure of verbs in the lexicon. Thus in addition to the active transitive verb *X love Y*, the lexicon contains the passive participle *loved (by X)* which can be predicated of *Y*. We agree with the intuition that the passive is a manipulation of

---

[1] As was recognized as early as Shopen (1972), but also by Brame (1978), Bresnan (1978), and many others subsequently.

argument structure, but we do not wish to localize it in the lexical entry of each verb. As we said in Chapter 1, we regard the lexicon as a long term memory repository of items that are learned and stored (possibly including predictable high-frequency material); this makes for a smooth transition between theories of competence and performance. In our view, what the lexicon should *not* include is material that can be freely constructed online through fully productive rules. Considering an extreme case, we would not want the thousands of forms of every Turkish verb (Hankamer 1989) to be stored in the lexicon; rather, when one learns a new verb, one can immediately produce any desired form online by freely combining the stem with a stored repertoire of affixes.

It is a rhetorical misdirection to say that the individual Turkish verb forms are in a "virtual" lexicon, which consists of anything that *might* be a word. One might equally claim that all of the possible auxiliary forms for an English verb (*will/can/might/should run, will/can/ ... have run, will/can/ ... be running, will/ can/ ... have been running*) are part of the "virtual" lexicon. Such a claim would be less persuasive, but only (we think) because in Turkish we are dealing with single words, and in English with formatives that allow intervening adverbs. But the same combinatorial considerations obtain: the (morpho)syntax allows a free combination of verb stems with a paradigm (see Ackerman and Webelhuth (1999) for discussion). We therefore think that the idea of a virtual lexicon is a mistake: free combinatoriality is free combinatoriality, whether phrasal or morphological. And free combination of items implies they are independent lexical items. (Recall the discussion of this point with respect to idiomatic VP constructions such as *V one's head off* in section 1.5.3.)

Turning back to the passive, the fact that one can immediately form the passive of a newly acquired transitive verb argues that the passive form is not learned verb by verb, once one has acquired the rule. Rather, it can be computed online. This conclusion requires us to regard the passive as a sort of constructional idiom, as in Construction Grammar. It is a piece of structure or a piece of interface stored in the lexicon, which has the effect of manipulating the argument structure of sentences in which it appears. The question is: Which argument structure does it manipulate?

The obvious choice is the argument structure of the verb. Instead of mapping the highest-ranked semantic argument of the verb to subject position, the passive could map the second-highest ranked to subject, and optionally map the highest ranked to an oblique position whose marker is *by*. This would work beautifully if we were dealing only with simplex sentences. But it founders when the surface subject of the passive is not a semantic argument of the verb (1a), and especially when the surface subject of the passive is a dummy such as *it* or *there*, hence not a semantic argument of anything (1b,c).

(1) a. John was believed to have left.
     b. It is believed to be possible to leave early.
     c. There are believed to be several difficulties with this analysis.

Similar considerations pertain to "raising to subject". One possible non-movement approach would say that a "raising" verb such as *tend* manipulates argument structure in the manner shown in (2).

(2) Map the highest-ranked semantic argument of my complement clause's verb into the highest-ranked syntactic position of my own clause, rather than into the highest-ranked position in the complement.

The effect is that the complement clause lacks a subject, and the main verb has a subject that is not its own semantic argument but rather a semantic argument of the complement—in fact the one that "belongs" in the complement's subject. Thus raising would be part of the syntax–semantics interface instead of an autonomous syntactic rule.

Such an approach to raising fails for the same reason as the parallel approach to passive does: there can be NPs in "raised" position that are not semantic arguments of the lower verb and in fact are not semantic arguments of anything:

(3) a. John tends to be believed to like ice cream.
     b. It tends to be possible to leave early.
     c. There tend to be lots of people here.

As we see it, the interface needs an extra degree of freedom: it needs to manipulate the status of *syntactic* arguments, irrespective of their semantic status and their syntactic position. Different frameworks have recognized this need in different ways. The most direct realization is in LFG, which posits a syntactic level of *functional structure* (or *f-structure*) that intervenes between semantic structure and phrase structure representation. The level of f-structure permits the grammar to manipulate the assignment of semantic arguments to the grammatical functions subject, object, and indirect object; and in turn grammatical function assignment determines syntactic position, case-marking, and agreement. Such a treatment escapes the problems illustrated above by virtue of the fact that (a) a phrase can be a semantic argument of one clause but have a grammatical function in another, and (b) a syntactic dummy can have a grammatical function without having a semantic function. Hence manipulations such as passive and raising, which affect grammatical functions, are not confined to semantic arguments of the clause being manipulated. Another virtue of grammatical functions is that they can map to different phrase structure realizations in different languages: in some languages such as English they map to fixed positions, while in other languages they map to structural case while leaving position free. Another version of the same insight is Relational Grammar (RG), which almost exclusively concerns manipulations on grammatical functions.[2]

A more indirect approach is Case Theory in GB/PPT, where structural case and verb agreement are assigned in terms of particular positions in phrase structure, and these phrase structure positions determine the eventual landing sites of arguments that move up through the tree. The effect is that the chain of positions successively occupied by an NP argument corresponds to the chain of grammatical functions assigned in the course of an RG derivation.[3] As observed by the early arguments for LFG and RG, such an approach is not conducive to a natural account of free phrase order, because structural position in the tree has to play the roles of both syntactic position and grammatical function. In order to account for free phrase order, the GB/MP approach has to first move all NPs to the structural positions where they can be case-marked and where verb agreement can be determined; then it has to "scramble" them into the desired surface order—where scrambling, as far as we know, has always been a formal wild card (see section 9.6.2).

Such a solution is necessary because (starting with Chomsky 1965: 68–74) MGG treats grammatical function, which determines case-marking and agreement, as implicit in phrase structure rather than as an independent dimension or tier of syntax. Consequently the theory misses the traditional insight that linear order, case-marking, and agreement are independent grammatical devices that each can be used to link phonological structure to meaning; none of them is dependent on the others, but in some languages they may cooccur redundantly. The desire to retrieve this insight in part motivated the divergence of RG, LFG, and RRG from mainstream generative grammar.

What all these theories have in common is that they pertain to only a restricted part of the syntax–semantics interface, i.e. to those semantic arguments that are realized as direct NP arguments. RG deals with three direct arguments—subject (numbered 1), object (2), and indirect object (3), plus oblique arguments and adjuncts. LFG distinguishes three functional roles: subject, object1, and object2; everything else is oblique. Both these theories

---

[2] According to David Perlmutter (p.c.), one of the originators of RG, in retrospect the original intent was to develop a constraint-based theory, a style of grammar at that time unknown; but given the ethos of the time, the machinery was invariably interpreted as derivational. His perception is however not universal (Paul Postal, p.c.). Arc-Pair Grammar (Johnson and Postal 1980), an outgrowth of RG, is more clearly constraint-based.

[3] Alsina (2001) develops the idea that Case in GF is a concealed notational variant of grammatical function.

provide principles that promote obliques to functional status (e.g. Bantu applicatives and the English "*for*-dative"), principles that demote arguments to oblique status (e.g. subjects to *by*-phrases in the passive), and principles that change the relative status of arguments (e.g. promotion of objects to subjects in the passive); but there are no rules that change obliques into other obliques. GB/PPT distinguishes two structural cases, nominative and accusative, and evinces some discomfort in dealing with indirect objects.[4] Hence, the system of so-called A-movements, the counterpart of the manipulations of RG, is essentially confined to subject and object positions, and excludes obliques.

6.2 The Grammatical Function tier and Raising

6.2.1 Some basic cases

The convergence of LFG, RG, and GB/PPT on the same phenomena—the disposition of direct NP arguments—suggests to us that there is a genuine insight about language captured by all three of them: there is a special system in language that concerns the realization of the direct NP arguments, of which there are at most three per clause. We will call this system the "grammatical function tier" or GF-tier. Section 6.3.3 will extend this system to the oblique arguments as well. Our approach appears to work nicely and capture the basic insights, at least for a first approximation. But we acknowledge that there are still many degrees of freedom in its formulation that we have not yet explored.

Confining ourselves for the moment to the direct NP arguments, the formal structure of the tier is the trivial hierarchy shown in (4), consisting of one to three ranked positions. These are *not* explicitly labeled subject, object, and indirect object, for reasons to be developed in the course of exposition; they are just ranked positions.

(4)   GF-tier: [$_{Clause}$ GF (> GF (> GF))]

Most of the interest of (4) lies in its interfaces with syntax and semantics. The basic idea is that semantic arguments to be expressed as direct NPs are correlated with positions in the GF-tier, which in turn are correlated with syntactic positions in phrase structure. In the most stereotypical case, the ranking of

---

[4] For example, Kayne (1984b) suggests that the indirect object is the subject of a small clause of which the direct object is the predicate; and, as noted in Ch. 2, Larson (1988) develops VP-shells largely to deal with the problems raised by indirect objects.

direct semantic roles in the thematic hierarchy ((47) in Chapter 5) is correlated with the ranking of GFs.[5]

(5) **Mapping of theta-hierarchy to GF-tier**
   $[\theta\text{-role}_i > \theta\text{-role}_j]_k \iff [_{Clause} GF_i > GF_j]_k$

So, for example, *John opened the door* will have CS and GF structures correlated as follows. (For greater perspicuity, we notate the connections for arguments by association lines as well as subscripts.)

(6)   [CAUSE (JOHN$_1$, [BECOME (DOOR$_2$,   OPEN)])]$_3$
              (agent)   (patient/theme)
                 | |
           [$_{Clause}$ GF$_1$ >   GF$_2$]$_3$

In English, the stereotypical mapping of the GF-tier onto syntax determines the placement of NPs in phrase structure as in (7a-c); subject–auxiliary agreement might be encoded as (7d). (As usual, roman type indicates the parts that the rule actually licenses, and italics denote contextual variables.)

(7) **Mapping of GFs to canonical syntactic positions and agreement**
   a. $[GF_i(> \ldots)]_k$ $\quad \Leftrightarrow \quad$ $[_S NP_i \ldots]_k$ $\qquad$ Position of subject[6]
   b. $[GF > GF_i > \ldots]_k$ $\Leftrightarrow$ $[_{VP} V NP_i \ldots]_k$ $\qquad$ Position of first object
   c. $[GF > GF > GF_i]_k$ $\Leftrightarrow$ $[_{VP} V\ NP\ NP_i \ldots]_k$ Position of second object
   d. $[GF_i(> \ldots)]_k$ $\quad \Leftrightarrow \quad$ $[_S \ldots T+agr_i \ldots]_k$ Subject-aux agreement

Thus a standard ditransitive clause would have the following structure.

---

[5] This formulation reflects the essence of such principles as the Theta Criterion of GB Theory and Lexical Mapping Theory of LFG. The notion of argument structure developed in Samek-Lodovici (2003), based in part on that of Grimshaw (1990), resembles our GF-tier, in that it is an unlabeled ranking.

[6] Do clauses functioning as subjects in English have a grammatical function? If so, we would want to add the following possibility:

i. $[GF_i(\ > \ldots)]_k \Leftrightarrow [_S CP_i \ldots]_k$

Such a move would allow clausal subjects to undergo raising just like NP subjects, as in *That you smoke tends to bother people*. If postverbal clauses by contrast disallowed a syntactic realization as objects, we could account for the ungrammaticality of **John believes [that you smoke] to bother people*. See e.g. Postal (1998: 111–20) and Huddleston and Pullum (2002) for arguments that this is the right way to characterize clausal arguments.

(8)

$$[\text{GIVE (PAT}_2 \quad \text{DAN}_3, [\text{BOOK; INDEF}]_4)]_1$$

$$[\text{GF}_2 > \quad \text{GF}_3 > \text{GF}_4]_1$$

$$[\text{NP} \ [_{\text{VP}} \text{V}_1 \ \text{NP} \quad \text{NP}]_1]_1$$

Pat   gave Dan   a book

In a free phrase order language with structural case, the counterpart of (7) might be (9); agreement would be identical with the English case.

(9) **Mapping of GF-tier to canonical structural case-marking**
  a. $[\text{GF}_i(> \ldots)]_k \quad \Leftrightarrow \ [_S \ldots \text{NP}_i + \text{nom} \ldots]_k$ Nominative subject
  b. $[GF > \text{GF}_i > \ldots]_k \Leftrightarrow \ [_S \ldots \text{NP}_i + \text{acc} \ldots]_k$ Accusative object
  c. $[GF > GF > \text{GF}_i]_k \Leftrightarrow \ [_S \ldots \text{NP}_i + \text{dat} \ldots]_k$ Dative indirect object[7]

French has a further interface rule along the following lines, which outranks (9b):

(10) **French object clitics**
  $[GF > \text{GF}_i > \ldots]_k \ \Leftrightarrow \ [_{\text{VP}} \text{Clitic}_i \ V \ldots]_k$

Thus in general Romance clitics occupy their position not through movement from a more canonical position, but rather through different linearization of the same grammatical function. Since the mapping rule for the clitic involves the GF-tier of the clause in which it is an argument, there is an immediate locality effect. Moreover, the linear order of clitics is stated in the grammar independently of the realization of a GF as a clitic, in the autonomous phrase structure rules. Hence clitic order does not reflect the order of full syntactic arguments.[8]

6.2.2 Absent subjects: Controlled VPs and pro-drop

It now proves convenient to let the subcategorization of direct arguments determine GFs rather than the position of NPs. Looking back to our motivation

---

[7] Actually, given the thematic hierarchy, which ranks recipients over themes, a better story might be the following instead of (9b,c). The idea is that nominative case goes with the first GF as before; accusative case goes not with the second GF but the *last* GF; and dative goes with the middle GF if there is one.

  i. $[\ldots GF > \text{GF}_i]_k \Leftrightarrow [_S \ldots \text{NP}_i + \text{acc} \ldots]_k$
  ii. $[GF > \text{GF}_i > GF]_k \Leftrightarrow [_S \ldots \text{NP}_i + \text{dat} \ldots]_k$

[8] The independence of clitic order from grammatical function was first noted by Perlmutter (1971); we think his solution in terms of a simple phrase structure template is essentially correct (and extends to clitic order in Balkan languages as well). Early treatments of Romance clitics took note of the restrictions on the position of the clitic with respect to the position of a full NP

for GFs, here is why. We want a verb to be able to stipulate that it has, say, two arguments, which in a declarative active tensed clause map into subject and object respectively. Yet we want the same stipulation to predict how this verb will behave under passive, raising, and so on. The traditional way is to call the canonical order of arguments "D-structure" or some such, and to achieve other configurations by movement. Since we do not have movement, we have to have a way of keeping track of a semantic argument for the purpose of mapping it into different grammatical roles. Our tack here will be to map the arguments onto a constant GF-tier whose syntactic realization is manipulated by various interface rules. The assignment of arguments to positions on the GF-tier is in effect an indexing of the arguments that allows us to state the relatedness between constructions.

Here are two immediate examples. First, consider controlled infinitival and gerundive VPs, such as the underlined parts of *Pat tried to sneeze* and *Robin thought about drinking beer*. Here, the semantic argument that would normally be destined for subject position is either a bound variable or a generic (so-called "arbitrary control") (see Chapter 12 for details of the semantics of control). In MGG, because of Interface and Structural Uniformity, this argument has to be expressed as a syntactic position, forcing the theory to posit an invisible NP in syntax, namely PRO. The Simpler Syntax Hypothesis (concurring with all the alternative frameworks) bids us to avoid such a null NP. One way to do this is to introduce a rule along the lines of (11).

(11)   **Controlled infinitival and gerundive VP**
$$[F \ldots [\alpha/\text{GEN}]_i, \ldots]_k \Leftrightarrow [\text{GF}_i(> \ldots)]_k \Leftrightarrow [_{\text{VP}} to/ing \text{ V} \ldots]_k$$

(11) says that if a bound variable α or a generic in conceptual structure corresponds to the highest-ranked GF of a clause k, then the clause can be realized as an infinitival or gerundive VP. The effect is that all the other GFs get

---

argument; Kayne (1975; 1984a) attributed them to locality constraints on movement. Sportiche (1996) deals with the problem by assuming that the clitics are heads base-generated adjoined to the verb, and that there is movement of the phonetically empty argument *pro* into the Spec of the clitic projection. This analysis provides no explanation for the details of clitic order, which must be independently stipulated, as Sportiche notes.

While locality restrictions on cliticization are empirically well motivated, exceptions have been noted in the literature over the years. These appear for the most part to involve constructions where an embedded predicate is incorporated into a higher predicate so that arguments of the lower predicates become arguments of the complex predicate. A typical example is Italian *Glielo voglio dare* [to-him-it I-want to-give] 'I want to give it to him.'; see Manzini (1983a). For important discussion of very different but related phenomena in West Germanic, see Evers (1975) and Wurmbrand (2001). The phenomena are complex, and in the interests of keeping this book to a reasonable size we do not try to explore them further here.

expressed within the VP in the normal way, but the S node, the tense, and the subject are absent—just as desired. (Note that the thematic role of the bound variable/generic in (11) is left unspecified. In canonical cases the highest ranking GF will be the highest ranked semantic role in the clause, but not if the clause happens to involve passive or raising (*Dana attempted not to be captured by the cops*; *Pat tried to appear to like mayonnaise*).)

For example, (12) shows what *Pat tried to sneeze* looks like.

(12)
$$[\text{TRY (PAT}_2{}^\alpha, ([\text{SNEEZE } (\alpha_4)]_3)]_1$$

$$[\text{GF}_2]_1 \qquad\qquad [\text{GF}_4]_3$$

$$\text{NP}_2 \; \text{V}_1\text{+past } [_{VP} \text{ to } \text{V}_3]_3$$

$$\quad\; \text{Pat} \;\; \text{tried} \qquad\qquad \text{to } \text{sneeze}$$

Each clause is assigned to a GF-tier. However, since only NP arguments are assigned to GFs, the GF-tier of the subordinate clause is not embedded in that of the main clause, but rather remains an independent entity. Because the semantic argument of *SNEEZE* is a bound variable, (11) licenses the clause being expressed as a subjectless infinitival.

A similar treatment suggests itself for "pro-drop" languages such as Italian. So-called "pro-drop" occurs when the highest-ranked semantic argument is anaphoric, or refers to speaker or addressee. This argument must receive a grammatical function for two reasons: first, it still determines verb agreement; and second, the next-ranked semantic argument must be prevented from becoming subject by default. However, this argument does not have to be expressed at all in syntax. (13) is a way of stating this rule. In this rule, *PRO* stands for the collection of semantic features that may map onto personal pronouns, and there is nothing in the syntax that corresponds to *PRO* or the designated GF. Nevertheless, because the GF is present, it can still determine subject–verb agreement in normal fashion.

(13) **Pro-drop**
$$[F(\text{PRO}_i, \ldots)]_k \;\Leftrightarrow\; [\text{GF}_i(> \ldots)]_k \;\Leftrightarrow\; [_S \ldots]_k$$

We see from these cases that although in the stereotypical case a GF is linked to both semantics and syntax, there are situations in which it is linked only to semantics. We will call the former cases 'doubly linked' GFs, and the latter 'CS-linked' GFs. In controlled and pro-drop clauses, the subject GF is CS-linked.

We note also that the GF-tier makes it straightforward for the grammar to refer to the subject of a clause: it is the highest GF, and if there is one GF, it is the only one. Hence it is possible to state fully general rules about subjects, along the lines of (11)–(13), without specifically referring to "subject".

6.2.3 *Dummy subjects*

What happens when there are no semantic arguments that map onto GFs? This arises in two situations: when the verb has no semantic arguments (e.g. *rain*, *drizzle*) and when the verb's semantic arguments map into non-NPs (e.g. *seem*). In either case the subject is of course the dummy *it*: *it's drizzling*; *it seems that* . . .

The standard story motivating dummy *it* is that a clause in English requires an overt NP subject. But the story has to be more complicated, because on one hand controlled infinitivals do not require overt subjects (14a), and on the other hand the dummy *it* can raise, leaving behind an infinitival (14b).⁹

(14) a. **To err** is human.   [generic control]
      b. **It** is likely **to rain**.

We propose a solution in terms of the GF-tier, which requires two stipulations. First, instead of requiring an overt NP subject, we suppose rather that English requires at least one licensed GF in the GF-tier of a clause. More formally,

(15) **Well-formedness condition on English GF-tier**
      [GF . . .]$_{Clause}$

As noted above, in the stereotypical case this GF is doubly linked, to both a semantic argument and subject position, but it can be just CS-linked as well, in which case it has the function of MGG's PRO or *pro*. We now add the possibility that a GF can also be licensed by a syntactic NP alone—what we will call an *S-linked* GF. The idea, then, is that in general a GF can be licensed by a semantic argument *or* a syntactic argument—or both. An example of licensing by only a semantic argument (CS-linking) is a controlled subject, where the clause lacks a subject position (*to err* in (14a). An example of licensing by only a syntactic argument (S-linking) is when the GF is licensed by the dummy *it* in syntax but does not express a semantic argument (*it's raining*). This yields the configuration in (16).

---

⁹ During a certain period of GB, this distribution of facts was accounted for with abstract case and the "PRO-theorem" (Chomsky 1981: 191): *it*, being overt, had to move to receive case, whereas PRO, being covert, did not need case and so could remain in situ.

(16)   [DRIZZLE]$_1$

                             [GF$_2$]$_1$
                                |
                             [NP$_2$ [$_{VP}$ V]$_1$]$_1$
                                | |
                               it   drizzles

Here, there is an S-linked GF that lacks a corresponding semantic argument—only the verb is linked to semantics. Hence the subject is realized as the dummy *it*. We will see more cases of S-linked GFs as we go along.

To see how this solution accounts for (14b), we next have to turn to raising.

6.2.4 *Raising*

The basic insight behind the "raising" construction in every syntactic theory is that certain NPs can have a grammatical function in one clause but a thematic role in the next clause down, and that this possibility is conditioned by the predicate of the upper clause. Since at least Fillmore (1963) and Rosenbaum (1967), MGG has treated the mismatch as a true match (i.e. uniform mapping) in underlying syntactic structure, distorted by a movement rule that moves the NP in question into the upper clause. LFG and HPSG treat it as a true mismatch, conditioned by lexical properties of the upper predicate. We will do something slightly different, using the GF tier in such a way that captures intuitions of both analyses. There are two parts to the solution. The first releases the subject from the infinitival clause, and the second licenses it in the matrix clause.

The crucial rule is (17), an alternative way of licensing a mapping from the GF-tier to syntax. Its effect is to realize the highest-ranking GF as an NP outside of its clause—as it were, it releases the subject from the clause, leaving an infinitival VP as remnant.

(17)   **"Raising" (removal of subject from infinitival clause)**
       [GF$_i$(> . . .)]$_k$ ⇔ NP$_i$ [$_{VP}$ to V . . .]$_k$

This is of course a violation of the Argument/Modifier Rule.

Now we must make provision for the released NP to be realized in the next clause up. Since it is an NP, it requires a GF in its new clause as well. In order for it to be assigned a GF, the upstairs clause has to license a GF—one that is not already occupied by one of the verb's semantic arguments. Such a situation occurs with a verb such as *seem*, which has no direct NP arguments. By rule (15), its clause must have at least one GF. This GF is therefore available to link to the NP from the lower clause.

(18) $[SEEM \ ([LIKE \ (JOHN_3, \ SCOTCH_4)]_2)]_1$

$[GF_3 \ ]_1$ $[GF_3 \ > \ GF_4 \ ]_2$

$[NP_3 \ [_{VP} \ V_1 \ [_{VP} \ to \ V_2 \ NP_4]_2 \ ]]_1$

John   seems   to like scotch

There are several noteworthy points here.

• The subordinate VP is not an NP argument, so it does not have a grammatical function (in our sense) in the matrix clause. Hence the two GF-hierarchies are independent.

• $JOHN_3$ in semantics maps canonically to GF_3 in its own clause, the GF-tier subscripted 2.

• However, the syntactic realization chosen for this clause follows rule (17), so that NP_3 cannot appear in clause 2.

• NP_3, now being forced to be realized in clause 1, requires a GF in clause 1. Not being an argument of clause 1, it cannot get its GF in the usual way.

• But clause 1 happens to have a spare GF that is not assigned to a semantic argument; were NP_3 not around, this GF would be connected to *it*, as in (16).

• The perfect marriage: NP_3 needs a GF in clause 1 and clause 1 has a spare GF, so they are connected.

• NP_3 is linearized in clause 1 in accordance with its role as the only GF, namely as subject. Were clause 1 embedded under something else (e.g. *John tends to seem to like scotch*), rule (17) could potentially kick NP_3 upstairs out of clause 1 as well.

Notice now that the GF tier contains two different GFs with the same index (a technical difference from the LFG treatment). This means that *John* is simultaneously subject of both clauses *on the GF-tier* (a variant of HPSG structure-sharing) while being subject of only the upper clause in phrase structure (i.e. it is S-linked here) and a semantic argument of the lower clause (i.e. it is CS-linked). This is precisely the desired result. The chain of coindexed GFs here thus plays the same role as the chain headed by a raised NP in the syntactic movement approach—it records the step-by-step connection from the semantic position that assigns the GF in the lowest clause to the syntactic position where the GF is finally realized.[10] (We will look at the consequences of this situation for binding in section 6.4.)

---

[10] Recent MP takes the position that movement is simply copying, and that normally the highest copy is the one that is spelled out in phonology. This too has a counterpart in the present approach: there is no movement per se, but one can think of GF_3 as having two copies in (18), only the upper of which is linked to an NP.

Here as usual we have been looking at this in terms of a semantics-to-syntax mapping. But it can go in the other direction as well. Suppose one encounters *John seems* in syntax. Since *seem* lexically does not allow a semantic argument, *John* has to be connected to semantics somewhere else. Rule (17), going from right to left, says that an NP can be interpreted as having the highest-ranked grammatical function in an infinitival—that is, its grammatical function is "passed down" to the lower clause, and the parser can try again to find it a semantic argument role there. This more or less parallels the HPSG interpretation of raising. In fact, (18) is *not* a derivation in *either* direction: it is the structure of the sentence, with all the requisite tiers placed in correspondence.

Since this whole system of GFs was motivated by the raising of dummy subjects, let us consider *it is likely to rain*. Abstracting away from some details of how adjectival complements work,[11] we get (19) as the structure.

(19) $[\text{LIKELY}([\text{RAIN}]_2)]_1$

$[\text{GF}_3]_1$ $[\text{GF}_3]_2$

$[\text{NP}_3 \ [_{\text{VP}} \text{V} \ \text{A}_1 \ [_{\text{VP}} \text{to} \ \ \text{V}_2 \ ]_2 \ ]_1$

it   is likely to rain

The trick here is that rule (17) doesn't care whether the GF in question is a semantic argument or not; it applies only to the GF–syntax mapping. So, although the lower clause requires a GF, (17) releases the NP that corresponds to this GF from the lower clause and installs it in the upper clause, where it acquires another GF. But since it is not mapped to a semantic argument, it is realized as the dummy *it*.

Now something interesting has happened: we can't tell whether NP_3 is realized as *it* in the lower clause and then moves up, or is installed in the upper clause and then realized as *it*. The question makes no sense. NP_3 never was *in* the lower clause, but it is realized as *it* because of the status of its grammatical function in the lower clause.

A nice consequence of the present analysis is a possible explanation of why nominals have control but not (or very marginally) raising from their infinitival complements. Raising depends on assigning a GF in the upper clause to an argument of the lower clause. It is plausible that the GF tier is inoperative or defective in nominals—that the linking of NPs is basically governed by purely semantic principles. Therefore there would be no way for an NP released from a clause to acquire a new GF in a nominal.

[11] For this example we'll assume that *be* is a light verb, inserted to fill the necessary verbal slot. Details follow in section 6.5.2.

How does a predicate determine whether it is a "raising" predicate? For instance, how do we account for the well-known difference between *likely* and *probable*?

(20) a. It is likely/probable that Bill left.
　　b. Bill is likely/*probable to leave.

The answer (as in LFG and HPSG) is that *likely* allows its argument to be realized as a tensed clause or an infinitival complement, whereas *probable* allows only the former. The possibility of raising then follows from syntactic subcategorization of the usual sort: only an infinitival complement can release its subject to be raised.[12] The analysis that we suggest thus differs radically from that of MGG, where raising is insensitive to the morphology per se but constrained by the configuration, which has covert morphological reflexes such as abstract Case.

Raising to object (a.k.a. ECM) follows from similar principles. Again the lower clause is realized in terms of (17), and so its subject has to find a GF in the upper clause. If the NP is to end up as the object of the upper clause, the GF tier of the upper clause has to fulfill two conditions: (a) it must have an extra GF that is not linked to a semantic argument; (b) there must be another GF in the upper clause that is thematically linked and therefore outranks the "spare" GF on the thematic hierarchy. The thematically linked GF will therefore be assigned to subject position and the "spare" to object position.

The spare GF has to be licensed by the verb of the upper clause—in traditional terms, the verb has to subcategorize a semantically unlinked NP. So here is the structure of raising to object with *believe*.

(21)　　　$[\text{BELIEVE}(\text{SUE}_3,$　　　　$[\text{LIKE } (\text{FRED}_4, \text{SAM}_5)]_2)]_1$
　　　　　　　　$|$　　　　　　　　　　$|$　　　$|$
　　　　　$[\text{GF}_3$　　$>$　　$\text{GF}_4]_1$　　$[\text{GF}_4 > \text{GF}_5]_2$
　　　　　　$|$　　　　　　　　$|$　　　　$|$
　　　　　$[\text{NP}_3 \ [_{\text{VP}} \ \text{V}_1$　　$\text{NP}_4 \ [_{\text{VP}} \text{ to } \ \text{V}_2 \ \text{NP}_5]_2]]_1$
　　　　　　$|$　　　　$|$　　　$|$　　　$|$　　$|$　　$|$
　　　　　Sue believes Fred　　to like Sam

Again the trick is that GF_4 has grammatical functions in both clauses; it is linked to syntax in clause 1 and to semantics in clause 2. If clause 2 happens to have no semantic link to its highest-ranked GF, then dummy *it* turns up in clause 1 just as it does in (19). An "object-raising" (or ECM) verb is one that subcategorizes an NP that is not semantically linked. Again this is quite parallel to the LFG/HPSG account. MGG, of course, does not condone raising to object (or didn't until

---

[12] This is true in English; however, Greek allows raising from tensed clauses as well (Joseph 1976). This difference will be reflected in the Greek counterpart of rule (17).

recently—see section 2.2.4), so that NP_4 is regarded as being in clause 2. However, the fact that in MGG *believe* governs NP_4 and therefore case-marks it corresponds to the fact that there is a GF_4 in the GF tier of the upper clause.

In some cases a verb may be ambiguous between raising and control, for example the well-known case of *begin* (Perlmutter 1970).

(22) *Looks like control*
    a. Sandy began to examine Robin.
    b. Robin began to be examined by Sandy. ($\neq$ (22a))

(23) *Looks like raising*
    a. There began to be a problem with the solution.
    b. It began to be obvious that the solution would not work.
    c. It began to rain.

Following Perlmutter's original observations, *begin* must have two semantic possibilities: one with an actor (the control case) and one without (the raising case). In present terms, the actor is an optional semantic argument. However, in both cases, the verb syntactically subcategorizes an infinitival or gerundive complement. When the optional semantic argument is present, it is controller for the subordinate clause; it is linked to the only GF in its clause, and therefore surfaces as subject. Thus the configuration is parallel to that with *try* in (12). When the optional semantic argument is absent, the infinitival complement still cannot express its subject, and the interface must resort to the "raising" rule. Fortunately the *begin* clause, lacking a semantically linked GF, has an available GF that maps into subject position, parallel to (18).

Similar phenomena occur in object position. Some verbs, such as *enable* and *force*, normally look like object control verbs, according to standard tests (24a,b); however, they can take dummy *it* as their objects, normally a symptom of raising (24c):

(24)   a. John enabled/forced the doctor to examine Sam.
      b. John enabled/forced Sam to be examined by the doctor. $\neq$ (24a)
      c. The cold weather enabled/forced it to snow (rather than rain) in Chicago.

A nice account of this emerges on our story. Looking first at semantic argument structure, these verbs definitely have an agent argument, and a situation that the agent influences. Suppose they have an optional patient argument, a character in the situation who is affected—this seems to be the role of *the doctor* and *Sam* in (24a,b). (24c) is a sentence in which this patient argument is absent. Next look at the syntactic argument structure. These verbs subcategorize for an NP (with a GF) followed by an infinitival. If the patient is present, it controls the infinitival. If there is no patient, the verb has a semantically unlinked NP/GF which can link to the highest-ranked GF of the infinitival, just like with *believe*. (This solution also applies to the case of *prevent*, discussed in section 2.2.4 as a counterexample to No Raising to Object.)

The one piece we might add to this account is that the actor argument with *begin* and the patient argument of *enable/force* are default: if the relevant NPs can be understood as having a thematic role in the main clause, they must be. Hence the "raising" interpretation will emerge most prominently when the downstairs subject is a dummy.

6.3 Passive

6.3.1 Standard cases and interaction with raising

The usual understanding of the passive views it as a construction that removes the subject, so that the object takes on the usual properties of subject such as preverbal position, nominative case, and/or agreement with the verb. Concurrent with this manipulation, the verb receives some special marking. The question is how to implement this perspective in present terms, in such a way that matters take their course most naturally.

Of course, the passive has different realizations in different languages. For example: There may be a special auxiliary as in English or a special verb conjugation as in Hebrew. There may have to be an object that moves up to subject position as in English, or passives may be formed from intransitive sentences as in German *Es wurde getanzt* 'It was danced', i.e. 'People danced'. The object may have to change position or it may have to change only case. Only immediately postverbal NPs can be promoted, or other arguments can be promoted as well. We would like our account to be in part neutral among these realizations, or to allow tweaking that produces these different realizations. A full account is well beyond the scope of this study. Here we will just suggest a preliminary account of English passive, with notes on how it might be adapted to other languages.

The essential issue is exactly what it means to "remove the subject". The notion 'subject' might be cashed out in terms of any (or any combination) of the three relevant tiers:

- In Conceptual Structure: "subject role" = the highest-ranked thematic role
- In the GF-tier: "subject GF" = the highest-ranked GF
- In phrasal syntax: "subject position" = the highest-ranked NP, i.e. the sister of VP

In MGG, passive omits the syntactic subject, vacating the position for the syntactic object to move into it. As we are trying to do without syntactic movement, this solution is unavailable to us.[13] We cannot remove the highest-ranked thematic role either, because that would radically change the meaning of the sentence. This leaves the highest-ranking GF as the only option. The approach is essentially that of RG; see Perlmutter and Postal (1983b). The intuition is that the highest-ranking GF is removed from play in the GF-tier by giving it a stipulated linking to an oblique (*by NP* in English); hence what would otherwise have been the second-rank GF acquires all the privileges of highest rank.

How is this to be formalized? In keeping with the way everything else in the interface has been treated, we wish to formulate the passive not as an operation that deletes or alters parts of argument structure, but rather as a piece of structure in its own right that can be unified with the other independent pieces of the sentence. The result of such a unification is an alternative licensing relation between syntax and semantics. (25) offers a possible treatment, in which the italicized parts are the "normal" structure of the sentence which serve as contextual specifications, and the non-italicized parts are an "overlay" on the normal structure.

(25) **Passive**

$[GF_i > [GF \ldots]]_k \iff [\ldots V_k + \text{pass} \ldots (\text{by NP}_i) \ldots]_k$

(25) has three effects. First, it adds a stipulated link between the highest-ranking GF in the existing GF-tier and an oblique NP, without disrupting the link between this GF and thematic roles. As is the default case with oblique arguments, it is optional in syntax if its content is contextually inferable (an aspect of oblique arguments we have not formalized). Second, it adds passive inflection to the existing verb (leaving it up to the syntax of the language in question as to how that is realized). Third, it adds a new pair of brackets to the existing GF-tier, such that the second-ranked GF is now adjacent to a left bracket. This means that all the linking rules that pertain to the syntactic realization of the leftmost GF now pertain to this argument: it turns up in preverbal position, it

---

[13] The movement analysis is attended by a number of auxiliary questions: Why can't the subject position be realized as empty? Why can't the subject position be realized as a dummy? Why does the object move to the subject position? Does the object have to move to the subject position and what happens if it doesn't? Why can't the object adjoin to a non-empty subject position? What is the role of the passive morphology? What arguments can move to what empty subject positions? Can there be empty non-subject positions that arguments move to in the same way? and so on. These (and similar) questions, while potentially interesting, contribute to the complexity of the MGG approach to passive in ways that are not paralleled in the approach that we sketch out here.

determines subject–auxiliary agreement, it receives nominative case, and it is a candidate for pro-drop, dummy *it*, and raising.[14]

Two examples comparing actives and passives. First a simple sentence:

(26)   a.   [DESIRE (BILL$_2$,   [SANDWICH; DEF$_4$]$_3$)]$_1$
             | |
             [GF$_2$ >   GF$_3$]$_1$
             | |
             [$_S$ NP$_2$ [$_{VP}$ V$_1$ [$_{NP}$ Det$_4$ N$_3$]$_3$]]$_1$
             | | | |
             Bill   desires   the   sandwich

       b.   [DESIRE (BILL$_2$, [SANDWICH; DEF$_4$]$_3$)]$_1$
             | |
             [GF$_2$ >   [GF$_3$]],
             _____
             [$_S$ [$_{NP}$ Det$_4$ N$_3$]$_3$ [$_{VP}$ V$_1$+pass [by NP$_2$]]]$_1$
             | | | | |
             the   sandwich   is desired   by   Bill

The thing to notice here is how the minimal difference in the GF-tier corresponds to radical differences in the syntax, all licensed by (25).

Next, notice that this formulation of the passive unproblematically yields a passive for ditransitives, as in *Bill was given a sandwich*. Rule (25) leaves open the possibility of a third GF, which by virtue of the rebracketing becomes the second GF and is thereby realized immediately after the verb.[15]

For a more complex example, let's see how to get a dummy *it* from a lower clause to turn up as the subject of a passive. (27a) shows the active. As in (19),

---

[14] This effect is our reason for making the GF tier a hierarchy without traditional labels such as subject/object/indirect object or 1/2/3. Our formulation of the passive works so nicely exactly because rank in the GF tier is only relative. Maybe this is just a notational trick, but we find it parallel to the reconceptualization of phonological stress in terms of relative rank instead of absolute values (Liberman and Prince 1977), which proved to be so useful in phonology. However, see section 6.3.4 for another possibility.

[15] Section 6.3.4 will offer some speculations on how to derive *A sandwich was given Bill*, which some speakers find acceptable; here the third GF instead of the second becomes subject.

The view that the indirect object is higher than the direct object in the GF hierarchy is not entirely uncontroversial. In the Keenan–Comrie Accessibility Hierarchy (1977) the indirect object is lower than the direct object; relativization of indirect object entails relativization of direct object, but not vice versa. In the HPSG Obliqueness Hierarchy (Pollard and Sag 1987), object1 (the direct object) is higher than object2. A similar hierarchy is assumed in LFG. On the other hand, in the Thematic Hierarchy of Jackendoff (1990a), the Recipient/Beneficiary (which is the typical indirect object) is higher than the Theme (which is the typical direct object), which in turn is higher than a spatial Goal. Finally, Kayne (1984b) treats the indirect object as syntactically superior to the direct object; a similar approach is taken by Larson (1988).

the dummy subject shows up in the GF-tier as a GF in the lower clause that is unlinked to semantics. Because of the effects of raising, this GF is coindexed with the "spare" GF provided by *believe*, just as in (24). (27b) shows the passive.

(27)   a.

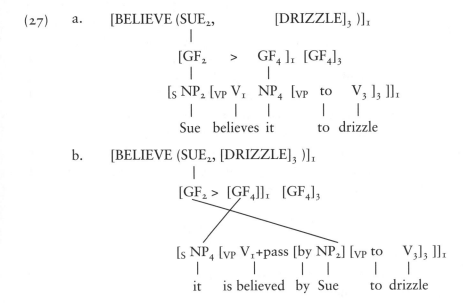

We note that this treatment of the passive does not "start" with an active and "derive" a passive; there are just alternative ways of linking certain GF tiers with syntax. The active is of course more broadly applicable and involves less structure on the GF tier, so it is certainly the default, but that does not give it any sort of derivational priority in any particular sentence.

We have conceptualized the passive in terms of how a GF-tier maps onto syntax, as though we are thinking of sentence production. But it can be conceptualized in the opposite direction as well. When one encounters a passive verb form in syntax, it calls for a GF-tier with the extra bracketing, so that the surface subject maps onto the second-ranked grammatical function. So like the rest of the interface rules, the passive is inherently nondirectional.

We also note that the outcome in (27b) is not a result of "ordering" passive, raising, and the insertion of dummy *it*. It is simply the result of using all three of these opportunities in linking the GF-tier with syntactic structure simultaneously, in such a way that everything ends up properly licensed. Thus there is no need for a cycle. We leave it as an exercise for the reader to derive the familiar examples with iteration of passive and raising.

As noted in Chapter 2, an important property of the movement analysis of passive and raising is that they are local. In the present framework, the locality property follows from the fact that these are constraints on the GF-tier, which encodes only intra-clause relationships. By contrast, the movement analysis of later MGG (after Chomsky 1973) does not allow for the possibility that the passive is constrained by reference to grammatical function (unlike RG) or lexical information (unlike HPSG and LFG). Consequently the locality property is inexplicable except as a constraint on movement across non-local domains, or a more general constraint against associating non-local positions in the syntactic structure. As we saw in Chapter 2, much of the development of this era in MGG, and especially the *Barriers* framework (Chomsky 1986a), is a consequence of this approach to non-locality.

This takes care of the standard cases of passive. The rest of this section deals, somewhat speculatively, with a variety of less stereotypical situations that a treatment of passive must ultimately account for.

6.3.2 *Passive VPs as complements and modifiers*

Section 2.2 pointed out a well-known difficulty for the movement treatment of passive: various contexts permit passive participial VPs without any overt passive sentence in evidence.

(28)   a. Robin got [arrested by the police] immediately after the rally began.
     b. We had Robin [arrested at the rally].
     c. The players heard insults [shouted at them by the fans].
     d. Many customers wanted their samples [handed to them by our employees].
     e. You may see/need your receipts [processed by the file clerk].
     f. With Robin [arrested by the cops], we'd better get out of here.
     g. The first person [arrested by the police] was Robin.
     h. [Arrested last night by the cops], Robin missed class today.

A possibility within MGG is to treat these as covert small clauses with a controlled PRO subject. Following a similar tactic, we can treat these much the way we treated controlled infinitivals, by introducing the linking principle set out in (29).

(29)   **Controlled passive VP**
$$[F \ldots [\alpha]_i, \ldots]_k \Leftrightarrow [GF > [GF_i(> \ldots)]]_k \Leftrightarrow [_{VP}V + \text{pass} \ldots]_k$$

This says that if the second GF in a clause is a bound variable, the clause can be realized as a passive VP. This only works if there is an independent way to dispose of the first GF by applying the passive.

In turn, the bare passive verb phrase must be licensed in syntax. The examples above present three possibilities: (a) the verb above it subcategorizes for it (28a–e); (b) the preposition *with* subcategorizes for it (28f); (c) there is some other construction such as passive relative (28g) or absolutive (28h) that licenses it. Each of these provides a way to bind the variable within the passive VP. Here is the structure of (28a).

(30)

$$[\text{GET } (\text{ROBIN}_2{}^\alpha, \quad [\text{ARREST } (\text{COPS}_4, \quad \alpha_5)]_3\,)]_1$$

$$[\text{GF}_2\,]_1 \qquad\qquad\qquad [\text{ GF}_4 > [\text{GF}_5]]_3$$

$$[\text{ NP}_2 \quad \text{V}_1 \quad [\text{V}_3 + \text{pass by} \quad \text{NP}_4\,]_3\,]_1$$

Robin got arrested by the cops

6.3.3 Prepositional passives; extension of the GF-tier to oblique arguments

The passive rule (25) as it stands applies only to direct NP arguments. It therefore offers no account of passives such as the following, which place an oblique argument in subject position and strand its designated preposition:

(31)   a. Robin was being stared at.
       b. Sandy can be relied on.
       c. Max is being talked about.

In our treatment so far, only direct NP arguments have been linked to GFs. If the passive is to be a manipulation of the GF-tier, (31) suggests that oblique NP arguments should also be linked to GFs.

Such a move permits us to make an interesting distinction. Not all objects of PPs adjacent to the verb can undergo passive:

(32)   a. *The kitchen was chatted in by the guests.
       b. *Tuesday was departed on by Bill.
       c. *This cane can be walked with by Mom.
       d. *The house was run past/around/through by all the joggers.
       e. *The ridge was climbed down/along/toward by Helen.
       f. *The tree was sat under/beside/in by Bernie.

The PPs in (32a–c) are locative, temporal, and instrumental adjuncts respectively. The PPs in (32d–f) are arguments—but true PP arguments, as can be seen by the fact that the choice of preposition is relatively free. This contrasts with the PPs in (31), whose prepositions are fixed by the verb. That is, in (31), the semantic argument is the NP, not the PP. It therefore appears that NP arguments can undergo passive, but the NP of a PP argument or adjunct cannot.

There is one exception, however. Many objects have a *proper function*, i.e. a canonical way they are to be used: beds are to sleep in, sofas are to sit on, telescopes are to look through, tables are to eat and work at. Prepositional passives seem generally possible when the verb and preposition together denote the (surface) subject's proper function.

(33)   a. This bed has been slept in/*under.
        b. The sofa has been sat on/*beside.
        c. The telescope is being looked through/*inside.
        d. The table was eaten at/*under for many years.

There have been treatments of the prepositional passive in terms of a syntactic restructuring which consolidates the preposition with the verb (e.g. Hornstein and Weinberg 1981). By virtue of this restructuring, the NP becomes a direct object and can undergo passive normally. The restructuring analysis has the unpleasant syntactic consequence that material between the verb and the preposition also must become a part of this restructured verb, as in the following examples.

(34)   Sandy was relied very heavily on.
        Jill was being looked intently at by Ann.

We find it implausible that *relied very heavily on* is a syntactic verb, but perhaps this is a matter of taste. Examples like (32) are more telling. The syntax per se does not distinguish between oblique NP arguments and PP arguments: they are both PPs, they are both are placed after direct NP arguments and particles, and they participate in extraction constructions the same way. Syntactic structure should not have to know which kind of semantic argument a PP is.

Still worse is the contrast illustrated in (33). The distinction between the good and bad cases depends on the detailed lexical semantics of nouns—what many would call "encyclopedic" information. Syntax cannot be expected to know that one canonically eats at but not under tables, and that one canonically looks through but not inside of telescopes. From the point of view of syntactic features, the prepositions are indistinguishable. Overall, then, it is clear that the need for this ad hoc restructuring operation is a direct consequence of a movement analysis of the passive, and may be seen as an argument against such an analysis. In the general approach of RG, which our analysis adapts, what is relevant for the analysis of the passive is the grammatical function of the argument, not the syntactic structure.

We conclude that autonomous syntax cannot make the proper distinctions between acceptable and unacceptable prepositional passives. Returning to our proposal in terms of grammatical functions, we extend the GF-tier, distinguishing oblique arguments as *GFo*. Then (31a) has a structure something like this (we improvise a bit on the realization of the stranded preposition, leaving details for a more thorough analysis).

(35)   [STARE-AT (INDEF$_2$, ROBIN$_3$)]$_1$
                      | |
                 [GF$_2$ > [GFo$_3$]]$_1$
                                   |
                         NP$_3$ V$_1$+pass   P$_1$
                           | | |
                         Robin   was stared   at

The CS of the examples in (32), however, is not susceptible to having the passive applied, because the NPs in question do not have grammatical functions:

(36)
a.   [CHAT (GUESTS); [IN (KITCHEN)]]   (KITCHEN is adjunct)
                   |
                 [GF]

b.   [RUN (JOGGERS, [PAST (HOUSE)])]   ([PAST (HOUSE)] is argument)
                   |
                 [GF]

This leaves the examples in (33). We conjecture that here a semantically/ pragmatically conditioned reanalysis is appropriate. What we have in mind is not a syntactic reanalysis but a conceptual reanalysis: By virtue of the object being used for what it is to be used for, it is conceptualized as a sort of honorary patient, adding this thematic role to its normal thematic role in the sentence. Since patient is the second role in the thematic hierarchy, the NP receives a grammatical function and therefore can undergo prepositional passive. The mechanics of such a solution are well beyond the scope of this work, but the semantics/pragmatics of the relevant distinction appear on the right track.

The idea that oblique NP arguments are assigned a grammatical function leads to a nice account of examples such as (37), whose underlined portions display the symptoms of raising to the object of a preposition. These are all taken from the Web.

(37) a. This morning I get up and there's no breakfast. That's freakin incon-
          siderate especially when some people have EXAMS and <u>depend on
          there to be BREAD in the morning</u>!!!!&^#&@#
      b. Whenever info here is good on a subject, <u>count on there to be highly
          specialized and better-more in depth info</u> on the sub communities.
      c. I can almost always <u>rely on there to be a group of students</u> playing
          Ultimate Frisbee every day at 3:30 in the afternoon.

As noted in Chapter 2, some discussions of raising have made a virtue of such
examples supposedly not existing. They are definitely impossible on standard
MGG accounts of infinitival complementation (Chomsky 1981: 99); for discussion see Postal and Pullum (1988). However, in the present account, the
verbs *count on*, *depend on*, and *rely on* behave just like the verbs *enable*, *force*,
and *prevent* illustrated above in (24), except that their second syntactic argument is oblique rather than direct. Normally this second argument expresses a
semantic argument, which therefore acts as controller of the subordinate clause.
But this semantic argument can be omitted, in which case the oblique GF is left
available for raising. Crucially for our account, the target of raising is not just
any PP, but a syntactic PP that expresses an NP argument obliquely. Thus the
relevant distinction is made in the GF tier rather than in syntactic structure
proper.

6.3.4 *Passives that skip over arguments*

Next consider passives like these:

(38) a. Bloffle Day is eagerly looked forward to by all Venusian children.
      b. Ozzie was taken advantage of by Harriet.

(38a) is relatively simple. The lexical entry stipulates not just a designated
preposition, but also the word *forward*, whose position in VP is fixed by the
idiom. Since *forward* is not an NP, it does not receive a GF. Hence the semantic
arguments of the verb are *Venusian children* (direct) and *Bloffle Day* (oblique).
This layout permits the reconfiguration imposed by the prepositional passive,
which simply ignores *forward* in the syntax.

The well-known case (38b) is a bit more complex, because we also have the
passive *Advantage was taken of Ozzie by Harriet*. Following the spirit of
Nunberg et al. (1994), we suggest that the idiom *take advantage* has two
alternative structures. In one, *advantage* is treated as an NP, in which case it
receives a GF and undergoes passive. In the other, *advantage* is treated either as
not an NP (like *forward*) or as an NP that for some reason fails to receive a GF.

In this case, *Ozzie* is assigned the second GF and undergoes prepositional passive.

The trick behind our analysis of the passive in (25) has been that by drawing a left bracket next to the second GF, it thereby becomes the leftmost GF. This trick won't work if something other than the second GF ends up in surface subject position. Unfortunately there exist such cases, even in English (for some speakers at least). Alongside the normal passives in (39a,b) are the "long" passives (39c,d).

(39) a. Bill was given a book.
      b. I have been shown nothing.
      c. A book was given Bill.
      d. Nothing has been shown me.

A possible solution takes a leaf from the analysis of raising, assigning duplicate but linked GFs to the semantic argument in question.

(40) $[$ GIVE (INDEF$_2$,   BILL$_3$, [BOOK; INDEF]$_4$]$_1$
                  | | |
         $[$ GF$_2$ > [GF$_4$ >   GF$_3$ > GF$_4$]]$_1$
                        | |
                      NP$_4$ V$_1$+pass   NP$_3$
                        | | |
                 A book was given Bill

The trick is that the left-hand GF$_4$ is only S-linked, and the right-hand one is only CS-linked. It is their coindexing that indirectly connects [*BOOK;INDEF*] to subject position. This begins to look like a notational variant of RG derivations and of passive A-chains in GB. Presumably this is no accident.

If this solution is along the correct lines, then it suggests that we revise the formulation of standard passive to yield structures like (41).

(41)   [KISS (PAT$_2$,   DANA$_3$)]$_1$
                          | |
                  [GF$_2$ > [GF$_3$ > GF$_3$]]$_1$

                  NP$_3$ V$_1$+pass by NP$_2$
                   | | | |
                  Dana was kissed by Pat

Here the lefthand GF$_3$ is S-linked and the righthand one is CS-linked. Since there is nothing between them, this degenerates in effect to the structure we had previously.

6.3.5 Things that don't undergo passive

As emphasized by Postal (2004), there are many exceptions to the supposedly totally regular passive. Moreover there is no great homogeneity among them, suggesting that there are multiple reasons why a verb might not passivize. Here we mention a number of cases, not with definitive solutions, but just with an eye to the degrees of freedom available for a solution.

Idioms.   *Kick the bucket* does not undergo passive, *let the cat out of the bag* does. The suggestion in Jackendoff (1997a) is that in *kick the bucket*, the syntactic object is not a semantic argument. Therefore its position cannot be stipulated on general principles but must be stipulated as part of the idiom—just like *forward* in *look forward to*. This fixes *the bucket* in object position, where it is S-linked to the GF-tier. But because its position is fixed, the GF-tier cannot be restructured by passive.

In *let the cat out of the bag*, however, *the cat* is a metaphorical argument, meaning a secret. Hence the idiom need not stipulate its syntactic position; rather *the cat* links to syntactic position in the usual way through the GF-tier, and therefore can be repositioned by passive. This distinction does not account for all idioms, but at least for a large proportion.

Predicate nominals and the like.   Predicate nominal arguments and arguments of measurement verbs crashingly fail to undergo passive.

(42)   *A doctor was been by Susan.
    *A rich man has been become by Frank.
    *Two tons are weighed by my car.
    *Fifty dollars are cost by this ring.

There are various possibilities. The thematic role of predicate nominal, exceptionally, might be a role that is not assigned to a GF. Predicate nominals would then (correctly) follow all the GF-assigned NPs in linear order. By virtue of lacking a GF, they could not be repositioned in the subject by the passive. Why might they lack a GF? It might have something to do with their being inherently nonreferential, but we see no immediate connection.

For-datives.   It was noticed as early as Fillmore (1965) that not all indirect objects undergo passive with equal comfort. The difference is linked to their alternation with PPs: *to*-datives undergo passive, *for*-datives do not.

Significantly, there is a second class of *to*-datives that don't undergo passive. (Note that these are not as violently bad as the previous examples.)

(43)   a. *Passivizable* to-*datives*
         Bill was given/sent/brought/served some cookies.
         (= Someone gave/sent/brought/served some cookies to Bill)
       b. For-*datives*
         ??Bill was baked a cake. (=Someone baked a cake for Bill.)
         ??Bill was fixed a drink. (=Someone fixed a drink for Bill.)
         ??Bill was sung *Stardust*. (=Someone sang *Stardust* for Bill.)
       c. *Non-passivizable* to-*datives*
         ??Bill was hurled/kicked the ball.
         (=Someone hurled/kicked the ball to Bill.)

Jackendoff (1990a) points out that there is a crucial difference in *semantic* argument structure. The verbs in (43a) are inherently three-argument verbs: you can't give something without giving it to *someone*. On the other hand, the indirect objects in (43b,c) are *not* inherent arguments of the verb. If you bake or sing something, it is not inherently with the intent of doing it for someone else's benefit. If you hurl or kick something, it is not inherently with the intent of someone else catching it. Hence these verbs are inherently *two*-argument verbs. Jackendoff (1990a) and Goldberg (1995) therefore argue that these indirect objects, despite their syntactic position, do not function as semantic arguments. Rather, they are semantic constituents of a conventionalized purpose modifier: in the case of *for*-datives, 'with the purpose of X (e.g. the cake) benefitting NP'; in the case of *to*-datives, 'with the purpose of NP receiving X (e.g. the ball)'. Jackendoff and Goldberg propose that these NPs are installed in indirect object position by a special VP construction that is sensitive to the semantics of the verb.

Within the present framework, this provides a wedge toward accounting for the fact that these verbs do not undergo passive. Because the indirect objects in (43b,c) are not arguments of the verb, they are not CS-linked to the GF-tier. Rather, the special construction bypasses the GF-tier and puts them directly in postverbal position. Now, either they remain unlinked to the GF-tier, or they are S-linked to the GF-tier. But in either case, if we try to apply passive to the GF-tier, we cannot remap these NPs to subject position, because the construction requires them to be postverbal. A diagram might help. (44a) is the active; (44b) is the attempted passive.

(44)a. [BAKE (INDEF$_2$,   CAKE$_3$); [PURPOSE: BENEFIT (BILL$_4$)]]$_I$

[GF$_2$ >   GF$_4$ > GF$_3$]$_I$

NP$_2$ V NP$_4$ NP$_3$

someone baked Bill a cake

b. [BAKE (INDEF$_2$,   CAKE$_3$); [PURPOSE: BENEFIT (BILL$_4$)]]$_I$

[GF$_2$ > [GF$_4$ >   GF$_3$]]$_I$

??NP$_4$ V$_I$+pass ??NP$_4$ NP$_3$

was baked   a cake

In the attempted passive, NP$_4$ is under two conflicting requirements: the construction requires it to be postverbal, and the GF-tier requires it to be subject. Hence there is no possible grammatical resolution.

Whether or not this is precisely the right technical approach, we have shown that in our framework the semantic distinctions necessary to account for the contrasts in (43) are naturally accessible to the rules of grammar, without building them into the syntax proper at all. In other words, it should be possible to maintain the Simpler Syntax Hypothesis.

Experiencer–object psych verbs. Stative psychological predicates with the experiencer argument in the object are uncomfortable in the passive. To a degree this is masked by the fact that (a) most of them have cognate nonstative forms and (b) many of them have cognate passive adjectives (Wasow 1977). The examples in (45) have been carefully chosen to avoid these confusions. Since in general oblique arguments can undergo prepositional passive, we have included a case in which the experiencer is an oblique argument marked by *to*—which also lacks the expected prepositional passive. By contrast, the passives of experiencer–*subject* verbs are fine.

(45) *Experiencer–object*
    a.   *Jill is struck by Jack as clumsy.
    b.   ??When did Bill start being pleased by the weather? (cf. When did Bill start being pleased *with* the weather?—passive adjective)
    c.   *Charlie is appealed to by chocolate.

Experiencer–subject
  d. Jack is regarded by Jill as clumsy.
  e. When was the weather around here enjoyed by anybody?
  f. Chocolate is liked by Charlie.

Again there is a potential solution in terms of linking. Recall from section 5.7 that there is something special about the linking of psychological predicates: it cannot be predicted in general from thematic roles. Rather, linking has to be specially stipulated by either experiencer–subject verbs (*regard, enjoy, like*) or experiencer–object verbs (*strike, please, appeal to*) or both. We have not yet talked about which verbs make the stipulation or how it is made. The peculiar behavior of experiencer–object verbs in the passive (and binding—see the next section and section 10.8.2) suggests that they are the ones with special properties.

Let us suppose, then, that the way *strike* stipulates its special linking is to say that its experiencer argument links to object position in syntax—note, *not* to a GF. Then we have exactly the same situation we had with the indirect object arguments in (44): because the verb fixes them in object position, they simply cannot be repositioned in subject position by manipulating the GF-tier.

We cannot pursue these matters any further here for want of space. However, the last four subsections have given a sampling of how the theory of passive as GF-tier manipulation might approach some of the well-known problem cases.

6.4 Binding of reflexives in the GF-tier

We now turn briefly to the treatment of reflexives and how they are bound to their antecedents. There are two independent questions: (a) At which level(s) of representation are binding relations instantiated: syntactic structure, Conceptual Structure, or the GF-tier? (b) At which level(s) of representation are the conditions that *license* binding stated? The answers to these questions might not be the same. For example, binding might be instantiated at CS but depend on conditions in syntactic structure, or vice versa.[16]

The answer to these questions in MGG[17] is that the binding relation is instantiated by coindexation in syntactic structure, and the conditions for

---

[16] Reinhart and Reuland (1993) offer an analysis of reflexives within the MGG framework that distinguishes syntactic and semantic conditions on reflexives; the specifics are quite different from those proposed here.

[17] This is true at least up until the Minimalist Program, whose position on binding is not so clear.

licensing binding are likewise stated over syntactic structure. There have been strains of dissent around the periphery of MGG, arguing that semantic conditions are also involved (Jackendoff (1972), Kuno (1987), among many others; see also references in Chapters 10–11). Here we will be working out the following position:

(46) a. The binding of reflexives can be instantiated in the GF-tier (*GF-binding*), in Conceptual Structure (*CS-binding*), or in both at once. If both apply, they must be consistent.

   b. The licensing conditions for GF-binding involve GF relations and syntactic structure. The licensing conditions for CS-binding involve CS relations and syntactic structure.

This position may seem unacceptably heterogeneous from the point of view of Occam's Razor. However, we will show why the facts push us in this direction. If we are correct, the heterogeneity of binding goes a long way toward explaining why binding theory has been so elusive for so long. This section will deal primarily with GF-binding; Chapters 10–11 will take up CS-binding in more detail, and Chapter 12 will deal with control.

Binding has to be heterogeneous because there are cases in which only the GF-tier is available for binding, and there are also cases in which only CS is available. For the first sort of case, consider verbs with pleonastic reflexive arguments such as *Paula perjured herself*, a number of which were listed in section 5.6. There is no evidence for such verbs having more than one semantic argument. The pleonastic syntactic argument is either semantically unlinked or else linked to the same semantic argument as the subject. Thus only in the GF-tier and syntactic structure are there are two separate arguments over which binding could be instantiated. Is GF or syntax the locus of binding? Consider an example like *It is dangerous to perjure oneself*. In the Simpler Syntax framework, there is no syntactic antecedent for the reflexive, in particular no invisible PRO subject. It is only in the GF-tier that both arguments are present, one CS-linked and one S-linked.

(47) $[\text{DANGEROUS} ([\text{PERJURE} (\text{GEN}_3)]_2)]_1$

   $[\text{GF}_4]_1$ $[\text{GF}_3 > \text{GF}_5]_2$

   NP_4 be A_1 to V_2 $\text{NP}[+\text{refl}]_5$

   it   is dangerous   to   perjure   oneself

This establishes the necessity for stating binding relations over the GF-tier rather than over syntactic structure. Further evidence will emerge shortly.

However, there are also reasons why the GF-tier cannot be the sole locus of binding. Fundamentally, binding is a *semantic* relation, fixing one phrase's reference in terms of another's. This relation is more general than reflexives, encompassing among other things quantifier scope. For instance, in *Each boy owns a bicycle*, the reference of *a bicycle* is determined by *each boy*, namely there is one bicycle per boy. Binding also encompasses control: for instance, in *Pat tried to leave*, the identity of the leaver is determined by the identity of the try-er. In addition, a reflexive-like semantic relation is essential to stating the lexical semantics of intransitive *wash*, *dress*, and *shave*. Recalling the discussion of optional and implicit arguments in section 5.6, these verbs have two inherent semantic arguments: you can't wash/dress/shave without washing/dressing/shaving *someone*, namely yourself. Thus these verbs, when intransitive, have a bound semantic argument with no reflexes in syntax or the GF-tier. For all these reasons, it is necessary to implement a form of binding in CS as well as in the GF-tier. In stereotypical cases such as *Kate dislikes herself*, both apply. Only in the less standard cases do they tease apart.

One of the original arguments for a raising transformation was based on the locality of reflexive binding. (48) shows the standard facts: A reflexive cannot be bound by an NP in a higher clause (48a), unless that NP has undergone raising from the reflexive's clause (48b) or controls the reflexive's clause (48c).

(48) a. *Sue thinks that I like herself.
      b. Sue seems to like herself. (← [e seems [Sue like herself]])
      c. Sue tries to [PRO like herself]

In the 1960s and early 1970s, before the introduction of traces into the theory, the cases involving raising were taken to show that reflexivization must be cyclic, so that the reflexive can be licensed before its antecedent is removed from the clause. After the advent of trace theory, it became possible for the reflexive to be bound to the trace of raising at S-structure.

The spirit of the latter solution can be preserved under the present treatment of raising as a GF-tier manipulation. Recall that raising involves coindexed GFs, one CS-linked to the lower clause, and the other S-linked to the upper clause. Similarly, a controlled VP has a subject GF which is CS-linked but not S-linked. Thus we get the following configurations.

(49)　　　　a.　　[SEEM ([LIKE (SUE$_3^\alpha$,　α_4)]$_2$)]$_1$
　　　　　　　　　　|　　　　　　　|
　　　　　　　　[GF$_3$]$_1$　　　　[GF$_3$ > GF$_4$]$_2$
　　　　　　　　　　|　　　　　　　|
　　　　　　　　Sue$_3$　seems to like　herself$_4$

　　　　　　b.　　[TRY (SUE$_2^\alpha$, [LIKE (α_4^β,　　β_5]$_3$)]$_1$
　　　　　　　　　　　|　　　　　　　　|　　　　|
　　　　　　　　　[GF$_2$]$_1$　　　　[GF$_4$ > GF$_5$]$_3$
　　　　　　　　　　　|　　　　　　　　|
　　　　　　　　　Sue$_2$ tries to like　herself$_5$

Here there is CS-binding for both reflexives and control, in addition to GF-binding. Following Jackendoff (1990a), this is notated with Greek letters: the antecedent is a superscript and the bound element is in normal type. So, in (49a), *SUE* CS-binds the second argument of *LIKE*, and the GF CS-linked to this licenses local GF-binding of the reflexive. Meanwhile, the syntactic position of *Sue* is S-linked to the coindexed GF in the higher clause. Thus the role in binding played by the trace in MGG is played here by the CS-linked GF in the lower clause.

　　In (49b), there are two instances of CS-binding. First, the subject of the upper clause controls the infinitive. Chapter 12 will show that control is properly treated in terms of binding in CS rather than in syntax; thus control is notated here in terms of *SUE* binding the first argument of *LIKE*, as notated by the αs. Second, the lower α serves as antecedent for the second argument of *LIKE*, as notated by the βs; the bound argument surfaces as the reflexive. Thus the role in binding played by PRO in MGG is played here again by the CS-linked GF in the lower clause.

　　At the same time, because a "raised" NP also has a GF in the upper clause, it can be bound to an NP there.

(50)　　　　[BELIEVE(SUE$_2^\alpha$,　　　　　　　[LIKE (α_4,　　SAM$_5$)]$_3$)]$_1$
　　　　　　　　　　|　　　　　　　　　　　　|　　　|
　　　　　　　　[GF$_2$　>　　GF$_4$]$_1$　[GF$_4$ > GF$_5$]$_3$
　　　　　　　　　　|　　　　　　　|　　　　　　　|
　　　　　　　Sue$_2$ believes　herself$_4$　to like　Sam$_5$

By contrast, the ungrammatical configuration in (51) lacks a local GF-relation between the reflexive and its antecedent.

(51)　　　　　　[THINK (SUE$_2^\alpha$, [LIKE　(I$_4$,　　α_5)]$_3$)]$_1$
　　　　　　　　　　　|　　　　　　　　　|　　　|
　　　　　　　　　[GF$_2$]$_1$　　　　　[GF$_4$ > GF$_5$]$_3$
　　　　　　　　　　　|　　　　　　　　　|　　　　　|
　　　　　　　　*Sue$_2$ thinks that I$_4$ like herself$_5$

So far this account looks rather like a notational variant of well-known treatments: an NP can be bound and expressed by a reflexive when its GF is subordinate to the GF of its antecedent.

The stories begin to diverge when we ask what happens with an NP that does *not* have a GF. Recall that an NP receives a GF only when it is an argument of a verb, either direct or oblique. GFs are not linked to NPs within true PP arguments or within adjunct PPs. We saw in section 6.3.3 that this makes a difference in the acceptability of prepositional passives: oblique NP arguments adjacent to the verb always allow passive, but NPs within other PPs require special semantic conditions. The same proves true of binding: oblique NP arguments are always bound by using a reflexive, but NPs that lack a GF are bound sometimes by a pronoun, and sometimes by either a pronoun or a reflexive.

(52) *Oblique NP arguments: reflexive has a GF*
    a. John$_i$ talked to me about himself$_i$/*him$_i$.
    b. John$_i$ looked at himself$_i$/*him$_i$.

(53) *PP (locative) arguments: reflexive lacks a GF*
    a. John$_i$ found/saw me beside him$_i$/*himself$_i$.
    b. John$_i$ had/held a rock under him$_i$/*himself$_i$.
    c. John$_i$ brought the blanket with him$_i$/*himself$_i$.
    d. John$_i$ pulled the blanket over him$_i$/himself$_i$.
    e. John$_i$ pulled the blanket next to him$_i$/??himself$_i$.

Cases like (53) have been known for a long time, going back to the example *John saw a snake near him(*self)*, attributed to Lakoff in the early 1970s. Our use of the GF-tier for oblique arguments, independently motivated for the passive, offers here an appealing solution to this old problem. The contrast in (53d–e) shows that the possibility of a CS-bound reflexive depends in part on delicate semantic conditions, which we will not try to characterize here.

Our sense, then, is that (53) represents situations in which the bound NP lacks a GF and therefore binding is CS-binding only. This enables us to state the following informal principles for GF-binding.

(54) **GF-binding conditions**
    a. A reflexive linked to a GF must be GF-bound to a more prominent GF-clausemate.   (GF Condition A)
    b. No other NP linked to a GF may be bound to a GF-clausemate: i.e. pronouns and R-expressions are free in a GF-domain.
                                       (GF Condition B-C)

These are the counterparts of the GB binding conditions for the situations where GF-binding applies. They also parallel the obliqueness hierarchy for binding in LFG and HPSG. Cases such as (53), where only CS-binding applies, are often problematic for GB binding theory. We return to CS-binding of reflexives in Chapter 10.

We now present a little more evidence that GF-binding has to be separate from CS-binding. Consider the stative psychological predicates with experiencer objects such as *please, strike, remind*, and *appeal to*. In the previous section, we suggested that these have Conceptual Structure parallel to that of experiencer-subject verbs such as *like, regard*, and *fear*, but they do not undergo the canonical mapping to syntax. Rather, they specify that their experiencer is linked to object or oblique position; this stipulation prevents them from undergoing passive. Significant in the present context is that these verbs also have unusual binding properties, as pointed out by Postal (1971). (The reflexives should be read noncontrastively.)

(55)   a. ??John finally started pleasing himself last week. (cf. John finally started liking himself last week)
       b. ??John appeals to himself.
       c. ??John strikes himself as intelligent. (cf. John regards himself as intelligent.)
       d. ??John seems intelligent to himself.
       e. ?John reminds himself of a gorilla.

Section 4.4.2 suggested that there are CS conditions on binding of reflexives that have to do with configurations of thematic roles. Because the experiencer-subject verbs do have acceptable reflexives (*John likes/fears himself*), we know that an experiencer argument can bind a stimulus argument. Therefore, if CS-binding of reflexives is asymmetric, like every other kind of binding, then a stimulus should not be able to bind an experiencer, which is the configuration required for (55) to be acceptable. In this case, even though GF-binding is licensed, CS-binding is not, and so the two are in conflict.[18]

Probing just a little farther, consider again some relevant examples from section 4.4.2.

---

[18] Hence there is something curiously right about Postal's idea that these are bad because of "crossover". The semantics (for him, Deep Structure) requires binding in one direction and the GF-tier (which reflects Surface Structure) requires it in the other direction. His "Psych Movement" transformation, along with that of Belletti and Rizzi (1988), simulates by movement the mismatch between prominence in CS and in the GF tier.

(56)   a.   *I mentioned Mary to herself.
       b.   I mentioned to Mary herself as a presidential candidate.

(56a) has the same problem as the psychological predicates: although its GF-binding is fine, its CS-binding calls for the wrong direction: the recipient of information is a kind of experiencer, and the information is a kind of stimulus. (For a more structured account, see section 10.8.) (56b), which is linearized by heavy shift, has the right linear order of antecedent and reflexive, and the right direction of CS-binding, but its GF-binding should be wrong, since the direct object *herself* ought to outrank the oblique. One possible solution would be that an NP in heavy shift position is not linked to the GF-tier. This would correspond to the standard intuition that it has been moved (or that it is a *chômeur* in the RG sense). Lacking a GF, the NP would be free to be CS-bound without conflict. If correct, this would be a case in which syntactic positioning distinct from the default voids GF-linking.[19]

In the other direction, we find that arguments of nominals in light verb constructions behave as though they are on the GF-tier of the verb. (57) presents an appropriate contrast.

(57)   a.   John$_i$ took a picture of himself$_i$/him$_i$ along to the party.
                                      [*picture* is argument of *take*]
       b.   John$_i$ took a picture of himself$_i$/*him$_i$.   [predicate is *take a picture*]

When *picture* is an ordinary argument of the verb, we have the choice of a pronoun or a reflexive, like some cases with NP objects of PP arguments such as (53d) above. But when the predicate is *take a picture*, only a reflexive is possible, as if it is a GF-clausemate. If correct, this would be a case where semantics forces something to have GF-linking where syntax alone would not permit it. We will see a little more of how this works in section 6.5.1.

This is only a rapid sketch of how a theory of GF-binding might work. We have taken it this far, albeit speculatively, in order to make a number of points.

• GF-binding takes over the function of the most robust cases of GB binding theory.

---

[19] The idea that a heavy shifted NP is possibly not a normal direct argument was anticipated in the discussion of the "freezing principle" in Wexler and Culicover (1980). They showed that shifted NPs, like adjuncts, are islands for extraction.

(i) . . . the celebrity who we gave a beautiful picture of t to the first twenty people who called in.
(ii) . . . ??the celebrity who we gave to the first twenty people who called in a beautiful picture of t

- It also provides a natural way to discriminate the robust cases from the more problematic cases, where either GF-binding does not apply or it conflicts with CS-binding.
- Finally, insofar as the GF-tier provides insight into binding, this provides further evidence for the essential role of the GF-tier in mediating the syntax–semantics interface.

6.5 Bells and whistles

This final section adds three special ways in which CS can be mapped to syntax: the light verb construction, VP constructions such as the sound+motion construction (*The trolley screeched around the corner*), and coercion. Other special devices will be added in subsequent chapters: sluicing and gapping (Chapter 7), VP ellipsis (Chapter 8), and long-distance dependencies (Chapter 9).

6.5.1 *The light verb construction*

The light verb construction in English is illustrated in (58b,c) and (59b,c).

(58) a. Pat blamed the accident on Dana.
     b. Pat put the blame for the accident on Dana.
     c. Dana received the blame for the accident from Pat.

(59) a. Sandy promised Chris to leave on time.
     b. Sandy gave Chris a promise to leave on time.
     c. Chris got from Sandy a promise to leave on time.

The a. sentences use *blame* and *promise* as ordinary verbs, whose thematic roles are mapped to syntax by the principles described in the previous sections. The b. and c. sentences, which are pretty much synonymous with the a. sentences (at least in terms of thematic roles), use *blame* and *promise* as nominals, and the main verb functions as a "light verb". How does the same semantics map into these different syntactic realizations? Or alternatively, how does such different syntax map into the same semantics?

As proposed in Jackendoff (1974), the general idea is that the nominal and the verb share thematic roles. The act of blaming involves a person making a speech act or having a thought that ascribes blame, a person being blamed, and a nasty situation for which the person being blamed is allegedly responsible. Crudely, the first two of these roles correspond to agent/source and recipient/goal respectively. When *blame* is used as a verb, it assigns syntactic positions to its arguments by the usual processes, as in (58a). When *blame* is used as a nominal, it undergoes role-sharing with the main verb. In (58b), *put* assigns an agent to subject position and a goal of motion to the PP complement. Thus the sharing of roles results in Pat being the blamer and Dana the blamee. In (58c), *receive* assigns a recipient to subject position and a source to the PP complement, so the sharing of roles ends up with the same interpretation, despite the switching of syntactic positions. (59) has a parallel analysis.

This basic analysis is refined and formalized by Jun (2003), in the context of Korean and Japanese light verbs.[20] Jun's idea is that the syntactic argument structure of the sentence is determined by the light verb, as usual—and in the present approach, the grammatical functions work out as usual too. However, the CS of the nominal, instead of serving as a semantic argument of the light verb, is unified with the CS of the verb as a whole. The composite CS has an argument structure that reflects the common arguments of the verb and the nominal, while allowing room for the nominal to include extra material not present in the light verb. Jun proposes to formalize this insight by coindexing both the light verb and the nominal to the same constituent of the CS of the sentence, approximately as in (60) (for a simple case).

(60)
$$[\text{WALK (JOHN}_2\,)]_{1,3}$$
$$[\text{GF}_2 > \qquad \text{GF}_3]$$
$$[_S \text{ NP}_2 \,[_{VP} \text{ V}_1 \qquad \text{NP}_3\,]]_1$$
$$\text{John} \quad \text{took a walk}$$

The CS of (60) correctly shows that John is understood as walking. The crucial question, though, is how this CS is carved into words such that it comes out as the syntactic structure in (60).

To see how (60) can be achieved by composing lexical entries, let us formulate the lexical entries for *take* and *walk*. (61) shows a straightforward treatment of the nominal. If its semantic argument were satisfied by the usual interface links, we would get something like *John's walk*, as in *John's walk satisfied him*.

(61) $[\text{WALK}(X)]_i \Leftrightarrow \text{N}_i \Leftrightarrow \text{walk}_i$

What about the light verb *take*? Its syntax is straightforward: it is a transitive verb. Its semantics is minimal: it denotes an action (of which walking is a special case). An action has at least one argument, namely an actor. This is linked to the

---

[20] Jun also considers numerous syntactically based analyses of light verb constructions (especially in Korean and Japanese), in many different frameworks, and shows what they miss. (Cf. Miyagawa 1989; Grimshaw and Mester 1988.)

syntactic subject, as usual. The trick that makes it a light verb lies in the linking of the syntactic object. It is not linked to a semantic argument; rather it is linked to the entire CS of the verb, as in (62).

(62) $[ACT(X)]_{j,k} \Leftrightarrow [V_j \; NP_k] \Leftrightarrow take_j$

As a result the direct object must be filled in by a noun whose meaning can unify with *ACT(X)*, namely an action nominal. When unification takes place, the common parts of the meaning coincide; in particular, *ACT(X)* plus *WALK(X)* unifies to *WALK(X)*. Thus the subject of *take* comes to satisfy the actor argument of *walk*, as desired. In short, what makes a verb "light" is that one of its syntactic arguments, instead of being linked to a semantic argument, is linked to the meaning of the verb as a whole.

Now consider the GF-tier associated with the light verb construction. Note that in (60), *walk* is not a semantic argument in CS. Hence its grammatical function is S-linked but not CS-linked, as shown in (60). On the other hand, consider the arguments of the nominal, such as *the accident* in (58b). Under our analysis, the CS for (58b) is *BLAME(PAT, DANA, ACCIDENT)*, which makes *the accident* eligible to be CS-linked to the GF-tier—even though it is not a syntactic argument of the main clause. This is the result we desired in the previous section in order to account for binding. The overall story, then, is that the nominal in a light verb construction receives an S-linked grammatical function, and the syntactic arguments of the nominal receive CS-linked grammatical functions. By virtue of their CS-linking, they are eligible for GF-binding, accounting for the obligatory reflexive in, e.g. *John_i gave a good account of himself_i/*him_i*.

As formulated so far, the CS of the sentence has segments that are mapped simultaneously to two lexical items. This mapping apparently violates the lexicalization constraint of section 5.3: "Given a CS to be expressed, every segment of it must be licensed by exactly one lexical item." Here the segment *WALK (X)* is apparently expressed by both the verb *took* and the noun *walk*. Suppose we wish to refine the formalization of this example so as to respect the lexicalization constraint. One way to do this is to treat the semantic content of the light verb as nothing but a selectional restriction on the nominal, i.e. to treat it as a contextual variable. As usual, we express this by notating the relevant parts in italics:

(63) $[ACT(X)]_{j,k} \Leftrightarrow [V_j \; NP_k] \Leftrightarrow take_j$

With this trivial change, the verb licenses no meaning of its own—it licenses only syntax and phonology. What it does in the semantics is provide a frame that can be aligned with the meaning of the nominal, so that the syntactic argument structures of the nominal and the light verb can be pooled to form a common semantic argument structure. But the semantics is actually licensed only by the content of the nominal, so that the lexicalization constraint is in fact satisfied. This is a rather nice realization of the traditional intuition that motivates the term "light verb": its meaning is "bleached out", though not removed entirely.

For a language to have a light verb construction, then, it basically requires a small repertoire of lexical items of the type illustrated in (63), which have these curious interface properties. There are obviously intricate issues to be worked out concerning the precise formulation of more complex light verbs such as those in (58) and (59), as well as issues concerning how light verbs develop historically from ordinary verbs. Some of these issues will arise in Chapter 12, in connection with control of complements of nominals in the light verb construction. For now we move on to another special way to construct VPs.

6.5.2 VP constructions

Section 5.3 showed how a CS can be realized as a lexical VP idiom such as *kick the bucket*. We repeat the analysis here, filling in the pieces we have developed in the interim. (64a) shows the form of the lexical entry; (64b) shows how it is integrated into a sentence.

(64)   a. $[\text{DIE (X)}]_2 \Leftrightarrow [_{VP} \text{V}_2 \, [_{NP} \text{Det}_4 \, \text{N}_5] \,]_2 \Leftrightarrow \text{kick}_2 \text{ the}_4 \text{ bucket}_5$

b. $[\text{PAST ([DIE (FRED}_3)]_2]_1$

$$[\text{GF}_3 \quad > \quad \text{GF}_5]_1$$

$$[_S \text{NP}_3 \, \text{T}_1[_{VP} \text{V}_2 \, [_{NP} \text{Det}_4 \quad \text{N}_5]]]_{12}$$

Fred$_3$ kick$_2$-d$_1$ the$_4$ bucket$_5$

What makes this an idiom is that the meaning of the whole does not decompose into word meanings: only the whole VP is coindexed to the meaning. In particular, the NP coindexed with *the bucket* in phonology does not coindex with anything in CS. As suggested in section 6.3.5, this NP has an S-linked grammatical function, but since the idiom stipulates its position, it cannot undergo passive.

More interesting are cases in which a standard phrasal construction such as (65a) can be paraphrased by a constructional idiom such as the sound+motion construction in (65b).

(65) a. The trolley went around the corner, squealing.
      b. The trolley squealed around the corner.

Chapter 1, following Goldberg (1995) and Jackendoff (1990a; 2002a), suggested that the sound+motion construction is an idiomatic lexical VP with an open verb position. Like other idioms, it is an interface rule with inherent syntactic structure. What is interesting about this construction is that it violates the Head Rule of section 5.4, in that the verb *squeal* functions not as the semantic head but rather as a manner modifier, just as in (65a). The actual semantic head is a predication of motion, unexpressed in the syntax, and it is this predication that licenses the path argument *around the corner*. Because this violates the Head Rule, it is a marked mapping. On the other hand, it has the virtue of cramming two clauses' worth of material into a single clause, so its value as (conventionalized) abbreviation apparently is sufficient to justify the nonoptimal mapping.

It is now straightforward to formalize the sound emission+motion construction. (66) shows how (65a) and (65b) carve up the relevant parts of the same CS.

(66) <u>Conceptual structure</u>   <u>Syntax</u>   <u>Phonology</u>

CS: [GO ([TROLLEY]$^\alpha$, [AROUND ([CORNER])])]; [SQUEAL (α)   ]]

a. i. [GO (*Object*,   *Path*   )   ]$_1$ V$_1$ go$_1$
   ii.   [SQUEAL (Z)]$_2$ V$_2$ squeal$_2$
b. i. [GO (*Object*$^\alpha$,   *Path*   ); [*EMIT-SOUND* (α)]$_i$]$_3$ [$_{VP}$ V$_i$ PP]$_3$
   ii.   [SQUEAL (Z)]$_2$ V$_2$ squeal$_2$

Realization (a) expresses the function *GO* as the main verb *go*; its arguments are the object in motion (*the trolley*) and a path, expressed as *around the corner*. The verb *squeal* is expressed as part of an adjunct; we will not deal here with how it gets the *-ing* affix. Importantly, in the CS to be expressed, the argument [*TROLLEY*] has the superscript α, which CS-binds the argument of *SQUEAL* to it, along lines already explored in section 6.4. The result is that *trolley* controls the gerundive adjunct *squealing*.

The interesting case here is realization (b). Line (ii) is the verb *squeal* again, unchanged. Line (i) is the sound+motion construction. Its meaning is the same as that of *go*, but with an extra modifier having to do with the object in motion emitting sound (the use of α again indicates that the two arguments are bound). The content of this added modifier, being in italics, is merely a selectional restriction on something that has to be filled in. Next notice the subscripts. The whole CS expression is coindexed with a VP in syntax; but the subscript on the modifier is a variable coindexed with the main verb of this VP. The result is that whatever fills in the modifier in semantics appears as a main verb in syntax.

Finally, notice that there is no phonology at all associated with the construction: all the phonology comes from its arguments. Here is how all the structures work out when everything is combined into (66a) and (66b). (For ease of reading we omit tense and determiners; there are enough subscripts to keep track of as is. Note that NP_6 does not receive a GF, because it is within a true PP argument.)

(67) a. [GO ([TROLLEY]$_4$α, [AROUND ([CORNER]$_6$)]$_5$; [SQUEAL (α)]$_2$]$_1$
      |
      [GF$_4$]
      |
      [NP$_4$ [vp V$_1$ [pp P$_5$ NP$_6$]$_5$ [vp V$_2$-ing]$_2$]$_1$]$_1$
        | | | | |
      trolley$_4$ go$_1$ around$_5$ corner$_6$ squealing$_2$

   b. [GO ([TROLLEY]$_4$α, [AROUND ([CORNER]$_6$)]$_5$; [SQUEAL (α)]$_2$]$_3$
      |
      [GF$_4$]
      |
      [NP$_4$ [vp V$_2$ [pp P$_5$ NP$_6$]$_5$]$_3$]$_3$
        | | | |
      trolley$_4$ squeal$_2$ around$_5$ corner$_6$

The verb *squeal* licenses the exact same part of the CS in both cases. The difference lies in whether the element that licenses GO in CS is the verb *go,* as in (67a), or the sound+motion construction, as in (67b). The consequences are of course radically different in the syntax. The lexicon of a language like Spanish lacks the constructional idiom (66b.i); hence only the more canonical mapping (67a) is available.

6.5.3 Coercions

The sound+motion construction creates a situation in which a piece of semantics has no corresponding piece in the syntax or phonology. Another class of such cases is now beginning to be fairly well understood (e.g. Briscoe et al. 1990; Pollard and Sag 1994; Pustejovsky 1995; Jackendoff 1997a): there are conventionalized principles of interpretation that permit unexpressed semantic operators when necessary for semantic/pragmatic well-formedness. Two well-studied cases are illustrated in the single sentence (68), discussed in Nunberg (1979) (see also Ward 2004). Note how the paraphrase differs just in containing the italicized material.

(68) [One waitress says to another:]
      The ham sandwich over in the corner wants another coffee.
      [= The *person contextually associated with a* ham sandwich wants
                                          another *cup of* coffee]

It is clear that *ham sandwich* does not lexically denote a person, and that *coffee* is lexically a mass rather than a count noun. The consensus in the literature (see Jackendoff 1997a and references therein) is that the parts of interpretation shown in italics are the product of auxiliary principles of interpretation. These are often termed "principles of pragmatics" and hence outside of grammar; yet they contribute material that makes the sentence semantically well-formed and that plays a role in the sentence's truth-conditions; Chapter 10 further demonstrates that they play a role in binding. However, as will be argued in detail in Chapter 10, the content expressed by italicized material in the paraphrase is present only in semantics, not in syntax; this, if anything, is the sense in which it is pragmatic.

Such a change in meaning for the sake of well-formedness is called a *coercion*. Viewed in the direction from semantics to syntax, it is a piece of meaning that can be left overtly unexpressed, leaving it up to the listener to reconstruct it. In the direction from syntax to semantics, it is a extra piece of meaning that can be optionally inserted into the interpretation in order to help it make sense.

It is important to recognize that coercions are conventionalized: it is not as if anything goes. For instance, the coercion responsible for the interpretation of *coffee* in (68) is sometimes called the 'universal packager'; but it is far from universal. It is truly productive only when applied to edible portions of liquid or semiliquid food (*water, pudding*, etc.). It is far less appropriate applied to, say, the portion of water necessary to fill a sprinkling can or to a truckload-sized portion of cement (in such a context, **I'll bring you a water/cement* is out), and under such circumstances it requires heavy contextual support. That is, generally a coercion is restricted to certain conventionalized contexts, within which it is fully productive.

(69) shows how a coercion works. In the normal composition of a sentence meaning, the meanings of the arguments satisfy the argument positions of the verb, as in (69a) for *John wants coffee*. However, *sandwich* cannot be integrated into the X argument of *want* (69b). Therefore the coercion (shown in boldface) is interposed as an 'adapter' that fits into the socket above and into which in turn the errant argument is plugged (69c).

(69)   a. WANT (X ,   Y)   ⇒ WANT (JOHN, COFFEE)
                      | |
                  JOHN   COFFEE

         b. WANT (X ,   Y)
                  **| |
              SANDWICH   COFFEE

c. WANT(X , Y) $\Rightarrow$ WANT ([PERSON WITH SANDWICH], COFFEE)]
| |
[PERSON WITH Z] COFFEE
          |
        SANDWICH

Put in terms of our format for showing how to carve a CS into words, the coercion looks like (70ii).

(70)   Conceptual structure   Syntax   Phonology
CS: [WANT ([PERSON WITH [SANDWICH]], COFFEE)]
  i.   [WANT (X , Y)]$_1$ V_1 want$_1$
  ii.   [PERSON WITH Z_i] N_i
  iii.   [SANDWICH]$_2$ N_2 sandwich$_2$
  iv.   [COFFEE]$_3$ $N_{\pm3}$ coffee$_3$

That is, the coercion is encoded as a lexical item with no phonology and no syntax aside from a contextual feature. All that shows up in syntax is the semantic argument of the coercion (*the sandwich*, indexed i in (70ii)). It thus appears as a syntactic argument of the head of which the coercion is a semantic argument, i.e. as the subject of *want*. This is in accord with the Argument/ Modifier Rule: semantic and syntactic embedding correspond insofar as there is anything to embed in syntax.

    A coercion can however have syntactic repercussions. Consider the second coercion in (68), the use of *coffee* to mean 'portion of coffee'. The aspectual feature on the lexical item *coffee* is MASS, but the aspectual feature on POR-TION is COUNT SINGULAR. It is the latter aspectual feature that makes it possible to use the determiner *another*. (71) shows some of the details. The coercion is (71i). We'll assume that *another* links to both the modifier OTHER and the feature INDEF; its contextual restrictions require a singular count noun in semantics.

(71)   Conceptual structure   Syn.   Phon.
CS: [PORTION ([COFFEE; MASS]); [OTHER]; INDEF, COUNT SING]
  i.   [PORTION ([X;   MASS]$_i$);   COUNT SING] N_i
  ii.   [COFFEE; MASS]$_3$ N_3 coffee$_3$
  iii.   [[OTHER]$_4$;INDEF$_4$,*COUNT SING]* Det$_4$ another$_4$

Similar considerations result in *three coffees*, where the plural affix attaches to the noun on the basis of the coerced interpretation. In other languages such adjustments can work differently. Wiese and Maling (2004) show differences in the way that number and grammatical gender play out in the counterpart of this coercion in Icelandic and German. In particular, in Icelandic the coercion imposes a grammatical gender, based on the gender of the particular noun implicit in the coercion.

(72) *Icelandic*
    a. annan   kaffi
        another$_\text{MASC}$ coffee$_\text{NEUT}$ [container: *bolli* 'cup', masculine]
    b. tvo   viski
        two$_\text{MASC}$ whiskey$_\text{NEUT}$
            [container: *sjússar* 'drinks', masculine](used for orders in a bar)]
    c. tvær   viski
        two$_\text{FEM}$ whiskey$_\text{NEUT}$ [container: *flöskur* 'bottles', feminine]

By contrast, the German coercion does not specify a grammatical gender, and the determiner takes its gender from the surface noun.

Fascinating though this all this, we will stop here. Coercions will play an important role in Chapter 10, where we will show that CS licensed by coercion plays a crucial role in binding, despite having no syntactic reflex. We will also make use of coercion in Chapter 12 to account for certain problematic cases of control.

6.6 Concluding remarks

We conclude this chapter with an overview of the syntax–semantics interface so far, as developed in this chapter and the last. We have seen that it has a sort of layered structure, in which each layer specializes or refines parts of the ones preceding it—in conformity with what we have called the Toolkit Hypothesis. The layers might be summed up like this:

• The CS to be expressed is carved up into lexical items. These include not only words but lexically listed affixes, idioms, constructions, light verbs, and coercions. Since each of these items is an interface rule, the result is a collection of corresponding syntactic units of varying sizes and their corresponding phonology.

• Where not otherwise stipulated by a construction or a lexical item with special properties (such as English tense), the Head Rule and Argument/Modifier Rule relate the CS embedding to syntactic embedding in a way consistent with the autonomous syntactic principles of the language.

• Linear order of heads and various other constituents is imposed by the autonomous syntactic principles (e.g. NPs precede PPs within VP). Further linear ordering is imposed by interface principles that distinguish arguments from adjuncts and that relate linear order to information structure.

• Linear order of NP arguments of verbs, however, is determined by the further subsystem of grammatical functions, the GF-tier. GF-tier ranking is sensitive to (a) the thematic hierarchy; (b) the need for tensed clauses to have a subject; (c) syntactic argument structure (subcategorization) of individual verbs that is mismatched with semantic argument structure (as in "raising" verbs).

• GF-tier organization can be further manipulated by constructions such as raising and passive, which result in further mismatches between syntax and semantics.

Thinking in engineering terms, each successive layer adds further precision and flexibility to the communication system offered by the layers above it. The first layer allows for nothing but an unstructured collection of words. The next one says that pieces of the same constituent will be adjacent to each other rather than scattered throughout the utterance; the third says that certain pieces will always be in predictable order.

If we only had this much of a grammar, and if all NP arguments were oblique, i.e. semantically case-marked, we could build a language along the lines of Case Grammar (Fillmore 1968), and perhaps there are languages that are more or less like that. However, if there are direct NP arguments, there has to be a way to identify which one is in which role. This is what the GF-tier accomplishes. Still, it could be that the GF-tier only stipulated a fixed order for the direct NP arguments. This would be a perfectly fine language. But in fact the GF-tier goes further: the manipulations such as raising and passive still allow the roles of NP arguments to be identified, while permitting more flexibility of position to meet other demands such as processing and information structure.

A progression of layers in the other direction would make no sense. Without words to provide a foundation for communication, none of the other interface principles are good for anything. And the most specialized layer, the GF-tier, pertains only to semantic constituents that have been identified by the other components as direct NP arguments—it does not pertain to adjuncts and only partially to oblique NP arguments. Thus it would be impossible to build a language just out of words and the GF-tier.

This logical relation among the layers has consequences for one's view of UG. Many of the phenomena that have been most robustly ascribed to "core" grammar fall under the aegis of the GF-tier, in particular all the so-called A-movements and the clearest cases of reflexive anaphora. It therefore is methodologically misguided to concentrate on "core" grammar as somehow primary and "temporarily" idealize away from the rest: the rest is the all-important substrate on which the GF-tier rides.

At the same time, the GF-tier is indeed a "hidden layer" of grammar that mediates between CS and surface syntax. It is far simpler than MGG's D-structure and Logical Form, but it is hidden nonetheless. As such, it presents the usual problem for learnability. Given that its properties depend heavily on the particular properties of the syntax–semantics interface, we do not see how it could possibly have been adapted from some other cognitive capacity. We conclude that the GF-tier is a part of the narrow faculty of language in Chomsky's sense, and that the ability to infer a GF-tier from primary linguistic data must be innate.

We speculate further, following Jackendoff (2002a) and Pinker and Jackendoff (2005), that the opportunities offered by the GF-tier for enhanced communication are what made it adaptive in the course of the evolution of the human language capacity. Given that the GF-tier logically depends on so much of the rest of the system being already in place, we would be inclined to see it as a relatively recent stage in the evolution of language.

We are far from done with the interface. The next three chapters add two important pieces: ellipsis and long-distance dependencies.

CHAPTER 7

Bare Argument Ellipsis and its Relatives

7.1 Introduction

Chapters 5 and 6 showed how a large class of argument structure phenomena can be accommodated within the Simpler Syntax Hypothesis, through use of a syntax–semantics interface somewhat richer than the homomorphism called for by Interface Uniformity. In particular, a substantial number of phenomena that MGG bundles under movement come to be treated as principles of linearization. Next, we pick up threads initiated in Chapters 1 and 4, and embark on a detour into a different class of phenomena: elliptical constructions. As we go along, we will see that these prepare the ground for a novel approach to A′ phenomena, which we address in more detail in Chapter 9.

The elliptical constructions we will discuss are of various sorts. Here are some examples, with the relevant parts in bold.

(1) a. A: What did Pat buy?
         B: **A motorcycle.**   [Bare Argument Ellipsis]
     b. A: When is Robin coming?
         B: **On Tuesday – and with Pat.**   [Bare Argument Ellipsis]
     c. Someone's coming with Bill, but I don't know **who.**   [Sluicing]
     d. Bill's coming, but I don't know **who with.**   [Sluice-stranding]
     e. Sam plays saxophone, and **Susan sarrusophone.**   [Gapping]
     f. Sam doesn't play saxophone, let alone/not to mention/never mind **sarrusophone.**   [*not . . . let alone*]
     g. A: Who wants to come along?
         B: **I do!**   [VP-ellipsis]

   h. Lenore gave $5000, but I could never **do that**.   [Do X anaphora]

   i. If you don't believe me, **you will the weatherman**.   [Pseudo-gapping]

These *fragments* (in the sense of Lappin and Benmamoun 1999) are distinguished from normal sentences in two ways. First, they are not well-formed full syntactic sentences, but rather strings composed of one or more well-formed nonsentential phrases. Second, their interpretation depends on their relation to an antecedent clause in the discourse. Thus (1a), for instance, is interpreted as though the speaker has said *Pat bought a motorcycle*.

The combination of these two properties has led to the widespread conclusion that at some underlying syntactic level, the fragments in (1) are indeed full sentences. This conclusion follows logically from Uniformity. Structural Uniformity says that the same structural principles should apply to all sentences. Since the sentence is taken to be the canonical category of an utterance, the apparently nonsentential utterances in (1) must actually be sentences too. Syntactocentrism says that the interpretation of an utterance is built from the meanings of the words plus the syntactic structure.[1] Since the interpretations of the fragments in (1) are fuller than their surface syntactic structure would permit, there must be hidden syntactic structure that is responsible for the full interpretation. Strong Interface Uniformity says that uniform factors in interpretation must stem from uniform syntactic sources. Since the interpretations of the fragments in (1) are propositional, they must follow from a syntactic structure that supports propositional interpretation, namely a full sentence. Thus everything converges on treating the fragments as the remnants of a fuller syntactic structure. We will term this approach the *deletion hypothesis* (Merchant (2003) uses the term *ellipsis approach*); versions of it vary in exactly what is taken to be deleted, as we will see later.[2]

An alternative view has maintained a minor presence in the field since the late 1960s: that the unexpressed parts of the fragment's interpretation are supplied not through underlying syntactic structure but via direct correspondence with

---

[1] e.g. Chomsky (1965:136), echoing Frege's doctrine of compositionality: "the semantic interpretation of a sentence depends only on its lexical items and the grammatical functions and relations represented in the underlying structures [or, in more recent versions, in the Logical Form—PWC/RJ] in which they appear."

[2] For analyses that take the position that the interpretation of fragments is determined by syntactic structure, see among many others, Pope (1971), Sag (1976), Williams (1977), Haik (1987), Hellan (1988), Lappin (1996), Fiengo & May (1994), Hestvik (1995), Phillips (2003), Wasow (1972), Hankamer (1979), Kitagawa (1991), Tancredi (1992), Wilder (1995), and Merchant (2001). For useful surveys and introductions to approaches to ellipsis, see Winkler and Schwabe (2003) and Merchant (2001).

the meaning of the antecedent sentence. Thus the answer in (1a) is interpreted by relating it to the interpretation of *What did you buy?* substituting the interpretation of *a motorcycle* for the interpretation of *what*, and changing the illocutionary force to declarative. We will call this approach the *direct interpretation hypothesis* (this time following Merchant 2001). There are still other possibilities, to be discussed in section 7.3.[3]

Sections 7.5 and 7.6 will motivate an approach we will call "indirect licensing", which, like direct interpretation, posits no more syntactic structure than appears at the surface, in conformity with the Simpler Syntax Hypothesis. It differs from direct interpretation in that the syntactic structure of the antecedent is relevant not only to the interpretation of the fragment but also to its syntactic well-formedness. This helps gives rise to the appearance that the fragment itself has hidden syntactic structure. The core of our argument is that if machinery exists that accounts for the interpretation of a fragment of one type, without appealing to covert syntactic structure containing the fragment, then that machinery is available for all types of fragments and constitutes the default hypothesis.

Finally, and crucially, in our approach the interpretation of the fragment or fragments does not require that the antecedent contain an identical constituent. Following a very substantial literature, we will argue that deletion under identity is not always possible in cases of well-formed ellipsis. Rather, fragments are interpreted by rules that match them up with the interpretation of antecedents in the discourse. We pay particular attention to the evidence that has suggested most strongly that the antecedent of the missing material is syntactic, since such evidence constitutes the main impediment to a general theory of fragment interpretation.

By this point in the development of syntactic theory, the literature on the interpretation of fragments is so vast that to adequately summarize the various contributions would require a substantial treatise (see notes 2 and 3 above for a sampling). We limit ourselves to the more modest goals of (a) establishing the feasibility of a theory of fragments based on indirect licensing, i.e. interpretation with reference to antecedent syntactic structure, and (b) dealing with some of the more problematic potential counter-examples.

---

[3] For analyses that argue for a strictly interpretive approach, see, among many others, Napoli (1983; 1985), Dalrymple et al. (1991), Hardt (1992; 1999), Jacobson (1992), Stainton (1994; 1998), Lappin (1996), Kehler (1993), and Hendriks and de Hoop (2001).

7.2. Nonsentential utterance types

The first thing we want to do is defuse the demands of Structural Uniformity—in this case the idea that underlying every elliptical utterance has to be a Sentence, i.e. a tensed clause. This task proves straightforward. As noticed as long ago as Shopen (1972) (and stressed by e.g. Fillmore et al. (1988)), English contains a wide range of free-standing utterance types that cannot be derived in any useful sense from sentences. Here are some:

(2) a. *Single-word utterances* (Jackendoff 2002a)
        Hello! Ouch! Wow! Allakazam!
     b. *PP with NP!* (Shopen 1972; Jackendoff 1973)
        Off with his head!
        On the porch with that trunk (, Mr. Stevenson, will you?)
     c. *NP, NP* (Shopen 1972)
        A good talker, your friend Bill.
        The best coffee in the world, that Maxwell House.
     d. *NP Pred!* (Shopen 1972)
        Seatbelts fastened!
        Everyone in the car!
        Books open to page fifteen!
     e. *How about NP/AP/Gerundive VP/S*
        How about a cup of coffee?
        How about a little shorter? [said by a hairstylist]
        How about going to the movies?
        How about we have a little talk?
     f. *(What,) NP+acc VP/Pred?* ("*Mad* Magazine sentences": Akmajian 1984)
        What, me worry?
        John drunk? (I don't believe it!)
        Him in an accident?
     g. *Salutation, Vocative NP*
        Hey, Phil!
        Excuse me, doctor.
        Hi there, handsome!
        Yoohoo, Mrs. Goldberg!
     h. *NP and S* (Culicover 1972, taken up again in Chapter 13)
        One more beer and I'm leaving.
        One more step and I'll shoot.
        Fifty years of generative grammar and what have we learned?

    i. *Expletive (P) NP!* (Dong 1971)
       Damn/Fuck syntactic theory![4]
       Shit on semantics!
       Three cheers/Hooray for phonology!
    j. *Scores: NP Numeral, NP Numeral*
       The Red Sox four, the Yankees three.

Two properties obtain in each of these constructions. First, it is impossible to find a plausible derivation from a canonical sentence. In particular, there is no tense and in most cases no verbal element. For the theorist to introduce an underlying verb, whether contentful or semantically empty, only to delete it in the course of the derivation, simply begs the question. From the point of view of learnability, the child must acquire the surface frame and the meaning, and that alone should be enough. There is no point in requiring the child also to learn a derivation of the surface frame from an abstract full sentence that explains nothing further about the interpretation (recall the parallel arguments in Chapter 1 regarding BAE and the position of *enough*).

The second property of these constructions is that they do not embed (except in direct quotes, of course):

(3) $\left\{ \begin{array}{l} \text{*Fred unfortunately doesn't realize (that)} \\ \text{*Steve is happy to} \end{array} \right\}$

$\left\{ \begin{array}{l} \text{hello} \\ \text{off with his head.} \\ \text{a good talker, your friend Bill.} \\ \text{yoohoo, Mrs. Goldberg.} \\ \text{hooray for phonology.} \end{array} \right.$

    *Ellen wondered whether him drunk.[5]

We conclude that these utterance frames are not of the category *S*. Instead, we might treat them as *sui generis* realizations of a more general category that might be called *Utterance* or *U*. This category, then, subsumes both *S* and a hodgepodge collection of other utterance frames, each with characteristic intonation and interpretation. Unlike the rest of the utterance frames, *S* can be embedded.

---

[4] Dong (1971) shows in detail that although some of the epithets in these examples are homophonous with verbs, they are not verbs, even on metaphoric interpretations. A representative piece of evidence is the contrast between *Fuck you*, with the epithet, and *Fuck yourself*, an imperative with the homophonous verb, which is altogether parallel to other imperatives such as *Stab yourself*.

[5] *Him drunk* does embed as a small clause (see section 4.5.3), but not as an indirect question in the sense required by the meaning of the free-standing construction illustrated in (2f).

This conclusion reduces Structural Uniformity to the more or less vacuous claim that every utterance is of the category *U*. Nothing in UG predicts the internal structure of *U*, aside from the trivial fact that it consists of words and phrases of the language. Every one of the constructions in (2) must be learned.

In turn, this conclusion opens the door to treating fragment constructions like those in (1) not as sentences manqués, but rather as species of noncanonical Utterance, in conformance with the Simpler Syntax Hypothesis. In particular, given the relative complexity of the frames in (2), there should be no problem allowing U also to license a single XP such as *a motorcycle* or *on Tuesday*—the canonical fragment of Bare Argument Ellipsis. Like the constructions in (2), these do not embed freely: **Fred doesn't realize (that) a motorcycle.*[6]

By contrast, the fragment in (1g) can embed freely, e.g. *Fred realizes that I will*. Thus it is a species of S. However, a special phrase structure rule is not needed to license it, provided VP is optional in the normal phrase structure rule for S, as proposed in section 4.7.

We conclude that in purely (Simpler) syntactic terms, each ellipsis construction in (1) is either a noncanonical species of Utterance or a permissible expansion of S. We do not need to amplify UG in order to allow the syntax of fragment constructions such as BAE to be licensed: UG needs this capability anyway, in order to permit constructions such as (2).

Of course, the ellipsis constructions in (1) differ from the constructions in (2) in that they are not free-standing: their interpretations are not a consequence purely of their own lexical items plus the meaning contributed by the construction. Rather, their interpretation depends on being related to an antecedent sentence, part of whose content is borrowed into the interpretation of the fragment. Thus, if we are to treat fragments according to Simpler Syntax, we must develop a satisfactory version of the interpretive hypothesis. We will see in 7.4 why a simple direct interpretive hypothesis is unsatisfactory; section 7.5 and 7.6 will develop an alternative and show that it leads to a novel treatment of A′ constructions such as *wh*-questions and topicalization. But first we have to work out some basic details of the treatment of fragments. The next sections will concentrate on Bare Argument Ellipsis, amplifying the treatment in Chapter 1. Sections 7.7–8.3 will extend the approach to other well-known fragment constructions, many illustrated in (1), including sluicing, gapping, VP-ellipsis, pseudo-gapping, and *one*-anaphora.

---

[6] There are, however, special cases such as *I wonder what Robin ate for breakfast—Fred thought cottage cheese* or the famous … *Spiro conjectures Ex-Lax*. These might well be a declarative counterpart of sluicing (i.e. on our analysis a form of embedded BAE), but we will not take them up here.

7.3. Problems for a syntactic account of bare argument ellipsis

Let us return to the examples of BAE from Chapter 1. B's responses in (4) are interpreted as abbreviations of the full sentences in (5).

(4)   a. A: I hear Harriet's been drinking again.
             B: i. Yeah, scotch.
                  ii. Scotch?
                  iii. Not scotch, I hope!
                  iv. Yeah, every morning.
      b. A: Has Harriet been drinking scotch again?
             B: i. No, bourbon.
                  ii. Yeah, bourbon too.
      c. A: What has Harriet been drinking?
             B: Scotch.
(5)   a.   i. Yeah, Harriet has been drinking scotch.
           ii. Has Harriet been drinking scotch?
           iii. I hope Harriet hasn't been drinking scotch.
           iv. Yeah, Harriet has been drinking scotch every morning.
      b.   i. No, Harriet's been drinking bourbon.
           ii. Yeah, Harriet's been drinking bourbon too.
      c. Harriet has been drinking scotch.

These examples show three different ways the response can be related to the antecedent.[7] In (4a.i–iii), *scotch* specifies an implicit argument of the verb *drinking* in the antecedent. In (4a.iv), *every morning* adds a modifier to the proposition expressed by the antecedent. In (4b), *bourbon* substitutes for the focus *scotch* in the antecedent; in (4c), *scotch* substitutes for the *wh*-phrase in the antecedent, which is usually taken in the literature to be a kind of focus as well. In addition, (4a.iii) and (4b.i) add negation to the interpretation of the fragment; (4a.ii) and (4c) change the illocutionary force of the antecedent.

What is responsible for these interpretations? Here are four possible solutions.

(6)   a. *Purely syntactic account*
         The responses in (4) have an underlying syntactic structure rather like (5), from which all parts repeated from A's sentence have been deleted in the course of deriving phonological form.
         e.g. (4a.i): Syntax: Harriet's been drinking scotch $\Longrightarrow$ scotch
                      Semantics: 'Harriet's been drinking scotch'

---

[7] A similar typology is noted for sluicing by Lori Levin (1982).

b. *Syntactic + interface account*
The responses in (4) have a syntactic structure rather like (5), except that all the parts that correspond to repetitions of A's sentence are represented as empty categories. The syntax–semantics interface supplies the interpretations of the empty categories through their correspondence with A's sentences.
e.g. (4a.i): Syntax: $[_{NP}$ e$][$ $[_{I}$e$][_{VP}[_{V}$ e$][_{NP}$ scotch$]$ $]$ $]$
Semantics: 'Harriet's been drinking scotch'

c. *Interface account*
The responses in (4) have just the syntactic structure present at the surface. The syntax–semantics interface supplies the rest of the details of the interpretation, relying on the structure of A's sentences.
e.g. (4a.i): Syntax: $[_{NP}$ scotch$]$
Semantics: 'Harriet's been drinking scotch'

d. *Purely semantic/pragmatic account*
The responses in (4) have just the syntactic structure present at the surface. The syntax–semantics interface derives an interpretation based only on this structure. The resulting interpretation does not form a proposition, so it is construed as part of a proposition whose content bears some relevant relation to A's sentence.
e.g. (4a.i): Syntax: $[_{NP}$ scotch$]$
Semantics/Pragmatics: 'scotch' $\implies$ 'Harriet's been drinking scotch'

Mainstream generative grammar has consistently favored solutions along the lines of (6a,b), where BAE arises from complete sentential syntax. Simpler Syntax, by contrast, favors solutions along the lines of (6c,d), where BAE has no further syntax beyond what appears at the surface. However, the choice of solution should not be merely a matter of theoretical preference: it should be defended both on empirical grounds and on the basis of its comparative complexity.

As observed in Chapter 1, the syntactic accounts allow concatenated constituents in a response to be combined into a unified underlying sentence:

(7)   A: (i) I hear Harriet's been drinking again.
          (ii) Has Harriet been drinking again?
      B: (i) Yeah, probably scotch.
              (from 'Harriet has probably been drinking scotch')
          (ii) Yeah, scotch, I think.
              (from 'Harriet has been drinking scotch, I think')
          (iii) Yeah, scotch this time. (from 'Harriet has been drinking scotch this time')

The interface and semantic accounts, by contrast, require the theory to countenance these simply as nonsentential concatenations of phrases. Within the
assumption of Structural Uniformity, this consequence is unpleasant. However,
the previous section showed that there is a wide range of nonsentential utterance types in English. We see no problem in principle in extending it to include
concatenated XPs—as long as a principle is available to give the resulting
structure an interpretation. So, in order to adopt either the interface or semantic
account, we have to assign the responses in (7) a paratactic structure like (8), in
which more or less random constituents are concatenated.

(8)

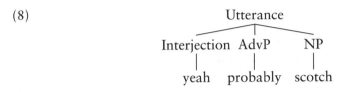

A proponent of a syntactic account might further argue that the pieces of
such responses can only be related to each other semantically if they are both
attached to a sentential structure. But such an argument would be unfounded: if
either the interface or a principle of construal is responsible for integrating
scotch into a propositional structure derived from the previous sentence, it is
equally capable of integrating both *scotch* and *probably*.

As pointed out in section 1.2, the syntactic accounts encounter problems
when the correspondence between the antecedent and the BAE interpretation is
less than perfect. For instance, the pronouns have to be adjusted: *you* substitutes
for *I* and vice versa. The illocutionary force has to be adjusted: statements in
response to questions and vice versa. Main clauses may have to be omitted, as in
B's reply in (4a.B:i), which means not 'I/You hear Harriet's been drinking scotch
again' but 'Harriet's been drinking scotch again'. The basis for these adjustments is semantic/pragmatic, not syntactic. In particular, whatever process is
responsible for omitting 'You hear' from the interpretation of the response, it is
exquisitely sensitive to factors of lexical semantics/pragmatics:

(9)   a. A: Ozzie said that Harriet's been drinking again.
          B: Yeah, scotch.   [= 'Harriet's been drinking scotch (again)' *or*
                              'Ozzie said that Harriet's been drinking scotch (again)']
       b. A: Ozzie mistakenly believes that Harriet's been drinking again.
          B: Yeah, scotch.   [= 'O mistakenly believes that H has been
                drinking scotch again'; ≠ 'H has been drinking scotch again']

    c. A: Ozzie doubts that Harriet has been drinking again.
          B: *Yeah, scotch.

Note that A's utterances in (9) are all syntactically parallel to (4a). The felicity of different interpretations of B's response clearly depends not on syntax but on details of the meaning of A's utterance (even if we don't understand how this is to be accomplished formally). In other words, there are clear semantic/pragmatic conditions on the felicity of responses, and these are necessary even in the syntactic account.[8]

Other cases arise in which the form of the antecedent and the form of the response are syntactically incompatible:

(10)   a. What did you do to Susan?
         —Kiss her.   [*I kissed her to Susan. / *I kissed Susan to her.]
     b. What's that frog doing in my tomato sauce?
         —Swimming. [*That frog's doing swimming in my tomato sauce.]
         [cf. What's that frog doing in my tomato sauce?—The backstroke.]

Semantics/pragmatics is even more deeply involved in instances of BAE where the syntactic relation between the antecedent and response is less direct. (11) repeats examples from Chapter 1 and adds some more (thanks to Ida Toivonen for (11i)).

(11)   a. A: Why don't you fix me a drink?
         B: In a minute, ok?
         [cf. infelicity of Why don't I fix you a drink in a minute? as response: response is understood as I'll fix you a drink in a minute]
     b. A: How about fixing me a drink?
         B: In a minute, ok?
         [response is understood as I'll fix you a drink in a minute, OK?]
     c. A: Let's get a pizza.
         B: OK—pepperoni?
         [cf. *Let's get pepperoni pizza?: response is understood as something like OK, should we get pepperoni pizza?]

---

[8] Further such cases arise in what Ginzburg and Cooper (2004) call Clarification Ellipsis. B's response in (i) has either of the readings in (ii) or (iii).

(i)   A: Bo finagled a raise. B: Bo?
(ii) Are you saying that BO (of all people) finagled a raise?
(iii) Who is Bo?

Here B refers to A's utterance metalinguistically, and discourse manipulation of some subtlety is taking place for which there is no warrant in the syntax of A's utterance. Ginzburg and Cooper come to conclusions similar to ours and, within an amplified version of HPSG, propose a formal treatment that goes far beyond ours here.

    d. A: Would you like a drink?
       B: i. Yeah, how about scotch?
          ii. No, but how about some lunch?
    [*cf.* *How about I would like a scotch/some lunch? *as well as other improbable variants*]
    e. A: Harriet's been drinking again.
       B: How stupid!   [= 'How stupid of Harriet to drink again']
    f. A: I hear there's been some serious drinking going on around here.
       B: i. Not Sam, I hope.
               [= 'I hope it's not SAM who's been drinking']
          ii. Not my favorite bottle of scotch, I hope.   [= 'I hope they haven't been drinking my favorite bottle of scotch.']
    g. A: Would you like a cookie?
       B: What kind?   [= 'What kind of cookie have you got/are you offering?'; ≠ 'What kind of cookie would I like?]
    h. A: Are you hungry?
       B: How about a cookie?   [What's the paraphrase?]
    i. A: Hey, look! There's John over there, reading *Moby Dick*.
       B: Are you blind? It's Sam and *Harry Potter*.

In short, a putative reconstruction of BAE as a copy of the antecedent is plausible just in case it is semantically or pragmatically plausible. Such a reconstruction has to be somewhat parallel to the antecedent in its syntax, but must deviate if necessary for the sake of plausible interpretation. (11g) is especially distant in this regard. Moreover, some cases of BAE such as (11d) are embedded in free-standing nonsentential constructions, into which it is impossible to embed any sort of relevant syntactic structure.

Of course, the semantic/pragmatic approaches have to make parallel adjustments; but these are appropriate adjustments for this level of interpretation. After all, similar—and more severe—accommodations of a Gricean or relevance-theoretic sort (Sperber and Wilson 1995) are necessary in any event to explain how full sentences are related in discourse, for instance how B's responses function as replies to A in (12).[9] In particular, (12b) directly parallels (11g), except BAE is not involved.

---

[9] Stainton (1994; 1998) proposes a relevance-theoretic account of BAE from a broadly philosophical rather than technical theoretical stance.

(12)   a. A: Would you like to go out for some lunch?
        B: i. It's raining.
           ii. There's a nice Italian place around the corner.
       b. A: Would you like a cookie?
        B: What kind of cookies have you got?

Let's push the syntactic accounts a bit further, for the moment restricting ourselves to the purely syntactic account (6a). In this approach, there is a rule that deletes the duplicated (or nearly duplicated!) structure. What is deleted is apparently not a constituent, since *Harriet has been drinking* is not a constituent of the putative underlying form for B's reply in (4a.B:i), *Harriet has been drinking scotch*. Suppose one tries to make the deleted portion a constituent by positing that prior to deletion the remnant has undergone extraction, such as *It is scotch that Harriet has been drinking*, *Scotch is what Harriet has been drinking*, or, in more contemporary approaches, [*scotch [Harriet has been drinking t]*]. This proposal runs afoul of the fact that the response may be a piece of structure that cannot be extracted (13).

(13)   a. A: What kind of scotch does Harriet drink?
        B: Expensive.   [= 'Harriet drinks expensive scotch']
        [*cf.* *It is expensive that Harriet drinks scotch; *Expensive is the kind of scotch Harriet has been drinking]
       b. A: Let's get a pizza.
        B: Pepperoni?
        [*cf.* *It is pepperoni that let's get a pizza; *Pepperoni is the kind of pizza that let's get]
       c. Did Susan say that she saw PAT Smith?
        —No, KIM.   [*cf.* *Kim, Susan said that she saw [t Smith].]
       d. Is that a Navy flight suit?
        —No, Army.   [*Army, that is a [t flight suit].]
       e. How many pounds does that pumpkin weigh?
        —Over a thousand.
                       [*Over a thousand, that pumpkin weighs [t pounds].]
       f. Is Sviatoslav pro-communist or anti-communist these days?
        —Pro.   [**Pro, Sviatoslav is [t-communist] these days.*]

Moreover, BAE is possible in situations where extraction would violate the usual island constraints on long-distance movement.[10] ((14d,e) are adapted from parallel sluicing examples in Chung et al. 1995.)

---

[10] Merchant (2001) assigns ungrammaticality judgments to similar examples, all of which we find reasonably acceptable given the appropriate focus intonation on the antecedent (high pitch maintained from the contrastively stressed word to the end of the sentence). In the following

(14) a. A: Harriet drinks scotch that comes from a very special part of Scotland.

　　　 B: Where?　　[*cf.* *Where does Harriet drink scotch that is from?]

　　b. A: John met a guy who speaks a very unusual language.

　　　 B: i. Which language?

　　　　　　　　[*Which language did John meet a guy who speaks t?]

　　　　　ii. Yes, Albanian.　[*Albanian, John met a guy who speaks t.]

　　c. A: John met a woman who speaks French.

　　　 B: i. With an English accent?　[*With an English accent, John met a woman who speaks French t.]

　　　　　ii. And Bengali?　[*And Bengali, did John meet a woman who speaks French t?]

　　d. A: The administration has issued a statement that it is willing to meet with one of the student groups.

　　　 B: Yeah, right—the Gay Rifle Club.

　　　　　[*The Gay Rifle Club, the administration has issued a statement that it is willing to meet with t.]

　　e. A: They persuaded Kennedy and some other senator to jointly sponsor the legislation.

　　　 B: Yeah, Hatch.　[*Hatch, they persuaded Kennedy and t to jointly sponsor the legislation.]

　　f. A: For John to flirt at the party would be scandalous.

　　　 B: Even with his wife?　[*Even with his wife, would for John to flirt t at the party be scandalous?]

---

examples from Merchant (2001), we indicate his judgments in parentheses, and we indicate focus with bold face.

(i)　a. Does Abby speak the same Balkan language that **Ben** speaks?
　　b. (*)No, **Charlie**.
　　c. No, she speaks the same Balkan language that **Charlie** speaks.

(ii)　a. Did Ben leave the party because **Abby** wouldn't dance with him?
　　b. (*)No, **Beth**.
　　c. No, he left the party because **Beth** wouldn't dance with him.

(iii)　a. Did Abby vote for a **Green** Party candidate?
　　b. (*)No, **Reform** Party.
　　c. No, she voted for a Reform Party candidate.

(iv)　a. Did Abby get "The Cat in the **Hat**" and "Goodnight Gorilla" for her nephew for his birthday?
　　b. (*)No, "The **Lorax**".
　　c. No, she got "The **Lorax**" and "Goodnight Gorilla" for her nephew for his birthday.

We have no account for why Merchant's judgments and ours differ.

Ross (1969a) points out facts like (14) in connection with sluicing, which will be shown in section 7.7 to be essentially a special case of BAE. His response is to propose that island constraint violations are cancelled by deletion. Merchant (2001; to appear), shows that the insensitivity of sluicing to island constraints is quite general, and offers a similar solution: "the PF interface cannot parse crossed island nodes", and "deletion of the island rescues the sluice from ungrammaticality" (Merchant, to appear). The technical details of these proposals would take us too far afield here, but the important point is that the solution fails to provide an explanation of the phenomenon. Rather, it crucially integrates into the account the observation that is to be explained: when there is no apparent movement because there is no apparent structure that contains a gap, there are no apparent constraints on movement.[11] In contrast, the Simpler Syntax solution is that there are no apparent constraints on movement because there is no movement, in fact no offending structure. The Simpler Syntax solution also accounts for the fact that there can still be BAE when there is no plausible syntactic source and when movement is simply impossible.

Next consider the more complex cases in which there are two BAs.

(15)   Harriet's been drinking again.
        a.   Yeah, scotch on the weekend.
        b.   *Yeah, on the weekend scotch.

In order to account for these facts under the syntactic approach, we would have to posit multiple topicalization, which (in English) is overtly impossible; hence we must arrange to allow multiple topicalization only when the rest of the source clause is deleted. Moreover, the order of constituents is what we would expect to find in the untransformed VP (16a), and not in a case of multiple topicalization ((16c), if at all good).

(16)   a.   Harriet's been drinking scotch on the weekend.
        b.   *Harriet's been drinking on the weekend scotch.
        c.   ??On the weekend, scotch Harriet's been drinking.
        d.   *Scotch on the weekend, Harriet's been drinking.

The only way that we can see of saving this analysis would be to posit that there is topicalization of the VP, with deletion of the V in the topicalized copy. This

---

[11] A question that is typically ignored in accounts of this type is why it should matter whether the offending syntactic configuration is overt or invisible. To say that the constraint is phonological, and therefore only holds for 'pronounced' structures, is sophistic, since it has yet to be demonstrated that the invisible structure actually exists (cf. the Emperor's new clothes). If cases such as (14) were ungrammatical, that would be far better evidence for the reality of the invisible structure.

could be accomplished by first extracting the V from the VP, then moving the VP, and then deleting the entire remnant IP—an Iterated Raising-style derivation of the sort discussed in Chapter 4.

(17)   Harriet's been [drinking scotch on the weekend] $\Rightarrow$
       Harriet's been drinking [~~drinking~~ scotch on the weekend] $\Rightarrow$
       [~~drinking~~ scotch on the weekend]$_i$ Harriet's been drinking [$_{VP}t_i$]$\Rightarrow$
       [~~drinking~~ scotch on the weekend]$_i$ ~~Harriet's-been-drinking~~ [$_{VP}t_i$]

While no doubt technically feasible, the analysis is ad hoc, in that there is no independent evidence that in general a VP from which the verb has been extracted can undergo topicalization.[12]

(18)   They said that Harriet will drink scotch on the weekends, and
       a.   drink scotch on the weekends she does.
       b.   *scotch on the weekends she drinks.

Next consider the syntax+interface account (6b), which posits a full syntactic structure in which all elements except for the BAE itself are empty. This avoids the problem of deleting nonconstituents, but at the price of admitting syntactic structures full of nothing. We can always rhetorically make a virtue of this (as did, for instance, Jackendoff (1972)), but the fact remains that the empty syntactic structure is there only to avoid positing nonsentential utterance structures like (8). The real work is done by the interface to semantics, which has to provide interpretations for all the empty nodes by looking at the previous sentence. But notice: the interface could do the same thing *without* the empty syntactic structure, since all the semantic content assigned to this structure comes from the preceding clause anyway. Why bother assigning it to specific nodes in an empty syntactic structure—especially when these nodes don't always correspond exactly to those in the antecedent? That is, account (6c), which accounts for the interpretation purely in terms of the interface, can do exactly the same thing without requiring phantom syntactic structure. In fact, since there need not be an exact match between the syntactic structure of the antecedent and the paraphrase of the response anyway, the interface is better off *not* worrying about the exact syntactic structure needed to encode the interpretation of the response.

---

[12] There have been arguments for extraction of V and subsequent topicalization for Stylistic Inversion (Culicover and Rochemont 1990) and for extraction of *be* (Akmajian and Wasow 1975). Whatever the merits of these analyses, they clearly do not extend to the general case we are considering here.

This leaves us with a choice between the two nonsyntactic accounts (6c) and (6d). For the moment we need not decide between them, as both conform to the tenets of Simpler Syntax. Like the syntactic approaches, of course, they have a price in the syntactic component, namely that we allow syntax to condone nonstandard structures like (8). But section 7.2 has shown that this price is not exorbitant, given that English has such structures in any event.

So here is where matters stand so far. BAE indisputably involves semantic/pragmatic conditions regarding the relation of the elliptical utterance to the previous sentence. All accounts must include these. Once these are taken care of—by whatever means—there is one thing left to say: that the *form* of the elliptical utterance is a string of constituents that may be syntactically unconnected. The syntactic account jumps through hoops by deleting the rest of a well-formed sentence (in dubious fashion at that). The syntax+interface account describes the form by means of an empty structure which is dispensible for semantic interpretation, and which of course has no role in phonology either. This syntactic structure is not necessary to mediate between sound and meaning; it is there only to preserve the regularity of syntactic form posited by Structural Uniformity. The two semantic accounts, by contrast, deal with the weird syntactic form of BAE by simply stating it as a bare fact: English just allows us to do these things in addition to normal sentences.

7.4. Reasons to believe syntax is involved in BAE

Structural Uniformity is not the only argument that BAE is derived from an underlying clause. Another argument goes back to Ross's (1969a) attack on a (hypothetical) interpretive account of sluicing. The same argument applies to BAE, as documented in detail by Merchant (2003), citing many other sources. The argument is that the fragment has syntactic features appropriate to its being a part of the antecedent sentence. For instance, in German, bare answers such as those in (19) have case-marking appropriate to the particular verb in the antecedent sentence.

(19) a. A: Wem   folgt   Hans?
              who$_{DAT}$ follows Hans 'Who is Hans following?'
          B: Dem   Lehrer.
              the$_{DAT}$ teacher 'The teacher.'
      b. A: Wen   sucht Hans?
              who$_{ACC}$ seeks Hans? 'Who is Hans looking for?'
          B: Den   Lehrer.
              the$_{ACC}$ teacher 'The teacher.'

Merchant adduces similar examples in Korean, Hebrew, Greek, Russian, and Urdu. A parallel phenomenon in English appears in (20).

(20) a. A: I hear Harriet has been flirting again.
         B: i.   Yeah, with Ozzie.
            ii. *Yeah, Ozzie.
      b. A: John is very proud.
         B: Yeah, of/*in his stamp collection. [*cf.* proud of/*in NP]
      c. A: John has a lot of pride.
         B: Yeah, in/*of his stamp collection. [*cf.* pride in/*of NP]

The verb *flirt* requires the 'flirtee' to be marked by the preposition *with*. Only this requirement can explain the need for the preposition in the fragment. The very close paraphrases (20b,c) push the point home further: they differ only in that *proud* requires its complement to use the preposition *of*, while *pride* idiosyncratically requires *in*. The replies, using BAE, conform to these syntactic requirements, just as if the whole sentence were there.

Merchant also adduces numerous binding effects in BAE, of which some of the simpler are illustrated in (21).

(21) a. A: I hear John$_i$ has become really enamored of someone.
         B: Yeah, himself$_i$/*him$_i$, as you might expect.
      b. A: John$_i$ is only sure of one thing.
         B: Yeah, that he$_i$/*the bastard$_i$ is a genius.
         [*cf.* John$_i$ is sure that he$_i$/*the bastard$_i$ is a genius.]
      c. A: John$_i$ is only sure of one thing.
         B: But he$_i$/the bastard$_i$ is a genius.

(21a) shows that a reflexive is appropriate in BAE just where it would be appropriate in a full sentence. (21b) deals with anaphoric epithets such as *the bastard*, which cannot have an antecedent in an immediately dominating clause. Similarly, they cannot be used within a BAE fragment just in case the BAE fragment would have been in the inappropriate position in a full sentence. (21c) checks this contrast: here B's response is not an instance of BAE, and the epithet can be used.

The conclusion from this and a wide range of similar evidence is that BAE cannot be based purely on a relation to the CS of the antecedent. Yet the previous section has shown that it cannot be based purely on a relation to syntax either, since the interpretation of BAE in the *general* case involves not a literal copy of the antecedent, but rather a pragmatic discourse relation to the antecedent. How are these two conflicting results to be resolved? One response would be to further syntacticize the meaning. But this way lies madness, we

believe: this direction was taken by the late developments in Generative Semantics, incorporating more and more of meaning and pragmatics into an increas-
ingly unwieldy and unprincipled underlying syntactic structure (cf. Newmeyer
1986). The direction urged by the Simpler Syntax Hypothesis is to let CS do as
much work as possible, since it is independently necessary to support inference,
and to admit only as much syntactic influence into BAE as is necessary.

There is evidence even within sentence grammar that this approach is on
the right track. The properties illustrated in (19)–(21) appear also in the foci
of clefts and pseudo-clefts, where they go under the rubric of "connectivity".
These constituents display the morphosyntactic and syntactic properties that
they would have if they appeared in a full syntactic structure in the position
occupied by the constituent that they correspond to. (22) illustrates parallels
to (20)–(21).

(22) a. It's with Ozzie that Harriet has been flirting.
      b. It's himself that John has become really enamored of.
      c. What John$_i$ is sure of is that he$_i$/*the bastard$_i$ is a genius.
      d. It's that he$_i$/*the bastard$_i$ is a genius that John$_i$ is sure of.

Such data led to early analyses (e.g. Hankamer 1974) in which the focus is
extracted to its surface position from an underlying position in the subordinate
clause. However, Higgins (1973) showed that precisely the same relations often
hold even when the first conjunct is a normal relative clause (23), from which
such extractions would be disallowed.

(23) a. The only thing that Robin ate was a bagel.
      b. The only one that John$_i$ has become enamored of is himself$_i$.
      c. The only thing that John$_i$ is sure of is that he$_i$/*the bastard$_i$ is a genius.

(24)

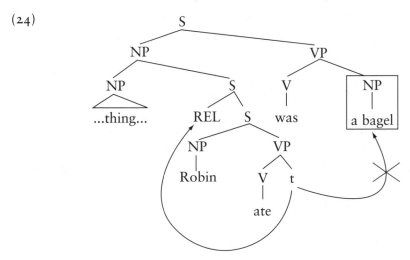

Because the focus in these cases appears to be a constituent of a relative clause, Higgins argued against a transformational account of the pseudo-cleft, where the focus constituent is extracted from the subject.

More recent formulations (e.g. Boškovic 1997, den Dikken et al. 2000) adopt a suggestion by Ross (1967) that the focus is actually a full clause with invisible or deleted material around the focus.[13] For instance, the structure of *What John ate was a banana* would be *What John ate was ~~John ate~~ a banana*. Many technical difficulties with the transformational analysis do not carry over to this approach. However, both approaches share the restriction that the focus must be licensed as part of a full clause. We have already seen many cases where a BAE is permitted but cannot be so embedded. Even in such cases, however, connectivity effects show up. The following examples amplify this point: the elliptical portions of (25) and (26) cannot be reductions of grammatical full sentences.[14]

(25) a. A: Ozzie$_i$ loves Harriet.
          B: But not himself$_i$/*him$_i$. [*But not Ozzie loves himself.]
      b. Ozzie$_i$ doesn't love Harriet, let alone himself$_i$/*him$_i$.
          [* . . . let alone Ozzie loves himself]

(26) A: Let's introduce Ozzie to someone interesting.
      B: a. How about himself$_i$/*him$_i$?
              [?How about let's introduce Ozzie to himself$_i$.]
          b. I was thinking along the lines of himself$_i$/*him$_i$.
              [*I was thinking along the lines of let's introduce Ozzie to himself$_i$.]

---

[13] Boškovic (1997) proposes a variant analysis in which the focus constituent is lowered at LF into the *wh*-clause.

[14] Den Dikken et al. (2000) argue that the syntax of the pseudo-cleft is the same as that of Question/Answer pairs, explained in terms of ellipsis. They argue that a syntactic approach is necessary for some connectivity effects, while there is another type of pseudo-cleft that lacks this syntactic analysis and may require semantic connectivity.

Interestingly, they note that case connectivity is not rigid in German (pp. 72f., their examples (105)–(107)).

(i)   a. was hat er schon immer kaufen wollen?
          what has he PRT   always buy   want
          'what has he always wanted to buy?'
      b. einen   Audi
          a-ACC Audi
      c. *ein   Audi
          a-NOM Audi

(ii) was   er schon immer kaufen wollte, ist ein/einen   Audi
      what he PRT   always buy   wanted is a(NOM)/a(ACC) Audi

(iii) was   er schon immer kaufen wollte, scheint ein   Audi/*einen   Audi zu sein
      what he PRT   always they   wanted seems a(NOM) Audi/*a(ACC) Audi to be

    c. It could be himself$_i$/*him$_i$, maybe.
      [*It could be let's introduce Ozzie to himself; *It could be himself that let's introduce Ozzie to.]

We note next that connectivity is not always strict. To be sure, the morphological form of the verb in an ellipted VP (27a,b) and in a pseudo-clefted VP fragment (27c,d) must be appropriate to the selectional context supplied by the antecedent.

(27)   a. A: What did you do?
        B: Eat/*Ate/*Eating the bagel.
    b. I can eat the hotdog but not eat/*ate/*eating the bagel.
    c. What I did was eat/*ate/*eating the bagel.
    d. What I am doing is eating/*eat/*ate the bagel.

But the choice of complementizer and tense for an ellipted or pseudo-clefted sentential complement (28a,b) is not as restricted as in full sentences (28c).

(28)   a. What did you want?
       i. —To leave.
      ii. —*(For) Robin to leave.
     iii. —That Robin leave.
     iv. —That Robin should leave.
    b. What I want is
       i. to leave.
      ii. *(for) Robin to leave.
     iii. that Robin leave.
     iv. that Robin should leave.
    c. I want
       i. to leave.
      ii. (?for) Robin to leave.
     iii. *that Robin leave.
     iv. *that Robin should leave.

Next we note that if the focus of a cleft or pseudo-cleft were part of a syntactically complete clause, it would be expected to preserve all relations within the embedded clause prior to extraction of the focus. As the following examples show, this prediction is falsified by negative polarity.[15]

---

[15] Some cases seem to show connectivity, e.g.

(i)   What I don't want is for anyone to borrow the lawnmower.

However, we may attribute *anyone* here to the irrealis interpretation of the complement; compare with

(29) a. ?? What Robin didn't buy was a picture of anyone.
         * It was a picture of anyone that Robin didn't buy.
         [*cf*. Robin didn't buy a picture of anyone.]
      b. ?? What no one did was give an inch.
         [*cf*. No one gave an inch.]
      c. ?? What no one believes are any of your stories.
         * It's any of your stories that no one believes.
         [*cf*. No one believes any of your stories.]
      d. ?? What Robin didn't do was anything stupid.
         [*cf*. Robin didn't do anything stupid.]
      e. ?? What Robin didn't think was that anyone called.
         [*cf*. Robin didn't think that anyone called.]

Consider also the contrast between the ordinary pseudo-clefts in (30) and the reversed pseudo-clefts in (31).

(30) a. *What she$_i$ heard on the radio was the recording that Valentina$_i$ had just made.
      b. *What she$_i$ heard on the radio was the report that Valentina$_i$ had just been named dean.

(31) a. The recording that Valentina$_i$ had just made was what she$_i$ heard on the radio.
      b. The report that Valentina$_i$ had just been named dean was what she$_i$ heard on the radio.

If the focus were the remnant of a larger structure, then this larger structure should appear in both forms of pseudo-cleft. For instance, we would have the following underlying forms for (30a) and (31a).

(32) a. *What she$_i$ heard on the radio was [~~she$_i$ heard on the radio~~ the recording that Valentina$_i$ had just made].
      b. *[~~She$_i$ heard on the radio~~ the recording that Valentina$_i$ had just made] was what she$_i$ heard on the radio.

If this were the correct analysis, however, (31) should be ungrammatical along with (30). In response, one might propose that the larger structure is present only in ordinary pseudo-clefts, (30). But there is no principled basis for assuming this difference.

(ii) a. For anyone to have to do that would be unfortunate.
      b. *For anyone to have to do that was unfortunate.
      c. What I don't want is for you to do something/??anything stupid.

In fact, where morphological connectivity effects occur, they occur regardless of the ordering of focus and antecedent. Compare the following with the examples (32a,b).

(33)   a. The one Ozzie$_i$ loves best is himself$_i$/*him$_i$.
       b. Himself$_i$/*He$_i$/*him$_i$ is who/the one that Ozzie$_i$ loves best.

Likewise, selection of complement type appears to be insensitive to the ordering.

(34)   a. That Leslie leaves/*leave right now is what Robin believes.
       a'. What Robin believes is that Leslie leaves/*leave right now.
       b. That Leslie leave/*leaves right now is what Robin demands.
       b'. What Robin demands is that Leslie leave/*leaves right now.

Given that the same connectivity effects hold regardless of the ordering, we would expect that there should be a uniform treatment of normal and reversed pseudo-clefts. From this we conclude that there is no full clausal structure surrounding the focus in clefts and pseudoclefts.

To sum up: There is a conflict between the fact that BAs obey syntactic licensing conditions and the substantial impediments to reconstructing a syntactic structure from the antecedent. When we put together all of the extra mechanisms that would have to be invoked to interpret BAE in terms of the syntactic structure of the antecedent, we find that pragmatics is deeply involved alongside syntactic licensing. (Ginzburg and Cooper (2004) arrive at the same position with respect to their "Clarification Ellipsis".) The same problems of connectivity arise for BAE, pseudo-cleft, answers to questions, and sluicing, among others. Thus there are good reasons to reject the view that there is a completely specified syntactic structure in which the syntactic licensing conditions on the fragment are directly satisfied.

7.5 The generalizations behind indirect licensing

We share with Ross and Merchant the intuition that BAE, sluicing, clefts and pseudo-clefts, and A' constructions such as *wh*-questions and fronted topics are all instances of the same grammatical mechanism at work. The question is what that grammatical mechanism is. The view that the mechanism is movement is largely a historical artifact of the order in which the constructions were approached: A' constructions were the first to be analyzed, then sluicing, which looks like the remnant of a *wh*-question (. . . *but I don't know **what** ~~Harriet's been drinking~~*), then BAE. Each extension was designed to build upon already existing analyses. Thus the machinery of sentence grammar was extended to account for BAE, a discourse phenomenon—in the absence of any independent theory of the syntax of discourse relations.

The difficulty with going in this direction is that, although A′ constructions share certain characteristics such as connectivity with BAE, there are several ways that they are more restricted. (i) A′ constructions are subject to all the well-known extraction constraints, while BAE and sluicing are not. (ii) A′ constructions and sluicing are constructions within a sentence, but BAE can be combined with nonsentential utterance frames, as in *How about pepperoni?* (iii) A′ constructions in English can extract only one constituent to the front, and sluicing (typically) permits only one remnant constituent, but BAE allows multiple fragments (e.g. *scotch, every night*). (iv) Not every language has A′ constructions, especially unbounded A′ constructions, but (according to Merchant at least) every language has BAE and (arguably) sluicing. These restrictions surface over and over again in our discussion above. In addition, we note that BAE can be used with a nonlinguistic context, such as in (35).

(35)   a. An eagle! [pointing]
       b. [Hostess:] Some more wine?
       c. [Hair stylist:] A little shorter?

One might extend this observation and speculate that children at the one-word stage are in effect using BAE, in that their single-word utterances are intended to be interpreted richly, with the context filling in the details.

These considerations suggest an alternative approach to BAE, which reverses its relationship with A′ constructions. Rather than taking A′ constructions to exemplify the basic phenomenon from which the others are derived, we could take BAE as the purest instantiation of the mechanism in question, and as the one that is most robustly supported by UG and pragmatics. A′ constructions would be a case in which further constraints are added to this mechanism, with some variation among languages; sluicing falls somewhere in between. In other words, BAE is not a special form of A′ construction; rather, A′ constructions are a special form of BAE.

The original arguments for A′ constructions involved the correlation of two facts: first, a phrase is in a place where it doesn't belong, as if it has been displaced; second, there is a gap in the position in the sentence where the phrase belongs. So the idea of movement is altogether natural. On the other hand, right alongside topicalization in English is left dislocation, which has a phrase where it doesn't belong, but lacks a corresponding gap in the "normal" position in the sentence (Postal 2004).

(36) a. *Topicalization*
      Green tomatoes, my gorilla used to throw at linguists.
   b. *Left Dislocation*
      Green tomatoes, my gorilla used to throw them at linguists.

The intonations and discourse functions of the two constructions are somewhat different, and most notably, as observed by Ross (1967), left dislocation is not subject to the extraction constraints. Nevertheless, in both sentences *green tomatoes* is in a place where it doesn't rightly belong. Ross proposed that the resumptive pronoun in (36b) is a remnant of copying *green tomatoes* into the dislocated position, leaving behind only its syntactic features; a more contemporary version of movement as copying plus PF deletion might attempt to revive such an approach. (37) shows that such a direction is untenable: instead of a resumptive pronoun there can be a resumptive epithet. As usual, an epithet contributes its own semantics to the sentence; thus it cannot be the remnant of a copy of the phrase at the front.[16]

(37) Professor X, my gorilla used to throw green tomatoes at the bastard/the poor guy.

Thus left dislocation, along with BAE, offers a challenge to the movement metaphor and to the formal machinery based on it.

   The generalization behind all these phenomena can be reconceptualized as follows: In each case there is a phrase whose syntactic position does not signal its semantic role in the propositional tier of the utterance (i.e. the aspect of meaning concerned with who did what to whom, as opposed to the information structure tier, concerned with topic and focus relations). Therefore the semantic role of the phrase has to be determined indirectly.

• In BAE, the bare argument is understood as embedded in a proposition, yet it constitutes the entire syntactic structure of the utterance.

• In clefts and pseudo-clefts, the position of the focus constituent marks its role in the information structure tier of the sentence, but not its role in the propositional tier.

• In sluicing, the sluiced *wh*-phrase is focus of an unstated question, in whose propositional structure the role of the *wh*-phrase is left inexplicit.

---

[16] Unless we are ready to go in the direction of Postal's (1972b) analysis of *the bastard* as derived from underlying *him, who is a bastard*. This of course presents problems of characterizing what predicate NPs license such a reduction and how, along lines discussed with *enough* in Ch. 1.

• *Wh*-movement, topicalization, and left dislocation all have a phrase hanging out on the left periphery of a clause; its role in the propositional structure of the clause is indeterminate.

We will call all of these "indirect licensing constructions" (IL-constructions); we will refer to the phrase that needs to be indirectly licensed as the "orphan".

The constructions differ in how the orphan phrase is integrated into a propositional structure. There are two parts to such integration: (1) identifying a proposition P in which the orphan plays a role; (2) identifying the exact role that the orphan plays in P. We consider these parts in turn.

• In BAE, P is a proposition that is pragmatically related to the antecedent sentence and/or the nonlinguistic context in some appropriate way (as discussed above).

• In clefts, P is identified as the meaning of the clause to which the orphan is connected by *be*.

• In pseudo-clefts, P is the meaning of the clause to which the free relative *wh*-phrase is adjoined. (e.g. *[Bill saw t]* in *What Bill saw was a banana*).

• In sluicing, P is identified as the meaning of some previous clause in the discourse.

• In *wh*-movement, topicalization, and left dislocation, P is identified as the meaning of the clause to which the orphan is left-adjoined.

Having identified the clause in terms of whose propositional structure the orphan is semantically integrated, the orphan's role in that proposition must be determined, via the clause's syntactic structure. There are three possibilities, which crosscut the IL-constructions:

• The orphan can be matched with an existing constituent of the clause. We will call this case "matching". (We underline the match.)
  In BAE: *Harriet's been drinking <u>scotch</u>.—No, bourbon.*
  In sluicing: *I know Harriet's been drinking <u>something</u>, but I don't know what.*
  In left dislocation: *That John, I don't like <u>him</u>.*
• The orphan can function as a supplemental constituent of the clause, either filling in an implicit argument or adding an adjunct. We will call this case "sprouting", following Chung et al. (1995).
  In BAE: *Harriet's been drinking.—Yeah, scotch.*   [implicit argument]
       Harriet's been drinking scotch.—Yeah, every night.   [added adjunct]
  In sluicing: *I know Harriet's been drinking, but I don't know what.*
                                                              [implicit argument]
       I know Harriet's been drinking, but I don't know how often.   [adjunct]

- The orphan can be matched with a trace in the clause.
  In A′ constructions: *Who$_i$ did you see t$_i$?*
  In free relatives (and hence in pseudo-clefts): *[$_{NP}$ what$_i$ [John needs t$_i$]]*
  In clefts: *It was scotch$_i$ that she was drinking t$_i$.*

All of these possibilities result in connectivity phenomena, as observed. Only those that involve matching with traces result in extraction constraints being imposed. Chapter 9 works out our treatment of A′ constructions.[17] We only note here that our use of traces does not imply an endorsement of movement. We will view a trace as rather like the constituent that satisfies a slash category in HPSG, and we will show why this is not simply a notational variant of movement.

7.6 A mechanism for indirect licensing

In order to see how indirect licensing might account for connectivity phenomena, let us return to BAE; the other cases will follow straightforwardly. The interpretation of the BAE utterance is the proposition P, related in some pragmatic way to the antecedent sentence; the orphan is integrated into the interpretation of P by either matching or sprouting. As a result, the orphan acquires all the semantic features and semantic relations that follow from its role in the interpretation. For instance, in our standard example (*Harriet's been*

---

[17] Chung et al. (1995) claim that sluicing also obeys extraction constraints, just in case the orphan plays an added role in the antecedent clause ("sprouting"). Although we agree with their judgments on the examples they adduce as evidence, we suspect there are other pragmatic and perhaps even logical factors involved. Here are examples of sprouted sluicing that seem to us impeccable, yet which violate constraints.

(i)   Bob found a plumber who fixed the sink, but I'm not sure with what.   [*complex NP*]
(ii) That Tony is eating right now is conceivable, but I'm having a hard time imagining what.   [*sentential subject*]
(iii) A: Does eating at a baseball game interest you? B: Depends on what.   [*sentential subject*]
(iv) Tony sent Mo a picture that he says he painted, but I can't imagine what with, given that Tony can't afford brushes.   [*complex NP*]

In addition, examples (14c,f) are cases where BAE involves sprouting and yet violates extraction constraints.
    The one case Chung et al. present that we find convincing involves indirect objects, which can be matched but not sprouted.

(v)   They served someone fish, but I don't know who.   [*matching*]
(vi) *They served fish, but I don't know who.   [*sprouting*]

We (perhaps rashly) believe this to be a garden-path parsing problem. Given the alternative subcategorization *serve NP to NP*, the process that seeks a gap where sprouting can be applied does not find one before *fish* in (vi), and anticipates the sluice-stranding completion *who to*.

drinking again—Yeah, scotch), the orphan *scotch* is understood as patient of drinking.

Thus far the story parallels the "direct interpretation" theory that Ross and Merchant criticize: It does not address the syntactic features of the orphan that depend on the syntax of the antecedent. We propose, therefore, that just as the orphan's semantic role is "indirectly licensed" at a distance by virtue of its connection to the antecedent, so are its syntactic features and relations. The relevant features and relations are basically of three types: inflectional features such as case in the German sentences in (19), preposition choice in examples like (20), and binding relations such as those in (21).

When an orphan is interpreted by matching—either to a full constituent or a trace—the syntactic features and relations can be matched along with the interpretation; hence this case presents no basic problem. The only difficulty arises in the case of interpretation by sprouting, where the syntax of the antecedent contains no pre-existing node from which the orphan can inherit its properties by indirect licensing. There are two cases: when the orphan is a "sprouted" VP adjunct, and when it is a "sprouted" optional argument.

Consider first the case in which the orphan is a "sprouted" VP adjunct (38).

(38)   A: Harriet's been drinking again.
         B: Yeah, every night/with Fred/in her bedroom/for fun.

The choice of preposition (and in case languages, the choice of case) has nothing to do with the verb: as seen in Chapter 5, an adjunct identifies itself by its preposition plus the meaning of its complement. So no syntactic features have to come from the verb.

This leaves the case of a sprouted implicit argument such as B's response in (39). This is the only problematic case.

(39)   A: Harriet has been flirting again.
         B: a.   Yeah, with Ozzie.
            b. *Yeah, Ozzie.

The preposition *with* is necessary because the verb *flirt* requires it. In the standard account, the only way *flirt* can license *with* is by virtue of a local relation, namely that the PP headed by *with* is a sister of the verb. This leads directly to the necessity for a phantom VP headed by *flirt* in the underlying form of B's response; in turn, if there is an underlying VP, there has to be a whole underlying sentence. Section 7.3 showed why such a solution cannot be constructed for the general case.

Towards an alternative, let's think more deeply about the proper way to state that *flirt* requires *with* for its oblique argument. The lexical entry for *flirt* says that it can be used intransitively; its subject is understood as its Agent. This use appears in A's sentence in (39). However, *flirt* has another obligatory semantic argument, the target of flirtation (you can't flirt with no one around). The lexical entry says that if this character is named, it has to appear as the object of *with*; that is, it is an oblique NP argument in the sense of section 5.6. Thus the lexical entry of *flirt* can be sketched as in (40) (as in Chapter 5, italicized parts are contextual features: selectional restrictions in semantics and strict subcategorization in syntax).[18]

(40)

Semantics	Syntax	Phonology
$[\text{FLIRT}_1(X, \{{}^{Y_3}_{\text{INDEF}}\})]$	$V_1([_{PP}P_2NP_3])$	$\text{flirt}_1(\textit{with}_2)$

The semantic structure of (40) allows the second semantic argument of the verb either to be expressed or to be left as an implicit indefinite. If it is expressed, it must be embedded in a *with*-phrase; if it is not expressed, it does not license a PP complement, because there is nothing in semantics to correspond to the index 3 in syntax.

Now we face an interesting technical problem that is worth exploring in some depth. Crucially, the full lexical entry of *flirt*, (40), is not present in A's utterance in (39), *Harriet has been flirting again*. Only the intransitive alternant actually appears in the sentence, and, to be sure, it is licensed by (40). But this alternant, the verb *as it is used in the antecedent*, specifies nothing about the potential syntactic realization of the implicit argument. Hence the structure of the antecedent alone cannot license the presence of *with* in (39a).

So what does license the presence of *with*? We find that it makes most sense to think of the licensing mechanism in processing terms. In the course of processing the antecedent, the lexical entry (40) is necessarily activated in memory. By virtue of this activation, we propose that (40) is also available to license the semantic role of the orphan—including the required syntactic features, in this case the preposition *with*. In other words, even though the relevant frame of *flirt* is not present in the antecedent, indirect licensing can also invoke additional features of the full lexical entry that licenses the antecedent. (Similar considerations will apply to case licensing in languages with case.)

The proposal that a lexical item contributes syntactic features without itself appearing in the structure of a sentence may sound outrageous, as if we are trying to have our cake and eat it too. However, such situations arise under

---

[18] This formulation is probably not quite right for dealing with our treatment of the prepositional passive in section 6.3.3. We leave the proper adjustments an open question.

other circumstances as well, where there is no alternative. Consider the use of a deictic whose syntactic features cannot be attributed to anything that has been uttered (41).[19]

(41) a. Would you hand me those, please?   [gesturing toward scissors]
      b. Those look great on you.   [gesturing toward pants]
      c. *Icelandic*
          Viltu   rétta mér   hana?
          will. you hand me-dat it-fem.acc
                                [pointing toward a book = *bókina* (fem.acc)]
      d. *Russian*
          Vy   mogli   by   mne   dat'   etu?
          you-pl.nom could-2.pl conditional me-dat give-inf that-fem.acc
                                [pointing toward a herring = *seljetku* (fem.acc)]
      e. *Serbo-Croatian*
          Možeš li mi   je   dodati?
          Can   Q me-dat fem.sg.acc hand
                                [pointing toward a book = *knjiga* (fem. acc.)]

Normally the deictic used for an object is *that*. The only possible reason for using *those* in (41a,b) is that *scissors* and *pants* are *syntactically* plural—despite the fact that these words are nowhere in the linguistic context. Similarly, the only reason the deictics in (41c–e) are feminine is that the words for *book* and *herring* happen to be feminine. There is of course the logical possibility that these words *are* present in underlying structure and deleted (perhaps in PF?). But this leads to massive and otiose syntactic ambiguity: does (42a), uttered while pointing to a car, have the underlying form in (42b), (42c), (42d), (42e), or the many other alternatives?

(42) a. Look at that!
      b. Look at that ~~car~~!
      c. Look at that ~~vehicle~~!
      d. Look at that ~~thing~~!
      e. Look at that ~~red VW Jetta coupe~~!

We therefore abandon this course.

---

[19] We are grateful to Joan Maling and Margret Jonsdottir for the Icelandic examples, to Vera Gribanov for the Russian, to Vedrana Mihalicek for the Serbo-Croatian, and to Roser Sauri for the Catalan (below). Icelandic also allows a neuter deictic, and Catalan lacks a gender-marked deictic. This shows that the determination of syntactic features by indirect licensing in this construction is partly language-specific. This is reminiscent of the language-specific differences in coercion noticed in section 6.5.3.

An alternative is to consider the utterance of (41) in a more psycholinguistic context. The production and perception of (41a), for example, involves a concomitant drawing of attention to an object in the environment; the perception of this object in turn primes the lexical entry for the word or words that can be used to denote the object. The lexical entry as usual is a complex of semantic, syntactic, and phonological structures. Thus in the case of (41a), the syntactic feature [*plural*] is ultimately primed by the *non*linguistic context.

The priming of the lexical entry for *scissors* might lead the speaker to utter *Could you hand me the scissors?*. But in this case it does not: the speaker instead settles on uttering a deictic pronoun. This deictic pronoun in turn needs to have its syntactic feature of plurality determined. In the default case this feature is doubly motivated: the semantics of single objects leads to singular syntax, and the lexical entries for most words for objects also link to singular syntax. In this particular situation, though, the plural syntax in the primed lexical entry *scissors* conflicts with the semantics and prevails over it. In other words, the lexical entry for *scissors* indirectly licenses the syntactic plural of *those*, without itself being a constituent of the sentence.[20]

Returning to BAE, then, if nonlinguistic context can determine syntactic features of a deictic via activation of a lexical entry, it is not so implausible that indirect licensing can make use not only of an antecedent S but also of a lexical entry activated by the antecedent sentence.

A slightly different case arises when the syntactic features of the orphan would be determined by a rule rather than a word. Possible instances are shown in (43) (crucial portions in boldface):

(43)   a. Ozzie took a picture.—Yeah, **Harriet's/of Harriet**.
  b. *Icelandic*
   A: Kisa   kom inn.
     kitty-nom-fem.sg came in
    B: Já, **rennblaut**.
     yes dripping.wet-fem.sg.nom
  c. *Serbo-Croatian*
   A: Onda je moj pas   utrcao u sobu.
     then be my dog-masc.sg ran in room.
    B: Da, **mokar**.
     Yes, wet (predicative)-masc.nom

---

[20] The situation is slightly more complex when there are two words for the same object that differ in syntactic features. For instance, syntactically plural *swim trunks* is a hyponym of syntactically singular *swimsuit*. In a situation where either is appropriate, one can say either *That looks good on you* or *Those look good on you*.

If these suggestions regarding priming are taken literally, they predict that there is psychological priming for lexical features of syntactic plurality and grammatical gender, simply on the basis of perception of the object, and that such priming could be detected experimentally.

d. *Catalan*
   A: El   go   va   entrar corrents   a l'habitació.
      the.masc dog past.3sg enter running-ADV to the room
   B: Si, **tot**   **moll.**
      Yes all.masc. wet.masc

In (43a), the orphan phrase *Harriet* is interpreted as being what is pictured. In order for it to have such an interpretation, two rules must be called into play. First, the Argument/Modifier Rule of Chapter 5 says that the semantic arguments of a noun (here, *picture*) should be constituents of the NP that the noun heads. Hence, in order for *Harriet* to be indirectly licensed as an argument of *picture*, it must have syntactic features appropriate for a constituent of NP. Second, the appropriate syntactic features are determined by either of two rules: the rule for possessive case-marking on a prenominal NP or the rule requiring *of* preceding postnominal NP. Indirect licensing imposes one or the other of these syntactic frames on *Harriet*. Similarly, in (43b–d), the interface rule that permits a postverbal AP to be interpreted as a depictive predicate requires the AP to agree in gender and number with its host. Thus if 'wet' is to be so indirectly interpreted, it must carry the relevant syntactic features.

Now notice that none of the rules in question is involved in the licensing of the antecedent sentence. They are invoked only to license the orphan. What makes their use indirect is that they involve a nonlocal connection to the antecedent. Again, such nonlocal connections have to be countenanced in the grammar anyway, in order to give discourse pronouns the right syntactic features. For instance, in order to use *them* to refer back to a use of *scissors* in earlier discourse, a nonlocal connection has to be established. It was a long time ago that we gave up believing that *them* is a reduced form of an underlying *the scissors* (as in Lees and Klima 1963)—and with good reason. We are now suggesting that the syntactic agreement of discourse pronouns is just the simplest case of nonlocal licensing of syntactic features.

We therefore arrive at the position that indirect licensing allows orphan phrases to be assigned syntactic features without licensers in the local context. The licensers may be either (a) in a previous sentence, (b) in a part of the lexicon activated by the previous sentence, (c) in a part of the lexicon activated by the nonlinguistic context, (d) in the rules of grammar that establish a syntactic connection appropriate to the orphan's semantic role in the antecedent.

The discussion in this section has concerned connectivity in assigning inflectional features such as case and grammatical gender and in assigning prepositions required for oblique arguments. This leaves the huge collection of connectivity phenomena associated with binding. There are two possibilities here, both probably operative in different situations. First, binding relations could be determined by syntactic rules applied nonlocally, rather like the depictive predicate in (43b). In the present framework such rules would be the rules of the GF-tier, in particular GF-binding in the sense of section 6.4. Second, to the extent that binding relations are established in semantics (CS-binding—see Chapters 10–11), they follow from the interpretation of the BAE without any nonlocal syntactic influence. We will spend much of Chapters 10–11 arguing that, aside from linear order, a significant portion of the binding conditions involve CS. We regretfully leave a full account of connectivity for future research, noting however that we have offered a framework with the appropriate degrees of freedom for such an account.[21]

It will be useful to have a notation for indirect licensing. We will superscript the fragment construction with *IL* ("indirectly licensed"), the antecedent sentence with *ANT*, and the orphan with *ORPH*. When there is a match for the orphan within *ANT*, we will superscript it with *TARGET*. When there is no match, we will notate the "sprouted" node in parentheses with the superscript *TARGET*. So our standard examples of BAE will be notated as in (44).

(44)   a. *Matching*

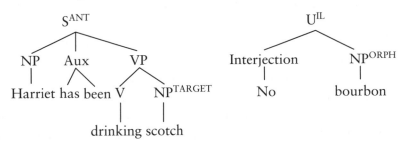

   b. *Sprouting*

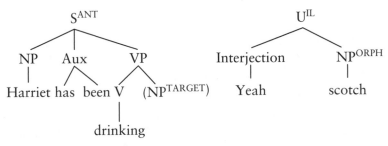

---

[21] The account of Clarification Ellipsis worked out by Ginzburg and Cooper (2004), which appeared as the present manuscript was about to go to press, appears to have many of the right characteristics for implementing indirect licensing more formally, including for example an invocation of the psycholinguistic priming literature to explain why indirectly licensed syntactic features are almost invariably from an immediately preceding sentence.

c. *Sprouting*

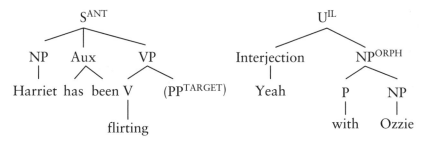

This notation is to be regarded as an abbreviation of all the machinery discussed in this section. It does not generalize immediately to the cases in which the interpretation of the BAE utterance is not directly built on that of the antecedent, as in *Would you like a cookie?—What kind?* Nevertheless, it will serve most of our purposes. In particular, note that the notation for sprouting is not meant to imply that the sprouted structure is actually in the tree for the antecedent.

The BAE construction can then be notated like this, for the case in which there is only a single orphan:

(45) **Bare Argument Ellipsis**
      Syntax: $[_U \text{XP}_i^{\text{ORPH}}]^{\text{IL}}$ Semantics: $[\mathscr{F}(X_i)]$

This says that an utterance consisting of an orphan XP can be interpreted as embedded in a larger indirectly licensed proposition. The superscripts *IL* and *ORPH* are triggers for the general rule of indirect licensing, which matches the IL-marked constituent to an antecedent and the orphan to a target within the antecedent. Having established an antecedent, the function $\mathscr{F}$ in the interpretation is constructed by reference to the antecedent. The examples in (44) then can be taken to show how indirect licensing annotates a pair of syntactic structures so that the first indirectly licenses the second.

In an important sense this notation expresses a generalized form of anaphora. The indirectly licensed constituent is taken as anaphoric to the antecedent, in that its sense is constructed on the basis of that of the antecedent. The orphan represents a piece of the indirectly licensed constituent that *differs* from the antecedent—that is, it is a specific part within the anaphoric constituent that is *non*-anaphoric. Ordinary definite discourse pronouns represent a degenerate case of anaphora in which there is no orphan and therefore no target, as in (46a). For the cases with only a deictic antecedent, we might use a notation like (46b).

(46) a. A: Fred^{ANT} is here.   B: Did you see him^{IL}?
      b. (scissors^{ANT}) Would you hand me those^{IL}?

As suggested in section 7.5, we can regard matching with a trace as a special case of indirect licensing. Here the orphan is a constituent on the left periphery of the clause, and the trace is the antecedent. The sentence as a whole is both the indirect licensee (in that its interpretation needs to be filled out) and the antecedent (in that its interpretation supplies the interpretation of the whole). Thus *wh*-questions can be notated as (47a). Left dislocation is similar but involves a pronoun rather than a trace (47b). Chapter 9 will work these out in more detail.[22]

(47)   a. *Wh-question*

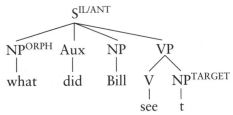

   b. *Left dislocation*

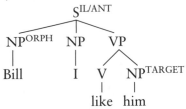

With all this in place, we now move on to other elliptical constructions.

7.7. Sluicing and sluice-stranding

Sluicing is typified by a bare interrogative phrase in a context where an indirect question would be expected.

(48)   a. Harriet is drinking something, but I don't know what.
   b. Harriet is drinking again, but I don't know what.
   c. Harriet is drinking scotch again, but I don't know why.
   d. Harriet is drinking scotch again, but I don't know what kind.

---

[22] Following our Simpler Syntax premises, we have made the top of the tree for *wh*-questions and left dislocation absolutely flat. Should there turn out to be evidence that the orphan is actually adjoined above the S node, we would have no problem replacing (47a) with something like [cpNP^ORPH Aux [s Bill see t]], for instance. Kuno and Takami (1993) argue that left-dislocated topics are adjoined above the S node but topicalized NPs are not.

> e. Harriet drinks scotch that comes from a very special part of Scotland, but I don't know where.
> f. Harriet either drinks scotch or smokes cigars, but I don't remember which.

Given that sluicing looks like a reduction of an indirect question, and given the uniformity assumptions of classical generative grammar, it is no surprise that the earliest account of sluicing, that of Ross (1969a), argued that it is produced by *wh*-movement and deletion of the remaining structure under identity with some antecedent. Oddly enough, though, the literature on sluicing has for the most part overlooked the overall generalizations with BAE (which Ross treated as a different rule, stripping). Even as late as Chung et al.'s (1995) thorough discussion of sluicing, all the examples resemble (48): a declarative conjoined with (or followed by) a clause containing a sluiced indirect question (we might call this configuration "classical sluicing"). They offer no examples in which the fragment is not embedded, and in which it is interpreted by reference to the previous sentence in the discourse: such examples look a lot more like BAE, as seen in (49–50) ((50a,b) repeats (14a,b)).

(49)   A: Harriet is drinking scotch again.
         B: a. What kind?
            b. Why?
            c. How often?

(50)   a. A: Harriet drinks scotch that comes from a very special part of Scotland.
            B: Where?
         b. A: John met a guy who speaks a very unusual language.
            B: Which language?
         c. A: Harriet either drinks scotch or smokes cigars.
            B: But which? I'm dying to know!

Merchant (2003) notices the connection between BAE and sluicing, and takes it to indicate that BAE, like sluicing, is a reduction of a full clause. We will take the opposite tack and treat sluicing as a special case of BAE, one in which the orphan is explicitly marked as a *wh*-question.

A deletion analysis is plausible in the case of examples like (48a): the missing material might be something like *Harriet is drinking t*, where *t* is the trace of the extracted *wh*-phrase and corresponds to *something* in the antecedent. But such an analysis is less plausible for the remaining examples, and quite problematic for those cases where extraction from full clauses is impossible. For instance, in (51a,b) the trace does not correspond to anything in the antecedent—it requires "sprouting"; in (51c,d) the syntactic extraction is impossible; in (51e) the putative underlying form is suspect.

(51)   a.   Harriet is drinking again, but I don't know what ~~Harriet is drinking t~~.
       b.   Harriet is drinking scotch again, but I don't know why ~~Harriet is drinking scotch again t~~.
       c.   Harriet is drinking scotch again, but I don't know what kind ~~Harriet is drinking [t scotch] again~~.
       d.   Harriet drinks scotch that comes from a very special part of Scotland, but I don't know where ~~Harriet drinks scotch [that comes from t]~~.
       e.   *Harriet either drinks scotch or smokes cigars, but I can't remember which ~~of drinks scotch or smokes cigars Harriet does~~.

                              [*or other less plausible possibilities*]

As mentioned earlier, Ross noticed cases like (51c,d) and suggested that they were possible because the offending extraction configuration is deleted. Along similar lines, Merchant (2001) proposes that some constraints are pragmatic rather than syntactic, that other constraints are undone by deletion of the syntactic material at PF, and that a third group of constraints do apply and that the data that suggest that they don't apply have a different interpretation. While many of his points are useful, we argued against this general approach in section 7.3. An approach in terms of indirect licensing is far simpler, in that the *wh*-phrase has no further underlying structure. In particular, it avoids Merchant's ad hoc assumption (echoing Ross's original proposal) that PF deletion can save island violations.

However, there is evidence that there is slightly more syntactic structure in embedded sluices than in BAE, namely a clausal node that dominates the fragment. The simplest piece of evidence is that sluiced phrases appear in positions normally occupied by clauses. The following examples come from Levin 1982. (52) shows that sluiced *wh*-phrases show up where CPs (but not NPs) go; and, like embedded questions in general, sluiced phrases govern singular agreement. The German examples in (53) show that the sluiced *wer* appears in postverbal position, which is a position for CP but not for NP.

(52)   We were supposed to do some problems for tomorrow,
       a.   *Sluicing*
            i.   . . . but which problems isn't (*aren't) clear.
            ii. . . . but it isn't clear which problems.
       b.   *Full indirect question*
            i.   . . . but which problems we were supposed to do isn't clear.
            ii. . . . but it isn't clear which problems we were supposed to do.

c. *NP argument*
  i. ... but the answers aren't clear.
  ii. * ... but it isn't clear the answers.

(53) *German*

Jemand   hat die Äpfel   gestohlen,
someone has the apples stolen

a. *Sluicing*
  i. ... und ich habe ihm   gesagt wer.
      and I   have to-him said   who
  ii. * ... und ich habe ihm   wer   gesagt.
      and I   have to-him who said

b. *Full indirect question*
  i. ... und ich habe ihm   gesagt wer kommt.
      and I   have to-him said   who comes
  ii. * ... und ich habe ihm wer kommt gesagt.

c. *NP argument*

Franz hat eine Frage   gestellt,
Franz has a   question asked

  i. ... und ich habe ihm   die Antwort gesagt.
      and I   have to-him the answer   said
  ii. * ... und ich habe ihm gesagt die Antwort.

In (54) (not to our knowledge mentioned before in the literature), the sluiced phrase *what*, like the clause *what he was doing* and unlike the NP *the answer*, can occur only after a particle and not before it.

(54) a. *Sluicing*
  i. He was doing something illegal, but I never found out what.
  ii. * ... but I never found what out.

b. *Full indirect question*
  i. I found out what he was doing.
  ii. *I found what he was doing out.

c. *NP argument*
  i. I found out the answer.
  ii. I found the answer out.

Example (55) shows that a sluiced phrase, like an indirect question, cannot appear in the subject position of a *for-to* complement, but can occur in extraposed position; an NP has just the reverse distribution.

(55) He will say something while he is lecturing,

a. *Sluicing*
  i.   but I expect very much for it to be unclear what.
  ii. *but I expect very much for what to be unclear.
b. *Full indirect question*
  i.   but I expect very much for it to be unclear what it's about.
  ii. *but I expect very much for what it's about to be unclear.[23]
c. *NP argument*
  i.   *but I expect very much it to be unclear his meaning.
  ii. but I expect very much for his meaning to be unclear.

We observe also that classical sluicing appears only in indirect question contexts, not for instance in relative clauses (an observation made by Kim (1997)).

(56)   *Pat knows a man who speaks Spanish and Terry knows a woman who ~~speaks Spanish~~.

Kim suggests that there is no sluicing in relative clauses because there is no focus and hence no focus movement in relative clauses. On this view, what is sluiced must undergo both *wh*-movement and focus movement. We suggest instead that sluicing is a construction whose utterance meaning is that of a *wh*-question. It therefore can be used only in contexts where an indirect question can be semantically licensed.

The structure that we propose for sluicing, then, is as shown in (57). The semantics contains a question operator Qx, which binds the semantics of the *wh*-word. This makes the meaning that of a *wh*-question. The function $\mathscr{F}$ is the propositional content of the question, to be filled in by indirect licensing. The syntactic category is S rather than U, in order to account for the distribution of sluicing shown above. (See section 9.2 for more detail of the treatment of questions and for sluices with pied-piping such as *to whom*.)

(57)   **Sluicing**
       Syntax: $[_S \; wh\text{-phrase}_i{}^{\text{ORPH}}]^{\text{IL}}$ Semantics: $Qx[\mathscr{F}(x_i)]$

Next we turn to sluice-stranding, discussed briefly in section 1.5.2. This construction, in which a stranded preposition follows the sluiced *wh*-phrase, appears both in classical sluicing contexts (58a) and in response to a previous sentence (58b). The fragment can correspond to an adjunct in the antecedent (58a) or to an implicit argument with a governed preposition (58b).

---

[23] This example has been carefully chosen to prevent the subordinate clause from being interpreted as a free relative, which is acceptable in this context.

(58)   a. Ozzie's been drinking again, but I'm not sure who with.
       b. A: Harriet's been flirting again.
          B: Who with?

Section 1.5.2 noted that, like ordinary sluicing, sluice-stranding occurs in contexts where extraction would violate the usual constraints.

(59)   a.   I saw a fabulous ad for a Civil War book, but I can't remember who by.
       b.   * ... but I can't remember by whom I saw a fabulous ad for a Civil War book.
       c.   * ... but I can't remember who I saw a fabulous ad for a Civil War book by.

We also noted that the acceptable combinations of *wh*-phrase and preposition are severely limited, and to some degree idiosyncratic for each *wh*-word. The list in (60a) is (as far as we know) exhaustive.

(60)   a. *Good*
           who of, who with, who to, who from, (?)who at, who for, who by;
           what of, what with, what to, what from, what at, what for, what on,
               what in, what about;
           where to, where from;
           how much for
       b. *Bad*
           who on, who in, who next to, who about, who beside, who before, ... ;
           what before, what into, what near, what beside, what by, ... ;
           where near;
           how much by, how much with;
           how many for, how many by, ... ;
           when before;
           which (book) of/with/to/from/next to/beside/ ... ;
           what book of/with/to/from/next to/beside/ ...

This pattern is reminiscent of semiproductive morphology. The class of acceptable *wh*-phrases is limited; some prepositions such as *to* and *from* occur with several of them, but for instance *by* sounds good only with *who*. The only case in which the *wh*-phrase is not a single word is *how much*, which occurs only with *for*; the parallel *how many* does not indulge in sluice-stranding at all. This pattern suggests that the acceptable cases of sluice-stranding, like irregular past tenses, are learned one by one, to some extent with the help of family resemblance to other cases. There is therefore not a general rule for sluice-stranding, but rather a collection of related idiomatic lexical entries. Such a solution of course precludes deriving sluice-stranding from full sentences by general processes of *wh*-movement and deletion, as is assumed in much of the literature (see section 1.5.2 for references).

A typical sluice-stranding fragment might be stated as (61). Note that it is essentially a variant of the more general rule (57) for sluicing.

(61) **Sluice-stranding** (one case)
      Phon: who$_i$ with$_j$ Syntax: $[_S wh\text{-word}_i \ [_{PP} P_j \ t_i]^{ORPH}]^{IL}$
                              CS: $Qx[\mathscr{F}([G_j([x; PERSON]_i)])]$

Let's decode this. The two words in the phonology correspond to the *wh*-word and the preposition in the syntax. The *wh*-word *who* corresponds also to the semantic variable [*x;PERSON*] that is bound by the Q operator. The differences from ordinary sluicing are in the syntactic and semantic treatment of the preposition.

First consider the syntax. We have adopted the conservative view that the preposition heads a PP that contains a trace bound to the *wh*-word— that is, that the *wh*-word is understood as the syntactic object of the preposition. However, since we are assuming that traces are not the product of movement (see section 9.2), the *wh*-word has in no sense moved from an underlying position as prepositional object. Because there is no underlying clause containing a trace bound to the PP, we do not have to explain why sluice-stranding does not observe extraction constraints. Moreover, since the *wh*-word is connected just to a trace inside the PP, extraction constraints do not apply here either.

Next consider the semantics. As in ordinary sluicing, the function $\mathscr{F}$ is the propositional content that comes from the antecedent sentence via indirect licensing. The function *G* is the meaning of the preposition; its argument is the meaning of the *wh*-word. The use of the function *G* encompasses two cases. In one case, the preposition is meaningful, for instance when it marks the fragment as an accompaniment expression in (58a). In the other case, as in (58b), the preposition is functional; because it does not alternate with other prepositions in this context, it carries no meaning independent of the verb. In this case *G* is the identity function.

Finally, turn back to the syntax. In normal sluicing (57), the *wh*-phrase is marked as the orphan. Here, however, the PP is marked as the orphan. The effect is that the PP rather than the *wh*-word has to fit into the interpretation of the antecedent, through either matching with a target or sprouting. This is in accord with the facts. In short, (61) is the prototype form for all the sluice-stranding idioms listed in (60a).

7.8 Gapping

7.8.1 Reasons why gapping cannot be syntactic deletion

In gapping, everything in a second conjunct is absent except for (usually) two constituents with contrastive focus intonation (Ross 1970; Jackendoff 1971; Stillings 1975; Kuno 1976; Pesetsky 1982).

(62)   a. **Robin** speaks **French**, and **Leslie**, **German**.
       b. **Robin** speaks **French** to Bill on Sundays, and **Leslie**, **German**.
       c. **Robin** wants to speak **French**, and **Leslie**, **German**.
       d. **Robin** wants to wake up in the morning and be able to speak **French**, and **Leslie**, **German**.
       e. **Robin** believes that everyone pays attention to you when you speak **French**, and **Leslie**, **German**.
       f. On **Sundays, Robin** speaks French to Bill, and on **Mondays, Leslie**.

(63)   a. **Robin** thinks that the New York **Times** will endorse George W. Bush, and **Leslie**, the Washington **Post**.
       b. **Robin** thinks that **Ferrari** are cool, and **Leslie**, **Maseratis**.
       c. On **Wednesday** Robin will leave the telephone in the **kitchen**, and on **Thursday**, in the **living** room.
       d. **Robin** is reading a book written by **John Updike**, and **Leslie**, **Ann Tyler**.
       e. **Robin** knows a lot of reasons why **dogs** are good pets, and **Leslie**, **cats**.

It is marginally possible to have three focus constituents, but as the number of foci goes up, the acceptability goes down.

(64)   a. Robin speaks French on Tuesdays, and Leslie, German on Thursdays.
       b. *With Yves, Robin speaks French on Tuesdays, and with Horst, Leslie, German on Thursdays.

We assume that the difficulty is due to processing the various constituents in the absence of an overt verb, and is not a deep syntactic fact.[24]

   It is sometimes believed that gapping only leaves behind clause-mates surrounding the verb, for instance the subject–object pairs in (62a,b). But (62f) shows that a topic and subject can serve as remnants of gapping; and examples

---

[24] See Stillings (1975) for many more examples exploring the effect of multiple foci on the acceptability of gapping.

such as (62c,d,e) and (63) suggest that more complex cases are simply more difficult to process but not fundamentally different in grammatical terms. (Such examples were known at least as early as Jackendoff 1971; see Sag et al. 1985 for discussion.)

Like BAE, gapping was originally approached within the framework of a classical transformational model that obeyed Structural and Interface Uniformity, so it was natural to think of it as derived from an underlying sentence. However, the construction has always been regarded as problematic, because it appears to be able to delete a non-constituent—and a discontinuous non-constituent at that (e.g. *speaks... to Bill on Sundays* in (61b) and *thinks that... are cool* in (63b). This in turn provides motivation for a movement analysis that consolidates the deleted material into a single constituent (albeit one containing traces). Consider, for example, (62e). Suppose that we topicalize *Robin* and *French* in the first conjunct, and *Leslie* and *German* in the second conjunct.

(65)   **Robin**$_i$ **French**$_j$ t_i believes that everyone pays attention to you when you speak t_j, and **Leslie**$_k$, **German**$_m$ t_k believes that everyone pays attention to you when you speak t_m.

The topicalizations produce identical structures in the two conjuncts, and we can delete the one in the right conjunct.

(66)   **Robin**$_i$ **French**$_j$ t_i believes that everyone pays attention to you when you speak t_j, and **Leslie**$_k$, **German**$_m$ t_k ~~believes that everyone pays attention to you when you speak~~ t_m.

In order to get the actual order of words in the left conjunct, we can subsequently move the clause containing the traces to the left of *French*—an Iterated Raising-style derivation—or perhaps more plausibly, we can assume that the movements shown in the left conjunct in (65) are "covert" but sufficient to license the deletion in the right conjunct (see Lasnik 1999a).

The obvious problem with such an approach, aside from its excessively stipulative nature, is that the movements in the right conjunct violate the usual extraction constraints as well as landing site constraints. In (62d), the lower NP *German* should move over the higher NP *Leslie*, if it moves at all. Moreover, as is well known, extraction from a subordinate adverbial is ill-formed in English.

(67)   *German, Leslie believes that everyone pays attention to you when you speak t.

Similar complexities arise in the case of examples such as (63). For instance, (63e) would require the following derivation.

(68) **Robin** knows a lot of reasons why **dogs** are good pets, and **Leslie**$_k$, **cats**$_j$, ~~t$_k$ knows a lot of reasons why t$_j$ are good pets~~.

Extraction of the subject of the embedded question to get *why t$_i$ are good pets* is clearly impossible in English. Again, one can of course stipulate that such impossible movements are allowed only if they are subsequently eliminated by deletion (perhaps along the lines of Merchant 2001), or that they occur only at LF. But such a move is less preferred as an explanation of these examples if there is a suitable interpretive procedure that captures the facts directly.

Further evidence against a movement approach comes from a construction within conjoined NPs that is very much like gapping (Jackendoff 1971).

(69) a. **Mike's** picture of **Bill** and **Sue's** of **Eva** resemble each other.
b. I enjoyed reading both **Kissinger's** criticism of **Hitchens** in the New York Times and **Hitchens'** of **Kissinger**.
c. **Yesterday's** story in the paper about **Bush** denouncing the press and **today's** about **Cheney** are equally intriguing.
d. Mike told **two** funny stories about **Harriet** and no less than **five** about **Ozzie** at the bar last night.

Again we see discontinuous nonconstituents missing from the second conjunct. A movement analysis along the lines of (65)–(66) has absolutely no independent motivation, since topicalization in NPs, like all A′-movement constructions, is totally unattested in English. To invoke some sort of covert topicalization to a phantom position in NP is patently nothing but a move to make the facts come out as one wants.

7.8.2 *Gapping as double BAE*

We propose to treat gapping as another special form of BAE, this time with two (or marginally more) concatenated orphan constituents. To see the relation between gapping and BAE, consider (70a.B:i), where a gapping-like construction appears in both conjuncts of the response to a multiple *wh*-question. (An unconjoined gapping-like construction is impossible in this context— (70a.B:ii).) The same structure appears in a nonsentential utterance frame mentioned in section 7.2, which is used to report scores of games (70b).

(70)   a.   A: Who plays what instrument?
    B: i.   Katie the kazoo, and Robin the rebec.
      ii. *Katie the kazoo.
   b.   The Red Sox six, the Yankees nothing.

Moreover, a gapping-like construction can appear on its own in a response, in place of a BAE construction (71a,b), as long as it is preceded by a conjunction. It can be conjoined with a BAE construction (71c), and can even appear on its own (71d).

(71)   a.   A: Are you going to visit Robin?
    B: Yeah, *(and) tomorrow night, Leslie.
   b.   A: I told you John's been drinking beer, didn't I?
    B: Yeah, *(but) not Sam, scotch.
   c.   A: Does Robin drink? B: Yeah, scotch, and Leslie, gin.
   d.   A: Does Robin speak French? B: No, Leslie, German.

Thus there is a more or less smooth transition between classical gapping like (62) and looser uses that are closer to BAE.

As has been noticed many times, the interpretation of gapping crucially involves paired contrastive foci. In fact, its intonation exactly parallels that of full clauses with paired contrastive foci, as indicated by the boldface type in (62)–(63). In particular, everything in the antecedent that follows the second focus has to be destressed (for instance *will endorse George W. Bush* in (63a) and *in the New York Times* in (69b). For a first approximation, then, we might formulate the gapping construction as in (72).

(72)   **Gapping**
  Syntax: $[\text{XP}_i{}^{\text{ORPH1}}\ \text{YP}_j{}^{\text{ORPH2}}]^{\text{IL}}$ CS: $[\mathscr{F}(\begin{bmatrix} X_i \\ \text{C-FOCUS} \end{bmatrix}, \begin{bmatrix} Y_j \\ \text{C-FOCUS} \end{bmatrix})]$

Again some decoding is in order. The syntax is a constituent consisting of two phrases, XP and YP, each of which is an orphan. These are connected to two constituents in semantics that are each marked as a contrastive focus. The function $\mathscr{F}$ in the semantics, of which these two constituents are arguments, is the part of the interpretation that is shared between the gapped clause and its antecedent. Since the two orphans are contrastive foci, they must contrast with matched foci in the antecedent. Thus, as in standard approaches to the semantics of gapping, $\mathscr{F}$ amounts to the presupposition of the antecedent, constructed by substituting variables for the two foci in the CS of the antecedent.

We leave open the question of the syntactic category of the fragment sequence. One attractive possibility is that it has no category at all, but is simply nondistinct in category from what it is conjoined with. Thus gapping could be conjoined with NP as well as S as in (69), and it could also appear in free-standing utterances such as (70a.B.i) and (71). Another possibility appears in section 7.8.3.

To work out an example, let us look at the simplest sort of case, (62a).

(73) **Syntax**

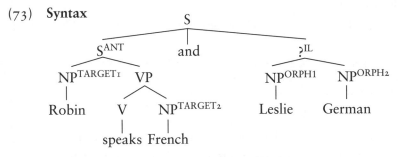

CS (before interpretation of $\mathcal{F}$ is filled in):

$$[[\text{SPEAK} \left(\begin{bmatrix} \text{ROBIN} \\ \text{C-FOCUS} \end{bmatrix}, \begin{bmatrix} \text{FRENCH} \\ \text{C-FOCUS} \end{bmatrix} \right)] \text{AND} [\mathcal{F} \left(\begin{bmatrix} \text{LESLIE} \\ \text{C-FOCUS} \end{bmatrix}, \begin{bmatrix} \text{GERMAN} \\ \text{C-FOCUS} \end{bmatrix} \right)]]$$

After matching the contrastive foci, the function F can be worked out by replacing the foci in the first clause by variables: [*SPEAK* (X, Y)]. Then the foci of the second clause are substituted, yielding the correct interpretation [*SPEAK* (*LESLIE, GERMAN*)] for the second clause.

Gapping typically applies in coordinate constructions, i.e. in coordination and paired discourse, as seen in all the examples above. We attribute this to the fact that gapping requires two matching contrastive foci in order for the interpretation to go through. The coordinate structures provide parallel semantic structure that satisfies this requirement. However, syntactic coordination is not sufficient for gapping, since in some cases syntactic coordination is not interpreted as semantic coordination (see Chapter 13).

(74) a. Robin saw Leslie and then/subsequently, Leslie, Robin.
b. *Robin saw Leslie and so/thus/consequently/therefore, Leslie, Robin.

In (74a), where the clauses refer to parallel and temporally connected events, gapping is possible. But in (74b) the events are causally linked, and in this case, gapping is not possible.

Gapping is of course not possible in most non-coordinating contexts (75). However, there is a range of connectives such as *as well as*, *but not*, *not to mention*, and *not . . . let alone* that are not conjunctions but still convey semantic parallelism. These permit gapping (76).

(75) a. *Robin speaks French, although/even though/despite the fact that
          Leslie, German.
      b. *Robin cooked lunch before Leslie, breakfast.
      c. *Robin's speaking French doesn't prevent Leslie's, German.
      d. *The teacher to whom Robin spoke French stared at the student to
          whom Leslie, German.

(76) a. Robin speaks French, as well as/but not/not to mention Leslie, Ger-
          man.
      b. Robin doesn't speak French, let alone Leslie, German.

Gapping is also possible in comparatives, which convey semantic parallelism.

(77) a. Robin speaks French better than Leslie, German.
      b. ?Robin thinks that it is harder to speak French than Leslie, German.
      c. ?Robin thinks that it is more fun to speak French than Leslie, German.
      d. Robin tried harder to learn French than Leslie, German.
      e. Robin no more speaks French than Leslie, German.

Plausibly, the comparative provides sufficient parallelism of conceptual structure to allow for the interpretation of the fragments.

7.8.3 The gapped fragment is not an S

We consider now two pieces of evidence that gapping involves not coordinate
Ss, but rather a sentence coordinated with a sequence of fragments. The first
type of evidence concerns asymmetric extractions.

(78) a. John can't eat steak and Mary just spam—it's not fair.
      b. Can John race cars and Mary, boats?

In these examples the modal *can't/can* takes scope over the composite actions
'John eat steak and Mary eat spam' and 'John race cars and Mary race boats'.
They do not have the interpretation in which there is a modal in each conjunct,
as in (79).

(79) a. John can't eat steak and Mary can't eat spam.
      b. Can John race cars and can Mary race boats?

It is possible for one of the fragments to be a VP:

(80) a. John can't eat steak and Mary, eat spam.
      b. Can John race cars, and Mary, cook lasagna?

Again, the modal takes scope over the entire conjoined structure. Similar examples involving negation are pointed out by Oehrle (1987).

(81) a. Kim didn't play bingo or Sandy sit at home all evening.
      b. Kim didn't play bingo and Sandy sit at home all evening.
         [*logically*: not (Kim play bingo and Sandy sit at home all evening)]

On our analysis, there is a single modal or negation that takes scope over the entire S, which includes both the antecedent and the fragment sequence as coordinate.

    Yet another such case is pointed out by McCawley (1993):

(82) a. Not every girl$_i$ ate a **green** banana and her$_i$ mother, a **ripe** one.
      b. Too many Irish setters are named Kelly and German shepherds, Fritz.
      c. Few cats eat Frolic or dogs Whiskas.

The theoretical strangeness of these cases arises from the fact that the quantifier in the left conjunct appears to take scope over the right conjunct. (82b,c) are particularly strange, because here the quantifier is a determiner of the subject of the first conjunct and appears to have been gapped from the subject of the second conjunct.

    Johnson (2000) offers an account of these cases in which there is across-the-board extraction of the material that is gapped in the right conjunct. Moreover, the subject of the left conjunct is asymmetrically extracted from it. Johnson assumes that the underlying coordinate constituents are VPs with internal subjects. A typical derivation is given in (83).

(83) [not every girl]$_i$ [Agr ate$_V$ Tense [$_{VP}$[$_{VP}$ t$_i$ t$_V$[a green banana]]
                              and [$_{VP}$ [her$_i$ mother] t$_V$ [a ripe one]]]

Johnson extends this analysis to cases like (82b,c) by assuming that the quantifier is similar to an adverb that takes scope over the conjoined VP.

(84) [few Tense [$_{VP}$[$_{VP}$ cats$_i$ eat$_j$ Frolic] or [$_{VP}$ dogs eat$_j$Whiskas]]] ⇒
      [[few cats$_i$] eat$_j$ Tense [$_{VP}$[$_{VP}$ t$_i$ t$_j$ Frolic] or [$_{VP}$ dogs t$_j$ Whiskas]]]

However, according to this proposal, *cats* has escaped the conjunction without being an across-the-board movement, in violation of the Coordinate Structure Constraint.

    We suggest instead that the gapped constituent is not in fact a clause, but a set of fragments adjoined to the first clause. The adjoined fragments together form a constituent of the main clause. Since there is only one clause, operators that take clausal scope take scope over the adjoined fragments as well.[25] What is special about these cases is that the interpretation of the adjoined fragments is that of a clause, which follows from indirect licensing, and that the quantifier in the subject of the main clause, which takes clausal scope, binds the gapped "subject". Whether this last property can be derived without stipulation depends on an independent account of the interpretation of bare NPs in the scope of a quantifier.[26] As (85a,b) show, this scoping occurs even when there is a single fragment adjoined to the main clause.

(85)   a. Few cats eat Whiskas, as well as dogs.
       b. Many cats eat Whiskas, but not dogs.

Suffice it to say that at worst, the interpretive account must make certain stipulations that mirror some of those in Johnson's syntactic account. We therefore see no reason to prefer the syntactic account over an interpretive one.

The second piece of evidence that the gapped constituent is not a clause involves *as well as XP*, which Huddleston and Pullum (2002) argue is an adjunct. It is similar to *and not* and *but not*: all three can be followed by NP, tenseless VP, CP, AP and PP (86), but not by tensed VP or IP (87).

(86)   a. Harriet drinks scotch, as well as/and not/but not gin.   [NP]
       b. Harriet will run the marathon, as well as/and not/but not train for the decathlon.   [VP]
       c. Ozzie thinks that Harriet is beautiful, as well as/and not/but not that she is without fault.   [CP]
       d. Harriet was angry, as well as/and not/but not shocked.   [AP]
       e. Ozzie has a house in Smallville, as well as/and not/but not in Palm Springs.   [PP]

(87)   a. *Harriet drinks scotch as well as/and not/but not eats key lime pie.   [tensed VP]

---

[25] However, see section 13.6 for a related construction in which such a solution is less attractive.

[26] Ackema and Szendrői (2002) argue, following Lin (1999), that ellipsis of determiners is possible without gapping, as illustrated in (i).

(i)   a. The boys drank whiskey and girls drank wine.
      b. Every boy drinks whiskey and girl drinks wine.

Johnson (2000: 105) claims that such sentences are not grammatical, citing cases such as the following (the judgments are his).

(ii) a. *Too many Irish setters are named Kelly and German shepherds are named Fritz.
      b. *Few cats eat Frolic and dogs eat Whiskas.

We tend to agree with Johnson in this regard.

b. *Ozzie said Harriet is beautiful as well as/and not/but not Ricky was
handsome.   [IP]

The fact that these connectives can be followed by a gapped phrase, as seen
above in (76a), suggests that the gapped phrase cannot be an IP. Hence it must
be a sequence of fragments.[27]

One might take another tack on these last cases of gapping. The fact *as well
as*, *and not*, and *but not* can be used with single phrasal fragments might
conceivably be taken as evidence that what follows them is a single constituent,
e.g. either IP or a VP with an internal subject. But the behavior of *and not/but
not* suggests that this would be the wrong conclusion. Suppose that *Leslie
German* is taken to be an IP in (88).

(88)   Robin speaks French and not Leslie, German.

We then have to assume that *not* originates in a position external or left-
adjoined to IP. But the evidence from *and/but not XP* suggests that the only
category to which *not* does not adjoin is IP. The analysis could be maintained
only by stipulating that *not* moves down into the IP. Such a stipulation is ad hoc,
and unprincipled in that it involves a lowering.

Alternatively, suppose that *Leslie German* is a VP with an internal subject.
This requires that the negative is external to the right-conjoined VP, as in (89).

(89)

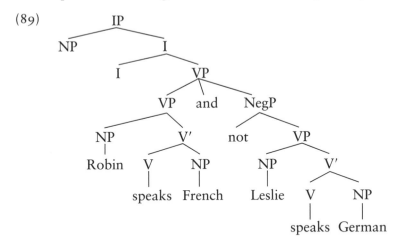

---

[27] This conclusion entails that in cases where what is in the right conjunct appears to be an
infinitival clause, it is actually a gapped sequence of fragments. This accords with the raising (or
raised) to object analysis, not the No Raising to Object of MGG (see section 2.2.4).

(i)   a. John expects Mary to leave but not Sam to stay.
      b. John expects Mary to leave as well as Sam to stay.

Notice that in this structure only *Robin* would move to a subject position, raising questions about how *Leslie* is licensed in situ. The latter position is a nominative case position, as examples like (90) demonstrate.

(90)   Susan loves John and/but not he, Susan/her.

Moreover, the conjoined structure in (89) is not parallel in category, which raises another set of challenging (although by no means technically unresolvable) problems.

So we conclude that gapped constructions are neither VP nor IP; rather they are paired fragments under a constituent of indeterminate category. We also conclude that the overall constraint on the distribution of gapped constituents is not syntactic, that is, gapping cannot be defined in terms of syntactic coordination.

CHAPTER 8

VP Ellipsis and its Relatives

8.1 *Do X* anaphora, *it happen* anaphora, VP ellipsis, pseudo-gapping, and *one*-anaphora

We now turn to a second major class of fragment constructions, those that stand in freely for canonical VPs. These played a major role in the argumentation concerning flat structure in Chapter 4. Within this class there are two major types, VP ellipsis (1a) and *do X* anaphora (1b); *X happen* anaphora (1c) is a variant of the latter. Pseudo-gapping (1d) is still another type. Within NPs, *one*-anaphora (1e) has characteristics parallel to *do X* anaphora.

(1) a. *VP ellipsis*
         Robin ate a bagel for breakfast, and Leslie did too.
     b. *Do X anaphora*
         Robin ate a bagel (on Thursday), and Leslie did so/that/the same thing/
         something similar/... (on Friday).
     c. *X happen anaphora*
         Robin got an A on the test on Thursday, and then it/that/the same thing/
         something similar/... happened (again) on Friday.
     d. *Pseudo-gapping*
         If you don't believe me, you will the weatherman.
     e. *One-anaphora*
         Leslie read a long book about Lincoln, and Steve read a short one about
         Stalin.

As already noted, the literature on ellipsis is vast, and we cannot attempt a comprehensive survey here. A useful summary is found in Kehler (2000), who with many others distinguishes between syntactic accounts that reconstruct the syntax of the missing VP in terms of the syntax of the antecedent, and semantic accounts that reconstruct the interpretation of the antecedent into the interpretation of the missing VP (see also notes 2 and 3 to Chapter 7). The literature shows that for most cases, either a syntactic account of ellipsis or a semantic account will suffice. There are a few arguments that the syntactic account is necessary, and section 8.2 will focus on defusing those.

8.1.1 *The facts*

First a review of the facts, many of which already appeared in section 4.4. *Do X* anaphora, of which we take *do so* as representative, requires its antecedent to be an action (2). *X happen* anaphora may denote any event, not just an action (3). And VP ellipsis is unrestricted (4). (We use negative examples in order to distinguish the *do* of *do so* ellipsis from *do*-support in VP ellipsis.)

(2) *Do so anaphora*
    a.   *Robin dislikes Ozzie, but Leslie doesn't do so.   [Stative]
    b. ?*Robin fell out the window, but Leslie didn't do so.
                                                   [Non-action event]
    c.   Robin read the newspaper today, but Leslie didn't do so. [Action]
(3) *X happen anaphora*
    a. *Robin dislikes Ozzie, but it doesn't happen with Leslie.   [Stative]
    b. Robin fell out the window, but that didn't happen with/to Leslie.
                                                   [Non-action event]
    c. Robin read the newspaper today, but that didn't happen yesterday.   [Action]
(4) *VP ellipsis*
    a. Robin dislikes Ozzie, but Leslie doesn't.   [Stative]
    b. Robin fell out the window, but Leslie didn't.   [Non-action event]
    c. Robin read the newspaper today, but Leslie didn't.   [Action]

In all three constructions, the elliptical clause may include one or more orphan constituents. Consider first orphans with *do so*, shown in (5)–(7). Chapter 4 showed that although the orphan usually is matched with a target at the end of the antecedent, it can also correspond to a target somewhere in the middle of the antecedent (7). Such cases are rendered more acceptable by focal or contrastive stress on both the target and the orphan.

(5) a. Robin smokes a pipe after dinner, and Leslie does so during breakfast.   [*do so* = smokes a pipe]
    b. Robin flipped the hamburgers with a spatula, and Leslie did so with a chef's knife.   [*do so* = flip the hamburgers]

(6)   Mary will cook the potatoes for fifteen minutes in the morning, and Susan
      a. will do so for twenty minutes in the evening.

                                        [*do so* = cook the potatoes]
      b. will do so in the evening.   [*do so* = cook the potatoes for 15 minutes]

(7)   a. Robin slept for **twelve** hours in the bunkbed, and Leslie did so for **eight**
         hours.   [*do so* = sleep . . . in the bunkbed]
      b. Robin cooked Peking duck on **Thursday** in order to impress Ozzie,
         and Leslie did so on **Friday**.
                        [*do so* = cook Peking duck . . . in order to impress Ozzie]

The orphan associated with *do so* may be an adjunct, as in all the above
examples and (8a), but it may not be an argument.

(8)   a.   Robin read a book on the train, while Leslie was doing so on the
           bus.   [*on the bus* = adjunct]
      b. *Robin put a book on the couch, while Leslie was doing so on the
           table.   [*on the table* = argument]
      c. *Robin ate a hot dog, while Leslie did so a pickle.
      d. *Robin said that syntax is wonderful, and Leslie did so that phonetics is
           even better.

However, there are two special adjuncts to *do X* that *can* be matched with
arguments of the antecedent: *to NP* can be used to match a patient, and *with NP*
can be used to match (roughly—we're not entirely sure) a theme.

(9)   a.   Robin broke the window (with a hammer) and Mary did the same to
           the vase.
      b.   John turned the hot dog down flat, but he wouldn't have done so with
           filet mignon.

X happen anaphora has the same possibilities for orphans, except that the
special *with*-adjunct can be matched to an agent as well as a theme.

(10) a.   John ate the cake, but it wouldn't have happened with the pizza/with
           Mary.
      b.   John shot Mary, but it wouldn't have happened to Sam.
                                             [= Sam wouldn't get shot]
           . . . , but it wouldn't have happened with Sam.
                                             [= Sam wouldn't shoot Mary]

Orphan adjuncts are also possible in VP ellipsis, though (to some speakers) not quite as acceptable (11). Orphan arguments are not acceptable (12). (The case with an orphan NP argument (12b) is pseudo-gapping, which we take up separately in section 8.1.4.) The special cases of *to NP* and *with NP* do not work very well with VP ellipsis (13).

(11) a. (?)Robin smokes a pipe after dinner, and Leslie does during breakfast.
     b. (?)Robin flipped the hamburgers with a spatula, and Leslie did with a chef's knife.
     c. (?)Mary will cook the potatoes for fifteen minutes in the morning, and Susan will for twenty minutes in the evening.
     d. (?)Robin slept for **twelve** hours in the bunkbed, and Leslie did for **eight** hours.
     e. (?)Robin cooked Peking duck on **Thursday** in order to impress Ozzie, and Leslie did on **Friday**.
(12) a. *Robin put a book on the couch, while Leslie did on the table.
     b. Robin ate a hot dog, while Leslie did a pickle.
                                 [OK—Pseudo-gapping]
     c. *Robin said that syntax is wonderful, and Leslie did that phonetics is even better.
(13) a. *Robin broke the window (with a hammer) and Mary did to the vase.
     b. ?John turned the hot dog down flat, but he wouldn't have with filet mignon.

Do this/that and *this/that happen* can be used deictically, even with an orphan attached.

(14) a. I bet you can't do **this**!   [*performing a handstand*]
     b. I bet you can't do this to the table top!
                             [*breaking a brick with one hand*]
     c. I bet you can't do this with a fork!   [*breaking a brick with a hammer*]
(15) a. **This** never used to happen when I was a kid!
                        [*gesturing at the mess in one's child's room*]
     b. If that happens again (to one of us) in the next ten minutes, I'm leaving.   [*gesturing at a waiter who has just spilled soup on someone*]

8.1.2 Reasons not to derive the constructions from full VPs

There are several reasons why these constructions cannot be derived by deleting constituents from a full VP, some of which we repeat from section 4.4. First

consider examples with VP-internal targets such as (7) and (11d,e). In order to
have a single constituent to delete under ellipsis, it is necessary to front the
focused constituent in both clauses, delete the VP in the second clause, then
somehow get the focused constituent in the first clause back into the right
position, perhaps by fronting the material that appears to its left (Iterated
Raising). We have argued already several times, especially in Chapters 2–4,
that such a treatment has no explanatory value: such machinery allows one to
move anything anywhere one wants.

Second, the phenomenon of 'vehicle change' illustrated in (16) (Fiengo and
May 1994) also can be taken as evidence against purely syntactic reconstruction. The form of the antecedent does not appear to inhibit interpretation of the
pro-VP, as the (16) shows.

(16)   Robin is eating frogs' legs, but I never could Ø/do so/do it/do that/do the
       same thing.

Here, the literal reconstruction is *eating frogs' legs,* but **I could never eating
frogs' legs* is impossible. Other mismatches between the target and the reconstructed ellipsis involve polarity.

(17)   a. Not many people bought anything, but Kim did ~~buy something/*any-
           thing~~.
       b. At first, the students wouldn't say anything, and then suddenly they
           started to ~~say something/*anything~~.

Here again, what is reconstructed cannot be strictly identical to the antecedent.

A third reason not to derive these constructions from full VPs comes
from certain variants of *do X* anaphora in which the element *X* has nontrivial
semantic content, for instance *do something else, do the opposite.* In such
cases the anaphoric expression cannot simply replace a deleted VP. Rather, if
there is an underlying VP, it must be a complement of *do X,* and its syntactic
form cannot correspond to that of the antecedent—if such a syntactic form
can be constructed at all (18a.iv). Parallel problems arise with *X happen*
anaphora.

(18)   a. Ralph inflated a balloon, and then Alice did something else/something
           similar/the opposite/something equally disgusting.
           i.   ... did something else beside inflate a balloon.
           ii. ... did something similar to inflating a balloon.
           iii. ... did the opposite of inflating a balloon.
           iv. ... *did something equally disgusting to inflating a balloon.

    b. The stove exploded Thursday morning, and then something else/
       something similar/something equally dreadful happened Friday night.
          i. ... and then something else besides the stove exploding happened
             Friday night.
         ii. ... and then something similar to the stove exploding happened
             Friday night.
        iii. ... *and then something equally dreadful to the stove exploding
             happened Friday night.

We return to these phenomena in Chapter 11.

A fourth reason that these constructions should not be derived from full syntactic structures is that the special *to-* and *with*-adjuncts used with *do X* and *X happen* anaphora cannot be integrated into a syntactically reconstructed VP (as pointed out by Chomsky (1971), following Kraak (1967)).

(19)   a. Robin broke the window (with a hammer) and Mary did so to the
       tabletop.
        * ... and Mary broke (the window) to the tabletop (with a hammer)
     b. John turned the hot dog down flat, but he wouldn't have done so with
       filet mignon.
        * ... but he wouldn't have turned (the hot dog) down flat with filet
        mignon
        * ... but he wouldn't have turned (the hot dog) with filet mignon
        down flat
(20)   a. John ate the cake but it wouldn't have happened with the pizza.
       * ... but John wouldn't have eaten (the cake) with the pizza.
     b. John shot Mary, but it wouldn't have happened with Sam.
       ... but John wouldn't have shot Mary with Sam [wrong meaning]

Finally, the deictic use of *do that* and *that happen* has no linguistic antecedent. Hence there is no basis for deleting the content of a VP under identity with something else.

A proponent of syntactic deletion might observe that the last three of our arguments pertain only to *do X* and *X happen* anaphora, not to VP ellipsis, and therefore might claim that although the former two are interpretive processes, VP ellipsis is still syntactic. However, such a claim would patently miss the clear generalizations among the constructions. If the interpretive machinery is necessary in any event for *do X* and *X happen*, the best theory of VP ellipsis is one that maximally exploits this machinery and introduces as little new machinery as possible. We return in section 8.2 to some recent arguments in the literature for a syntactic treatment of VP ellipsis.

8.1.3 *Treatment of the constructions in terms of indirect licensing*

Our treatment of BAE, sluicing, and gapping suggests an approach to VP ellipsis, *do X* anaphora, and *X happen* anaphora based on indirect licensing. These constructions differ from BAE, sluicing, and gapping in that the indirectly licensed expression is a VP or S rather than a relatively unstructured fragment. But, like the other indirect licensing constructions, each of them permits an orphan expression that represents what is *not* the same in the interpretation of the fragment and the antecedent, and in each case focus plays a role in establishing a match between the orphan and the target. Accordingly, we will adapt the formalism from the previous sections to these cases.

Do *so* anaphora is shown in (21). Notice how it basically just adds more structure to the principles for BAE.[1]

(21)   **Do so anaphora:**
         Syntax: $[_{VP}[_{V}do][_{?}so] < YP_i^{ORPH} >]^{IL}$ CS: $[_{Action} \mathscr{F}(\dots); \dots < Y_i > \dots]$

The syntax is straightforward: it is a VP consisting of *do so* plus an optional YP (in < >) marked as an orphan (more generally, there can be multiple orphans). The VP is connected by indirect licensing to an antecedent; the orphan is connected to a target within the antecedent. In the semantics, the interpretation of *do so* is stipulated as an Action (which is likely inherited from the lexical semantics of the verb *do*); this restricts the antecedent to Actions as well. Within the CS, there is the familiar open function $\mathscr{F}$ whose content is filled in from the antecedent by indirect licensing, and the optional semantic constituent Y corresponding to the orphan falls within the domain of $\mathscr{F}$.[2]

However, unlike our previous cases, it is necessary to designate the orphan as a modifier rather than an argument, in order to account for the distinctions illustrated in (8). Chapter 4 argued that there is no syntactic difference between arguments and adjuncts in VP: they are all simply attached to a flat VP in the

---

[1] Counter to our usual practice, we have entered *do so* into the syntactic structure of the expression, rather than putting it in the phonology. This is partly just for convenience, but also partly to finesse the question of how the irregular conjugation of the verb is achieved in the lexical entry. The same question arises in the treatment of idioms with irregular verbs, such as *take NP for granted*, and it is orthogonal to our concerns here.

[2] The interpretation of the VP alone will leave $\mathscr{F}$ still with one open argument corresponding to the subject. This is instantiated by the usual processes for integrating subjects into the interpretation—including those associated with control and raising. See Chapter 6.

appropriate linear order. However, the difference is reflected in the semantics: syntactic arguments correspond to semantic arguments, and syntactic adjuncts correspond to semantic modifiers. To notate this difference in CS, we place the arguments in parentheses and separate the modifiers off by a semicolon, as in Chapter 5. In (21), the notation stipulates that the orphan constituent Y falls in with the modifiers. This achieves the desired distinction somewhat artificially; perhaps there is a more insightful solution.

In order to treat the special *to-* and *with-*adjuncts, it is necessary to stipulate additional subcases of (21) that map these adjuncts into the appropriate thematic roles within the semantic argument structure of the function $\mathscr{F}$. We will not work out the formalization of these cases here.

A treatment of *it happen* anaphora runs along similar lines, except that the anaphoric element is a clause rather than a VP, and the category of the CS is Event rather than the more restrictive category Action.

(22) **It happen anaphora** (first attempt)

Syntax: $[_S it [_{VP} [_V happen] <YP_i^{ORPH}>]]^{IL}$ CS: $[_{Event}\mathscr{F}(\ldots);\ldots<Y_i>\ldots]$

This is not quite right, as it is too stipulative about the use of *it* in subject position. As stated, it would prohibit *it* from undergoing raising, as in ... *it seems to happen to Bill too often*, and it prohibits deictic subjects such as in *that* [pointing] *better never happen at home*. A subtler approach might build on our analysis of light verb constructions in section 6.5.1. We observe that the sentence as a whole refers to an event, and the subject refers to the very same event—in other words the subject and the verb are coindexed to the same constituent in CS. Thus *happen* is a sort of light verb. This leads to the following formulation of *it happen* anaphora.

(23) **It happen anaphora** (second attempt)

Syntax: $NP_j [_{VP} happen_j <YP_i^{ORPH}>]^{IL}$ CS: $[_{Event}\mathscr{F}(\ldots);\ldots<Y_i>\ldots]_j$

The subscript *j* has the effect of linking both the clause headed by *happen* and its subject with the Event in CS. The fact that the syntactic attachment of the NP is not stipulated allows it to be positioned by general principles of linking— including raising.

The semantics of VP ellipsis is the same as *do so* anaphora, except that its category is Situation, which encompasses both Events and States. The syntax is a little tricky. What should be the constituent marked for indirect licensing? The obvious candidate is VP. But when there is no orphan, there is no evidence aside from the interpretation for the presence of a VP constituent. We could just this once allow an empty VP constituent, as in (24), but such a solution grates against our Simpler Syntax sensibilities.

(24)   **VP ellipsis** (first attempt, with potentially empty VP)
        Syntax: $[_{VP} <YP_i^{ORPH}>]^{IL}$ CS: $[_{Situation}\mathscr{F}(\dots); \dots <Y_i> \dots]$

An alternative is to do without an empty VP and attribute indirect licensing to whatever constituent contains the Auxiliary. If this constituent is S, then the subject functions as an additional orphan that has to be matched syntactically with the subject of the antecedent. However, VP ellipsis also takes place in infinitivals such as... *but no one expected her to*. To incorporate this case, we might treat *to* as the Auxiliary, following Huddleston and Pullum (2002). With these assumptions in place, we might state VP ellipsis as in (25).

(25)   **VP ellipsis** (second attempt, without empty VP)
        Syntax: $[<NP_i^{ORPH1}> Aux <YP_j^{ORPH2}>]^{IL}$
        CS: $[_{Situation}\mathscr{F}(<X_i> , \dots); \dots <Y_j> \dots]$

This formulation would give us the syntactic structure shown in (26) for a typical instance of VP ellipsis.

(26)

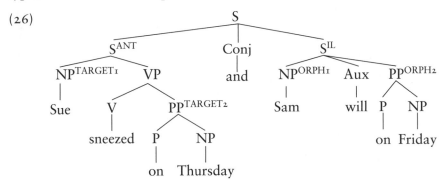

Note that there is no need for the orphan *on Friday* to be in a VP, any more than there is for an orphan in BAE to be in a VP. It is attached to whatever node is handy; the only place that requires parallel structure is CS.

While we are at it, we can state a rule for *one*-anaphora. As observed in section 4.6.1, *one*-anaphora allows for orphans of various sorts.

(27)   a. John listened to [a terrible recording of the Moonlight Sonata by Horowitz] today, and tomorrow he'll go out and buy [(a much better) one (by Rubinstein)].
        b. I'm not fond of [that silly picture of Robin from Mary that was on the table], but I adore [this (artful) one (of Leslie)(from Fred)(that I just found)].

Like *do so* anaphora, *one*-anaphora is often uncomfortable with orphan arguments (Jackendoff 1977):

(28)   a. *The king of England hates the one of France.
                    [*cf.* The king from England hates the one from France.]
       b. *The destruction of Chicago was scarier than the one of New York.
       c. *The meaning of life has been known for years, but the one of death is still unclear.
       d. ?I'll bring a bottle of red wine if you'll bring one of sparkling water.

When the NP is definite, the slack can be taken up by *that*+orphan anaphora:

(29)   a. The king of England hates that of France.
       b. The destruction of Chicago was scarier than that of New York.
       c. The meaning of life has been known for years, but that of death is still unclear.

Section 4.6.1 gave a number of arguments why *one*-anaphora cannot be derived by deletion from a full NP, so we will content ourselves here by stating the rule in a format parallel to the VP anaphora rules. (We ignore the complex and irregular morphological details that fuse various determiners with *one*, e.g. *my+one = mine, some+ones = some*, etc.; see Jackendoff 1977.)

(30)   **One-anaphora**
       Syntax: $[_{NP} <\text{Det/NP}_i{}^{ORPH_1}><\text{YP}_j{}^{ORPH_2}> \text{one} <\text{ZP}_k{}^{ORPH_3}>]^{IL}$
       CS: $[\mathscr{F}(\ldots);\ldots <X_i> ,<Y_j> , <Z_k>\ldots]$

8.1.4 *Pseudo-gapping*

Lasnik (1999a) discusses sentences of the form shown in (31).

(31)   If you don't believe me, you will ~~believe~~ the weatherman.

Lasnik proposes that raising extracts the direct object to a Case-licensing position, and then deletion applies to the remnant VP under identity with an antecedent VP. The derivation, which has the by now familiar character of Iterated Raising, involves leftward movement of *the weatherman* within VP, then deletion or phonological nonrealization of the remnant VP.

(32)   …you will $[_{VP}$ believe [the weatherman]] $\Rightarrow$
       …you will $[_{VP}$[the weatherman]$_i$ $[_{VP}$ believe t$_i$]] $\Rightarrow$
       …you will $[_{VP}$[the weatherman]$_i$ $[_{VP}$~~believe t$_i$~~]]

As Lasnik notes, pseudo-gapping appears superficially to delete discontinuous parts of a VP.

(33) Robin will cook the potatoes quickly, and Leslie will ~~cook~~ the beans ~~quickly~~.

His account in terms of extraction allows what is deleted to be a VP at the point of deletion.[3]

(34) Robin will cook$_i$ [the potatoes]$_j$ [t$_i$ t$_j$ quickly] and Leslie will [the beans]$_k$ ~~[cook t$_k$ quickly]~~

On the other hand, this fact might suggest instead that, as in the other constructions discussed in this chapter and the previous one, the internal syntactic structure of the VP is simply not relevant to this construction.

It turns out that Lasnik's treatment works only for a particular subset of the possible examples. Many other derivations that are predicted by Lasnik's treatment are in fact not possible with pseudo-gapping. Some examples are given below, with the putative derivations under Lasnik's treatment.

(35) a. *Robin will slowly cook the potatoes, and Leslie will quickly the beans.
   b. Robin will slowly cook$_i$ [the potatoes]$_j$ [t$_i$ t$_j$] and Leslie will quickly [the beans]$_k$ ~~[cook t$_k$]~~

(36) a. *Slowly, Robin will cook the potatoes, and quickly, Leslie will the beans.
   b. Slowly, Robin will cook$_i$ [the potatoes]$_j$ [t$_i$ t$_j$] and quickly, Leslie will [the beans]$_k$ ~~[cook t$_k$]~~

(37) a. *Robin will try to cook the potatoes, and Leslie will try (to) the beans.
   b. Robin will try to cook$_i$ [the potatoes]$_j$ [t$_i$ t$_j$], and Leslie will try [the beans]$_k$ ~~to [cook t$_k$]~~

(38) a. * Robin might like the potatoes, and Leslie is likely (to) the beans.
   b. Robin might like$_i$ [the potatoes]$_j$ [t$_i$ t$_j$], and Leslie is likely [the beans]$_k$ ~~to [like t$_k$]~~

While we could conceivably rule out (35) on the grounds that there are two fronted constituents in VP, such an account will not work for (36), since in the latter case, only *the potatoes/beans* is VP-initial. Regarding (37) and (38), while some of the details of the pseudo-gapping analysis remain unclear and may perhaps be further specified in order to deal with such sentences, it appears

---

[3] Lasnik argues that the deleted verb must delete when it is not raised, because its features are not checked.

that the range of possibilities allowed for by movement and deletion of the remnant VP is somewhat larger than the set of actually occurring expressions. As we have noted many times already, it is always possible to adopt an Iterated Raising analysis that yields a coherent constituent for the cases that allow deletion and to stipulate constraints that block certain configurations, so we will not attempt to argue that such an approach to pseudo-gapping is technically impossible.

However, it is also possible to construct pseudo-gapping examples for which there appears to be no reasonable source on the derivation proposed by Lasnik. Consider (39) (using appropriate contrastive focus intonation).[4]

(39) **Robin** will bet an entire fortune that the **Mets** will win the pennant, and **Leslie** will ~~bet an entire fortune~~ that the **Braves** will win.

In (39), the constituent that must be moved out of VP prior to ellipsis is a CP, *that the Braves will win*. It is highly unlikely that such movement can be motivated on the grounds of feature checking, given the overwhelming evidence in languages such as Dutch and German that even where there putatively is overt movement of NP to the Spec position of a functional head to the left of the V, a CP does not undergo such movement (see Zwart 1997).

The heightened intonation necessary in (39) is reminiscent of gapping, and suggests that pseudo-gapping is a sort of hybrid of gapping and VP ellipsis. And in fact we find the distribution of pseudo-gapping resembles that of gapping more than VP ellipsis. For instance, while VP ellipsis permits long distance dependencies, similar to the interpretation of pronouns and other pro-VPs, pseudo-gapping does not.

(40) *VP ellipsis*
      a. Robin will vote for Bush and Leslie will too.
      b. Robin will vote for Bush if Leslie did.
      c. A student who spoke French met another student who didn't.
      d. Whenever you want to, go ahead and taste the soup.

(41) *Pseudo-gapping*
      a. Robin will vote for Bush and Leslie will (for) Nader.
      b. *Robin will vote for Bush if Leslie did (for) Nader.
      c. *A student who spoke French met another student who didn't/did German.
      d. *Whenever you want to the salad, first go ahead and taste the soup.

---

[4] Examples of this sort are due to Robert Levine (p.c.). They are OK for PWC, terrible for RJ.

(42) *Gapping*
    a.   Robin will vote for Bush and Leslie (for) Nader.
    b.   *Robin will vote for Bush if Leslie (for) Nader.
    c.   *A student who spoke French met another student who German.
    d.   *Whenever you the salad, first go ahead and taste the soup.

And like gapping, pseudo-gapping can appear in the right conjunct of a parallel conjoined structure (as in all the good examples above) or in the comparative (43).

(43) a. Robin speaks French better than Leslie does German.
    b. Robin thinks that it is harder to speak French than Leslie does German.

However, pseudo-gapping is somewhat more liberal than gapping:

(44) *Pseudo-gapping*
    a.   Whenever Robin speaks French, then Leslie does German.
    b.   Because Robin speaks French, Leslie does German.
    c. ? Leslie will not speak German, because Robin does French.
    Gapping
    d.   *Whenever Robin speaks French, then Leslie, German.
    e.   *Because Robin speaks French, Leslie, German.
    f.   *Leslie will not speak German, because Robin French.

Another difference is that the constituent in which pseudo-gapping applies is an S. This is shown by the fact that the second fragment can topicalize.

(45) If you don't believe **me**, the **weatherman**, you **will**.

    Leaving aside the issue of the exact distribution of pseudo-gapped clauses, we can state a preliminary version of pseudo-gapping.

(46) **Pseudo-gapping**

Syntax: $[_S \text{ NP}_i{}^{ORPH1} \text{ Aux}_k \text{ NP}_j{}^{ORPH\pm2}]^{IL}$

CS: $[M [\mathscr{F}(\begin{bmatrix} X \\ C\text{-}FOCUS \end{bmatrix}_i, \begin{bmatrix} Y \\ C\text{-}FOCUS \end{bmatrix}_j)]]_k$

This is similar to gapping, in that it stipulates two contrastive foci. However, it is also like VP ellipsis in that it stipulates that the syntax is a clause, and it stipulates the presence of a subject and an auxiliary. In the best examples of pseudo-gapping, the syntax takes the form *NP Aux NP*, and the second NP is construed as an argument rather than an adjunct. This is the way we have coded it here; more exotic examples such as (39) will require extensions in the statement of the rule.

8.2 Some arguments that VP ellipsis must be syntactic deletion

We now turn to two recent arguments that there is syntactic structure in the ellipted (that is, invisible) part of the ellipsis construction. We consider first an argument of Kehler's that while semantic reconstruction of ellipsis is adequate for most cases, there are some cases where syntactic reconstruction is required, and for principled reasons. Then we turn to an argument of Kennedy's that extraction constraints hold even when there is ellipsis.

Kehler (2000) argues that there are three basic types of coherence relation between sentences in discourse—Resemblance/Parallelism, Cause/Effect, and Narration—and that evidence for syntactic reconstruction occurs only in the first of these. In other words, there is syntactic reconstruction when the syntactic structure is needed to license discourse coherence. We will argue here that for the cases that motivate such syntactic reconstruction, the purely *syntactic* information is information about linear order, which is consistent with our proposals about flat structure in Chapter 4. The relevant hierarchical information is available in the semantic reconstruction from Conceptual Structure. So while there is reconstruction, it is consistent with the Simpler Syntax Hypothesis.

Here are the key examples. It is well known that ellipsis of a VP containing a referential NP yields a condition C violation when the subject of the ellipsis is a coreferential pronoun. Consider (47) (adapted from Lappin 1993, cited by Kehler (2000: 534)).

(47)   *Susan defended Bill$_i$, and he$_i$ did too.   [*did = defend Bill$_i$*]

It is argued that the Condition C violation can be explained if *defended Bill$_i$* is reconstructed into the empty VP position prior to evaluation by Condition C. In contrast, there are similar cases without Condition C violations; according to Kehler this is because in these cases there is no parallelism and hence no syntactic reconstruction: see (48) (from Dalrymple 1991, cited by Kehler (2000: 536)).

(48)   ?I expected Bill$_i$ to win even when he$_i$ didn't.

[*didn't = didn't expect Bill$_i$ to win*]

In order to show that there is no syntactic reconstruction, we will show that there are examples syntactically parallel to (47), in which Condition C violations do not occur. The difference between Kehler's examples and ours is that ours are constructed to facilitate a contrastive focus interpretation. We will see therefore that the problem with his examples is not a Condition C violation, but rather insufficient contrast to license the pronoun.

To begin, notice that (48) can be improved by replacing *he* with *he himself*, although without ellipsis, *he himself* would normally produce a Condition C violation (49b).

(49) a.   I expected Bill$_i$ to win even when he$_i$ himself didn't.
      b.   *He$_i$ himself thinks that Bill$_i$ will win the race.

The violation in (49b) can be ameliorated by increasing contrast. This is achieved by deaccenting *Bill* and placing heavy stress on *self*.

(50) ?I was talking to Bill$_i$ on the phone and found out that he$_i$ him**self** thinks that Bill$_i$ will win the race.

With these facts in mind, compare (47) above to (51a), which is good with or without ellipsis. We can also make examples such as (47) quite acceptable by using other devices that strengthen the contrast between *he* and *Susan*.

(51) a.   **Susan** defended Bill$_i$ because **he**$_i$ (himself) couldn't (defend Bill$_i$).
      b.   Susan defended Bill$_i$, but **he**$_i$, being a lawyer himself, would have if necessary.

Furthermore, notice that the same pattern occurs when the pro-VP is not ellipsis, but *do so/it/that/the same thing/likewise*.

(52) *Susan defended Bill$_i$, and he$_i$ did so/it/that/the same thing/likewise (too).

In this case, syntactic reconstruction is not a plausible option. Yet the judgment is the same as that of (47). When we highlight the contrast, the judgment improves.

(53) Susan defended Bill$_i$, but **he**$_i$, being a lawyer him**self**, would have done so/it/that/the same thing/likewise if necessary.

The fact that it is possible to affect the acceptability judgment by manipulating accent and contrast suggests that Kehler's account does not really provide support for a syntactic account of ellipsis interpretation, even in a restricted set of cases. We conclude, therefore, that the resolution is purely semantic.

We now turn to the argument of Kennedy (2003), who notes examples such as (54) (p. 30).

(54) a.   Dogs$_j$, I understand t$_j$, but cats$_i$, I don't [~~understand t$_i$~~]
      b.   *Dogs$_j$, I understand t$_j$, but cats$_i$, I don't know anyone who does [$_{VP}$ ~~understand t$_i$~~]

Kennedy's argument is based on the assumption that *cats* is extracted from an elliptical VP in both examples. The ungrammaticality judgment in (54b) is taken to show that the syntactic structure of the ellipted VP is still present, since without the trace, there is no configuration that would violate subjacency. (Note that this is a case where PF deletion would *not* abrogate island violations, unlike BAE and sluicing!)

But there is an alternative analysis, which as far as we can tell is empirically equivalent. Suppose that examples such as (54a) are instances not of VP ellipsis but of pseudo-gapping, in which the verb is deleted but the object is not. In this particular case, the direct object is topicalized, parallel to (45) (... *but the weatherman, you will*); thus the structure of the ellipted clause in (54a) would be a topicalized version of the pseudo-gapped construction (55a) below. The complete syntactic structure would be (55b). Under this analysis, the second clause of (54b) would have the syntactic structure (55c), in which the trace is improperly bound, accounting for its unacceptability.

(55)   a. ... but I don't cats.
       b. ... but cats$_i^{ORPH}$ I don't t$_i$
       c. ... but cats$_i^{ORPH}$ I don't know anyone [who does t$_i$]
                                                    [improperly bound trace]

If this latter analysis is in fact possible, the subjacency violations do not show more generally that ellipsis constructions have syntactic structure.

8.3 Summary of Chapters 7 and 8

Our approach to fragment constructions has taken them all to be special instances of the mechanism of indirect licensing. We motivated this mechanism on the basis of bare argument ellipsis, arguably the most primitive and unrestricted fragment construction, and one that, more than the others, often relies on pragmatics and nonlinguistic context for its interpretation. Indirect licensing involves the following considerations:

• IL is discourse-based, i.e. it is not strictly a part of sentence grammar.

• An IL construction receives its interpretation by reference to an antecedent elsewhere in the discourse, or possibly in the nonlinguistic context.

• The interpretation of IL can be mediated by reference to lexical items and rules that are not present in either the IL construction or the antecedent.

• The IL construction can contain one or more orphan constituents which need not be syntactically attached to the IL construction in any canonical way.

- The orphan is interpreted as a part of the IL construction that differs from the antecedent. It can be localized in the interpretation either (a) by matching it with a corresponding constituent in the antecedent, often as contrastive focus, or (b) by "sprouting" an appropriate position in the antecedent to which it can be matched.

- The orphan inherits syntactic features from the position in the antecedent with which it is matched.

Each of the constructions we have considered can be treated similarly to bare argument ellipsis, except that the indirectly licensed constituent has more elaborate structure. We have suggested that definite discourse pronouns and deictic pronouns can be treated as degenerate cases of indirect licensing, in which there is no orphan constituent. Furthermore, we have suggested that the connection of a "displaced" constituent to a trace is a particular elaboration of indirect licensing, an issue we take up in detail in Chapter 9.

We have repeatedly contrasted indirect licensing with the more traditional deletion approach to ellipsis constructions. In every construction we find that the same considerations arise:

- Deletion cannot be licensed by identity with a part of the antecedent, either because the interpretation of the ellipsis construction is not the same as the corresponding part of the antecedent, or because the syntax of the ellipsis construction imposes different syntactic constraints than the syntax of the antecedent.

- Many of the adjustments necessary to align the relevant parts of the antecedent with the interpretation of the fragment belong in pragmatics and discourse theory, not in syntax. They therefore cannot be captured in the deletion theory per se.

- In many cases, the portion purportedly deleted is not a syntactic constituent of the antecedent, nor is it even a continuous string. It is therefore necessary to posit extensive and otherwise unmotivated rearrangement of the antecedent and the ellipsis construction, so that there is a single constituent that can serve as target of deletion. Such movement in turn requires considerable syntactic structure for which there is no independent motivation. Moreover, such movement often violates extraction constraints, which must then be mitigated by claiming that the constraints apply to PF after deletion takes place.

- Where independent arguments have been offered for the necessity of deleted syntactic structure, we have been able to show that the evidence actually concerns semantic rather than syntactic structure—with one sort of exception.

• This exception is the syntactic features of fragments such as case, gender, governed prepositions, and GF-tier binding. We have proposed that these features are supplied by indirect licensing. We have shown that similar features can appear in bare argument ellipsis whose antecedent is nonlinguistic context, and therefore that they cannot be uniformly supplied by syntax in any event.

Finally, we have confronted the fact that some fragment constructions such as bare argument ellipsis, gapping, and sluicing look syntactically weird. The prevailing ethos, falling back on the presumption of Structural Uniformity, has been that they must be sentences at some underlying level. We have argued that they are *propositions* at the level of Conceptual Structure, but they are not syntactic sentences. Rather, the syntax of English requires a collection of non-sentential utterance frames in any event, so adding these fragment constructions is not an overwhelming burden on UG.

What does have to be added to UG in our approach is the mechanism of indirect licensing, and, to be sure, our description still leaves many questions open. In particular, there are the issues of how an antecedent is identified, how a target within the antecedent is identified, and how "sprouting" works. But parallel issues arise in the deletion approach and are in principle less tractable for the reasons we have outlined. On the other hand, in compensation for adding indirect licensing to UG, we save huge amounts of abstract structure and covert derivation, all of which has a cost in the theory of UG and in particular in the theory of learnability. In our approach, essentially all a learner has to learn is the surface syntactic form of a fragment construction; the rest comes from the general process of indirect licensing. In short, although we have hardly covered all the bases, we hope to have shown that the approach is well worth consideration.

CHAPTER 9

Discontinuous Dependencies

Chapter 7 laid the groundwork for a treatment of discontinuous (or long-distance) dependencies such as *wh*-fronting and topicalization in terms of indirect licensing. The present chapter develops this treatment in more detail and works out some of its consequences for various well-known phenomena. In particular, we continue our survey of phenomena that MGG has treated in terms of movement, showing that such treatment is not the only possibility and in fact leads to empirical and theoretical problems.

As with passive and raising, the case for a non-movement approach to discontinuous dependencies has been under active development in the field for many years, with the most extensive contributions occurring within GPSG and HPSG. The goal of this chapter is to show how a wide range of discontinuous dependencies, many of the type referred to in the literature as A'-constructions, can be accounted for within the type of architecture that we are proposing. We discuss not only *wh*-questions (with extraction and with *wh*- in situ), but relative clauses of various types, topicalization, left and right dislocation, *tough* movement, heavy shift, and scrambling. Several critical points should be highlighted.

• The way that the grammar deals with constituents adjoined to a sentence in A'-position is a special case of the way it deals with Bare Argument Ellipsis—that is, through indirect licensing.

• The chain that links a constituent in A'-position with the corresponding gap is defined by a syntax–semantics correspondence rule. There are a number of such rules that define chains. They share many properties, but they are different rules and may differ in other respects.

• Constraints on these chains can and must be formulated in terms of the percolation through the syntactic structure of the dependencies between the constituent in A′-position and the trace, as well as in terms of semantic dependencies.

• Since there is no movement, there are no intermediate traces.

9.1 There is no A′-movement

Consider the initial PP *with whom* in (1).

(1)   With whom is Terry flirting?

The *with*-phrase is licensed by the verb *flirt*, even though it is not in the canonical argument position prescribed by *flirt*. Considerations such as this (and there are many of them) form the basis for the conclusion in MGG that *with whom* is moved from its canonical position to clause-initial position, a conclusion that is so routine as to be a given in MGG. On this approach, the PP is licensed after it is combined with *flirt*, but before it is dislocated. As we saw in Chapter 2, there have been various implementations of this general idea, but the core notion of movement is preserved throughout the course of development of MGG, including the Minimalist Program.

The Simpler Syntax Hypothesis suggests that we look elsewhere for an account of "displacement" phenomena that have been treated in terms of movement in MGG. On the basis of our analysis of bare argument ellipsis in Chapter 7, we argued that there are two ways in which the syntactic properties of a phrase may be licensed. One is direct licensing, where there is a local connection between the licenser and licensee. The second is indirect licensing (IL), where the licenser is in a noncanonical position with respect to the licensee, including being in a preceding sentence—or even just being primed by nonlinguistic context. In particular, indirect licensing accounts for case-marking and syntactically governed prepositions such as the *with* in a discourse such as *Terry is flirting.—Yeah, with Sandy.*

Indirect licensing thus provides an alternative to movement for deriving the syntactic properties of phrases that are not in direct licensing positions—including A′-constructions. Given an overabundance of resources, Occam's Razor urges us to eliminate one or the other. As shown in Chapter 7, it is impossible to derive all the cases of BAE by movement. Hence it behooves us to try to develop a theory of A′-constructions that relies on indirect licensing rather than movement, and to try to eliminate movement from the theory.

Chapter 7 suggested that it is possible and natural to view cases of apparent A'-movement as special cases of IL. After all, recall what "A'-position" means: a position where phrases do not have a local licenser—precisely the context for IL. Under this approach, the "fronted" constituent in A'-constructions is to be considered the indirectly licensed orphan in the sense of Chapter 7. The context that supplies the licensing (the antecedent in the sense of Chapter 7) is the clause at whose left periphery the orphan is located. The orphan is licensed by being linked to a *target* position in the antecedent. In the case of a *wh*-question such as (1), such a linking relationship would be that of a chain, in which the orphan *with whom* is the head of the chain, and the target, the tail of the chain, is a trace in the position to the right of the verb, as in (2). It is the linking through a chain, terminating in a trace, that makes *wh*-fronting grammatically more complex than BAE.

(2)   [with whom]$_i^{\text{ORPH}}$ is Terry flirting t$_i^{\text{TARG}}$.

We wish to be careful about the status of the trace, which again is so straightforward in MGG as to be taken for granted. In constructions such as topicalization and *wh*-questions, there is typically a gap that marks the syntactic function of the displaced constituent. For us, the trace represents this syntactic gap; it is emphatically *not* to be thought of as something left behind by movement. Rather, the trace represents the presumptive position of a constituent which is linked to a CS constituent through direct licensing and which serves as the target for indirect licensing of the *wh*-phrase. Note however that the justification for a syntactic gap is only theory-internal when what is in A'-position is an adjunct or a complement that is optionally subcategorized.[1] Moreover, there are other A'-constructions, such as left dislocation, which link a resumptive pronoun or epithet instead of a gap to the constituent in A'-position.

What we are suggesting here is of course altogether familiar from the literature. Researchers have been seeking alternatives to movement at least as early as Brame (1978). Non-movement proposals for *wh*-questions play a central role in

---

[1] There have been attempts to demonstrate the syntactic reality of traces, but these have not been entirely convincing. The most prominent is the argument that the trace of movement blocks the contraction of *want* and *to* to *wanna* in English. For review and discussion, see Pullum (1997). There is also some psycholinguistic evidence that there are traces, e.g. Swinney and Fodor (1989), Nicol et al. (1994), Kluender and Kutas (1993), Swinney et al. (1996), Zurif et al. (1993). It is important to recognize that evidence for the activation of a fronted constituent somewhat later in the processing of a sentence is not in itself evidence for a trace. It is simply evidence for the linking of the fronted constituent with something at the point of the activation (i.e. some kind of chain effect). For some discussion of this particular issue, as well as an interesting argument that what is activated is not a chain, see Pickering and Barry (1991).

a number of influential "monostratal" accounts, including Gazdar et al. (1985), Pollard and Sag (1994), Bresnan (1982b), and Ginzburg and Sag (2000). Our account will borrow freely from these earlier approaches, with HPSG as our most prominent influence. Our emphasis will be on the broader conceptual issues surrounding the debate, not on the technical details. The reader interested in pursuing the latter should consult Ginzburg and Sag (2000), which contains a fully explicit analysis of the syntax and semantics of *wh*-questions in the HPSG framework. It is far too detailed for us to be able to summarize here, although we will note several points of contact as we proceed.[2]

It is important to note that what we are up to here is not simply to demonstrate that a non-movement account of A′-phenomena is *possible*. This has been known for many years, as the references just cited attest. Rather, we wish to argue that a non-movement account of A′-phenomena is possible using in part descriptive devices that are *independently motivated* for the description of bare argument ellipsis.

By the same token, we are not trying to demonstrate here that a movement account of A′-phenomena cannot be developed in principle.[3] Given the greater descriptive power of movement (compared for example with linearization), it would be quixotic to attempt such a demonstration—especially since, as observed in Chapter 4, *any* configuration of linear relationships can be derived by well-chosen applications of Iterated Raising to well-chosen underlying structures. Rather, in the spirit of minimalism, we are arguing that in order to justify movement there has to be something about A′-phenomena that *requires* that they be derived through movement; otherwise movement should be abandoned as an otiose component of syntactic theory.[4]

Before we get into the details, let us review the range of constructions of English that have been considered the likeliest candidates for movement within a sentence. Not all of these will require or permit an analysis in terms of IL;

---

[2] There have also been attempts to construct traceless accounts of movement phenomena, including Sag (1998), Sag and Fodor (1994), Blevins (1994), and Bouma, et al. (2001). Whether these and other proposals are truly traceless or somehow include at least the functional equivalent of traces is a complicated matter that we cannot go into here. At issue is not only whether there is a phonetically empty constituent in the gap position, but also the character of the formal devices through which the fronted material is linked to the gap.

[3] There have been attempts over the years to show that movement is not correct as an account of A′-dependencies. See e.g., Bresnan (1977), which we discuss below. More recently, Levine and Sag (2003a; 2003b) have argued that multiple gap constructions, such as parasitic gaps, cannot be accounted for by movement.

[4] One could of course invoke the rhetorical strategy of arguing for the existence of movement from "conceptual necessity" in the absence of factual necessity. For instance, Chomsky (2001: 8–9, n. 29) takes the existence of A′-phenomena to be evidence for movement *tout court*: "Recourse to any device to account for the displacement phenomena also is mistaken, unless it is independently

rather, as proposed in Chapters 5 and 6, there are at least three other mechanisms that create the illusion of movement. The first, discussed in section 5.5, involves alternative linearizations of daughters of the same constituent. This option encompasses simple free phrase order alternations such as (3a,b), particle "movement" (4a,b), heavy shift alternations (5a,b), and lexically idiosyncratic positioning (6a,b). (We return to heavy shift, perhaps the most controversial of these, in section 9.6.1.)

(3) a. We talked with our students about the war on Tuesday.
     b. We talked on Tuesday about the war with our students.
(4) a. We looked the answer up.
     b. We looked up the answer.
(5) a. We discussed the war with the students.   [*canonical order*]
     b. We discussed with the students the injustices caused by the war.
                                                        [*Heavy shift*]
(6) a. This book is too long.
                         [*canonical order of degree phrase + adjective*]
     b. This book is long enough.
                         [*lexically specific order of* enough + *adjective*]

A second source of apparent movement is the reconfiguring of embedding in extraposition from NP, discussed in section 5.4. Like heavy shift, this noncanonical order is motivated by linking to more favorable prosody and/or by the preference for postponing focus to the end of the sentence.

(7) a. Three people who had the same birthday came to the meeting.
                                                        [*canonical order*]
     b. Three people came to the meeting who had the same birthday.
                                                        [*extraposed*]

A third source of apparent movement involves reconfiguring the GF-tier through such constructions as passive and raising, as discussed in sections 6.1–6.3. For instance, subject position in syntax is normally linked to the the most prominent grammatical function slot in GF-structure, but in the passive it is not. Rather, subject position in a passive is linked to the next most prominent GF slot, which normally links to object position. The alternation does not involve movement, and there is no need to mediate the licensing of the subject

---

motivated (as is internal Merge). If this is correct, then the radically simplified form of transformational grammar that has become familiar ('Move a' and its variants) is a kind of [*sic*] conceptual necessity, given the undeniable existence of the displacement phenomena." Saying that it is conceptually necessary does not make it so, of course. For discussion and criticism, see Postal 2004.

of the passive by way of an "underlying" syntactic object position. Hence there is no need for a syntactic chain and no need for a trace. The semantic relation of active and passive sentences is established through the link to CS. There is the *illusion* of movement based on the fact that the same argument may be realized in more than one syntactic position. A similar argument applies to raising.

Turning to constructions that involve indirect licensing, not all call for a chain containing a trace. Constructions such as left dislocation and right dislocation instead have as target a resumptive pronoun in the clause.

(8)   a. *Left dislocation*
         [That guy that I was telling you about]$_i$, he$_i$ called me yesterday on my cellphone.
      b. *Right dislocation*
         He$_i$ called me yesterday on my cellphone, [that guy that I was telling you about]$_i$

We will look more closely at (English) left and right dislocation in section 9.4.5, comparing them to topicalization. We will suggest that in some respects these constructions are closer to BAE than they are to *wh*-questions or to topicalization. We merely note at this point that in English they are not sensitive to island constraints; and in languages that have overt morphological case, they do not appear to form syntactic chains with the resumptive pronoun, in that they often have a case different than that of the resumptive pronoun. (Some languages have left dislocation constructions that do obey island constraints; we mention these briefly in section 9.4.5.)

In suggesting that there are multiple sources of "displaced" constituents, we seem to be flouting Occam's Razor ourselves. As we noted in Chapter 1, a major theme of MGG has been to reduce the number of distinct computational mechanisms in grammar, and here we are indeed multiplying entities. However, we remind ourselves that Occam's Razor says "Do not multiply entities *beyond necessity*", and the qualification is crucial. It has been known for years that different kinds of "movement" have different properties, for example that some are strictly local and some can invoke long-distance dependencies; that some (such as raising) depend on properties of particular verbs and some do not; that some are to the left and some are to the right. As noted in Chapter 2, MGG has incorporated these differences through technical devices such as abstract Case, government, barriers, special properties of [Spec, CP], and so on. In effect the heterogeneity has been hidden in the inner workings, at the same time making structures and derivations more complex. As Chapter 2 has shown, the effort to provide such an account inevitably has led to complex auxiliary assumptions that undermine the alleged simplicity and elegance of the approach. In other words, multiplying entities *is* necessary, *somewhere* in the grammar. We have belabored this point enough in earlier chapters and will not go through it again here.

In contrast, Simpler Syntax seeks to take the heterogeneity of displacement phenomena as a starting point, and to parcel out the description of the grammatical possibilities directly into a somewhat richer set of fundamental grammatical phenomena, each of them highly constrained to produce the particular properties in question. This is the Toolkit Hypothesis of Chapter 1. In such an approach, *wh*-fronting is characterized by the fact that there is an indirectly licensed *wh*-phrase in initial position; to be licensed it must be linked to a trace. By contrast, as we will see, displacements such as heavy shift and left and right dislocation do not require appeal to traces, i.e. different tools are involved.

We might add that eschewing movement leads to a more direct relation between the theory of linguistic structure and a theory of processing. Despite the intuitive appeal of movement for a story about language production ("To ask a question, you move the *wh*-word to the front"), we are always reminded as students that a grammatical description in terms of movement does not correspond to anything *actually* moving in processing—movement is "just a metaphor". As argued in Chapter 1, achieving a more direct relation between the theories of competence and performance is a desideratum of explanation in linguistic theory. And, as pointed out there, a monostratal constraint-based formalism, because of its neutrality as to direction of application, is more suited than a movement approach to account with equal facility for both perception and production.

We begin our examination of long-distance dependencies with *wh*-constructions, which are the most widely studied and for us the canonical case. We show how to form syntactic chains and how to express constraints on the well-formedness of these chains. We then go on to other constructions for which movement analyses have been entertained in the literature, including topicalization, left and right dislocation, *tough*-movement, heavy shift, and scrambling.

9.2 *Wh*-questions

9.2.1 *Simple wh-questions*

Within *wh*-constructions, we start with the case of simple *wh*-questions, then generalize to *wh*-questions with pied-piping and to relative clauses and free relatives. Along the way, we begin to separate the general structure of long-distance dependency constructions from the idiosyncrasies of each construction and to show how they are encoded.

In CS, a *wh*-question might be encoded roughly along the lines of (9). Qx is the question operator, which applies to a proposition and binds the variable x within the proposition. (9b) is a more or less conventional notation with a restricted variable; section 9.2.3 will develop an alternative that has certain advantages.

(9)   a.   General form: Qx[F(. . . x . . .)]
                    'What is the x such that F(. . . x . . .)?'
      b.   Example: Who will John see?
                    Q[x_{PERSON}] [FUTURE [SEE (JOHN, x)]]
           'What is the x, x a person, such that John will see x?'

The conceptual problem here is that it is impossible to relate the parts of the CS one-to-one to parts of the linguistic expression. The question operator Q is associated both with the proposition and with the variable; the variable x is associated both with the question operator (let us call this occurrence of x the "operator variable") and with its role as an argument of *SEE* (the "bound variable"). A movement approach accounts for the dual roles of the variable by starting it in its argument position and moving it to the operator, leaving behind a trace. It accounts for the dual roles of the operator by having a covert syntactic category Q (i.e. an interrogative complementizer) whose specifier is the variable and whose complement is the proposition:

(10)   Syntax: [[who$_i$] Q [will John see t$_i$]]

The outcome is that *who* corresponds to the operator variable in CS and the trace corresponds to the sentence variable.

In terms of the Simpler Syntax Hypothesis, four parts of this are suspect. First is the syntactic element Q, which is covert. Second, the movement of *who* presupposes a covert level of syntax in which *who* is the object of *see*. Third, the inversion of subject and auxiliary is also taken to be a case of movement, perhaps adjunction of *Tense* or *Modal* (here, *will*) to Q, again requiring a covert level of syntactic structure. Fourth is the trace. We will attempt to get rid of the first three but will accept the fourth as a necessary complexity. The first three are interdependent, in that the covert syntactic element Q, corresponding to the semantic element Q, is supposed to be what triggers (or licenses) movement of both the wh-word and the *Tense*. How it does that has varied over the years, but this basic story (minus the trace) originates as long ago as Katz and Postal (1964).

Section 5.5 proposed that subject–auxiliary inversion is an interface rule that licenses a non-default linearization of S, based on the presence of (*inter alia*) the semantic operator Q. Thus there is no need for a *syntactic* operator Q to condition inversion, and no need for the syntax to "start" in the canonical order and undergo movement.[5] There remains the issue of the variable. We propose (for a first approximation) that the discontinuous complex of operator variable and bound variable in CS maps as a whole into a chain in syntax, here consisting of the *wh*-phrase and the trace. That is, instead of a one-to-one mapping, there is a "two-to-two" mapping that preserves the discontinuous structure of CS in syntax. The position of the trace in syntax is determined by the position of the bound variable in CS plus normal rules of linking. The open proposition in CS over which the semantic operator Q takes scope corresponds to the clause in syntax at whose left edge the *wh*-phrase is located. Hence the basic physiognomy of *wh*-questions is accounted for by (a) the structure of questions in CS, (b) the constructional idiom that stipulates inversion in the semantic context of questions, and (c) the mapping of operator+bound variable into a syntactic chain. There is no covert syntactic Q and no movement. The only new rule type is (c), which we will modify somewhat in section 9.2.2.

Here is the structure of *Who will John see* under this proposal. We have notated the CS–syntax correspondence by means of the usual indices, adding association lines for perspicuity in showing how the variable-chain correspondence works.[6]

(11)

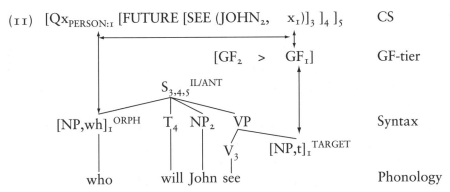

The two occurrences of *x* are coindexed with each other in CS, and with the *wh*-phrase and the trace in syntax. Thus it does not make sense to say which of

---

[5] The fact that inversion takes place only in main clause questions and that it does not take place when the subject is questioned are facts about the statement of inversion. They are independent of whether there is a Q in syntax or not, and of whether inversion is raising to C, as in contemporary MGG accounts, or an alternative linearization, as we have proposed. We therefore leave the exact formulation of inversion aside.

[6] In accordance with our commitment to flat structure, we depart from convention in not requiring the *wh*-phrase to be a sister of a single constituent containing the rest of the sentence and ultimately the trace. As we noted in Ch. 4, we are happy to revert to the more traditional Chomsky-adjoined structure if independent evidence for it emerges.

the xs corresponds to the *wh*-phrase and which to the trace: the two elements in CS and the two in syntax form a unit. Notice also that the entire sentence is subscripted to three nested constituents in CS: those headed by the Q operator, by *FUTURE*, and by *SEE*. Thus the syntax collapses the nesting in semantics, having three semantic co-heads. Finally, the syntactic structure is marked for indirect licensing in the manner suggested in Chapter 7: the *wh*-phrase is marked as an orphan and the trace as target. The sentence is both the constituent that is indirectly licensed (i.e. it contains the orphan) and the antecedent in which the target is to be found.

It is useful to see how (11) is carved into its parts, along the lines of section 5.3. The treatments of *FUTURE*, *SEE*, and *JOHN* are familiar from Chapter 4 and should not be problematic. (12.iv) is the lexical entry for *who* and again offers no new challenges.

(12)   Conceptual structure   Syntax   Phonology
$[Qx_{\text{PERSON}:1}$ [FUTURE [SEE (JOHN, x_1)]]]
  i.   [FUTURE [*SITUATION* $]_4$ $[T/M]_4$ will$_4$
  ii.   [SEE (X, Y)]$_3$ V_3 see$_3$
  iii.   JOHN$_2$ NP$_2$ John$_2$
  iv. [x;PERSON]$_6$ [NP,wh]$_6$ who$_6$

  v. $[Qx_1$ $[\mathscr{F}(\ldots$ $x_1)]]_5$ $[_S[\text{wh}]_1^{\text{ORPH}} \ldots [t]_1^{\text{TARG}} \ldots]_5^{\text{IL/ANT}}$

The tricky part is (12.v), the lexical entry for the *wh*-question construction. The semantics contains the Q operator and the variables; the variables are linked to both the *wh*-phrase and the trace in syntax. Within the scope of the Q operator is the open function $\mathscr{F}$ familiar from other rules for indirect licensing; this is filled in by the content of the rest of the sentence. The *wh*-phrase and the trace are not specified for syntactic category, which comes from the choice of *wh*-phrase, e.g. *who* (NP), *where* (PP), *how* (AdvP). Likewise, there is no phonology: the phonology also comes from filling in the *wh*-phrase. The only covert syntactic structure is the trace.

The syntactic structure of (12.v) is marked for indirect licensing in the manner suggested in Chapter 7 for other such constructions such as BAE. The linking of the trace to the *wh*-phrase allows the syntactic properties of the trace to be associated with the *wh*-phrase as well. For example, in a case language the counterpart of (10b) would mark the trace with accusative case by virtue of its GF-role, which would then be transmitted to the *wh*-phrase by indirect licensing.

It should be pointed out that all the overlapping coindexation in the analysis of this example is characteristic of "structure-sharing" formalisms such as HPSG; see Ginzburg and Sag 2000 for a particular analysis.

Finally, it is useful to compare (12.v) with our structure for sluicing from section 7.7, repeated below in a compatible format.

(13) **Sluicing**

$$[Qx_I[\mathscr{F}(\dots x_I \dots)]]_2 \quad [_S[wh]_I{}^{ORPH}]_2{}^{IL}$$

Notice that the semantics is exactly the same, but the syntax is less complex, lacking both the trace and any further syntactic content in the sentence. It is by virtue of the mapping of the CS variable to a chain that *wh*-constructions are more grammaticized than BAE and sluicing: instead of indirect licensing passing features through a separate CS constituent in the antecedent or through pragmatics, the orphan and the trace are coindexed directly with the same CS constituent.

9.2.2 *Comparison of movement and non-movement*

Not surprisingly, our account of simple *wh*-questions in terms of indirect licensing resembles the standard transformational account in many respects. A more detailed comparison is in order, so that the differences also become sharper.

Contemporary versions of the traditional transformational account derive *wh*-questions by A′-movement to Spec,CP, as in (14).

(14)

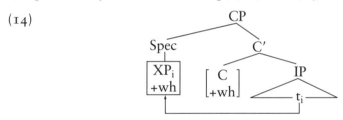

The crucial property of the construction is the chain that links the *wh*-phrase and its trace. In a movement analysis, the trace must be created so as to agree with the moved constituent, and the moved constituent must appear in clause-initial position. The function of [C,+wh] is to mark this position in the structure, and the movement is typically triggered by a licensing condition that requires agreement between [C,+wh] and something in its specifier position (e.g. May 1985; Rizzi 1996; Chomsky 1995).

In the present account, the counterpart of the syntactic [C,+wh] is the semantic operator Q: Q is the semantic co-head of the clause whose left edge determines the position of the *wh*-phrase. Q is not present in syntax, and there are no CP and C′ nodes above IP.

Let us consider what it takes to derive a phrase in initial position that is linked with a gap in (14). On a movement account in MP terms, a derivation would go as follows.

(15) what   [Select *what* from the numeration]
      write what   [Merge *write* with *what*; stipulate order]
      John write what   [Merge *John* with *write what*; stipulate order]
      [C,+wh] John write what
                          [Merge [C,+wh] with *John write what*; stipulate order]
      what [C,+wh] John write t_{what}
                          [Copy *what*, Re-Merge *what* with [C,+wh] *John write t_{what}*]

This derivation involves three essential devices. First is the merging of [C,+*wh*] in the initial position. Second is the crucial step of copying *what* and adjoining the copy to the clause in the position of [Spec, [C, +*wh*]], which is tantamount to movement. Third, in the MP, this adjunction is conditioned by the requirement that some features of the functional head (here represented as *wh*) be matched with the features of the adjoined constituent; this matching produces movement into the specifier configuration.

In our account, the position of Q in semantics is determined by the meaning of the sentence. The counterpart of copying *what* and re-Merging, thereby creating a chain, is the double linking of the variable in CS to the chain in syntax. The counterpart of matching features of the adjoined phrase to [C,+*wh*] is the semantic binding of the variable by the operator. Only the first of these involves syntax at all.

Another way to achieve the effect of movement syntactically is simply to produce the *wh*-phrase and its trace together as a pair. Either the chain is created as a primitive (much as we have done in our own analysis), or there is a chain creation operation that applies to a phrase in situ; these appear to be equivalent operations from the perspective of economy.

(16) what   [Select *what* from the numeration]
      what | t_{what}   [Create Chain/Copy]
(17) whose book   [Merge *whose* and *book*]
      whose book | t_{whose book}   [Create Chain/Copy]

The creation of *what* paired with t_{what} is the foundation of *wh*-movement, although not equivalent to it unless the *wh*-phrase is positioned in a position that is not adjacent to the trace.[7] Suppose that subsequent Merges may leave

---

[7] In fact, one might suggest in a minimalist framework that *wh* in situ differs from *wh*-movement simply in where the *wh*-phrase ends up. The pairing of the *wh*-phrase and the (silent) trace could be common to movement and non-movement.

what on the left periphery. This allows the rest of the structure to be built up, with *what* always being in a leftmost position. This is more or less how Tree-Adjoining Grammar (Frank and Kroch 1995) produces *wh*-constructions. Continuing on from the derivation in (16):

(18) what | write t_{what} [Merge *write* with t_{what}]
      what | John write t_{what} [Merge *John* with *write* t_{what}]

This derivation avoids movement, adjunction, and intermediate copies of the *wh*-phrase. It is essentially the same as our construction of the syntactic structure, except that it treats all of the individual sublinearizations as ordered steps rather than simultaneous constraints. While minimalist with a vengeance, it differs crucially from the transformational derivation of A′-movement, because *what* does not in fact get to initial position by movement.

In short, in Simpler Syntax we do not map phrase structures into phrase structures; rather we map CS-representations into phrase structures. There are no syntactic operations of Move, Copy, or Merge that distinguish the linearization of an interrogative direct object in clause-initial position from the linearization of a non-interrogative direct object in postverbal position. They are both accomplished by interface rules that map constituents onto particular positions depending on their syntactic properties and semantic roles. Furthermore, the binding of the clause-initial *wh*-phrase to the trace is not accomplished by copying, Merge, and deletion, as in the MP, but by creation of the chain, linking both its members to the bound variable, and positioning of the head of the chain in clause-initial position. Aside from the presence of the chain, everything is done in the semantics and the syntax–semantics interface.

9.2.3 *In situ wh- and pied-piping*

The account given thus far calls for some revision when we consider in situ *wh*-questions and *wh*-questions with pied-piping. For the former, we could consider languages in which in situ *wh* is the normal form for questions, and we will look at such languages briefly in section 9.3.3. But for the moment it's easier to consider English echo-questions and "quizmaster/pedagogical" questions, which have different conversational pragmatics but the appropriate syntax.

(19) a. Echo question:
         You saw **who** last night? [*upward intonation*]
      b. Quizmaster/pedagogical question:
         The election of 1848 brought **who** to the presidency?
                                                        [*downward intonation*]

The formalism for *wh*-questions in the previous section is easily adapted to these constructions. Let us call the CS operators for these types EQ and QQ respectively, to distinguish them from ordinary Q. The difference between these and standard *wh*-questions is that the *wh*-word is in its canonical position and there is no trace. Thus there is no need for indirect licensing either. These constructions also stipulate links to prosody that produce the characteristic intonation.

(20)   **Echo question**
$$[EQx_1[\mathscr{F}(\ldots x_1 \ldots)]]_2 \qquad [_S \ldots [wh]_1 \ldots]_2$$
$$\text{[upward terminal intonation]}_2$$

   Quizmaster/pedagogical question
$$[QQx_1[\mathscr{F}(\ldots x_1 \ldots)]]_2 \qquad [_S \ldots [wh]_1 \ldots]_2$$
$$\text{[downward terminal intonation]}_2$$

English in situ *wh*-questions do not observe so-called extraction constraints. Section 9.2.3 takes up the question of the different status of in situ *wh*-questions with respect to such constraints.[8]

More problematic is the formulation of the *wh*-construction to permit pied-piping, when not just a *wh*-word but a constituent containing the *wh*-word appears at the front of the question. The problem is that the complex of operator variable + bound variable does not match the complex of fronted constituent + trace.

(21)   Whose book did John read?
   Syntax: $[_{NP}[_{NP} \text{ who}]_2 + \text{poss book}]_1$ did John read t_1
   CS: $Qx_{PERSON:2} [\text{READ (JOHN, } [\text{BOOK; ASSOC-WITH } x_2]_1)]$
   'What is the *x*, *x* a person, such that John read *x*'s book?'

Thus the two-to-two mapping of subscripts illustrated in (11) will not work for this case.

The crucial problem is that the fronted *wh*-phrase corresponds not to the bound variable in CS, but to a constituent $G(\ldots x \ldots)$ that *contains* the bound variable, here 'book associated with *x*' (i.e. a book that *x* owns or *x* wrote or some other pragmatically appropriate connection). Thus the index that links the operator variable to the bound variable has to be dissociated from the one that

---

[8] English multiple *wh*-questions also show *wh*- in situ, as in *Who bought what? Where did you put what?* We discuss these briefly in section 9.3.1.
   The distinction between the operators EQ and Q can be demonstrated by a sentence that contains both: *What did WHO buy?* [upward intonation]. This has the CS $[EQ^\alpha[Q^\beta[BUY(\alpha,\beta)]]]$. The echo-question takes scope over the ordinary question: its force is "what x is such that you asked the question 'what did x buy?'?"

links $G(\dots x \dots)$ to the *wh*-phrase and the trace. The result is a structure along the lines of (22), in which $G(\dots x \dots)$ is linked to an initial YP containing the *wh*-word and to the trace.[9]

(22) **Wh-question, second approximation**
$$[Qx_1[\mathscr{F}(\dots[G(\dots x_1 \dots)]_2 \dots]]_3 \Leftrightarrow$$
$$[_S[_{YP} \dots [wh]_1 \dots]_2^{ORPH} \dots [t]_2^{TARG} \dots]_3^{IL/ANT}$$

Rule (22) needs to be illustrated with a diagram (we omit *Tense* and the GF-tier for simplicity).

(23) $[Qx_1 [READ (JOHN_4, [BOOK; ASSOC-WITH x_1]_2)]_3]_5$

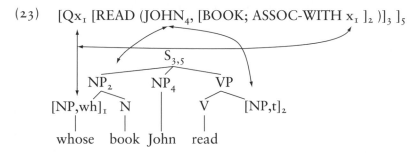

This has a two-to-one linking from the two occurrences of the variable in CS to the *wh*-word (index 1), and a one-to-two linking from the CS constituent containing the bound variable to the chain of *whose book* and the trace (index 2). In simple *wh*-questions, the function G is the identity function and YP is the category of the *wh*-word, so that (22) reduces to (12.v).

Consider also the case of an oblique NP argument whose preposition has pied-piped along, such as (1), *With whom is Terry flirting?* Here, since *with* contributes no independent meaning, the semantic function G is the identity function, but $YP = PP$. Thus the formulation in (22) allows for pied-piping in the case of oblique arguments as well.

However, it's still pretty horrible. In order to improve on it, we need to back up a little and look from a larger perspective. So far, we have notated variable binding along conventional lines familiar from formal logic. However, section

---

[9] As our rule stands, the [wh] can be indefinitely deeply embedded in the clause-initial constituent. This is probably too free, although examples like (i), along lines suggested by Ross (1967), suggest that there is considerable freedom, at least in formal speech registers:

(i)   The lettering on the covers of which books did Bill design?

However the limits on pied-piping are stipulated, they are no worse in the present framework than in others. For discussion of the formal mechanism for implementing pied-piping in the minimalist framework, see Koster (2000).

6.2.2 introduced a different notation for binding in connection with control, and section 6.4 applied the same notation to reflexives:

(24)   a. Pat tried to sneeze: [TRY (PAT$^\alpha$, [SNEEZE (α)])]
       b. Pat shot herself: [SHOOT (PAT$^\alpha$, [α; FEM])]

Here a superscripted Greek letter marks the binder, and a matching normal-type Greek letter marks its bindee. The intent of the notation is that the reference of the bindee is determined by that of the binder. Suppose we generalize this notation to the sort of binding we are dealing with here, so that the operator variable is a Greek superscript and the bound variable is the matching normal-type Greek letter:

(25)   a. Who will John see?   [Q$^\alpha$ [SEE (JOHN, α)]]
       b. Whose book did John read?
                    [Q$^\alpha$ [READ (JOHN, [BOOK; ASSOC-WITH α])]]

For a first approximation this is nothing but a notational change. However, it points up a conceptual distinction between the indices used for binding variables in CS and those used for linking to syntax. The function of the former is to mark referential dependency among CS constituents; the function of the latter is to mark relations between CS constituents and syntactic constituents. The two functions should be kept distinct, and we will henceforth do so by using Greek letters for CS-binding and numerals for CS–syntax linking.

Going back to diagram (23), we therefore replace the CS expression with that in (25b), which uses Greek letters to connect Q and the bound variable. Now the question arises as to whether Q$^\alpha$ or α—or both—should carry the subscript that links to *whose*. The operator variable (the superscript α) is of course at the edge of the CS expression, the correct position for mapping straightforwardly to the linear position of the fronted *wh*-phrase. Moreover, in the conventional notation (9b), the restriction on the variable ('for which x, x a person...') is a component of the operator variable, again suggesting that this is the one that should be linked to syntax.

On the other hand, the present notation suggests the opposite, for four reasons. First, the superscripted α is no longer a CS constituent—it is just a marker that ties the bound variable to the operator. It is therefore not a candidate for linking.[10] Second, in in situ *wh*-questions, the *wh*-phrase falls in the position where one would expect it under normal linking, and therefore it clearly is the one that links to syntax. Third, consider how referential binding

---

[10] Unless of course we play notational games with the superscripts and indices for which there is no apparent motivation.

works. The binder and the bindee each have their own links to syntax (in the case of a controlled bindee, to the GF-tier alone—see section 6.2). Crucially, the superscripted index on the binder plays no role at all in the mapping from the binder to syntax. For instance, PAT maps to *Pat* in (24) regardless of whether it binds anything. By parallelism, the superscripted operator variable in questions should not play a role in linking, either. Fourth, consider the reflexive in (24b). The fact that *Pat* is female is indicated not by the antecedent but by the reflexive: the CS of *herself* is $[\alpha; FEM]$. Thus in the case of reflexive binding, the restriction on the bound variable is part of the content of the bound variable, not part of the operator variable. By parallelism, the CS of *who* and *whose* ought to be $[\alpha; PERSON]$. Thus again the operator variable plays no role in the mapping to syntax.

With all these considerations in mind, we arrive at a structure like (26). The superscript on the operator binds the bound variable, and in turn the bound variable is linked to syntax. The pied-piped phrase *whose book* is built up in the usual way; both it and the trace are linked to the CS constituent containing the bound variable. The positioning of *whose book* is determined by the operator Q: it is at the front of the clause linked (here, by index 5) to the CS constituent that Q heads. (We notate the dependence of the bound variable on the operator redundantly by the Greek letters and by a directed arrow within CS.)

(26) $[Q^{\alpha}[\text{READ (JOHN}_4, [\text{BOOK; ASSOC-W } [\alpha;PERSON]_1]_2)]_3]_5$

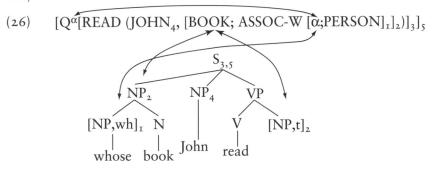

This leads to a final revision of the rule for wh-questions, (27a). For consistency, we also restate as (27b,c) the rules of sluicing (including pied-piped sluicing, which we did not state in Chapter 7) and echo-questions.

(27)   a. **Wh-question** (final revision)

$$[Q^{\alpha}[\mathscr{F}(\ldots[G(\ldots\alpha_1\ldots)]_2\ldots]]_3 \Leftrightarrow$$
$$[_S[_{YP}\ldots[wh]_1\ldots]_2{}^{ORPH}\ldots[t]_2{}^{TARG}\ldots]_3{}^{IL/ANT}$$

   b. **Sluicing**

$$[Q^{\alpha}[\mathscr{F}(\ldots[G(\ldots\alpha_1\ldots)]_2\ldots]]_3 \Leftrightarrow [_S[_{YP}\ldots[wh]_1\ldots]_2{}^{ORPH}]_3{}^{IL}$$

c. **Echo-question**

$$[EQ^{\alpha}[\mathscr{F}(\ldots\alpha_{I}\ldots)]]_{2} \Leftrightarrow [_{S}\ldots[wh]_{I}\ldots]_{2}$$

It is important to see how (27a) creates the illusion of movement. The semantic operator Q is co-head of a particular clause in syntax, along with the verb and the tense. The *wh*-phrase YP is positioned at the front of the clause co-headed by Q, and the trace is in a position determined by the normal rules of argument and modifier linking. Hence we get the characteristic syntactic structure of A′-constructions through a direct mapping from semantics.

Under this account, the semantic parallelism among the three forms of questions in (27) is due to the common form of their conceptual structures. Because of this semantic parallelism, MGG is forced by Interface Uniformity to treat sluicing and echo-questions also as cases of movement—the former as movement followed by deletion, the latter as covert LF-movement—even though in these constructions there is not even the illusion of movement. Simpler Syntax, by contrast, allows the superficially simpler constructions to be genuinely simpler.

A further note is in order on the notation proposed here for the CS of questions. We have proposed a common formalism for referential binding and for the binding of variables by operators such as Q. It is important to see how this notation works in a sentence where both types of binding are involved. A more or less conventional approach might look like (28).

(28) a. Who shot herself? $Qx [SHOOT (x, x)]$
   b. Who does Fred think shot herself?

$$Qx[THINK (FRED, [SHOOT (x, x)])]$$

Here both arguments of *shoot* are bound to the Q-operator. However, recall how we encoded combinations of control and reflexive binding in section 6.4:

(29) Sue tries to like herself. $[TRY (SUE^{\alpha}, [LIKE(\alpha^{\beta}, \beta)])]$

This keeps the binding relations distinct: the control relation is indicated by the αs, and the bound variable α in turn serves as binder for the reflexive binding, indicated by the βs. Applying this approach to the examples in (28), we get the following:

(30) a. Who shot herself? $Q^{\alpha}[SHOOT(\alpha^{\beta}, \beta)]$
   b. Who does Fred think shot herself?

$$Q^{\alpha}[THINK (FRED, [SHOOT(\alpha^{\beta}, \beta)])]$$

Returning to pied-piping: The *wh*-question rule as stated allows pied-piping to be optional. Thus it should be possible to map *whose* alone onto initial position, yielding *Whose did John read t book*, a violation of the Left-Branch condition (Ross 1967). Similarly, alongside *How long is the book,* with pied-piping, we should get *How is the book t long*. An attractive way to incorporate this condition into the grammar is to stipulate that in English, for whatever reason, the configurations $[_{NP}\ t\ N]$ and $[_{AP}\ t\ A]$ are not legitimate structures. English contrasts with Russian and Latin, in which the word-for-word translation of *whose read John [t book]* is perfectly all right.[11]

(31) a. *Russian*
　　　 Č'ju$_i$　ty　čitaješ $[_{NP}$ t$_i$　knigu] ?
　　　 whose　you are-reading　book
　　　 'Whose book are you reading?'
　　 b. *Latin*
　　　 Cuius$_i$ legis　　　$[_{NP}$ t$_i$　librum] ?
　　　 whose　you-are-reading　book
　　　 'Whose book are you reading?'

There are of course many languages that do not permit preposition stranding, for instance German.

(32) *German*
　　 a. *Wem　　geht Katharina　ins　　Kino　　[mit t]?
　　　　 who-dat goes K.　　　　 to-the　movies　with
　　 b. Mit wem geht Katharina ins Kino?

The impossibility of P-stranding in such languages has the same formal status as the impossibility of extracting *whose* from *whose book* in English. That is, these languages prohibit the configuration $[_{PP}\ P\ t]$.[12]

How are these configurations excluded? Going back to Chomsky (1964a) and Ross (1967), MGG assumes that *wh*-movement is totally free, and extrinsic constraints such as the Left-Branch condition are needed to restrict it. Since it would take negative evidence to learn these constraints, they must be part of UG. Given the variability among languages, the constraints must be moreover parameterized. We propose an alternative: syntactic configurations containing a trace are by default excluded unless there is positive evidence for them. In other words, the *permissible* configurations for "extraction" are learned. We take this hypothesis up in slightly more detail in section 9.4.

---

[11] For discussion and analysis of examples such as these, see Corver (1990; 1992).

[12] We might also note, following Culicover (1999), that there are individual prepositions in English that prohibit stranding for no apparent semantic reason:

(i) Which talk did you arrive in time for/*during?
　　 Who did you stay home in spite of/*despite?
　　 *Which couch did you rescue the pen from under? [Huddleston and Pullum 2002: 630, 10i]

9.3 Other *wh*-constructions

9.3.1 *The signature of a long-distance dependency*

The comparison of *wh*-questions, sluicing, and echo-questions paves the way for a more general examination of long-distance dependency constructions. They all have in common a CS in which an operator binds a variable within its scope. They differ in the permissible configurations at the front of the clause, which we will call the "signature" of the construction in question. A signature is a pairing of syntactic and CS properties which, taken together, define a particular construction. For example, English tensed relative clauses permit a *wh*-phrase, *that*, or null in the signature; free relatives permit, among other things, *wh+ever* in their signature (*whoever Bill sees*); exclamations permit *what a N* and *how Adj* in their signature, and unlike *wh*-questions, do not invert the auxiliary in main clauses. A well-known difficult case is the infinitival relative clause in English, which stipulates an infinitival inflection, and permits a *wh*-PP, a *for*+subject NP, or null in the signature, but not other combinations.

(33) a. a person [with whom to work]
  b. a person [for Bill to work with]
  c. a person [to work with]
  d. *a person [who(m) to work with]
  e. *a person [with whom for Bill to work][13]

  As can be seen from the cases we have mentioned, the signature for a construction involves not just the "fronted" phrase but its interaction with properties of the complementizer, the subject, and the inflection (including the possibility or necessity of inversion). Instead of encoding these peculiarities in terms of the movement of a constituent to Comp (the standard approach in MGG), we adapt a treatment of long-distance dependencies advanced in differing versions by HPSG (Pollard and Sag 1994; Sag 1997; Ginzburg and Sag 2000), Construction Grammar (Fillmore and Kay 1993), and Tree-Adjoining Grammar (Frank and Kroch 1995). In these frameworks, the grammar contains a general treatment of long-distance dependencies in terms of the relation between a gap (or trace) within a clause and a constituent or operator in front of the clause. This constituent, along with properties of Comp, subject, and Infl of the uppermost clause of the construction, are the construction's signature,

---

[13] Ginzburg and Sag (2000: 7ff.) provide a formalized constructionist account of the various signatures found in English and the relationships between them. One might use inheritance hierarchies to capture the similarities among the constructions, as in Fillmore and Kay (1993), Michaelis and Lambrecht (1996), and Sag (1997).

and the construction is defined in terms of its signature. The signature is regarded as base-generated, not as moved from some underlying syntactic position; hence it can be described directly in phrase-structure terms. Its relation to the trace is regarded as a constraint on surface configuration.[14]

The definition of any particular long-distance dependency construction, then, involves (a) specifying its signature, including the structure of the fronted constituent and Infl features of the clause to which the signature is adjoined (e.g. tensed, infinitival, inverted), and (b) inheriting all the general properties of long-distance dependencies from the constraints on the relation of signatures to traces. Proposals of this sort have been in the literature, even within mainstream tradition, for years (e.g. Brame 1978; Koster 1978; Brody 1995). Nevertheless, the movement analysis has been predominant, often introducing empty operators or equivalent devices in order to have something to move (e.g. Chomsky 1977).

9.3.2 Other wh-constructions in English

Remaining for a moment within the domain of questions, consider multiple *wh*-questions such as *What did Bill read when?* The Q operator must be marked as binding two distinct variables, perhaps along the lines of (34); but the signature for English *wh*-questions permits only one A′-position at the front. Therefore the other *wh*-phrases must remain in situ.

(34)   What did Bill read when? $Q^{\alpha,\beta}[\text{READ (BILL, } \alpha);[_{\text{Time}} \beta]]$

For a language such as Bulgarian, in which all *wh*-phrases appear in initial position, the signature permits multiple fronted phrases.[15]

---

[14] See section 14.4 for discussion of the intricate signatures of fronted degree expressions such as *so...that, all the more,* and *the more.*

We recall as graduate students in the 1960s trying to write transformations to make the signatures come out right for each construction following movement to the front. This proved a tricky and unreliable enterprise; and interestingly enough (speaking a little ironically), it was largely abandoned in MGG once A′-movement came to be treated as a unitary process. By contrast, a treatment in terms of construction-specific phrase structure is eminently tractable—and learnable.

[15] The semantics of multiple *wh*-questions is somewhat complex. On the one hand, in English, at least, they presuppose a list of tuples. For example, *Mary bought a book* is not an appropriate answer to *Who bought what?*—in contrast to Japanese (Citko and Grohmann 2001). On the other hand, multiple *wh*-questions with *which* do allow a single pair answer (Dayal 2002). Moreover, it is open to question whether the appropriate representation of the multiple *wh*-question is that of two variables bound by the same *wh*-operator, as in (i), or one variable bound by the *wh*-operator, and the other variable bound by the first variable, as in (ii), or both.

Turning to relative clauses, the CS has a different operator. Section 5.2 introduced the lambda operator, adapted from traditional lambda-extraction, as a way of recasting a Situation as a Property of a character in that Situation. Revising the notation along the lines worked through in section 9.2.3, the semantics of a relative clause comes out like (35).

(35)   a book that John read: [BOOK; INDEF; [$_{\text{Property}}\lambda^{\alpha}$[$_{\text{Situation}}$READ (JOHN, α)]]]

In English, there are three alternative signatures for tensed clauses that express this CS: with a *wh*-phrase, with the complementizer *that*, and with nothing. Only the first of these maps to a chain and permits pied-piping. They can be formulated as (36a–c).

(36)   <u>Conceptual structure</u>   <u>Syntax</u>
       a. ***Wh-relative***
       [$_{\text{Property}}\lambda^{\alpha}$[$\mathscr{F}$(...[G(...$\alpha_{\text{I}}$...)]$_2$...]]$_3$ ⇔ [$_{\text{S}}$[$_{\text{YP}}$...[wh]$_{\text{I}}$...]$_2^{\text{ORPH}}$...[t]$_2^{\text{TARG}}$...]$_3^{\text{IL/ANT}}$
       b. ***That-relative***
          [$_{\text{Property}}\lambda^{\alpha}$[$\mathscr{F}$(...$\alpha_{\text{I}}$...)]]$_3$ ⇔ [$_{\text{S}}$ that...[t]$_{\text{I}}$...]$_3$
       c. ***Zero relative***
          [$_{\text{Property}}\lambda^{\alpha}$[$\mathscr{F}$(...$\alpha_{\text{I}}$...)]]$_3$ ⇔ [$_{\text{S}}$ NP...[t]$_{\text{I}}$...]$_3$

Notice that only the *wh*-relative requires indirect licensing, for only here is there something at the front of the clause that must be related to the trace. In the other two, there is not even the illusion of movement, unless we require it by analogy with *wh*-relative clauses, bolstered by Interface and Derivational Uniformity. On the present account, again the superficially simpler forms come out formally simpler.[16]

Free relatives such as those in (37a) have posed a technical problem within traditional frameworks, in that the *wh*-word looks on one hand as though it has been fronted from the clause and on the other as though it is the head of the whole NP. Thus there are conflicting analyses in the literature along lines such as (37b,c) (for discussion, see Bresnan and Grimshaw 1978).

(i) a. Q$^{\alpha,\beta}$[$\mathscr{F}$(...α,β,...)]
(ii) b. Q$^{\alpha}$[$\mathscr{F}$(...α^{β},β,...)]

Because of these and other complexities, a discussion of multiple *wh*-questions requires a far more detailed analysis than we can devote to them here. We therefore leave them aside, but do not wish to suggest by doing so that they are either uninteresting or straightforward. Rudin (1988) has discussion of multiple *wh*-questions in the Slavic languages, and the papers in Boeckx and Grohmann (2003) analyze multiple *wh*-questions in a range of languages. See also Ginzburg and Sag (2000).

[16] (36c) stipulates that the clause must begin with an NP, in order to account for *the man *(that) saw Bill* in the standard dialect; there are dialects that lack this restriction. There are doubtless other ways to state this restriction.

(37)   a. What you see is what you get.
     b. *Wh moves; empty NP head:*
        [$_{NP}$ e [$_{CP}$ what$_i$ [you see t$_i$]]]
     c. *Wh is head of NP; covert operator OP moves:*
        [$_{NP}$ what$_i$ [$_{CP}$ OP$_i$ [you see t$_i$]]]

The conflict is forced by Interface and Derivational Uniformity: whenever the symptoms of long-distance dependency appear, they must be due to movement of something or another to [Spec, CP], leaving behind a trace (recall the quote from Chomsky to this effect in section 2.1.2).

In the present framework, there is nothing in principle to prohibit the trace from being bound to a *wh*-word that serves as head of the NP. In order to formulate the rule, we need a CS for free relatives. There seem to be (at least) two possible CSs, which we might call "definite" and "indefinite" free relatives. For the "definite" form in (38a), a possible operator is Russell's iota, 'the x such that F(x)', shown in (38a). An alternative notation for this reading might decompose the iota operator into a definite plus a relative clause, 'the entity that you see', shown in (38b) (where the head has only the content NEUTER, plus a definiteness feature and a modifier). The "indefinite" free relative uses the *wh-ever* form, e.g. *whatever you see*, for which a reasonable paraphrase is *anything you see*. This suggests that the operator for this form is something like *any*. Given that we have not treated quantifiers, the formulation in (38c) is very tentative; the parallel to (38b) is attractive.

(38)   a. what you see: [ι^α[SEE (YOU, α)]]
     b. what you see: [NEUT; DEF; [$_{Property}\lambda^\alpha$[SEE (YOU, α)]]]
     c. whatever you see: [α; NEUT; ANY$^\alpha$;[$_{Property}\lambda^\beta$[SEE (YOU, β)]]]

The crucial point for syntax is that the *wh*-word is indirectly licensed by a trace within the free relative, but it is also directly licensed by the clause in which the free relative is embedded. For instance, *what you see* has to appear in an NP position, because *what* is a noun, but *wherever you go* has to appear in a PP position, because *where* is a preposition. In the structure-sharing formalism available to us, such double constraints are not problematic: we just have to locate the *wh*-word in head position in the XP, so that direct licensing will apply to it. (39) states a version of the rule, using the CS format of (38a). (There is no pied-piping in free relatives, so the structure is simpler than ordinary relatives.) (40) shows the structure of an example.

(39)   **"Definite" free relative**
     [ι^α[$\mathscr{F}$(...α_1...)]$_2$]$_3$ $\Leftrightarrow$ [$_{XP}$[wh]$_1$[$_S$...[t]$_1$^{TARG}...]$_2$^{ANT}]$_3$^{ORPH}

(40)

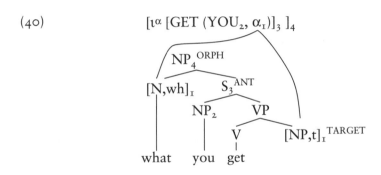

The structure in (39–40) captures the desired properties of free relatives without any covert structure of the sort seen in (37b,c). The dual properties of the *wh*-phrase—as a head of the NP and as the antecedent of the trace—follow from the way the bound variable maps to syntax plus the properties of indirect licensing. In particular, the entire free relative is treated as the orphan, leading to the desired matching of features.

Some further cases of long-distance dependencies will be discussed in sections 9.4.5 and 9.5.

9.3.3 Chains and wh in situ

One of the most salient characteristics of non-echo *wh*-questions of the English type is how the CS information about the operator and the variable *wh*-phrase is distributed over the chain. The scope of the operator is indicated by the position of the *wh*-phrase in the sentence, the restriction on the variable is indicated by the form of the *wh*-phrase, and the position of the variable is indicated by the position of the trace.

The same information must be represented in *wh* in situ constructions in languages such as Chinese and Japanese. In the case of in situ *wh*, the scope may be determined by the position of a scope marker, as in Japanese, or it may be implicit, as in Chinese and French. In the case of a scope marker, there is a syntactic component to such a determination of scope, in the sense that the *wh* in situ must be related to the scope marker across some syntactic structure. In Japanese, the scope marker *-ka/-no* is attached to the verb that heads the sentence over which the interrogative takes scope—just where we would expect it, given its semantic scope.

(41) a. [anata-wa John-ga   dare-o   aisiteiru-ka] sitteiru.
          you-Top   John-Nom   who-Acc   love   Q know
          'You know who John loves.'

b. [anata-wa John-ga   dare-o   aisiteiru to] omotteiru-no?
   you-Top John-Nom who-Acc love COMP think   Q
   'Who do you think that John loves?'
c. [Robin-wa   Kelly-ga   nani-o   mottekita-ka] itta-ndesu-ka?
   Robin-TOP Kelly-NOM what-ACC brought- Q   said-POLITE-Q
   'Did Robin say what Kelly brought?'
d. [Robin-wa   Kelly-ga   nani-o   mottekita-to] itta-ndesu-ka?
   Robin-TOP Kelly-NOM what-ACC brought-that said-POLITE-Q
   'What did Robin say that Kelly brought?'

There are clearly processing issues here, as there are in the case of *wh*-extraction (Miyamoto and Takahashi 2001). The fact that *wh*-questions in languages such as Japanese do not appear to obey movement constraints such as subjacency (Watanabe 1992) suggests that the processing complexity for *wh* in situ is different from *wh*-extraction. At the same time, computing the relationship between the *wh* in situ and the scope marker is a nontrivial task, and we would expect to find processing complexities that are particular to it. But we would not necessarily expect the processing requirements to be the same as in the case of chain formation of the English type.

As noted, Chinese also has *wh* in situ. But in Chinese, there is nothing to mark the scope of the *wh*. Thus it is formally (but not pragmatically) similar to the English case of "quizmaster" questions and "leading-the-witness" questions, mentioned in section 9.2.3, where the hearer can be reasonably expected to know the answer. Consider the following, which do not have an echo intonation.

(42) a. For $100, Martha Washington was married to which American president.
     b. ...and after you received the money, you went right out and spent it on what.

In English the *wh*-phrase must have widest scope. We cannot understand (43a), for example, as (43b).

(43) a. ...and then you said that he had been smoking what.
     b. ...and then you said what he had been smoking.

The reason for the impossibility of the interpretation (43b) is, presumably, that in English, intermediate scope must be overtly marked by a *wh*-phrase at the front of the embedded question. Similar observations hold for French, which uses *wh*-in situ much more freely than does English (Rizzi 1996), but overtly marks the beginning of interrogative complements.

However, Chinese uses *wh* in situ and does not mark the beginning of interrogative complements. Rather, a *wh*-phrase may take scope over any clause that allows an interrogative interpretation. For instance, in (44a), the *wh*-phrase is in the main clause and naturally takes scope over it. In (44b,c) the verb obligatorily selects a *wh*-question as its complement; therefore the *wh*-phrase takes scope over that complement. In (44d,e) the verb selects a non-*wh*-complement; therefore the *wh*-phrase takes wide scope. In (44f) the verb optionally selects a *wh*-question as its complement, and therefore the *wh*-phrase may take either scope.

(44) a. Ni   xihuan shei?
         you like   who
      b. Zhangsan wen wo   [shei mai-le shu].
         Zhangsan ask me   who   bought books
         "Zhangsan asked me who bought books.'
      c. Zhangsan wen wo   [ni   maile   shenme]
         Zhangsan ask me   you bought what
         'Zhangsan asked me what you bought.'
      d. Zhangsan xiangxin [shei mai-le shu].
         Zhangsan believe   who   bought books
         'Who does Zhangsan believe bought books?'
      e. Zhangsan renwei [ni   maile   shenme]
         Zhangsan think   you bought what
         "What does Zhangsan think you bought?'
      f. Zhangsan zhidao [shei mai-le shu].
         Zhangsan know   who   bought books
         i. 'Who does Zhangsan know bought books?'
         ii. 'Zhangsan knows who bought books.'
   [Huang 1982a]

As the examples from Japanese and Chinese show, in the case of *wh* in situ, there is no problem with determining the propositional function of the interrogative phrase, in contrast to what happens when there is a chain. However, a computational problem arises in determining the scope of the Q operator. In Japanese this is marked overtly by a fixed morpheme; in Chinese it is a matter of the semantics of the verbs in question plus pragmatics. The Simpler Syntax Hypothesis suggests that *wh*-chains and *wh* in situ are syntactically distinct, do not share the syntactic mechanisms such as movement and constraints on movement that follow from a Uniformity approach, and require different mechanisms for interpretation. In particular, there is no need for a syntactic chain or indirect licensing for in situ *wh*. And there is certainly no evidence aside from Uniformity for movement.[17]

9.4. Island constraints

9.4.1 *Against intermediate traces of movement*

As mentioned briefly in section 9.2, the predominant assumption about long-distance dependencies is that they are fundamentally free, and that ungrammatical long-distance movement is prohibited by constraints extrinsic to the process of movement itself. From Chomsky (1973) through MP, MGG seeks to constrain movement by the use of intermediate traces that mark out discrete steps of movement. On this view, an intermediate trace is the reflex of a maximally short movement, ending at a landing site at the front of a constituent which dominates the trace and which is in turn a constituent of the clause to which the *wh*-phrase will eventually move. In pre-MP, all longer movements are simply prohibited. In MP, any longer movement would be ruled out as uneconomical relative to the shortest movement; since movement is actually Copy and Merge, each successive movement leaves behind a trace in the site of the previous adjunction.

The device of intermediate traces, which is central to the analysis of long movement in Chomsky (1981; 1986a; 1986b), and much other work, is not available to us under the Simpler Syntax Hypothesis. This is in fact the right result, since there is no independent syntactic evidence for intermediate traces, at least in English and many other well-studied languages (though see n. 19 below). Two arguments point to this conclusion.

First, the original motivation for step-by-step movement (Chomsky 1973) was its explanation for Ross's (1967) Complex NP Constraint, which prohibits extraction out of complement clauses within definite NPs (** What did you learn the fact that Ida ate t?*). The idea was that NP lacks a landing site for the *wh*-phrase as it attempts to move to the top of the tree. Such a landing site, if it existed, would be a counterpart of C at the front of sentences. The difficulty is

---

[17] There are also languages, such as Hungarian, Hindi, and (dialects of) German, that show varieties of "partial *wh*-movement". The *wh*-phrase in such cases does not appear at the edge of the clause, but at the edge of an embedded clause, while the main clause contains an expletive that realizes the scope of the question (see e.g. McDaniel 1989, Müller 1997, and Horvath 1997). Such cases would appear to require some complication in stating where the *wh*-phrase goes in the syntax but are not otherwise problematic for our approach, as far as we can tell.

that it is indeed possible to question a constituent of an NP, as well as a constituent of a gerundive, infinitival, or small clause (in the sense of section 4.5.3), even though there is no concrete evidence for an 'escape hatch' position in such constructions. The kind of evidence that we would look for would be that such a complement may have a topic or fronted adverbial adjoined in initial position. The following examples illustrate.

(45)   *Complements of NPs*
    a.   I bought a picture of [NP Santa Claus in the bathtub].
    b.   Who did you buy [a picture of t in the bathtub]?
                                      [*who* can escape from NP]
    c.   *I bought [in the bathtub [a picture of Santa Claus] t].
                                       [PP cannot be fronted in NP]
    d.   In the bathtub I discovered [a picture of Santa Claus] t.
                                       [PP can be fronted in S]

(46)   *Gerundive complements*
    a.   I talked about [Ger Leslie singing the Marseillaise in German last night].
    b.   What song did you talk about [Leslie singing t in German last night]?   [*wh* can escape from gerundive]
    c.   *I talked about [last night Leslie singing the Marseillaise in German t].   [*last night* cannot be fronted in gerundive]
    d.   Last night Leslie sang the Marseillaise in German t.
                                     [*last night* can be fronted in S]

(47)   *Infinitival complements*
    a.   Mary expected John [to sing the Marseillaise tomorrow night].
    b.   What did Mary expect John [to sing t tomorrow night]?
                                       [*wh* can escape from VP]
    c.   *Mary expected John [tomorrow night to sing the Marseillaise t]
                                [*tomorrow night* cannot be fronted in VP]
    d.   *Mary expected [tomorrow night John to sing the Marseillaise t]]
                           [*tomorrow night* cannot be fronted in clause (if it is one)]

(48)   *Small clauses*
    a.   John imagined [SC Mary singing the Marseillaise tomorrow night].
    b.   What did John imagine [Mary singing t tomorrow night]?
                                       [*wh* can escape from SC]
    c.   *John imagined [tomorrow night [Mary singing the Marseillaise t]].
                                 [*tomorrow night* cannot be fronted in SC]
    d.   Tomorrow night Mary will sing the Marseillaise t.
                                  [*tomorrow night* can be fronted in S]

As far as we can determine, the only motivation for a left adjunction site in NPs, infinitivals, gerundives, or small clauses is Structural and Derivational Uniformity.[18]

In the absence of overt evidence for such left adjunction sites, Simpler Syntax suggests that they do not exist.[19] If they do not, there is no way that we can leave behind intermediate traces in them as the moving constituent lands in them on the way to the initial position. The only traces that are permitted are those that correspond to actual gaps in the syntactic structure, as defined through the syntactic realization of CS. We will discuss shortly an alternative way to establish the chain relation between the filler and the gap: the device of slash-categories, a central innovation of GPSG.

A second argument against intermediate traces was presented by Bresnan (1977). It involves the phenomenon of 'comparative subdeletion', illustrated in (49) (from Bresnan (1977: 162–3)).

(49) a. Why were there more women on tv than there were men?
      b. There weren't as many women on tv as there were men.

Bresnan argues that there must be an unbounded link between the comparative (e.g. *more women* in (49a)) and the unexpressed quantifier of the second NP (e.g. *men*). While Bresnan discusses the relationship in terms of deletion, we can express it just as well in terms of a chain linking the two quantifier phrases, as in (50a). Crucially, there can be no *wh*-"movement" from the position of the trace (50b), because it violates the Left-Branch condition.

(50) a. There weren't [[as many]$_i$ women] on tv as there were [t$_i$ men].
      b. *[How many]$_i$ were there [t$_i$ men]?

---

[18] In addition, there is no independent evidence in English (or, as far as we know, in any other language that uses an A'-construction for *wh*-questions) that adjunction of a *wh*-phrase to VP is possible. This is perhaps one of the reasons why the formulation of movement in Chomsky (1986a), which utilizes adjunction to VP, was not widely adopted in subsequent work.

[19] There is overt evidence from Afrikaans, Romani, Frisian, and German for adjunction of a copy of an initial *wh*-phrase to an intermediate complement (Felser 2003). Our account does not rule out the possibility of such a construction, but simply argues against intermediate traces in languages in which there is no evidence for it. Similarly, there is linguistic (Chung 1982) and psycholinguistic (Gibson and Warren 2004) evidence that extraction from a subordinate clause may affect the form and the processing of the clause, even if there is no evidence of adjunction of anything to its left edge. The fact that something has been extracted from a sentential complement can be formally marked in other ways, e.g. percolation of a feature corresponding to the trace or slash-features (see below). Such percolation also plays a role in the formulation of island constraints; see Koster (2000).

The possibility of this chain is a property of the construction of comparative subdeletion; it is the "signature" of the construction, in the sense that we introduced earlier. Bresnan shows that the subdeletion chain is subject to all of Ross's movement constraints (except the Left-Branch Condition); here is just one example, involving the Complex NP Constraint (from Bresnan (1977: 165)).

(51)   *Why have they produced only half as many job applicants as they believe the claim that there are__jobs?

Bresnan draws the natural conclusion: in our terms, Ross's constraints are constraints on operator-trace configurations, not on movement. Chomsky (1977: 118ff.) argues against Bresnan's conclusion on the grounds that subdeletion displays a somewhat different pattern of grammaticality judgments than does *wh*-movement across a range of complex cases. While the facts may be correct, the argument is misdirected. Even if subdeletion is different in certain respects from *wh*-movement, it still falls under the generalization that accounts for (51) and similar examples that traditionally involve movement. Moreover, Chomsky provides no alternative account of subdeletion; to simply relegate it to the periphery is basically to disregard the data. As usual, the construction must be learned, and the fact that it resembles the other A′-movements in crucial respects argues that it partakes of the same machinery.

9.4.2 *Slash-categories*

By now it should be becoming clear that what MGG has termed "constraints on movement" are in the present account general constraints on the connection between an A′-operator and a gap. On this analysis, constraints subsumed under subjacency in Chomsky (1986a) and other constraints must be formulated in terms of the well-formedness of adjacent node configurations in the syntactic structure. Whatever the motivation for these constraints, they can be represented descriptively in terms of the slash-category formalism of GPSG and HPSG. Following essentially the conventions of G/HPSG (though with slightly different notation), a slash-category XP/t_{YP} designates an XP which dominates somewhere within it a trace of category YP. The trace, which has syntactic features [YP,t], is the lowest slash-category in the tree and satisfies or saturates the slash; and all the constituents dominating it up to the signature are also slash-categories. The chain of slash-categories can be as long as we like. The constituent marked ANT is at the top of the chain of slashes, so that a typical syntactic tree for a *wh*-question may be filled out as in (52).

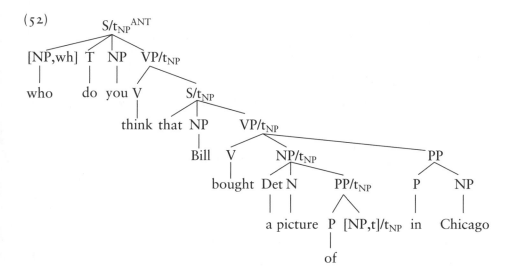

This syntactic structure captures the essential properties of the G/HPSG account of A'-constructions. For a first approximation, it does the same work as the chain of intermediate traces in MGG, but it does not require syntactic positions that have no independent justification, and it does not rely on an ordered derivation. On the other hand, it comes with a price: an enrichment of the theory of syntactic categories to include slash-categories. One might justify this price on the grounds of parsing: upon encountering (or producing) a *wh*-phrase at the front of the sentence, the parser has to keep track of the fact that it requires a gap that licenses the *wh*-phrase. The passing of the slash-feature down the tree might be taken to represent this anticipation of a gap, and to result in increased working memory load. Proposals along these lines go back as far as Wanner and Maratsos (1978) and have been a staple of the psycholinguistic literature since (see Kluender 1998 and Gibson 1998 for recent discussion).[20]

Note that a *wh*-phrase is not needed at the front in order to set up a chain of slash-categories. All that is necessary is a signature that marks a long-distance dependency construction. For example, in an English relative such as *the house I bought*, the signature is the subject of the relative jammed up against the head noun. Here there is no chain in syntax, just a trace. But the chain of slash-categories is present nevertheless, marking the dependence between the signature and the trace position.

---

[20] Recall that in a language like Japanese, the processing problem is, having heard a *wh*-phrase in situ, to find the operator that binds it at the end of a clause. As we have said, in such languages there is no chain with a trace at the bottom. However, slash-categories might still be an appropriate way to encode the processing problem. For example, *XP/wh* might denote an XP node dominating a *wh*- whose operator has not yet been found; the slash would percolate up to the node dominating the operator, where it would be saturated.

In terms of this formalism, constraints on extraction can be viewed as prohibitions on the transfer of the slash across a particular configuration. For instance, the Complex NP Constraint can be stated as (53a), and the Sentential Subject Constraint as (53b).

(53)   a.   *NP/t   (e.g. *who did you deny [NP the claim [s that Amy likes t]])

                   |

                S/t

          b.   *S/t   (e.g. *[s who did [NP a picture of t] fall on Harry]

                   |

                NP/t

Thus this formalism provides a satisfactory substitute for the intermediate traces of MGG, one that does not require movement or unjustified intermediate landing sites. For discussion, see Pollard and Sag (1994).

9.4.3 *Where do constraints come from?*

Still, a treatment of constraints as prohibitions on the formation of chains of slash-categories is not so much better than a treatment in terms of prohibitions on movement: they are still artificial stipulations that must come from somewhere. Similarly, we have noted the artificiality of ruling out preposition stranding through a prohibition on the configuration *[pp P t]. So let us consider the status of "extraction" constraints more closely. As mentioned earlier, the conventional approach in MGG is to assume that the rule for extraction is maximally general. This reflects the assumption that it is natural for a learner to generalize whenever possible, and that other things being equal, the most general formulation of a relation is preferred. Pursuing this approach to generality, the most general movement rule is one with no context and no landing site specified, and with a minimally restrictive description. This idea developed historically from individual movement rules for each long-distance dependency construction, to produce first a general rule of *wh*-fronting (from any syntactic context), then simply *Move wh* (to any position), and then *Move α*, where α is anything. This very general formulation of the rule is taken to be part of Universal Grammar and not learned—after all, what can be learned if the formulation is maximally general? The learned differences between languages are then attributed to variations in a finite number of parameters, e.g. whether the language allows *wh* to move or not. Since rules such as *Move α* overgenerate wildly, it is necessary to posit constraints that disallow certain types of application of the rules. The constraints themselves are not learned, either, though they too may be parameterized.

Against this view it has been argued (Culicover 1999; Pullum and Scholz 2002; Culicover and Nowak 2003; Culicover 2004; Tomasello 2003) that while learners generalize, they generalize on the basis of what they are exposed to, and they do not generalize more broadly than is warranted by their experience. On this view, anything that is not known to be possible is ruled out because the learner has not (yet) incorporated it into his/her grammar. Clearly, novel utterances per se do not fall under this type of prohibition, since they can be predicted from well-supported generalizations about structure and categories. But such generalizations can be limited by experience and can be constrained by complexity of structure. Thus, if we assume that the learner is a conservative generalizer, the learner's experience of *wh*-dependencies in simple sentences does not warrant a conclusion that the language permits *wh*-dependencies in complex sentences. Generalizing to the conclusion that the language allows *Move wh* (or even more generally, *Move α*) is warranted only if learners are predisposed to generalize wildly beyond their experience. We see no reason to believe that learners are so predisposed.

A converging line of thought is developed by Postal (1997c). He observes that, although extractions can indeed be unbounded in scope, in fact the constraints on extraction sharply limit the actual range of configurations that support unbounded dependencies. He suggests that if we take the trouble to enumerate these configurations, we may find it easier to characterize them positively rather than negatively—to say what *can* be extracted rather than what *can't* be. From our perspective, Postal's proposal suggests a learning procedure for extraction configurations: assume you can't extract from anyplace and then learn the possibilities in your language from positive evidence (Culicover 1999). Thus one does not need to learn a rule *[P t] in German or a rule *[$_{NP}$ t N] in English. Rather, one just has no occasion to learn [P t] or [$_{NP}$t N], so there is no way to license such configurations.

The generalization of such learning might be guided by something along the lines of the crosslinguistically motivated Accessibility Hierarchy proposed by Keenan and Comrie (1977) for relative clauses; see also Hawkins (1994). Very roughly: there is a hierarchy of structural positions on the order of (54).

(54) subject > direct object > indirect object > oblique argument > adjunct

Some languages have constructions that permit only extraction of subjects. But if a construction permits extraction of subjects and something lower on the hierarchy, it permits extraction of everything in between. Keenan and Comrie also note that many languages have special constructions that pertain only to positions lower on the hierarchy. These do not necessarily generalize upward. Looking to more complex situations, extraction from main clauses is probably higher on the hierarchy than extraction from inside infinitival complements, which is higher than extraction from embedded tensed clauses. Thus if learners hear a construction that extracts from a position low on the hierarchy and also from subjects, they can assume that all positions higher on the hierarchy can be extracted. However, if a learner lacks evidence for a particular complex extraction chain, generalization on the basis of simpler chains will not subsume the more complex case. Thus crosslinguistic differences are to be expected, but in a relatively constrained fashion.

It remains to be seen if the strategy of learning long-distance dependencies from positive evidence, guided by the Accessibility Hierarchy, can be made to work empirically. If it can, it is an improvement in the theory of UG, in that it does not posit a lot of specific technical constraints that have to be parameterized, all carried on the genome. There still remains the question of where the Accessibility Hierarchy comes from. Does *it* have to be carried on the genome instead? Keenan and Comrie suggest that it is motivated by a hierarchy in processing complexity, so it might prove to be functional rather than formal in nature. Specifically, in the present context, chains contribute to complexity in the mapping between syntax and CS, because of the displacement of the head of the chain to the position marked by the operator. Of course the specification of what constitutes greater complexity is far from trivial; see Hawkins (1994), Culicover (1999), Culicover and Nowak (2002) for discussion. Nonetheless, such an approach bolsters the Simpler Syntax hypothesis, since the complexity introduced by constraints is not part of the syntax per se but is rather stated in terms of syntax–CS correspondences.

9.4.4 *Semantic constraints on long-distance dependencies*

The discussion in this section has proceeded thus far under the standard MGG assumption that the constraints on long-distance dependencies are purely syntactic in nature—that they concern the syntactic connection of the head of the chain and its trace. But there has also been a long tradition in the field arguing that at least some constraints on long-distance dependencies are semantic, arising from the relation between the operator and the variable that it binds.

An early piece of evidence to this effect was pointed out by Erteschik (1973): manner-of-speech verbs are more resistant to extraction than ordinary speech verbs.

(55) a. How many bottles of beer did Frank tell you/say to you that his guests drank?

  b. ?*How many bottles of beer did Frank mumble/yell/groan to you that his guests drank?

Erteschik classifies verbs into "bridge verbs", which permit extraction, and "non-bridge verbs". The distinction can be made clearly on semantic grounds, and there is no obvious syntactic difference aside from the extraction possibilities. To our knowledge, no convincing syntactic explanation has ever been given of this difference because in fact it is not a syntactic phenomenon.[21]

A semantically based solution to this and other cases is proposed in different versions by Kuno (1987), Erteschik-Shir (1979), Kluender (1992), Kuno and Takami (1993), Van Valin (1998), Csuri (1996), and Goldberg (to appear). Suitably generalized, the idea is this: an operator imposes a referential dependency on the variable it binds. For instance, the question operator asks the hearer to establish the reference of the variable, such that the clause in the scope of the operator is true. The lambda operator (for relative clauses) establishes the property of being a particular character in a situation denoted by the clause in the scope of the operator, so that the identity of the character is fixed by the situation. Suppose, however, that a variable happens to be in a position in CS where its reference is independently fixed. In such a configuration, it cannot be subject to the desired referential dependency. The outcome will reveal itself in syntax as an improper extraction of the phrase corresponding to the variable.

Let us illustrate. Factive verbs like *regret* presuppose the truth of their complements, whereas nonfactive verbs like *think* do not:

(56) a. Ginny regrets that Don bought a Porsche. → Don bought a Porsche.
      b. Ginny doesn't regret that Don bought a Porsche. → Don bought a Porsche.
      c. Ginny thinks/doesn't think that Don bought a Porsche → [no entailment about Don buying a Porsche]

Since the event in the complement of *regret* is presupposed, characters within this event are presumed to exist. Hence they cannot be referentially dependent on Ginny's having regrets about this event. Therefore extraction from the complement of *regret* should be impossible (or at least difficult), and this turns out to be the case (57a). By contrast, the identity of the event in the complement of *think* is dependent upon the act of thinking, so the characters in it can be referentially dependent on this event as well, and extraction is of course possible (57b).

---

[21] Chomsky (1981: 303–4) alludes to this phenomenon without so much as giving an example. He tentatively suggests accounting for the difference in terms of whether verbs permit a movement from S to S', a purely stipulative distinction, and he does not bring up the obvious semantic difference. After that, as far as we know, the phenomenon quietly disappears from the canon.

(57)   a. ??What does Ginny regret that Don bought?
       b.   What does Ginny think that Don bought?

In order to make (57a) acceptable, it is necessary to set up a discourse scenario in which the regretting is presupposed and the content of the regret is what is being questioned, thereby permitting the referential dependency.[22] This requires special contrastive intonation, for instance:

(58)   a. I **know** Ginny regretted that **Harry** bought a **tuba**, but what did she
          regret that **Don** bought?
       b. I **know** Ginny didn't regret that Don bought a **tuba**, but what **did** she
          regret that he bought?

A similar analysis pertains to "definiteness effects" on extraction from NPs. Consider:

(59)   a. She bought/didn't buy that picture of Richard → There is a picture of
          Richard that she bought/didn't buy.
       b. She bought a picture of Richard. → There is a picture of Richard that
          she bought.
       c. She didn't buy a picture of Richard. → [no implication that there is a
          picture]

In these examples, *that picture of Richard* fixes a reference independently of whether she bought it or not, whereas *a picture of Richard* does not. Therefore a referential dependency between the character in the picture and the act of buying can be established only in the indefinite case:

(60)   Who did she buy a/*that picture of?

For one more case, (61a) is a typical violation of the Complex NP Constraint. But (61b), with the same apparent syntactic structure, is perfectly acceptable.

(61)   a. *Who did Phyllis hear/deny/believe the claim that Bob is dating?
       b.   Who did Phyllis make the claim that Bob is dating?

The difference is that in (61a), *the claim* has a fixed reference independent of whether Phyllis heard it or not; but in (61b), with a light verb construction, the event of *making the claim* is the very same event as the claiming (see section 6.5.1). Hence in the latter case, characters in the claim can be referentially dependent on the event in the scope of the question operator.

---

[22] We are following here a line of argument initiated by Kroch (1989).

These examples (and many others offered in the references cited above) suggest that extractions may be subject not only to syntactic conditions but also to semantic conditions. In each case, there are minimal pairs that differ in only one lexical item, preserving syntactic structure but changing the referential properties of the domain of extraction. The possibility of extraction may to some extent be sensitive to special choices of focus, as seen above, because focus interacts with referential properties and referential dependencies (e.g. focus, as new information, fills out the proposition truthfully in accordance with the constraints of the old information).[23]

To the extent that conditions on extraction are semantic, they are sensitive to the CS configuration of operator/bound variable, not to the syntactic chain of [Spec,CP] and trace or to blocked slash-category configurations. Thus they should not be sensitive to how the dependency is expressed in syntax. Such constraints should be expected to apply equally to operator constructions that involve a fronted constituent, like English *wh*-questions, to constructions that involve an in situ expression of the variable, like Chinese and Japanese questions (see section 9.3.3), and to constructions that have no overt expression of either the operator or the variable, like English zero relative clauses.[24] There is no need for covert morphemes and covert movement to establish the commonality of all these constructions. The parallelism is in the formal properties of the meaning.

The idea that there are both syntactic and semantic conditions on extraction, and that they produce different effects, is a natural one if we take the view that they stem ultimately from different sources. Semantic conditions stem from the inherent nature of reference and referential dependencies. Syntactic conditions stem from the temporally organized nature of the mapping between form and meaning. In the latter case, it is not controversial that complexity arises in the identification of the gap corresponding to a signature at the beginning of a clause, although the exact nature of this complexity is still open to question. If there is an A′ constituent, its function is indeterminate if it is an unmarked NP; if it is case-marked or a PP, then its general function may be determined (e.g.

---

[23] This particular way of phrasing semantic constraints on extraction fits naturally into the account of the "Referential Tier" of CS sketched in Jackendoff (2002a), based on Csuri (1996). It should be readily translatable into the terms of Discourse Representation Theory (Kamp and Reyle 1993). The other accounts cited above phrase the constraints in terms of Information Structure—focused information vs. backgrounded information, but in a similar spirit. It remains to be seen which of these approaches is more robust in the long run.

[24] The fact that English echo- and quizmaster questions are not subject to extraction constraints presumably has something to do with their meaning as well. We know of no account of the semantic differences.

where denotes a place or direction), but in any case, the verb that determines its precise interpretation (and that defines the gap) has yet to be encountered.

Finally, under this account, nothing has to be said in UG about semantic constraints, and nothing has to be coded on the genome. The constraints simply follow from the logic of referential dependencies, the complexity of the structures in which the dependencies are embedded, and the meaning of the operators.

In summary, we believe that there is a case for constraints arising out of both syntactic and semantic structure. In Chapter 13 we discuss in detail a case in English, having to do with the Coordinate Structure Constraint, which we think leads to a division of labor between syntactic and semantic constraints. We leave the issue here, having established that there are several promising ways other than movement to account for extraction constraints.

9.4.5 Topicalization, left and right dislocation, and connectivity

As a further illustration of the present approach to extraction constraints, it is useful to compare topicalization with left and right dislocation. Topicalization resembles *wh*-questions, since it is an A'-construction (62a). However, it also resembles left dislocation (LD) (62b).

(62) a. That book$_i$, I have never read t$_i$.
      b. That book$_i$, I have never read it$_i$.

Traditional and contemporary critiques of movement analyses in general and of topicalization in particular (e.g. Postal 2004) have emphasized its similarity to left dislocation. This construction shows that it is independently necessary to allow constituents to appear in A'-position without having been moved there. As pointed out by Ross (1967), topicalization obeys extraction constraints but LD does not.

(63) a. *LSLT, I don't know any young linguists who have read in its entirety.
         *LSLT, I wonder how many linguists have read in its entirety.
      b. LSLT, I don't know any young linguists who have read it in its entirety.
         LSLT, I wonder how many linguists have read it in its entirety.

This difference emerges from the approach adopted here. The structure of topicalization is parallel to *wh*-questions. The operator comes from the information structure tier of CS. For convenience we call this operator TOP, but in fact it offers a number of different semantic and pragmatic possibilities, as shown for example by Prince (1998).

(64)   Inf Str: [TOP$^\alpha$]$_3$
          Prop Str: [READ (I$_1$, [α; BOOK; THAT$_4$]$_2$)]$_3$

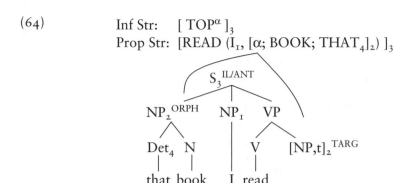

Left dislocation has essentially the same structure as topicalization, except that instead of a gap there is a proform (or, as noted earlier, an epithet) linked to the constituent in A'-position. Hence, although there is still indirect licensing and the constituent at the front is an orphan, there is no bound variable and no chain. (Again the term "topic" is too crude, but the proper range of discourse functions can be filled in appropriately.)

(65)   Inf Str: [TOP: [BOOK; THAT$_4$]$_2$]$_3$
          Prop Str: [READ (I$_1$, [3SG NEUT]$_5$)]$_3$

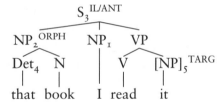

Because there is no bound variable and no chain, it follows that, as in BAE and sluicing, neither semantic nor syntactic island constraints obtain. Right dislocation (RD) is syntactically and semantically identical to LD, except that the interface rule localizes the right dislocated constituent in clause final position.

Returning to a point raised in sections 7.5 and 7.6, connectivity effects pertain to topicalization and left dislocation equally, because of indirect licensing. The trace per se need play no role. In particular, a constituent of the phrase at the front can be bound regardless of whether the construction in question is a *wh*-question, topicalization or LD. Thus we get some of the familiar reconstruction and strong crossover effects unproblematically.

(66)   a. [Which picture of himself$_i$]$_j$ does John$_i$ really like t$_j$?
           (cf. John really likes this picture of himself.)
       b. [This picture of himself$_i$]$_j$, John$_i$ really likes t$_j$.
       c. [This picture of himself$_i$]$_j$, John$_i$ really likes it$_j$.

(67)   a.   *Who$_i$ does he$_i$ think that Mary will laugh at t$_i$?

      b.   *John$_i$, he$_i$ thinks that Mary will laugh at t$_i$.

      c.   John$_i$, he$_i$ thinks that Mary will laugh at him$_i$.

         [*OK because interpreted with* he *anaphoric to* John, him *anaphoric to* he]

(68)   a.   *[That John$_i$ would win]$_j$, he$_i$ scarcely dared to hope t$_j$.

                   [*cf.* *He$_i$ scarcely dared to hope that John$_i$ would win.]

      b.   *[That John$_i$ would win]$_j$, he$_i$ scarcely dared to hope it/so$_j$.

As we said in section 7.6, there are two possible reasons for connectivity of binding in these constructions. First, to the extent that binding principles are syntactic, the property of being in a syntactic binding domain could be transmitted by indirect licensing. The clearest case is GF-binding, which depends on a phrase having a GF. We know that indirectly licensed topics and *wh*-phrases receive GFs through indirect licensing, since they receive case appropriate to their GF. Therefore, since a topicalized direct object still has the GF of a direct object, it can be a GF-bound reflexive, as in *Himself, John likes*. To the extent that other principles of binding involve syntactic domains, being in a syntactic binding domain might also count as a syntactic feature for purposes of indirect licensing, so that connectivity would obtain for these other relationships as well.

At the same time, since the fronted phrase is in a different syntactic position from the target (trace or pronoun as the case may be), some syntactic binding relations might apply to it differently, so that different binding might be licensed. We see such cases in anti-reconstruction contexts (69) and also with certain picture-noun reflexives (70).

(69)   a.   [Which book that John$_i$ wrote]$_j$ did he$_i$ sign t$_j$?

                   [*cf.* *He$_i$ signed every book that John$_i$ wrote.]

      b.   [Every book that John$_i$ has written]$_j$, he$_i$ has signed t$_j$.

      c.   [Every book that John$_i$ has written]$_j$, he$_i$ has signed it$_j$.

(70)   a.   [which picture of himself$_i$]$_j$ did John$_i$ deny that Mary had painted t$_j$?

                   [*cf.* *John denied that Mary had painted a picture of himself.]

      b.   That picture of himself, John denied that Mary had painted.

      c.   That picture of himself, John denied that Mary had painted it.

Examples of anti-reconstruction bring to mind the account of anaphora proposed originally by Langacker (1969): an anaphoric expression may not both precede and command its antecedent (where everything in an S commands everything in the same or a lower S). Condition C rules out an anaphor being higher in the tree than its antecedent; whether this is a syntactic or a CS condition is difficult to determine (though see Chapter 11). But the facts of anti-reconstruction suggest that linear order can sometimes override Condition C. Such an approach to anaphora has been proposed at times in the literature (e.g. Lasnik 1976, Kuno 1987, Van Valin 1990), but has been far less developed than the purely configurational approach that has dominated the study of binding.

The conflict between connectivity and linear order is further illustrated by the fact that for some speakers of English, certain argument NPs within constituents in A′-position cannot be antecedents of a pronoun that follows them; for these speakers, the b-sentences below are as bad as the a-sentences (Lebeaux 1990).

(71) a. *He$_i$ vigorously denied the allegation that John$_i$ raided the company treasury.
  b. (*)The allegation that John$_i$ raided the company treasury, he$_i$ vigorously denied.

(72) a. *She$_i$ really dislikes inaccurate stories about Mary.
  b. (*)Inaccurate stories about Mary$_i$, she$_i$ really dislikes.

(73) a. *He$_i$ likes the oldest of Sam$_i$'s kids the best.
  b. (*)Which of Sam$_i$'s kids does he like the best?

However, the present authors' own experience suggests that the judgments are somewhat variable across speakers and unstable within speakers. For the speakers who find the b-sentences bad, connectivity overrides linear order; for those who find them acceptable, linear order wins out.

Consider finally the possibility that some licensing conditions for binding are stated over semantic configurations, as we will argue in Chapters 10 and 11. If this is the case, constructions with a trace (e.g. *wh*-questions and topicalization) potentially diverge from constructions with pure indirect licensing (e.g. LD). In the former case, the orphan and the trace in syntax are linked to the same CS constituent, namely the bound variable. Therefore any binding relations that pertain to the semantic position of the trace also pertain to that of the orphan, and so we expect pure "reconstruction" with respect to such binding relations, as we have seen. In the latter case, the orphan and the target have separate CS positions, so they might have different potential for semantic binding: the orphan would inherit possibilities through indirect licensing but also have extra possibilities of its own. This would result in a possible divergence between topicalization and LD with respect to binding. Keeping in mind the variability of judgment in the topicalization case just noted, the examples in (74–76) suggest that there may be some difference between the two.

(74) a. (*)[Mary$_i$'s dissertation]$_j$, she$_i$ is trying to publish t$_j$ before the end of the summer.

b.   [Mary$_i$'s dissertation]$_j$, she$_i$ is trying to publish it$_j$ before the end of the summer.

(75) a. (*)[The evidence that George$_i$ was mistaken]$_j$, I could never convince him$_i$ of t$_j$.

b.   [The evidence that George$_i$ was mistaken]$_j$, I could never convince him$_i$ of it$_j$.

(76) a. (*)[This picture of John$_i$]$_j$, I would never show him$_j$ t$_j$.

b.   [This picture of John$_i$]$_j$, I would never show it$_j$ to him$_j$.

In all the cases of chains we have explored here, a variable in CS is doubly linked to a fronted orphan and to a target trace. But there is also the possibility that a variable might be linked instead to a fronted constituent and a resumptive pronoun or clitic. In such a case, what looks superficially like LD might behave more like topicalization (in situations where the two diverge). And indeed such constructions exist. In contrast to the English type of LD (often called Hanging Topic Left Dislocation), languages such as Italian, Greek, Dutch, Arabic and German have Contrastive (CLD) or Clitic Left Dislocation (CLLD), which like English topicalization preserve binding relationships (Anagnostopoulou et al. 1997).

9.5 *Tough* movement

We next turn to one of the historically more problematic cases of long-distance dependency, *tough* movement (TM).

(77) This construction$_i$ is tough to analyze t$_i$ in terms of movement, for theoretical reasons.

As is well known, TM appears to be movement (a) because the presence of an NP in the subject position of the *tough*-predicate correlates with a gap elsewhere in the infinitival complement and (b) because there is often an almost synonymous form in which the NP in question appears somewhere inside the infinitival complement (78).

(78) It is tough to analyze this construction in terms of movement, for theoretical reasons.

Moreover, the gap can (within limits) be as deeply embedded as we like, paralleling other long-distance dependencies:

(79)   This construction is tough to believe that anyone could analyze t in terms
        of movement.
        This construction is tough to convince anyone that they should analyze t
        in terms of movement.
        This construction is tough to expect anyone to be convinced that they
        should try to analyze t in terms of movement.

So the *tough*-construction seems to parallel raising to subject (*NP seems to VP*
= *it seems that NP VP*), except that the raised constituent is a *non*-subject of the
infinitival and in fact potentially deep within the infinitival. Like raising,
the possibility of using the construction is determined by the choice of main
clause predicate: verbs like *tend* and *seem* for raising, predicates like *tough* and
fun for TM.

However, as Lasnik and Fiengo (1974) demonstrate, there are many similar
cases where the object may be overt. Those in (80) involve complements of the
degree modifiers *too* and *enough*.

(80)   a. This problem is too abstract for Bill to solve (it).
                                            [Lasnik and Fiengo 1974: 538]
        b. This problem$_i$ is specific enough for there to be a solution to it$_i$.
                                            [Lasnik and Fiengo 1974: 558]

Moreover, there are many well-known grammatical examples of the *tough*-
construction that cannot plausibly be derived by movement.

(81)   a.   This is a hard construction for us to try to solve t.
        b.   *It is a hard construction for us to try to solve this.
(82)   a.   The President is a real jerk to talk to t at parties.
        b.   *It is a real jerk to talk to the President at parties.

Lasnik and Fiengo therefore propose that basic form of TM is like that of
(80a)—in other words, that the *tough*-construction is more like control. For
them, in some lexically determined cases, deletion of the object is obligatory; in
others it is optional.

In our view this is still the most satisfactory analysis of TM, in spite of
persistent efforts over the years to analyze it in terms of movement. Chomsky
(1977) recognizes that the subject of TM in fact plays a semantic role with
respect to the *tough*-predicate, that is, he acknowledges Lasnik and Fiengo's
point. But in order to maintain a movement analysis, he posits a *wh*-operator
that moves to the front of the complement and then is deleted.

(83)   this construction is tough [$_s$OP$_i$ for us to try to analyze t$_i$]

Of course, Simpler Syntax finds such an analysis objectionable, in that it has a covert operator that moves just in order to preserve the generalizations of *wh*-movement under Derivational Uniformity.

A little attention to the semantics of *tough*-predicates yields a more natural account within the present framework. Consider what the adjective *tough* means. It fundamentally expresses a property of a task: the difficulty of the task for a performer (*tough, easy*) or the affective quality of the task for a performer (*fun, a gas*). Thus the semantics of the adjective is most transparently expressed in the syntactic frames in (84), and the semantics should have basic structure along the lines of (85). (84d) shows a case in which the clausal argument is not a task but a situation. In this case *for* can be replaced by *on*.

(84)   a.   This job/task is tough/easy/fun/a gas for Robin.

     b.   [Analyzing this construction] is tough/easy/fun/a gas for Robin.
              —————task—————   *performer*

     c.   It is tough/easy/fun/a gas for Robin   to analyze this construction.
                    performer   —————task—————

     d.   It's tough for/on Robin to be so tall.

     e.   *Yiddish:* S'iz shver tsu zayn a yid. (old saying)
               it is hard to be   a Jew

(85)   [$_{\text{Situation}}$ BE ([$_{\text{Action/Situation}}$ X], [$_{\text{Property}}$ TOUGH ([$_{\text{Individual}}$ Y])])][25]

The default actor in the action/situation argument is the individual for whom the task or situation is tough/easy/etc. That is, there is a default control relation between the individual and the action. This is notated in (86) as a binding relationship between the Individual argument and the Actor role of the action—as usual, a Greek superscript on the controller and an ordinary Greek letter in the controllee position.

(86)   It is tough for Robin to analyze this construction:
     [$_{\text{Situation}}$ BE ([$_{\text{Action}}$ ANALYZE (α, CONSTRUCTION)],
                                        [$_{\text{Property}}$ TOUGH (ROBIN$^{\alpha}$)])]

If the *for*-phrase is absent, the implicit argument is a generic performer, along lines familiar from our discussion of psych predicates in section 5.6: the task is tough *for people*. This can be encoded by replacing *ROBIN* with *GEN* in (86).

---

[25] We are treating the CS of adjectives here as the Property in the complex *[BE ([INDIVID-UAL], [PROPERTY])]*. The individual of whom the Property is predicated is either not a semantic argument of the adjective or else a semantic argument that must be realized as the syntactic argument of an external predicate such as *be* or *become*. A more conventional account would treat the CS of adjectives as the entire Situation *[BE-PROPERTY ([INDIVIDUAL])]*, i.e. as a one-place predicate. Readers more comfortable with the conventional treatment should feel free to translate throughout this section.

Alternatively, it is possible for the Action to be performed by someone other than the affected individual, in which case there is a *for*-phrase within the complement:

(87)   It's harder for/on me [for you try to clean up] than for me to do it myself.

Next consider an expression like *a construction [AP tough to analyze in terms of movement]*. Here the AP expresses a property of the construction: the construction is such that the task of analyzing it is tough for a generic performer. That is, the property of being *tough to analyze* is not a property of a task but of the construction. What is the relation of this meaning and the meaning shown in (85–86)? We can derive this sense by doing a lambda-extraction on the form in (86), binding the object of analysis to the lambda operator (β in (88)). Intuitively, the meaning of *tough to analyze* might be expressed in "logicalese" by 'such that it is tough for people to analyze it'.

(88)   This construction is tough to analyze:
[$_{\text{Situation}}$ BE (CONSTRUCTION, [$_{\text{Property}}$ λ^β [$_{\text{Situation}}$ BE
    ([$_{\text{Event}}$ ANALYZE (α, β)], [$_{\text{Property}}$ TOUGH (GEN$^\alpha$)])])])]

A CS tree structure (89) makes this structure clearer. The lambda operator in this structure binds a variable, and the variable is somewhere within the complement of *be tough*. Hence the usual properties of variables bound by operators emerge in this construction. Thus there is a sense in which Chomsky's analysis with the invisible OP is correct. There is indeed an invisible operator that binds a variable in this construction. But it is the lambda-operator in CS, not a covert operator which then undergoes movement in syntax. Again the commonalities of long-distance dependency constructions emerge in their CS; the syntactic parallelisms, such as they are, reflect the parallel semantics.

(89)

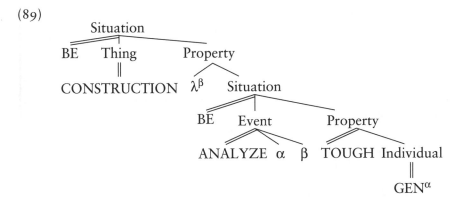

Under this analysis, the two forms *It is tough to analyze this construction* and *This construction is tough to analyze*, despite their (near-)synonymy, do not express the same CS: compare (86) to (88). This might be seen as a flaw in the analysis. However, consider the relation between the two CSs. They parallel the following pair exactly:

(90)   a. Harry bought a heckelphone.
          [BUY (HARRY, HECKELPHONE)]
       b. A heckelphone is what Harry bought.
          [BE (HECKELPHONE, [ι^α [BUY (HARRY, α)]])]

In each case, the semantic relation between the two members of the pair arises from the logic of lambda/iota extraction.

In the case of the *tough*-predicates, the two readings are lexical possibilities for the adjective itself. Both readings occur in the syntactic context *X is tough*, so it is hard to tease them apart. The paradigm in (91) points up the differences.[26]

(91)   a. Tough *predicated of tasks and situations (CS 85–86)*
          This job/work is tough for me.
          *This cat/milk is tough for me.
       b. Tough *predicated of anything, in reference to a situation in which it is a character (CS 88)*
          This job/work is tough for me to finish.
          This cat is tough for me to live with.
          This milk is tough for me to drink.

Summarizing, the two lexical forms for *tough* can be sorted out as follows:

(92)   a. *Simple form—CS (85–86)*
          [$_{Property}$TOUGH([$_{Individual}$X])]
       b. *Complex form—CS (88)*
          [$_{Property}\lambda^\alpha$[BE([$_{Situation/Action}$Y($\ldots\alpha\ldots$)],[$_{Property}$TOUGH ([$_{Individual}$X])])]]

---

[26] The situation is still more complicated because many nouns denote objects with a "proper function"—the standard use to which they are put. When some such nouns appear in a "simple" *tough*-context (91a), they coerce the reading into the "complex" reading:

(i)   This book is tough = 'tough to read/understand'
      This problem is tough = 'tough to solve'
      This sonata is tough = 'tough to play'
      But:
      *This pen is tough = 'tough to write with'

It is not clear to us what distinguishes the nouns that coerce the *tough*-construction from those that do not.

The latter is a lexical form that contains an operator and a bound variable, accounting for the fact that this construction, unlike other long-distance dependencies, is lexically specific.[27]

9.6 Other candidates for movement

We conclude this chapter with brief notes on two more phenomena that MGG takes to be movement: heavy shift and scrambling.

9.6.1 *Heavy shift*

There are two main cases of heavy shift (HS). First, if a verb obligatorily subcategorizes an NP argument, then the failure of that argument to appear immediately adjacent to the verb suggests that there is a trace.

(93)   The car crushed (t) under its tire [the seed that had fallen from the tree].

The second case is when there are two PP arguments or adjuncts.

(94)   a. Terry talked to the students about the homework.
       b. Terry talked about the homework to the students.

As argued in Chapter 5, the second case has a natural characterization in terms of linearization of the constituents of VP, involving preferential conditions on processing, prosody, information structure, and discourse structure (Ross 1967: 63; Hawkins 1994; Wasow 1997). Thus no special rule of heavy shift appears necessary for it.

For the first case, however, it would seem natural to posit an interface rule similar to topicalization, except with the orphan on the right. Such a counterpart to topicalization is given in (95), essentially the rightward version of (64). We use the operator FOC for the heavy shifted constituent, since HS is often a

---

[27] This analysis does not account for *The president is a real jerk to talk to*, which has a different semantic structure. We assume, however, that this structure, whatever it is, also contains a lambda-extraction.

Tough movement, like subdeletion, has properties that distinguish it from standard long-distance dependencies. For example, *tough* movement typically disprefers a gap in a *that*-clause, and disallows a subject gap in a tensed complement:

(i)   ?? These books would be tough to prove that everyone in the class has looked at t.

(ii)   *Those students would be tough to prove t have read every book that was assigned.

Such lack of complete uniformity is precisely what we would expect if the constructions are distinct, but related through their use of an operator/bound variable complex, rather than being instances of a common movement operation, as Chomsky (1977) originally proposed.

type of focusing construction (Rochemont and Culicover 1990). (On the other hand, Chapter 5 cited cases in which HS was motivated primarily on prosodic grounds; in such cases it would be harder to justify a FOC operator.)

(95) Inf. Str. $[FOC^\alpha]_3$
       Prop. Str. $[WRITE (JOHN_1, [\alpha_2; BOOK]); [_{Time} YESTERDAY]_4]_3$

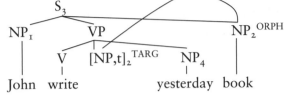

The interface rule says to place the focused constituent in final position. This will work for the simple cases.

However, there are several problems with this formulation of HS. First, if the heavy shifted constituent appears medially in VP, as in (96), a formulation such as (95) will be inadequate.

(96)   Richard rolled t into the room [the cart with all of the presents on it] using his nose.

That is, unlike topicalization, HS does not require that the dislocated constituent be at the periphery of the phrase.

Second, HS does not apply to the complement of a preposition, even when it expresses an argument of the verb.

(97)   *Mary looked at t without fear [the tiger that was slowly approaching].

In this regard HS is not symmetrical with topicalization, which allows preposition stranding.

The third problem is that in general subjects cannot undergo HS and leave a trace.

(98)   a. *t_i walked into the room [the man that I was telling you about]$_i$.
       b. *I told you [t_i walked into the room [the man that I was telling you about]$_i$].

But topicalization and *wh*-questions can apply to subjects.

(99)   a. This book$_i$, I told you [t_i really disturbed me].
       b. Which book$_i$ did you tell me [t_i really disturbed you]?

A fourth problem is that in HS the focus does not appear to adjoin to the S, but to the VP. To see this, consider the *that*-clause associated with the degree word *so*, as in *He's so tired that he can't eat*. Williams (1975: 266) shows that if *so* is in the subject, the *that*-clause is attached at the end of S (100a). A heavy-shifted NP must occur before this *that*-clause, not after it (100b,c).

(100) a. So many people visited the museum founded by Rockefeller in 1953 that we had to charge admission.

       b. So many people visited last week the museum founded by Rock-efeller in 1953 that we had to charge admission.

       c. *So many people visited last week that we had to charge admission the museum that Rockefeller founded in 1953.

A fifth problem is that the formulation of HS illustrated in (95) allows for an unbounded dependency, like topicalization. But this is incorrect, since (as noted by Ross (1967)), the focused constituent cannot appear outside the clause in which it "properly" belongs:[28]

(101) *John said [that he was going to fix t][to anyone who would listen] [the stove that he found at the dump].

The standard explanation of this fact in MGG is that there is no landing site to the right, and no escape hatch for movement. This constraint can be accomplished by stipulation, or by building it into the basic architecture of the phrase structure. For example, Kayne takes all branching to be rightward and all movement to be leftward. Hence there is no possibility of a rightward movement to a structure-preserving position. Assuming this, HS as a movement would have to be movement to the left and then movement of the remnant phrase further to the left (an instance of Iterated Raising). It will still be necessary to explain why HS to the left cannot involve long movement; this is a stipulation at a deeper level. In Simpler Syntax, our goal is to avoid building such complexity into the syntactic descriptions. For us, the impossibility of long-distance HS is due to the fact that HS is a matter of linearization within VP.

---

[28] Under certain very restricted circumstances, a heavy shifted constituent may appear to the right of a constituent of the higher clause. These cases all involve infinitival complements of *want* and temporal adjuncts, e.g.

(i) I have wanted [to know ___$_i$]] for many years [what happened to Rosa Luxembourg]$_i$.

We hypothesize that these cases have a reanalysis (perhaps at the level of GF-structure) in which *want to know* is the main verb. Such an analysis ties together with clitic climbing and coherent infinitives. The phenomena are sufficiently complex that they will require special treatment in any approach to syntax and do not constitute a particular difficulty for the approach that we are advocating.

Some of these problems may be accommodated while maintaining a structure like (95) that incorporates a trace. For example, Culicover and Levine (2001) suggest that the reason for the prohibition on HS out of subject position has to do with independent conditions on the distribution of subject traces. However, the fact that other constraints on long-distance HS seem purely stipulative suggests that HS is actually limited to constituents of a single VP. Such a formulation of HS would explain (101), since the complement of a preposition is not a constituent that is linearized in the VP; the PP is. It would also account for the fact that HS is bounded within the VP (setting aside the exceptions in n. 28). Thus we conclude that Chapter 5 was essentially correct in treating heavy shift as a principle of linearization in the VP rather than an indirect licensing construction.

9.6.2 *Scrambling*

Another candidate for movement mentioned in Chapter 5 is scrambling, in which arguments and adjuncts appear in various orders. In some languages, e.g. Serbian (Godjevac 2000), scrambling is highly correlated with information structure. In others, e.g. Japanese, it appears to be freer. In any case, our concern here is whether scrambling needs to be understood as movement or whether it can be accounted for in terms of linearization, as mandated by Simpler Syntax.

The issue is somewhat difficult to resolve, because the question of whether scrambling is movement or linearization is rarely addressed directly. Most of the literature on scrambling (again following Ross (1967)) simply assumes that it is movement and tries to work out the technical details. Theorists are typically concerned with other issues, for example: Why does scrambling show both A-and A′-properties? What accounts for the optionality or apparent optionality of scrambling? Can optional scrambling be formalized as an obligatory movement in the MP framework? Why do some languages have scrambling and others do not? How can the discourse and information structure properties of scrambling be represented syntactically? (For some recent discussion, see the papers in Karimi 2003.)

While these are not at all straightforward questions to resolve, we find nothing in the facts of scrambling to suggest that linearization along the lines discussed here is ruled out as a way of accounting for the basic syntax of the construction.[29] On the one hand, A-scrambling appears to be linearization within the domain of a VP or a clause, as proposed here for English PPs within VP. Linearization offers a trivially simple account for the fact that A-scrambling

---

[29] For a recent review that confirms this conclusion, see Haider (2000).

is clause-bound, since the clause is the default domain of linearization in the absence of scopal operations such as topicalization. A-scrambling has all of the properties that we find in the case of the passive construction: locality, no reconstruction, quantifier scope determined strictly by the superficial linear order, no weak crossover violations, and so on (see Mahajan 1990, Webelhuth 1989).

On the other hand, A'-scrambling is not clause bound (Mahajan 1990), shows reconstruction effects, including scope reconstruction (Tada 1990), and weak crossover. A'-scrambling therefore falls under a variant of the analysis that we have proposed for topicalization; it is A'-scrambling (and not A-scrambling) in virtue of the chain that the scrambled constituent forms with a trace.

What may distinguish scrambling (including A'-scrambling) from English-type passive and topicalization is that scrambling may apply to more than one constituent. Thus it is necessary to properly linearize the scrambled constituents with respect to one another. The notion of "syntactic field" provides a natural way to refer to the position in a sentence where one or more scrambled constituents may be located (see Kathol 2000). However, scrambling is subject to different restrictions in different, even closely related languages. For example, in German, the arguments of a verb may appear in any order to the left of the verb, while in Dutch the subject must precede the indirect object, which must precede the direct object; PPs and adverbs in Dutch are freer in their distribution (Haider 2000: 21–2); Jun (2003) shows very intricate interactions between scrambling and case-marking within Korean nominals. Hence it is reasonable to hypothesize that scrambling is a type of linearization that may refer to CS, discourse structure and the GF-tier in ways that are particular to the individual language.

9.7 Summary

We conclude that the phenomena uniformly analyzed as movement in MGG divide into a number of distinct classes, each falling under a different tool in the UG toolkit. Such divisions have been recognized from the beginning of the attempts to draw them all under a single umbrella of movement. However, in MGG the differences have been forced into the background by the relentless demands of Derivational Uniformity and by invocations of Occam's Razor without assessment of the true costs.

The present chapter has focused on long-distance dependency constructions as a distinct type. The innovation in our approach has been to approach them as a special case of indirect licensing, a type of grammatical phenomenon not previously recognized explicitly in the literature. Such phenomena as BAE and sluicing, because of their similarities to topicalization and *wh*-questions, have often been treated as special cases of long-distance dependencies. We have proposed reversing the relationship: BAE and sluicing are basic cases of indirect licensing, and topicalization and *wh*-questions are the special cases. What makes them special is that (a) their indirect licensing is intrasentential (a property they share with left dislocation); (b) they express an operator-bound variable complex; (c) the bound variable is expressed as a chain consisting of a fronted constituent plus a trace; (d) the fronted constituent is the orphan of indirect licensing and the trace is the target.

Other constructions express an operator-bound variable complex without using a chain or indirect licensing, for instance English zero relative clauses. There is a gap in the clause, but there is no overt evidence for a displaced constituent. Therefore Simpler Syntax does without one. The reason such constructions have been assimilated to A′-movement, of course, is Derivational Uniformity, plus the fact that they, like the constructions with true chains, observe "extraction" constraints. Here we have proposed several mechanisms, mostly already in the literature, that do the work of "extraction" constraints. They depend not on movement but on allowable configurations containing traces, on allowable slash-category configurations, and—crucially—on permissible operator/bound variable configurations in CS.

We find then that long-distance dependencies involve two overlapping mechanisms: operator/variable complexes and intrasentential indirect licensing. *Wh*-questions and topicalization partake of both; zero relatives are operator/variable complexes without indirect licensing of a fronted constituent; left dislocation is intrasentential indirect licensing without an operator/bound variable complex. It is the operator/bound variable complex that is responsible for "extraction" constraints. Therefore left dislocation, like BAE and sluicing, does not obey the constraints.

There is a price for this solution: we do have to enrich UG. In CS, we must add the machinery of operator/variable complexes. However, much of this is independently necessary for quantification and perhaps for information structure as well. In syntax, it is necessary to add traces. In the interface, it is necessary to add the machinery to link a variable bound by an operator to a chain consisting of a fronted constituent and a trace. These are indeed complications in the theory of UG. Along with the GF-tier and its properties, these seem to be the main ways that the theory of syntax and the syntax–semantics interface goes beyond a bare minimum that would seem necessary to provide a canonical and functionally flexible syntax–semantics mapping.

PART III

Binding and Control

CHAPTER 10

Mme Tussaud Meets the Binding Theory

10.1 Introduction

This chapter and the next concern constructions of English that present challenges to the approach to binding adopted in mainstream generative grammar. In each case, we show that Interface Uniformity cannot be maintained without loss of generality, and that the correct solution involves enrichment of the syntax–semantics interface rather than enrichment of syntactic structure. As a consequence, it is possible and in fact preferable to maintain the Simpler Syntax Hypothesis, in which there are no hidden elements or levels of syntactic structure.

This chapter is specifically concerned with some phenomena concerning the coding of coreference relations with reflexive pronouns. The issue is the choice between the two following positions:

Syntactic Binding Theory. Coreference relations are coded by coindexation in syntax (redundantly with the semantics, where coreference is necessarily

---

This chapter has been revised from its original version (*Natural Language and Linguistic Theory* 10: 1–31) to reflect innovations in the present study. In particular, section 10.8 is largely new, in response to the introduction of GF-binding in Ch. 6. The original version was inspired by Fauconnier (1985), where examples similar to (8)–(13) are presented in a quite different grammatical framework. The discussions of Fauconnier's work took place in a 1990 seminar with RJ whose members were (in reverse alphabetical order) Cheryl Zoll, Saeko Urushibara, Hubert Truckenbrodt, Vieri Samek-Lodovici, Feargal Murphy, Gyanam Mahajan, Bill Isham, Henrietta Hung, Piroska Csuri, Strang Burton, Maria Babyonyshev, and John Aberdeen. In particular, Truckenbrodt, Csuri, and Babyonyshev did pieces of (unpublished) work that clarified the issues a great deal. Jane Grimshaw, Joan Maling, David Dowty, Craige Roberts, Noam Chomsky, Fritz Newmeyer, and two anonymous readers also offered important contributions to the argument.

encoded to derive inference); the possibility of coreference is conditioned by syntactic structure.

Semantic + Interface Theory. Coreference relations are coded in semantics alone; the possibility of binding is conditioned by some combination of semantic and syntactic structural conditions (the latter including the Grammatical Function tier).

We argue that the latter approach is correct. Chapter 11 continues this line of argument and extends it to the coding of scope of quantification, showing that no purely syntactic level can uniformly express relations of quantifier scope. Since the syntactic level of Logical Form was originally proposed as a way of syntacticizing quantifier scope in accordance with Interface Uniformity (Chapter 2), we conclude that the justification for such a level is severely undermined—again in accord with the Simpler Syntax Hypothesis.

10.2 The problem

Suppose you and I go down to the wax museum and I am guiding you through the statues. I may say,

(1)   Look! Here's W. C. Fields, and here's Mae West, and, wow, over here are the Beatles: This one's John, and this one's Ringo.

We see from (1) that there is a principle of language use that can be stated very informally as (2). For convenience we'll call it the "statue rule".

(2)   (**Statue rule**) It is legitimate to identify a statue by using the name of the person the statue portrays.

What kind of principle is (2), i.e. in which component of knowledge of language should it (or a suitable generalization of it) belong?

The statue rule is one of a considerable number of "reference transfers", in which one phrase (the *source phrase*) is used to denote a related entity (the *target entity*). Here are examples of some others:[1]

(3)   a. While he was driving to the studio, a truck hit Ringo in the left front fender.   [*Ringo* denotes his car]

---

[1] Reference transfers of the types (3b) and (3d) were mentioned in section 6.5.3 as examples of coercion. See Nunberg (1979; 2004), Ward (2004) for more extensive discussion of reference transfers.

    b. [*One waitress says to another:*]
       The ham sandwich in the corner needs another cup of coffee.
       [*ham sandwich* denotes person contextually related to ham sandwich]
    c. Plato is on the top shelf.   [*Plato* denotes book(s) by Plato]
    d. I'll have three coffees, please   [*coffee* denotes portion of coffee]
    e. That store has an incredible number of Portuguese wines.
                              [*wine* denotes kind of wine]

There is also a principle with an effect approximately opposite to that of the statue rule: one can use a deictic expression, pointing to Ringo's statue, and say *He/That guy* [pointing]—*I forget his name—used to be the drummer of the Beatles*. Here the statue stands in for the person it portrays.

Though the present chapter is concerned with the statue rule in particular, we will have reason to compare it with some of these other reference transfers as we go along. They turn out to have quite distinct grammatical and semantic properties, which makes the problem all the more interesting: it appears there is not a unified solution to what appears superficially a unified class of processes.

To state the problem somewhat more carefully, *Ringo* in (1) is understood not to denote its ordinary reference, the person Ringo, but rather a statue. For ease of exposition, we will use the notation *<plain> Ringo* to stand for 'the phrase *Ringo* used in reference to the actual person' and *<statue> Ringo* to stand for 'the phrase *Ringo* used in reference to a/the statue of the person'. The latter is the case in which the statue rule is operative.

In order for the difference between these two readings to be available for forming inferences, there must be at least one level of linguistic structure, that which encodes the contextual understanding of sentences, in which the representations corresponding to the morpheme *Ringo* differ in (1) and (4).

(4)   Ringo was the Beatles' drummer when they made *Sgt. Pepper.*

Since the phonological sequence *Ringo* is identical in the two sentences, there must be some point in the mapping from contextual understanding to phonology where the difference is neutralized—or, seen in the direction from phonology to contextual understanding, where the two readings come to be differentiated. The statue rule can be seen as the principle that licenses this neutralization or differentiation. So the issue can be stated more precisely as (5).

(5)   At what levels of linguistic structure is *<statue> Ringo* differentiated from
     <plain> Ringo?

The form of the solution is shown schematically in (6).

(6)   contextual understanding of S   [readings differentiated]

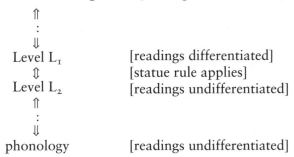

Level L$_1$	[readings differentiated]
	[statue rule applies]
Level L$_2$	[readings undifferentiated]

phonology   [readings undifferentiated]

So (5) can be rephrased as (7).

(7)   What are the levels L$_1$ and L$_2$ in (6), such that the statue rule is part of the mapping between them?

Here are some possibilities.

• **Pragmatic Option.** L$_1$ is the level of contextual understanding and L$_2$ is the level of sentence meaning, the aspect of meaning constructed compositionally from the lexical items in the sentence and their syntactic structure. The statue rule is therefore a principle of pragmatics, a way of mapping from sentence meaning onto the world; it deals only with sentence use, and has nothing to do with grammar per se.

• **Syntactic Option.** L$_1$ and L$_2$ are both levels of syntactic structure; the statue rule is a rule of deletion or movement that reduces the syntactic structure *statue of X, portrait of X*, etc. simply to *X*.

• **Interface Option.** L$_1$ is the level of sentence meaning and L$_2$ is a level of syntactic structure. The statue rule is a rule of interpretation that licenses the optional matching of a syntactic structure X with a semantic/conceptual structure that is more fully expressed as 'visual representation of X'.

Sections 10.4–10.6 will work through these possibilities in turn. The impulse of many syntacticians will be to favor the Pragmatic Option, because sentences like (1) don't seem to bear on anything normally considered syntactic. The Syntactic Option, which preserves Interface Uniformity, sounds like something out of the 1960s; nobody really considers such idiosyncratic deletions any more. Section 10.5.3 will, however, work out a variant perhaps more palatable to current tastes. The intent of the Interface Option is to put the statue rule within the domain of knowledge of language, but as a coercion in the syntax–CS interface, along lines suggested in section 6.5.3. This option enriches the interface and keeps the syntax simple. Eventually, we are going to suggest that the Interface Option is correct. But that is not all that is going to happen: first the plot thickens considerably, as we now see.

10.3 Interaction of the statue rule with binding

Consider a slightly more elaborate scenario. The other day I was strolling through the wax museum with Ringo Starr, and we came upon the statues of the Beatles, and...

(8)   ...All of a sudden I accidentally stumbled and fell on Ringo.

(8) is ambiguous: I may have fallen either on the actual guy or his statue. The ambiguity turns on whether the last NP of (8) is *<plain> Ringo* or *<statue> Ringo*.

   Next, the same scenario, but

(9)   ...All of a sudden Ringo started undressing himself.

(9) too is ambiguous: he could be taking off his own clothes or those of the statue.[2] The latter reading is problematic for a standard theory of referential anaphora, in that the anaphor, *<statue> himself*, does not have the same reference as its antecedent, *<plain> Ringo*. We return to this issue shortly.

   Now consider (10).

(10)   ...?All of sudden Ringo stumbled and fell on himself.

This is not quite as good as (9), but it clearly means that the real guy falls on the statue. The same problem occurs with the anaphora as in the parallel reading of (9).

   Next, still under the same scenario,

(11)   ...All of a sudden I accidentally bumped into the statues, and John toppled over and fell on Ringo.

This is ambiguous: the statue of John could have fallen either on the statue or the real guy. Now the crucial case:

(12)   ...All of a sudden I accidentally bumped into the statues, and
           *Ringo toppled over and fell on himself.

---

[2] Noam Chomsky (p.c.) and an anonymous reader say that they do not find (9) particularly acceptable in the desired interpretation. However, in discussing this material with a large number of colleagues, we have encountered little skepticism with it or with the more crucial examples to follow. Another example in which the reading in question is perhaps more prominent is (i).

(i)   Ringo was looking for himself among the wax statues.

Evidently there are differences among speakers either in how free they are in applying the statue rule, or in the degree to which a more salient reading interferes with the desired reading in which the statue rule applies. In order to lessen such interference, we have taken care to set up reasonably plausible contexts, which are often essential for these judgments.

Pragmatically, the only possible interpretation of (12) is that the statue falls on the guy—but, surprisingly, this reading is impossible. (Even for speakers who find (10) odd, (12) is clearly far worse.) What's going on?

Stripping away all the *mise-en-scène*, the problem is that sentence (13) is (pretty) good when the subject is *<plain> Ringo* and the object is *<statue> himself*, a reading paraphrased by (13a). But (13) is unacceptable when the subject is *<statue> Ringo* and the object is *<plain> himself*, as paraphrased in (13b).

(13)   Ringo fell on himself.
      a. = 'The actual Ringo fell on the statue of Ringo.'
      b. ≠ 'The statue of Ringo fell on the actual Ringo.'

One's initial impulse might be to look for a fairly trivial explanation, perhaps something like a prohibition on "statue" readings in subject position. However, this solution won't work, for it incorrectly predicts that (11), whose subject is *<statue> John*, should also be bad. Rather, the problem seems to have something to do with the binding of the reflexive.

If this is the case, then it follows that

Readings (13a) and (13b) must be structurally differentiated at the level at which binding applies.

That is, binding must apply at L1 or above in (6). What are the consequences?

10.4 The Pragmatic Option

Consider the alternative for the statue rule that is probably most people's initial guess: the Pragmatic Option. This claims that the difference between *<plain> Ringo* and *<statue> Ringo* is encoded not as part of grammar, but rather as part of general world knowledge or pragmatics or language use (e.g. a kind of metonymy). If this claim is correct, then readings (13a) and (13b) are not differentiated at any level of the grammar of English. In order for binding theory to access the difference between these readings, then, it must contain a component that is not part of grammar either.

Such a conclusion is impossible under the assumption that binding theory belongs to syntax, i.e. the Syntactic Binding Theory of section 10.1. Rather, readings (13a) and (13b) must be structurally differentiated somewhere within the syntax of English. In turn, this means that the statue rule, which is responsible for both of them taking the form (13), must also be situated somewhere within the syntax of English. That is, we cannot simply assume the Pragmatic Option and thereby permit syntactic theory to ignore phenomena like the statue rule.

One possibility for preserving the Pragmatic Option (suggested by Craige Roberts and an anonymous reader) is to claim that binding theory is not responsible for the unacceptability of (13b). Rather, binding is merely concerned with the coindexing of NPs, and there also exist conditions on coreference, which apply to contextual understanding of sentences. In this approach, both readings of (13) undergo binding in syntax, but the difference between them shows up in the conditions on coreference. The idea might be that these conditions tolerate binding between non-coreferential NPs just in case the reference of the anaphor is an "extension" (or extended part) of the reference of the antecedent. Under this account, Ringo's statue might be considered an "extension" of Ringo, just as Ringo's car is construed as an "extension" of Ringo in (3a). In this case, reading (13a) would be acceptable; but reading (13b) would not, because Ringo (the reference of the anaphor) is not an "extension" of Ringo's statue (the reference of the antecedent). Such an approach would be conceivable in the present framework, if we consider the syntactic aspect of binding to be GF-binding (section 6.4). GF-binding does not have to do with coreference per se, since it applies even to pleonastic arguments such as the reflexive in *This approach lends itself to abuse.*

Although we think there is a grain of insight in this approach, which we will capture later on, it is important to ask whether such a solution can get us off the hook—whether we can regard the principles of "pragmatics" concerning "referential extension" as really outside of grammar. We must not be satisfied to posit such principles and then excuse them from serious study because they are not syntax. Rather, it is important to explore the properties of reference transfers further. First, notice that the use of *Ringo* by extension for Ringo's car has quite different semantic/pragmatic properties from the 'statue' use of *Ringo.* The former seems to be limited roughly to cases where Ringo is driving (or parked), or where Ringo's car is otherwise in a relation that is stereotypical for cars, such as getting gas.

(14)   a.   A truck hit Ringo in the fender when he was momentarily distracted by a motorcycle.

 b.   ? A truck hit Ringo in the fender while he was recording *Abbey Road.*

 c.   ? I'm going to the gas station to fill Ringo up.

 d.   * A truck hit Ringo in the fender two days after he died.

 e.   Ringo squeezed himself [i.e. the car he was driving] between two buses.

 f.   * Ringo repainted himself [i.e. his car].

 g.   * I saw Ringo [i.e. his car] down at the mechanic's having an oil change.

h. *We sat in/on/under Ringo until the storm was over.

i. *The dog just peed on Ringo.

j. *I scratched Ringo with my key.

k. *John listed Ringo in the classifieds.

l. *Paul took Ringo for a drive.

[*i.e. where Ringo is the car, not the person*]

m. Someone seems to have run into/*stolen/*borrowed Ringo.

The proposed "pragmatic" account basically depends on the idea that in certain circumstances, a part of Ringo's car can be considered a part of Ringo by "extension". Note that in (14a), *he* refers to *<plain>* Ringo and *Ringo* refers to the car or *<*"extended"*>* Ringo—and anaphoric reference is possible; in (14e) the reverse configuration is possible. However, configurations parallel to (14a) are not felicitous when the "extension" pertains to Ringo's statue:

(15) a. ?? When Ringo quit the Beatles, a disgusted fan went down to Mme. Tussaud's and hit him [*i.e. his statue*] in the nose.

b. ?? When a disgusted fan defaced *<statue>* Ringo in the wax museum, *<plain>* he cried.

And a personal pronoun is freer referring to the statue than to the car:

(16) a. Hey, that's Ringo parked over there [*pointing to Ringo's car*]! Isn't *he/?it beautifully painted!

b. Hey, that's Ringo standing over there [*pointing to statue of Ringo*]! Isn't he/*it beautifully painted!

These differences show that the statue rule cannot be immediately assimilated to whatever rule of "referential extension" accounts for (14a). As we will see, other rules that shift reference have still different effects on discourse and anaphora. Without investigating their typology in detail, it is merely handwaving to assert that they all fall out of an as yet unarticulated theory of pragmatics. For the moment we are not concerned with such rules in general, some of which might well fall under the Pragmatic Option: we are interested specifically in the limited class that includes the statue rule, and *its* implications for binding theory. We return to some other reference transfers in section 10.8.1.

More generally, this account of (13)—like any solution based on the Pragmatic Option—admits the possibility that syntactic binding theory is not the only source of structural conditions on anaphora. However, the complexity of the data already presented indicates that the Pragmatic Option cannot be pursued without a more serious theory of pragmatics and contextual understanding. It therefore does not provide any sort of convenient escape from investigating the interaction of the statue rule with formal grammar.

10.5 The Syntactic Option

Now let us hold our noses and consider the Syntactic Option. (We will review the reasons for its unpleasant odor in section 10.5.2, but for the sake of argument let's grin and bear it.) Basically, the Syntactic Option claims that L_1 and L_2 in (6) are both levels of syntax: reading (13a) has the derivation (17a) and reading (13b) has the derivation (17b), conforming nicely with Interface Uniformity.

(17)   a. Ringo fell on [$_{NP}$ a/the statue (of) himself] $\Rightarrow$ <*plain*>Ringo fell on <*statue of*> himself

   b. [$_{NP}$ A/the statue (of) Ringo] fell on himself $\Rightarrow$ *<*statue of*>Ringo fell on <*plain*>himself

The statue rule, then, is a syntactic deletion that removes *a/the statue (of)* in the course of deriving L_2 from L_1. If readings (13a) and (13b) are differentiated at level L_1, then the binding theory, applying at this level, can explain the difference in grammaticality.

   Such an approach has two favorable consequences. First, it solves the problem noted in connection with example (9): the fact that the anaphor apparently refers to the statue while its antecedent refers to the actual person. If <*statue*> *himself* has the structure *statue (of) himself* at level L_1, then the anaphor actually refers to the person, so it is coreferential with its antecedent, as desired. There is therefore no need for an extended theory of anaphora-without-coreference, of the sort necessary in the Pragmatic Option.

   Second, the statue rule is optional, of course. If it does *not* apply, the underlying structures in (17a) and (17b) emerge unaltered at level L_2, as (18a,b).

(18)   a.   Ringo fell on a statue of himself.
   b. *A statue of Ringo fell on himself.

(18a) is grammatical and (18b) is not, because of Principle A: in the former, *himself* is bound by a c-commanding constituent in its governing category and in the latter it is not. At L_1, however, (18a) is structurally identical to (17a), and (18b) is identical to (17b). Hence (17b) and (18b) are ungrammatical for the very same reason. In other words, this account directly predicts the desired distinction between the readings of (13).

   But let's not get too optimistic. There are two major classes of problems with the Syntactic Option, one having to do with the proper interaction of the statue rule with the binding theory, and the other having to do with the implementation of a syntactic deletion for *statue (of)*. (Counterparts of these problems also arise with a more up-to-date variant of the Syntactic Option, which we will work out in section 10.5.3. But they are easier to explain in this version, so we beg the reader's indulgence.)

10.5.1 Interaction of the Syntactic Option with binding

Let us try to identify which particular syntactic levels are L_1 and L_2 in (6). Suppose Principle A of the binding theory applies at S-structure, which therefore equals L_1. In this case, the only place where *statue (of)* can delete is in the mapping from S-structure to PF; PF therefore must equal L_2.[3]

Let us set aside the fact that the mapping from S-structure to PF is a component in which few if any syntactic rules have yet been firmly established, despite over twenty years' assumption that this component exists. This throws doubt on such a solution on general grounds. But in addition, there are strong reasons to believe that readings (13a) and (13b) are already identical at S-structure. Most importantly, *<statue> Ringo* behaves syntactically as though its head is *Ringo*, not *statue*. Notice the contrasts in (19)–(21):

(19) *Case-marking*
       a. He [*pointing at <plain> Ringo*] is cute.
       b. The statue of him [*pointing at statue of Ringo*] is cute.
       c. He/*him [*pointing at statue of Ringo*] is cute.

(20) *Number agreement*
       a. The four oxen [*pointing at <plain> four oxen*] are cute.
       b. The statue of four oxen is cute.
       c. The four oxen [*pointing at single sculpture of four oxen*] are/*is cute.

(21) *Pronominal agreement*
       a. Look at *<plain> Ringo* over there. Isn't he cute!
       b. Look at the statue of Ringo over there. Isn't he/it cute!
       c. Look at *<statue> Ringo* over there. Isn't he/?? it cute!
       d. Look at *<statue>* the four oxen over there. Aren't they/??Isn't it cute!

These examples show that *<statue> Ringo* falls in with *<plain> Ringo* and not with *statue of Ringo* with respect to case-marking (19), number agreement (20), and pronominal agreement (21). In other words, these three processes behave as though *Ringo*, not *statue*, is the head of *<statue> Ringo*. If L_1 is S-structure and L_2 is PF, then case marking, number agreement, and pronominal agreement

---

[3] The original version of this chapter was written prior to the advent of the Minimalist Program, which eliminates D-structure and S-structure as possible levels for implementing the binding conditions. The MP only makes the absence of viable options more acute.

must take place (or be checked) somewhere in the mapping from S-structure to PF. But this conclusion is implausible, and we abandon this line of attack.

Let's try other possibilities for L_1 and L_2. Suppose L_2 is S-structure, so that case marking and agreement work out properly. Then L_1 could be either D-structure or LF. Can it be D-structure? No, because binding theory cannot apply to D-structure—it is known to depend on the outcome of movement. Can L_1 be LF? Assuming the direction of derivation is S-structure to LF, we then have to construe the statue rule as a rule that *inserts* material on the way from S-structure to LF. But this is impossible, because then *statue* would be absent in D-structure, even though it marks a θ-role, namely that of *Ringo*. So we end up with no possible pair of syntactic levels that can serve as L_1 and L_2, despite the initial plausibility of the proposal.

It should be mentioned that, as observed by Abusch (1989), the counterparts of (20)–(21) come out differently with another class of reference transfers, called by Fauconnier (1985) "closed connectors". These are the well-known "ham sandwich" cases pointed out by Nunberg (1979), where a waitress refers to a customer by what (s)he ordered, or a nurse refers to a patient by his/her symptoms:

(22)   a. [One waitress to another:]
           The ham sandwich in the corner needs more coffee.
       b. The french fries at table five want(s) a glass of water.
       c. [One nurse to another:]
           The measles in Room 426 needs/*need a fresh IV.

(22b,c) show that number agreement in this case can be triggered by either target entity—the singular person who has the french fries or the measles—or in some cases by the source phrase, *french fries*. This is distinct from the statue cases in (20c), where agreement is clearly triggered by the source phrase *four oxen* and not by the singular target entity. (Abusch shows parallel phenomena in Hebrew gender agreement.) Similarly, the appropriate pronominal form in (23) is that for the target entity—the person, not the measles or the ham sandwich.

(23)   a. The ham sandwich in the corner needs his/*its bill.
       b. The measles in Room 426 has a fever. Could you look in on her/
           *them?

This is again the reverse of (21c,d), where even in referring to a singular neuter target entity one preferably uses an animate or plural pronoun that agrees with the source phrase.

As in the "car-for-person" case, this contrast shows that one cannot treat these reference transfers as a unified class; each requires its own analysis. This gives us a sense of how specialized the statue rule might be; its properties are not going to follow from general considerations alone.

10.5.2 A deletion can't work anyway

Even if we could solve the technical problems that arise in accounting for (19)–(21), the standard old-time reasons still militate against a syntactic rule deleting or inserting *statue (of)*: the statue rule has clear semantic content. It applies to a semantically delimited class of nouns that denote physical objects containing either visual representations (*picture, portrait, statue, photograph*) or, more marginally, auditory representations (*tape, record, CD*). Lexical innovation creating a new term in this class, say *CD*, produces results typical of the class. For instance, (24a) is a lot better than (24b):

(24) a. ?All the CDs were lying around on the floor. Carelessly, I stepped on Beethoven and Ringo stepped on himself.[4]
   b. *All the CDs fell off the shelf. Beethoven fell on me and Ringo fell on himself.

On the other hand, the statue rule does not apply to abstract nouns that denote representations, such as *description, legend, tale,* and *account*:

(25) a. Harry gave us a description/an account of Ringo ≠ *Harry gave us Ringo.
   b. Now we're going to hear the tale/legend of Ringo ≠ Now we're going to hear Ringo.

---

[4] Abusch (1989) points out a considerable context-dependence on the acceptability of sentences like these. Sentences (i) and (ii) are better than (24a), which has been chosen for comparability with (24b). But in turn (24a) is better than the relevant reading of (iii).

i. There were a lot of CDs in the bookcase. Out of curiosity, I listened to Beethoven and Ringo listened to himself.
ii. There were a lot of CDs in the store. Out of curiosity, I bought Beethoven and Ringo bought himself.
iii. A lot of CDs were sitting on the shelf. Maliciously, I threw Beethoven on the floor and *Ringo threw <CD-of> himself out the window.

This gradation is more evident with recordings than with pictures or statues. Intuitively, greater acceptability seems to have something to do with how centrally the recorded content of the object is involved in the action described by the sentence, but we have no principled explanation to offer.

The nouns *picture* and *sketch* can be used to denote either a physical object containing a visual representation or a brief description. Only on the former reading can they undergo the statue rule:

(26) a. Bill was doing charcoal sketches of the Beatles, and to my delight he gave me Ringo.

   b. *Bill was giving us quick (verbal) sketches of the new employees, and to my surprise he gave us Harry.

The fact that the statue rule is highly constrained by idiosyncratic semantic factors suggests that it cannot be a component of autonomous syntax.

   At the risk of preaching to the converted, let us push the argument one step further. Using either the statue rule or a closely related principle, an actor portraying a character in a play can be referred to by using the name of the character alone:

(27) In the new production of Shakespeare at the Colonial Theater, Hamlet is a woman.

(27) is ambiguous: it can mean either that the character Hamlet is a woman (drastically changing the plot) or that the actor portraying Hamlet is a woman (as has actually happened). The latter reading is the one of interest here. Adapting an example from Fauconnier (1985), suppose Richard Nixon had gone to see John Adams's opera *Nixon in China* (yes, this is a real opera!), in which James Maddalena played Nixon. Then (28a,b) would be possible but (28c,d) would not. That is, this locution creates exactly the same problem with binding as the *<statue>* X locution.[5]

(28) a. Nixon listened to himself singing to Mao. '*<plain>* Nixon listened to Maddalena'

---

[5] The authors have some disagreement on these judgments, RJ finding (28c,d) impossible, PWC finding them possible though difficult to get. As has been seen above, this variability seems characteristic of reflexives in such examples. In any event, the differences in acceptability are systematically asymmetric, and it is the reasons for this asymmetry that we are trying to characterize.

   Fauconnier observes that another application of this principle (or of a closely related one) is to people's counterparts in dreams. David Dowty has suggested therefore that (i), a notorious example of James McCawley's from the late 1960s, might be relevant to the analysis.

(i) I dreamed I was Brigitte Bardot, and *I* kissed *me*.

This case is more complex because the italicized pronouns are both dream-counterparts; also, for strict analogy with the present cases, the object pronoun should be reflexive, as in (ii), which also seems acceptable.

(ii) I dreamed I was Brigitte Bardot, and I kissed myself.

    b.   Sitting in the audience, Nixon spotted himself in the crowd on stage.

    c.   *Nixon listened to himself snoring in the audience. 'Maddalena listened to <plain> Nixon'

    d.   *When he came out on stage, Nixon spotted himself in the audience.

However, in this case there is no good syntactic source from which material can be deleted to produce the surface form. (29a) is ungrammatical; (29b) is marginal, because *portrayer* is barely acceptable as a word (at least with the desired meaning); (29c) implausibly involves deletion of not only the head but part of the modifier:

(29)   a.   *actor of Nixon

      b.   ??portrayer of Nixon

      c.   actor portraying/playing Nixon ?? ⇒ Nixon

These problems are altogether parallel to those pointed out by Chomsky (1970) in his discussion of putative syntactic sources for deverbal nouns like *destruction*: they are semantically idiosyncratic and often there are no plausible syntactic underlying forms. Hence, if we are not prepared to return to transformationally derived nominals, with all the entailed loss of constraints on the syntax, we should not be prepared to accept a deletion for the statue rule either.

10.5.3 *An apparently better version of the Syntactic Option*

Suppose that we retreat from the syntactic deletion analysis, but retain a syntactic difference between <plain> Ringo and <statue> Ringo, for instance by giving the latter an empty head, as in (30). This preserves certain virtues of the deletion analysis. Compare structures (31a) and (31b), which on this proposal encode readings (13a) and (13b) respectively:

This seems to mean that in the dream, Bardot kissed McCawley, not the other way about. Changing the sentence to third person yields a wealth of incomprehensible data (the judgments here are very difficult, and we offer them with some uncertainty—and disagreement between the two of us):

(iii)   McCawley dreamed he was Bardot, and (in the dream)

      a.   *she kissed him (i.e. McCawley).

      b.   *he (i.e. McCawley) kissed her (i.e. Bardot).

      c.   *she kissed herself (i.e. McCawley).

      d.   he (i.e. Bardot!) kissed himself (i.e. McCawley).

      e.   *he (i.e. McCawley) kissed himself (i.e. Bardot).

Cases (d) and (e) are the closest parallel to our statue examples here, but we hesitate to offer an analysis, especially since PWC thinks (d) is bad too.

(30) <*statue*> Ringo = [$_{NP}$ e [$_{NP}$ Ringo]]

(31) a. [$_{NP}$ Ringo]$_i$ fell on [$_{NP}$ e [$_{NP}$ himself]$_i$]

           = '<*plain*>Ringo fell on <*statue*>himself'

    b. *[$_{NP}$ e [$_{NP}$ Ringo]$_i$] fell on [$_{NP}$ himself]$_i$

           = '<*statue*>Ringo fell on <*plain*>himself'

(31b) violates Principle A in exactly the same way as (17b) (**A** *statue of Ringo fell on himself*). Furthermore, the acceptable case of binding is again between coreferential terms, so an extended notion of anaphora-without-coreference need not be added to the theory.

However, return to the case-marking and agreement facts in (19)–(21). In order for these to work out properly, the empty category in (30) would some-how have to be "transparent" to case-marking and agreement, while still being "visible" to binding. It is probably impossible to argue against all the conceivable ways that this could be accomplished, but let us go through a couple that are suggestive of the complications that would arise.

First, the fact that the extra structure is "transparent" to case-marking and agreement but "visible" to binding cannot be a matter of general convention. Let us compare the <*statue*> X locution with another construction that argu-ably has a structure much like (30): bare possessives such as *Ernie's* in (32):

(32) Bert's oatmeal is lumpy, but Ernie's is runny.

The structure of this construction appears to be (33), where *e* is an empty anaphoric element (Jackendoff 1977: 114–25, esp. n. 8).[6]

(33) [$_{NP}$ [$_{NP}$ Ernie]+gen [$_{N'}$ e]]

Unlike in the statue examples, *Ernie* in (32) is genitive, not nominative; this shows that the empty structure in (33) *is* visible to case-marking. Similarly, note that the verb in the second clause of (34a) agrees with the plural antecedent *cookies*, not with the singular *Cookie Monster*; and that the pronoun in (34b) agrees with its neuter antecedent *picture*, not with the masculine *Ernie*:

(34) a. Bert's cookies are ugly, but Cookie Monster's are/*is truly hideous.

    b. I don't know about *your* picture, but Ernie's is famous. Do you want to look at it/??him?

---

[6] Following section 8.1, the structure might even be as simple as (i), with no empty head.

[$_{NP}$[$_{NP}$ Ernie]^{ORPH} + gen]^{IL}

For the moment, we will assume the empty head is present; this is the position most consistent with the view of reference transfer we are arguing against here.

And of course binding is sensitive to the embedding of the genitive NP:

(35)   Big Bird's picture fell on Bert, but *Ernie's fell on himself.

Ernie is ineligible as an antecedent for *himself* because it does not c-command it. In short, the empty head *e* in the bare possessive construction is visible to case-marking, number agreement, and pronominal agreement, as well as to binding. Accordingly, it is hard to see why the empty head in (30) for *<statue> Ringo* should be visible to binding but transparent to the other three processes.

An explicit way to accomplish this effect would be to claim that (30) undergoes head-to-head movement, moving *Ringo* into the empty head. Thus at S-structure the structure would be (36), permitting case-marking and agreement to work properly:

(36)   [$_{NP}$ Ringo$_i$ [$_{NP}$ t$_i$]]

However, there are two problems with this solution. First, binding would have to take place at some level other than S-structure, in particular while *Ringo* is still embedded. This leads to the same problems we saw in the deletion analysis in section 10.5.1: the structure would have to be (30) both at D-structure, where the θ-role of *Ringo* is marked, and at LF, where binding would have to apply. Yet S-structure, where the structure is (36), falls between them in the derivation.

Second, the process that eliminates the *e* can't be head-to-head movement anyway, because of examples like (37a), whose subject would have the structure (37b): the whole constituent *little mermaid braiding her hair* (referring to the individual portrayed by the statue) would have to undergo raising.

(37)   a. The little mermaid braiding her hair is cute.
        b. [$_{NP}$ (the) e [$_{NP}$ (the) little mermaid braiding her hair]]

In addition to these technical difficulties, there is a serious conceptual difficulty: structure (30) does not solve our original problem, namely how *Ringo* comes to be understood as *statue of Ringo*. That is, the statue rule is no longer localized in the syntax. Rather, the empty head *e* in (30) has to receive some interpretation at the level of sentence meaning. But it cannot be interpreted by general convention; the possibilities are strictly constrained semantically, as we saw in section 10.5.2. A specialized principle of interpretation is necessary, of approximately the form (38).

(38)   The syntactic structure [$_{NP}$ e [$_{NP}$...]] may correspond to the semantic/conceptual structure STATUE (X), where X is the ordinary interpretation of the inner NP.

We will return to the details of (38) in the next section, where we will articulate a related but simpler principle. For the moment, let us simply observe that proposing structure (30) for *<statue> Ringo* merely provides a syntactic structure that mimics the function–argument structure of the interpretation STATUE (X), without actually providing the semantic content of the interpretation. The structural aspect of Interface Uniformity is maintained, but the interface still has to be enriched by rule (38) in order to supply the semantics.[7] Hence this proposal actually has the worst of both worlds, requiring the complications of both the Syntactic Option and the Interface Option.

Since structure (30) raises tricky syntactic problems and is a variant of the Interface Option anyway, it is time to move on more seriously to the Interface Option.

10.6 The Interface Option

The most straightforward version of the Interface Option is that the syntactic structure of *<statue> Ringo* is (39) at *all* levels, in conformance with the Simpler Syntax Hypothesis. The statue rule may be stated informally as the interface rule (40); we will develop a more formal treatment in the rest of the chapter.

(39)   [$_{NP}$ Ringo]

(40)   The syntactic structure NP may correspond to the semantic/conceptual structure *PHYSICAL REPRESENTATION (X)*, where X is the ordinary interpretation of NP.

In (40), the expression *PHYSICAL REPRESENTATION (X)* (henceforth abbreviated as *REP (X)*) is intended to capture the semantic features that pictures, statues, recordings, and portraying actors have in common, while excluding descriptions, tales, and legends (which are not physical) as well as cars (which are not representations).[8] For the moment, the notation is intended as a stand-in for whatever formalism for semantic structure the reader may favor, be it predicate calculus, any variety of model-theoretic semantics, semantic networks, or a more psychologically based theory.

---

[7] Note how this parallels the argument in section 7.3 against a treatment of ellipsis in which all the syntactic structure is present but filled with empty nodes.

[8] To be more explicit, this rule leaves it up to contextual understanding to decide exactly what kind of physical representation is being referred to: a statue, picture, recording, etc. But this is altogether parallel to leaving it up to contextual understanding to decide what particular kind of object is referred by the phrase *that thing*—so it presents no new sort of problem.

Seen from the point of view of the mapping from syntax to sentence meaning, (40) licenses adding a chunk to the interpretation of the NP that is not expressed anywhere in the syntax. Alternatively, from the point of view of the mapping from sentence meaning to syntax, (40) licenses abbreviating the intended meaning, leaving the function *PHYSICAL REPRESENTATION* unexpressed or implicit.[9]

How does this differ from the Pragmatic Option? In the Pragmatic Option, *<statue> Ringo* has the same *meaning* as *<plain> Ringo*, but this meaning is applied to objects in the world differently. In the Interface Option, *<statue> Ringo* and *<plain> Ringo* have different meanings, which in turn result in different conditions of application to the world. At the same time, both options take the view that the difference is not reflected syntactically.

Under the Interface Option, it follows without further ado that there should be no difference between *<statue> Ringo* and *<plain> Ringo* in agreement and case marking—the stumbling block for the Syntactic Option. It also follows that there should be a specialized bit of meaning in "statue" readings, since such a specialized bit is stipulated as part of the rule. Note how the Interface Option differs crucially from the Syntactic Option in this respect: a rule like (40), which establishes a correspondence between syntax and semantics, can very naturally stipulate semantic particulars, while, by contrast, an autonomous syntactic deletion cannot. Finally, it is no problem that cases such as (27)–(28) have no syntactic paraphrase from which a segment can be plausibly deleted (cf. (29)); the unexpressed piece of meaning is never present in syntax anyway.

A more formal statement of the statue rule would treat it as a coercion—a conventionalized piece of meaning that can be omitted from syntactic expression. Following the approach to coercion sketched in section 6.5.3, a coercion can be treated as a lexical item that licenses a CS but not associated syntax or phonology (parallel to epenthetic *of* or dummy *it*, which have syntax and phonology but no semantics). In carving a CS into words and morphemes, the coercion licenses a piece of the semantics without connecting it to syntax and phonology. The scenario in (41) illustrates.

---

[9] Could (40) be thought of instead as some sort of lexical rule that assigns additional interpretations to words? No: the derived reading involves compositional structure of the NP, not just the reading of the head noun. For instance, *four oxen* in (20) denotes a sculpture of four oxen, not four sculptures of oxen, and *little mermaid braiding her hair* in (37) denotes a sculpture of a little mermaid braiding her hair, not a little sculpture of a mermaid that is performing the sculptural counterpart of braiding to sculptured hair. In other words, (40) cannot just enrich the meanings of individual lexical items; it must add information at the level of N′ or NP. Thus it cannot be a lexical rule. (Notice that this parallels the argument in section 10.5.3 that a syntactic version of the rule cannot involve head-to-head movement.)

(41)   I saw <*statue*> Ringo.

Conceptual structure		Syntax	Phonology
[PAST [SEE ([I], [STATUE ([RINGO])])]]			
i. [PAST [*Situation*	$]_2]_1$	V_2-T_1	Wd_2-d_1
ii. [SEE (X, Y	$)]_2$	V	see
iii. [I]$_3$		[NP1sg]$_3$	I$_3$
iv. [RINGO]$_4$		[NP3sg]$_4$	Ringo$_4$
v. [REP (Z_i)]		XP_i	

Up to the last line, everything proceeds as in Chapter 5. The last line is the crucial difference. It has the meaning REP (Z), but it does not link to the syntax; only its argument does. The result is that RINGO is expressed as the direct object of the verb, and REP is not expressed at all. This approach generalizes nicely for all the coercions described in Jackendoff (1997a: ch. 3), which include aspectual coercions, mass-count coercions, Pustejovsky's (1995) co-compositional coercions (*John enjoyed the beer*), and Grimshaw's (1990) implicit indirect questions (*I asked the time*). We will use this approach again in Chapter 12, when we deal with coercion in control phenomena.

The main problem with this version of the Interface Option, sad to say, is the interaction with binding theory. On this account, <*plain*> *Ringo* and <*statue*> *Ringo* are indistinguishable at every level of syntax, so there is no way for a syntactic binding theory to predict the different grammaticality of readings (13a) and (13b).

So we seem to be at an impasse. The Pragmatic Option requires supplementing the syntactic binding theory with a theory of non-coreferential anaphora at the mysterious level of contextual understanding. The Syntactic Option, despite some initial promise, turns out to raise tricky technical problems, and it neither interacts properly with binding theory nor preserves the autonomy of syntax. The Interface Option eliminates the syntactic technicalities at the price of also eliminating the necessary interaction with binding theory. The variant of the Interface Option stated in section 10.5.3 restores the interaction with binding theory, though still problematically, and it reintroduces the syntactic technicalities. Where do we go from here?

10.7 Reconceiving binding theory

We suggest that the proper solution is to reconsider the nature of binding theory. Around the corners of the literature, one encounters from time to time suggestions that binding conditions for reflexives and *PRO* are sensitive to semantic configurations as well as syntactic ones (e.g. Jackendoff 1972; 1974; 1990a;

Cantrall 1974; Schachter 1976; Culicover and Wilkins 1984; Cattell 1984; Williams 1985; Chierchia 1988; Farkas 1988; Grimshaw 1990; Sag and Pollard 1992 and, within a broader range of traditions, Kuno 1987, Fauconnier 1985, Langacker 1991, Van Hoek 1992, and Van Valin 1990; see also Chapter 12 for control). Let's explore this possibility in conjunction with the Interface Option, in which readings (13a) and (13b) are structurally different in semantic/conceptual structure, but not in syntax. If binding theory can be revised so that it is sensitive to this semantic/conceptual difference, then it will be possible to account for the difference in grammaticality.[10]

What structural difference in meaning might there be? (42) gives the semantic structures for readings (13a) and (13b), assuming a basic predicate calculus-like treatment of CS, supplemented by binding indices. The structures should be self-explanatory, and the reader is free to substitute his or her own favorite formalism. We will elaborate these structures shortly.

(42)   a. *<plain>* Ringo fell on *<statue>* himself =
          FALL (RINGO$_i$, ON (REP (SELF$_i$)))
       b. *<statue>* Ringo fell on *<plain>* himself =
          FALL (REP (RINGO$_i$), ON (SELF$_i$))

Thus, if binding theory is stated in part over semantic/conceptual structure, it will be able to distinguish (42a) from (42b), ruling the latter ill-formed. Before going into the considerations involved in stating binding theory this way, we will give two arguments for the plausibility of this approach.

First, like the Syntactic Option, it does not require binding between an expression denoting *<plain>* Ringo and one denoting *<statue>* Ringo. Rather, the binding in (42a) relates two semantic constituents that refer to *<plain>* Ringo. Thus binding theory does not need to be supplemented by a theory of anaphora-without-contextual-coreference.

Second, consider (18a) and (18b), repeated here:

(18)   a.   Ringo fell on a statue of himself.
       b. *A statue of Ringo fell on himself.

These will have semantic/conceptual structures identical to (42a,b) respectively, except that *PHYSICAL REPRESENTATION* will be augmented by some

---

[10] For readers who find this possibility intuitively objectionable, recall that the Pragmatic Option requires binding/coreference to be sensitive not only to syntax but also to completely unspecified contextual conditions. If the reader is willing to consider such a move in order to save the traditional syntactic binding theory, it should not seem so awful to introduce much more explicit semantic conditions instead.

modifiers that distinguish statues from portraits, photographs, recordings, and so forth. Hence, any condition on semantic structure that rules out reading (13b) will also rule out (18b). In other words, like the Syntactic Option, this approach captures the generalization between (13) and (18).

This way of relating (13) and (18) leads to an interesting situation. In the mainstream analysis, (18b) is blocked by a syntactic configuration, namely that the anaphor is not syntactically bound by a c-commanding constituent in its governing category. We are now proposing that (42b) is ruled out by a principle stated over conceptual structure—and that (18b) is ruled out by the very same principle. But then, what work is the syntactic principle doing? In order to explore this question, we have to be more explicit about how parts of binding theory might pertain to semantics.

The approach we will adopt is proposed as part of the theory of conceptual structure in Jackendoff (1987; 1990a). The essential idea is that (43a), the standard notation for binding, is to be considered an abbreviation for the formal treatment (43b):

(43)   a. NP_i binds [NP, anaphor]$_i$

      b.   CS: X_i^α binds [α;Y]$_j$
          corresponds to | |
          Syntax: NP_i [NP;anaphor]$_j$

That is, the apparent syntactic binding of an anaphor actually consists of three relations:

• CS-binding: A binding constituent in CS binds a variable, as notated by the Greek letters.

• Antecedent realization: The binder corresponds to an antecedent in syntax.

• Anaphor realization: The bound variable corresponds to an anaphor in syntax.

(43b) is not just a complicated notational variant of (43a). Jackendoff (1987; 1990a: ch. 3) shows that a notion of binding over conceptual structure is independently necessary to encode the lexical entries of verbs whose syntactic arguments occupy more than one thematic role, for instance *undress* and *sell* in (44). Here the antecedent is realized in syntax but the anaphor is not.

(44)   a.   Ringo undressed. (*Ringo* is agent and patient; compare to *Ringo undressed George*)[11]

---

[11] Because the second argument is not expressed in syntax, there is no way to apply coercion to it, so as to mean <*plain*> Ringo undressed <*statue*> Ringo.

b. Ringo sold a book to Paul for five pounds. (*Ringo* is agent, source of *book*, and goal of *five pounds*; *Paul* is goal of *book* and source of *five pounds*)

Control offers another such case. Section 6.2.3 proposed that controlled infinitival and gerundive complements do not have an invisible NP subject, PRO. That is, the structure of *John tried to leave* is not *[John tried [PRO to leave]*, as Structural Uniformity would demand, but rather just *[John tried [to leave]]*. The CS corresponding to the infinitival clause has a bound variable as its thematically most prominent argument; this maps to the most prominent grammatical function on the GF-tier but has no syntactic realization.

(45) $[\text{TRY (JOHN}_2^{\alpha}, [\text{LEAVE } (\alpha_4)]_3)]_1$
                          | |
                  $[\text{GF}_2]_1$ $[\text{GF}_4]_3$
                          |
                  $[\text{John}_2 \text{ tried [to leave]}_3]_1$

In other words, again there is CS-binding and the antecedent (here the controller) is realized syntactically, but the bound variable is not realized in syntax.

Binding of the form (43b) is then the particular case of CS-binding in which both the bound variable and its binder are syntactically explicit. Thus the formulation in (43b) leads to a more general theory of binding.

In standard binding theory, reflexive anaphors are licensed by Principle A, whose overall form, ignoring structural details for the moment, is (46):

(46)   **Principle A**: A reflexive anaphor must be bound in syntactic domain D.

In order to see how this can be recast in terms of conceptual structure binding, let us first restate it slightly as (47):

(47)   **Principle A′**: A reflexive anaphor must be bound. The binding relation (43a) is well-formed (or licensed) iff the anaphor is in syntactic relation R to its antecedent.

(47) involves only syntactic structure. However, in a theory of CS-binding, the licensing of anaphors may involve both syntactic and conceptual structure. It is therefore reasonable to assume that conditions on both structures may play a role. The counterpart of Principle A′ then takes the general form (48):

(48)   **Principle A$_{CS}$**: A reflexive anaphor must be bound. The following conditions must obtain in order to bind it:

   a. Syntactic condition: If the antecedent is expressed in syntax, it must be in relation R_{SS} to the anaphor.

   b. GF tier condition (cf. section 6.4): If the reflexive anaphor has a GF, its antecedent must have a more prominent GF clausemate.

   c. CS condition: If the reflexive anaphor has a CS, it corresponds to a bound variable, whose binder must be in relation R_{CS} to the variable.

Condition (48b) is stated as a conditional. This is because not every reflexive has a GF—only those that are arguments of verbs. For example, the reflexive in *John bought a picture of himself* does not have a GF, so condition (48b) does not apply to it. Similarly, (48c) is a conditional because not every reflexive anaphor has a CS: for instance the reflexive in *John behaved himself* is a pleonastic argument that has a GF but no CS.

   Among potential conditions involved in defining R_{SS}, the *syntactic* relation between a reflexive and its antecedent, are presumably standard ones such as dominance, linear order, c-command, and bounding categories.[12] What sorts of structural condition over conceptual structure might be available for defining R_{CS}? Here are six possibilities:

• *Thematic prominence.* A recurring idea in the literature cited above is that one argument can be distinguished from another by virtue of being higher on a Thematic Hierarchy. In Jackendoff (1990a) such a hierarchy is defined in terms of structural conditions on conceptual structure, so it is less arbitrary than it may have appeared in previous work. In particular, thematic prominence plays a major role in mapping between semantic and syntactic argument structure (Chapter 5).

• *Specific thematic configurations.* Kuno (1987) argues that a reflexive pronoun can be licensed in a "logophoric" context: the antecedent is a perceiver or thinker of some situation or information or object, and the reflexive is a character in that situation or information or object (e.g. *picture of himself*).

• *Dominance.* Just as in syntax, a conceptual constituent X can be said to dominate a constituent Y if Y is a constituent of X.

• *Argument/modifier distinctions.* Arguments and modifiers of a particular conceptual constituent are attached in distinct fashion inside the constituent, and binding relations might depend on this difference.

• *Bounding conceptual constituents.* Particular conceptual categories like *THING* and *EVENT* might, like syntactic bounding categories, block binding relations into them. Alternatively, one might define a notion of bounding

---

[12] For a concrete proposal along these lines incorporating both syntactic and semantic conditions, see Reinhart and Reuland (1991; 1993).

conceptual constituents in terms of constituents that determine an independently specified reference. The latter possibility played a role in our discussion of semantic conditions on extraction in Chapter 9, and similar "definiteness effects" have been observed to block reflexive anaphora.[13]

• *Information structure conditions.* Kuno (1987) and others argue that the antecedent of a non-focused anaphor (reflexive or pronominal) cannot be both focused and to its right. The intuitive basis for such a constraint is that it is impossible for old information to be referentially dependent on new information. This accounts, for example, for the necessary stress pattern in *That Sue$_i$ is happy* **bothers** *her$_i$* (vs. **That Sue$_i$ is happy bothers* **her**$_i$): the unstressed pronoun is backgrounded information.

The empirical problem in working out Principle A_{CS} is the same as that for working out Principle A: to find the correct characterization of the binding domain in terms of available structural principles. Principle A_{CS} poses the additional problem of properly distributing the conditions among three levels of grammar (and multiple tiers within CS). This issue is especially interesting because syntactic and conceptual conditions can very closely mimic each other. For example, because of the Argument–Modifier Rule in the interface component (section 5.4), syntactic embedding fairly closely parallels conceptual embedding. Hence any condition involving dominance (such as c-command) may appear plausible as part of either component. Similarly, as observed in section 5.7, it has frequently been suggested that the syntactic prominence of an argument is determined (or largely determined) by its thematic prominence (Carter 1976; Anderson 1977; Ostler 1979; Marantz 1984; Foley and Van Valin 1984; Carrier-Duncan 1985; Grimshaw 1987, 1990; Bresnan and Kanerva 1989; Jackendoff 1990a). Hence the subject of a sentence is (as a rule) more thematically prominent than all other arguments. Consequently, any syntactic condition referring to the external argument will closely duplicate a conceptual condition referring to the thematically most prominent argument (see especially Grimshaw 1990 for arguments bearing on this issue).

The same sort of mimicry is possible with the other conceptual structure conditions mentioned above. The argument–modifier distinction is very close to but not identical to the syntactic argument–adjunct distinction (section 5.4); on the other hand, Chapter 4 wiped out the argument–adjunct distinction as a structural principle of syntax. Finally, a definition of bounding conceptual

---

[13] Such conditions lend themselves to statement in terms of the *referential tier* of CS proposed in Jackendoff (2002a: ch. 12), which resembles many aspects of Discourse Representation Theory. We forgo this extra elaboration in the interest of keeping the course of the argument here reasonably within bounds.

structure constituent in terms of dominating *THING* or *EVENT* is close to a syntactic definition in terms of NPs and IPs, since NPs canonically express *THING*s and IPs canonically express *EVENT*s.

Thus it may be the case that, in the absence of an articulated theory of conceptual structure, syntactic conditions on Principle A have seemed plausible (and the only available possibility) because their effects are so similar to parallel conceptual structure conditions which are in fact the correct choice. Given the complexity of the problem, this is not the place to develop a detailed theory of conceptual structure binding conditions; that would be the subject matter of a much larger work. Our intent here is only a preliminary exploration of the issues, in the service of showing what questions a detailed theory would have to address. However, at this point enough conceptual structure phenomena are understood on independent grounds that we can state some interesting options and test them with some rigor. The next section will begin to work out one line of attack.

10.8 Formalizing and generalizing parts of Principle A_CS

10.8.1 The 'statue' sentences and other coercions

(49) and (50) repeat the sentences we have been primarily concerned with so far, along with their conceptual structures, now expressed in the CS formalism of previous chapters. The claim is that (49a,b) share conceptual structure (49c), and that (50a,b) share structure (50c).

(49)	a.	Ringo fell on a statue of himself.	(= 18a)
	b.	*\<plain\>* Ringo fell on *\<statue\>* himself.	(= 13a)
	c.	[FALL (RINGO$^\alpha$, ON [REP (α)])]	(= 42a)
(50)	a.	*A statue of Ringo fell on himself.	(= 18b)
	b.	* *\<statue\>* Ringo fell on *\<plain\>* himself.	(= 13b)
	c.	[FALL ([REP (RINGO$^\alpha$)], [ON α])]	(= 42b)

Our hypothesis so far is (a) that, in conformance with the Simpler Syntax Hypothesis, the 'statue' reading of (49b) does not have any extra syntactic structure; (b) that (50b) is ungrammatical because of a condition on its conceptual structure; (c) that (50a), the overt paraphrase of (50b), violates the same condition. This means that (50a) is ungrammatical because of a condition in R_CS rather than (or in addition to) something having to do with c-command. A very narrow statement of the condition might be stated as (51a); (51b) states it more concisely as a linking condition between CS and syntax. We will generalize the condition shortly.

(51) **Part of R_{CS} in Principle A_{CS}**

    a.   A reflexive anaphor cannot correspond to a bound variable α in the configuration

        $F\ ([REP\ (X^{\alpha})],\ G(\alpha))$,

        where X is linked to the antecedent of the reflexive.

    b.   (more concisely)

        $*\ [F\ ([REP\ (X_{i}^{\alpha})],\ G(\alpha_{j}))] \Leftrightarrow \ldots NP_{i} \ldots [NP,refl]_{j} \ldots$

Before we consider our work done, however, we must also account for some further variants on (49)–(50), in which the coerced version diverges in grammaticality from the non-coerced version. (52) is a different configuration of reflexive and antecedent, and (53)–(55) replace the reflexive with a pronoun.

(52) a.   A statue of himself fell on Ringo.

     b.   *<statue> Himself fell on <plain> Ringo.

     c. $[FALL\ (REP\ (\alpha),\ [ON\ RINGO^{\alpha}])]$

(53) a.   ?Ringo fell on a statue of him.

     b.   *<plain> Ringo fell on <statue> him.

     c. $[FALL\ (RINGO^{\alpha},\ ON\ [REP\ (\alpha)])]$ $(=(49c))$

(54) a.   A statue of Ringo fell on him.

     b.   *<statue> Ringo fell on <plain> him.

     c. $[FALL\ ([REP\ (RINGO^{\alpha})],\ [ON\ \alpha])]$ $(=(50c))$

(55) a.   A statue of him fell on Ringo.

     b.   *<statue> He fell on <plain> Ringo.

     c. $[FALL\ (REP\ (\alpha),\ [ON\ RINGO^{\alpha}])]$ $(=(51c))$

These appear to be counterexamples to the hypothesis so far: the (a) cases and the (b) cases are claimed to have the same conceptual structure, yet they differ in grammaticality. The solution to their difference lies in the GF-tier. We repeat here the conditions on GF-binding from section 6.4.

(56) **GF-binding conditions**

    a. A reflexive linked to a GF must be GF-bound to a more prominent GF-clausemate.   [GF Condition A]

    b. No other NP linked to a GF may be bound to a GF-clausemate.

       (I.e. pronouns and R-expressions are free in a GF-domain.)

                               [GF Condition B–C]

Unfortunately we have to go through all the examples in detail, tedious though that may be. First consider the (a) sentences, in which coercion has not taken place. In (49a, 52a, 53a, 55a), the anaphor is embedded in a *statue* NP, so it lacks a GF, and GF-binding conditions do not apply to it. Rather, GF-binding conditions apply between *Ringo* and *statue of him(self)*, which are correctly not GF-bound to each other. This leaves two cases without coercion: (50a) and (54a). In (50a), the GF-binding conditions apply between *a statue of Ringo* and *himself*. If GF-binding has to be consistent with CS-binding, then *himself* cannot be CS-bound to *Ringo*, as in the desired interpretation. Condition (51) rules out this CS-binding as well, so it is doubly bad. In (54a), the GF-binding conditions apply between *a statue of Ringo* and *him*, correctly marking them not bound; and evidently CS-binding condition (51) applies only to reflexives, not to pronouns. Hence (54a) is acceptable.

Now look at the (b) sentences, the coerced versions. In (49b) and (50b), GF-binding occurs between *Ringo* and *himself*; however, CS-binding condition (51) applies to (50b), ruling it out. (52b) is not ruled out by a CS-binding condition, as we can see from (52a); but it *is* ruled out by GF-binding, since *himself* is linked to the highest GF in the clause. In (53b,54b,55b), the intent is for *him* to be CS-bound to *Ringo*, but it can't be, because it has a GF and therefore cannot be GF-bound to *Ringo*. In short, all the differences between the (a) and (b) sentences are a consequence of GF-binding.

Let us next look at "ham-sandwich" coercions, which we analyzed in section 6.5.3 as having the structure (57).

(57)   The ham sandwich wants coffee. =
         [WANT ([PERSON ASSOC-W [HAM SANDWICH]], COFFEE)]

Again, only the CS argument of the constituent [*PERSON ASSOC-W (X)*] shows up in syntax.[14] There is one essential difference between this coercion and the "statue" coercion: it does not permit pronouns to be coerced. Thus (58b) is a "statue" coerced version of (58a), but the parallel (58d) is not an acceptable "ham sandwich" coerced version of (58c). This restriction on coercion is also seen in (58e) with a non-reflexive pronoun.

(58)   a.   Ringo admires the statue of himself.
        b.   *<plain>*Ringo admires *<statue>* himself.
        c.   The ham sandwich didn't suit the person who ordered it.
        d.   **<plain>*The ham sandwich didn't suit *<person assoc-w>* it(self).

---

[14] Interestingly, modifiers can pertain either to the person (i) or the sandwich (ii); the coercion is slightly less comfortable if modifiers are mixed (iii, iv, v).

(i)   The blonde ham sandwich with a big hat wants coffee.
(ii) The rare roast beef with mustard wants coffee.
(iii) ?The blonde ham sandwich with mustard wants coffee.
(iv) ?The rare roast beef with a big hat wants coffee.
(v)   ?The blonde rare roast beef wants coffee.

e. If the ham sandwich starts to act fresh, kick him/*it out of the restaurant.

With this difference in mind, consider the parallels to (49–50).

(59) a. *The ham sandwich didn't suit the person who ordered itself.   [*GF-binding]
      b. *<*plain*>The ham sandwich didn't suit <*person assoc-w*> itself.
                                                                          [*coercion of pronouns]

(60) a. *The person who ordered the ham sandwich ate itself.
                                                                          [*GF-binding, *CS-binding]
      b. *<*person assoc-w*>The ham sandwich ate <*plain*>itself.
                                                                                        [*CS-binding]

Thus both cases of coercion are ungrammatical here, but for different reasons.[15] The crucial case, in which nothing but CS binding putatively stands in the way of grammaticality, is (60b), paralleling (50b). Its structure is (61).

(61) [EAT ([PERSON ASSOC-W [HAM SANDWICH]$^\alpha$], α)]

Parallel facts obtain with the "car-of" coercion. We observed in section 10.4 that this coercion has approximately the meaning *[VEHICLE DRIVEN BY X]*, or perhaps more formally (62).

(62) [VEHICLE; λ^α[DRIVE (X, α)]]

We don't fully understand the conditions under which this coercion can be applied to personal pronouns, but the relevant cases are shown in (63). For pragmatic plausibility, let us suppose this time that Ringo is not in the car, but rather the car is radio-controlled by Ringo.

(63) a. <*plain*>Ringo squeezed <*car-driven-by*>himself into a tight parking spot.
      b. *<*car-driven-by*>Ringo ran over <*plain*>himself.

---

[15] One further case ought to be mentioned, and here the two coercions are parallel:

(i)   <*person assoc-w*>The ham sandwich scratched <*plain*>himself.
(ii) <*robot*>Ringo shook <*plain*>itself to bits.

The CS-binding is licit in (i), because the person, not the sandwich, is the antecedent. The GF-binding is licit as well, since the reflexive is GF-bound to the NP that refers to the person. The same analysis pertains to (ii). Note that <*robot*>*Ringo shook himself to bits* is also all right, but <*person assoc-w*>*The ham sandwich scratched itself* is bad because the reflexive cannot be coerced to refer to the person.

The structure that (61) and (63b) have in common with (50c) is (64), where *H* is a variable function that in one case is *REP*, in another *PERSON ASSOC-W*, and in a third *VEHICLE DRIVEN BY*.

(64) $[F ([H(X^\alpha)], G(\alpha)]$

So a plausible hypothesis is that condition (51) is a special case of the more general (65).

(65)   **Part of R_{CS} in Principle A_{CS}**
       $*[F([H(X_i^\alpha)], G(\alpha_j)] \Leftrightarrow \ldots NP_i \ldots [NP,refl]_j \ldots$

A crucial feature here is that *H(X)*, the constituent that contains the binder, is more prominent in CS (i.e. higher on the thematic hierarchy) than *G(α)*, the constituent that contains the bound variable. This begins to resemble a CS counterpart of c-command; we might call it the CS-command condition.

10.8.2 *Verbs whose meanings involve representations or information*

So far we have used CS-binding condition (65) only to account for the ungrammaticality of certain coercions. But it can be used to our advantage elsewhere. Let's consider a well-known recalcitrant case in the theory of reflexives, dating back to Postal (1971), and mentioned in Chapters 4 and 6:

(66)   a.   I talked to Ringo about himself.
       b.   *I talked about Ringo to himself.

Postal accounts for the ungrammaticality of (66b) in terms of a violation of his Crossover Principle, which prohibits coreference if the antecedent and reflexive have been moved so as to reverse their linear order. However, (66) parallels (67) semantically, and (67b) cannot have arisen through movement.

(67)   a.   I told Ringo about himself.
       b.   *I mentioned Ringo to himself.

The real generalization, we believe, has to do with the semantic content of the verbs. Recall the suggestion in section 6.4 that (67b) is a case where GF-binding and CS-binding impose conflicting requirements. We are now in a position to be more specific. Let us work out the conceptual structures of the verbs in (66)–(67), incorporating the idea that they express transfers of information. (*INF (X)* may be read 'information pertaining to X'.)

(68)   a. I talked to/told Ringo about himself =
                      [CAUSE (I, [GO ([INF (**α**)], TO (RINGO$^\alpha$)])]

b. *I talked about/mentioned Ringo to himself =

$$[\text{CAUSE (I, [GO ([INF (RINGO}^{\alpha})], \text{TO } (\alpha)])]$$

The part of (68a) in bold is structurally parallel to (52c), except that it has *INF* (an abstract kind of representation) where (52c) has *REP* (physical representation); similarly, the part of (68b) in bold is structurally parallel to (50c).[16] Thus (68b) violates condition (65).

The striking difference between this and the coercion cases has to do with where in the sentence the function *INF* comes from. In (50a) and (52a), *REP* is contributed by the noun *statue*; in (50b) and (52b), it is contributed by the statue rule, i.e. a coercion. But in (68), *INF* is contributed by the meaning of the verb—this function is what makes *talk*, *tell*, and *mention* verbs of communication rather than verbs of causation of motion.

However, the part of binding theory that pertains to conceptual structure does not care at all about the way a conceptual structure is syntactically expressed. It cares only about the conceptual structure itself. Hence, (65) rules out (68b) for the same reason that it rules out (50b), despite the fact that their syntactic forms are altogether different.[17]

For another well-known old case, consider the pair in (69), a syntactic account of which drives Larson (1988) to rather extreme lengths of innovation (see Chapters 2 and 4):

(69) a. I showed John himself in the mirror.
　　　b. *I showed John to himself in the mirror.

Under a fairly reasonable conceptual analysis of the verb, *X shows Y to Z* and the "dative-shifted" version *X shows Z Y* mean roughly "X causes Z to (visually or mentally) experience Y". In turn, "Z experiences Y" might be decomposed as "mental representation of Y comes into Z's mind". Under this (admittedly contentious) analysis, we get the analyses in (70).

---

[16] The whole of (68a) is parallel to a causative version of (13), *I pushed Ringo into himself*. As expected, this is good in the reading 'I pushed *<plain>* Ringo into *<statue>* himself,' but bad in the reading 'I pushed *<statue>*Ringo into *<plain>*himself.'

[17] Kuno (1987) has a similar account of the semantics of these verbs but a different account of the constraint on anaphora. He proposes (p. 178) a "Humanness Hierarchy": the antecedent of a reflexive should be at least as human as the reflexive. Thus (68b) is bad because the antecedent, being information, is less human than the reflexive. This approach would also account for our examples with "statue" coercions. Note that his account depends implicitly on adopting the view (which we have rejected) that reflexives need not be coreferential with their antecedents. With this in mind, we see that his account founders on our example from note 16, involving the "ham sandwich" coercion: *The ham sandwich scratched himself*. Here the antecedent (on Kuno's account) is the inanimate *ham sandwich*, less human than the reflexive *himself*, yet the example is acceptable.

(70) a. I showed John himself.
          [CAUSE (I, [GO ([REP (α)], TO (MIND (JOHN$^\alpha$)))])]
      b. *I showed John to himself.
          [CAUSE (I, [GO ([REP (JOHN$^\alpha$)], TO (MIND (α)))])]

Again the bad configuration is in violation of CS condition (65). Consequently, no syntactic condition is necessary to account for the ungrammaticality of (69b).

Another case with semantics similar to (67) appears in (71).

(71) a. The war concerns/preoccupies Richard.
      b. Rumors about himself concern/preoccupy Richard.
      c. *Himself concerns/preoccupies Richard.
      d. *Richard concerns/preoccupies himself.
      e. Richard concerns/preoccupies himself with the war.
      f. Richard concerns/preoccupies himself with himself.
      g. Richard is concerned/preoccupied with himself.

(71c) is of course ungrammatical because of GF-binding. Although GF-binding is proper in (71d), the sentence is out because it means "information/representations of Richard cause concern to himself", which violates (65) again. What is interesting about these verbs is that they have another argument realization, shown in (71e), in which a reflexive object is acceptable. The reason is that in this realization, the experiencer is in subject position, the object is a pleonastic reflexive, and the information argument is in the *with*-phrase.[18] Thus CS-binding plays no role and GF-binding is acceptable. (71f) pushes the point still further: the object of *with* is the content of Richard's preoccupation, so it can be CS-bound by the experiencer argument in a fashion consonant with GF-binding. Finally, (71g) shows the passive adjective form, which is another way of reversing the order of arguments in (71c), and which again provides a way to bring GF- and CS-binding into alignment.

The important point here is that the syntactic relation of the reflexive and its antecedent is the same in (71d) and (71e); what differs is how the subject and object correspond to *semantic* roles, and hence how CS-binding applies differently, accounting for the difference in grammaticality.

In turn, the frame in (71d) is closely parallel to the better-known stative psychological predicates such as *please*, *strike*, *remind*, and *appeal to*, also proposed in section 6.4 as cases where GF-binding and CS-binding conflict. To the extent that a semantic analysis along the lines of (70) is on the mark,

---

[18] This alternation is close to the one with *fill*: *Water filled the tank/The tank filled with water*, except that it adds the pleonastic reflexive.

these cases now all fall under the generalization that accounts for the "statue" sentences, namely principle (65).

Returning to the *talk about* verbs, what we cannot yet account for is the ungrammaticality of (72).

(72)   *I talked about himself to Ringo.

This is identical to (68a) except that the two PPs are in reverse order. From the synonymy of *I talked to Bill about Harry* and *I talked about Harry to Bill*, we infer that the difference between (68a) and (72) cannot be one of conceptual structure. Thus the ungrammaticality of (72) cannot follow from the part of binding theory that applies to conceptual structure. However, this case may well be out because of a *syntactic* condition on binding. One possibility is that GF-binding rules it out. However, our current theory of GF gives no criteria for ranking oblique arguments, such that *about-NP* would outrank *to-NP* in (72) but the reverse would be the case in (68a)—other than linear order. A plausible alternative is therefore (73), which makes direct use of linear order, following the lead of early theories of anaphora (and revived by Barss and Lasnik (1986); see section 4.4).

(73)   **Part of R_{SS} in Principle A_{CS}**
       If an anaphor and its antecedent are within the same minimal governing category (or c-command each other), the antecedent must be to the left of the anaphor.

Condition (73) rules out backward anaphora in (72), but allows it in (52a) (*A statue of himself fell on Ringo*) because in the latter, the antecedent is outside the NP which serves as minimal governing category for the reflexive.[19] Section 4.4.2 offered examples involving heavy shift where (73) plays a role:

(74)   a.   *John showed herself as a young girl to Mary.
       b.   John showed to Mary herself as a young girl.

Condition (73) will be redundant with the conditions on GF-binding in many cases, but not all.

---

[19] A note on what counts as a minimal governing category (or relevant domain for c-command): our assumption is that it includes S and NP, but not PP, so that *himself* and *Ringo* count as being in the same minimal governing category in (68). Other possible candidates for minimal governing categories are small clauses (i) and *with-* and *without*-adjuncts (ii–iii), all of which can contain a reflexive whose antecedent is outside of them and to the right.

(i)   Himself as treasurer would annoy Bill.
(ii)   With only himself to blame, Bill's getting very upset.
(iii)   Without himself as a candidate, Bill doesn't know who to vote for.

10.8.3 Final remarks

What we see, then, is that the contrasts like (66)–(67) with "information" verbs are not due to differences in syntax; the relevant difference is in conceptual structure. Moreover, their difference in conceptual structure is exactly the same as that in the coercion cases such as the 'statue' readings in (13). Hence the same semantic condition (65) in Principle A_{CS} accounts for both sets of cases, despite the considerable difference in the syntax of the two pairs.

This result is significant because in the case of the information verbs, superficial syntax has proven insufficient for a solution. Past research within MGG has for the most part reacted to the difficulties of these cases by proposing more elaborate underlying syntax. Here we have shown that *no* plausible syntactic elaboration can account for the coercion cases, which have not been addressed within MGG. The present approach renders such elaborations unnecessary, in compliance with the Simpler Syntax Hypothesis. Our account, along with much past literature, suggests that MGG has been barking up the wrong tree in seeking a purely syntactic account of binding, and that some substantial part of the traditional syntactic content of binding theory really belongs in conceptual structure.

More generally, what we have done here is of course far from a comprehensive reanalysis of binding theory. Given the size and complexity of the literature, this will necessarily be a vast enterprise. To mention only one glaring omission, we have not looked here at what component of Principle A_{CS} might contain the locality conditions on anaphora, such that (75) is ruled out, but long-distance counterparts in other languages (e.g. Japanese *zibun* and Norwegian *sig*) are acceptable.[20]

(75) *John said that Mary kicked himself.

Moreover, many crucial cases depend on conceptual structure analyses that are as yet far from secure. However, we have been able to work out the overall shape of a revised theory and propose concrete analyses for a number of phenomena; succeeding chapters will further support our approach.

We suspect that our conclusion will strike many readers as madness. Why consider discarding long-established analyses and starting over? We submit, however, that the present situation is an artifact of history. As discussed in Chapter 2, the development of binding theory began at a time when there was no articulated notion of semantic structure to work with, so there was no possibility of developing a formally acceptable mixed theory of binding. In

---

[20] For extensive discussion of these and other cases, see the papers in Koster and Reuland (1991).

addition, the early days of binding theory followed close on the heels of the discrediting of generative semantics, when anything that smacked of a mixture of syntax and semantics was ideologically suspect. Those times are gone, and we ought now to be willing to consider mixed alternatives when the facts push us that way, as they do here in the wax museum.

CHAPTER 11

Something Else for the Binding Theory

This chapter examines another binding phenomenon outside the treatment of "core" binding in MGG: the behavior of the obviative element *else* in English and related referentially dependent elements. Our goal is to clarify the nature of the referential dependency that *else* expresses as well as the proper formulation of this dependency within the grammar. As in Chapter 10, we will explore a number of alternative analyses; we will show that the best one on empirical grounds is one that conforms to the Simpler Syntax Hypothesis, in that no covert syntactic structure is associated with *else*. Along the way, our exploration will uncover evidence that casts doubt on the generality and hence theoretical usefulness of a covert syntactic level of Logical Form in the sense of MGG, again providing support for Simpler Syntax.[1]

11.1 Introduction

The use of *else* is exemplified in the following sentence.

(1) Mary thinks that someone else will win.

Two interpretations of *someone else* are possible in (1). On one reading, *someone else* refers to an individual different from some individual mentioned

We are grateful to Marc Authier, Georgia Green, Jim McCawley, Urpo Nikanne, Ken Safir, and two LI referees for important comments on earlier versions of this chapter. We have also benefited from opportunities to present this material at McGill University, Harvard University, SUNY Buffalo, and Stanford University.

[1] An early discussion of *else* in the generative literature can be found in McCawley (1975); see also McCawley (1988a).

earlier in the discourse. On the other reading, *someone else* refers to an individual different from Mary. This shows that *someone else* is a referentially dependent expression, and that it is possible to pick out a specific antecedent for it in the sentence or discourse.

We introduce a provisional notation to distinguish these two readings, shown in (2a,b).

(2)   a. Mary$_i$ thinks that someone else$_{j \neq DA}$ will win.
      b. Mary$_i$ thinks that someone else$_{j \neq i}$ will win.

(2a) is the reading in which *someone else* is distinct from some (here unmentioned) discourse antecedent. It parallels the reading of the discourse pronoun in *Mary thinks that he$_{DA}$ will win*. (2b) is the obviative reading in which *someone else* is distinct from Mary. It parallels the reading of the pronoun in *Mary$_i$ thinks that she$_i$ will win*.

Someone else belongs to a larger family of expressions *X else*, for instance *anything else*, *everywhere else*, and *nobody else*. All of these are obviative in some sense, and the question arises as to how they acquire this interpretation. There are a number of possibilities. Standard GB binding theory claims that the referential dependency of anaphoric elements is represented by syntactic coindexing at S-Structure and/or LF, and that the syntactic indices are semantically interpreted either as identity of reference or as a bound variable. *Else*, which seems to require some sort of "contra-indexing" that marks it as referentially distinct, does not immediately fall under this theory, but a suitable extension might be devised.

For example, several readers of an earlier version of this chapter have suggested that Universal Grammar might contain a strictly syntactic "narrow" binding theory that applies only to pronominals and anaphors within single sentences, plus an altogether distinct "broad" binding theory that accounts for the behavior of all other referentially dependent elements in terms of semantics or pragmatics. We might base such a semantic or pragmatic theory on Evans's (1980) and Neale's (1990) approach to the referential dependency of "E-type" pronouns, i.e. all referentially dependent elements except those pronouns and anaphors that are c-commanded by their antecedents. E-type pronouns, on this analysis, include all discourse pronouns; they can be linked with a definite description that is "recoverable" (in Neale's sense) from an expression in prior discourse. We will provide arguments against such a divided approach to *X else*, in that it seamlessly incorporates features of both "narrow" bound anaphora and "broad" discourse anaphora.

Whether there is a natural extension of standard binding theory to elements other than pronouns and reflexives is of course an empirical question. The literature does suggest, in fact, that there are numerous referentially dependent elements in natural language that are quite distinct from the familiar English-type pronouns and reflexives. Nevertheless, their behavior is syntactically constrained, and they should therefore fall under a properly extended binding theory. For example, Keenan (1988) and Partee (1989) discuss a class of "extended anaphors", including terms such as *local* and *enemy* that are implicitly related to an antecedent. Partee observes (1989: 349) that their distribution is "either just like the constraints on the corresponding uses of pronouns or slightly less restrictive", and goes on to argue against treating the implicit anaphors as empty pronouns in the syntax. Both of these accounts propose a unification of standard pronominals and anaphors with these extended expressions, but in terms of semantic rather than syntactic structure. Our approach ends up close in spirit to these.

For another case, Saxon (1984) shows that the element *ye* in Dogrib must have an antecedent within the sentence but cannot be locally bound; it thus shares some features of pronouns and other features of reflexives. On this basis, Enç (1989) proposes a rather far-reaching reformulation of the binding theory, one that crucially dissociates the syntactic constraints on referential dependency from the semantics of the dependency. This proposal is in some respects parallel to the direction we went in Chapter 10.

We will however go further. As in our study of ellipsis in Chapters 7 and 8, we will show that in some crucial cases the antecedent of *X else* is not a syntactic expression in the standard sense. We will therefore argue that the level of representation at which *X else* generalizes with more standard anaphoric expressions is not a level of syntax but rather a level of semantic/pragmatic representation in which it is possible to access both lexical semantic decomposition and decomposition of the sentence in terms of information structure, i.e. the level of Conceptual Structure.

Given that conditions on binding are shared between *X else* and other anaphoric expressions, and given that at least some of these conditions must be stated over Conceptual Structure, the question arises of how much of binding theory in general should be treated as syntactic. As mentioned in Chapter 10, the possibility of reformulating all or part of binding theory as a semantic theory has been raised by many researchers. A uniform approach to referential dependency would suggest that the semantic properties of all referentially dependent expressions would be accounted for at CS, and that the syntactic relations between all referentially dependent expressions and their antecedents would fall under a generalized binding theory that is not restricted to pronouns and reflexives. This is, we believe, the general view of Enç (1989), and this chapter provides additional evidence in support of it.

In saying that certain conditions on binding must be stated over Conceptual Structure, our idea, following Chapter 10, is that the traditional notation for binding, (3a), can be regarded as an abbreviation for the three-part relation, (3b).

(3)   a. NP_i binds [NP, anaphor]$_i$

     b. $[X]_i^\alpha$ binds   [α; Y]$_j$ conceptual structure

       | | corresponds to

      NP_i [NP, anaphor]$_j$ syntactic structure

That is, the antecedent NP expresses a conceptual structure X, the anaphor NP expresses a conceptual structure Y, and the actual binding relation obtains between X and Y. The binding is notated by the Greek letters: a superscripted Greek letter indicates a binder, and the corresponding Greek letter within brackets indicates a bindee.

In order to show that (3b) rather than (3a) is the proper way to conceive of binding, it is necessary to find cases in which syntactic mechanisms alone are insufficient to characterize the relation between anaphors and their antecedents. Chapter 10 and the literature cited there present a range of such cases; the present chapter works out another.

Under this conception of binding, what should the counterpart of GB binding theory look like? If the relation between syntactic anaphors and their antecedents is mediated by both syntactic and conceptual structure, we would expect a "mixed" binding theory whose licensing conditions involve both structures (plus the GF-tier), as proposed in Chapter 10. More specifically, when the anaphor and antecedent are syntactically explicit, as in standard binding examples, we would expect both syntactic and conceptual conditions to be invoked. On the other hand, (3b) presents the possibility of anaphoric relations that are not expressed in the syntax, but only in the meaning of the sentence. Chapter 10 reviewed some such examples: the implicit reflexive argument in *John washed* and the implicit controlled argument in *John tried to leave*. Here we might expect syntactic conditions not to apply, as there is nothing to apply them to.

It is conceivable that *all* apparent syntactic conditions on binding are simply reflections of the interface between syntactic structure and conceptual structure, i.e. that all conditions on binding are semantic. However, we do not at the moment find this possibility persuasive. In particular, sections 4.4 and 10.8 argued that linear order in syntax plays a role.

The problem for a general theory of binding, then, is to tease apart the complexities of binding into syntactic conditions, GF-tier conditions, and conceptual structure conditions. Our approach in this chapter is to "deconstruct" binding theory, looking for seams between syntax and conceptual structure, using as a testing ground the class of anaphors *X else*.

11.2 How *else* behaves

First, some data. We will show that *else* displays referential dependencies parallel to those of the full set of pronominals: reflexives, pronouns, and *one*, in both bound and discourse contexts.

Local antecedents

In (4a), the direct object *someone else* is referentially dependent on the subject of the same clause, parallel to the reflexive in (4b).

(4)   a. John$_i$ loves someone else$_{j \neq i}$
       b. John$_i$ loves himself$_i$

This suggests that *someone else* may have a local antecedent. However, it might be objected that the interpretation in (4a) is conceivably due not to a local referential dependency between *someone else* and *John*, but rather to a pragmatic referential dependency between *someone else* and some instance of *John* in prior discourse. To eliminate this possibility, consider the following examples, the latter of which might be considered a hypothetical footnote to this chapter:

(5)   a. John$_i$ carefully ignores everyone else$_{j \neq i}$ while doing yoga.
       b. Frankly, we$_i$ don't expect anyone else$_{j \neq i}$ to like this chapter, but we're publishing it anyway.

X else in these examples is in a position where it can be locally bound by the subject, with no necessary prior context. Hence there need be no discourse antecedent. To our ears, the intended interpretation for these sentences is as readily available as when *else* is nonlocally bound, as in (6).

(6)   We$_i$ don't expect that anyone else$_{j \neq i}$ will like this chapter.

Nonlocal antecedents

(7) shows that *someone else* can have a nonlocal antecedent in the sentence. The nonlocal antecedent may c-command *someone else*, as in (7), but need not.

(7) a. Mary$_i$ was elected President and someone else$_{j \neq i}$ was elected Vice President.
  b. John$_i$ thought that someone else$_{j \neq i}$ would win.
  c. John$_i$'s mother thought that someone else$_{j \neq i}$ would win.
            [*John* does not c-command *someone else*]

In this respect *someone else* functions just like the pronouns in (8).

(8) a. Mary was elected President and she was not elected Vice President.
  b. John thought that he would win.
  c. John's mother thought that he would win.

And, like a pronoun, *someone else* can take a split antecedent.

(9) a. John$_i$ told Mary$_j$ that they$_{i+j}$ were going to be asked to do the work.
  b. John$_i$ told Mary$_j$ that someone else$_{k \neq i+j}$ was going to be asked to do the work.

Deictic antecedents

Someone else, like a pronoun, can have a deictic antecedent.

(10) a. [Pointing to John entering the room:] Oy, why did you get **him**?
                                    [i.e. John]
  b. [As John enters the room:] Oy, can't you find someone else?
                                    [i.e. someone other than John]
  c. [As John enters the room:] See, I got someone else.
        [i.e. John is someone other than unspecified discourse antecedent]

Quantifier binding

We have seen that, like a reflexive, *X else* is referentially dependent on an NP. When the antecedent is a quantifier in the same clause, we also get a legitimate interpretation—that is, (11a) and its bound interpretation (11b) exactly parallel (12). ((11b) also has a discourse antecedent interpretation, of course.)

(11) a. Everyone (here) loves someone else.
  b. $\forall x, \exists y, y \neq x, x$ loves y

(12) a. Everyone (here) loves herself.
  b. $\forall x, x$ loves x

And like a pronoun, *else* can be referentially dependent on a quantifier outside of its local environment.

(13)   a. Everyone (here) thinks that someone else will win.
       b. $\forall x$, x thinks that $\exists y$, $y \neq x$, y will win
(14)   a. Everyone (here) thinks that she will win.
       b. $\forall x$, x thinks that x will win

This shows that at least some cases of *X else* do not function like "E-type" discourse pronouns. Rather, they function like bound variables and hence fall under the c-command cases of referential dependency, like anaphors and pronominals.

Another such case is (15), in which *everyone else* is referentially dependent on *who*.

(15)   a. Who$_i$ tried to prevent everyone else$_{j \neq i}$ from having ice cream?
       b. which x is such that x tried to prevent [$\forall y$, $y \neq x$, y have ice cream]

This requires precisely the sort of binding found with pronouns bound by *wh*-expressions, so it cannot fall under an E-type analysis.

To sum up so far, the distribution of *X else* is essentially the union of that of anaphors and pronominals. In this respect it parallels the Turkish pronoun *kendisi* discussed by Enç (1989), which likewise needs no sentence-internal antecedent, but can be bound either locally or nonlocally within its sentence. Enç in fact notes (p. 58, n. 6) that this pronoun behaves similarly to the English expression *the others*, which is of course semantically related to *X else*.

Sloppy identity

Strikingly, *X else* displays a strict/sloppy identity ambiguity. Compare the standard case shown in (16) to the example in (17) with *else*.

(16)   Bill went to his house, and John did too.
       read as:
       a. ... and John went to Bill's house   [strict identity]
       b. ... and John went to John's house   [sloppy identity]
(17)   Bill went to his house, but John went somewhere else.
       read as:
       a. ... but John went somewhere other than to Bill's house
                                                                 [strict identity]
       b. ... but John went somewhere other than to John's house
                                                                 [sloppy identity]

The possibility of sloppy identity with *else* turns out to be of crucial importance to our analysis. One reason of particular relevance here is that sloppy identity further undermines the possibility that the interpretation of *else* always involves an E-type strategy, i.e. the construction of a definite description pragmatically based on a discourse antecedent. If this were the case, *X else* could fall entirely outside the treatment of anaphors and pronominals under binding theory. However, as is well known (see Reinhart 1983), sloppy identity occurs only in the context of binding. Example (18) shows that, under sloppy identity, *else* may even have a quantifier phrase antecedent.

(18)   The teacher went immediately to his house, but every student went somewhere else.
       read as:
       a. ...but every student went somewhere other than to the teacher's house   [strict identity]
       b. ...but every student went somewhere other than to his own house   [sloppy identity]

It follows, therefore, that *X else* falls under binding theory in most of the same contexts that anaphors and pronominals do.

Crossover

A difference between pronouns and *X else* is that, given proper pragmatics, the latter is not subject to Condition C or Strong Crossover, as seen by comparing the paired examples in (19) and (20). While the examples with *X else* in (20) are marginal, they are not nearly as bad as those with pronouns. (We are grateful to Ivan Sag for pointing out these cases.)

(19)   *Condition C*
       a. *He$_i$ wrote all of Shakespeare$_i$'s plays.
          Someone else$_{j \neq i}$ wrote all of Shakespeare$_i$'s plays.
       b. *He$_i$ is going to have to undo everything that Bush$_i$ did.
          Someone else$_{j \neq i}$ is going to have to undo everything that Bush$_i$ did.
       c. *He$_i$ thinks Nader$_i$ will win.
          No one else$_{j \neq i}$ thinks that Nader$_i$ will win.

(20)   *Strong Crossover*
       a. *Whose$_i$ plays did he$_i$ write?
          ?Whose$_i$ plays did someone else$_{j \neq i}$ probably write?
       b. *How many of Shakespeare$_i$'s plays did he$_i$ write?
          How many of Shakespeare$_i$'s plays did someone else$_{j \neq i}$ write?
       c. *Who$_i$ does he$_i$ think will win?
          ??Who$_i$ does no one else$_{j \neq i}$ think will win?

We may take these observations as showing one of two things. (a) Either *X else* is a primitive anaphoric element that, although it shares many properties of bound anaphora, violates certain conditions of binding theory; or (b) *X else* is compositional and contains an anaphoric element (e.g. *else*) that does not produce Condition C and Strong Crossover effects for reasons that are predictable because of its compositional structure. We will argue in section 11.3 for the second alternative.

Obviation of sense

Not only does X else display most properties of reflexives and pronouns, it also behaves like an obviative counterpart of identity-of-sense *one*. Consider (21).

(21)   John saw a red balloon but Bill saw something else.

This sentence has two interpretations, paraphrased in (22).

(22)   a. John saw a red balloon and Bill saw something other than **that red balloon** (which, for all I know, might have been another red balloon).
       b. John saw a red balloon and Bill saw something other than **a red balloon**.

Interpretation (22a) is the sort we have been considering so far, in which *else* parallels definite pronouns and reflexives; it expresses distinctness from some previously mentioned individual. However, interpretation (22b) parallels the indefinite pronoun *one*, as in . . . *and Bill saw one too*: it expresses distinctness of category (or type) from that of some previously mentioned individual. We can think of it as "non-identity-of-sense anaphora".

Do- and happen-ellipsis

Finally, just like a pronoun and other anaphoric expressions, *else* can appear with *do* and with *happen* to express event-anaphora.

(23)   a. John [went to the supermarket], and then Bill [did {it/that/the same thing/so}].
       b. John [went to the supermarket], and then Bill [did something else].

(24)   a. The phone woke me up, but {it/that/the same thing} wouldn't have happened if the bell had been turned down.
       b. The phone woke me up, but something else would have happened if the bell had been turned down.

Summarizing, the evidence shows that *X else* can be licensed in any environment that licenses either a pronoun, a reflexive, or anaphoric *one*. (We will deal with the differences in Condition C and Crossover cases in section 11.3.3.)

It thus appears that X *else* is not a simplex element that falls under the category "pronoun" or "reflexive", yet it falls somehow under binding theory.

11.3 Contra-indexing and extended anaphora

11.3.1 Against contra-indexing

How is the binding of X *else* to be represented and licensed? On the standard GB view, binding theory accounts for the distribution of reflexives and pronouns in terms of the following notion of "binds", formulated in terms of referential indices.

(25) α binds β iff
a. α c-commands β and
b. α and β are co-indexed.

Suppose we want to extend this definition of binding to account for *someone else*. The most obvious way to do this would be to allow the binding relation to obtain when *someone else* is contra-indexed with its antecedent, i.e. when its index is different from all the other indices used in the sentence. That is, parallel to the formulation (3a) for ordinary anaphors, we might adopt Hypothesis 1 as the formulation of how X *else* is bound.

(26)   **Hypothesis 1**
NP binds [X else] iff
a. NP c-commands [X else] (or whatever the structural conditions are) and
b. NP and [X else] are contra-indexed.

This leads to representations like (27).

(27)   Mary$_i$ thinks that someone else$_j$ will win. [= (1)]

Unfortunately, this notation does not distinguish the two observed interpretations of this sentence, in which the antecedent of *someone else* is either *Mary* or a discourse antecedent, because *someone else* and *Mary* are contra-indexed in either case. To make this clearer, consider the more complex case in (28), where $i \neq j \neq k$.

(28)   Hillary$_i$ thinks that Bill$_j$ voted for someone else$_k$.

(28) is three ways ambiguous: Bill may have voted for someone other than Hillary, someone other than himself, or someone other than some discourse antecedent. Suppose that this referential dependence were formally expressed

by the contra-indexing given in (28). Then its indices would turn out to have exactly the same form as (29).

(29)   Hillary$_i$ thinks that Bill$_j$ voted for George$_k$.

George$_k$ too has an index that is different from all of the other indices used in the sentence, since it is a different name from the other names in the sentence, and by Principle C, it is therefore free of the other NPs. The contra-indexing encodes this fact.

However, there is a fundamental difference between the interpretations of *someone else* and of *George*. *George* is not understood as referentially dependent on any other NP in the sentence, but *someone else* is. Moreover, the representation in (28) does not tell us that *someone else* is distinct specifically from either *Hillary* or *Bill*: it is contra-indexed equally with both of them. Hence, the standard indexing notation is not expressive enough to make the distinctions necessary to encode the meaning of *someone else*.

Consider also example (30).[2]

(30)   Almost everyone thought George would win, but Teresa predicted to John that someone else would win: John himself.

This example shows that *someone else* need not be contra-indexed with every NP in the sentence. Here *someone else* is dependent on *George*, but it is contingently coreferential with *John*. (Related problems for co-indexation, involving the reciprocal *each other*, are discussed by Farmer (1987).) It thus appears that the relation of *referential dependency* must be dissociated from that of *co-indexing-as-coreference*, just as is argued for example by Higginbotham (1985) and Enç (1989).[3]

11.3.2 *Quantifier* + else *is compositional*

A natural alternative would be to say that *somone else, nothing else*, etc. are members of the class of "extended anaphors" such as *local* and *foreign*, in the sense of Keenan (1988). What it means to say that *local* is an extended anaphor is that it has to be interpreted in terms of somebody's location. For instance, in *Pat always goes to a local bar*, the bar is local with respect to Pat's location (or perhaps the speaker's). Under this approach, *X else* might be an extended anaphor with the special property that it is contraindexed with its antecedent.

---

[2] We thank Jim McCawley for suggesting this example to us.

[3] We could say, for example, in Higginbotham's terms, that in (27) *someone else* has the index *j*, but is linked to the antecedent *Mary$_i$*. But then binding (i.e. referential dependency) is not equivalent to coindexation under c-command.

In fact, Keenan suggests such a treatment for other obviative extended anaphors such as *someone other than himself* and *someone other than him*. Such a theory of extended anaphora might be expressed in terms of Higginbotham's (1985) notion of referential dependency.[4] This could be formalized for *X else* along the lines of the notation we have been using here:

(31)   **Hypothesis 2**
       NP_i binds $[X \text{ else}]_{j \neq i}$ iff structural conditions $C_1, \ldots, C_n$ obtain

Here, the non-coreference is encoded by giving the entire unit *X else* an index *j* distinct from that of its antecedent. Its referential dependence is encoded by explicitly marking—as part of the index—that *j* is unequal to *i*. Hence *X else* is both referentially dependent on and non-coreferential with its antecedent.

However, Safir (1991) argues that the anaphoric behavior of complex expressions like *someone other than him* should not be treated as a primitive property; rather it should follow from the behavior of the simple anaphors embedded within them. In fact, like these cases, the class of *X else* expressions clearly shows compositional behavior, in that the meaning as well as the morphology of the expression is a function of X and *else*: {*some/every/any/no*} + {*one/thing/body/place/where*} + *else*.[5]

To make this point clearer, notice that *everyone else* can bind an indefinite or another quantifier, just like *everyone* (32a), and *nobody else* can condition negative polarity items, just like any other negative (32b).

(32)   a. John bought a red balloon, but everyone else bought a teddy
          bear.   [*a teddy bear* is bound by *everyone else*]
       b. Nobody else has ever bought anything like that.

Furthermore, *else* appears in combination with wh-words: *who else*, *what else*, *where else*, etc., and the meaning is clearly compositional.[6]

A subtler piece of evidence comes from a difference between *someone else* and *something else*. Only the latter can be used for obviation of sense anaphora, even for animates:

---

[4] Partee (1989) suggests a similar notion for expressions like *local* and *foreign*, but in non-syntactic terms.

[5] This observation parallels Heim et al.'s (1991) argument that *each other* is compositional.

[6] Still, the combinations are somewhat idiosyncratic: *how else* exists but **somehow else* does not. Also (as pointed out to us by Victor Manfredi), *somewhere else* can be replaced by *elsewhere*; this possibility does not exist with any of the other combinations. This suggests that although the morphology and meaning are combinatorial, lexical listing of *X else* expressions must somehow play a role as well—not unlike the acceptable combinations of sluice-stranding discussed in sections 1.5.2 and 7.7.

(33) Bill is a poet, but Susan wishes he were something/*someone else.

This difference follows from an independent difference between *X-one* and *X-thing*: only *X-thing* can be used to denote a profession. This can be seen in examples like *Bill wishes to be something/*someone like a poet, Bill is nothing/ *no one like a poet* (cf. also *A poet is what/*who Bill wants to be*). Thus it clearly misses a basic generalization to take *someone else* as an unanalyzed expression with anaphoric properties.

If the contribution of *X* is the normal sense of a quantifier + indefinite proform (*someone, nowhere*, etc.), what role does *else* play? Provisionally, we can see its contribution as *other than* α, where α is an anaphor that can be marked coreferential (or identical in sense) with its antecedent. Hypothesis 3 expresses this treatment of how *X else* is bound.

(34) **Hypothesis 3**
       NP_i binds [X other than α_i] iff structural conditions $C_1, \ldots, C_n$ obtain

This analysis offers the promise of keeping binding theory simple, making the notion of "extended anaphora" unnecessary, as Safir urges. In addition, it eliminates the troublesome mechanism of contraindexed binding. The obviative properties of *X else* instead follow from the semantic content of 'other than α', where α is an ordinary coindexed anaphor.

11.3.3 *Condition C and Crossover*

A closer consideration of the Condition C and crossover phenomena discussed in section 11.2 supports Hypothesis 3. Suppose that *X else* is an unanalyzed

---

Additionally, the syntax of *else* deserves closer scrutiny than we can give it here, in view of paradigms like the following:

(i)   a.   someone else
       b.   someone tall
       c.   ?someone else tall
       d.   *someone tall else
       e.   someone else as tall
       f.   *someone as tall else

Note too that *much else* functions as a polarity item, and *many else* does not exist.

(ii)   a.   How much/*many else did you look at?
       b.   Did you look at much else?
       c.   I didn't look at much else.
       d.   *I always looked at much else.

How this use of *else* is related to the cases that we are concerned with in this chapter is an open question.

extended anaphor (Hypothesis 2). We would then expect that Condition C violations would arise when *X else* c-commands its antecedent. But the examples in (19), repeated here, show that they do not.

(19) a. Someone else$_{j\neq i}$ wrote all of Shakespeare$_i$'s plays.
    b. Someone else$_{j\neq i}$ is going to have to undo everything that Bush$_i$ did.
    c. No one else$_{j\neq i}$ thinks that Nader$_i$ will win.

On the other hand, suppose the actual anaphor is embedded, as in Hypothesis 3. Then the structure of (19c), for example, is (35a), parallel to (35b) with an ordinary pronoun.

(35) a. [no one other than α$_i$] thinks that Nader$_i$ will win
    b. [no one other than him$_i$] thinks that Nader$_i$ will win

Condition C does not apply in (35b), because *him* does not c-command *Nader*. Similarly, then, it should not apply in (19c)—in accordance with the actual judgments. (Note that in both (35b) and (19c), *Nader* has to be unstressed.) Thus this compositional account of *X else* automatically accounts for the difference in Condition C behavior between *X else* and ordinary pronouns.

In addition, under Hypothesis 2, we would expect that crossover with *X else* could yield degrees of ungrammaticality typical of both Strong Crossover (36a) and Weak Crossover (36b). However, (37) shows that both *someone else* and *someone else's mother* produce the lesser degree of ungrammaticality typical of Weak Crossover. This follows automatically if the actual anaphor in *someone else* is embedded, as in Hypothesis 3.

(36) a. *Who$_i$ does he$_i$ love?   [Strong Crossover]
    b. ??Who$_i$ does his$_i$ mother love?   [Weak Crossover]

(37) a. ??Who$_i$ does someone else$_{j\neq i}$ love?
        (= Who$_i$ does [someone other than α$_i$] love?)
    b. ??Who$_i$ does someone else's$_{j\neq i}$ mother love?
        (= Who$_i$ does [someone other than α$_i$]'s mother love?)

Sam Epstein has pointed out to us that the "strong" cases with *X else* get better as the *wh*-phrase becomes more definite or specific, a possible instance of Pesetsky's (1987) D-linking. For instance, (38a), which can for example be used as a sort of quiz-show question, is better than (38b), which has no such use.

(38) a. Which famous playwright$_i$ did everyone else$_{j\neq i}$ imitate?
    b. ?Who$_i$ did everyone else$_{j\neq i}$ imitate?

This parallels distinctions in Weak Crossover with pronouns:

(39)   a.   Which famous senator$_i$ do his$_i$ constituents despise?
       b.   ??Who$_i$ do his$_i$ constituents despise?

By contrast, Strong Crossover shows no such distinctions:

(40)   *Which famous senator$_i$/Who$_i$ does he$_i$ love?

Thus again the appropriate generalization for *X else* crossover appears to be with Weak Crossover, as suggested by Hypothesis 3.

11.3.4 Sloppy identity

The facts of sloppy identity also suggest that Hypothesis 3 is to be preferred over Hypothesis 2. We note first that sloppy identity with *else* finds a close parallel with so-called "paycheck pronouns" (Karttunen 1969), such as the boldfaced pronoun in (41a).

(41)   a.   John spent his paycheck on food but Bill spent **it** on clothes.
       b.   John had dinner with his kids but Bill had dinner with **someone else**.

A typical (although by no means the only) account of such constructions invokes a "reconstruction" of the proform, so that *it* in (41a) is "reconstructed" as *his paycheck* at some level of syntax such as LF (see e.g. Fiengo and May 1994).[7] The ambiguity of strict and sloppy identity then follows from the ambiguity of the pronoun *his* in the first clause. If *his* is an ordinary pronoun (or, in some accounts, "reconstructed" in the first clause as *John*), then copied over in the course of reconstructing *it*, the interpretation is strict identity: *it* refers to John's paycheck.[8] On the other hand, if *his* is a bound pronoun, then when it is copied into the second clause it comes to be bound to *Bill*, yielding the sloppy reading 'Bill's paycheck'.

Within this scenario, the most plausible possibility for *someone else* in (41b) is to treat it as *someone other than* α at the level of reconstruction, then to reconstruct α as a "paycheck pronoun". This will result in the expression *someone other than his kids* at this level. For the moment deferring the question of what this level of reconstruction might be, we will now show how the distinction between strict and sloppy identity then depends on whether *his* in the reconstruction is referentially dependent on *John* or *Bill*.

---

[7] We hasten to point out that this use of "reconstruction" is different from that used in connection with the interpretation of phrases in A-bar position, discussed in Ch. 9; see Barss (1986). In the present framework, however, they do both show up as side effects of indirect licensing.

[8] In the Evans–Neale account, this is an "E-type" pronoun that is c-commanded by its antecedent. It is not clear to us whether Evans and/or Neale actually permit such a possibility.

For concreteness, let us suppose that the reconstruction in question is computed as follows. *It* is interpreted as formally identical to its antecedent *his$_x$ paycheck*, and then the variable index x is set to the index of the c-commanding antecedent. We can break down the steps of the sloppy interpretation as follows (we notate the binding of a pronoun of index x by setting the index equal to that of the antecedent):[9]

(42)   John$_i$ spent [his$_x$ paycheck]$_k$ on food but Bill$_m$ spent it$_n$ on clothes
            (reconstruction of *it*) $\Rightarrow$
        John$_i$ spent [his$_x$ paycheck]$_k$ on food but Bill$_m$ spent [his$_x$ paycheck]$_n$ on clothes
            (setting values for variable indices) $\Rightarrow$
        John$_i$ spent [his$_{x=i}$ paycheck]$_k$ on food but Bill$_m$ spent [his$_{x=m}$ paycheck]$_n$ on clothes

An essentially identical sequence of steps will produce the correct indexing for (41b), *ceteris paribus*, if we assume that *someone else* is represented as *someone other than α*, with anaphoric α.

(43)   John$_i$ had dinner with [his$_x$ kids]$_k$ but Bill$_m$ had dinner with [someone else]$_n$
            (expansion of *someone else*) $\Rightarrow$
        John$_i$ had dinner with [his$_x$ kids]$_k$ but Bill$_m$ had dinner with [someone other than α]$_n$
            (reconstruction of α) $\Rightarrow$
        John$_i$ had dinner with [his$_x$ kids]$_k$ but Bill$_m$ had dinner with [someone other than [his$_x$ kids]]$_n$
            (setting values for variable indices) $\Rightarrow$
        John$_i$ had dinner with [his$_{x=i}$ kids]$_k$ but Bill$_m$ had dinner with [someone other than [his$_{x=m}$ kids]]$_n$

Thus the view of *someone else* as a complex, one of whose constituents is the anaphoric element, leads to a natural account of sloppy identity that completely parallels that with ordinary pronouns.

11.4 *Else* is not *other than* α in syntax

The price of a successful account of sloppy identity involving X *else* is an appeal to reconstruction. But now let us ask how reconstruction is really to be formulated. In particular, Hypothesis 3 claims that *else* is represented at some

---

[9] We note that the arrows in these steps are not meant to imply that the steps are ordered in a derivation. The connections can equally be instantiated in terms of constraint satisfaction.

level of syntax as *other than* α, where α is a proform that can be subjected to reconstruction. This parallels the "Syntactic Option" in the account of "statue" coercions in Chapter 10. As we did in Chapter 10, we now must ask what level of syntax this might be.

On the face of it, it is plausible that the level in question is LF, as is usually assumed for the operation of reconstruction (see e.g. Fiengo and May 1994). However, this possibility recedes considerably in light of the evidence to be presented in this section. We will conclude that the level we are looking for is not syntactic but rather Conceptual Structure. But in turn, if the obviation of *else* in standard binding contexts is not represented at LF, then neither should anaphoric relations in general in such contexts, since the treatment of *else* has proven to be just a special case of anaphora.[10]

11.4.1 *Syntactic reconstruction is not possible with "extended anaphors"*

If reconstruction takes place in LF, then *else* must be represented as *other than* α prior to LF in the syntactic derivation. In order to achieve this representation, we must invoke a lexically idiosyncratic syntactic substitution in the course of mapping from S-structure to LF, changing the single morpheme *else* into the syntactically complex *other than* α (alternatively, a substitution of *else* for *other than* α between S-structure and PF). If only this one particular case were at issue, we might be able to live with such a consequence.

But now let us recall the existence of "extended" anaphoric expressions such as *local*, *foreign* (Partee 1989) and *home* (Fillmore 1992; Jackendoff et al. 1993). For instance, as observed earlier, the adjective *local* must have an "antecedent", the individual whose neighborhood is being picked out by the adjective. *Local* can even be bound by a quantifier, as in *The mayor of every city likes to hang out in a local bar*, so it falls under the theory of bound variable anaphora, part of standard binding theory. Moreover, *home* has locality properties reminiscent of reflexives: *John persuaded Bill to go home* may mean only that Bill went to Bill's home, not to John's.[11] This locality condition shows that

---

[10] We rule out as *prima facie* theoretically undesirable a theory in which some anaphoric elements are accounted for in terms of their semantics or pragmatics while others are accounted for in the syntax, if identical structural relations obtain in the two cases.

[11] Jim McCawley suggested to us that the preferred reading for such cases depends on the verb in the embedded infinitive. While Bill's house is preferred in *John persuaded Bill to go home*, John's house is preferred in *John persuaded Bill to come home*. Such preferences appear to be pragmatic, since they can be easily manipulated by changing the context. See Jackendoff et al. (1993) for discussion of such cases; in particular, our judgment is that in the latter example the home may well be John's, but it is Bill's as well (or at least Bill is a house guest of John's).

home falls under a further condition normally attributed to standard binding theory.

If *else* is reconstructed in LF as a complex expression containing a standard anaphor, then these expressions must be too. For example, *local* has to be represented prior to LF as something like 'nearby α'; *home* as something like 'residence of α'. According to Barker (1995), the number of such expressions is very large, since it includes all nouns that have a relational sense, such as *enemy*, *glove compartment* (of a car), body parts, and family members. Given the number of such expressions, each of which requires a lexically idiosyncratic substitution, a treatment involving syntactic reconstruction at LF becomes more objectionable. The grounds are altogether parallel to those that initially motivated the Lexicalist Hypothesis (Chomsky 1970)—and parallel to some of our grounds for rejecting the Syntactic Option for "statue" coercion in Chapter 10. Partee (1989) offers no "conclusive arguments" against such a syntactic approach, but gives a number of "reasons for being skeptical about it" (p. 350), among them the fact that in many cases there is no syntactically identifiable antecedent for the anaphoric element (an issue to be raised in section 11.4.3). Carlson (1987) provides similar arguments against an LF treatment of *same* and *different*. Crucially, the treatment of *else* falls in with this class.

11.4.2 *Syntactic reconstruction is impossible because there need be no possible syntactic realization*

The class of anaphoric expressions that require reconstruction is still more problematic. It was pointed out to us (by a member of an audience at McGill University whose identity has been forgotten; similar facts are noted by Carlson 1987) that expressions such as *someone stronger, everything less expensive*, and *anyplace just as beautiful* have a distribution quite similar to that of *X else*.

(44) a. Mary thinks that **someone smarter** will win.
                    [someone smarter than Mary/discourse antecedent]
      b. Everyone predicted that **someone stronger** would win.
                    [for all x, x predicted that someone stronger than x would win]
      c. Mary's mother thinks that **someone just as rich** will win.
                                              [i.e. just as rich as Mary]
      d. John went to dinner with his uncle, but Bill went to dinner with **someone less closely related**.   [note sloppy identity]
      e. John kissed Mary yesterday, but **nothing as bizarre** will happen today.

The referential dependencies of these phrases can conceivably be captured in syntax by applying reconstruction at LF to such forms such as *someone smarter than α, someone just as rich as α,* and *someone less closely related than α.*

However, there are related expressions for which syntactic reconstruction of an overt anaphor is less plausible. We give examples in E-type contexts with NP and S-anaphora ((45a,b) respectively) and in a bound context (45c). (Partee (1989) discusses similar difficulties for reconstruction with some of the expressions she cites.)

(45)   a. Bill bought a llama, and Harry bought something equivalently/comparably/ similarly exotic.
> [*equivalently/comparably/similarly exotic to α;
> *exotic equivalently/comparably/similarly to α]

      b. John kissed Mary yesterday, but nothing equivalently/comparably/ similarly unpleasant will happen today.
> [*equivalently/comparably/similarly unpleasant to α;
> *unpleasant equivalently/ comparably/similarly to α]

      c. Each of the guys imagined that Mary must have fallen for someone equally/comparably rich.
> [*equally/comparably rich to α; *rich equally/comparably to α]

The problem with such syntactic reconstruction is that *equivalently, comparably,* and *similarly,* being adverbs, do not license syntactic complement structures in which the implicit anaphor can be realized at LF. On the other hand, the conceptual structures of *equivalently, comparably,* and *similarly* clearly must include implicit arguments that encode the basis of equivalence, comparison, and similarity. These arguments are part of the meaning—whether or not they are expressible in syntax.

11.4.3 *The reconstructed antecedent of else need not be a constituent in syntax*

In the cases just pointed out, there is no syntactic position where the reconstructed material can be attached. Another piece of evidence against syntactic reconstruction comes from examples in which reconstruction cannot be based on a plausible syntactic constituent. These largely recapitulate evidence from sections 4.5 and 8.1, adding *else* into the mix: *do something else* and *something else happen* ellipsis. First consider examples with *do something else,* paralleling *do it/so/that.*

(46)   a. Mary swam in the river, and Bill did {it/so/that} too.
      b. Mary swam in the river, but Bill did something else.

In the case of (46b), it is feasible to generalize the reconstruction approach to VP ellipsis, interpreting the anaphor through reconstruction at LF, *à la* Reinhart (1983).

(47)   Mary swam in the river, but Bill did something other than swim in the river.

Hence so far reconstruction can in principle be carried out at the syntactic level of LF.

Consider however what happens when we add an orphan *to-* or *with*-phrase to the ellipted VP. The examples in (48) are parallel to examples in Chapters 4 and 8 which show the difficulty of establishing a syntactic antecedent for *do so*.

(48)   a. John patted the dog, and Sam did something else to the cat.
       b. Mary put the food in the container, and then Susan did something else with the trash.

As in the corresponding standard *do so* cases, there is no antecedent VP that can be reconstructed in order to get the interpretation for *do something else*: none of the conceivable possibilities in (49)–(50) are grammatical.[12]

(49)   a. *John patted the dog, and Sam did something other than pat (the dog) to the cat.
       b. *John put the food in the container, and then Susan did something other than put (the food) in the container with the trash.

That is, *something else* cannot be paraphrased by overt reconstruction as *something other than* α. A parallel difficulty arises in reconstructing *something else happen* anaphora:[13]

---

[12] It is possible that there are other factors contributing to the ungrammaticality in some of these cases, such as the internal embedding of clausal constituents. The general pattern of ungrammaticality nevertheless casts doubt on the notion that the anaphor X has a syntactic antecedent in the *do X to Y* construction.

[13] As Jim McCawley and Georgia Green have pointed out to us, the ungrammatical examples here can be improved by changing the syntactic structure of the reconstructed anaphor. For example, (50b) is somewhat improved if we use *that John kissed Mary* or *John kissing Mary*.

(i)   a ?? John kissed Mary, but something other than [α that John kissed Mary] happened to Sue
      b ?? John kissed Mary, but something other than [α John kissing Mary] happened to Sue

The important point here, made in more detail in Chapters 7 and 8, is that the interpretation of the anaphor is in some sense constructed from the antecedent, but is not syntactically identical to it, as would be required by a syntactic theory of reconstruction.

(50) a. John kissed Mary, but something else happened to Sue.
  b. * ..., but something other than John kissed (Mary/her) happened to Sue.

(51) a. John won $50 in a poker game, but something else happened with Bill.
  b. * ..., but something other than (John) won $50 in a poker game happened with Bill

This outcome is exactly like what we found in Chapters 4 and 8 with standard *do it* and *it happen* anaphora. Let us review. Following Chomsky (1971) and Akmajian (1973), the proper interpretation of *do it* and *it happen* anaphora requires matching the *to-* or *with*-phrase (the orphan) with a target in the antecedent clause; the orphan and target are typically contrasting foci. The antecedent clause is "reconstructed" in the meaning of the elliptical expression—i.e. indirectly licensed—by substituting the interpretation of the orphan for that of the target. Reconstruction along such lines is not feasible in syntax, say at LF, in part because there are many contrastive foci that cannot be syntactically extracted. (52) is a smattering of examples adapted from Chapter 7.

(52) Harriet doesn't drink **expensive** scotch, she drinks **cheap** scotch.
  The pumpkin doesn't weigh **three** hundred pounds, it weighs **six** hundred pounds.
  That isn't a **navy** flight suit, it's an **army** flight suit.
  For John to flirt with his **wife** at a party would be scandalous, but not with his **sister.**
  etc.

Chapters 7 and 8 concluded that the only place in the grammar where indirect licensing can be worked out is CS. In particular, the information structure tier has to be used to match the orphan (e.g. *to Sue* in (50a)) with its target (*Mary*).

If this is the appropriate solution for *do it* and *it happen* ellipsis in general, we must apply it to the present case with *do X else* and *X else happen* as well. In other words, we should not attempt to appeal to LF extraction to isolate a syntactic constituent that can serve as antecedent for LF reconstruction in (48), (50), and (51). Rather, we must apply indirect licensing to account for the interpretation of these cases, which depends on CS relations between the anaphor and antecedent.

11.4.4 *Putting the pieces together*

If these complex cases of *someone else* are interpreted at CS, then the more straighforward cases must be as well. In turn, since *someone else* shares so much with "core" cases of binding, then "core" binding must also belong in CS, in accordance with the approach advocated in Chapter 10.

As has come up before in the discussion in this chapter, one might object that the problematic examples of reconstruction in sections 11.4.2 and 11.4.3 are cross-sentential, so that they might have no bearing on "core" intrasentential binding theory. However, now let us return to the reconstruction of sloppy identity. (53b) is the reconstruction of (53a). (The reconstructed part is indicated in bold and should now be considered only an informal rendering of the requisite CS into pseudo-English.)

(53) a. John had dinner with his kids, but every other guy had dinner with
         someone else.
      b. John$_i$ had dinner with [his$_i$ kids]$_k$ but every other guy$_x$ had dinner with
         [someone other than [his$_{y=x}$kids]$_p$]

Crucially, because the antecedent of the reconstructed *his* is a quantified NP, this binding falls under standard binding theory. However, we have just shown that the reconstructed material is in general not present in LF or any other syntactic level. Therefore even reconstruction that determines the interpretation of an anaphor bound by a quantifier, surely a "core" case of binding, must rely on CS.

Our overall conclusion, as in Chapter 10, is that

Anaphoric dependencies, even those belonging to standard binding theory, cannot in general be determined in syntactic structure—that is, the relation of binding does not belong to syntax (though it may have some syntactic licensing conditions).

In addition, referential dependence on quantifiers depends on reconstruction, which depends on information structure; hence

Quantifier scope cannot be determined in syntactic structure.

This being the case, there is no need for *else* to have the structure 'other than α' at any level of syntax. Rather, we are led to the following treatment:

(54) *Hypothesis 4*

$$[X]^\alpha_i \text{ binds } [\text{OTHER THAN } \alpha]_j \quad \text{iff} \quad C_1, ..., C_n$$
$$\quad | \qquad\qquad\qquad\quad | $$
$$\text{NP}_i \qquad\qquad\quad \text{else}_j$$

That is, the apparent syntactic binding of *else* is a reflection of an "implicit anaphor" α hidden in the lexical conceptual structure of *else*. This anaphor is bound by virtue of being marked identical with the superscript on its antecedent in CS. The conditions $C_1, \ldots, C_n$ might be partly syntactic and partly semantic, as in the treatment of Principle A_{CS} in Chapter 10.

With Hypothesis 4 in mind, consider again the "extended" anaphors of section 11.4.1. If the anaphoric properties of *else* are encoded by means of an implicit anaphor in its CS, then, similarly, the lexical conceptual structure of *local* is [*NEARBY* α], that of *home* is [*RESIDENCE OF* α], and so forth. This should seem perfectly natural. After all, it is altogether usual for a lexical item to be conceptually composite and equivalent to a larger expression (*go toward* = *approach*, *go across* = *cross*) because of equivalences in CS. The only innovation with *else* and these other expressions is that their lexical conceptual structure (LCS) contains an anaphor.[14] And even this is not so unexpected: we know of verbs such as intransitive *wash* and *shave* that have an implicit reflexive argument. Thus Hypothesis 4 solves the problem of the extreme variety of "extended anaphors": such variety is just what one would expect of lexical items.

Hypothesis 4 also solves the problem of referential dependencies that cannot be expressed syntactically, such as (45): *equally* and *comparably*, like some verbs we have encountered, have semantic arguments that are not expressed syntactically. What makes these cases more interesting is that the semantic arguments in question are impossible to express because of gaps in the autonomous syntax of English adverbs. It so happens, though, that these implicit arguments are anaphoric and require reconstruction. Now that reconstruction is in CS, there is no need for the implicit arguments to be present in syntax.

Hypothesis 4 retains certain advantages of Hypothesis 3: syntactic structure contains a family of complex anaphors subject to binding theory, and they all reduce to expressions containing an implicit simple anaphor α—except now the implicit anaphor is in CS. There is therefore no need for contraindexing within binding theory: the semantic content of *else* leads to the obviative interpretation.

However, recall the differences between *X else* and pronouns with respect to Condition C and Crossover, discussed in section 11.3.3. Hypothesis 3 accounted for these differences naturally by virtue of the fact that the implicit anaphor was embedded within *X else*. If we are to try to retain that advantage, we must explore a theory in which Condition C and Crossover are phenomena stemming from CS configurations rather than syntactic structure. Section 9.3

---

[14] In fact, this offers an attractive variant on Enç's (1989) account of Dogrib *ye*: suppose it has the same decomposition as *someone else*, namely 'other than α'; but like *home*, it carries a feature requiring syntactic locality (parallel to Enç's feature +L). This appears to yield the right results.

also pointed in that direction for Crossover, in accounting for extraction constraints. We leave such exploration for future research.[15]

11.5 Summary

Recapitulating our argument:

• *X else* has all the properties expected of an anaphoric element, and therefore, like pronouns, it should fall under binding theory.

• In seeking the proper way to generalize binding theory to include *X else*, we have rejected the use of simple contra-indexing (Hypothesis 1), as it does not distinguish *X else* from names. We have also rejected a generalized notion of referential dependency *à la* Partee and Keenan for *else* (Hypothesis 2), as it does not account for the apparent compositionality of *X else*.

• The proper treatment of *X else* appears to decompose it as *X other than α*, where *α* is an anaphoric element that is coreferential with its antecedent (or identical in sense in the identity-of-sense cases). This treatment permits us to account for the difference between ordinary pronouns and *X else* in crossover, and, through the reconstruction of *α* as a "paycheck pronoun", for the existence of sloppy identity with *X else*.

• However, the class of morphemes to which *else* belongs is substantial and varied enough that it does not seem feasible to simply replace *else* by *other than α* in syntax. In addition, adverbs like *comparably* display "extended" anaphora for which no plausible well-formed syntactic form can be reconstructed. Therefore, the compositionality of *else* is most plausibly encoded in its lexical conceptual structure, in accordance with the Simpler Syntax Hypothesis. The anaphor *α* can be regarded as an "implicit anaphor", an element not present in syntax at all, but rather part of the lexical structure of the word *else*. Partee's cases of "complex anaphors" appear to be reanalyzable as similar cases in which an anaphor implicit in syntax is overt in conceptual structure; we have adduced further cases with similar properties. Thus none of these anaphors have covert syntactic structure, and we can maintain the Simpler Syntax Hypothesis.

• This conclusion forces us to treat the binding of *α* as a property of conceptual structure, as in Hypothesis 4.

---

[15] On a more theory-internal plane, we have not worked out precisely how *X else* composes semantically with the *do X* and *X happen* constructions, such that indirect licensing works out properly.

• The reconstruction of *else* in general includes cases of *do X else* and *X else happen* anaphora. Some of these cases are bound variables, and some are E-type anaphora. These fall in with cases of ordinary *do it* and *it happen* anaphora, with the same properties discussed in Chapters 4 and 8. The level at which reconstruction should take place is therefore one at which the antecedent of indirect licensing can be determined, which involves among other things information structure—again not a level of syntax, but the level of CS.

• We would like an account of *else* that unifies it with the account of the pronoun *it*, such that binding conditions apply at the same level for all cases. This suggests that the "core" relation of binding is imposed at Conceptual Structure, where syntactically implicit anaphors are structurally present.

Our argument consequently opens a giant can of worms: how are the parts of binding theory addressed by GB to be reformulated in terms of conceptual structure instead of (or in addition to) syntactic structure? The same questions arise as in Chapter 10: which of the traditional binding conditions pertain to conceptual structure, and which are retained in syntax? How are pronominals, anaphors, and reciprocals to be differentiated, and how are differences among languages in their repertoire of anaphoric elements to be formulated? What consequences might such reformulation have on the nature of syntactic structure, in particular on the nature of extraction?

We leave these questions as fascinating challenges for future research. As a spur to such research, we conclude with three observations.

• Since the proper account of crossover (section 11.3.3) depends on treating the implicit anaphor in *else* as embedded, it appears that the account of crossover too must be stated at a level of representation at which the implicit anaphor is explicit, e.g. CS rather than LF or S-structure. Such an account will of course require a suitable CS analogy of c-command; Chapter 10 begins to motivate such an analogue in the context of cases where not even reflexives can be properly accounted for in syntax. Partee (1989) points out the analogue to c-command in a Discourse Representation Theory framework.

• Since implicit anaphors can be quantified, the appropriate level for stating quantifier binding would appear to be one at which such anaphors are structurally present, namely CS rather than than LF.[16]

---

[16] Partee (1989) suggests that the proper representation may be a discourse representation in which contexts are quantified over. We leave open here the question of how the quantification is to be formally implemented.

• Since the primary original motivation for LF (Chomsky 1976; May 1977; 1985) was to explicitly encode quantifier binding in syntax, our conclusions cast doubt on the existence of such a level, in concurrence with the desiderata of the Simpler Syntax Hypothesis.

CHAPTER 12

The Semantic Basis
of Control in English

12.1 Introduction

The binding phenomena examined in the last two chapters might be considered "peripheral" in language, perhaps only because they have hardly been noticed (let alone intensively studied) in the context of mainstream syntactic theory. We have shown, however, that in each case there are important implications for the theory of grammar: a treatment of binding in terms of syntax alone does not "scale up" as it should to the phenomena in question, while a treatment that brings into play conceptual structure and the syntax–semantics interface does. Moreover, in each case the syntactic analysis we arrive at is that predicted by the Simpler Syntax Hypothesis: structures are flat, there are no hidden levels made of syntactic units, and, aside from traces of long-distance dependencies, there are no terminal nodes that are not realized phonologically.

The present chapter turns to a phenomenon, addressed in passing in Chapter 6, which has been absolutely central to mainstream theory for forty years: control. The problem of control concerns how to determine the understood subject of infinitival or gerundive VPs that lack an overt local subject, for instance the bracketed constituents in (1).

(1) a. John$_i$ likes [to $_i$dance with Sarah]
    b. John$_i$ enjoys [$_i$dancing with Sarah]

We would like to thank Sten Vikner, Ian Roberts, and members of the audience at University of Stuttgart, where some of the material in this chapter was presented, for helpful comments and questions. We also thank Adele Goldberg for useful discussion of many of these issues, and Brian Joseph, Richard Oehrle, Klaus-Uwe Panther, Idan Landau, and two anonymous readers for many important comments on earlier versions.

    c. John$_i$ talked to Sarah$_j$ about [$_{i/j/i+j/gen}$dancing with Jeff]

    d. John$_i$ urged Sarah$_j$ [to $_{j/*i/*i+j/*gen}$dance with Jeff]

In (1a,b), John is understood as the character whose dancing is under discussion; *John* is said to *control* the complement VP or be its *controller*. We notate this relation by co-indexing *John* with the verb it controls.[1] In (1c), either *John* or *Sarah*—or both together—can be understood as the dancer(s) under discussion; the last of these possibilities is notated with the subscript $i + j$. John may also be talking about dancing with Jeff in the abstract, with no particular dancer in mind; this interpretation is generally called "arbitrary control" and is notated here with the subscript *gen* (generic). Like (1c), (1d) presents two potential controllers in the main clause. But in this case only *Sarah* can be construed as controller, and joint and generic control are impossible. Solving the control problem thus requires identifying the factors that determine possible controllers in any given circumstance.

One tradition in approaching control, beginning with Rosenbaum (1967) and continuing to such works as Chomsky (1981), Bresnan (1982b), Manzini (1983b), Larson (1991), Hornstein (1999), Landau (2000), and Wurmbrand (2001), contends that the solution to the control problem involves primarily syntactic factors (while generally acknowledging that semantics plays some role). Another tradition, beginning with Jackendoff (1969c) and continuing through Jackendoff (1972; 1974), Růžička (1983), Nishigauchi (1984), Williams (1985), Dowty (1985), Farkas (1988), Chierchia (1988), Sag and Pollard (1991), Pollard and Sag (1994), and Van Valin and LaPolla (1997), focuses on the importance of semantic factors, in particular the lexical semantics of the predicate that selects the infinitival or gerundive complement.

The intent of the present chapter, in the face of a persistent tradition of studying control in purely syntactic terms, is to reiterate the fundamental importance of semantics in the control problem, and to articulate some of the semantic factors more precisely than has heretofore been possible. At the same time, we also pinpoint some syntactic factors relevant to control. We can by no means solve all the complexities of the control problem here, but we do cover a rich and important subclass of cases in detail, demonstrating their semantic basis. This chapter thus illustrates yet again the overall theme of this book: a

---

[1] We use this notation rather than the conventional null pronoun *PRO* so as not to prejudice whether the infinitive has a genuine syntactic subject. Some theories of control, notably those in the mainstream tradition, assume the presence of *PRO* and an S or IP node above the VP; others such as Lexical-Functional Grammar and some formal semantics approaches (e.g. Dowty 1985) assume the infinitival is simply a subjectless VP in phrase structure. While the Simpler Syntax Hypothesis favors the latter approach (see Ch. 6, also e.g. Culicover and Wilkins 1986, Jackendoff 1990a), the arguments in this chapter are largely neutral on this issue.

syntax–semantic interface more flexible than that demanded by Interface Uniformity is necessary. Given such an interface, syntax can be radically simplified but it does not wither away altogether.

A quick survey of where we are headed. Section 12.2 briefly presents some of the obstacles to a theory of control based on syntactic binding, then sorts out some aspects of control which are nevertheless purely syntactic and presents a descriptive typology of control. Most of the rest of the chapter is devoted to unique (or "obligatory") control, as in (1d): sections 12.3 and 12.4 show that in a very large class of cases of unique control, the controlled VP denotes an action—usually a voluntary action—and the controller is the character who has the onus for that action. Section 12.5 begins to formalize the semantics, showing how the descriptive generalizations follow from the formal character of predicates that select actions as arguments. As a consequence, we begin to approach the goal of explaining much of control directly from the lexical decomposition of the matrix verb.

Section 12.6 deals with a well-known class of exceptions to the conditions of unique control, and proposes that they are cases of coercion, in which extra conventionalized semantic material is added that is not present in syntax. Section 12.7 proposes a further instance of coercion to account for the phenomenon of partial control discussed at length by Landau (2000). Sections 12.8 and 12.9 assess the situation, in particular making clear how much is left to explain.

Our study suffers from the limitation that it is restricted to English. Our impression from the literature (e.g. Van Valin and LaPolla 1997) is that control behaves crosslinguistically in much the same fashion (within limits: cf. Růžička 1999, Panther and Köpcke 1993), but we will not verify this here. On the other hand, we make frequent appeal to control in English nominals, a phenomenon which is seldom cited in the literature (exceptions are Jackendoff (1972; 1974), Williams (1985), Sag and Pollard (1991), and Pollard and Sag (1994)) but which proves exceptionally revealing.

12.2 A typology of control

12.2.1 Motivation for pursuing a semantic solution

Let us begin with some relatively simple observations, most of which have appeared several times in the literature (yet are often neglected). First, theories of control based predominantly on syntax (e.g. Chomsky 1981, Manzini 1983b) treat control as a subcase of syntactic binding. In conformance with Structural and Interface Uniformity, this requires a syntactic NP (usually called

PRO) to serve as the subject of the controlled VP, plus a syntactic NP that serves as the antecedent of PRO, to which PRO can be bound. In this approach, (1a) is notated as

(2)   John$_i$ likes [PRO$_i$ to dance with Sarah]

This elegant solution has a price: the problem immediately arises of how to confine PRO to the subject of controlled complements and prohibit it in other NP positions. A considerable literature has been devoted to this problem alone (e.g. Chomsky (1981), Wurmbrand (2001), and many of the papers in Larson et al. (1992)).

A different syntactic approach has been prominently espoused by Hornstein (1999; 2001) (less-known versions of this approach include Bowers (1981) and O'Neil (1997)). Hornstein proposes that the controller originates in the position of subject of the controlled VP (where PRO is in (2)), and moves up to the controller position. (For critiques, see Culicover and Jackendoff (2001), Landau (2003); for responses, see Boeckx and Hornstein (2003; 2004).)

One argument against either of these treatments of control is that on occasion there is no independently motivated NP that can serve as controller. Postal (1969) points out examples like (3), in which a derived adjective instead of an NP plays the role of controller.

(3)   a. an American attempt to dominate the Middle East
       b. the Anglo-French agreement to respect each other's territorial claims

(3b) presents a particular problem in that there is no obvious derivation of *Anglo-French* from a plausible NP source such as *England and France*.

The difficulty of identifying an NP controller is more severe in examples like (4). (4a,b) appear in Williams (1985); (4c) appears in Sag and Pollard (1991); the type in (4d) appears in Cantrall (1974) but to our knowledge has not been discussed since.

(4)   a. Any such attempt [to leave] will be severely punished.
       b. Yesterday's orders [to leave] have been canceled.
       c. How about [taking a swim together]?
                                    [controller is speaker and hearer jointly]
       d. Undressing myself/yourself/ourselves in public may annoy Bill.

In (4a,b), the specifiers of the nominals *order* and *attempt* preclude an independent NP controller in the appropriate position. One could stipulate a phantom position in the specifier that can never be realized by anything but a null NP; alternatively one could stipulate a null *by*-phrase in (4a) and a null *to*-phrase in (4b). However, such stipulations have no independent syntactic motivation. They are patently motivated by the desire to provide a syntactic controller (as well as by theory-internal considerations such as the theta-criterion, which ultimately amount to Structural and Interface Uniformity). In (4c,d) the situation is still worse, since the controller is the speaker and/ or hearer, nowhere overtly mentioned in the discourse. Unless one is willing to resurrect Ross's (1970) theory of performative deletion, long in disgrace (see Newmeyer 1986: ch. 5), there is no way to provide a syntactic NP as the controller.[2]

A second sort of argument against a purely syntactic account of control— whether or not there is a PRO—comes from the fact that the choice of controller can be doubly dissociated from syntactic configuration. On one hand, the same syntactic configuration can be associated with different controller choice, as seen in (5). On the other hand, the controller can appear in different syntactic configurations, while preserving meaning, as seen in (6).

(5)   a. $John_i$ persuaded $Sarah_j$ to $_{j/*i}$dance.
      b. $John_i$ promised $Sarah_j$ to $_{i/*j}$dance.
      c. $John_i$ talked about $_{i/gen}$dancing with Jeff.
      d. $John_i$ refrained from $_{i/*gen}$dancing with Jeff.

(6)   a. Bill ordered $Fred_i$ [to $_i$leave immediately]
      b. $Fred_i$'s order from Bill [to $_i$leave immediately]
      c. the order from Bill to $Fred_i$ [to $_i$leave immediately].
      d. $Fred_i$ received Bill's order [to $_i$leave immediately].

Should one wish to find a relevant syntactic difference between (5a) and (5b) and between (5c) and (5d), it has to be motivated by the dogma that control is syntactic; there is no independent motivation. Intuition suggests that the differences are a consequence of what the verbs mean; we will be able to be more explicit later on. On the other hand, the syntactic differences among (6a–d) are blatant; what remains constant is that Fred is recipient of the order, a constancy at the level of thematic role. Many more such cases will appear below.

We therefore seek a treatment of control as a relation stated over the level of conceptual structure rather than over syntactic structure. We will show that CS is an appropriate level for stating control for three reasons:

• At the level of CS, syntactically implicit arguments are explicit, so that an antecedent is readily available for cases like (4).

---

[2] As stressed by Culicover and Jackendoff (2001), these situations where an NP controller is absent are especially problematic for Hornstein's (1999) movement account of control, in which the controlled NP moves to the position of the controller.

- At the level of CS, the meanings of verbs are explicitly represented, in such a way that they can directly bear on control relations without special added machinery.
- Finally, the association of control with constant thematic roles is most natural at CS, the level at which thematic roles are structurally represented.

No other level of linguistic structure offers these possibilities. Syntactically implicit arguments are indeed explicitly encoded in LFG's level of functional structure (Bresnan 1982a), Grimshaw's (1990) level of argument structure, Levin and Rappaport Hovav's (1999) event structure, the GB/MP level of Logical Form (Chomsky 1981), and standard formal semantics logical representations (e.g. Bach 1979, Chierchia 1988). But the structured meanings of verbs and the structural representation of thematic roles are not explicit in these levels. Thus they all require control to be handled in terms of item-by-item lexical marking (or diacritics such as "object-control verb" or "Agent-control verb") rather than as an organic part of meaning. Our own intuition (shared by Dowty (1985), Farkas (1988), Sag and Pollard (1994), and Van Valin and LaPolla (1997)) is that the control behavior of *persuade* and *promise* is an essential part of their meanings; there could not be a verb that meant the same thing as *persuade* but that had the control behavior of *promise*. This requires a level of representation where the requisite aspects of meaning are structurally explicit: conceptual structure. We will show in section 12.5 why a diacritic labeling of verbs is descriptively inadequate in any event.

12.2.2 *One purely syntactic dimension: possibility of a local subject*

It is well known that some infinitival and gerundive complements permit a local subject and others do not. (7–12) present some minimal pairs, selected to present as close a semantic parallelism as possible.

(7)   a. John attempted (*for his kids) to have a better life.
      b. John strove (for his kids) to have a better life.[3]

(8)   a. Sally beseeched Bill (*for his kids) to leave.
      b. Sally begged Bill (for his kids) to leave.

(9)   a. Fred hoped (for Sally) to leave.
      b. Fred's hopes of (*Sally's) leaving

---

[3] Richard Oehrle has pointed out to us that the difference in (7) correlates with some difference in syntax and semantics of the verbs' nonclausal complements: *John attempted a somersault* vs. *John strove for happiness.*

(10) a. Vera left George so as (*for Fred) not to go crazy.
     b. Vera left George in order (for Fred) not to go crazy.

(11) a. Before (*John('s)) mentioning Harry, Bill was already nervous.
     b. Without (John('s)) mentioning Harry, Bill was already nervous.

(12) a. the best place at which (*for you) to buy hummus
     b. the best place (for you) to buy hummus

(7) and (8) contrast semantically related verbs; (9) contrasts a verb and its nominal; (9) and (10) contrast semantically parallel subordinating conjunctions. (12) is the well-known case of infinitival relatives, where the contrast turns on whether there is an overt *wh*-phrase.

It is hard to imagine anything in the semantics of these pairs that could be responsible for the syntactic distinction, particularly since each pair represents a different semantic class. We therefore conclude that this distinction is a matter of lexically determined syntactic selection, cutting broadly across semantic classes. Some heads such as *attempt, beseech*, and *so as* select a simple *to-VP* complement; others such as *strive, beg*, and *in order* select a *(for-NP)-to-VP* complement. We know of no heads that require *for-NP* before an infinitive complement.

Using the pretheoretical terminology of Baker (1995), we will call the former case an Infinitival Phrase (InfP) and the latter an Infinitival Clause (InfC). Thus, *attempt* selects an InfP and *strive* an InfC. Similarly, *before* selects a Gerundive Phrase (GerP) and *without* a Gerundive Clause (GerC). With a fronted *wh*-, an infinitival relative requires an InfP; without a *wh*-, it permits the more liberal InfC. Exactly how this distinction is formalized need not concern us here; different syntactic theories will account for these possibilities for selection in different ways.

The early literature (e.g. Rosenbaum 1967, Lakoff 1965/70) used terms such as "obligatory subject deletion" and "obligatory Equi" for the prohibition of a local subject with the infinitive or gerund. More recent literature (beginning as early as Williams (1980) and extending to Hornstein (1999) and Landau (2000), among many others) recognizes two major types of control, Obligatory Control (OC) and Nonobligatory Control (NOC) (Bresnan (1982b) uses instead "functional" and "anaphoric" control in much the same sense). However, this more recent use of "obligatory" does not align with the earlier use, as we will see next.

12.2.3 *Free control, nearly free control, and unique control*

A more complex dimension of variation in control, and the one that concerns us here, is the choice among "free", "nearly free", and "unique" control. Two other dimensions of variation, "exhaustive" vs. "partial" control and "obviative" vs.

"non-obviative" control, will be discussed in sections 12.7 and 12.8.2 respectively.

Many complements in subject position (and extraposed subject position) have the broadest range of possible controllers, as illustrated in (13). The gerund in (13) can be controlled by either NP, by both jointly (split antecedent control), or by an implicit generic person. The literature often calls this range of possibilities "non-obligatory control"; since there prove to be so many ways that control can be non-obligatory, we will call this case "free control".

(13) a. Amy$_i$ thinks that $_{i/j/i+j/gen}$dancing with Dan intrigues Tom$_j$.
      b. Amy$_i$ told Tom$_j$ that $_{i/j/i+j/gen}$dancing with Dan might be fun.

Notice that *Amy* is outside the minimal clause that contains the controlled complement (and in (12b) *Tom* is too). This configuration for control was called "Super-Equi" in the early literature (Grinder 1970); Ladusaw and Dowty (1988) call it "remote control"; it is now generally termed "long-distance control", which is what we will call it here.

As observed by Bresnan (1982b), the controller in this configuration can be a discourse antecedent (14a). Cantrall (1974) observes that the controller can also be the speaker and/or hearer (14b). The speaker and an NP in the sentence can also jointly control the complement (14c).

(14) a. Brandeis$_i$ is in a lot of trouble, according to today's newspaper. Apparently, $_i$firing the football coach has turned off a lot of potential donors.
      b. Here's the thing: undressing myself/yourself/ourselves [=you and me] in public could cause a scandal.
      c. Here's the thing: it might really upset Tom to have to undress ourselves [=Tom and me] in public.

Speaker/hearer control is also the usual option in the curious construction illustrated in (4c) above, as seen in (15a). Richard Oehrle has suggested the final sentence of the dialogue (15b) as a case where this construction has split discourse antecedents.

(15) a. How about undressing myself/yourself/ourselves in public?
      b. How about the girls taking a swim?—Okay.
         How about the boys taking a swim?—Well, okay.
         How about taking a swim together? [i.e. boys and girls]

In short, free control is a configuration in which the range of possible controllers includes (a) any NP in the sentence or surrounding discourse plus the speaker and hearer, (b) the possibility of split antecedents, and (c) the possibility of a generic controller.

Free control is not confined to subject complements; it also appears in certain object complements:

(16) a. Amy thinks that what you propose beats undressing herself/oneself/myself/yourself/ourselves [=you and me, Amy and me] in public. [also *outranks, entails, is as good as*]
  b. Fred makes undressing himself/oneself/myself/yourself/ourselves [=you and me, Fred and me] in public almost appealing.

Landau (2000: 109–11), citing previous literature, discusses some cases where the controller is not an argument of the main verb but is rather embedded in an argument, for instance:

(17) a. It would help Bill$_i$'s development to $_i$behave himself in public.
  b. $_i$Finishing his work on time is important to John$_i$'s development/ ??John$_i$'s friends.
  c. It would ruin Steve$_i$'s figure/career to $_i$eat so much ice cream.

Given that *help*, *important*, and *ruin* all take subject complements with free control, our inclination is to see these as further examples of free control.

A slightly less free version of control occurs in a class of object complements such as (1c) above. Here the controller may be either of two NPs in the sentence; split antecedents and generic controllers are also possible (18a). However, the options in (14) are not available: long-distance control (18b), a discourse controller (18c), and control by the speaker and/or hearer (18d). Discourse control is, however, possible in circumstances such as (18e) (pointed out by Sag and Pollard (1991), based on Higgins (1973)). Here the InfC is indirectly licensed (in the sense of Chapter 7), and so control follows from connectivity, not from syntactic configuration.

(18) a. John$_i$ talked to Sarah$_j$ about $_{i/j/i+j/gen}$taking better care of himself$_i$/herself$_j$/themselves$_{i+j}$/oneself$_{gen}$.
  b. *Amy$_k$ knows that John$_i$ talked to Bill$_j$ about $_k$taking care of herself$_k$.
  c. *Brandeis$_i$ is in a lot of trouble. John talked to Sarah about $_i$firing the football coach.
  d. *John talked to Sarah about undressing myself/yourself in public.

e. A: John$_i$ talked to Sarah$_j$ about something.

   B: What was it?

   A: It was probably $_{i/j/i+j/gen}$taking better care of himself$_i$/herself$_j$/ themselves$_{i+j}$/oneself$_{gen}$.

[also *think about, speak to NP about,* many others]

We will call this case "nearly free control". It occurs consistently as a complement of verbs of communication and thought and of nouns that denote information-bearing objects, such as *book* and *hypothesis*. The controlled complement always denotes a proposition being communicated, considered, or contained in an information-bearing object (as in *a book about defending oneself*). The controlled complement is typically a gerund serving as complement of *about*, but it also occurs as the direct object complement of the verbs *mention* and *discuss*:

(19) a. John mentioned/discussed Sally('s) taking care of herself.

   b. John$_i$ mentioned/discussed $_{i/gen}$taking care of himself/oneself.

   c. John$_i$ mentioned to/discussed with Sally$_j$ $_{i/j/i+j/gen}$taking care of herself/himself/themselves.

   d. A: I think John mentioned/discussed something important.

      B: What was it?

      A: It might have been taking care of himself.

   e. *Amy$_i$ thinks that John mentioned $_i$taking care of herself.

   f. *John discussed undressing myself in public with Sally.

We believe the distinction between free and nearly free control has not been made clearly in the literature before, both usually being taken to fall under nonobligatory control.

The most restricted form of control is generally called "obligatory control" in the literature; it appears in many object complements and in adjunct clauses under *in order to, before, without,* and so on. Standard examples appear in (20a,b): there are two possible targets of control in the matrix clause, but only one of them can serve as controller. There can be no split antecedents (20c), generic control (20d), long-distance control (20e), or speaker/hearer control (20f).

(20) a. Sally persuaded Ben to take better care of himself/*herself.

   b. Sally promised Ben to take better care of herself/*himself.

   c. *Sally promised/persuaded Ben to take better care of themselves.

   d. *Sally promised/persuaded Ben to take better care of oneself.

   e. *Amy thinks that Ben promised/persuaded Fred to take better care of herself.

   f. *Ben promised/persuaded Fred to take better care of myself/yourself.

We will call this situation "unique control". A major question is how the unique controller is determined. Most of the present chapter concerns the way that many important cases of unique control are determined by the semantics of the head that selects the controlled complement.

A further type of control occurs in infinitival indirect questions in object position: there is a choice between a single controller in the main clause and generic control, but the other options available in free and nearly free control are excluded (21a). If the *wh*-word is *whether*, generic control is excluded (21b). However, infinitival indirect questions in subject position can behave like free control (21c).

(21) a. Harry$_i$ told Sally$_j$ how to $_{j/gen/*i/*i+j}$defend herself/oneself/*himself/ *themselves/*myself.
      b. Harry asked Sally whether to take care of himself/*oneself/*herself.
      c. Amy$_i$ knows that how to take care of herself/oneself/myself/yourself/ ourselves [=you and me, Amy and me] is a tough question.

We might call the situation in (21a) "unique+generic control"; we will have nothing to say about it here (though not for lack of interest!).

We emphasize that the syntactic position of a complement plays no direct role in the type of control it displays, contrary to a frequently cited claim of Manzini (1983b). One half of her claim is that object complements require a controller (i.e. unique control) within the immediately dominating clause. But we have already seen examples of postverbal complements with free control (16), nearly free control (19), and unique control (20). The other half of her claim is that, in our terms, subject complements all have free control. We disprove this claim in section 12.4.2, where we discuss some subject complements with unique control.

Our claim, by contrast, is that the type of control a complement displays is a consequence of the semantic role it is assigned by the head that selects it, not a consequence of its syntactic position or that of its controller.

12.2.4 *Control in adjunct clauses*

One point in control theory where some syntactic constraint seems unavoidable is in the control of adjuncts. As we observed in (10)–(11), some subordinating conjunctions that introduce adjuncts (e.g. *in order*) select for InfC, and some (e.g. *so as*) select for InfP. Similarly, some (e.g. *without*) select for gerundives with or without overt subjects, and others (e.g. *after*) select for subjectless gerundives. In every case, if the adjunct lacks an overt subject, the surface subject of the main clause, whatever its thematic role, is always the controller. A generic interpretation is never possible; a split antecedent is never possible.[4]

(22) a. Helen$_i$ examined Bernie$_j$ in order/so as to $_{i/*j/*gen/*i+j}$vindicate herself/ *himself/*oneself/*themselves.
      b. Bernie$_j$ was examined by Helen$_i$ in order/so as to $_{*i/?j/*gen/*i+j}$vindicate ?himself/*herself/*oneself/*themselves.
      c. Helen examined Bernie in order/*so as for us to vindicate ourselves/ *herself/*himself.

(23) a. Helen$_i$ liked/pleased Bernie$_j$ without/after $_{i/*j/*gen/*i+j}$compromising herself/*himself/*oneself/*themselves.
      b. Bernie$_j$ was liked/pleased by Helen$_i$ without $_{*i/??j/*gen/*i+j}$compromising ??himself/*herself/*oneself/*themselves.
      c. Helen liked Susan without/*after Bernie's compromising himself/ *herself.

However, some nonsyntactic influence is necessary even in these cases. For one thing, these adjuncts can be controlled by implicit arguments, where there is no evident syntactic position for a covert controller.

(24) a. Such a brutal interrogation of the suspect without considering the legal repercussions could lead to disaster.
      b. That sort of flattery of your professors, just in order to curry favor, is frowned upon at this institution.

The subject of *consider* is necessarily understood as the individual who is interrogating the suspect. Yet, because of the form of the determiner, there is no apparent place to cram an Agent NP into the specifier of *interrogation*. Similarly, the subject of *curry favor* is necessarily understood as the flatterer, yet there is apparently no NP position available in the specifier of *flattery* where an appropriate controller could be located.

There are two possible solutions. First, one can try to find a position for a null subject in the NP, in violation of the (quite complex) surface constraints on English determiners. Or one can admit the possibility of an implicit controller, present only at a level such as argument structure or conceptual structure.

There is also a deeper semantic influence on control specifically with *in order to* clauses. Since *in order to* denotes a purpose, it must be controlled by an

---

[4] It is interesting that another use of *without* does not have the same restriction: like depictive predicates such as *drunk*, it can apply to either the subject or the object.

(i) a. Helen examined Bernie drunk. [either one is drunk]
     b. Helen examined Bernie without her/his glasses on.

individual capable of having a purpose. When the subject of the matrix is not such an individual, two options are available for controller. First, if the matrix is a passive, the explicit or implicit agent of the passive controls the *in order to*, as in (25a). Second, in the absence of any explicit or implicit agent in the matrix clause, the *in order to* clause can be controlled by an implicit "stage manager" or "playwright" who has control over the course of action. Examples appear in (25b,c).

(25) a. The ship was sunk (by the owners) in order to collect the insurance.
                                                  [Owners collect the insurance.]
      b. The ship sinks in order to further the plot.
                          [Playwright furthers the plot by making the ship sink.]
      c. This story appears on the back page in order not to embarrass
          the president.   [Editors keep the president from being embarrassed
          by putting story on back page; *or* Editors keep the story from embar-
          rassing the president by putting it on the back page.]

12.3 Actional complements

Most of the rest of this chapter is devoted to developing the following hypothesis, which is prefigured in the literature as early as Lasnik and Fiengo (1974):

Unique Control of Actional Complements (UCAC) Hypothesis
Infinitival and gerundive complements that are selected by their head to be of the semantic type Voluntary Action have unique control. The unique controller is the character to which the head assigns the role of actor for that action—whatever its syntactic position. (This does not preclude other sources of unique control, however: see section 12.8.1.)

The notion of Voluntary Action is relatively familiar, but we take a moment to make our use of it clear. We use the term "situation" for any sort of state or event. "Actions" are a special subclass of situations, detectable by the standard test *What X did was*.

(26) a. *Actions*
          What Roberta did was run the race/read a book/think about physics.
      b. *Non-actions*
          What Roberta did was ?grow taller/*strike Simmy as smart/*realize it
          was raining.

When the actor of an action is animate, the default interpretation is that the action is performed voluntarily. Voluntary actions can be detected by standard tests such as the imperative and the adverbials *voluntarily* and *on purpose*.

(27) *Voluntary actions*
  a. Run the race!
    Roberta ran the race voluntarily.
  b. Be quiet!
    Roberta was quiet voluntarily.
  c. Be examined by a doctor!
    Roberta was examined by a doctor voluntarily.
 Non-voluntary (non-)actions
  d. *Grow taller!
    *Roberta grew taller voluntarily.
  e. *Strike Simmy as smart!
    *Roberta struck Simmy as smart voluntarily.
  f. *Realize it's raining!
    *Roberta realized it was raining voluntarily.

As observed as long ago as Fischer and Marshall (1969), the possibility of a VP expressing a voluntary action is heavily conditioned by pragmatics. For example, passives are normally nonvoluntary, but the well-worn example *be examined by a doctor* can be voluntary; as an imperative it is understood as *get yourself examined by a doctor*. Similarly, *be hungry* cannot be voluntary, but *be quiet* can, under the interpretation *make yourself quiet*. *Growing taller* is not usually voluntary, but there are "Alice in Wonderland" scenarios in which a character voluntarily grows taller by eating a mushroom, and perhaps less spectacular examples of taking hormones. We will therefore use the sign # throughout the exposition of this chapter to convey the judgment "ungrammatical, barring special scenarios".

We will call complements that express voluntary actions "actional" complements and those that express situations (which include actions) "situational" complements. Some verbs select specifically for voluntary actions; some for any kind of action; others, still less choosy, permit their complements to be any sort of situation. The verb *urge*, for instance, selects voluntary actional complements: its complement must be something one can do voluntarily (28a), and this complement has unique control (28b). By contrast, *talk to NP about NP* allows its complement to be any state or event (29a), and control is nearly free (29b). (The residue of situations that are *not* actions does not appear to form a natural semantic class; there is no verb that selects for only such complements.)

(28) a. Miriam urged Norbert to dance with Jeff/*be six years old.
  b. Miriam$_i$ urged Norbert$_j$ to $_{j/*i/*i+j/*gen}$dance with Jeff.

(29) a. Miriam talked to Norbert about dancing with Jeff/being six years old.
  b. Miriam$_i$ talked to Norbert$_j$ about $_{i/j/i+j/gen}$dancing with Jeff.

This illustrates the basic generalization claimed by the UCAC Hypothesis.

Section 12.6 will show that various interesting cases of control arise when the semantic type of a complement diverges from the type selected by the verb. Under such conditions the semantic composition of the sentence is subject to coercion, which inserts extra semantic material to establish well-formedness. Such coercions account for some well-known apparent exceptions to the UCAC hypothesis, as well as for some cases not previously cited.

As part of our argument that control is essentially a semantic phenomenon, we need to show that the selection of actional vs. situational complements cannot be reduced to some sort of syntactic selection—that the two do not correlate precisely.

• Can actional vs. situational be correlated with infinitivals vs. *that*-complements? No. Some verbs, such as *wish*, *hope*, and *claim*, select *that*-complements and infinitival complements, both of which are situational.

(30)   a.   Nancy wishes/hopes that she will run the race/that she will realize it's raining.
       b.   Nancy wishes/hopes to run the race/to realize it's raining.
       c.   Beth claims that she ran the race/that she has realized it's raining.
       d.   Beth claims to have run the race/to have realized it's raining.

Plan selects either a *that*-complement or an infinitival, both of which are actional.

(31)   a.   Hilary planned that she would run the race/#that she would realize it's raining.
       b.   Hilary planned to run the race/#to realize it's raining.[5]

And some verbs, for instance *tell* and *persuade*, select situational *that*-complements and actional infinitival complements.[6]

---

[5] Richard Oehrle has pointed out to us that this characterization pertains only to *plan to VP*, as the complement in (i) is clearly a situation. This difference appears to correlate with the difference between (ii) and (iii).

(i)   Hilary planned for there to be thirty people at the meeting.
(ii) Hilary planned a meeting.
(iii) Hilary planned for winter.

In (31b) and (ii), the complement denotes an action Hilary is planning to carry out; in (i) and (iii), the complement denotes a situation whose contingencies are addressed by Hilary's plans.

[6] This class of verbs provides an important piece of evidence for the semantic difference between situational and actional complements. The infinitival complements in (32b) have a close paraphrase with a *that*-clause: *Nancy told/persuaded Ben that he should run the race.* However, as observed by Searle (1983), Klein and Sag (1985), Jackendoff (1985), and Bratman (1987), among others, the two forms are not entirely equivalent, since we can without contradiction juxtapose each with the negation of the other:

(32)   a. Nancy told/persuaded Ben that he could run the race/that he would
          realize it's raining.
       b. Nancy told/persuaded Ben to run the race/#to realize it's raining.
       [also *swear, decide, forget, occur to NP, teach, learn*]

Thus the distinction between situational and actional complements does not
correlate with *that*-clauses vs. infinitivals in syntax.

• Can situational vs. actional be correlated with selecting InfC vs. InfP? No. At
first glance this might seem promising. As seen above, *hope* and *wish* take
situational complements; they also allow InfC. By contrast, *try* and *attempt*
require actional complements and allow only InfP.

(33)   a. Bill hoped/wished (for Harry) to run the race/to realize it's raining.
       b. Bill tried/attempted (*for Harry) to run the race/#to realize it's
          raining.

However, *plan* allows an InfC but requires an actional complement (34a), and
lucky and *unlucky* allow a situational complement but require an InfP (34b).

(34)   a. Hilary planned (for Ben) to run the race/#to realize it's raining.
       b. Norman is lucky/unlucky (*for Ben) to have run the race/to have
          grown taller.

Thus there is no correlation here either.

• Finally, both situational and actional complements can be expressed as gerunds. Gerundive complements of verbs such as *discuss* and *mention* express
situations, but gerundive complements of verbs such as *refrain from* and *pressure into* require voluntary actions.

(35)   a. Sue discussed/mentioned running the race/growing older.
       b. Sue refrained from running the race/#growing older.
       c. Sue pressured Joe into running the race/#growing older.

   Still, despite all this variation, there are strong tendencies: the default situational complement is a tensed *that*-clause, and the default actional complement is an InfP. InfC, GerC, and GerP seem to fall somewhere in between.
Although many verbs are lexically marked with a nondefault syntactic selection, no verb totally reverses the default case, assigning a situational complement to an infinitival and an actional complement to a *that*-clause.

 (i)   Nancy persuaded Ben to run the race, but she never persuaded him that he **should** run it.
 (ii) Nancy persuaded Ben that he should run the race, but she never actually persuaded him to
       run it.

With the notion of selection of actional complements in place, we return to the UCAC Hypothesis: predicates that select actional complements require unique control. (36)–(38) offer examples of the generalization.

(36) Free control predicates: not restricted to actional complements
    a. *Voluntary actions*

$$\left.\begin{array}{l} \text{Running the race} \\ \text{Being quiet} \\ \text{Being examined by a doctor} \end{array}\right\} \text{annoys Max/is a drag}$$

    b. *Non-voluntary actions*

$$\left.\begin{array}{l} \text{Growing taller} \\ \text{Striking Simmy as smart} \\ \text{Realizing it's raining} \end{array}\right\} \text{annoys Max/is a drag}$$

(37) Nearly free control predicates: not restricted to actional complements
    a. *Voluntary actions*

$$\text{Marsha spoke to Ed about} \left\{\begin{array}{l} \text{running the race} \\ \text{being quiet} \\ \text{being examined by a doctor} \end{array}\right\}$$

    b. *Non-voluntary actions*

$$\text{Marsha spoke to Ed about} \left\{\begin{array}{l} \text{growing taller} \\ \text{having struck Simmy as smart} \\ \text{realizing it's raining} \end{array}\right\}$$

(38) Unique control predicates: restricted to actional complements

$$\left.\begin{array}{l} \text{Fred promised (Louise)}\ldots \\ \text{Fred persuaded Louise}\ldots \end{array}\right\}$$

    a. *Voluntary actions*

$$\left.\begin{array}{l} \text{to run the race} \\ \text{to be quiet} \\ \text{to be examined by a doctor} \end{array}\right\}$$

    b. *Non-voluntary actions*

$$\left.\begin{array}{l} \text{\#to grow taller} \\ \text{\#to strike Simmy as smart} \\ \text{\#to realize it was raining} \end{array}\right\}$$

As further confirmation of the generalization, notice that some verbs such as *tell*, *shout* and *call* (belonging to a class to be discussed in section 12.4.2) show an alternation in their complement types. When they occur with *about*+gerund, they select situations and take nearly free control. When they occur with infinitives, they select voluntary actions and take unique control.

(39)   a. Fred$_i$ told/shouted to/called to Louise$_j$ about $_{i/j/i+j/gen}$running the race/
           growing taller.
       b. Fred$_i$ told/shouted to/called to Louise$_j$ to $_{j/*i/*i+j/*gen}$run the race/
           #strike Simmy as smart.

12.4 Unique control by objects and by subjects

We now differentiate some of the cases of unique control. Among the standard
cases of unique control are transitive verbs for which the object is unique
controller, such as *persuade* (20a), and transitive verbs for which the subject is
unique controller, such as *promise* (20b). The *promise* class was Rosenbaum's
(1967) leading exception to his proposed Minimal Distance Principle (MDP),
which claimed to determine the controller uniquely on the basis of counting
nodes from potential controller to the complement in syntactic structure. This
class retains its exceptional status in Hornstein's (1999) approach to control,
which seeks to derive the MDP from constraints on movement.[7] Of course the
MDP fails to account for long distance control in subject complements and for
free and nearly free control in object complements (e.g. *John talked to Sarah
about defending himself*). This suggests that, whatever its attractions, the MDP
should be abandoned forthwith. The question is therefore what accounts for the
difference in controller choice with *persuade* and *promise*.

   The touchstone of semantically based analyses of unique control (see references in section 12.1) is that the difference has something to do with the
meanings of these predicates. Section 12.4.1 reviews the evidence that the
difference between *persuade* and *promise* has to do with semantics, not syntax;
section 12.4.2 reviews two classes of communication verbs and a class of
adjectives with unique control, driving the conclusion home further.

12.4.1 Unique control is determined by semantic roles

The verbs that require their objects to be unique controller span a number of
semantic classes, some of which are shown in (40a–c). There are also verbs and
nominals whose unique controller is the object of a PP complement, seen in
(40d,e).

---

[7] Boeckx and Hornstein (2003), replying to criticisms of Hornstein (1999) in Culicover and
Jackendoff (2001), propose to account for the exceptionality of *promise* by claiming that the
postverbal NP is actually within a PP headed by a null P or by a *to* deleted in PF. However, they
ignore the fact that when there is an *actual* preposition in this position, it does not properly
distinguish between subject control (*vow to NP to VP*) and object control (*depend on NP to VP*);
examples of this sort appeared in Culicover and Jackendoff (2001).

(40) a. John$_i$ forced/helped/enabled/pressured Susan$_j$ to $_{j/*i/*gen}$take care of herself/*himself/*oneself.

b. John$_i$ kept/prevented Susan$_j$ from $_{j/*i/*gen}$taking care of herself/*himself/*oneself.

c. John$_i$ ordered/instructed/encouraged/reminded Susan$_j$ to $_{j/*i/*gen}$take care of herself/*himself/*oneself.

d. John$_i$ counted on/relied on/called upon Susan$_j$ to $_{j/*i/*gen}$take care of herself/*himself/*oneself.

e. John$_i$'s order/instructions/encouragement/reminder to Susan$_j$ to $_{j/*i/*gen}$take care of herself/*himself/*oneself

(41) verifies that the verbs in (40) select for actional complements.

(41) #John forced/helped/enabled/pressured Susan to be tall.
#John kept/prevented Susan from being tall.
#John ordered/instructed/encouraged/reminded Susan to be tall.
#John counted on/relied on/called upon Susan to be tall.

There seems to be only one transitive verb, *promise*, that requires the subject to be the unique controller (42a). But there are several other verbs and adjectives that take PP complements and assign unique control to the subject (42b,c). The nominals of these verbs (42d)also require unique control by the subject, as do quite a few semantically related nominals (42e).[8]

(42) a. John$_i$ promised Susan$_j$ to $_{i/*j/*gen}$take care of himself/*herself/*oneself.

b. John$_i$ vowed to/pledged to/agreed with/is obligated to Susan$_j$ to $_{i/*j/*gen}$take care of himself/*herself/*oneself.

c. John$_i$ learned from Susan$_j$ to $_{i/*j/*gen}$take care of himself/*herself/*oneself.

d. John$_i$'s vow to/pledge to/agreement with/obligation to Susan$_j$ to $_{i/*j/*gen}$take care of himself/*herself/*oneself

e. John$_i$'s offer/guarantee/oath /commitment to Susan$_j$ to $_{i/*j/*gen}$take care of himself/*herself/*oneself

---

[8] Why has the size of this class not been previously recognized? The reason seems to be that people have not looked at the nominals. Most of the verbal counterparts of the nominals in (42e) do not *syntactically* license the relevant argument structure. They do allow an InfP (i); and they do allow an indirect object plus some other complement (ii–iv). But for some reason they exclude the combination of indirect object plus InfP (v); this is presumably a fact of syntactic selection.

(i)   John offered/pledged to leave.
(ii)   John offered a cookie to Susan; John offered Susan a cookie.
(iii) John guaranteed Susan that Fred would come.
(iv)   John pledged to Susan that Fred would come.
(v) * John offered/guaranteed/pledged (to) Susan to leave.

(43) shows that the verbs in (42) select actional complements.

(43) #John promised Susan to be tall.
   #John vowed to/pledged to/agreed with/is obligated to Susan to be tall.
   #John learned from Susan to be tall.

Since (40) and (42) are completely parallel in syntactic constituency, there is no overt syntactic basis for the difference in control. Manipulation of the nominals makes this even clearer. Compare (44), with *order*, and (45), with *promise*.

(44) a. the $_i$order$_j$ to Susan$_j$ from John$_i$ to $_{j/*i}$take care of herself/*himself
   b. John$_i$ gave Susan$_j$ some kind of $_i$order$_j$ to $_{j/*i}$take care of herself/ *himself.
   c. Susan$_j$ got from John$_i$ some kind of $_i$order$_j$ to $_{j/*i}$take care of herself/ *himself.
   d. A: Susan got an order from John. [*or* John gave Susan an order.]
     B: What was it?
     A: I think it was to take care of herself/*himself.
  [also *instructions, encouragement, reminder, invitation, advice*]

(45) a. the $_i$promise$_j$ to Susan$_j$ from John$_i$ to $_{i/*j}$take care of himself/*herself
   b. John$_i$ gave Susan$_j$ some sort of $_i$promise$_j$ to $_{i/*j}$take care of himself/ *herself.
   c. Susan$_j$ got from John$_i$ some sort of $_i$promise$_j$ to $_{i/*j}$take care of himself/ *herself.
   d. A: John made/gave Susan a promise.
     B: What was it?
     A: I think it was to take care of himself/*herself.
  [also *vow, offer, guarantee, pledge, oath*]

These completely elude a solution in terms of syntactic structure: the controller is in too many different positions—including in a previous sentence. The clear generalization is that the complement is controlled by the recipient of the order and the giver/maker of the promise, wherever that character may be located in the syntax. Minimal Distance clearly has nothing to do with what is going on here. (The thematic roles giver and recipient are notated by pre-subscripts and post-subscripts respectively on the nouns. See section 6.5.1 for how the thematic roles of the light verbs are correlated with those of the nominals.)[9]

---

[9] Note that, as in section 12.1, we have given *order* and *promise* in (44b,c) and (45b,c) a specifier that precludes a genitive NP (**John's some sort of order*, *some sort of John's promise*), so it is impossible to treat the controller of the complement as a null NP in the specifier of *order*.

The two paradigms together show that no principle based on syntactic structure can account for controller position, since apart from control the paradigms are syntactically identical. All that varies is the lexical semantics of the nominals *order* and *promise*. Control with the verbs *order* and *promise* follows the same generalization. With both verbs, the role of giver falls in subject position, and recipient falls in object position; hence *order* has object control and *promise* has subject control.[10]

Order of course undergoes a normal passive, in which case the surface subject is controller (46a). This case alone cannot show us whether control is syntactic or semantic. However, *order* and some other verbs in this class permit an impersonal passive of the form (46b)—for which there is no corresponding active (46c).

(46) a. Susan was ordered by John to take care of herself.
      b. It is ordered/advised/encouraged by the authorities not to shoot oneself/*themselves.
      c. ??The authorities order/advise/encourage not to shoot oneself.

The controller in (46b) is not the syntactically overt argument, but rather an implicit generic argument that functions as recipient of the order, advice, or encouragement.

As is well known, the verb *promise* is exceptional in that (47a), the passive of (42a), is ungrammatical—despite the fact that another subcategorization frame of *promise* does passivize (47b), and despite the fact that the corresponding nominal passive (47c) is grammatical. We take this to be a syntactic fact, but have no further explanation.[11]

(47) a. *Susan was promised by John to take care of himself/herself.
      b. Susan was promised a new bike by John.
      c. the promise to Susan by John to take care of himself/*herself

---

Rather, control has to be passed down via conceptual structure, where the giver of the promise is explicitly represented. (This argument appeared in Jackendoff 1974 and Williams 1985.)

[10] This conclusion also has as a consequence that constructional meaning (*à la* Fillmore et al. 1988 and Goldberg 1995) has little to do with the control problem. It is true, as Takagi (2001) observes, that there is a strong bias toward interpreting *NP V NP to VP* as object control, and this may be a default constructional meaning that makes it hard for some speakers (especially young ones, as shown by C. Chomsky (1969)) to get subject control readings. But in the end the choice of control type is a matter of predicate and complement semantics, as revealed especially by the nominals.

[11] The literature recognizes the absence of the passive (47a) as 'Visser's Generalization' (Bresnan 1982b). Pollard and Sag (1994) offer an explanation in terms of their version of binding theory, but they have no explicit solution for why the corresponding nominal (47c) is good.

However a passive *is* possible in the very special case (48) pointed out by Hust and Brame 1976; here, exceptionally, the controller is the surface subject of the passive—the recipient of the promise.

(48)   Susan$_j$ was promised (by John$_i$) to $_{j/*i}$be allowed to take care of herself/ *himself.

Hust and Brame (and many subsequent writers) take this as a fatal counter-example to the thematically based theory of control in Jackendoff (1972); but a little further examination is revealing. The relevant configuration is strikingly narrow: it is fully acceptable only when the complement is a passive verb of permission, as seen from the contrast between (48) and (49a). (49b) shows that the same complement shifts control to the recipient of the promise in the nominal construction. (49c), pointed out by Bresnan (1982b), shows an impersonal passive, closer in form to (49b). (49d,e), from Sag and Pollard (1991), are in our judgment less acceptable than (48) and (49b,c), but certainly better than (49a). We find the previously uncited (49f) better than (49d,e).

(49)   a. * Susan was promised $\left\{ \begin{array}{l} \text{to permit John to leave} \\ \text{to get permission to leave} \\ \text{to leave the room} \\ \text{to be hit on the head} \end{array} \right\}$

     b.   the promise to Susan to be allowed to take care of herself

     c.   It was promised to Susan to be allowed to take care of herself.

     d.   ?Grandma promised the children to be able to stay up for the late show.

     e.   ?Montana was promised (by the doctor) to be healthy by game time on Sunday.

     f.   Susan was promised to be helped/encouraged/enabled to take care of herself.

Thus, if anything, this exceptional case depends *more* heavily on semantics than do the cases cited in (45). In particular, to the extent that (49d–f) are acceptable, it is because the situation described by the complement is more plausible for the recipient of the promise than for the promiser (the source). This case generalizes with a paradigm to appear in section 12.4.2; we will work on a solution in section 12.6.[12]

---

[12] Note, by the way, that the other predicates in this class, *vow*, *guarantee*, and *be obligated*, cannot be substituted into (48), because they do not allow passive of their recipient argument at all. Some of the nominals, such as *offer*, can be substituted into (49b) with no problem; others, such as *obligation*, cannot.

Our other example of a subject control verb, *learn from* (42c), assigns control not to the source (the teacher), but to the recipient, which happens to fall in subject position. Examples like (50) following demonstrate this dependency.

(50) a. It was learned from Susan to take care of ?oneself/*herself.
       b. A: John learned something from Susan.
           B: What was it?
           A: I think it was to take care of himself/*herself.

(*Oneself* in (50a) presumably is appropriate because the impersonal passive has an implicit generic source.)

Further light is thrown on the contrast between the *promise* and *persuade* classes by four predicates that allow either subject or object control: *contract with, bargain with, arrange with*, and *make a deal with*—not surprisingly, semantically related to each other. (51b) shows that these predicates do not have nearly free control, since split antecedents and generic control are not possible.

(51) a. John$_i$ contracted with Susan$_j$ to $_{i/j}$take care of himself/him.
       b. *John$_i$ contracted with Susan$_j$ to $_{i+j/gen}$take care of themselves/oneself.
       [also *bargain with, arrange with, make a deal with*]

Larson (1991) attributes the curious control behavior of the verb *promise* to its occurring syntactically in the ditransitive construction, as in *I never promised you a rose garden.* He compares *promise* to numerous other verbs that do not occur in the ditransitive construction and do not take subject control. However, there are three important omissions in his account. (1) He does not look at all at the behavior of the nominal *promise*, in particular at the facts adduced here, which in fact have been in the literature since at least Jackendoff (1972). (2) He does not look at the verb *pledge*, which, as shown in (42b), does not allow an indirect object with its infinitival complement but still allows subject control. (3) He does not consider the verb *tell*, which has almost the same syntactic distribution as *promise*, in particular occurring in a ditransitive with optional indirect object (*tell (Bill) a story*), yet has object control (section 12.4.2).

The syntactic peculiarities of *promise* are amplified in its evil twin, *threaten*. In particular, when the recipient is present, the complement is gerundive rather than infinitival ((iii)–(iv), (vi)–(viii)); and control can switch to the (underlying) object given the right semantics.

   (i)   Susan threatened Bill.
   (ii)   Susan threatened to punish Bill.
   (iii) * Susan threatened Bill to punish him.
   (iv)   Susan$_i$ threatened Bill$_j$ with *$_i$punishing him/?$_j$being punished.
   (v)   Bill was threatened with being punished/??leaving the room.
   (vi) * Susan's threat to Bill of punishing him/being punished
   (vii) Susan's threat to punish Bill
   (viii) the threat to Bill of being punished
   (ix)   What Susan$_i$ threatened Bill$_j$ with was $_j$being made fun of/??$_i$making fun of him.

We have no explanation of this distribution, which so far as we know has not been explored in the literature.

We think that these verbs, like *rent* (*rent X to Y*/*rent X from Y*), have ambiguous thematic roles. One reading of *contract with* parallels *hire*: the object gets paid by the subject and controls the complement (52a). The other reading parallels *hire oneself out*: the subject gets paid by the object and controls the complement (52b). (52c,d) are another pair with exactly parallel semantics and different syntax.

(52)   a. John$_i$ hired Susan$_j$ to $_{j/*i}$take care of him/*himself.
       b. John$_i$ hired himself out to Susan$_j$ to $_{i/*j}$take care of her/*herself.
       c. John$_i$ gave Susan$_j$ $500 to $_{j/*i}$take care of him/*himself.
       d. John$_i$ got $500 from Susan$_j$ to $_{i/*j}$take care of her/*herself.

In each case the recipient of the money is controller of the complement. We can see no independent motivation for a syntactic difference between the two control possibilities in (51a), nor any plausible candidates for alternative structures.

12.4.2 *Some communication verbs and some adjectives with unique control*

A class of verbs pointed out by Perlmutter (1971) has a paradigm like (53). With infinitival complements, these verbs all express communication of an order or advice, and control generally goes with the addressee, expressed as the object of *to* (53b).

(53)   a. John shouted (to Sally) for Harriet to leave.
       b. John$_i$ shouted to Sally$_j$ to $_{j/*i}$take care of herself/*himself/*themselves.[13]
       [also *say, yell, call, signal*]

Moreover, they all occur with a *that*-complement; many of them also take a gerundive complement with nearly free control. As seen in (39), repeated below, the infinitival complements are restricted to voluntary actions, but the gerundives can be any situation.

---

[13] The complement in (53b) has another reading in which *himself* is acceptable: as a purpose reading, *(In order) to take care of himself, John shouted to Sally*. We are concerned here however with the reading of (53b) in which the complement expresses the content of the speech act.

   We also note the possibility of indirect control, as in *Sherman shouted to Lt. Jones not to fire*, where the order is for the troops to fire, not Lt. Jones himself. However, this case falls under more general phenomena of indirect agency, as in *Sherman/Lt. Jones fired on Atlanta*, so we need not make special provision for it here.

(39)   a. Fred$_i$ shouted/called to Louise$_j$ about $_{i/j/i+j/gen}$running the race/growing taller.

   b. Fred$_i$ shouted/called to Louise$_j$ to $_{j/*i/*i+j/*gen}$run the race/#realize it's raining.

Semantically, *tell* also belongs in this class; but syntactically it differs, in that when it takes a clausal complement, the addressee is expressed as an indirect object.

(54)   John told (*to) Sally to take care of herself.

Control here might be construed here as an ordinary case of the Minimal Distance Principle. However, given the failures of the MDP demonstrated in the previous subsection (especially (44)–(45)), we might instead seek a semantic explanation. In fact, when the addressee is implicit, as in (55), the MDP and semantic accounts make different predictions. The MDP predicts that control should shift to the subject, while the semantic account correctly predicts that control is still assigned to the addressee. (We take it that *yourself* in (55) refers to the implicit addressee.)

(55)   John$_i$ just shouted to $_{j \neq i}$look out for him$_i$/yourself/*himself$_i$/*oneself.

Sag and Pollard (1991: 93) present further examples of this sort, for instance (56a,b) (their (89)). Moreover, if the sentence is explicitly marked as generic, a generic implicit addressee immediately becomes possible (56c).

(56)   a. Mary realized that John had signaled to position herself near the door.

   b. Mary was on the alert. John had signaled to position herself behind the door.

   c. John always signals to position oneself/yourself near the door.

This paradigm closely resembles free control. However, for a number of reasons we believe it is not free control but rather unique control, as our analysis above predicts. First, free control permits any NP in the main clause or above to function as controller; by contrast, the present case specifically excludes control by the subject, who is the agent and source of the communicative act denoted by the verb. Second, free control permits generic control; the present case permits it only in a generic sentence. Third, the interpretation of a communication verb always includes an intended addressee, whether explicit or implicit. When the complement is an infinitival, the controller always turns out to be the addressee, even if determined by pragmatic factors in the discourse. Consider a case like (57).

(57)   John was waving out the window in the direction of some police$_k$ down
        the street. Mary$_j$, standing next to John, realized that he$_i$ was signaling to
        $_{k/*j}$rescue her/*herself.

The context fixes the implicit addressee as *the police*. Consequently the controller must be *the police*, not *Mary*, despite the fact that *Mary* is in the same
structural position as in (56a). We conclude that the discourse effects in (55)–
(57) are due to the pragmatics of determining the implicit addressee, not to how
control is determined.[14]

Paradigms involving nominals, parallel to those for the *promise* and *persuade*
classes, confirm this thematic assignment of control.

(58)   a. the signal from Mary$_i$ to John$_j$ to $_{j/*i}$look out for himself/*herself
        b. Mary$_i$ made some kind of $_i$signal$_j$ to John$_j$ to $_{j/*i}$look out for himself/
            *herself.
        c. John$_j$ got some kind of $_i$signal$_j$ from Mary$_i$ to $_{j/*i}$look out for himself/
            *herself.
        d. A: John got some kind of signal from Mary.
            B: What was it?
            A: I think it was to look out for himself/*herself.
        [also *shout*]

Another class of communication verbs is illustrated in (59); here the complement expresses the content of a request. As with the *shout* class, control
generally goes with the addressee (59a), and the infinitival must express a
voluntary action (59b). The major difference from the *shout* class is that
when the addressee is implicit, control shifts to the source of the speech act
(59c). (Of course, this may look like a classic case of the MDP; we hope that by
now the MDP is sufficiently discredited that we don't have to argue specifically
against it here.)[15]

---

[14] As Sag and Pollard (1991) point out, (55) is an immediate counterexample to what they call
"Bach's generalization" (Bach 1979): that object control verbs do not permit omission of their
object. We therefore disregard various attempts in the literature to account for this nonfact. One
such attempt is that of Manzini (1983b), who posits a null NP serving as addressee in such
examples, thereby saving both Bach's generalization and her own claim that object complements
must have controllers in the immediately dominating clause; we have addressed this claim above in
section 12.2.3 and return to it in a moment.

[15] *Ask* is unusual in this class in also permitting a gerundive complement with nearly free
control, as in *Bill asked Sue about taking care of herself/himself/themselves/oneself*; the other verbs
in this class do not. *Scream* seems ambiguous between this class and the *shout* class, presumably
related to the fact that screaming is more readily construed as a request for help than shouting is.

(59)   a. John$_i$ asked Sally$_j$ to $_{j/*i}$take care of herself/*himself.
       b. John asked Sally to run the race/#realize it's raining.
       c. John$_i$ asked to $_i$take care of himself$_i$/*him$_i$/*oneself/*yourself.
       [also *request*, *beg*]

(60)–(62) add further members of the class with different syntactic properties but parallel semantics and identical control properties.

(60)   a. John pleaded (with Sally) for Harriet to leave.
       b. John$_i$ pleaded with Sally$_j$ to $_{j/*i}$take care of herself/*himself.
       c. John$_i$ pleaded to take care of himself$_i$/*him$_i$/*oneself/*yourself.

(61)   a. John prayed (to Athena) for Harriet to leave.
       b. John$_i$ prayed to Athena$_j$ to $_{j/*i}$take care of herself/*himself.
       c. John$_i$ prayed (to be able) to $_i$take care of himself.
       [also *appeal*]

(62)   a. John beseeched *(Sally) (for Harriet) to leave.
       b. John$_i$ beseeched Sally$_j$ to $_{j/*i}$take care of herself/*himself.
       c. *John beseeched to leave. [bad because addressee is syntactically obligatory]

As with various other classes we have examined, the syntactic variation among these verbs and the overlap of their syntax with other classes preclude a syntactic solution to control. In particular, suppose one were to adopt a solution to the *shout* verbs (like that of Manzini (1983b)) in which a null addressee in syntax controlled the infinitive structurally. Then, by parallelism, the *ask* verbs in (59)–(62) should also have a null addressee in syntax, and it too should control the infinitive. The contrast between (55) and (59c) shows that this is the wrong solution; hence we have another case where syntactic structure cannot determine control.

Again we can test for thematically determined control, using situations in which the controller varies its syntactic position but retains its thematic role.

(63)   a. the plea by John$_i$ to Athena$_j$ to $_{j/*i}$take care of herself/*himself
       b. Athena$_j$ received a $_j$plea$_j$ from John$_i$ to $_{j/*i}$take care of herself/*himself.
       c. John$_i$ made a $_i$plea$_j$ to Athena$_j$ to $_{j/*i}$take care of herself/*himself.
       d. A: John made a plea to Athena for something.
          B: What was it?
          A: I think it was to take care of herself/*himself.
       [also *request*, *prayer*]

In addition to switching control with an implicit addressee, these verbs are also capable of shifting control even when the addressee is explicit—if the VP

complement is of a certain sort (64a); the same complements are simply ungrammatical with the *shout* class (64b)—unless the verb is construed pragmatically as conveying a request.[16]

(64) a. John$_i$ asked/begged/beseeched Sally$_j$ to $_{i/*j}$be allowed to defend
          himself/*herself.
          John$_i$ pleaded with Sally$_j$ to $_{i/*j}$be allowed to defend himself/*herself.
          John$_i$ prayed to Athena$_j$ to $_{i/*j}$be allowed to defend himself/*herself.
      b. *John shouted/said/yelled/signaled to Sally to be allowed to defend
          himself/herself.

A parallel contrast appears in the corresponding nominals.

(65) *Indirect requests*
      a. John$_i$'s request to Sally$_j$ to $_{j/*i}$defend herself/*himself
      b. John$_i$'s request to Sally$_j$ to $_{i/*j}$be allowed to defend himself/*herself
      Indirect orders or advice
      c. John$_i$'s shout to Sally$_j$ to $_{j/*i}$defend herself/*himself
      d. * John's shout to Sally to be allowed to defend herself/himself

Strikingly, the complements that permit this shift of control are the same ones
that allow shift of control in the *promise* class:

(66) a. John$_i$ asked Sally$_j$ to $_{i/*j}$be allowed/able/encouraged/helped/enabled to
          leave.
      b. He$_i$ begged me$_j$ to $_{i/*j}$be able to stop taking German.
                                                [recorded in conversation]

   The usual tests with nominals show that the shift of controller is thematic, i.e.
to source, not to subject:

(67) a. a plea to Sally$_j$ from John$_i$ to $_{i/*j}$be allowed to defend himself/*herself
      b. John$_i$ offered a $_i$prayer to Athena$_j$ to $_{i/*j}$be able to defend himself/
          *herself.
      c. Athena$_j$ received a $_i$request$_j$ from John$_i$ to $_{i/*j}$be able to defend himself/
          *herself.
      d. A: John offered a prayer to Athena for something.

---

[16] In some examples in the literature there appears to be controller shift:

(i) The car signaled to turn left. (Sag and Pollard 1991)
(ii) The goalkeeper signaled (to the coach) to be replaced. (Růžička 1999)

We find (i) interpretable but a bit strange. In (ii), the goalkeeper is requesting an action, so *signal* is
being used pragmatically as a verb of the *ask* class—thereby predicting this behavior.

B: What was it?

A: I think it was to be able to defend himself/*herself.

Sag and Pollard (1991), as part of their thematically based theory of control, propose a solution to the controller shift in passive permission complements of *ask* and *promise* verbs. We agree with the spirit of their solution but find it needs some emendation. We return to this problem in section 12.6.

For a final case of unique control, consider a class of adjectives that select voluntary actions as subject complements. These clearly fall into a couple of relatively delimited semantic classes.

(68) a. ᵢCalling Ernie/#Growing taller was rude/thoughtful of Bertᵢ.
      b. It was rude/thoughtful of Bertᵢ to ᵢcall Ernie/#ᵢrealize it's raining.
      [also *polite, considerate, helpful, boorish, stupid, wise, smart, clever*]

The UCAC Hypothesis predicts that these selected actional complements should have unique control, and in fact they do.

(69) Amyⱼ thinks that ᵢ/*ⱼ/*ᵢ₊ⱼ/*ₘₑₙcalling attention to himself/*herself/*them-selves/*oneself/*myself was rude of Bertᵢ.

This observation is fatal to the second half of Manzini's (1983b) putative generalization: that, in our terms, control in a subject complement is always free control. Control is semantically parallel in an alternate syntactic form with an object complement (70a), as well as in the nominal form (70b).

(70) a. Amyⱼ thinks that Bertᵢ was rude to ᵢ/*ⱼ/*ᵢ₊ⱼ/*ₘₑₙcall attention to himself/*herself/*themselves/*oneself/*myself.
      b. Amyⱼ ignored Bertᵢ's rudeness in ᵢ/*ⱼ/*ᵢ₊ⱼ/*ₘₑₙcalling attention to him-self/*herself/*themselves/*oneself/*myself.

Thus unique control again appears to be correlated with the semantic type of the predicate, and not with the syntactic position of the complement and controller; here control goes with the actor of the clause or NP dominating the complement.

The semantic nature of control here is further confirmed by situations in which the actor is implicit in the clause dominating the complement.

(71) a. Bertᵢ doesn't realize that ᵢ/ₘₑₙcalling attention to himself/oneself is rude.
      b. Amyⱼ is in big trouble: Bertᵢ feels that ⱼtalking to himᵢ that way was rude.
      c. Amyⱼ is in big trouble: Bertᵢ can't stand such rudeness in ⱼtalking to himᵢ that way.

This looks superficially like free control. However, notice that in every case the controller is the person who is being rude—i.e. the controller is still the actor, a character explicit in conceptual structure but implicit in syntax.[17] In short, the apparent free control in (71a) is actually due to freedom in assigning the implicit actor role. This precisely parallels the account of implicit addressee controllers with the verbs of communication such as *shout*.

12.5 Toward a semantically based theory of unique control

The previous section has established two descriptive generalizations. First, heads (verbs, nouns, and adjectives) that select actional complements govern unique control. Second, the unique controller is determined by the thematic roles that the head assigns to its arguments. However, the thematic role that identifies the controller differs from one semantic class of heads to the next. We now work out a somewhat deeper account of these generalizations.

First consider the conceptual structure associated with a controlled VP. Because all the arguments of the verb are saturated except the subject, the overall form of the conceptual structure is a function of one variable. A subset of such VPs denote actions. For present purposes it is not critical how this subset is formalized; let us use the notation $x\ ACT$ for action VPs.[18] Then a predicate that selects for an actional complement will designate the semantic argument in question as of the type $[x\ ACT]$.

What semantic predicates select for actional complements? One of the insights of Pollard and Sag (1994) and of Van Valin and LaPolla (1997) is that the lexical items that govern unique control fall into a delimited number of semantic classes, and that each class determines a particular thematic role that serves as controller. We attribute this fact to the existence of a limited number of basic predicates in CS that select actions as arguments; each of these can serve as a component of the meaning of verbs, nouns, and/or adjectives. Crucially for our purposes, each basic predicate establishes a control relation—a type of semantic binding—between its action argument and one of its other arguments. The syntactic control behavior exhibited by a particular word containing one of

---

[17] And this character cannot be represented in syntax by a null NP: we have chosen the form of (71c) to preclude an NP in the relevant position.

[18] *ACT* can be understood as a general cover term feature for actions, as a feature of action predicates, or as the name of the category that contains actions, depending on one's theory of semantic decomposition. In the notation of Jackendoff (1990a), the relevant class of VPs are those that contain *AFF(x,)* on their action tier.

these basic predicates is then a consequence of how the arguments of the basic control predicate are mapped into syntax.[19]

Let us enumerate some of the more prominent cases of basic semantic predicates that select actional complements. Perhaps the simplest to explicate is *intention*. Contrast your *believing you will do X* (a situational complement) with your *intending to do X* (an actional complement). The difference is that in the case of an intention you are committed to playing an active role in making X take place—to executing the intention. Now, although someone else can *believe* you will do X, no one else can *execute your intention* to do X. That is, someone who holds an intention is necessarily identical with the individual who executes the intended action. (An apparent counterexample is *A intends for B to do X*. But in fact this sentence implicitly conveys an intended action on the part of A to *bring it about* that B does X. We deal with this case and other potential counterexamples in section 12.6.)

The predicate *intend* is thus a two-place function, one of whose arguments is an animate entity, the intender, and the other of which is an action. The point of the above observation is that the Actor of the action argument of *intend* is necessarily bound to the intender. (See Jackendoff (1995; to appear, a: ch. 6) for a more detailed analysis of intending and its relation to believing.)

The structure of the predicate can thus be notated something like (72). In (72a), as in Chapters 5 and 6, we notate argument positions and the semantic restrictions on them (selectional restrictions) in italics. As in Chapters 6, 10, and 11, a bound position is notated by a Greek variable, which corresponds to a superscript on the binder. (72a) uses the notation for predicates and their arguments used throughout this study so far. (72b) says the same thing in a slightly simplified notation that will help us get through the thickets of embedding to come: instead of enclosing both arguments in parentheses after the function, the first argument comes before the function and the second argument comes after it.

(72)   a. standard notation: $[INTEND\ (X^{\alpha},\ [ACT(\alpha)])]$
       b. simplified notation: $X^{\alpha}\ INTEND\ [\alpha\ ACT]$

As a consequence of the inherent binding within the predicate *intend*, any verb that contains this predicate as part of its meaning will have a control

---

[19] Pollard and Sag's Control Theory (1994: 288, 302) enumerates three such predicates: influence (including causation), commitment (including intention and promising), and orientation (including desire and expectation). We think this approach is on the right track, but that one need not extract a special principle of grammar called "control theory". Rather, we would like the control properties of heads to follow insofar as possible directly from their meanings, couched in terms of conceptual structure.

equation in which the intender uniquely controls the actional complement. Besides the verb *intend* itself, this class includes *decide* 'come to intend', and *persuade* 'cause to come to intend'. In the latter case, the intender appears in object position and therefore the verb exhibits object control.

Another predicate that selects an actional argument is obligation. This is a function of three arguments: person A is obligated to person B to perform some action. One cannot be obligated to perform someone else's action; i.e. the action is necessarily bound to the person under obligation. Person B is the person who benefits from the obligation being performed; this may or may not be the same person who has imposed the obligation on A (Jackendoff 1999; to appear, a: ch. 9). Note that obligation is not a special case of intention: one can have an obligation with no intention of carrying it out, and one can intend some action without being obliged to do it.

More formally, the basic semantic structure of obligation is therefore something like (73a); a more ramified notation like (73b) makes explicit the connection of the beneficiary to the action.[20]

(73)   a. X^α OBLIGATED $[\alpha\ ACT]$ TO Y

   b. $\begin{bmatrix} X^\alpha \text{ OBLIGATED } [\alpha\ ACT]^\beta \\ \beta \text{ BENEF Y} \end{bmatrix}$

The notion of obligation plays a rich role in control verbs. *Ordering* involves an individual in authority imposing an obligation on someone to perform an action. The person under obligation falls in object position, so the verb *order* is an object control verb. *Instructing* someone to do something conveys a similar sense (though instructing someone *how* to do something is different). For a different configuration, *promising* is undertaking an obligation to the promissee. Since in this case the person under obligation falls in subject position, this is a subject control verb. Most of the subject control predicates of section 12.4.1 are of this type: *pledging*, *vowing*, *taking an oath*, *guaranteeing*, and so on. Verbs like *contract with*, *hire*, and *hire oneself out* describe a transfer of money in exchange for an obligation to perform an action; the character that receives the money undertakes the obligation, and is therefore the controller.

Another basic semantic predicate that selects an actional argument is ability—a relation between an entity and an action. One cannot have an ability with respect to someone else's performance of an action; that is, the person with the ability must be bound to the actor position in the action:

---

[20] In the notation of Jackendoff (1990a), the beneficiary role is indicated by the Y argument in the function $AFF^+(,Y)$ on the action tier.

(74) X^α ABLE $[\alpha$ ACT]

This predicate is a component of the adjective *able*, the noun *ability*, and the root modal *can*. It is also a component of one sense of *learn to VP*, roughly 'come to be able to VP' and *teach NP to VP*, roughly 'cause to come to be able to VP'. Thus *learn* is a subject control verb and *teach* ('instruct how to') is an object control verb.

Another sense of *learn to VP* involves normativity, as in *Elmer learned not to wear sneakers to work*. This implies both that Elmer learned that it is a norm not to wear sneakers to work, and also that he came to comply with that norm. Another sort of normativity appears in *remind NP to VP*, which carries the sense that NP is supposed to VP (because of either obligation or social norm); similarly, *remember to VP* and *forget to VP* carry the presupposition that the subject is supposed to VP. The basic predicate for normativity appears to range over the various senses of the root modal *should*. Again there is an inherent control equation: one cannot, by performing some action, comply with the norm that someone else is supposed to perform that action. So the predicate looks something like (75).

(75) X^α SHOULD$_{root}$ $[\alpha$ ACT]

The consequence is that *learn to, is supposed to, remember to,* and *forget to* are subject control predicates and *remind to* is an object control predicate.

A slightly more complicated case involves the class of force-dynamic predicates (Talmy 1985; Jackendoff 1990a). These include predicates of causing, preventing, enabling, and helping; they also include variants in which the outcome is uncertain, such as pressuring and hindering; they include predicates both in the physical domain such as pushing and in the social domain such as encouraging. Talmy and Jackendoff analyze all of these as featural variants of a basic configuration: one character, the antagonist or agent, is involved in influencing the execution of an action by another character, the agonist. The features include:

(76)   a. Agent is working toward the execution of the action (e.g. causing, forcing) vs. Agent is working against the execution of the action (e.g. preventing)

   b. Action is completed (causing, forcing) vs. possibly incomplete (pressuring, hindering)

   c. Agonist, in absence of agent's influence, would not (attempt to) execute action (e.g. forcing), vs. agonist would naturally (attempt to)

execute action (e.g. helping), vs. Agonist would be unable to execute
action (e.g. enabling, permitting)

The basic configuration looks like (77), where CS is the basic predicate to which
the feature distinctions in (76) are applied.

(77)   X CS Y$^\alpha$ [α ACT]

This is of course the control configuration in all the causative verbs like *force,
help, assist, enable, prevent, hinder, pressure, encourage, discourage, permit,
allow,* and so on. Because the agent always maps onto subject position, these are
all object control verbs.[21]

What more conventional thematic role is assigned to the agonist? When the
Agent is working against the agonist's natural tendencies (the first option in
(76c), the agonist passes the standard test for patients (78a). When the agent is
working with the agonist's natural tendencies (the second and third options in
(76c), the agonist behaves like a beneficiary (78b).

(78)   a. What Pat did to/#for Stan was force him to leave/pressure him to quit/
           prevent him from talking.
       b. What Pat did for/#to Stan was help him leave/enable him to quit/allow
           him not to talk.

This observation will play a role in the next section.

The communication predicates like *shout* and *signal* now fall under our
analysis. The meanings of these verbs appear to have two parts. First, the

---

[21] At least some force-dynamic predicates display another configuration as well. In *The gas
caused an explosion, The gas prevented a fire,* and *The window lets the light come in,* the subject is
not acting *on* anything, it is just causing or preventing an event pure and simple. In this case there is
no independent agonist; rather the agonist and the action are coalesced into a simple event, the
Effect, as in (i).

(i) X CS [EVENT]

This provides an explanation of cases like (ii).

(ii) a. Bill prevented there from being an explosion.
      b. The new phone system enabled tabs to be kept on our private calls.

Here the expletive NP and the idiom chunk are obviously not arguments of the main verb; they
play a role only in the interpretation of the subordinate clause. Thus, although these verbs are
usually control verbs, here they look like raising to object or ECM verbs. The explanation is that
the raising/ECM configuration is a mismatch between semantic argument structure, where there is
a single situational argument such as that in (i), and syntactic argument structure, where there is an
NP plus infinitive. The NP has no argument role in the main clause, only in the subordinate clause.
This is the standard HPSG/LFG account; see also the discussion of *prevent* and *begin* in section 6.2
and the discussion of *tough*-movement in section 9.6.

speaker is trying to influence the addressee to perform the action denoted by the complement—i.e. these verbs are in part force-dynamic verbs. The addressee, being agonist, is controller. Second, the speaker's means of exerting influence is by communicating either an order or advice described by the VP complement. An order is the imposition of an obligation on the addressee; by (73), the person under obligation is controller of the action. Therefore the addressee of the order has to be controller. Advice is normative: you *should* do such-and-such. So conveying advice invokes schema (75), and again the addressee is controller. Requesting is also attempting to influence the addressee to perform some action, so once again the addressee is the controller. However, asking someone to do something is neither conveying an order nor giving advice. What seems to make requesting different is that the requester is saying 'do such-and-such *for me*': the addressee of a request is the actor of the action as usual, but in addition the speaker is explicit or implicit beneficiary of the action. Using the notation for beneficiary in (73b), we arrive at the rather complex schema in (79).

$$(79) \quad X^\alpha \text{ REQUEST } Y^\beta \begin{bmatrix} [\beta \text{ ACT}]^\gamma \\ \gamma \text{ BENEF } \alpha \end{bmatrix}$$

This says that the requested act is performed by the addressee of the request (indexed β), and that the act itself (indexed γ) is for the benefit of the requester (indexed α). Complexity on this order seems inescapable in a description of what it means to request (and there are undoubtedly subtleties we have not yet captured).

Finally, the adjectives with unique control have the curious characteristic of ascribing the same property to an actor as to his or her action. Spitting in public is a rude action; so someone who spits in public is a rude person. It is not clear how to formalize this, but the control equation is intuitively obvious: one cannot have such a property on the basis of someone else's action. So control follows from the semantics again.

Let us contrast the basic predicates in (72)–(79), which select actional complements, with the nearly free control predicates. As observed in section 12.2, nearly free control occurs in gerundive complements of verbs of communication and thought and in complements of nouns that denote information-bearing objects such as *book* and *hypothesis*, usually but not always with the preposition *about*. The controlled complement always denotes a proposition being communicated, considered, or contained in an information-bearing object (as in *a book about defending oneself*). Crucially, the characters transmitting and receiving information need bear no relation to the content of the information being transmitted. Thus there is no necessary semantic constraint on control as there is in the predicates in (72)–(79).

Let us also re-examine the situations with true free control presented in section 12.2.3. Complements with free control occur both in object complements (80a–c) and in subject complements (80d,e).[22]

(80)   a. Jeff thinks that this outcome beats undressing himself/oneself/myself/ yourself/ourselves [=you and me, Jeff and me] in public.

[also outranks, is as good as, feels like]

       b. Jeff thinks that this outcome entails undressing himself/oneself/myself/ yourself/ourselve's [=you and me, Jeff and me] in public.

[also requires]

       c. Jeff makes undressing himself/oneself/myself/yourself/ourselves[=you and me, Jeff and me] in public almost attractive.

       d. Undressing himself$_i$/oneself/myself/yourself in public wouldn't help Jeff$_i$.

          Jeff$_i$ is in big trouble. Undressing himself$_i$ in public has caused a big scandal.

       e. It wouldn't help Jeff$_i$ to undress himself$_i$/oneself/myself/yourself in public.

          Jeff$_i$ is in big trouble. It's caused a scandal to undress himself$_i$ in public.

These predicates select situational complements: examples like *Being taller wouldn't help Jeff* and *Jeff's being fat caused a scandal* are grammatical. Thus our generalization correctly predicts that they do not have unique control. These complements are also not understood in the way characteristic of nearly free control: as information being conveyed or understood by one of the characters in the sentence.

The predicates in (80a) compare one situation to another; those in (80b) describe contingencies between two situations. Now notice that the remaining three verbs in (80) are force-dynamic verbs: *cause, help,* and *make*.[23] However, here the complement clauses do not correspond to the Effect argument, as they do in the standard cases such as *X forced Y to VP*. Rather, the subject complements in (80d,e) are the agent/causer argument—a situation is causing or

---

[22] The standard examples of free control are subject complements of experiencer predicates, e.g. *Amy thinks that undressing herself in public would bother Tom.* We have used examples here with non-experiencer predicates, because we suspect that experiencer predicates have special control properties, requiring at least defeasibly that the experiencer control the complement. It is also possible that experiencer predicates fall under what Kuno (1987) and Williams (1992) call "logophoric control"; since logophoricity depends on semantics, such a solution supports our overall argument. But we have not worked through the details and this chapter is long enough already.

[23] Under Talmy's construal of force-dynamics, *entail* and *require* are also force-dynamic verbs, in the logical rather than the physical or social domain.

helping something to happen; and the object complement in (80c) is the agonist/patient argument—Jeff is making this situation become attractive.[24] The basic schema for force-dynamic verbs (77) says nothing to restrict control in these arguments, so they govern free control. The contrast between these cases and the standard cases (e.g. *Mary made John shoot himself/*herself*) shows that control cannot be determined by simply marking a verb "object control": it is a particular *argument configuration* of the verb rather than the verb as a whole over which the control equation is defined.

To sum up this section, we have shown how unique control is determined by the meanings of the predicates that govern it. For example, *promise* means 'undertake an obligation', and its control behavior follows from the inherent control equations of its constituent basic predicates. The verb could not mean the same thing and display different control. In particular, controller position is determined by semantic argument structure and not syntactic position. Moreover, we have explained the connection between unique control and actional complements: a variety of basic predicates that select actional complements have inherent control equations. We have not by any means dealt with the whole range of control predicates, but we have shown the plausibility of our approach in a significant range of cases.

12.6 Coercion that shifts control

According to the story of unique control so far, a basic predicate that selects an actional argument inherently assigns control of this argument to a particular one of its other arguments. We now deal with two cases in which the designated

---

[24] We should also remember a class of examples observed by Postal (1970) in which the predicates come from the classes in (80a,b), and both the subject and object are controlled VPs. Significantly, control in the two must match (ii).

(i)   Amy knows that shaving herself/myself/oneself is like torturing herself/myself/oneself.
(ii) * Amy knows that shaving herself is like torturing myself/oneself.

In (iii) the two freely controlled complements are both in the VP and again control must match. (iv) has yet another combination, not quite the same.

(iii) Fred makes shaving myself like torturing myself/*oneself/*himself.
(iv) Shaving himself reminds Fred of torturing himself/oneself.
     Shaving oneself reminds Fred of torturing oneself/*himself.

We have no explanation for either this need for matching or for the asymmetry in (iv). More complex cases are cited by Chomsky (1972) (though he does not note the possible asymmetry):

(v)   Shaving himself makes John think of torturing himself/oneself.
(vi) Shaving himself brings to John's mind the idea of torturing himself/oneself.
(vii) Shaving himself appears to John as pointless as torturing himself/oneself.

character does not end up as controller. The second of these cases includes the exceptions with *promise* and the control shifts with *ask*. Following the approach of Sag and Pollard (1991), Pollard and Sag (1994), and Panther and Köpcke (1993), we argue that each of these cases is indicative not of defects in the basic theory, but rather of further complications going on in the syntax–semantics interface that fall under the class of specialized coercions.

12.6.1 *The* bring about *coercion*

According to the description of intention in the previous section, a verb of intending should not permit a local subject, since an intender cannot intend some else's action. However, this prediction is immediately counterexemplified by the most basic verbs of intending, *intend* and *plan*. Both allow an InfC (81a); *intend* also allows a *that*-subjunctive (81b) and *plan* a *that*-indicative complement (81c). What's worse, such complements can describe non-voluntary situations as well as actions (81d–f).

(81)   a. Hilary intends/plans for Ben to come along to the party.
       b. Hilary intends that Ben come along to the party.
       c. Hilary plans that Ben will come along to the party.
       d. Hilary plans for Ben to understand physics.
                                    [*Ben voluntarily understands physics.]
       e. Hilary plans for the cat to be fed.   [*The cat is voluntarily fed.]
       f. Hilary plans for there to be more light in here.
                                    [*There is voluntarily more light in here.]

   The resolution to this apparent anomaly comes from observing that these sentences can be paraphrased approximately by (82).

(82)   a. Hilary intends/plans *to bring it about* that Ben comes along to the party/understands physics.
       b. Hilary plans *to bring it about* that the cat be fed.
       c. Hilary plans *to bring it about* that there is more light in here.

Hilary's intended action in (81), then, is understood to be a bringing about of the situation expressed in the complement. These *are* actions that Hilary can execute, restoring the generalization that one's intentions can be executed only by oneself.

   We can verify this analysis by noting that the *InfC* and *that* complements of *intend* and *plan* have to be situations that *can* be brought about by voluntary actions. So, for instance, in (81), *Ben understands physics* and *the cat is fed* are not voluntary actions, but they can be voluntarily brought about (by someone other than Ben and the cat respectively). By contrast, a situation that cannot be voluntarily brought about by *anyone* is still unacceptable in these complements (except under a scenario where, say, Nancy is a calendar reformer and Louise is casting a movie):

(83)   a. #Nancy intends for next year to be 1636.
       b. #Louise plans for Fred to be six years younger.

This contrasts with true situational complements, in which such situations are still normally acceptable:

(84)   a. For next year to be 1636 would be astounding.
       b. Louise wished for Fred to be six years younger.

This notion of bringing about is not explicitly present in any of the sentence's lexical items. Where does it come from? Any time we find a paraphrase relation like that between (81) and (82), where the paraphrases differ only in the presence of some extra material, we have the marks of a *coercion*—a conventionalized omission of semantic material in syntactic expression. The mechanisms for licensing such extra material in the interpretation are discussed in section 4.12.3.[25]

In the *intend/plan* cases, *intend* and *plan* select semantically for a controlled actional complement, but they select syntactically for the marked complements illustrated in (81), which denote noncontrolled situations. This creates a conflict in composing the meaning, shown in (85a). Thus the principle of coercion must step in, reinterpreting the complement as the action 'bring about Situation'. Formally the content of the coercion is our old friend *CAUSE* (probably in the two-argument version of n. 21 above). And now the control equation of *intend* can be imposed on *this* action, as shown in (85b). Thus control of the VP diverges from the intender just in case there is a coercion. (As in section 6.5.3, the notation in (85) is a way of reflecting how the meaning of a sentence is carved into its parts.)

---

[25] Pollard and Sag treat the coercion involved in control as a lexical rule that adds the semantic material in question to the head verb before it combines with the rest of the sentence. We do not find such an approach conducive to a general treatment of coercion. For instance, it is odd to think of *ham sandwich* as undergoing a lexical rule to form a new lexical item that means *person with a ham sandwich*. Our preference is to see the coerced material as a conventionalized but freely available piece of semantic structure that is inserted to avoid anomaly. In any event, we concur with Pollard and Sag in emphatically *not* regarding coercion as the deletion of *words* from a syntactic structure, as in old-fashioned transformational grammar, nor as the deletion of empty nodes from syntax. See Jackendoff (1990a: ch. 3) for discussion.

(85) a. X^α INTEND   *[α ACT]*
             ⇑   *⇑
             HILARY   [BEN COME]

      b. X^α INTEND   *[α ACT]*
             ⇑   ⇑
             HILARY   *[Y CAUSE [SITUATION]]*
                                  ⇑
                                  [BEN COME]

This solution comes with an interesting price. *Intend* and *plan* both select semantically for actional complements. But they select syntactically for a broader range of complements, some of which cannot serve as appropriate semantic arguments of the verb except through the use of coercion. The effect is that the relatively narrow selectional restrictions of these verbs are masked by the broader range of coerced complements—situations that can be voluntarily brought about. In other words, we are forced to accept a more severe mismatch between syntactic and semantic argument structure than is generally admitted.

12.6.2 *The* someone allow *coercion*

Consider now (86), a case from section 12.4.2.

(86)   John asked/begged/pleaded to take care of himself.

Section 12.4.2 and 12.5 argued that the predicates of requesting take an actional complement whose controller is normally the addressee. However, we noted that this class has an unusual shift of control—for instance in (86) the speaker is controller. We now attempt to explain this shift.

One might suggest applying the *bring about* coercion to this case, so that (86) is interpreted as (87) (implicit material in boldface).

(87)   John asked **someone to bring it about that he** take care of himself.

In (87) the implicit addressee controls the action, as it should. Since the control equation is discharged by the implicit addressee, the subject of the complement is therefore free to bind to *John*.

However, under this solution, we should also predict that the coercion also applies to the verbs of communication such as *shout*. That is, *John shouted to go* should have the possible (and plausible) meaning 'John$_i$ shouted to someone to bring it about that he$_i$ go'. But it doesn't: it can only mean 'John shouted to someone$_i$ that he$_i$ should go'. What is responsible for the difference?

We believe that the difference arises from the difference between requests on one hand and orders or advice on the other. *John asked to go* is a report of a request for permission: 'May I go?' By contrast, in the absence of context, *John shouted to go* is a report of an imperative: 'Go!' Thus a better paraphrase of (86) is (88). (88b) spells out the addressee implicit in (88a), and, as we would expect, the addressee controls the action.

(88) a. John asked **to be allowed** to go.
      b. John asked **someone to allow him** to go.

This suggests that the coercion with *ask* abbreviates not the semantic material '...bring it about that...' but rather a different force-dynamic relation: '...allow/enable X to...', where X is bound to the asker in conceptual structure.[26]

Why should such a coercion be more plausible with asking than with shouting? Panther and Köpcke (1993) suggest that the difference has to do with the role of the beneficiary. An asker, unlike a shouter, is a beneficiary of the addressee's action, and the character to whom permission is granted is also a beneficiary. An attempt at formalizing this coercion appears in (89). (89a) shows the individual pieces and where they are plugged into each other, with the coercion in boldface; (89b) shows the composed semantic structure (in which coinciding binding indices are resolved into a single index).

(89) John asked to take care of himself

$$
\text{a.} \quad X^\alpha \quad \text{REQUEST } Y^\beta \quad \begin{bmatrix} [\beta \ ACT]^\gamma \\ \gamma \ BENEF\alpha \end{bmatrix}
$$

$$
\Uparrow \qquad\qquad\qquad\qquad \Uparrow
$$

$$
\text{JOHN} \qquad\qquad \begin{bmatrix} [Z \ \textbf{ENABLE } W^\delta \ [\delta \ ACT]]^\in \\ \in \textbf{BENEF } \delta \end{bmatrix}
$$

$$
\Uparrow
$$

$$
[\zeta \ \text{TAKE CARE OF SELF}]
$$

$$
\text{b. JOHN}^\alpha \ \text{REQUEST } Y^\beta \quad \begin{bmatrix} [\beta \ \textbf{ENABLE } \alpha \ [\alpha \ \text{TAKE CARE OF SELF}]]^\gamma \\ \gamma \ \textbf{BENEF } \alpha \end{bmatrix}
$$

---

[26] Růžička (1999) is largely concerned with explaining such shifts with *ask* and *promise*. Lacking the notion of coercion, he resorts to (what we find) complex and unintuitive conditions on theta-grids. Eventually, though, he adverts (p. 61) to "silent" *be allowed*, without any characterization other than conventionally motivated compression or conceptual-pragmatic "reconstruction", which is essentially our solution here. What is interesting about his account is his claim that (in our terms) languages differ in whether they permit (or have conventionalized) these coercions involved in control, a point made also by Panther and Köpcke (1993) (see below). It is also our impression that Farkas's (1988) insightful treatment of control in terms of responsibility is somewhat loose because the mechanism of coercion was not known at the time of her work.

Thus the standard semantics of *ask* assigns control for the action to its addressee (index β in (89a)), and binds the asker to the beneficiary of the action (index α). When the coercion is plugged into the requested action, the addressee becomes the enabler and the asker becomes the enablee. In turn, the coercion imposes its own binding conditions: the enablee performs the action enabled (index δ). Thus through this chain of binding, the asker comes to control the complement.

The crucial piece that establishes connection between the asker and the complement is the beneficiary role. It is the fact that this role is connected both to the asker and the enablee that permits the asker to be connected to the enablee and therefore to control the complement. This piece is missing with the *shout* verbs, which is why such a coercion does not work with these verbs.

This solution suggests a direct connection to the other problematic case with the *ask* verbs:

(90)   John asked Susan to be allowed to take care of himself.

Sag and Pollard (1991) observe that *to be allowed to take care of himself* is not a voluntary action, and therefore that it does not satisfy the semantic selection of *ask*. They propose to invoke the *bring about* coercion, claiming that the coerced form of (90) is the interpretation (91).

(91)   John asked Susan *to bring about that he* be allowed to take care of himself.

While we agree that the interpretation of (90) involves a coercion, we disagree with Sag and Pollard's invocation of the *bring about* coercion, for the same reasons we argued against it in (87): it is too broadly applicable. It predicts incorrectly that (92) should be acceptable, under the interpretation shown.

(92)   *John asked Susan to be forced to leave.
         (= 'John asked Susan to *bring it about that* he be forced to leave')
       *John asked Susan to understand physics.
         (= 'John asked Susan to *bring it about that* he understand physics')

Our proposal is that in this case the complement is unified with (or overlaid on) the *allow/enable* coercion, instead of being plugged into its variable. The pieces of the interpretation are shown in (93a), and the composed structure appears in (93b).

(93) John asked Susan to be allowed to take care of himself.

$$\text{a. } X^\alpha \text{ REQUEST } Y^\beta \begin{bmatrix} [\beta \ ACT]^\gamma \\ \gamma \ BENEF \ \alpha \end{bmatrix} \qquad\qquad [X \text{ ask } Y \text{ to act}]$$

$$\underset{\text{JOHN}}{\Uparrow} \qquad \underset{\text{SUSAN}}{\Uparrow} \quad \begin{bmatrix} [Z \ ENABLE \ W^\delta \ [\delta \ ACT]]^\epsilon \\ \epsilon \ BENEF \ \delta \end{bmatrix} \qquad \begin{matrix} [\text{coercion: } Z \text{ enable} \\ W \text{ to act}] \end{matrix}$$

$$\begin{bmatrix} [U \ ENABLE \ V^\zeta \ [\zeta \ ACT]]^\eta \\ \eta \ BENEF \ \zeta \end{bmatrix} \qquad [V \text{ be allowed by } U \text{ to act}]$$

$$\Uparrow$$

$$[T \text{ TAKE CARE OF SELF}]$$

$$\text{b. } JOHN^\alpha \text{ REQUEST } SUSAN^\beta \begin{bmatrix} [\beta \ ENABLE \ \alpha \ [\alpha \ TAKE \ CARE \ OF \ SELF]]^\gamma \\ \gamma \ BENEF \ \alpha \end{bmatrix}$$

This solution helps explain why the coercion is restricted to a delimited class of complements. As mentioned earlier, the only complements that we find really acceptable in this context are listed in (94):

(94) John asked Susan to be allowed/encouraged/helped/enabled to take care of himself.

What *encourage*, *help*, and *enable* have in common with *allow* is that they are force-dynamic verbs whose Agonist is a beneficiary rather than a patient, as shown in (78) above. The fact that just these verbs are permitted in (94) gives us an idea of the tolerances of the coercion—how closely an overlaid complement has to match the coerced material. Sag and Pollard's examples (95) are variations on this theme; they are less acceptable, we believe, because they fit the template less rigorously.

(95) a. ?The children asked Grandma to be able to stay up for the late show.
                [*to be able* here = 'be permitted by Grandma']
      b. ??Montana asked the doctor to be healthy by game time on Sunday.
                [=Sag and Pollard (1991: 42e,f)]

A remaining puzzle is precisely how the application of the coercion is regulated. For instance, *John asked Susan to leave the room* could potentially undergo the coercion and mean 'John asked Susan to allow him to leave the room'. In our dialect it cannot, but Farkas (1988) and Landau (2000) report that some speakers accept this reading (especially if there is an implied authority relation, as in *The student asked the teacher to leave the room* or *The goalkeeper asked the coach to be replaced*). Also, there seems no reason why *John asked to go* could not also have a reading that did not undergo the coercion, and

therefore meant 'John asked [discourse addressee]ᵢ to ᵢgo'. We do not understand the mechanics of coercion well enough yet to predict these exact results.[27]

Next consider the *promise* class, where control can shift to the recipient of
the promise just in case the complement involves permission or enabling. We
repeat the relevant examples from section 12.4.1 in (96)–(97).

(96)   Susan was promised (by John) to be allowed to take care of herself/
       *himself.

(97)

   a.   *Susan was promised $\left\{ \begin{array}{l} \text{to permit John to leave} \\ \text{to get permission to leave} \\ \text{to leave the room} \\ \text{to be hit on the head} \end{array} \right\}$

   b.   the promise to Susan to be allowed to take care of herself

   c.   It was promised to Susan to be allowed to take care of herself.

   d.   ?Grandma promised the children to be able to stay up for the late
       show.

   e.   ?Montana was promised (by the doctor) to be healthy by game time on
       Sunday.

   f.   Susan was promised to be helped/encouraged/enabled to take care of
       herself.

The arguments against a *bring about* coercion apply here just as they did with
the *ask* verbs: the possibilities are too broad. However, the fact that the same
complements appear in the problematic cases with *promise* and in the *ask*
coercion suggests that the specialized *allow to* coercion can be generalized to
the *promise* class. To argue that this is plausible, it is necessary to show that *ask*
and *promise* have some relevant semantic factor in common.

As observed by Panther and Köpcke (1993), again the relevant factor appears
to be the presence of a beneficiary. The asker is beneficiary of the requested
action; the *recipient* of a promise is the beneficiary of the promised action. Thus,
just as the beneficial granting of permission goes to the asker in (93), it should
go to the recipient of the promise—as it in fact does in (96) and (97b–f). In
short, we think the generalization is that control of the *be allowed to* coercion is

---

[27] There is some variation among verbs of asking which suggests that the matter may ultimately
be a lexical one. For example, (i) and (ii) are ambiguous, while (iii) is not, to our ears.

  (i) John pleaded with Mary to go to the football game.
  (ii) John begged Mary to go to the football game.
  (iii) John asked Mary to go to the football game.

The variable here appears to be the strength of the benefit to the asker.

determined by the beneficiary role in both cases. Significantly, this role is missing in the *shout* and *persuade* classes, and they do not undergo this coercion.

This still leaves the puzzle of why the *promise* coercion is so severely restricted—much more so than the *ask* coercion (see n. 12 above for the parallel but more severe problems with *threaten*). Whatever accounts for these further restrictions, we believe that the *promise* class too is subject to a semantically specialized coercion.

Panther and Köpcke point out that it is just the cases we have characterized as coercion that are subject to crosslinguistic and cross-speaker variation (the latter of which they study experimentally). In particular, the German (98a) is better than its literal English translation (98b), and (99a) is understood like English (99b), not like its word-for-word translation (99c).

(98) a.   Jürgen$_i$ verspricht Harry$_j$ befördert zu $_j$werden
           J.   promises H.   promoted to become
      b.   ?*Jürgen$_i$ promises Harry$_j$ to $_j$be promoted.

(99) a.   Die Mutter$_i$ bat   das Geschirr $_j$abzuwaschen.
           the mother asked the dishes   to.wash
      b.   The mother$_i$ said to $_j$wash the dishes.
      c.   The mother$_i$ asked to $_i$wash the dishes.

But we are not prepared to go any farther at this point.

To sum up this section: three important exceptions to thematically based control prove to be constrained by very precise semantic conditions. We have proposed accounting for them in terms of two specialized coercions that license extra semantic material in the interpretation that is not present in syntactic structure. Once we recognize the presence of this material, we see that the semantic conditions on control are preserved—it is just that the relevant elements are not visible in syntax.

12.7 Partial control and the joint intention coercion

We now turn to another dimension in the control problem, developed in detail by Landau (2000). This dimension cuts across the distinction among free, nearly free, and unique control. It is detectable when the complement contains a verb such as *meet*, which, when used intransitively, requires a collective subject: *John and Bill/the group met at six*, but **John met at six*. Naturally, when such verbs appear in a controlled complement, one expects that the controller should be collective, and so it must be—at least sometimes, as in (100a). Surprisingly, though, many predicates, such as those in (100b,c), do permit noncollective controllers of a collective complement. Köpcke and Panther (2002) point out a German counterpart of (100c), with parallel properties.

(100) a. John and Bill/*John managed to meet at six.
           The committee/*the chair dared to gather during the strike.
       b. John wanted to meet at six.
           The chair was afraid to gather during the strike.
       c. The teacher promised the parents to take a class trip to Greece.

The interpretation of (100b,c) is that the controller performs the action *in association with others*. These others may be determined pragmatically from context or may be present as discourse antecedents. Landau calls this situation 'partial control', contrasting it with the 'exhaustive control' shown in (100a).

It is important to distinguish partial control from split antecedent control. Split antecedent control permits a plural reflexive in the infinitive complement; but partial control does not. (Following Landau, we notate partial control with the subscript$_{i+}$.)

(101) *Split antecedent control*
       a. John$_i$ talked to Sarah$_j$ about $_{i+j}$meeting each other$_{i+j}$ at six.
       b. Amy$_i$ figured that John$_j$ would discuss $_{i+j}$protecting themselves$_{i+j}$ during the strike.

(102) *Partial control*
       a. *John$_i$ knows that Sarah$_j$ wanted to $_{j+}$meet each other at six.
       b. *Amy$_i$ figured that John$_j$ was afraid to $_{j+}$protect themselves during the strike.

The problem is to figure out exactly what partial control means, and why it is available only with certain matrix predicates.[28]

The key to understanding partial control, we believe, comes from the idea of 'collective intention' first proposed (to our knowledge) by Searle (1995); a similar idea is Clark's (1996) notion of a "joint activity". Consider Amy and Beth together carrying a long table, one at each end. Amy does not simply intend to carry one end of the table, although that is all she is doing. Rather, according to Searle, her intention should be characterized as directed toward

---

[28] One exception to this generalization is the verb *vote*, cited by Landau as an example of partial control pointed out as long ago as Lawler (1972). Oddly, it *does* permit plural reflexives in the complement. The semantically related predicates *propose*, *opt for*, and *be in favor of* have the same property:

(i) I$_i$ voted to $_{i+}$immolate ourselves, but I was overruled.
(ii) I$_i$ {proposed/opted for/was in favor of} $_{i+}$immolating ourselves, but I was overruled.

We have no explanation for these exceptions, but they certainly do form a natural class.

the activity 'We will carry the table, and my role is to carry this end'. Similarly, a member of a team has an intention directed toward 'We will win the game, and my role in this activity is to do such-and-such'. Note that although one can *hold* an intention toward a joint activity, one cannot *execute* it; one can only execute one's own role in the joint activity. (And one's understanding of others' roles may be less precise than that of one's own role.)

It is presupposed in an intention toward a joint activity that the other participants share it. Of course this presupposition may be false, leading to various possibilities for misunderstanding, defection, and deception. Clark shows how these possibilities play out in the context of conversation, which he describes as a particular sort of joint activity.

Establishing a jointly held intention toward a joint activity requires some overt signal on the part of each partner; Clark calls these signals "offer" and "uptake". They may be as elaborate as a contract or as simple as shaking hands, saying "okay", or giving a nod. Consider the situation in (103) (based on an example of Landau's).

(103) John and Mary have agreed to learn the same language, but they haven't decided which one yet.

Each participant must internally describe the plan as 'We agree to learn the same language'. But the choice of language cannot be established unilaterally; it must be established by offer and uptake: 'How about Romanian?' 'OK.'

Our hypothesis is that partial control occurs in contexts where the controller holds an intention with respect to a joint activity described by the complement. This hypothesis makes a number of predictions. First, complements exhibiting partial control should be voluntary joint activities. This is clearly true of *meet* and *gather* in (100b), and appears to be true in all the many examples cited by Landau. By contrast, collective states and collective nonvoluntary events do not appear to be felicitous as complements of partial control. Consider (104)–(106).

(104) a. Hildy and I formed/constitute an alliance.
b. Hildy told me that she$_i$ wants to $_{i+}$form/#$_{i+}$constitute an alliance.

(105) a. ?George told Dick that he$_i$ looked forward to $_{i+}$being jointly examined by the doctor.
b. #George told Dick that he$_i$ looked forward to $_{i+}$being jointly elected by the voters.

(106) a. The chair$_i$ hopes to $_{i+}$adjourn shortly after calling a vote.
b. #The chair$_i$ hopes to $_{i+}$adjourn shortly after receiving a bomb threat.

In (104), *forming* an alliance can be understood as an activity, but *constituting* an alliance is only a state; the latter is decidedly worse as a complement with partial control. Likewise, in (105), one can voluntarily be jointly examined by the doctor, but one cannot voluntarily be jointly elected by the voters; hence the latter is worse with partial control. Finally, in (106), adjourning after a vote is more of a preplanned voluntary action than adjourning in reaction to a bomb threat; hence the latter is worse with partial control.

A second prediction concerns Landau's observation about the temporal properties of complements that allow partial control. Verbs that prohibit partial control in their complements time-lock the complement to the main clause (107), whereas the complements of verbs that allow partial control are non-past-oriented with respect to their main clause (108).

(107) a. *No partial control*
           *Dan managed/dared/was unwise/was rude to meet at 6.
       b. *Time-locked*
           This morning, Dan managed/dared/was unwise/was rude to run the race (?right then/*tomorrow/*yesterday).

(108) a. *Partial control*
           Dan intended/planned/agreed to meet at 6.
       b. *Nonpast-oriented*
           This morning, Dan intended/planned/agreed to run the race right then/tomorrow/*yesterday.

Landau suggests that the complements exhibiting partial control have a covert tense in their syntax, and he attempts to derive the phenomena of partial control from this stipulation. Since partial control infinitives look exactly like nonpartial control infinitives, we take a different tack, as usual eschewing syntax that doesn't turn up at the surface. Rather, (on our account) partial control involves an intention toward a joint activity, and intention is by its nature nonpast directed. Hence the temporal properties of partial control follow directly from the semantics. No distinction whatsoever need be made in the syntax.

Exploring a bit further, recall that although one can *hold* an intention toward a joint activity, one cannot *execute* it alone. Now consider two senses of *dare*. Intransitive *dare*, shown in (107), has a time-locked complement and entails that the complement is executed—daringly. Thus it cannot involve an intention toward a joint activity—only the execution of an intention—and hence partial control is impossible. By contrast, transitive *dare* concerns the formation of an intention to act in the future—which *can* be a joint action; thus this use of the verb permits partial control (but not split antecedents):

(109)   Frankie dared Johnnie$_i$ to $_{i+}$meet/kiss (*each other) in the alley.

Similarly, *rude* and *unwise* in (107) characterize the execution—not the intention—of a voluntary action, and therefore prohibit partial control. By contrast, *be eager*, unlike intransitive *dare*, characterizes an attitude toward a future action or situation and can therefore tolerate partial control when the complement is a joint action.

(110)   Frankie thinks Johnnie$_i$ is eager to $_{i+}$meet/kiss (*each other) in the alley.

It remains to figure out exactly what semantic structure to attribute to intention toward joint action, such that it makes partial control possible. Joint action is certainly an aspect of meaning that is not expressed directly in syntax—we can see it only indirectly through its effects on control and so forth. This suggests that it is introduced by another coercion. Without a formal account of joint action, it is difficult to determine exactly what material this coercion would introduce. However an informal guess would be (111), in which the coerced material is in boldface.

(111)   JOHNNIE$^\alpha$ INTEND/BE EAGER
                                        [[GROUP INCLUDING α]$^\beta$ [β KISS]]

The crucial part of this is *group*: Johnnie's intention is directed toward the joint action of the group rather than just his own.

Landau points out that the subject of partial control, despite being semantically plural, is syntactically singular; *group* has the requisite property. Note that, like partial control complements, *group* permits collective predicates (112a) but not plural pronouns or reflexives (112b):[29]

(112)   a.   The group gathered/met/disbanded at 6.
             The group formed an alliance.
             The group has ten children altogether.
             The group was jointly elected by the voters.
         b.   *The group met/kissed each other at six.
             *The group has ten children among them.

The composition of the group introduced in (111) would have to be determined pragmatically, as partial control indeed requires. A discourse antecedent is a prime candidate for another member of the group, as observed in partial control. Furthermore, the application of this coercion would be automatically constrained by the semantics of intention toward joint action; the introduction

---

[29] Although, as Richard Oehrle has pointed out, our analysis might also predict that *The chairman moved to disband itself* is acceptable, where the antecedent of *itself* is the implicit group.

of a group into a control equation would be ill-formed except in the very special cases described above.

12.8 Further problems

Many questions about control still remain. This section enumerates a few.

12.8.1 Four more cases of control

First, we have said nothing here about control in infinitival relative clauses. Second, we have given no reason why information complements have a slightly more restricted distribution of controllers than free control complements—in particular, disallowing just the case of speaker/hearer control.

Third, selected actional complements are not the only instances of unique control. Verbs like *hope* and *wish* take situational infinitival complements, but they exclude generic, long-distance, and speaker/hearer control. And *remind* and *strike* present two possible controllers in the clause, of which only one is actual controller.

(113)   a. Judy$_j$ thinks that Henry$_i$ hopes/wishes to $_{i/*j/*gen}$redeem himself/ *herself/*oneself/*myself.
      b. Judy$_j$ reminds Henry$_i$ of $_{i/*j}$being much younger.
      c. Judy$_j$ strikes Henry$_i$ as $_{j/*i}$being much younger.

Thus there are sources of unique control other than being a selected actional complement. We suggest that these reasons too should be sought in the semantics of the verbs in question—in these cases, perhaps because they are experiencer verbs.

Fourth, infinitival indirect questions all express voluntary actions.

(114)   Fred asked/Sally told Fred
      a. how to win the race/ how to realize it's raining
      b. what to talk about/ what to resemble
      c. when to leave/ when to understand physics

Our account of voluntary action suggests therefore that they should have unique control, tied to the recipient of the answer (*Fred* in both cases of (114)). Yet there is also the possibility of generic control:

(115)   Fred asked/Sally told Fred
      a. how to defend oneself
      b. what to promise oneself under these conditions
      c. when to excuse oneself

It is not clear to us where this possibility comes from.

12.8.2 *Obviative vs. non-obviative control*

A further distinction in control has not to our knowledge been noted in the literature. Consider the predicates that that permit a local subject (i.e. that select InfC/GerC). Suppose that when the complement is *to VP*, its normal controller is NP_i. Then the question is, when the complement is *for NP to VP*, can the NP be a pronoun bound to NP_i? In the context in (116a,b) it can; in (116c,d) it cannot.

(116) a. $Nelda_i$ discussed $_i$leaving early.   [controller is *Nelda*]
       b. $Nelda_i$ discussed her_i leaving early.   [*her* can corefer with *Nelda*]
       c. $Beth_i$ hopes to $_i$leave early.   [controller is *Beth*]
       d. $Beth_i$ hopes for her_{*i} to leave early.   [*her* cannot corefer with *Beth*]

The ungrammaticality of *her = Beth* in (116d) has the flavor of a Condition B violation (the inability of a nonreflexive object pronoun to corefer with the subject, as in $Beth_i$ saw her_{*i}). We might call the situation in (116c,d) "obviative control", and that in (116a,b) "non-obviative control". (117)–(118) offer further examples, in a variety of syntactic configurations. (These represent our judgments; apparently speakers differ.)

(117) *Non-obviative control*
       a. (For her_i) to $_i$have to leave early wouldn't bother Susan.
       b. Amy_i thinks it's possible (for her_i) to $_i$leave early.
       c. Amy_i mentioned the possibility of (her_i) $_i$leaving early.

(118) *Obviative control*
       a. Diane begged $Daniel_i$ to $_i$leave early.
          Diane begged $Daniel_i$ for him_{*i} to leave early.
       b. $Fred_i$ is eager to $_i$leave early.
          $Fred_i$ is eager for him_{*i} to leave early.

Curiously, obviative control contexts still permit a bound pronoun if it is conjoined with something else (a fact pointed out to us by Joan Maling):

(119) a. $Beth_i$ hopes for Amy and her_i to leave early.
       b. Diane begged $Daniel_i$ for him_i and his friends to come home early.
       c. $Louise_j$ thinks $Fred_i$ is eager for the two of $them_{i+j}$ to leave early.

This differs from standard Condition B contexts such as (120a,b), which shows that obviative control should not be assimilated to Condition B. However, a reader has pointed out that certain verbs do permit such conjoined configurations (120c).

(120) a. Beth$_i$ likes Amy and her$_{*i}$.
      b. Louise$_j$ thinks Fred$_i$ likes the two of them$_{*i+j}$.
      c. Bill$_i$ differentiated between Mary and him$_i$.

It is not clear to us whether the distinction between obviative and non-obviative control is determined by syntax or semantics. However, given our prejudices stated in section 12.1 and the semantic factors in binding identified in Chapters 10 and 11 (and references there), we would be most inclined to seek semantic factors.

12.8.3 Parallels with reflexives

The most prominent cases of reflexive anaphora are those that involve GF-binding (section 6.4). Setting these aside, we find a residue of purely CS-bound reflexives, such as those in *picture*-noun complements. When we put *picture*-nouns in contexts that permit free control, we find almost the same range of antecedents:

(121) *Control*
      a. Amy$_i$ thinks that $_{i/j/i+j/gen}$dancing with Dan intrigues Tom$_j$.
      b. Amy$_i$ told Tom$_j$ that $_{i/j/i+j/gen}$dancing with Dan might be fun.

(122) *Picture-noun reflexives*
      a. Amy thinks that a picture of herself/himself might intrigue Tom.
      b. Amy told Tom that a picture of herself/himself was hanging in the post office.

(123) *Control*
      a. Brandeis$_i$ is in a lot of trouble, according to today's newspaper. Apparently, $_i$firing the football coach has turned off a lot of potential donors.
      b. Here's the thing: undressing myself/yourself/ourselves [=you and me] in public could cause a scandal.
      c. Here's the thing: it might really upset Tom to have to undress ourselves [=Tom and me] in public.
      d. How about undressing myself/yourself/ourselves in public?

(124) *Picture-noun reflexives*
      a. Amy is in a lot of trouble. Apparently, a compromising picture of herself came into Tom's hands.
      b. Here's the thing: a picture of myself/yourself/ourselves in public could cause a scandal.

  c. Here's the thing: it might really upset Tom to have a picture of ourselves in the post office.

  d. How about a picture of myself/yourself/ourselves hanging in the bathroom?

(125) *Control*

  a. Amy thinks that what you propose beats undressing herself/oneself/ myself/yourself/ourselves [=you and me, Amy and me] in public.

  b. Fred makes undressing himself/oneself/myself/yourself/ourselves [=you and me, Fred and me] in public almost appealing.

(126) *Picture-noun reflexives*

  a. Amy thinks that what you propose beats a picture of herself/oneself/ myself/yourself/ourselves hanging in the bathroom.

  b. Fred makes a picture of himself/oneself/myself/yourself/ourselves hanging in the bathroom almost appealing.

(127) *Control*

  a. It would help Bill$_i$'s development to $_i$behave himself in public.

  b. $_i$Finishing his work on time is important to John$_i$'s development/ ??John$_i$'s friends.

  c. It would ruin Steve$_i$'s figure/career to $_i$eat so much ice cream.

(128) *Picture-noun reflexives*

  a. A better picture of himself would help Bill's development/*Bill's friends.

  b. Another picture of himself in the paper would ruin Steve's career.

This suggests, as many have long suspected, that there is some deep unity between control and reflexives. However, it has been masked by the cases where there are additional restrictions on control such as unique control and by the cases where there are additional restrictions on reflexives such as GF-binding. In (121)–(128) we are seeing the purest, least restricted form of binding, and here control and reflexives coincide. The puzzle, of course, is to develop a binding theory that captures this unity and these constraints.

12.8.4 *Control of nominals*

The control problem should ultimately be embedded in a larger inquiry, that of determining the arguments of any head that lacks local syntactic arguments. Well-known cases include long-distance depictive predicates such as (129a), adjunct predicates such as (129b), and light verb constructions such as (129c,d). (We notate argument assignment again by cosubscripting; the subscript before the nominal in (129c,d) indicates the agent, and those after the nominal crudely indicate the other arguments.)

(129)   a. Susan$_i$ appreciates Bill$_j$ (only)(when) $_{i/j}$drunk.
   b. Bill$_i$ examined Susan$_j$ without glasses on$_{i/j}$.
   c. Harry$_i$ put [the $_i$blame$_{j,k}$] on Sam$_j$ for the disaster$_k$.
   d. Sam$_j$ got/received/was assigned [the blame$_{j,k}$] for the disaster$_k$.

(129a) is ambiguous as to who is drunk during Susan's appreciation of Bill, although there seems to us to be a preference for Susan; (129b) is ambiguous as to who was not wearing glasses. In (129c) it is clear that Harry is doing the blaming, Sam is being blamed, and the blame concerns the disaster; in (129d), despite the difference in syntactic configuration, Sam is still being blamed.

The case of nominals differs importantly from control in that all arguments of a nominal, not just the subject, can be satisfied nonlocally. A good contrast is (130).

(130)   a. *Nominal*
      Kathy$_i$ promised Ted$_j$ a $_i$hug$_j$.
   b. *Control*
      Kathy$_i$ promised Ted$_j$ to $_i$hug *(him$_j$).

But there are other differences as well. (131) and (132) offer some cases where a controlled complement alternates with a nominal or adjunct predicate, with what would seem to be similar interpretations. Yet thematic role assignment is quite different. In (131), *shoot* is controlled by the attempter, as usual. In (131a), *Bill* controls the verb *attempt(ing)*. However, in (131b), the most likely interpretation is that the person who is attempting to shoot is not Bill.

(131)   a. *Control*
      Bill$_i$ avoided/resisted $_i$attempting to $_i$shoot himself$_i$.
      Bill$_i$ expected to $_i$attempt to $_i$shoot himself$_i$.
      Bill$_i$ anticipated $_i$attempting to $_i$shoot himself$_i$.
   b. *Nominal*
      Bill$_i$ avoided/resisted $_{j\neq i}$attempts to $_j$shoot him$_i$.
      Bill$_i$ expected an $_{j\neq i}$attempt to $_j$shoot him$_i$.
      Bill$_i$ anticipated an $_{j\neq i}$attempt to $_j$shoot him$_i$.

Similarly, in (132a), the gerundive complement of *without* is controlled by the subject. However, in (132b), the complement of *without* does not have an overt verb (perhaps it is a small clause), and here the person with glasses on can be either the subject or the object.

(132)   a. *Control*
        Bill$_i$ examined Susan$_j$ without $_{i/*j}$having glasses on$_{i/*j}$.
      b. *Adjunct predicate*
        Bill$_i$ examined Susan$_j$ without glasses on$_{i/j}$.

We do not have an account of this difference, but we are sure that such an account must be a part of a complete treatment of control.

12.9 Conclusions

Our goal here has been to show that most of the factors involved in solving the control problem are semantic rather than syntactic. One factor has proven clearly syntactic: the choice of selection between InfC, InfP, GerC, and GerP. On the other hand, this does not correlate precisely with semantic selection; and it is semantic selection, not syntactic position, that determines whether a predicate governs free, nearly free, or unique control.

In all the cases of unique control we examined in section 12.4, the controller is determined by thematic role, not by syntactic position. Moreover, the choice of thematic role is not an arbitrary diacritic. In the cases we were able to analyze in section 12.5, the meaning of the matrix predicate determines which thematic role serves as controller, through the inherent control equation of the basic predicate(s) embedded in its lexical decomposition. Thus the theory of unique control reduces to the theory of the content of basic predicates that select actional arguments.

The systematic exceptions to thematically determined control are the outcome of a number of coercions—pieces of semantic structure that are not expressed syntactically. In every case that we have treated in terms of implicit arguments and coercion, a syntactic account must make heavy use of idiosyncratic covert elements that violate the natural texture of syntactic distribution.

Our conclusion can be put a bit more dramatically. In the cases we have examined here, the only thing syntax can "see" that pertains to control is that there is some infinitival or gerund lacking a local subject. It cannot see what kind of control is possible, nor, if there is unique control, what the controller should be. All these factors are determined by conceptual structure, in particular the verb meaning interacting with the meaning of the complement.

More generally, we take these results to be confirmation of the Simpler Syntax Hypothesis, where we take it that syntax is the minimal structure necessary to mediate between semantics and phonology. Although for a first approximation syntax mirrors semantic structure, on closer examination it has its own semi-autonomous patterns of distribution. As a consequence, the syntax–semantics interface is somewhat dirty. As argued in Chapter 1 and Jackendoff (2002a), this is what is to be expected in a mentalistic theory of language: it is characteristic of the way the brain connects its disparate functions to each other.

PART IV

Connections Between Clauses

CHAPTER 13

Semantic Subordination Despite Syntactic Coordination

13.1 Introduction

This chapter and the next explore syntactic constructions in which the syntactic connection between clauses does not match their semantic connection. We will draw the general conclusion that it is possible to separate genuine syntactic conditions on linguistic form from the reflexes of semantic conditions that only indirectly constrain syntax. In particular, these constructions will again show that binding conditions are most generally stated over CS, not syntax. At the same time, it will become apparent that some syntactic conditions are not reflexes of CS conditions. Syntax is therefore autonomous, in that it is not reducible to semantic structure, confirming the conclusions of Chapters 10 and 11 that there is no level of syntactic structure such as LF that has a uniform interface with semantic structure with respect to such phenomena as binding and quantification.

The construction of concern in this chapter is coordination with what we will call "left-subordinating" *and* (*LS-and* or *and*$_{LS}$). The notion that there are both coordinate and subordinate interpretations of *and* is not new. This point was made by Culicover (1970; 1972) in connection with "OM-sentences" (*one more*...) such as (1). Such sentences were cited in section 7.2 as among the noncanonical utterance frames of English.

We would like to express our thanks to Paul Postal, an audience at UCLA (including Tim Stowell and Anna Szabolcsi), and two anonymous reviewers for their extremely helpful and constructive comments on an earlier version of this chapter.

(1) One more can of beer and I'm leaving.

(1) has an interpretation in which the left conjunct functions semantically as if it were a subordinate clause. It can be used, for example, as a paraphrase of *If you have one more can of beer, I'm leaving*. However, the antecedent of the implicit conditional in (1) is vaguer than this possible paraphrase, in that it can also be used in a vast variety of other contexts somehow involving one more can of beer. We will not pursue here the question of precisely how to characterize the meaning of the antecedent. Culicover (1972) proposed that it is simply "vague"; Paul Postal has suggested to us (p.c.) that it has the specifically vague meaning 'If something happens involving one more can of beer'. In the terms of Chapters 7 and 8, this might be formalized as (2), in which $\mathscr{F}$ is an indirectly licensed function to be filled in pragmatically from linguistic or nonlinguistic context.

(2) IF [$\mathscr{F}$(ONE MORE CAN OF BEER)]

However OM-sentences manage to get their interpretation, their existence constitutes a *prima facie* case for a semantic representation whose structure diverges significantly from that of the corresponding syntactic structure. Culicover argues that the structure of OM-structures is coordinate, i.e. of the form *NP and S*. There is no apparent syntactic or morphological basis for taking the first conjunct in an OM-sentence to have the structure of a subordinate clause or to be embedded in an invisible clause with such a structure.

A different case involving conjunction is addressed by Goldsmith (1985), in connection with asymmetric extractions from coordinate constructions with the interpretation 'and nonetheless'.

(3) How many courses can we expect our graduate students to teach *t* and (still) finish a dissertation on time?

Such examples must be structurally distinguished from standard coordination, which permits only across-the-board extraction. Goldsmith argues that the distinction is syntactic: the second clause has been reanalyzed as a subordinate clause in the syntax, allowing the extraction to take place from the first clause without violating the Coordinate Structure Constraint. Postal (1993) elaborates the point, arguing that where there is an apparent violation of the CSC, there is not really a coordinate structure, but rather a subordinate structure of some sort. (On the other hand, Sag et al. (1985) treat *all* coordination as syntactically subordinate, so that the desired distinction cannot be in the syntax.)

Others, beginning with Ross (1967) and including Grice (1967/76), Schmerling (1975), Lakoff (1986), and Deane (1992), have also observed that *and* can be used asymmetrically, in the sense that the order of conjuncts cannot be reversed without affecting the meaning of the sentence. The typical case is that *A and B* is taken to mean either that B follows A, or that B in some sense results from A; other interpretations are also possible, as discussed by Lakoff and Deane. Although all of these writers make the point that *and* can induce subordinate interpretation, none explores explicitly the possibility argued by Culicover with respect to OM-sentences, namely that the syntactic structure of a sentence with subordinate *and* is still coordinate despite its semantics. Moreover, none, including Culicover, provides evidence that subordinate *and* maps onto a level of linguistic representation at which subordination is formally represented. What they all do show is that asymmetric conjunction, unlike standard conjunction, can be taken to have a meaning that is paraphrasable by subordination. We return to some of these other asymmetrical uses of *and* here and there, but especially in section 13.7.

Our goal here is to demonstrate that there is at least one use of asymmetric conjunction which is coordinate in syntactic structure, just the way it looks, in conformance with the Simpler Syntax Hypothesis, but which corresponds explicitly to subordination at the level of CS.[1]

13.2 A conditional reading of *and*

Example (4) illustrates a class of sentences that are semantically related to OM-sentences, in that they contain a conjunction that is interpreted like a conditional.

(4)   a. You drink another can of beer and I'm leaving.
                              [= If you drink another can of beer, I'm leaving.]
        b. Big Louie sees you with the loot and he puts out a contract on you.
              [= If Big Louie sees you with the loot, he'll put out a contract on you.]

Let us call this use of *and* "left-subordinating *and*" (*LS-and* or *and$_{LS}$*) to distinguish it from normal coordinating *and* (*C-and* or *and$_C$*). The intuitive judgment that conditionals with *if* are an appropriate paraphrase grounds our claim that the left conjunct in (4) is semantically subordinate. To be more explicit: there is some relation in conceptual structure between an *if*-clause and its consequent clause, which we take to be reflected overtly by subordination in syntactic structure; we are claiming that the same relation obtains in conceptual structure between the left and right conjuncts in (4), but without

---

[1] Taking a similar tack, Napoli and Hoeksema (1993) argue that there is a construction involving *so* that is syntactically paratactic but semantically subordinate.

overt syntactic subordination. As will seen, the parallelism between the two constructions is very strong.

Examples very similar to (4) can also be constructed with *or* instead of *and*, for example *You drink another can of beer or I'm leaving* (= *If you don't drink another can of beer, I'm leaving*). However, on closer examination they turn out to have somewhat different properties, so we defer their discussion to section 13.7.

Left-subordinating *and* is quite restricted in its distribution. For instance, if the tense is changed to perfect, the conditional reading is lost.

(5) a. You've drunk another can of beer and I've left.
> [≠ If you've drunk another can of beer, I've left.]

   b. Big Louie has seen you with the loot and he's put out a contract on you.
> [≠ If Big Louie has seen you with the loot, he has put out a contract on you.]

We will frequently use the perfect tense as a test to rule out the possibility of *LS-and*.[2]

The conditional reading is also lost in a tripartite conjunction of the form *X, Y, and Z*.

(6) a. (*)You drink another can of beer, Bill eats more pretzels, and I'm leaving.
> [≠ If you drink another can of beer, (and if) Bill eats more pretzels, I'm leaving.]

   b. (*)Big Louie sees you with the loot, you look guilty, and he puts out a contract on you.
> [≠ If Big Louie sees you with the loot, (and if) you look guilty, he puts out a contract on you.]

Although the conditional reading can appear in a subordinate clause (7a), it is lost if both conjuncts contain the complementizer (7b). That is, this reading appears only with IP conjunction, not CP conjunction.

(7) a. You know, of course, that you drink one more beer and you get kicked out.
> [= ...that if you drink one more beer you get kicked out.]

   b. You know, of course, that you drink one more beer and that you get kicked out.
> [≠ ...that if you drink one more beer you get kicked out.]

---

[2] A reader has pointed out a plausible example where perfect tense occurs in the first conjunct only: [context: I'm about to open the door to find out whether or not you've broken anything] *You've broken another vase and I'm leaving.* Tom Wasow suggests the following context for perfect in the second conjunct: [An alcoholic says:] *I take one little drink and I've fallen off the wagon.*

This reading also does not appear in VP conjunction.

(8)   a.   Big Louie sees you with the loot and puts out a contract on you.
            [≠ If Big Louie sees you with the loot, he puts out a contract on you.]
      b.   Big Louie has seen you with the loot and put out a contract on
           you.   [*Perfect forces coordinate interpretation only.*]

(Note that another asymmetric conjunction, the right-subordination conjunction that expresses causal connection, *does* allow VP conjunction, as seen for instance in (3).)

Whereas *C-and* constructions can of course undergo right node raising (9a), *LS-and* constructions cannot (9b), parallel to *if*-constructions (9c).

(9)   a.   Big Louie found out about ___, and_C Big Louie put out a contract on,
           that guy who stole some loot from the gang.
      b.   *Big Louie finds out about ___, and_{LS} Big Louie puts out a contract on,
           that guy who stole some loot from the gang.
           [*cf.* Big Louie finds out about that guy who stole some loot from the
                           gang, and_{LS} Big Louie puts out a contract on him.]
      c.   *If Big Louie finds out about ___, then Big Louie puts out a contract on,
           that guy who stole some loot from the gang.

Similarly, whereas *C-and* constructions can undergo gapping (10a), *LS-and* constructions cannot (10b), paralleling *if*-constructions (10c). (The restriction of gapping to *semantic* coordination was noted in section 7.8.)

(10) a.   Big Louie stole another car radio and_C Little Louie the hubcaps.
      b.   *Big Louie steals one more car radio and_{LS} Little Louie the
           hubcaps.   [*Okay perhaps as generic or implied future
                                        coordination but not as conditional.*]
      c.   *If Big Louie steals one more car radio, then Little Louie the
           hubcaps.

It should also be noted that *LS-and* paraphrases only a restricted subset of the uses of *if*. For instance, there is no *LS-and* paraphrase of irrealis conditionals such as (11a) or conditionals with abstract stative clauses (11b).

(11) a.   If Bill hadn't come, we would have been sad.
                          [≠ *Bill didn't come, and_{LS} we were sad.]
      b.   If x is less than y, the derivative of f(x) is positive.
                  [≠ *X is less than y, and_{LS} the derivative of f(x) is positive.]

13.3 *LS-and* is not a subordinating conjunction

The obvious question is: what syntactic structure is associated with *LS-and*? A plausible account, following Interface Uniformity, would be that, parallel to the conditional paraphrases, there is a syntactic structure in which the first clause is subordinate to the second.

There are at least four arguments against such a proposal, of which we consider two in this section and two more in sections 13.5 and 13.6. Consider first the syntactic structure that would have to be assumed for a sentence such as (4b).

(12) [s [s [s Big Louie sees you with the loot] and$_{LS}$] he puts out a contract on you]

On this view, *Big Louie sees you with the loot and$_{LS}$* is a subordinate clause adjoined to the left of *he puts out a contract on you*; *LS-and* is some kind of subordinating conjunction. Schematically, the structure is (13).

(13) [S$_1$ and$_{LS}$] S$_2$

This structure is wrong for two obvious reasons. First, the normal position of a subordinating conjunction in English is clause-initial, as shown by the distribution of *after, before, since, when, until, if, unless, although, though, because,* and so on:

(14) ... because it is raining
      ... *it is raining because

While languages exist in which subordinating conjunctions are clause-final, there is no independent reason to believe that English is such a language.[3]

Second, a subordinate clause in English can appear either to the left or to the right of the main clause (15a). But *S$_1$ and$_{LS}$* cannot appear to the right of S$_2$ (15b).

(15) a. Big Louie will put out a contract on you if he sees you with the loot.
      b. *[s Big Louie puts out a contract on you, [s [s he sees you with the loot] and$_{LS}$]

Suppose that we tried to make *LS-and* more plausible as a subordinating conjunction by generating it in D-structure as an ordinary subordinating conjunction in the ordinary place, i.e. clause-initially (conforming with Structural

---

[3] Here we use the traditional terminology, and not the more principled terminology of Huddleston and Pullum (2002), where *after, because,* etc. are prepositions and *after it rains, because it is raining,* etc. are prepositional phrases.

Uniformity). Then a special movement rule would be necessary to move just this particular conjunction (plus subordinating *or*) to the end of its clause, and output conditions would be necessary to guarantee that this particular kind of subordinate clause always precedes its main clause. It would also then be an accident that this subordinating conjunction occurs in S-structure in precisely the position where the homonymous coordinating conjunction *C-and* appears. That is, a great deal of otherwise unmotivated machinery would be invoked to account for what the theory would end up treating as a curious coincidence—a classic case of a syntactic generalization being missed.

In short, *LS-and* would be highly anomalous syntactically as a subordinating conjunction, whereas everything in the syntax per se is consistent with its being an ordinary coordinating conjunction that happens to have a noncanonical subordinating interpretation under certain conditions. That is, given the two alternative hypotheses in Table 13.1, these very gross syntactic considerations argue against the "Matching Hypothesis" and for the "Mismatching Hypothesis".

Under the Matching Hypothesis, the differences between the two kinds of *and* follow automatically, since *LS-and* is not a coordinating conjunction and therefore does not participate in typical coordinate constructions. However, the price is the totally anomalous nature of this subordinating conjunction, as just noted.[4] Under the Mismatching Hypothesis, a special interface rule must say that under certain conditions, syntactic *and* can be interpreted as subordinating, with the first clause taken (roughly) as a condition on the occurrence of the

Table 13.1 Matching versus Mismatching Hypotheses

	Syntactic structure	Conceptual structure
Matching Hypothesis		
Coordination	C-and	C-and
Subordination	if, since, LS-and	if, since, LS-and
Mismatching Hypothesis		
Coordination	C-and, LS-and	C-and
Subordination	if, since	if, since, LS-and

---

[4] Interestingly, none of the cases of asymmetric *and* cited by Ross, Goldsmith, Lakoff, Deane, and Postal permits this argument. In all of their cases, the clause interpreted as subordinate is on the right rather than the left, so that the necessary syntactic structure is the unobjectionable (i).

(i) [S [and [S]]

Thus *LS-and* constitutes a more serious syntactic challenge to the Matching Hypothesis than do these previous cases.

event in the second. (Such a rule might be conceived of as the lexical entry for *LS-and*, just as with other semi-anomalous items as *enough* discussed in section 1.5.) These conditions are precisely when there are two full, nongapped IP conjuncts whose tenses are appropriate. The two solutions are of approximately equal complexity.

The Matching Hypothesis does considerable violence to the syntactic treatment of subordinating conjunction, as just observed. The Mismatching Hypothesis does a certain amount of violence to Interface Uniformity, i.e. the assumption that syntactic and conceptual structures are matched. But much of the present study has proven it necessary in any event to abandon (or at least modulate) that assumption, so it is unclear that there is anything else objectionable about Mismatching; it depends on how mismatched syntax and CS can be in general.

A hint toward the full extent of mismatches is provided by the OM-construction, a case closely related in its semantics to *LS-and*-conjoined clauses. We have already cited Culicover's demonstration that a full *syntactic* conditional cannot be constructed for this sense. Once something as ill-matched as the OM-construction is admitted into the syntax–CS correspondence, it should not seem especially problematic to interpret syntactic coordination as subordination more generally, particularly when *and* has a parallel conditional interpretation in OM-sentences.

Another hint comes from a colloquial construction with a conditional meaning similar to *LS-and* constructions, in which there is no apparent syntactic relation at all between the clauses, beyond bare parataxis. (We mark rising intonation with ↑ and falling intonation with ↓.)

(16)   Mary listens to the Grateful Dead↑, she gets depressed↓.
         [≈ Mary listens to the Grateful Dead and she gets depressed;
          ≈ If/when Mary listens to the Grateful Dead, she gets depressed.]

This construction can be embedded, though not as freely as the *LS-and* construction. (We find it helpful to put an intonation break after *that*, here indicated by a comma, in order to prevent a garden-path interpretation of the first clause.)

(17)   a. ?I really think that, Mary listens to the Grateful Dead↑, she gets depressed↓.
            I really think that Mary listens to the Grateful Dead and she gets depressed.
        b. ?I'm not shocked by the idea that, Mary listens to the Grateful Dead↑, she gets depressed↓.

I'm not shocked by the idea that Mary listens to the Grateful Dead and she gets depressed.

c. *It is not entirely obvious whether, Mary listens to the Grateful Dead↑, she gets depressed↓.

It is not entirely obvious whether Mary listens to the Grateful Dead and she gets depressed.

d. *I want to explain exactly why, Mary listens to the Grateful Dead↑, she gets depressed↓.

I want to explain exactly why Mary listens to the Grateful Dead and she gets depressed.

Unlike the *LS-and*-construction, this construction can concatenate more than two clauses.

(18)   You kill a cop↑, you go to jail↑, you don't get out↓. [*Law and Order*]

Chapter 14 will discuss another construction in which the only syntactic connection between two clauses is parataxis, yet there is a clear conditional connection in the semantics. The overall picture that emerges is that mismatches between syntactic and semantic subordination are hardly confined to the *LS-and* construction.

13.4 Interactions with binding

It turns out that *C-and* and *LS-and* differ in their binding properties. Binding with *LS-and*, either with an IP-conjunction (19a) or with an OM-sentence (19b), parallels a paraphrasing *if*-construction (19c), not a *C-and* construction (19d). (Note, by the way, the use of *right*-subordinating conjunction conjoining VPs in these examples, alongside of *LS-and*.)

(19)   a.   Another picture of himself$_i$ appears in the newspaper and$_{LS}$ Susan thinks John$_i$ will definitely go out$_{RS}$ and get a lawyer.

b.   Another picture of himself$_i$ in the newspaper and$_{LS}$ Susan thinks John$_i$ will definitely go out and$_{RS}$ get a lawyer.

c.   If another picture of himself$_i$ appears in the newspaper, Susan thinks John$_i$ will definitely go out and get a lawyer.

d.   *Another picture of himself$_i$ has appeared in the newspaper, and$_C$ Susan thinks John$_i$ will definitely go out and get a lawyer.

The grammaticality of (19a,b) shows that, under the subordinating interpretation, an anaphor in the left conjunct can be bound by an antecedent in the right conjunct; the ungrammaticality of (19d) shows that such binding does not occur under the coordinating interpretation.

The reflexives in (19a–c) can be replaced by *him* without affecting grammaticality. On the other hand, not all cases involving *LS-and* do allow both a pronoun and a reflexive, for instance (20a,b,c). Compare to (20d,e,f).

(20)   a. Another picture of him(*self) (appears) in the paper and$_{LS}$ Susan will think John is famous.
   b. Another picture of him(*self) (comes out) in the paper and$_{LS}$ Susan divorces John.
   c. Another picture of him(*self) (appears) in the paper and$_{LS}$ John will get arrested.
   d. Another picture of him(self) (appears) in the paper and$_{LS}$ John leaves.
   e. Another picture of him(self) (comes out) in the paper and$_{LS}$ Susan thinks John will definitely be offended.
   f. Another unflattering picture of him(self) (appears) in the paper and$_{LS}$ early retirement will begin to appeal to John.

We are not entirely clear about the conditions that distinguish these examples, but the reflexive seems to be available only roughly when there is a logophoric connection in the sense of Kuno (1987)—when the antecedent's attitude or volition is expressed in the second conjunct. For example, in (20d–f), the pragmatic connection between the clauses is that John is reacting to seeing the picture or to learning of it. This connection is unavailable in (20a–c), because the second conjunct cannot be construed as an action on John's part that depends on his awareness of the picture. Whatever the conditions, they precisely parallel those in paraphrasing *if*-constructions.

(21)   a. If there is another picture of him(*self) in the paper, Susan will think John is famous.
   b. If another picture of him(*self) comes out in the paper, Susan will divorce John.
   c. If another picture of him(*self) appears in the paper, John will get arrested.
   d. If there is another picture of him(self) in the paper, John will leave.
   e. If there is another picture of him(self) in the paper, Susan thinks John will definitely be offended.
   f. If another unflattering picture of him(self) appears in the paper, early retirement will begin to appeal to John.

Moreover, a reflexive is not permitted in *C-and* constructions syntactically parallel to (20d–f). On the logophoric story, this is because the coordinate constructions establish no causal connection between John's action or attitude and the *picture*-noun.[5]

(22) a. Another picture of him(*self) has appeared in the paper and$_C$ John has left (—so let's have a party).

b. Another picture of him(*self) has come out in the paper and$_C$ (in addition) Susan has decided John will definitely be offended.

c. Another unflattering picture of him(*self) came out in the paper yesterday, and$_C$ (what's more) early retirement has begun to appeal to John.

In the Matching Hypothesis, all this asymmetry of binding is consistent with a syntactic characterization of the antecedent–anaphor relation—but, as observed in section 13.3, at the cost of a thoroughly unsatisfactory account of the bare-bones syntax of *LS-and*. The Mismatching Hypothesis, however, is inconsistent with a syntactic account of binding, since in particular (19a) and (20d,e,f) are syntactically indistinguishable from (19d) and (22a–c) in the relevant respects.

In order to save the Mismatching Hypothesis, it is necessary to conclude that the sort of binding illustrated here is sensitive to relations of subordination in CS, for then the *semantic* subordination of the first conjunct to the second can license the anaphor in the first conjunct. However, such a conclusion is not unprecedented, given the quite different cases discussed in Chapters 10 and 11 (and in the references there). Following our treatment there, the reflexives in these examples are not GF-bound (in the sense of section 6.4), because they are within *picture*-noun phrases and therefore lack a GF. Hence their binding is exclusively CS-binding. Like other CS-bound reflexives, they can be replaced by *him* without affecting grammaticality. As we have seen in Chapters 10 and 11, the licensing conditions for CS-binding involve some mixture of syntactic and CS relationships. In particular, on no one's account can logophoric connections be defined in strictly syntactic terms, so sooner or later semantic conditions must be invoked for at least some cases of binding. We are just advocating sooner rather than later.

A similar problem arises in the binding of pronouns by quantifiers. It is standardly argued that a quantifier must c-command a pronoun in order to bind it. In most cases, S-structure c-command is sufficient.

---

[5] We acknowledge that some of these judgments may be difficult. For our purposes it is sufficient that one's judgments for (20) parallel those for (21) and differ from those in (22).

(23) a. Every senator$_i$ at the party thought that he$_i$ would have no trouble getting elected.

b. *Every senator$_i$ was at the party and he$_i$ was worrying about getting elected. [no c-command]

However, as with the obviative expression *X else* discussed in Chapter 11, the behavior of *LS-and* constructions suggests in fact that the relevant level for quantifier binding is CS. Consider the following sentences.

(24) *LS-and/OM*

a. ((You) put) enough pressure on him$_i$ and every senator$_i$, no matter how honest, will succumb to corruption.

b. (You) come up with a few more juicy stories about him$_i$ and every senator$_i$ will change his vote in your favor.

c. (You) give anyone$_i$ too much money and he$_i$ will go crazy.

(25) *If*

a. If you put enough pressure on him$_i$, every senator$_i$, no matter how honest, will succumb to corruption.

b. If you come up with a few more juicy stories about him$_i$, every senator$_i$ will change his vote in your favor.

c. If you give anyone$_i$ too much money, he$_i$ will go crazy.

(26) *C-and*

a. *We have put enough pressure on him$_i$ and every senator$_i$, no matter how honest, has succumbed to corruption.

b. *We came up with a few more juicy stories about him$_i$, and sure enough, every senator$_i$ changed his vote in our favor.

c. *You have given anyone$_i$ too much money and he$_i$ has gone crazy.

Under the *LS-and* interpretation in (24a,b), the quantifier in the right conjunct binds the pronoun in the left conjunct, exactly parallel to the corresponding conditionals in (25a,b). (26a,b) show that under the coordinate interpretation, a quantifier in the right conjunct cannot bind a pronoun in the left conjunct. Furthermore, (24c) shows that *any* can be licensed in the first clause by *LS-and*, just as it is licensed by *if* in (25c).

Again, the Matching Theory would predict this automatically under a standard theory of quantifier binding at LF—but at the price of requiring the unnatural subordinating conjunction *LS-and*. The Mismatching Theory is not consistent with a syntactic theory of quantifier binding, since *LS-and* is indistinguishable from *C-and* in syntax. If, however, the conditions on quantifier binding are stated in terms of Conceptual Structure, the Mismatching Theory can be maintained.

Now notice that the binding of variables by quantifiers must appear in CS in any event, since it is involved in deriving inferences—a prime function of CS, and one that cannot be carried out over any level of syntax, even LF. Therefore in principle there is no problem with putting conditions on variable binding at CS rather than (or in addition to) at LF.

In short, in the CS of *LS-and* sentences, the first clause displays semantic properties normally associated with clauses that are syntactically subordinate. Thus any theory of binding that accounts for the CS properties of subordinate clauses should apply to these cases as well. (For instance, see Chierchia (1995), who accounts for binding relations in sentences with subordination in terms of a modification of Discourse Representation Theory.)

13.5 Extraction

The evidence from anaphora and quantifier binding constitutes a strong argument for treating the left conjunct of *LS-and* as subordinate to the right conjunct at some level of linguistic structure. The arguments of section 13.3, however, are intended to show that the left conjunct is not a subordinate clause in the syntactic sense, although it clearly has a subordinate interpretation. We have therefore tentatively concluded that the notion of subordination that is relevant to the anaphor and quantifier binding facts is a semantic one. But the arguments of section 13.3 against syntactic subordination are not overwhelmingly conclusive; it is still possible, though highly implausible, that English has a special kind of syntactic subordination that would allow us to account for the facts of section 13.4 in syntactic terms, say at LF. In this section and the next we show that such a proposal cannot be right. That is, we show that the construction with *LS-and* must be syntactically coordinate.

The arguments turn on extraction. Consider what happens when we try to extract from conjoined structures with *C-and* and *LS-and*. The canonical case of extraction from conjoined structures, of course, is subject to Ross's (1967) Coordinate Structure Constraint (CSC), which in general requires across-the-board (ATB) extraction.

(27) a. This is the senator that I voted for *t* and$_C$ Terry met *t* in
          Washington.   [*ATB extraction*]
      b. *This is the senator [that I voted for *t* and$_C$ Terry met Bill Clinton in
          Washington].   [*left-conjunct extraction*]
      c. *This is the senator that I voted for Bill Clinton and$_C$ Terry met *t* in
          Washington.   [*right-conjunct extraction*]

If the CSC were a syntactic constraint, and if *LS-and* were truly a coordinating construction, we would expect the same pattern to occur with *LS-and*. However, in fact ATB extraction sounds decidedly strange.

(28)　a.　You just point out the thief and$_{LS}$ we arrest her on the spot.
　　　b.　?This is the thief that you just point out *t* and we arrest *t* on the spot.

On the other hand, *LS-and* violates the CSC, in that it *does* allow extraction independently from either conjunct. The examples in (29a,b) are not wonderful, but they are much better than their *C-and* counterparts in (29c,d).[6] (Here and elsewhere we intend for the diacritics *, ??, and ? to indicate ungrammaticality relative to the unmarked examples, which themselves may sometimes be mildly problematic. We indicate relative judgments by using < to mean 'is worse than'.)

(29)　a.　?This is the loot that you just identify *t* and we arrest the thief on the
　　　　　spot.　　　　　　　　　　　　　　　　　*[left-conjunct extraction]*
　　　b.　??This is the thief that you just identify the loot and we arrest *t* on the
　　　　　spot.　　　　　　　　　　　　　　　　*[right-conjunct extraction]*
　　　c.　*This is the loot that [you have identified *t* and we have arrested the
　　　　　thief on the spot].　　　　　　　　　　　　　　　　*[< (29a)]*
　　　d.　*This is the thief that you have identified the loot and we have
　　　　　arrested *t* on the spot.　　　　　　　　　　　　　*[< (29b)]*

The asymmetric *and* that expresses causal connection also allows single-clause extraction, as seen in (30a). *Both* occurs only with *C-and* and thus allows us to produce the minimally contrasting (30b), where extraction is impossible.

(30)　a.　This is the senator that the Mafia pressured *t* and (consequently) the
　　　　　senate voted for health care reform.

---

[6] We assume, following standard analyses of relative clauses, that the landing site of extraction is outside the clauses conjoined by *LS-and*. A reviewer has pointed out that one might suppose instead that the landing site in (29a) is within the first conjunct, so that CSC is violated only in (29b). However, the extraction is good even in (i), where movement clearly must go beyond the first conjunct (see also (34a)).

(i) ?This is the loot that the chief says you just identify *t* and they arrest the thief on the spot. [= the loot such that the chief says they arrest the thief on the spot if you identify it]

This point is important, because the next section will argue that matters are different in extraction from main clauses conjoined by *LS-and*.

　Incidentally, the reader may notice that all of the examples of relative clauses in this section are in predicate NPs. For reasons unclear to us but probably connected to their modality, these types of relative clause are strongly ungrammatical in referential NPs:

(ii) *I'll bring in the loot that you just identify and we arrest the thief on the spot.

   b. *This is the senator that both the Mafia pressured *t* and the senate
      voted for health care reform.

Under the Mismatching Hypothesis, since the left conjunct of *LS-and* is
syntactically coordinating, there is only one way to account for this distribution
of facts: the CSC is a semantic constraint (as argued e.g. by Goldsmith (1985)).
The CSC then requires ATB extraction from a semantically coordinate construction, and allows asymmetric extraction from either main clause conjunct
when semantic parallelism does not obtain.

This conclusion may not be entirely welcome. But this time the Matching
Hypothesis does not come to the rescue. It correctly predicts that, if the CSC is
syntactic and *LS-and* is a subordinating conjunction, the CSC should not apply
to it and ATB extraction should be impossible. But it also predicts, incorrectly,
that extraction is impossible from the left conjunct alone, since adjunct clauses
are islands, falling under the CED.[7] Compare (29a) and (30a) with the corresponding examples in (31).

(31)   a. ??This is the loot that if you identify *t*(,) we will arrest the thief on the
        spot.   [< *(29a)*]
   b. *This is the senator that when the Mafia pressured *t*(,) the senate
        voted for health care reform.   [< *(30a)*]

To make the contrast between *LS-and* and *if* clearer, notice that *LS-and*-
constructions are if anything slightly degraded by replacing the trace with a
resumptive pronoun, while *if*-clauses are if anything slightly improved. (We use
the symbol ≤ to mean 'is equal to or worse than' and ≥ to mean 'is equal to or
better than'.)

(32)   a. ?This is the loot that if you identify it, we will arrest the thief on the
        spot.   [≥ *(31a)*]

---

  [7] The CED is the Condition on Extraction Domains, due to Huang (1982b): "No element can
be extracted from a domain that is not properly governed." A related account is given in Chomsky
(1986a) in terms of barriers. The condition has the effect of permitting extraction from a governed
complement, but blocking extraction from an adjunct.

We do not employ a notion of government in Simpler Syntax. If we wish to treat this condition
as a syntactic constraint, we must nevertheless formulate it in syntactic terms. For example, we
might try to distinguish between an argument and an adjunct by appealing to whether there is
linking to GF. (But note that at least in the version developed in Ch. 6, clausal complements do not
receive GFs.) An alternative approach is to take constraints such as the CED to be reflexes of the
complexity of syntactic processing; see e.g. Hawkins (1994), Culicover (1999), and Culicover and
Nowak (2002). Such constraints would be syntactic to the extent that the processing crucially
involves constructing syntactic representations as part of the mapping between syntax and CS.
Unfortunately, we can do little more than speculate on these possibilities here.

    b.   ?This is the senator that when the Mafia pressured him, the senate voted for health care reform.   [≥ *(31b)*]

    c.   ??This is the loot that you identify it and we arrest the thief on the spot.   [≤ *(29a)*]

    d.   ??This is the senator that the Mafia pressured him and the senate voted for health care reform.   [≤ *(30a)*]

The following examples demonstrate the point further. (33a) is the *LS-and*-construction with a trace; (33b) is the *if*-construction with a trace; (33c,d) replace the traces with resumptive pronouns.

(33)   a.   That is one rock star that I see another cover story about *t* and I'll scream.

      b.   ?That is one rock star that if I see another cover story about *t* I'll scream.

      c.   ??That is one rock star that I see another cover story about him and I'll scream.   [≤ *(33a)*]

      d.   (?)That is one rock star that if I see another cover story about him I'll scream.   [≥ *(33b)*]

Clear differences also are found with extraction of an interrogative *wh-*.

(34)   *Extraction*

      a.   ?Who did John say Mary goes out with *t* and her father disinherits her?

      b.   *Who did John say her father disinherits her if Mary goes out with *t*?

      c.   *Who did John say(,) if Mary goes out with *t*(,) her father disinherits her?

(35)   *Resumptive pronoun*

      a.   ??Who$_i$ did John say Mary goes out with him$_i$ and her father disinherits her?   [≤ *(34a)*]

      b.   ?Who$_i$ did John say Mary's father disinherits her if she goes out with him$_i$?   [≥ *(34b)*]

      c.   ?Who$_i$ did John say, if Mary goes out with him$_i$, her father disinherits her?   [≥ *(34c)*]

Differences in judgments are if anything sharper when an adjunct is extracted instead of an object NP. In this case, extraction from the left conjunct is not problematic, while extraction from the left-adjoined subordinate *if*-clause produces a violation of ECP as well as CED.[8]

---

[8] We have kept the terminology of the original version of this chapter, including reference to ECP, which in GB theory constrains extraction of adjuncts from adjuncts, and also accounts for the *that-t* effect (Lasnik and Saito 1992). It is not clear what form the constraints would take in Simpler Syntax; see n. 7 above for some discussion.

(36) *LS-and*

    a. You can just wave your hands like *this* and we arrest the whole gang.

    b. You blow your nose during this aria and the next day Big Louie goes ballistic.

    Extraction from LS-and

    c. ?This is the way (that) you can just wave your hands *t* and we arrest the whole gang.

    d. This is the famous aria during which you blow your nose and the next day Big Louie goes ballistic.

(37) *If*

    a. If you just wave your hands like this we arrest the whole gang.

    b. If you blow your nose during this aria, the next day Big Louie goes ballistic.

    Extraction from if

    c. *This is the way that if you just wave your hands *t*, we arrest the whole gang.

    d. *This is the way that we arrest the whole gang if you just wave your hands *t*.

    e. *This is the famous aria during which if you blow your nose, the next day Big Louie goes ballistic.

How can we account for the difference in extraction in these cases? There must be a difference *somewhere* between *LS-and* and subordinating conjunctions, a difference denied by the Matching Hypothesis. The Mismatching Hypothesis, in fact, permits an elegant account. On this theory, the *if*-clauses in (31), (33b), (34b), and (37) are genuine syntactic adjuncts, and extraction from a syntactic adjunct clause is constrained by some form of the CED—a *syntactic* constraint (see n. 7 above). By contrast, although the initial clauses in (29a), (30a), (33a), (34a), and (36) are semantically subordinate, they are syntactically coordinate; hence the CED does not block extraction from them. At the same time, because they are semantically subordinate, the ATB requirement of the (semantic) CSC does not apply. Hence it is possible to extract from a single conjunct of a syntactically coordinate construction, just in case its interpretation is asymmetric. This constitutes a clear demonstration of the autonomy of (some form of) the CED as a syntactic constraint, one that is not reducible to any notion of semantic subordination. Table 13.2 (next page) sketches the essentials of our solution.

Such conclusions about extraction have been anticipated in the literature; see especially Goldsmith (1985) and Lakoff (1986). Goldsmith and Lakoff both show that asymmetric extraction from a coordinate structure can occur when

Table 13.2 Application of constraints within the Mismatching Hypothesis

Syntactic structure	Conceptual structure
a. S_1 and$_C$ S_2	P_1 AND P_2
CED permits extraction	CSC requires ATB extraction
from either clause	from both propositions
b. S_1 and$_{LS}$ S_2	IF P_1 THEN P_2
CED permits extraction	CSC does not apply
from either clause	
c. If S_1, S_2	IF P_1 THEN P_2
CED permits extraction	CSC does not apply
from S_2 but not S_1	

there is a semantic connectedness between the conjuncts. Their cases involve coordination that implies causal connection:

(38) How many counterexamples can the Coordinate Structure Constraint sustain t and still be assumed? (Lakoff 1986)

Here there is a shared subject (*the Coordinate Structure Constraint*), and extraction is from the left conjunct of a conjoined VP.

Let us briefly consider the implications of our results for the understanding of island phenomena. Postal (1993) shows that a clause from which asymmetric extraction is possible is a "selective" island, in that, among other properties, it allows extraction of NP arguments but not of adjuncts and PPs:

(39) a. They sat around all day drinking and played with the cat.
      b. ?This is the cat that they sat around all day drinking and played with t.
      c. *This is the cat with which they sat around all day drinking and played t.

Examples (39b) and (39c) show that the NP argument but not the PP can be extracted from the right conjunct.[9] Postal makes a strong case that asymmetric extraction is subject to different conditions than ATB extraction. In effect, he shows that CSC applies only when there is semantic parallelism, confirming Goldsmith's point and supporting our conclusion.

---

[9] On the other hand, our examples (36c) and (36d) appear to violate this generalization. They are, to our ears, somewhat worse than the examples with extraction of objects such as (29a) and (30a); that is why we had to set them up with their unextracted counterparts, (36a) and (36b). Still, they are better than the corresponding extractions from *if*-clauses. We leave open a deeper account of these subtle distinctions.

It is not just a terminological point whether the CSC is "syntactic", as Postal suggests, or "semantic". There is no question, it seems to us, that the conditions under which CSC applies are just those where there is semantic parallelism; *ipso facto* it is a semantic constraint, albeit with syntactic consequences. By extension, since selective islands appear when there is no semantic parallelism, these are "semantic", in the same sense.

In contrast, as noted by Cinque (1990) as well as Postal, extraction from subjacency islands is not affected by the argument/non-argument distinction, in the sense that extraction of arguments as well as non-arguments produces ungrammaticality. We suggest therefore that these are genuine syntactic islands (though with caveats—see section 9.4.4). But now the question remains: what is it about the semantic properties of selective islands that allows asymmetric extraction of arguments only? At the moment we have no satisfactory answer to this question; we wish to stress, however, that if our account is correct in its essentials, the answer to this question will constitute a semantic account of selective island phenomena, in contrast to the syntactic approach taken by Cinque (1990) and Rizzi (1990). We note that the approach to extraction that we developed in Chapter 9 allows a very natural account of both syntactic and semantic constraints.

13.6 Inversion and extraction within main clause S-and$_{LS}$-S

Further evidence for the Mismatching Hypothesis and for the semantic character of the CSC comes from another remarkable property of *LS-and*-constructions. In all our previous examples of extraction, the entire *LS-and*-construction has been subordinated. However, if it is a main clause, subject–auxiliary inversion can occur in either the left conjunct (40) or the right (41). (The latter case, (41), appears to have the force of a rhetorical question rather than a normal *wh*-question; nevertheless, inversion operates in the usual fashion.)

(40)   a. Who does Big Louie visit and the whole gang goes nuts?
       b. What does he mention and she kicks him out of her office?

(41)   a. Big Louie sees this mess and who's he going to yell at?
       b. You so much as mention the Minimalist Program and how loud does she scream?

If the left conjunct were in fact a subordinate clause, we would not expect it to support inversion. Compare (40) to the feeble attempts in (42).

(42)   a. *Who does if Big Louie visit, the whole gang goes nuts?
           *Who if does Big Louie visit, the whole gang goes nuts?
           *If who does Big Louie visit, the whole gang goes nuts?
       b. *What does if he mention, she kicks him out of her office?
           *What if does he mention, . . .
           *If what does he mention, . . .

Under the Matching Hypothesis, in which *LS-and* is subordinate in syntax as well as Conceptual Structure, the presence of inversion in (40) cannot be explained. By contrast, under the Mismatching Hypothesis, the first conjunct of (40) counts as a main clause for purposes of syntax, and therefore permits inversion.

The possibility of such asymmetric inversion turns out to depend on an asymmetric interpretation of *and*. *C-and* does not support asymmetric inversion (43a,b), but it does allow parallel inversion in both clauses at once (43c,d).

(43)   a. *What has Bill seen and he has heard the bad news.
       b. *Bill has seen the broken window and what has he heard?
       c. What has Bill seen and what has he heard?
       d. Who was at the party and what were they wearing?

Again the Mismatching Hypothesis provides a way out. Notice that in (43), nothing is extracted from the conjuncts—movement is entirely internal to the conjuncts—so the CSC in its standard form does not apply. However, a possible generalization of the ATB constraint would require that semantically coordinate constituents be of parallel (logical) form. The relevant notion of parallelism remains to be further explored, but ATB extraction would be the particular case where both conjuncts contain a variable bound by the same operator. Extending the account in Table 13.2, then, such a parallelism constraint would apply to symmetric conjunction but not to asymmetric conjunction, creating the difference between the symmetric (43) and the asymmetric (40) and (41). On the other hand, the difference between (40) and (42) would be a *syntactic* difference: inversion is restricted to syntactically main clauses.

What is the position of the *wh*-word in (40)? We wish to show that it is positioned at the front of the conjunct, not at the front of the entire sentence. That is, the syntactic structure is (44a) rather than (44b,c).

(44)   a. [who does Big Louie visit] and [the whole gang goes nuts]
       b. *who [does Big Louie visit] and [the whole gang goes nuts]
       c. *who does [Big Louie visit] and [the whole gang goes nuts]

One reason we believe (44a) is the correct structure is that in the parallel examples (41a,b), a *wh*-word is positioned at the beginning of the second conjunct. That is, we would like to think that *wh*-extraction and inversion apply identically in the two conjuncts—and in both at once in symmetric conjunction such as (43c,d).

However, in main clause S-*and*_LS-S constructions, a *wh*-phrase from the second conjunct can also be positioned at the front of the entire construction. In such a situation, it conditions inversion not in the second conjunct, as in (45a), but rather in the first conjunct. (45b) is not wonderful, but with a more specific *wh*-phrase (45c) it does not seem so bad.

(45) a. **What you just walk into his office and does he start blabbing about *t*?

   b. ?*What do you just walk into his office and he starts blabbing about *t*?

   c. ?Which topic do you just walk into his office and he starts blabbing about *t*?

We will not speculate here on the derived structure of (45c), which seems problematic, to say the least—nor on how inversion is licensed. (Flat structure at the top of the clause, as advocated in Chapters 4 and 9, would seem to make these configurations more feasible than if a lot of projections of I and C have to be manipulated—but the problem is still not trivial.)

This situation raises the possibility that the *wh*-phrase in (40) is positioned outside the entire construction as well (structure (44b or c)). However, notice that extraction from the second conjunct is subject to a specificity constraint, as seen from the contrast (45b,c). Thus, under the reasonable assumption that extraction possibilities are symmetrical in the two conjuncts, extraction from the first conjunct to outside the entire construction ought to be subject to a similar constraint. It is not: the *wh*-phrases in (40) are no more specific than that in (45b), yet the examples are much more acceptable. Hence, if the specificity constraint has to do with extraction from the entire S-_LS*and*-S construction, the *wh*-phrases in (40) must be within the first conjunct. In addition, extraction from the second conjunct is subject to a striking prohibition on removing the subject (46a); yet a subject in the first conjunct can easily be questioned (46b).

(46) a. *Which linguist do you just walk into the room and *t* starts blabbing about Optimality Theory?

   b. Who just walks into the room and John starts blabbing about OT?

Again, this suggests that the *wh*-phrase in (40) and (46b) remains within the first conjunct. (Still, extraction to outside the entire construction is possible with a more specific *wh*-phrase bound to a trace in postverbal position in the first conjunct.)

Having established the position of the *wh*-phrase in (40), we now observe a semantic mismatch. Even though this phrase is within the first conjunct, its semantic scope is the entire sentence, not the first conjunct alone, in the sense that the entire sentence is being questioned. This can be made clearer by comparison to a barely acceptable paraphrase with an *if*-clause—which unlike (42) is rescued from a CED violation by the barbaric resumptive pronoun—or by a paraphrase with *such that* and a resumptive pronoun.

(47)   a. ??Who$_i$ does the whole gang go nuts if Big Louie visits him$_i$? ($\geq$ (42a))
          ?Who is such that Big Louie visits him and the whole gang goes nuts?
       b. ??What$_i$ does she kick him out of her office if he mentions it$_i$? ($\geq$ (42b))
          ?What is such that he mentions it and she kicks him out of her office?

To the extent that these are interpretable as intended, we can see that they paraphrase (40a,b) and that the scope of the *wh*-word is the entire sentence.

The upshot is that the *wh*-phrases in (40) are syntactically inside the first conjunct but semantically take scope over the entire sentence—yet another example of the syntax–semantics mismatch in these constructions, violating Interface Uniformity. It may be recalled that we saw similar mismatches in gapping in section 7.8.3, with examples like

(48)   a. Can John race cars and Mary boats?
       b. Few cats eat Frolic or dogs Whiskas.

In these examples an auxiliary (48a) and a quantifier (48b) take scope over both conjuncts despite being inside the first conjunct. Since gapping occurs only with coordinate *and*, not LS-*and*, these scope effects must have to do with syntactic coordination, not with semantics. So we find some combination of syntactic and semantic licensing conditions for quantifier binding as well as for anaphoric binding and extraction.

13.7 Asymmetric coordination $\neq$ semantic subordination

We have argued thus far that sentences with *LS-and* have nonmatching representations in syntax and CS: the first conjunct is a main clause in syntax but is subordinate in CS. The relationship between the two representations is expressed by an interface rule; as suggested in section 1.5 for similar cases, this rule may be the lexical entry for *and$_{LS}$* itself. We have also alluded to other asymmetric uses of *and*. In this section we wish to return to other cases of asymmetric coordination and show that they do not display exactly the same semantic behavior.

The first type of example involves coordination where the event denoted by the second conjunct is understood as temporally following the first. Sometimes the second event is understood as a consequence of the first as well.

(49) a. John came home and his kids kissed him.
b. Mary bought the newspaper after work and she read it on the train.

The temporal inferences are very strong. In (49a), for example, we understand that John's children kissed him after he came home. In addition, we understand the two events as being connected as parts of a larger event; they did not occur independently, on different 'occasions', so to speak. Similar observations hold for (49b). Consequently, the coordination is asymmetric, in the sense that the conjuncts cannot be reversed in order without changing meaning (even adjusting the pronouns):

(50) a. John's kids kissed him and he came home.   [≠ (50a)]
b. Mary read the newspaper on the train and she bought it after work.   [≠ (50b)]

Crucially, however, we do not want to claim that these sentences have a subordination structure in CS, with either the first or second conjunct treated as subordinate. The binding facts suggest that they are in fact coordinate structures, as seen in (51).

(51) a. *Attempted quantifier binding from left conjunct into right conjunct*
*Everyone$_i$ came home and his$_i$ kids kissed him$_i$.
[*Cf*. Everyone$_i$ went to work after his$_i$ kids kissed him$_i$.)
b. *Attempted anaphora binding from left conjunct into right conjunct*
*John won the contest and a picture of himself appeared in the paper.   [< ??John won the contest because a picture of himself appeared in the paper.]
c. *Attempted quantifier binding from right conjunct into left conjunct*
*He$_i$ came home and everyone$_i$'s kids kissed him$_i$.
[*Cf*. When he$_i$ comes home, everyone$_i$'s kids kiss him$_i$.]
d. *Attempted anaphora binding from right conjunct into left conjunct*
*A picture of himself$_i$ appeared in the paper and John$_i$ was very proud.   [*Cf*. When a picture of himself appeared in the paper, John was very proud.]

We conclude that these are coordinate structures in both syntax and semantics, and that their asymmetric properties are consequences of their (very strong) invited entailments, along lines suggested by Grice (1967/76) and by Relevance Theory (Sperber and Wilson 1995).

A case much closer to the main topic of this chapter concerns the use of *or* in sentences parallel to OM- and *LS-and-* constructions. These usually have interpretations as conditionals with an *unless-* or negated *if*-clause, often with an implied sense of threat (but not always, as seen in (52e)):

(52) a. Another beer or I'm leaving.
                        [≈ Unless I/you have another beer, I'm leaving.
                        ≈ If I/you don't have another beer, I'm leaving.]
     b. You hide that loot right now or we're in big trouble.
                        [= Unless you hide that loot right now, we're in big trouble.
                        = If you don't hide that loot right now, we're in big trouble.]
     c. Little Oscar makes himself scarce by midnight, or Big Louie gets real mad.
     d. The money will be on the table when I open my eyes, or someone is going to be real sorry.
     e. Fuel cap must be on pump side of car or hose will not reach.
                                                    [*sign in gas station*]

Like *LS-and*, this subordinating *or* does not appear in perfect aspect (53a); it can be subordinated, but only as IP-conjunction, not as CP-conjunction (53b); it does not appear in VP conjunction (53c); nor does it gap (53d).

(53) a. Little Oscar has made himself scarce, or Big Louie has gotten real mad.   [*no conditional threat interpretation*]
     b. Georgie warned us that Little Oscar makes himself scarce by midnight or (*that) Big Louie gets real mad.
     c. Big Louie gets the payoff or *(he) gets real mad.
     d. You kill Georgie, or Big Louie *(kills) your dog.

Subordinating *or* does not behave like *LS-and* with respect to binding and licensing of *any* (54).

(54) a. Put another picture of himself$_i$ on the wall and/*or John$_i$ will get upset.
     b. Give him$_i$ enough bribes and/*or every senator$_i$ will vote for the President's proposal.
     c. Say anything and/*or I'll call the police.
     d. Be nice to anyone$_i$ and/*or he$_i$'ll resent you.

Also, although superficially imperative clauses appear in the first conjunct with both *LS-and* and threat-*or*, only with the latter do they permit the semantic trappings of true imperatives. (To the extent that *and* is acceptable in (55), it is not LS-*and*.)

(55) a. Sit down, please, or/??and I'll call the police.
      b. Sit down, won't you, or/??and I'll call the police.
      c. Do sit down, or/??and I'll call the police.
      d. Sit down, or/*and else.

(56) shows that, more generally, subordinating *or* expresses the unpleasant consequence of not doing something, even when the first conjunct cannot be paraphrased with an *unless* or *if not* conditional.

(56) a. I order you to sit down or I'll call the police.
                    [≠ Unless I order you to sit down, I'll call the police;
                     ≠ If I don't order you to sit down, I'll call the police.]
      b. You should sit down or I'll call the police.
                    [≠ Unless you should sit down, I'll call the police;
                     ≠ If you shouldn't sit down, I'll call the police.]
      c. It is imperative that you sit down or I'll call the police.
                    [≠ Unless it is imperative that you sit down, I'll call the police;
                     ≠ It is imperative that unless you sit down, I'll call the police.]
      d. Fuel cap must be on pump side of car or hose will not reach.
         [≠ Unless fuel pump must be on pump side of car, hose will not reach;
          ≠ If fuel pump must not be on pump side of car, hose will not reach.]

These facts suggest that, despite the blatant asymmetry of subordinating *or*, its first conjunct—unlike that with *LS-and*—is not subordinate in CS, and that the paraphrase with an *unless* or *if not* conditional reflects a more distant relation of implicature or invited inference. However, we will not speculate on the subtleties of CS that would permit such a situation.

On the other hand, as coordinate structures with a suitably asymmetric interpretation, threat-*or* sentences should allow asymmetric extraction and inversion. The following examples show that this prediction is correct. (We leave it to the reader to verify that replacing the trace by a resumptive pronoun degrades the subordinate *or* sentences but improves the parallel conditionals, just as with *LS-and*.)

(57) a. This is the loot that you hide *t* right now or we're in big trouble.   [*Cf.*
         ??This is the loot that unless you hide *t* right now, we're in big trouble.]

    b. That is one linguist that you take *t* seriously or you risk your career.   [Cf. ??That is one linguist that unless you take *t* seriously you risk your career.]

    c. ?Midnight is when you make yourself scarce *t* or the next day Big Louie gets real mad.   [Cf. *Midnight is when unless you make yourself scarce, the next day Big Louie gets real mad.]

    d. Which kind of candy do you spit *t* right out or you get real sick?   [cf. ??Which kind of candy do you get real sick unless you spit *t* right out? *Which kind of candy, unless you spit *t* right out, do you get real sick?]

If anything, this evidence presents an even more severe challenge for a syntactic theory of binding and the CSC. There is no reason to distinguish *LS-and* and subordinate *or* in syntactic structure other than their differences in binding. But if one attempts to create a syntactic difference to account for binding, say by making the first conjunct of *LS-and* subordinate and that of subordinate *or* coordinate, then there is no way to account for the parallelism in extraction behavior. Moreover, if subordinate *or* creates a coordinate structure, it should not violate CSC in any event. By contrast, under the approach proposed here, where binding and the CSC are semantic conditions, there is at least the possibility of accounting for the facts—provided one can come up with a suitable CS for subordinate *or*, not necessarily a straightforward task.

13.8 Summary

This chapter has explored the extent to which the subordinating reading of *and* challenges Interface Uniformity. Section 13.3 showed that one can postulate that *LS-and* is subordinating in syntax as well as in semantics, preserving Interface Uniformity, but at a price: one must assume that this conjunction violates all the usual canons for position with respect to the clause it governs and for freedom of position for subordinate clauses.

On the other hand, section 13.2 illustrated a number of phenomena which the Matching Hypothesis predicts automatically but which the Mismatching Hypothesis must add as extra conditions on the interpretation of *and*. Moreover, section 13.4 showed that binding conditions are dependent on the distinction between *LS-and* and *C-and*, again predicted by the Matching Hypothesis under standard versions of binding theory. The price for the Mismatching Hypothesis is that at least part of binding theory must consist of conditions over conceptual structure; but there is independent evidence that this is the case in any event.

Sections 13.5 and 13.6 finally demonstrated a decisive difference between the two hypotheses. Although *LS-and* does not permit ATB extraction, consistent with its being a subordinate conjunction, it *does* allow extraction from and inversion within its subordinate conjunct, so it does not parallel ordinary subordinating conjunctions either. The Matching Theory has no room for this distinction. However, the Mismatching Theory has a wedge of opportunity to distinguish *LS-and* from subordinating conjunctions: it is coordinating in syntax, where the (syntactic) CED applies, but subordinating in semantics, where the (semantic) ATB requirement applies. Section 13.7 showed, however, that asymmetric interpretation of conjunction does not automatically imply that one clause is semantically subordinated.

Our final conclusion is that it is possible to separate genuine syntactic conditions on linguistic form from the reflections of semantic conditions in the syntax. The aspects of syntax that prove actually to be reflections of semantics are more numerous than are generally assumed within mainstream generative grammar—but syntactic conditions do not wither away altogether. There is still need for an autonomous syntax, as well as for an autonomous conceptual structure.

The View from the Periphery: The English Comparative Correlative

14.1 Introduction to the CC construction

Two major themes of the present study are the importance of "peripheral" phenomena to linguistic theory and the pervasiveness of syntax–semantics mismatches, in violation of Interface Uniformity. This chapter illustrates both of these themes through an exploration of a construction of English that we will call the Comparative Correlative (CC), exemplified in (1a). It has a meaning roughly paraphrased by (1b).

(1) a. The more you eat, the less you want.
      b. If/when/as you eat more, you want correspondingly less.

We find the paraphrase with *as* the closest. In particular (as pointed out by a reader), *if*-clauses but not *as*-clauses may be counterfactual (2a) or contain superlatives (2b). The CC construction follows the *as*-clauses in this respect (2c,d).

(2) a. If/*as you had eaten more, you would want less.
      b. If/*as you eat the most, you want the least.
      c. *The more you would want, the less you would eat.
      d. *The most you want, the least you ate.

We are grateful to James McCawley (to whose memory the original version of this chapter was dedicated) and to two reviewers for *Linguistic Inquiry* for useful comments and suggestions on earlier versions of this chapter.

This construction was noted first in the generative literature by Ross (1967: §6.1.2.6). It is treated briefly by Fillmore et al. (1988), who argue that it is idiosyncratic and meaning-bearing. McCawley (1988b), who calls the construction the Comparative Conditional, expands their argument, showing how the construction inherits properties from both the comparative construction and the conditional. McCawley also examines parallel constructions in German and Mandarin, showing how they have similar properties relative to their host languages. Beck (1997) proposes a formal semantics-style account of the construction's meaning, concentrating on German and English; she also cites examples from Dutch, French, Maltese, and Korean.[1] Den Dikken (2004) discusses how the comparative correlative is realized in a variety of languages; in each case the special meaning of the construction is conveyed, but the syntax shows some variation from language to language. Borsley (2003) argues that the English version of the construction receives a particularly natural treatment within the HPSG framework. Michaelis (1994) shows that in Latin the semantics of the comparative correlative are transparently realized in its syntax, unlike in English. In investigating the syntax of CC in more detail, we will essentially confirm and refine the conclusions of Fillmore et al. and McCawley, showing how they bear on our more global concerns.

We call the two parts of CC the "clauses" of the construction: the first clause (*the more you eat* in (1a)) is C_1 and the second (*the less you want*) is C_2.

For the moment, let us call the node dominating the entire construction simply CC. Then we get an overall structure along the lines of (3a), using conventional treatment of the CP/IP distinction, or (3b) using the flatter structure of Chapters 4 and 9.

(3)

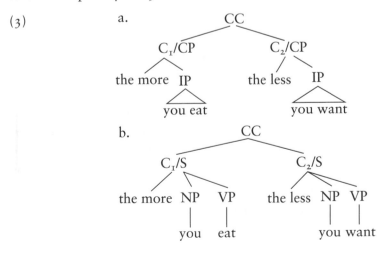

---

[1] Beck bases her analysis on parallels with *if*-conditionals but does not mention *as*-correlatives. We suspect that her analysis could be easily adapted to the latter.

For the moment staying with (3a), it labels each clause as a CP. This is motivated by the fact that (as noted by Fillmore et al. 1988: 508) the complementizer *that* can occur in either clause, perhaps with a sense of a more colloquial register.

(4)　The more (that) you eat, the less (that) you want.
　　　The angrier (that) Sue gets, the more (that) Fred admires her.

Now it might be that CC is a completely idiomatic category. However, it can be embedded in a complement construction, suggesting that actually CC = IP.

(5)　a. I think that the more you eat, the less you want.
　　　b. I'm not shocked by the idea that the more you eat, the less you want.
　　　c. It is obvious that the more you eat, the less you want.
　　　d. It is not entirely clear if/whether the more you eat, the less you want.
　　　e. I want to explain exactly why the more you eat, the less you want.

Another option is that in (3), the node CC = CP, and that therefore the use of CC in (5) is an instance of CP recursion. Still another possibility is that CC is semantically propositional, whatever its syntactic category, and by virtue of this alone it can appear as the complement of CP. In any event, we are faced with the uncomfortable choice of either inventing an entirely new syntactic category just for CC, as in (3), or else permitting an unconventional expansion of IP or CP into two CPs. We will tentatively call CC an IP or CP, and explore some possible ways to alleviate its apparent anomaly.

If CC is IP or CP, what is its internal structure? We will be exploring two main possibilities:

Hypothesis A (Paratactic Hypothesis)
C_1 and C_2 are paratactic clauses forming an IP or CP.

(6)　$[_{IP/CP}[_{C_1}$ the more you eat$]$ $[_{C_2}$ the less you want$]]$

This is the "what you see is what you get" approach, in conformance with the Simpler Syntax Hypothesis. C_1 and C_2 are main clauses jammed together paratactically in an idiosyncratic configuration that, like constructions observed in Chapters 4 and 7 such as small clauses, gerundive NPs, sluicing, and gapping, is anomalous from the point of view of X-bar theory.

Hypothesis B (Left-Subordinate Hypothesis)
C_2 is a main clause, C_1 a left adjunct.

(7)　$[_{IP/CP}[_{CP/C_1}$ the more you eat$]$ $[_{IP/C_2}$ the less you want$]]$

This gives the construction a somewhat more canonical structure, with a main clause and a preposed adjunct.[2]

Three other logical possibilities might occur to the systematic investigator:

Hypothesis C (Right-Subordinate Hypothesis)
C_1 is a main clause, C_2 a right adjunct.

(8) $[_{IP/CP}[_{IP/C_1}$ the more you eat] $[_{CP/C_2}$ the less you want]]

This is the mirror image of the left-subordinating hypothesis and shares all its virtues and vices so far.

Hypothesis D (Empty Conjunction Hypothesis)
C_1 and C_2 are IPs conjoined by an empty conjunction.

(9) $[_{IP}[_{IP/C_1}$ the more you eat] Conj $[_{IP/C_2}$ the less you want]]

This is a potential refinement of the paratactic hypothesis. It eliminates the apparent anomaly of paratactic clauses at the cost of introducing a necessarily empty conjunction. However, it still does not solve the node-labeling problem of the left-subordinate hypothesis: IP/C_1 and IP/C_2 are both IPs that directly dominate CPs. As far as we can tell, then, this is at best a notational variant of the paratactic hypothesis and can be disregarded.[3]

Hypothesis E (Empty Verb Hypothesis)
C_1 and C_2 are arguments of an empty main verb.

(10) $[_{IP}[_{C_1}$ the more you eat] Infl $[_{VP}$ V $[_{C_2}$ the less you want]]]

In this hypothesis, CC is headed by an empty Infl and an empty V; C_1 is the specifier and C_2 the complement of the empty V; C_1 and C_2 are both

---

[2] Interestingly, Beck (1997) calls C_1 a subordinate clause, presumably because of its semantics, which she treats along the lines of *if*-clauses. However, when she draws a syntactic tree, it is symmetrical, like (6). She does not comment on the apparent mismatch—which is the main point of the present chapter.

[3] In Italian, however, it is possible to have *e* 'and' between C_1 and C_2.

(i) Più   si mangia (e)   più   si ingrassa.
    more SI eats   (and) more SI gets-fat
    'The more you eat, the fatter you get.'

This does not, in our view, constitute evidence about the correct analysis for the English construction, which differs from the Italian one in a number of respects. The most obvious difference is that English uses the idiosyncratic *the more* while Italian uses the adverbial *più* 'more' in clause-initial position. Similar observations pertain to Den Dikken's (2004) evidence that the syntax of the comparative correlative is somewhat more transparently related to its semantics in other languages than it is in English. Den Dikken demonstrates how to assign to the comparative correlative in English a syntax that makes it entirely transparent as well, but it is still necessary to say for English that *the more* is a special form with a special interpretation.

subordinate clauses. This has the virtue of giving CC a relatively normal IP structure. The price is an empty verb and empty Infl whose only purpose is to make this normal structure possible.

14.2 Evidence for the left-subordinate hypothesis

We might rule out Hypothesis E just on methodological grounds, because of its unmotivated verb and Infl. However, we have stressed that the Simpler Syntax Hypothesis should always be empirically justified. Fortunately, there is simple empirical evidence against both Hypothesis E and Hypothesis C. This evidence shows that if anything is the main clause of CC, it has to be C_2, as proposed in the left-subordinate hypothesis.

First, when CC is the complement of a verb or adjective that governs the subjunctive, subjunctive morphology may appear on C_2 (11a). (Since in our dialect the subjunctive is only optional in these contexts, indicative in both clauses is also possible.) It may not appear on C_1 (11b).

(11)   It is imperative that/I demand that
   a.   the more John eats, the more he pay(s).
   b.   *the more John eat, the more he pay(s).

It is also possible to form a tag question based on C_2 (12a), but not one based on C_1 (12b,c).

(12)   a.   The more we eat, the angrier you get, don't you.
   b.   *The more we eat, the angrier you get, don't we.
   c.   *The more we eat, don't we, the angrier you get.

Hypothesis E incorrectly predicts that subjunctive should appear on the empty verb, which is the main verb of the construction, and that tags should echo the empty Infl and contain a pronoun counterpart of the whole clause C_1. Hypothesis C incorrectly predicts that the subjunctive should appear on C_1, and that tags too should be based on C_1. Thus these data rule out both Hypotheses C and E: they appear to show that C_2 is a main clause and C_1 is a subordinate clause.

The paraphrase relationship illustrated in (1) and (2) further suggests that C_1 is interpreted as a subordinate clause; more evidence to this effect will appear in what is to follow, especially section 14.5. Hence, given the evidence that the antecedent in a comparative correlative is semantically subordinate,[4] Interface

---

[4] There are of course other possible semantic accounts of comparative correlatives, which we will ignore here. Actually, our argument goes through under *any* semantic analysis of the comparative correlative: the point is that it is expressed in two apparently distinct ways in syntax. At least one of these, therefore, must either present a syntax–semantics mismatch or else have a covert syntax matching the other.

Uniformity urges us toward the left-subordinate hypothesis. Moreover, the left-subordinate hypothesis correctly predicts the use of subjunctive in (10) and the form of the tag in (11).[5]

Both clauses of CC begin with a constituent bearing comparative morphology; let us call this clause type a "CC-clause". A variant of the construction, which we will call the Inverted Comparative Correlative (ICC), is shown in (13). Its second clause is a CC-clause, but its first clause retains the comparative phrase in its normal position.

(13)   Mary got angrier and angrier, the more pictures she looked at.

The paraphrases in (14) show that the first clause of an ICC, the one that bears normal order, plays a role parallel to C_2 in a CC.

(14)   a. The more pictures she looked at, the angrier Mary got.   [=(13)]
       b. If/when/as she looked at more pictures, Mary got correspondingly
           angrier.   [≈(13)]

We will therefore call the first clause of an ICC C_2 and the second C_1, in order to preserve the semantic parallel. The fact that C_2 is in the form of a normal clause suggests again that it is a main clause and C_1 is subordinate.

This hunch is verified by the subjunctive and tag versions of ICC: the first clause in an ICC parallels the behavior of C_2 in a CC.

(15)   It is imperative that /I demand that
       a. John pay more, the more he eats.
       b. *John pays more, the more he eat.
(16)   a. You get angrier, the more we eat, don't you.
       b. *You get angrier, the more we eat, don't we.

We next note that it is possible to construct direct questions based on CCs. In such questions, *the* in C_2 is replaced by *how much*, and inversion takes place in C_2 if appropriate. The interpretation closely parallels that of sentences with *when/as*-clauses such as (17c).[6]

(17)   a. The harder it rains, how much faster do you run?
       b. The harder it rains, how much faster a flow do you see in the river?

---

[5] In Swedish, according to Verner Egeland (p.c), the second clause in the corresponding construction displays V2 effects while the first clause does not. To the extent that crosslinguistic evidence is telling in such constructions, this is a further piece of evidence that the second clause is a main clause and the first is subordinate. For discussion of V2 effects in the comparative correlative, see Den Dikken (2004).

[6] The complementizer *that* cannot appear in C_2:

(i)   The hard (that) it rains, how much faster a flow (*that) appears in the river?

c. When/as it rains harder, how much faster a flow appears in the river?

In principle, C_1 might also yield question forms. But it turns out that a question of the requisite form has the semantics of an ICC. For instance, (18a) approximately paraphrases (18b), the conditional paraphrase expected of ICC. In other words, the questioned clause in (18a) is C_2, even though it comes first.

(18)   a. How much harder has it rained, the faster a flow you see in the river?
       b. How much harder has it rained, when you see a faster flow in the river?   [≈(18a)]

Again this shows that C_2 is the clause with main clause force, in both the CC and ICC constructions.

Consider also the imperative construction. Standard imperative form, where the subject is omitted, is impossible in a CC (19a). However, with the proper kind of generic subject in C_2 and the proper pragmatics, a moderately acceptable imperative can be formed (19b). As might by now be expected, though, C_1 cannot have imperative form (19c). Again, this parallels the semantics of imperative conditionals (whose subject is however optional (19d)). We note also that an ICC can form imperatives on C_2; as befits the normal clause structure of C_2, the subject can be omitted (19e)). Evidently the subject is obligatory only in CC-clauses.

(19)   a. *The more John eats, the tighter keep your mouth shut about it.
       b. ?The more John eats, the tighter everyone keep your mouth shut about it, ok?/if you would.
       c. *The more everyone eat, the more John keeps his big mouth shut about it, ok?
       d. If/when/as John eats more, (everyone) keep your mouth shut tighter, ok?   [parallels (19b)]
       e. (Everyone) keep your mouth shut tighter, the more John eats, ok?

Within the left-subordinate hypothesis, the facts in (18) and (19) follow automatically from standard assumptions. Within the paratactic hypothesis, we must say that the possibility of questions and imperatives follows from the semantics of main clause force, which is usually reflected in the syntax— but not here.

In a further surprising variant of the CC construction, C_2 (and more marginally, C_1 as well) takes the form of an accusative-gerundive complement of verbs. Its distribution as complement of verbs like *imagine* suggests that it is a small clause in the sense of section 4.5.3.

(20) a. ?I can well imagine the more he eats, the fatter him getting.
     b. ?? I can well imagine the more him eating, the fatter him getting.

Like imperative CCs, gerundive CCs must have an overt subject. There is no form (21b) parallel to the subjectless gerundive (21a).[7]

(21) a. Bill can well imagine getting fat.
     b. *Bill can well imagine the more he eats, the fatter getting.

The ICC construction also appears in gerundives. Because its C_2 is a normal clause rather than a CC-clause, it can be subjectless.

(22) Fred can well imagine (Joe) getting fatter, the more he eats.

The small clause CC appears to be an isolated instance of a tenseless CC. For instance, a CC cannot appear as an infinitival complement, with or without an overt subject in C_2. (23a,b) explore a number of conceivable configurations, all of which prove grossly ungrammatical. On the other hand, an ICC, with the normal clause first, is acceptable here (23c).

(23) a. *It is important (for) the more you (to) eat, the more careful ((for) you) to be.
     b. *It is important (for) the more to eat, the more careful to get.
     c. It is important [(for you) to be more careful, the more you eat].

To sum up, a wide variety of constructions in which CCs can be embedded suggest that the CC construction is asymmetric, with C_2 behaving as a main clause. More evidence will appear in section 14.5.

14.3 Evidence for the paratactic hypothesis

As mentioned in section 14.1, the paratactic hypothesis on the face of it seems unlikely, given the absence of parataxis from core constructions of English, not

---

[7] (20) presents an additional challenge. Usually a small clause gerundive construction permits no fronted subordinate constituent (except possibly with exaggerated intonation breaks), as seen in (i). In particular, a fronted conditional clause is out (id):

(i) a. ?*I can well imagine on Tuesday him leaving. [i.e. he leaves on Tuesday]
   b. *I can well imagine quickly Mary answering the question.
   c. ?*I can well imagine with a hatchet Mary destroying the Jeep.
   d. ?*I can well imagine if he eats more, him getting fat.

Hence it does not appear that C_1 can be a (normal) fronted subordinate clause in (20). A possible escape is provided by the paratactic hypothesis, in which C_1 is not a subordinate adjoined constituent. However, formulating the constraints on the small clause construction to admit this possibility is a challenge that we must leave for future research.

to mention the subordinate clause interpretation of C_I extensively documented in section 14.2. Nonetheless, we will argue eventually that the paratactic hypothesis is correct, and that the CC construction is an example of a syntax–semantics mismatch: paratactic (i.e. quasi-coordinate) syntax with conditional semantics. This section presents some initial plausibility arguments for such a position. What we take to be the crucial facts, however, are postponed till section 14.6.

We begin by recalling the colloquial conditional construction mentioned in Chapter 10, in which parataxis is about the only conceivable relation between the clauses.

(24)   Mary listens to the Grateful Dead↑, she gets depressed↓.
       [≈ If/when Mary listens to the Grateful Dead, she gets depressed.]

This construction gives some independent motivation for the existence in English of paratactic syntactic structures whose interpretation parallels sentences with preposed adjuncts. This lends the paratactic hypothesis for CC a somewhat greater patina of legitimacy than it might have had in isolation.

We also recall that (24) shows a semantic alliance with the *LS-and* construction that was the main topic of Chapter 13.

(25)   Mary listens to the Grateful Dead and she gets depressed.
       [= If/when Mary listens to the Grateful Dead, she gets depressed.]

Chapter 13 showed that the most plausible account of *LS-and* is as a syntactically ordinary conjunction that maps onto a subordinate interpretation of C_I, i.e. as a syntax–semantics mismatch. Since this construction shows that a conditional interpretation need not entail syntactic subordination, we tentatively conclude that the semantics of the CC construction does not constitute immediate grounds for ruling out the paratactic hypothesis.

A further consideration concerns the ordering of the clauses. Typically, subordinate clauses can occur either before or after their main clauses:

(26)   a. If/when Mary listens to the Grateful Dead, she gets depressed.
       b. Mary gets depressed if/when she listens to the Grateful Dead.

(An exception, of course, is the *if–then* construction, which cannot be reordered into a *then–if* construction.) By contrast, neither a CC, nor an ICC, nor either of the constructions in (24)–(25) can be reordered. In the cases where reordering is grammatical, the conditional meaning is reversed.

(27)   a. The angrier Mary got, the more she looked at pictures.
       [≠ The more she looked at pictures, the angrier Mary got.]

    b. *The more pictures Mary looked at, she got angrier and angrier.

    c. *Mary gets depressed↓, she listens to the Grateful Dead↑.

    d. Mary gets depressed and she listens to the Grateful Dead.   [≠(25)]

Thus, in their dependence on linear order, the CC and ICC constructions parallel these other nonsubordinating constructions, rather than standard constructions with adjunct subordinate clauses. (However, the behavior of *if–then* keeps this from being an altogether decisive argument in favor of the paratactic hypothesis. Perhaps *if–then* constructions are paratactic too.)

We thus find ourselves in an interesting tension. On the one hand, all these constructions have approximately the semantics of the conditional. On the other hand, although the conditional itself syntactically subordinates the *if*-clause, these other constructions (CC, ICC, and (24)–(25)) show no overt syntactic subordination. If semantic parallelism were always to require syntactic parallelism (following Interface Uniformity), we would be forced to assimilate all these latter constructions to subordinating syntax, at whatever price in the naturalness of syntactic derivations. The alternative is to accept complexity in the syntax–semantics interface, with the advantage of rendering the syntactic component simpler. So, as usual in the present study, the basic issue is in which component—the syntax itself or the syntax–semantics interface—the necessary complexity is to be localized. Our position is that there is no cut-and-dried answer; the question must be decided on a case-by-case basis.

The paratactic hypothesis, of course, has one particularly pointed consequence for this issue. In the previous section, subjunctive, tag, question, and imperative configurations showed that C_2 in a CC has main clause force, and that C_1 is subordinate. If, as the paratactic hypothesis proposes, this subordination occurs only in semantics, we have to conclude that the notion "main clause force" is based on the semantics of the CC construction, not on its syntax; by extension the same would have to be the case in ordinary sentences as well. For the moment we will leave the issue in tension, keeping both the left-subordinate and the paratactic hypotheses alive.

We now turn away temporarily from the choice between these two and address the balance between idiosyncrasy and regularity *within* C_1 and C_2.

14.4 The internal structure of CC-clauses

14.4.1 *The subject requirement and* be-*omission in CC-clauses.*

We noticed in section 14.2 that a subject is obligatory in C_2 of imperative and gerundive CCs ((19a) and (21)). By contrast, the subject can be omitted in C_2 of imperative and gerundive ICCs ((19e) and (22)). We ascribed this to the fact that C_2 in CC is a CC-clause, but C_2 in ICC is a normal clause. Hence part of the syntactic characterization of a CC-clause must be the obligatoriness of its subject.

McCawley (1988b) points out another curious aspect of CC-clauses: the verb *be* can be omitted under certain conditions. (28a) illustrates with both clauses of the CC construction. (28b) shows that *be*-omission is a characteristic of CC-clauses rather than of the CC construction as a whole: in a ICC, *be* can be omitted in the CC-clause C_1 but not in the normal clause C_2. McCawley further observes that the subject of the clause must have a generic or variable interpretation. (28c), with a specific subject, illustrates: *be* cannot be omitted. As Tom Wasow has pointed out to us (p.c.), the remnant in the CC-clause cannot be an anaphoric pronoun (28d).

(28) a. The higher the stakes (are), the lower his expectations (are).
      b. $\left\{ \begin{array}{l} \text{His expectations are lower,} \\ \text{*His expectations lower,} \end{array} \right\}$ the higher the stakes.
      c. $\left\{ \begin{array}{l} \text{The more obnoxious Fred is,} \\ \text{*The more obnoxious Fred,} \end{array} \right\}$ the less attention you should pay to him.
      d. The richer John's friends get, the richer he *(is).

Since CC-clauses look a bit like comparatives, we might think this omission is related to that in ordinary comparatives such as (29a). However, (29b) shows that *be*-omission in ordinary comparatives does not depend on whether the subject is specific or not, and (29c) shows that the remnant in the comparative clause can be an anaphoric pronoun.

(29) a. His expectations are always lower than mine (are).
      b. John was lots more obnoxious than Fred (was).
      c. John's friends are all richer than he/him.

Hence *be*-omission in CC is probably not related directly to that in comparatives. Rather, the specificity restriction in CC-clauses appears more closely related to a parallel restriction in the complements of *no matter* and *wh-ever*, discussed by Culicover (1999). Note that these, like CC-clauses, have fronted predicates.

(30) a. You should always lock your door, no matter how fancy the hotel (might be).
      b. I don't plan to lock the door, no matter how fancy this hotel *(is).

    c. I'm going out, whatever the weather.

    d. I'm going out, wherever that hurricane *(might be).

    e. You should never trust your mother, no matter how wise she *(is).

Although we suspect this omission is related to the semantics as well as the syntax of these constructions, we have no explanation to offer at this point. We note, however, that the constructions in (30) are very close in meaning to the CC construction: while CC asserts a dependency of C_2 on C_1, these cases assert that the main clause has *no* dependency on the situation described in the free relative.

    Again, however this *be*-omission is characterized, it appears to be a feature of CC-clauses, in this case shared with *no matter* and adverbial *wh-ever* clauses. Given this and the subject requirement, to some extent CC-clauses seem to constitute a special construction of English.

14.4.2 *The usual constraints on long-distance dependency*

CC-clauses appear to have a long-distance dependency between the comparative phrase at the front and a gap within the CP. Indeed, the gaps in the two clauses show the typical constraints on long-distance dependencies. (31)–(35) illustrate with gaps in C_1; (36)–(40) illustrate in C_2. We will assume for the moment that the antecedent of the trace is the *the more*-phrase.

Constraints in C_1

(31)   [The more counterexamples]$_i$ Mary says that Bill has helped Fred to discover t_i, the less I believe her.   *[unbounded dependency in C_1]*

(32)   a. *[The more food]$_i$ Mary knows a man that eats t_i, the poorer she gets.   *[CNPC, ECP]*

     b. ?[The more great books]$_i$ he makes the claim [that he has read t_i], the more suspicious I become of him.   *[CNPC]*

     c. *[The fatter]$_i$ he goes to a doctor when he gets t_i, the more he eats.   *[CED, ECP]*

     d. *[The fatter]$_i$ that [that he gets t_i] bothers him, the more he eats.   *[Subject Condition, ECP]*

     e. ?[The more books]$_i$ I ask whether he'll read t_i, the angrier he gets.   *[weak wh-island]*

     f. *[The more books]$_i$ I ask to whom$_j$ he will give t_j t_i, the more he reads.   *[strong wh-island]*

     g. *[The more people]$_i$ I ask what$_j$ he will give t_i to t_j, the more he reads.   *[strong wh-island, crossing dependency]*

(33) a. [The more carefully]$_i$ he words the letter t_i, the safer he'll be.
      b. *[The more carefully]$_i$ he knows a man that worded the letter t_i, the safer he'll be.   [CNPC, ECP]

(34) a. The more geniuses John meets the angrier he gets.
      b. *[The more]$_i$ John meets [t_i geniuses]], the angrier he gets.
                                                 [Left Branch Condition]

(35) a. [The more people]$_i$ you say t_i will buy tickets, the happier I'll be.
      b. *[The more people]$_i$ you say that t_i will buy tickets, the happier I'll be.   [that-t effect]
      c. [The more people]$_i$ you say that right after the show opens t_i will buy tickets, the happier I'll be.   [adverb effect]

Constraints in C_2

(36) The more I talk to Joe, [the less about linguistics]$_i$ I am inclined to think Sally has taught him to appreciate t_i.   [unbounded dependency in C_2]

(37) a. *The more he eats, [the poorer]$_i$ he knows a woman that gets t_i.   [CNPC, ECP]
      b. ?The more he eats, [the poorer]$_i$ he makes the claim that he gets t_i.   [CNPC]
      c. *The more he eats, [the fatter]$_i$ he goes to a doctor when he gets t_i.   [CED, ECP]
      d. *The more he eats, [the fatter]$_i$ that [that he gets t_i] really bothers me.   [Subject Condition, ECP]
      e. ?The more books he buys, [the more books]$_i$ I wonder whether he'll read t_i.   [weak wh-island]
      f. *The more he reads, [the more books]$_i$ I wonder to whom$_j$ he will give t_j t_i.   [strong wh-island]
      g. *The more he reads, [the more people]$_i$ I wonder what$_j$ he will give t_i to t_j.   [strong wh-island, crossing dependency]

(38) a. The sooner you call, [the more carefully]$_i$ I will word the letter t_i.
      b. *The sooner you call, [the more carefully]$_i$ I know a man that will word the letter t_i.   [CNPC, ECP]

(39) a. The richer John gets, [the more geniuses]$_i$ John meets t_i.
      b. *The richer he gets, [the more]$_i$ John meets [t_i geniuses].
                                                 [Left Branch Condition]

(40) a. The more articles he reads, [the fewer people]$_i$ he thinks (*that) t_i will go into linguistics.   [that-t effect]
      b. The more articles he reads, [the fewer people]$_i$ he thinks (that) under the current circumstances t_i will go into linguistics.   [adverb effect]

In CCs the gap can also be in subject position in C_1 (41a) or C_2 (41b).

(41)   a. The more people that *t* arrive, the louder (that) it gets.
        b. The more people (that) you give beer to, the more people that *t* get sick.

In such cases, some speakers cannot omit *that* after the comparative phrase. Consider C_1 in (42a) and C_2 in (42b).

(42)   a. The more people arrive, the louder (that) it gets.
        b. The more people (that) you give beer to, the more people get sick.

In (41a), what is compared is the number of people that arrive. Some speakers (including RJ) find (42a) ambiguous between this interpretation and one in which what is compared is the extent to which people arrive (as in *the more that people arrive...t...*). Other speakers (including PWC) find that (42a) cannot paraphrase (41a), and only the latter interpretation is possible. For these speakers, *that* cannot be absent before a covert subject, just as in a standard relative clause.[8]

(43)   a.   The man that arrived on the ten fifty-three was my brother.
        b.   *The man arrived on the ten fifty-three was my brother.

14.4.3 *The upper end of the long-distance dependency*

Consider the structure of the comparative phrase. *More* and *less*, as usual, are quantifiers; they can occur in the specifier of NP (44a), AP (44b), AdvP (44c), or PP (44d), or alone as an adverbial modifier of VP (44e) (Jackendoff 1977: ch. 6). (*More* is of course subject to the usual morphological alternations of the

---

[8] The two clauses in CC also show exactly the reconstruction and anti-reconstruction effects of topicalization (section 9.4.5). Compare the topicalization examples in (i) with the CC examples in (ii).

(i)   a.   [The pictures of himself$_i$ in the living room]$_j$, John$_i$ bought t$_j$ in Paris.   [*reconstruction*]
       b.   [The pictures that John$_i$ owns]$_j$, he$_i$ hung t$_j$ in the living room.   [*anti-reconstruction*]
       c.   (*)[The pictures of John$_i$ in the living room]$_j$, he$_i$ likes t$_j$ the best.   [*anti-reconstruction*]
(ii)   a.   [The more pictures of himself$_i$]$_j$ that John$_i$ buys t$_j$, the more arrogant he becomes.
                                                                                      [*reconstruction*]
       b.   [The more pictures that John$_i$ buys]$_j$ that he$_i$ likes t$_i$, the more arrogant he becomes.
                                                                                      [*anti-reconstruction*]
       c.   (*)[The more pictures of John$_i$]$_j$ that he$_i$ buys t$_j$, the more arrogant he becomes.
                                                                                      [*anti-reconstruction*]

It is well known that adjuncts moved into an A′-position do not reconstruct. Hence in (ib), for example, *he$_i$* and *John$_i$* can be coreferential, even though *he$_i$* c-commands the trace of the constituent containing *John$_i$* and would otherwise be expected to produce a Condition C violation. On the other hand [for some speakers, e.g. PWC but not RJ], an argument does reconstruct, so that

comparative, yielding forms such as *bigger, fatter,* and the suppletions *better* and *worse.*)

(44)   a. (much/far/a lot) more/less custard
      b. (much/far/a lot) more/less beautiful
      c. (much/far/a lot) more/less quickly
      d. (much/a lot) farther [= more far] down the road
      e. sleep (much/far/a lot) more/less

The appears to be a specifier of *more* and *less*, in alternation with other specifiers such as *much, far,* and *a lot.* (Jespersen (1949: 509–12) points out that it bears no diachronic relation to the definite article. There are a few related relics in the language, such as *none/not much the wiser* and *all the more;* we return to the last of these in section 14.4.4.)

So the overall structure of the comparative phrase is roughly (45) (except for (44e), where the topmost XP and X′ are absent).

(45)

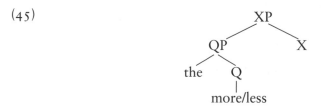

As with fronted *wh*-phrases, fronted comparative phrases carry along everything of which *the more* is a left branch.

What is the position of the comparative phrase? The structures in (31)–(40) assume that there is a direct dependency between the comparative phrase and the trace position. In the usual movement theory of long-distance dependencies, this amounts to saying that the comparative phrase moves to the Spec of CP. In a non-movement theory such as HPSG or that developed in Chapter 9, the

---

(ic) is a Condition C violation. The same pattern appears in the CC construction, which is precisely what we would expect if this were an instance of A′-movement.

    CCs also license parasitic gaps.

(iii)   a. The more people he talks to *t* without inviting *pg* to the party, the more embarrassed he becomes.
      b. The more timid he feels, the more people he interviews *t* without asking questions of *pg*.

Curiously, CCs do not license parasitic gaps where the parasitic gap is contained within a relative clause that precedes the true gap.

(iv)   a. *The more people everyone who likes *pg* pays attention to *t*, the happier we all are.
      b. *The later it gets, the more people everyone who likes *pg* pays attention to *t*.

We have no explanation for this fact.

comparative phrase is generated in Spec of CP (or, in the flat structure of Chapters 4 and 9, as a leftmost daughter of S), and a connection is formed between it and the empty category. The most plausible structure is thus roughly (46a) or (46b), paralleling for instance indirect questions.

(46)

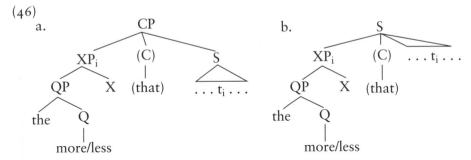

14.4.4 *Behavior of* the more *compared to other specifiers of QP*

For a further basis of comparison, let us examine yet another construction semantically related to the CC construction, illustrated in (47), in which *all the* appears as a specifier of *more* or *-er*, parallel to *much*, *far*, and *a lot*. Crucially for the parallel, *all the* can appear as specifier in C_2 of a ICC (47c); *much*, *far*, and *a lot* are less felicitous here (47d).

(47) a. Whenever Bill smokes, Susan hates him {all the more/much more/far more/a lot more}.
      b. Once Janet left, Fred became {all the crazier/much crazier/far crazier/a lot crazier}.
      c. Fred became all the crazier, the more often Janet left.
      d. Fred became {*much crazier/?far crazier/*a lot crazier}, the more often Janet left.

All the more can front, unlike *much*, *far*, and *a lot*. When it occurs at the front, it is accompanied by the entire projection of which it is the specifier, and it requires subject-aux inversion (48). Coincidentally, such inversion occurs marginally in CCs as well, in C_2 but not C_1 (49):

(48) a. When Bill smokes, all the more/*much more does Susan hate him.
          Once Janet left, all the crazier/*much crazier did Fred become.
      b. *When Bill smokes, all the more Susan hates him. [*no inversion*]
          *Once Janet left, all the crazier Fred became.

(49) a. ?The more Bill smokes, the more does Susan hate him.
      b. ?The more often Janet leaves, the angrier does Fred become.

    c. *The more does Bill smoke, the more Susan hates him. [inversion in
       C_1]

    d. *The more does Bill smoke, the more does Susan hate him.

The degree specifier *so* also triggers inversion, but *how* (in indirect questions)
does not.

(50)   a. so much did you eat that...
      b. so fast did you run that...
      c. so intelligent a dog did you buy that...

(51)   a. I know how much you ate.
      b. I know how fast you ran.
      c. I know how intelligent a dog you bought.

    There are still more distinctions. First, as seen in (47), *all the more* need not
appear in clause-initial position; the same is true of *so* (52). By contrast, *the
more* must appear in clause-initial position (53a–c), like *how* (53d).

(52)   a. He ate so much that he got sick.
      b. So much did he eat that he got sick.

(53)   a.   The more you eat, the more you want.
      b. *You eat the more, the more you want.
      c. *The more you eat, you want the more.
      d. *I wonder you ate how much.

Second, unlike these other specifiers, *the more* in initial position permits the
presence of the complementizer *that*, as observed earlier. (Under a standard
analysis, this is a violation of the Doubly-filled COMP filter.)

(54)   a.   the faster that you eat,...
      b. *...all the faster that do you eat
      c. *so much faster that did you eat that...
      d. *how much faster that you eat

Third, *the more* does not allow pied-piping of a preceding preposition. *All the
more* is marginal here, and *so* and *how* are of course acceptable.

(55)   a.   *to the more people Bill talks,...
      b. ?*...to all the more people will Bill talk
      c.   to so many people does Bill talk that...
      d.   I wonder to how many people Bill talks

    On the whole, then, (46) represents a reasonable structure for CC-clauses:
they fall together in many respects with other constructions that involve mater-

ial in A′ positions. On the other hand, like the CC construction's unusual IP-over-CP phrase structure, its long-distance dependencies appear to some extent *sui generis*. In particular, one must deal with (a) the obligatory positioning of the *the more*-phrase at the front, in contrast with the optional positioning there of *so* and the nearly synonymous *all the more*; (b) the optional presence of the complementizer *that* in what appears to be a main clause (at least C_2, and, we will argue, C_1); (c) the marginal possibility of inversion in C_2, in contrast with the obligatory inversion with *all the* and *so* and its impossibility in indirect questions and C_1; and (d) the failure of a preposition to pied-pipe with *the more*.

One may of course attempt to use the PPT/MP technology of functional heads, strong features, and attraction to describe these idiosyncratic properties of the CC construction; but as far as we can see, these properties are not in any interesting sense reducible to those of other constructions in the language. It would be equally natural—in fact more natural from a theory-neutral perspective—to say simply that these are the properties of the construction, without reference to formal devices that have no particular explanatory role here. In short, this system of specifiers has the peculiar sort of idiosyncratic properties of the "syntactic nuts" discussed in section 1.5.

In the framework for long-distance dependencies developed in Chapter 9, there is no movement of the *the more*-phrase. Rather, it is syntactically licensed in A′ position, and along with the trace it is linked to a bound variable in CS. Its relation to the rest of the clause, like that of *wh*-phrases and topics, comes via indirect licensing. All the peculiarities of the *the more*-phrase and related fronted phrases with *all the* and *so* are "signatures" of these constructions, in the sense of Chapter 9. Their idiosyncratic properties resemble those of other signatures, only if anything they are still more idiosyncratic.

We have concluded that the internal structure of CC-clauses presents a number of idiosyncrasies: the obligatoriness of the subject in imperatives and gerundives, the possibility of omitting *be* with a nonspecific nonpronominal subject, and the peculiar configuration in the specifier of the comparative phrase. The last of these is pretty much within the range of variation for constructions in which a specifier motivates positioning a phrase at the front of a clause. On the other hand, CC-clauses help point up how peculiar this range of variation is, a fact neglected in recent mainstream tradition.

14.5 Binding

We return now to a fuller investigation of the relationship between C_1 and C_2. Sections 14.2 and 14.3 presented evidence that C_1 functions as a subordinate clause and C_2 functions as a main clause. This section will provide additional evidence to support this conclusion.

The evidence concerns binding of reflexives and pronouns. As in Chapter 13, we will argue here that evidence of this sort does not lead to the conclusion that the subordinate clause is syntactically subordinate (i.e. an adjunct), but simply supports the conclusion that it is subordinate at least at the level of conceptual structure. In the next section we will in fact argue that the *syntactic* evidence shows that the clauses are paratactic, and that C_1 is subordinate *only* at the level of conceptual structure.

McCawley (1988b) points out that in the CC construction, pronouns in C_1 can have antecedents in C_2 (56a), paralleling fronted subordinate clauses (56b). Furthermore, in the ICC construction, pronouns in C_2 cannot have antecedents in C_1 (56c), so the ICC construction parallels sentences with *if*-clauses at the end (56d).

(56) (=McCawley's (6))
    a. The longer he has to wait, the angrier John gets.
    b. If he has to wait, John gets angry.
    c. ??He$_i$ gets angrier, the longer John$_i$ has to wait.
    d. *He$_i$ gets angry if John$_i$ has to wait.

Next let us consider the binding of a reflexive. As shown in Chapter 13, a reflexive complement of a picture-noun can have an antecedent in another clause if the following conditions hold:

• The reflexive is in a clause subordinate to the clause that contains its antecedent;
• The reflexive is logophoric, i.e. (roughly) its antecedent is understood as having an attitude toward the situation described by the clause containing the reflexive.

Reviewing the evidence, (57)–(58) show that this relationship holds both in standard conditionals and in sentences with *LS-and*, but does not hold in ordinary conjoined clauses.

(57) a. *Conditional with logophoric reflexive*
        If another picture of him(self)$_i$ appears in the news, (Susan's afraid that) John$_i$ will really get angry.
    b. *LS-and with logophoric reflexive*
        Another picture of him(self)$_i$ appears in the news and (Susan's afraid that) John$_i$ will get really angry.

    c. *Ordinary conjunction with logophoric reflexive*
      Another picture of him(*self)$_i$ appeared in the news yesterday, and unfortunately (Susan's afraid that) John$_i$ will really get angry.

(58) a. *Conditional with non-logophoric reflexive*
      If another picture of him(*self)$_i$ appears in the news, (Susan suspects) John$_i$ will be arrested.

    b. *LS-and with non-logophoric reflexive*
      Another picture of him(*self)$_i$ appears in the news and (Susan suspects) John$_i$ will get arrested.

On the basis of examples such as these, Chapter 13 argued that the first condition above must be stated over CS representations, since it is at this level where the conditional and *LS-and* share the subordinate character of the clause containing the reflexive. Furthermore, inasmuch as logophoricity inherently involves aspects of clause meaning, it is impossible in any event to state the second condition in purely syntactic terms.

    Similar examples can be constructed for CC-sentences, with the reflexive in C_1, the putative subordinate clause.

(59) *Logophoric reflexive*
    a. The more pictures of him(self)$_i$ appear in the news, the more embarrassed John$_i$ becomes.
    b. The more (frequently) that pictures of him(self)$_i$ appear in the news, the more embarrassed John$_i$ becomes.

(60) *Non-logophoric reflexive*
    a. The more pictures of him(*self)$_i$ appear in the news, the more likely John$_i$ is to get arrested.
    b. The more (frequently) that pictures of him(*self)$_i$ appear in the news, the more likely John$_i$ is to get arrested.

(61) shows that a logophoric reflexive cannot appear in C_2, the putative main clause—even though it *follows* its antecedent. (For some reason, it is not easy to find an example that is clearly logophoric; we think (61) is a reasonable case.)

(61) The more that John$_i$ gets upset by them, the more that stories about him(*self)$_i$ seem to show up on the evening news.

    In the ICC construction, where C_2 comes first, still the reflexive can only appear in C_1. Again logophoricity is necessary.

(62) a. John$_i$ is more embarrassed, the more pictures of him(self)$_i$ appear in the news.

   b. John$_i$ is more embarrassed, the more (frequently) that pictures of him(self)$_i$ appear in the news.

   c. John$_i$ is more likely to get arrested, the more (frequently) that pictures of him(*self)$_i$ appear in the news.   [*non-logophoric*]

   d. Stories about him(*self)$_i$ seem to show up more on the evening news, the more that John$_i$ gets upset by them.   [*logophoric reflexive in* C_2]

Another type of binding evidence that supports the conclusion that C_1 is a subordinate clause at some level of representation involves the binding of a pronoun by a quantifier. (Examples adapted from Chapter 13.)

(63) a. If you put enough pressure on him$_i$, every senator$_i$ will succumb to corruption.   [*conditional*]

      b. You put enough pressure on him$_i$, and every senator$_i$ will succumb to corruption.   [*LS-and*]

      c. *We put enough pressure on him$_i$ and, sure enough, every senator$_i$ succumbed to corruption.   [*ordinary conjunction*]

(63b) shows that a coordinate structure whose first conjunct has a subordinate interpretation allows leftward binding by *every*, parallel to preposed *if*-clauses; a semantically coordinate structure such as (63c) does not. In addition, fronted conditionals and left-subordinating *and* allow rightward binding by *any* (but not *every*) out of the first clause.

(64) a. If you put enough pressure on any/*every senator$_i$, he$_i$ will succumb to corruption.

      b. You put enough pressure on any/*every senator$_i$ and he$_i$ will succumb to corruption.

      c. * We put enough pressure on any/every senator$_i$ and, sure enough, he$_i$ succumbed to corruption.

  CC sentences have a similar pattern (65).

(65) a. The more lobbyists he$_i$ talks to, the more corrupt every senator$_i$ seems to become.

      b. The more lobbyists wine and dine him$_i$, the more every senator$_i$ is susceptible to improper influence.

      c. The more time that any (*every) senator$_i$ spends with lobbyists, the more likely he$_i$ is to succumb to corruption.

The pattern for ICC (66a,b) parallels postposed *if*- or *as*-clauses (66c,d).

(66) a. Every/any senator$_i$ becomes more corrupt, the more lobbyists he$_i$ talks to.

b. *He$_i$ seems to become more corrupt, the more lobbyists every/any senator$_i$ talks to.

c. Every/any senator$_i$ seems to become more corrupt, if/as he$_i$ talks to more lobbyists.

d. *He$_i$ seems to become more corrupt, if/as every/any senator talks to more lobbyists.

To sum up this section, we have found confirming evidence from anaphora and binding that C$_1$ in a CC is interpreted as a subordinate clause. Under the assumption that binding is determined (entirely) by syntactic configuration, this would constitute a strong argument for the left-subordinate hypothesis of CC. But if binding has (in part) a semantic basis, as argued in the four previous chapters (see also references in Chapters 10 and 11), then this evidence does not distinguish the left-subordinate hypothesis from the paratactic hypothesis. In the next section we provide evidence that the subordination is not in syntactic structure.

14.6 Extraction from CC

If C$_1$ is a subordinate clause and C$_2$ is a main clause, as suggested by the data discussed in sections 14.2 and (perhaps) 14.5, we would predict—at best—that extraction from C$_2$ would be unproblematic while extraction from C$_1$ would produce CED violations. Moreover, since both clauses contain long-distance dependencies parallel to those in indirect questions and free relatives, we might predict *both* clauses to be islands by virtue of their internal structure.

Both these predictions turn out to be incorrect. Extraction from C$_2$ is indeed possible; and, more surprisingly, so is extraction from C$_1$. In fact, if anything, extraction from C$_1$ sounds better to our ears, perhaps because it does not involve intervening clausal material.[9]

(67)   *"Base" sentence*

---

[9] It is also possible to extract from both clauses simultaneously.

(i) This is the problem that the quicker you solve t, the quicker you'll be able to tell your friends about t.

This might be seen as ATB extraction, even though the two clauses are not (superficially) coordinate conjuncts. However, we suspect that one of the extractions is actually a parasitic gap of the sort found when both extractions are independently possible; this situation would be similar to multiple extractions from two complements of the same verb, as in (ii).

(ii) a. Who did you tell t that you would pay a call on t?
     b. Who did you give pictures of t to friends of t?

The sooner you solve this problem, the more easily you'll satisfy the folks up at corporate headquarters.

(68)   *Relative clause*
   a. This is the sort of problem which$_i$ the sooner you solve t_i, the more easily you'll satisfy the folks up at corporate headquarters.

[extraction from C$_1$]

   b. The folks up at corporate headquarters are the sort of people who$_i$ the sooner you solve this problem, the more easily you'll satisfy t_i.

[extraction from C$_2$]

(69)   *Topicalization*
   a.   This problem$_i$, the sooner you solve t_i, the more easily you'll satisfy the folks up at corporate headquarters.   *[extraction from C$_1$]*

   b. ?The folks up at corporate headquarters$_i$, the sooner you solve this problem, the more easily you'll satisfy t_i.   *[extraction from C$_2$]*

(70)   *It-cleft:*
   a.   It is this problem$_i$ that the sooner you solve t_i, the more easily you'll satisfy the folks up at corporate headquarters.

[extraction from C$_1$]

   b. ?*It is the folks up at corporate headquarters$_i$ (not the ones here at the regional office) who$_i$ the sooner you solve this problem, the more easily you'll satisfy t_i.   *[extraction from C$_2$]*

Wh-questions should also be possible with CCs, but the simplest cases are not, as seen in (71).

(71)   a. *Which problem does the sooner (that) you solve t, the more easily you'll satisfy the folks up at corporate headquarters?
   b. *Which problem the sooner (that) you solve t, will the more easily you satisfy the folks up at corporate headquarters?

One possible reason for this ungrammaticality is that the clause-initial comparative phrase blocks inversion in main clauses. However, when the *wh*-phrase is a subject, and hence need not cause inversion, a CC construction is still impossible (except as an echo-question).

(72)   a. *The harder it rains, the faster who runs?
   b. *The louder who talks, the angrier you get?

Given the possibility of examples such as (ii), the possibility of parasitic gaps in CC or ICC cannot serve as a diagnostic for structure.

This suggests that both (71) and (72) are bad because the comparative phrase occupies the initial position in the clause, blocking the *wh*-phrase from having this status—the signatures for the two constructions cannot both be satisfied at once. In (72), the *wh*-phrase is thus forced to be positioned in situ, where it cannot get the necessary wide scope interpretation. This analysis is confirmed when we recall that direct questions can be posed in C_2 by substituting *how much* for *the*. Notice that in this case inversion is acceptable.

(73)   The harder it rains, how much faster a flow do you see in the river?

Here *how much* simultaneously satisfies the signature for both the *wh*-question construction and the CC construction, so that a single initial position suffices.

Embedded *wh*-questions and "long *wh*-movement" turn out to be possible, evidently because they do not raise these problems.[10]

(74)   a.   They failed to tell me which problem the sooner I solve *t*, the quicker the folks up at headquarters will get off my back.
                                              [*extraction from C_1*]

        b.   ??I finally worked up enough courage to ask which people at headquarters the sooner I solve this problem, the quicker I'll get free of *t*.   [*extraction from C_2*]

(75)   a.   Which problem do you think that the sooner you solve *t*, the quicker you'll be able to tell the folks up at headquarters to buzz off?

        b.   ??Which people at headquarters do you think that the sooner you solve this problem, the quicker you'll be able to tell *t* to buzz off?

What are we to make of these facts? In Chapter 13 we found that extraction is the one place where *LS-and* differs from its conditional paraphrase: although as usual one cannot extract from an adjunct *if*-clause, one can extract from either clause conjoined by *LS-and*. (Again we use > to mean "better than" and < to mean "worse than".)

(76)   a.   ??This is a problem that you'll be able to tell the folks up at corporate to buzz off if you solve *t*.

        b.   ?This is a problem that you solve *t* and$_{LS}$ you'll immediately be able to tell the folks up at corporate headquarters to buzz off.   [> *(76a)*]

---

[10] Note, however, that *which problem* in (74a) does precede the comparative phrase, a configuration which we found impossible in (71). There are at least two possible accounts of this difference. First, it might be that main clauses beginning with *the more* lack a further initial position in which a *wh*-phrase could be placed, but such a position is available with subordinate *the more* clauses. Second, it might be that comparative clauses lack a position before *the more* in which Infl could be positioned when a fronted *wh*-phrase makes inversion necessary. The exact solution is not crucial to our general point.

c. ?Those are the folks that you just solve *this* problem and$_{LS}$ you'll be
able to forget about *t*.   [> *(76a)*]

Though admittedly the judgments are delicate, we find that *if*-clause extraction
is improved by a resumptive pronoun, but extraction from left-subordinating
conjunction becomes worse.

(77) a.   This is a problem that you'll be able to tell the folks up at headquar-
            ters to buzz off if you solve it.   [> *(76a)*]
      b.   ??This is a problem that you solve it and$_{LS}$ you'll be able to tell the
            folks up at headquarters to buzz off.   [< *(76b) and (77a)*]
      c.   ??Those are the folks that you just solve *this* problem and you'll be
            able to forget about them.   [< *(76c)*]

Our reasoning in Chapter 13 was

• Constraints on binding and quantification apply at the level of conceptual
structure, where conditionals and left-subordinating coordination are equivalent;

• The coordinate structure constraint applies at the level of conceptual structure, where standard coordinating conjunction is a coordinate structure but left-
subordinating coordination is not—hence the CSC does not apply to left-
subordinating coordination;

• Left-subordinating coordination is however still coordination in syntactic
structure; and

• The constraints on extraction from adjunct clauses apply at the level
of syntactic structure, so that they apply to *if*-clauses but not to left-
subordinating coordination.

We concluded that this is the only possible way to partial out the constraints
that enables us to account for the facts. The consequence is that left-
subordinating conjunction is a case of a syntax–semantics mismatch: coordinate in syntax but subordinating in semantics.

    On the basis of the fact that extraction is possible from both C_1 and C_2 in
CCs, we arrive at a conclusion parallel to that for left-subordinating conjunction: C_1 is not an adjunct, despite all the evidence for its subordinate semantics.
As noted in section 14.1, there is no evidence that it is a conjunct, either, in the
sense of being linked to C_2 by an obligatorily empty conjunction. In fact,
the most plausible hypothesis on these grounds is the paratactic hypothesis:
C_1 and C_2 are paratactically linked to form an IP or CP. And this is the
hypothesis best in tune with the Simpler Syntax Hypothesis.

It is not clear to us why the CC construction permits extraction from what appears to be a complex construction along the lines of an indirect question or free relative; such constructions are normally islands to extraction. The uniqueness of the construction makes it difficult to find analogous cases elsewhere in the language. One potential hypothesis is revealed by attempting extraction from a ICC. To our ears, extraction from the normal clause C_2 is perfectly acceptable, as might be expected, but extraction from the CC-clause C_1 turns out to be fairly bad.

(78) You'll beat the competition more easily, the sooner you solve this problem.   [*"base" sentence*]

(79) a. They failed to tell me who I'll beat *t* more easily, the sooner I solve this problem.   [*extraction from C_2*]

  b. ??They failed to tell me which problem I'll beat the competition more easily, the sooner I solve *t*.   [*extraction from C_1*] [< (74a,b)]

(80) a. These are the guys that you'll beat *t* more easily, the sooner you solve this problem.

  b. ??This is the problem that you'll beat the competition more easily, the sooner you solve *t*.   [< (68a,b)]

This suggests that in a ICC, C_2 is syntactically a main clause and C_1 is subordinate, matching the semantics. (However, our judgments are indeterminate as to whether a resumptive pronoun improves (79b) and (80b), as it does (76a).) If these admittedly delicate judgments are correct, CCs differ from ICCs because of the total symmetry of their clauses in syntax; just as in a coordinate construction, there is no syntactic evidence for one clause being subordinate to the other. Such an analysis would comport with the treatment of left-subordinating *and*, where there is also no evidence in the syntax for an asymmetry between the conjoined clauses, and where, as we have argued, extraction acts as though both are main clauses rather than conjuncts.[11]

---

[11] It is also worth noting that when the complementizer *that* is present, the possibilities for extraction are more restricted. Consider the following contrasts.

(i) This is the kind of rice that the quicker (*that) you cook *t*, the better it tastes.
(ii) This is the kind of rice that the more pounds (??that) you cook *t*, the longer it takes.

To our ears, the insertion of *that* with an adjunct extraction from CC, as in (i), produces ungrammaticality, while it has a weaker effect when an argument is extracted, as in (ii). We might speculate that the presence of *that* produces a reanalysis in which the head *quicker* or *more pounds* is treated like the head of a relative clause. The difference in (i)–(ii) brings to mind the classical argument/adjunct asymmetries and, although it does not resolve the question of extraction raised in the text, may shed some additional light on it.

14.7 Summary and consequences for UG

Recapitulating, then, the CC construction is *sui generis*, in that its basic para-tactic structure does not conform to the general patterns of X′ theory. The clauses that make up this construction have many of the properties of CP (though we noted idiosyncratic possibilities and restrictions in section 14.4.1), and the comparative phrase is linked to a trace by a classic long-distance dependency. However, the specifier of the comparative phrase in both clauses is sufficiently idiosyncratic that there is no natural way to subsume it completely under normal *wh*-movement or under the fronting of other degree specifiers such as *all the* and *so*. Finally, C$_1$ has the interpretation of a subordinate clause, and C$_2$ has the interpretation of a main clause; but from the perspective of extraction, both clauses have the status of coordinate clauses, that is, neither is an adjunct or argument of the other.[12]

(81) sums up some details of the construction, distinguishing the *sui generis* parts of the structure from the parts that follow from more general principles. (81a) shows the structure with a conventional CP; (82b) shows it in terms of flat structure in the clause.

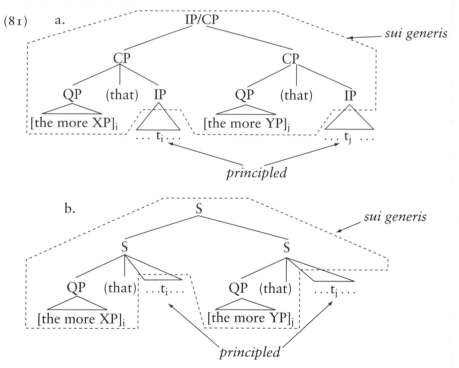

---

[12] An interesting question remains. Recall from section 14.3 that the paratactic analysis leads to an unsettling consequence: the notion of "main clause force", necessary to determine where subjunctive appears and on which clause imperatives, tags, and *how much* questions can be formed, is not a syntactic matter under this analysis. Rather, "main clause force" distinguishes

Overall, then, the CC construction is another case that confirms the general perspective of the present study concerning the relationship between syntactic structure and semantic structure. On our view, syntactic structures may reflect to a greater or lesser degree the semantic structures they express. On the plausible assumption that conceptual structure is universal, universals of conceptual structure will in the default case project invariantly into syntactic universals. Such a default projection may be able to explain, for example, why all languages have nouns and verbs, why verb phrases have more or less the same form across languages, why adjuncts appear external to the arguments of a phrase cross-linguistically, and other apparent but not entirely rigid universals of X' theory. The dogmas of Structural and Interface Uniformity attempt to assimilate all aspects of syntax to this default situation.

At the other extreme, however, the mapping of syntactic structure onto conceptual structure is more or less arbitrary. This aspect of syntactic structure is autonomous and unpredictable, insofar as it is *not* a projection of universal conceptual structure. The CC construction is one such case, we argue. Although the internal structure of the construction's individual clauses follows the standard principles of semantics–syntax mapping, its syntax at the level above the clause and its mapping into conceptual structure is *sui generis* and follows from no general principles, as far as we can tell, as shown in (81).

In this light, let us consider the status of the extraction constraints observed in sections 14.5 and 14.6. Section 14.5 showed that extraction of the comparative phrase *within* the clauses of a CC is subject to the usual constraints; but section 14.6 showed that extraction from the clauses of a CC to *outside* of CC is not so constrained. On this basis we argued that the clauses of a CC below the level of the adjunction site of the comparative phrase have normal clausal structure, but that the two clauses of a CC are connected paratactically.

The question naturally arises as to how a learner could possibly acquire this information. A learner would be unlikely to have enough experience with CCs to be able to identify its crucial properties. It is especially striking that speakers judge C_1 to be syntactically a main clause in the absence of evidence, given that, as shown in sections 14.2 and 14.5, this clause receives a subordinate interpretation.

One possibility is that UG permits parataxis as a generally available syntactic option in natural language, making available paratactically connected clauses that are individually accessible to extractions just as simple clauses are. On the

---

C_2 from C_1 only in the semantics. We are not clear to what extent this forces reconsideration of many deeply-held beliefs about syntactic structure. For now, we must leave such reconsideration, important though it may be, for future research.

view that syntactic constraints on extraction are simply a product of the relative syntactic complexity of the configuration (see section 9.4.3 and the references there), nothing more needs to be said about extraction from such clauses. In particular, if a construction exhibits no syntactic subordination, then it will contribute no extraordinary complexity to extraction. What will remain are any semantic constraints on extraction, of the sort discussed in section 9.4.4. In the CC construction, the subordinate interpretation of one of the clauses is only a *semantic* fact, and hence irrelevant to syntactic complexity for purposes of extraction. This view is confirmed by the existence of the paratactic conditional construction marked only by intonation, which also semantically subordinates the first clause.[13]

In fact, it is plausible to view parataxis as grammatically the most primitive way to combine linguistic elements, one that leaves the semantic relations among the elements to be determined by their inherent semantic possibilities or by pragmatic considerations coming from the discourse or nonlinguistic context. It is *more* primitive than the Minimalist Program's primitive Merge, in that it does not designate one of its elements as syntactic head. This comports with the position advocated in Chapters 4 and 5, where for instance arguments and adjuncts in VP and NP are connected paratactically. Their semantic relations (especially in a noncase language like English) are established only by their linear order and by the way they can combine semantically and pragmatically with the head of the phrase and each other. Similarly, the paratactic conditional establishes the connection by using topic-focus intonation, which creates an interpretation "close enough" to the conditional. Just as case-markers and the prepositions of oblique arguments are grammaticizations of semantic connections of an argument to its head, devices such as subordinating conjunctions are grammaticizations of semantic/pragmatic connections among clauses. By virtue of this conventionalization, they make possible reordering of the clauses.

On this view, what the child must learn is not the possibility of parataxis but rather the particular semantics to associate with the paratactic CC construction and its counterparts in other languages. It is surely significant that many other languages have similar constructions expressing the comparative correlative reading found in CCs, although specific syntactic properties of the constructions differ from language to language. It is as though universal semantics has a kind of meaning to express—the comparative correlation of two scales of magnitude, which involves relating two bound variables. Standard default mapping to syntax does not provide a complete solution; and languages therefore are forced

---

[13] Why the intonationally marked paratactic conditional prohibits extraction altogether is beyond us.

to "cobble together" some kind of mechanism to express it. Because of its meaning, it is likely to involve two long-distance dependencies, but their syntactic connection and the signature of the long-distance dependencies is liable to be highly variable. We have not explored the extent to which such comparable constructions provide evidence for or against paratactic syntax. But in many cases the constructions are superficially unusual in just the way the English construction is, often appearing paratactic and often inheriting properties of comparatives and/or conditionals, as McCawley (1988b) and Beck (1997) have documented. In other cases, the construction is transparent, as Michaelis (1994) argues for Classical Latin. At the moment we are unable to be more explicit about this intuition, or about its consequences for the theory of UG. More crosslinguistic work is called for on this and other idiosyncratic constructions (for instance left-subordinating *and*, which appears to be widespread).[14]

Let us close by reflecting on the consequences of the CC construction for Interface Uniformity and the core-periphery distinction. The CC construction has proven in numerous respects to behave unlike more familiar "core grammar". Yet it *is* learned; and its details emerge as surprisingly robust, given the surely minimal exposure any speaker has to such exotica as imperative CC and extraction from embedded CC. Although we are far from solving all the puzzles that the CC construction poses, we have seen clearly the rich interaction of the totally idiosyncratic with the more general that this construction exemplifies. The moral of these results, amplifying our position in Chapter 1 and illustrated to some degree throughout this study, is that the "periphery" cannot be neglected in the study of UG.

We also conclude, as we have in the rest of this study, that although syntactic form reflects and to an extent depends on semantic representation, syntax and semantics are independent systems of representation with their own nontrivial autonomous principles of organization, principles that remain to be discovered by research in both domains. Under such a view, the structure of the interface between the two levels must be regarded as nontrivial and constitutes a further important domain of research on UG, again in contrast to more standard approaches.

---

[14] Den Dikken (2004) proposes a structure in which C_1 is a subordinate clause, based on analogy with subordinating constructions in other languages. As far as we can tell, there is no evidence that the syntactic structure for the English construction must be subordinating. He also provides evidence that correlative comparatives show a high degree of syntactic similarity across languages but morphosyntactic variability. We attribute the former to the fact that the construction expresses the same CS relation across languages, and the latter is precisely the type of *sui generis* matter that does not follow from general principles. Beyond this, it is expected that the particular morphosyntax that a language uses for this construction would be related to the morphosyntax that the language uses in general.

CHAPTER 15

What Is Language Like? Moving On

15.1 Where have we gotten?

Three fundamental insights of early generative grammar were (a) that language is to be regarded as a mental capacity, (b) that the creativity or unlimitedness of language is one of its most important features, and (c) that there is a lot more to linguistic structure than is apparent on the surface. For nearly fifty years these insights, echoing the Cartesian linguists, have guided inquiry into the nature of language. Under their influence, linguistics and the related cognitive sciences have flourished.

The present study, without relinquishing these insights, proposes a substantial revision of the basic organization of language laid out by mainstream generative grammar. Many aspects of our revision have been in currency in one or another of the alternative frameworks such as LFG, HPSG, Cognitive Grammar, Construction Grammar, Role and Reference Grammar, Autolexical Syntax, and so on, and we have tried to bring out the similarities when we are aware of them. In fact we have a sense of an implicit consensus among the alternative frameworks—not a monolithic consensus by any means, but one with more of a family resemblance character. We highlight important elements of this consensus in this summary of our conclusions.

A useful starting point in laying out our revision is the status of syntax. From the beginning of generative grammar, syntax was seen as the distinctive characteristic of language—the component that provides language with its creative properties, and the one in which resides the lion's share of complexity and abstractness. It has been in terms of syntax that the central problems of acquisition and innateness have been framed and argued. Phonology and morphology, while recognized as important to language, have decidedly played second fiddle (and viola) to syntax. Insofar as semantics (the mysterious cello?) cannot be coded in syntactic terms, mainstream generative grammar leaves it either to the formal semanticists (who for the most part do not concern themselves with the mental character of language and language acquisition) or to vague invocations of unformalizable "knowledge of the world", "about which little is known".

This view of syntax certainly served the field well in its early days. Our sense, though, is that it is time to move on. Syntax, on our view, is simply one component of language among several, each of which contributes to the creativity, complexity, and abstractness of language, and each of which poses problems for acquisition. Syntax is still central "geographically", in that it serves as a major conduit between semantics and phonology. But it is no longer central conceptually. It is no longer to be considered a success to show that some bizarre phenomenon can be accounted for by expressing it in terms of a sufficiently abstract theory of syntax. Success lies in showing how the properties of the phenomenon are properly parceled out among syntax, semantics, phonology, morphology, and the interfaces among them.

The alternative frameworks concur with this judgment in varying degrees. HPSG, Role and Reference Grammar, and some versions of Functional Grammar and Construction Grammar divide the work of building linguistic structure into syntactic and semantic components, and both components contribute liberally to the licensing of phrases and sentences (there is less discussion of phonology). Cognitive Grammar and related versions of Functional Grammar and Construction Grammar also reject the hegemony of syntax, but they downplay its importance in favor of semantics. We find this an overreaction: it is not necessary to reject syntax altogether in order to dethrone it. As we have said at many points in this study, we doubt that semantics does all the work, and we stress that the balance is an empirical matter to be decided by careful weighing of alternatives in each case.

Like most of the alternative frameworks, we have made a major break with the formal tools of mainstream syntax. There are three parts to this break. First, rather than seeing syntactic structure as built up algorithmically through a sequential derivation, we see it as licensed by constraints, all of which can be applied simultaneously. In many cases this approach permits more flexible analyses in terms of "structure-sharing": a particular element meets disparate constraints simultaneously—or represents a compromise among conflicting constraints—instead of having to be put together from disparate abstract parts, each of which embodies a single constraint. This difference has come up, for example, in our analysis of constituent order in the VP (Chapter 5), in the interaction of raising and passive in the GF-tier (Chapter 6), in our treatment of chains in long-distance dependencies (Chapter 9), and in our discussion of simultaneous GF- and CS-binding (Chapters 10 and 11).

The second part of this break with mainstream tradition, shared universally with the alternative frameworks, is more radical: the rejection of syntactic movement. Syntactic movement is of course the most prominent formal tool of generative grammar, and the one that was touted in the early days of the field as what most clearly distinguished generative grammar from more traditional "taxonomic" grammar. Hence a rejection of movement has often been seen as repudiating everything that generative grammar holds most dear. "Transformational grammar" and "generative grammar" were taken as more or less coreferential terms, and for this reason many alternative frameworks have been loath to call themselves varieties of generative grammar. Yet in the sense of "generative grammar" originally intended—namely a formally explicit account of grammar, part of whose brief is to explain the unlimited expressive capacity of language—all the alternative theories are every bit as much generative grammar as the mainstream.

In the present study we have stressed that the choice between movement and nonmovement accounts is an empirical one, not just a matter of preference or ideology. In one case after another, we have counterposed syntactic analyses in terms of movement with alternative accounts in terms of a combination of phrase structure, semantic structure, and the syntax–semantics interface. In every case we have found the movement approach insufficient. We have proposed a variety of formal mechanisms that account for the "illusion of movement", including alternative linearizations of constituents (Chapter 5), manipulations of the GF-tier (Chapter 6), indirect licensing (Chapters 7 and 8), and direct generation of chains and signatures of long-distance dependencies (Chapters 9 and 14). There is no rearrangement of constituents, only arrangement.

One of the most seductive features of syntactic movement is that it makes it possible to posit a "hidden level" of syntactic structure in terms of which syntactic regularities can be coded. In the *Aspects* theory this level was Deep Structure; in GB there were two such levels, D-Structure and LF; in the Minimalist Program there is LF. The promise held out by these theories was that the hidden level of syntax could provide a direct mapping onto meaning—what we have called here Interface Uniformity. Thus "deep" syntax could provide a key to the structure of thought.

Without movement, of course, such hidden levels of syntax are impossible, and with their banishment goes all hope of a simple mapping from syntax to meaning. Again the issue is not a matter of preference or dogma, it is empirical.

Throughout this study, especially in Chapters 2, 3, 4, 7, and 9, we have traced how the logic of Interface Uniformity and the tools of movement have led mainstream theory into ever more abstract syntactic structures and ever more elaborate derivations, aided and abetted by an aesthetic that considers such results to be a conceptual advance. What we (along with the alternative theories) have shown is that these results are often brittle: they do not generalize as they should to the full range of evidence. A prime case studied here was the treatment of sluicing and sluice-stranding (Chapters 1 and 7), which look like and are interpreted like elliptical *wh*-questions, which therefore by Interface Uniformity must *be wh*-questions in all respects, and whose violation of extraction constraints is therefore an unexplained anomaly. We have shown here that the most insightful generalizations for these constructions are with bare argument ellipsis, for which an account in terms of Interface Uniformity is unworkable once one considers the full range of data. Likewise, we have spent considerable effort (Chapters 10–14) showing that anaphoric binding and control cannot receive an insightful account in terms of syntactic structure alone. And we have shown (Chapters 11 and 13) that covert movement in LF, originally developed to syntacticize quantifier scope, cannot account for the full range of phenomena, because quantifier scope depends on lexical semantics, on information structure, and on semantic relations of subordination that cannot be insightfully coded in syntactic terms.

Interface Uniformity has a methodological advantage: you don't have to know anything about the structure of meaning in order to do syntax. Rather, every semantic judgment simply is rendered into "hidden" syntactic terms by one stratagem or another, and then the principles of movement are adjusted so as to allow a derivation to the surface form. By contrast, a theory that eschews movement lacks this shortcut and has to make concrete proposals about the structure of meaning. In the early days of generative syntax, not enough was known about meaning for this to be possible, so it was necessary basically to handwave about meaning. For this reason, the "Interpretive Semantics" of the late 1960s and early 1970s never took off. Thirty-five years later, however, proposals about semantic structure have a great deal more independent motivation and the tools of semantic analysis have a great deal more precision. Hence it is now possible to use semantic analyses to ground syntactic investigation.

The theory of Conceptual Structure used here is only one of a number of possibilities available for this purpose. However, we think it is ideally suited for investigating the extent to which the syntax–semantics interface is uniform and the extent to which it is littered with mismatches. In particular, because it assumes a continuity between the generative mechanisms behind word meanings and behind phrasal composition, it allows us to explicitly show the interplay between syntactic phenomena and details of word meaning, as we did especially in our studies of argument structure (Chapters 5 and 6), prepositional passives (Chapter 6), binding (Chapters 10 and 11), and control (Chapter 12). In this respect it differs from most versions of formal semantics and concurs with the spirit of treatments in Cognitive Grammar.

We conclude, then, that the notion of syntactic movement can no longer be considered the most promising formal device for revealing how language works. Fifty years ago there was no coherent notion of meaning that could function as the necessary hidden level, and Deep Structure looked like a suitable proxy. Movement and deletion were therefore an altogether natural way to simulate the flexibility of the syntax–semantics interface within syntax alone. Indeed, had transformational grammar not been invented, the field would have had no tools for clearing away the debris of syntax–semantics mismatches pointed out for centuries by philosophers of language, and, crucially, there would have been no way to get at the underlying regularities of grammar. Transformational grammar has been a phenomenally effective vehicle for motivating the explosion in research on language of the past half century—not only theoretical syntax but also phonology, semantics, psycholinguistics, neurolinguistics, and first- and second-language acquisition. We think, though, that the time has come for the field to find ways to live without syntactic movement as its most productive metaphor.

There is a third way in which we (and some of the alternative frameworks, especially Construction Grammar and HPSG) have broken with mainstream generative grammar. This one is more subtle, but perhaps even more consequential than the rejection of movement. It concerns a feature of traditional grammar that has been preserved throughout all incarnations of mainstream generative grammar: the strict distinction between grammar and lexicon. Chomsky (1965: 214, n. 16) approvingly cites Bloomfield (1933: 274): "The lexicon is really an appendix of the grammar, a list of basic irregularities" and Sweet (1913: 31): "grammar deals with the general facts of language, lexicology with the special facts." As far as we can tell, this conception has persisted throughout the history of mainstream generative grammar. The emphasis has been on finding ever larger regularities in grammar, to the point that the "essence" of grammar has been distilled in the Minimalist Program to Merge and Move, or perhaps only to Internal and External Merge.

In the course of this distillation of the grammar, the constructions of traditional grammar such as the passive and *wh*-questions have been subsumed into the larger generalizations of movement. This has been considered a virtue, as it removes more of the superficial idiosyncrasy of language. Chomsky has asserted (e.g. Chomsky 2002: 95, 105) that this is a greater advance over early transformational grammar than the latter was over traditional grammar. Yet much of the fine detail of the traditional constructions has ceased to garner attention—recall our discussion of the passive in Chapter 2, for instance. The appeal to parameterization has accounted for some of the crosslinguistic differences; but as we have seen, the intricacies in the "syntactic nuts" of English defy plausible finite and innate parameterization. The loss of empirical coverage has also been rhetorically justified by appeal to an ever-shifting distinction between "core" and "periphery", the latter considered (at least for the foreseeable future) of comparably little interest in comparison to the real quarry, the maximally general and perhaps "perfect" core.

The alternative frameworks will have none of this (and we share this sense). They continue to value the idiosyncrasies of language, often in the interest of demonstrating the effects of semantics and pragmatics on syntactic structure, but often in the interest of just seeing how a language works down to the last little detail. A particular focus has been the behavior of individual words in governing the structures in which they reside, for example how the intricate specifics of argument structure are coded in the lexicon and implemented in phrase structure. It has turned out that constraint-based formalisms lend themselves readily to encoding this material. This is because, within these formalisms, a word can carry pieces of contextual structure in its lexical entry (what we have called here "contextual variables"), and these can be used directly to constrain or even build the context in which the word appears. By contrast, the mainstream derivationally-based formalism treats a lexical item as completely self-contained, and it interacts with its context only by such formal devices as moving to check features.

But now there is a striking consequence, which various constraint-based approaches have come upon independently. Once one sees a word as carrying external structure with it, it is a short step to constructing lexical entries for idioms, even discontinuous idioms, in the same format. And from there it is another short step to seeing complex syntactic structures as constructions, i.e. as abstract idioms that may or may not carry phonological or morphological markers. Like other idioms, they may carry meaning—or (at least in our approach but not in some others) they may be purely structural. Thus the traditional strict divide between grammar and lexicon has been breached, and replaced with a multidimensional continuum between the idiosyncrasy of individual words and general principles such as X-bar theory, verb position, and the possibility of long-distance dependencies. We brought this point out in Chapter 1, and it has been a theme throughout, especially in our discussion of argument structure (Chapters 5 and 6), VP constructions (Chapter 6), noncanonical utterance forms (Chapter 7), ellipsis constructions (Chapters 7 and 8), long-distance dependency constructions (Chapter 9), coercions (Chapters 10 and 12), and paratactic constructions (Chapters 13 and 14).

We believe that this emerging "constructionist" view represents a deep and true discovery about the nature of language. Like traditional grammar but unlike mainstream generative grammar, it acknowledges and captures the rich interaction of semantics with the use of constructions. And, as we have mentioned in several places, it has deep consequences for the problem of acquisition, for now the acquisition of rules can be seen as a principled extension of the acquisition of words, guided by generalizations over the contextual restrictions of individual words. The mystery of classical generative grammar was how the child could acquire all the strange and idiosyncratic rules. Principles and Parameters theory cut the Gordian knot by advocating very general universal principles of structure and movement, differentiated by parameters. This was taken to be a major advance. However, the constructionist approach offers a different and potentially better way to cut the knot, namely by finding a way to make rules learnable—without relegating any of their idiosyncrasy to an ill-defined periphery.

We find it significant that this discovery became possible in large part because of the adoption of constraint-based formalism, whose affordances for representation lend themselves to discovering and formalizing the continuum between words and rules. Thus, as stressed in the early foundational work in generative syntax and phonology, the choice of formalism plays an important role in theory development—in what it leads the theorist to regard as natural and unnatural. The wrong formalism can hobble development. Again, we think it is time to stop thinking in terms of derivations—a conceptual holdover both from the traditional theory of computation in algorithmic Turing-machine-like terms, and also from traditional morphology, which thinks in terms of complex words being "derived" by putting together smaller morphemes.

We stress that none of this makes the overarching issues of mental representation, creativity, and acquisition go away. They are the same problems as ever, just approached with a different technology that affords different sorts of insights—insights that we judge to bring us closer than mainstream generative grammar to what language is really like.

15.2 Special properties of the present approach

Within this broad constructionist view of language, the approach we have developed here has a number of special properties. Like everyone else, we have phrase structure built out of lexical and phrasal categories that observe some version of X′ theory. Like many of the alternative frameworks, our phrase

structure is relatively flat and multiple branching. In particular, phrasal categories are only two nodes deep: NP immediately dominates N, AP immediately
dominates A, and so on. The only exception is S, which dominates VP, which
dominates V. There is no "Chomsky-adjunction"; there are no phrasal nodes
projected from functional categories, especially covert functional categories;
and S = IP = CP (i.e. no separate complementizer phrase). Chapter 4 argued
extensively for this approach in contrast to the articulated Spec and Comp levels
of mainstream theory, and especially in contrast to the strictly binary branching
favored over the last decade.

In addition, like the alternative frameworks, we have strenuously avoided the
use of covert syntactic elements that are present only to satisfy semantic constraints or to guide the organization of overt elements. We have argued against
such null elements in ellipsis (Chapters 4, 7, and 8), coercion (Chapters 6, 10,
and 12), operators in long-distance dependencies (Chapter 9), binding (Chapters 10 and 11), and control (Chapter 12), showing not only that one can do
without them, but that their use leads ultimately to impossible complications.
The only null elements we have retained from mainstream generative grammar
are the traces of long-distance dependencies. Such dependencies are a crucial
defining characteristic of human language, and traces are a convenient formal
device for characterizing them.

The upshot is Simpler Syntax, a syntactic component that maintains the
standard insights about phrase structure but lacks movement, null elements,
projections of functional categories, and all other excess nodes. By virtue of its
simplicity and, particularly, its overtness, it presents fewer problems for acquisition that force one into positing complexity in the innate genetic component of
language. Thus it also sharpens and simplifies the problems of the evolution of
the language capacity—though it hardly makes them go away.

Whereas our constructionist position brings us closest in many respects to
HPSG and Construction Grammar, we differ from them in our views on the
autonomy of syntax. HPSG stresses the Saussurean sign—a complex of phonological, syntactic, and semantic features—as the fundamental building block of
linguistic structure, and Construction Grammar stresses the meaningfulness of
all constructions. We have taken a more flexible view, allowing lexical entries to
constrain/license only one or two of the parallel structures of language. Thus
not every construction involves phonology (e.g. coercions, raising, the
sound+motion construction); some involve the interaction of prosody and
information structure (e.g. marking focus by intonation); some have phonology
and syntax but no semantics (pleonastic reflexives, default *of* in NPs); some
involve the interaction of syntactic ordering and prosody (heavy shift). In
short, we have found it useful to take the Saussurean sign as simply the

stereotypical case of a lexical item, and to allow a broader range of possibil-ities.[1] Among these possibilities are constructions that involve the constituency and/or ordering of syntax alone (e.g. V final or initial in VP). These are the classic locus of autonomous syntax in mainstream generative grammar, and we see no reason to rule them out on general principle (say just because mainstream theory has stressed them too much). As always, we are seeking the right balance of power between components, on empirical grounds.

Any theory of syntax without movement requires a syntax–semantics inter-face that takes over much of the work that mainstream theory attributes to movement. The minimal conception of such an interface has surface syntactic structure, semantic structure, and a set of interface principles that establish the correspondence between the two. Among the interface rules, on a construction-ist conception, are the words of the language, which establish relatively idio-syncratic correspondences. Beyond the words we seek the most general account possible of phrasal correspondences. In Chapter 5 we skimmed off the relatively easy cases of head/modifier relations, the treatment of adjuncts, and the order of non-NP arguments. We were then confronted by a tougher problem in the position of NP arguments of verbs. This could not be solved entirely in semantic terms, because dummy arguments behave in many respects just like semantic arguments. We were therefore forced to introduce the Grammatical Function Tier (Chapter 6), a small "hidden level" that deals only with the positioning of NP arguments of verbs.

A grammar incorporating a GF-tier is by no means an *a priori* optimal solution. But we observed that every theory of syntax has a counterpart—most notably in LFG and Relational Grammar, where it is the central innov-ation, but also in the obliqueness hierarchy of HPSG and (for the most unwieldy treatment) abstract Case in mainstream generative grammar. And in each of these theories this little system is responsible for the prominent constructions of raising and passive. In our approach it is also responsible for the core cases of intraclause binding, and it differentiates the most rigid cases of reflexives such as direct objects from more flexible cases such as picture-noun constructions and logophoric reflexives.

---

[1] HPSG admits such possibilities as well, by leaving one or more components of a sign unspecified. We are uncomfortable less with the formalism than with the emphasis on the sign. For instance, it is hard to think of a coercion as a sign—if anything, a coercion licenses the *absence* of a sign. Similarly, it is hard to think of a rule such as V-final in VP or a preference for heavy prosodic constituents at the end as signs, since they do not signify anything; they only linearize the other signs. Yet all of these are natural constraints within the formalism of the parallel architec-ture.

Given that no one has found a way to avoid these problems, and that everyone has a solution with the same flavor despite radically different formalisms, we are inclined to think that the GF-tier and its counterparts in other theories are also capturing something deep and true about language. It does have the uncomfortable consequence of letting back in some of the classical problems of acquisition: how can the child be expected to figure out that there is a GF-tier, if linguists can't agree on it? Thus we are pressed into the position of claiming there is something innate about it—it is one of those things that has to be carried on the genome. But this is the way empirical science goes. Maybe there will be a deeper explanation for it and maybe there won't. Our conjecture is that it is a late evolutionary add-on to the syntax–semantics interface, hardly inevitable but affording adaptive advantages in efficiency and reliability of communication (see below). At the same time, we have pared its structure down to a bare minimum, compared to the fully fleshed-out f-structure of LFG, so there is less for evolution to account for.

Another important feature of our approach is the introduction of indirect licensing into the theory of grammar, with bare argument ellipsis as its simplest exemplar (Chapter 7). The basis of indirect licensing is the grammatically primitive process of interpreting fragmentary utterances in terms of the pragmatics of the discourse and nonlinguistic context. This is probably something that children do prior to the acquisition of grammar, and that adults do in interpreting these children's utterances. Pidgins too make heavy use of such pragmatic effects. What makes indirect licensing grammatical rather than just pragmatic is that it transmits syntactic properties such as case, gender, and syntactic (GF-) binding properties from the discourse antecedent to the fragment, giving rise to connectivity effects. Indirect licensing is further grammaticized by being incorporated into more complex constructions as diverse as gapping, sluicing, VP ellipsis, *ones*-ellipsis, and left dislocation.

The most grammaticized instances of indirect licensing are those involving long-distance dependencies, where the fragment is the "fronted" phrase and the antecedent or "target" is a trace to its right (Chapter 9). Here indirect licensing interacts with another important interface device, the binding of an operator–variable configuration in semantics to a chain in syntax. Following especially the approach of HPSG, a chain associated with a particular long-distance dependency construction consists of a trace in a position associated with the bound variable plus a "signature" phrase structure configuration at the position associated with the operator (e.g. a *wh*-phrase followed immediately by tense in main clause questions, *that* in one variety of relative clause, *what a* in exclamations, and so on). The characteristic island constraints are not products of movement, as in MGG, but a consequence of the construction of chains in syntax (as in HPSG) plus semantic constraints on operator-variable configurations (as in many different non-mainstream schools of thought).

Finally, we have shown that binding theory has components both in syntax—specifically in the GF-tier—and in semantics. Chapter 6 developed the position that GF-binding is limited to NP arguments of verbs within a single clause; all other cases are CS-binding alone. Chapter 10 developed the position that GF-binding and CS-binding can come into conflict, leading to ungrammatical reflexives in positions where they would be expected—both in cases of coercion and in cases where the semantic violations come from the verb meaning. We do not feel anywhere near solving the problem of binding, but we believe we have established parameters for a proper solution, again following in the footsteps of many others.

15.3 Two aesthetics

We end up with a rather heterogeneous theory. It includes a considerable variety of tools in place of the simplicity of Merge and Move: the machinery of constructions, which is an extension of the machinery for words and idioms; the linearization of hierarchical structure; the "hidden level" of the GF-tier; indirect licensing; and the linking of operator-variable complexes to chains with all their peculiar syntactic properties. On the other hand, each tool is relatively constrained, and we have managed to do without complex and abstract auxiliary assumptions, including movement and all the constraints on it, LF, null elements, and parameters. And we have been able to maintain a very lean notion of syntactic structure.

We have learned, mostly through the grapevine, that our approach to syntax has met in some quarters with the reaction: "If this approach is right, then syntax isn't interesting." We find this reaction disconcerting and feel it calls for some speculative exegesis.

We begin by looking at the rhetoric behind the predicate "interesting". It belongs to a class of psychological and evaluative predicates that we mentioned briefly in section 5.6. The inherent semantic argument structure involves two characters: the entity characterized as interesting and the individual in whom this entity evinces interest. The latter can be expressed overtly in "Syntax isn't interesting to me" or "Syntax doesn't interest me", or it can be left implicit, in which case the implicit argument is generic, roughly "Syntax isn't interesting to people". When used in this latter way, it presents the uninterestingness of syntax as though it is an objective inherent property of syntax, not a property of an interaction between syntax and an observer. Thus the invited inference of "... then syntax isn't interesting" is that if you happen to be interested in this approach to syntax, there is something wrong with you. We reject this invited inference and submit that interestingness is to some degree in the eyes of the observer—baseball cards and poodles interest some people and not others, and the same is true of Simpler Syntax.

This reaction of course typically comes from someone committed to the Minimalist Program, which has cultivated a particular aesthetic of what is interesting. The basic question of the Minimalist Program is "How optimal is the design of language?" where "optimal" is defined in terms of providing the "best possible" mapping between sound and meaning. And the conjecture is that if we work hard enough at it, we will find that language is indeed optimal, despite all its apparent imperfections. What constitutes the "best possible mapping"? One that uses the fewest and most general principles and that squeezes out every bit of redundancy.

Chomsky (2002) says that our ability to meaningfully ask this question is another major breakthrough in our understanding of language. He implies that any approach that does not take this question as basic misses the point of the last fifty years of linguistics and, being mired in mere description, simply cannot be compared with the Minimalist Program. This is the sense, we think, in which our minimalist critics find other approaches "not interesting": only the questions, style of argumentation, and ultimately the style of solution of the MP are "interesting".

We have several lines of reply. First, theories can and should be compared for their *results*, whatever their stated goals of explanation. As we observed in Chapter 3, the Minimalist Program is notably lacking in empirical coverage compared even to its predecessor, Government-Binding Theory. The response that it is still just a "program", a way of asking questions, may have been justifiable in 1995, but a decade later it rings hollow.

Second, as we observed in Chapter 1, there are other definitions of optimality besides formal elegance and lack of redundancy. To be sure, scientific standards demand predictiveness and generality, and Occam's Razor should always be on the ready to slice away unneeded machinery. However, another criterion for optimality, the one we have explored here, is minimization of structure, especially covert structure. As we have stressed in the course of this study, this is not always consistent with minimization of principles. Moreover, optimization must be consistent with adequate coverage of the facts; we have been at pains to show that the derivations of late PPT and MP are not up to the task. Here we concur with the many critics of the MP who have come forward especially in recent years (e.g. Johnson and Lappin 1999, Lappin et al. 2000, Newmeyer 2003, Postal 2004, Pullum 1996, Seuren 2004, Pinker and Jackendoff 2005).

Yet another criterion for optimality is effectiveness for actual use by humans as a system for communicating thoughts to each other. Yes, Chomsky has denied that adaptivity for communication has anything to do with the design of language, but we find this position almost perverse; (see Pinker and Jackendoff (2005) for discussion). A system designed for optimal communication will most likely be full of redundancy in order to enhance reliability; and indeed language features alternative systems for conveying the same thing, such as word order, agreement, and case. Still another criterion for optimality is optimality for acquisition, which again would favor redundancy. And another is optimality for brain storage and processing, about which we know little, but it is a good bet that it again favors redundancy. Thus the design criteria for language are quite different from the austere logical optimality that the Minimalist Program seeks.

A third line of reply to the goals of the Minimalist Program is to acknowledge the importance of asking how optimal or perfect language is, but also to recognize that a language is under very different constraints from those of a physical system like a galaxy or a molecule. It has to be carried in brains, and its structure has to be created anew in each speaker. The reason there are lots of languages rather than a single Universal Language is that a human language requires too much information to be carried on the genome. In particular, there are too many words for them all to be innate. Or, seen from a different angle, for language to be entirely innate would have required a far more extensive evolutionary process than humans have undergone.[2] The innate language faculty has evolved just enough tricks for learners to be able to pick up the rest relatively quickly, and for the result to be a communication system that does the job more effectively than if the innate parts had not been there.

Languages may have adventitious, nonoptimal properties for a number of reasons. They are products of imperfect transmission through a society over historical time, subject to cultural forces, language contact, and so on. These effects may be "peripheral" in Chomsky's sense, but the languages still are learned. Moreover, speakers may be tolerant of "imperfections" such as ambiguity, because they have pragmatics to help guide interpretation. A tolerance for

---

[2] This point is missed by Baker (2001), who sees linguistic diversity as socially adaptive for group identification. He therefore conjectures that evolution selected for the system of innate parameters in the service of increasing linguistic diversity. Our argument is that it would be impossible to select for linguistic *uniformity*, because the genome isn't big enough and evolution hasn't had enough time. Linguistic diversity is an inevitable consequence of the insufficiency of the genome. The use of language as a badge of group membership is a natural exaptation: people use anything they can (even badges) as badges of group membership.

ambiguity in turn may make it possible to communicate in less time and with less effort to achieve precision.

A deeper reason for "nonoptimality" in languages is that the learning of languages is guided by brains whose language capacities are the product of adaptation from an ape prototype over evolutionary time. Adaptation may result in more or less optimal structures in response to environmental constraints, for example the streamlined shape of fish and dolphins. But it is hard to argue that, say, the human reproductive system is "optimal" in any engineering sense, apart from the fact that it is more or less the best achievable compromise, given the form from which it evolved (e.g. the baby's head has to fit through the mother's pelvis, often endangering the lives of both).

The genetic component of language might be like that: a collection of innovations, each of which improved the kind of communication system that could be learned through cultural transmission. Such a conception is very much in line with the Toolkit Hypothesis. Following the spirit of the sequential evolutionary scenario in Jackendoff (2002a): if you start with words alone, it's an improvement to have phrase structure so you can group words reliably. If you have phrase structure, it's an improvement to add the possibility for canonical order, case-marking, and agreement so you can tell the semantic roles of each phrase. From there, it's an improvement to add the GF tier, because you have an even more reliable way to mark the roles of NPs, the quintessential arguments. In another, possibly simultaneous, line of development, if you have words, it's an improvement to have indirect licensing so you can connect the sense of one utterance to the next. If you have indirect licensing plus syntax, it's an improvement to add syntactic properties to indirect licensing, so as to make elliptical utterances less ambiguous. If you have indirect licensing plus syntax, it's an improvement to use long-distance dependencies with traces, because that frees you up to express both focus and thematic role at the same time by using a chain.

The redundancy of linguistic systems in this light is perhaps not so surprising. We know that the visual system is full of partially redundant tricks for accomplishing the same goal, for example depth and shape perception, and that these tricks can be teased apart by experiment. The language capacity has done the experiment for us by giving us languages with an abundance of morphology and without, languages with tone and without, languages with overt long-distance dependencies and languages without—and they all permit us to say the same things.

We see no inevitability in this series of developments, especially its later stages. If language didn't have a GF-tier, would it be less perfect, less optimal? Is there another way that the same or greater advantage might have been gained? If languages had a GF-tier but no GF-binding, would that be better or worse? We can't say. But perhaps, following the Minimalist mode of inquiry, these questions are worth at least keeping in mind.

Is this bad? It is not the beautiful elegant "Galilean" outcome envisioned by Chomsky. We agree that a simple Grand Unified Theory of language would be an amazing scientific achievement. On the other hand, given that language is situated in the brain, itself a product of evolution, we find ourselves willing to back off from a Grand Unified Theory and to acknowledge that language is as riddled with eccentricities as every other part of the biological world, arising through contingencies of evolutionary history. This leads to a different aesthetic for the form the theory should take. We submit that, along with derivations, movement, and the lexicon/grammar distinction, it's also time to give up on the Galilean aesthetic and learn to live with this new one.

Of course, good science still demands that we try to reduce to a minimum the internal resources for learning language, with a minimum of eccentricity. But if at some point we have tried in many possible ways, and we keep coming up with the same somewhat eccentric resources, just reconceived in different technologies, it is scientifically most responsible to recognize this clearly as the best tentative answer, and not try to hide it in the inner workings of a putatively Galilean system. This is what we have tried to do here. Taking such a tack does not preclude doing one's best to make each component and each interaction among components maximally general and beautiful—again, this is just good science. But good science also involves judging when the situation is not ideally beautiful, and then searching for the most productive compromise. In our experience, making such judgments and thereby deciding to break with tradition are among the most difficult choices in one's professional life, taking on an almost moral character. Through the present work we hope to have laid down some new paths to explore and to draw attention to some relatively neglected ones. If we have also encouraged others to create still more new paths, that would be a bonus.

15.4 Where do we go from here?

The present study, despite its undoubtedly excessive length (whew!), is only a beginning at reconceiving syntax and its interfaces with the rest of grammar. We have drawn on everything we know from nearly forty years each in the field, but the full enterprise is way beyond the capacities of two guys who are nearing retirement. Here is a wish list of directions in which we could envision research proceeding. The list is hardly exhaustive.

• We have looked at many phenomena on which there is a vast literature that goes far beyond our discussion. To what extent can the results of other frameworks be translated into ours, and when there are differences, what is the best way to resolve them?

• We have from time to time mentioned phenomena in other languages (and in English) without being able to provide a serious analysis. How does the present framework fare with such well-known syntactic phenomena as agreement within phrases, clitic and contrastive left dislocation, clitic climbing, coherent infinitives, ergativity, floating quantifiers, internally headed relatives, pro-drop, quirky case, scrambling, small clauses, subject-aux/verb agreement, superiority, unaccusativity, verb second, verbless sentences, weak crossover?

• We have looked not at all at morphology. How does it integrate into the system? What are the implications for the structure of the lexicon?

• We have repeatedly brought up prosody as a force on syntactic structure. How influential is it? (Steedman 1996 and Hartmann 2000 come to mind as the sort of work we would welcome.)

• We have sketched a ramified space of possibilities for binding theory but hardly have made concrete proposals for the licensing conditions for binding. Do the possibilities we have laid out make it possible to make further progress on an adequate binding theory?

• We have speculated on the possibility of unifying the treatment of quantification, anaphora, and the variables of long-distance dependencies through a uniform notation for binding. Can this be carried through and what does that tell us about the nature of language? We would guess that the answer would come through a more fundamental treatment of referential dependencies, via some variant of Discourse Representation Theory or the referential tier of CS in Jackendoff (2002a).

• We have shown repeatedly that syntactic distribution is driven by the lexical semantics of heads and the combinatorial semantics of phrases. The current theory of Conceptual Structure has taken us a certain distance, but there are many important words and constructions whose semantics we do not understand at all. (The psychological predicates, which have played a role here and there in our discussion, are perhaps at the cusp of our understanding.) In order to go deeper, we also need a far subtler theory of semantic combination, including coercion, integration of context, and cocomposition in the sense of Pustejovsky (1995).

• How does indirect licensing work? We have suggested that it involves principles of conversational coherence, which take us still further into the details of semantics and pragmatics.

• We have not explored the implications for processing and for acquisition here, although Jackendoff (2002a) and Culicover and Nowak (2003) have suggested some plausible directions. However, we suspect that our approach ought to lend itself to experimental investigation, which we would welcome.

On another plane, our wish list would include some change in the way people do syntax. Above all, we think we have shown that syntax cannot be studied without simultaneously studying its interaction with semantics (not to mention prosody). It is true that semantics is hard and much of it is ill-understood, and the way has often been obscured by philosophers who have quite different goals in mind than linguists (see Jackendoff 2002a: chs. 9, 10). Syntax seems so much more concrete, tractable, like a hard science. But science is not about playing it safe.

We have suggested as well that an adequate theory of syntax should connect in a natural way to an account of how humans produce and understand sentences. It has been a dogma in the field that a syntactic theory should not be viewed as a theory of how language is processed, and that a theory of linguistic competence should be free of performance considerations. But we believe that it is essential to understand the role that processing plays in explaining the form of language and the character of speakers' judgments. We do not want to substitute a competing dogma that all of the properties of a language can be explained in terms of how it is processed. But not to look into processing as a possible source of explanation is short-sighted, to say the least. The interaction between syntactic theory and psycho-/neurolinguistics should be a two-way street.

Finally, we think there must be more of an effort to transcend the technology. The standard genre for papers in syntax gives an account of some phenomenon within a particular framework, and perhaps suggests some tweaks within the framework. We would like to see more investigation that compares frameworks dispassionately, for it is only by doing such comparisons that we pit them against each other scientifically rather than merely sociologically. In particular, most of the alternative frameworks conceive of themselves primarily in opposition to mainstream generative grammar and not in comparison to one another—despite the evident conceptual affinities among them that we have reviewed above. The goal of such comparison would be to distill out of each framework the essence of what it thinks language is like, free of the peculiarities of its formalism. Again, this is hard: it's tough enough to master one framework, much less know two or more well enough to do a comparison. But it can be done, especially in the context of collaboration. Given the fragmentation of frameworks that prevails today, such integration is crucial for the future of the field. Again, we hope the present work has helped set the stage.

References

Abney, S. (1987). 'The Noun Phrase in Its Sentential Aspect'. Doctoral dissertation, MIT.

Abusch, D. (1989). 'Reflexives, Reference Shifters, and Attitudes', in E. Fee and K. Hunt (eds.), *WCCFL 8*. Stanford, Calif.: Stanford Linguistics Association, 1–13.

Ackema, P., and Szendröi, K. (2002). 'Determiner Sharing as an Instance of Dependent Ellipsis', *Journal of Comparative Germanic Linguistics* 5: 3–34.

Ackerman, F., and Webelhuth, G. (1999). *A Theory of Predicates*. Stanford, Calif.: CSLI.

Akmajian, A. (1973). 'The Role of Focus in the Interpretation of Anaphoric Expressions', in S. R. Anderson and P. Kiparsky (eds.), *A Festschrift for Morris Halle*. New York: Holt, Rinehart & Winston.

—— (1975). 'More Evidence for an NP Cycle', *Linguistic Inquiry* 6: 115–29.

—— (1984). 'Sentence Types and the Form–Function Fit', *Natural Language and Linguistic Theory* 2: 1–23.

—— and Wasow, T. (1975). 'The Constituent Structure of VP and AUX and the Position of the Verb BE', *Linguistic Analysis* 1: 205–45.

Alsina, A. (2001). 'Is Case Another Name for Grammatical Function? Evidence from Object Asymmetries', in W. Davies and S. Dubinsky (eds.), *Objects and Other Subjects*. Dordrecht: Kluwer, 77–102.

Anagnostopoulou, E., van Riemsdijk, H., and Zwarts, F. (eds.) (1997). *Materials on Left Dislocation*. Amsterdam: Benjamins.

Anderson, S. R. (1977). 'Comments on the Paper by Wasow', in P. W. Culicover, T. Wasow, and A. Akmajian (eds.), *Formal Syntax*. New York: Academic Press, 361–77.

—— (2000). 'Some Lexicalist Remarks on Incorporation Phenomena', *Studia Grammatica* 45: 125–42.

Asaka, T. (2002). 'A Lexical Licensing Analysis of the Adjectival Noun Construction', *English Linguistics* 19: 113–41.

Atkinson, M. (2001). 'Minimalism and First Language Acquisition', *Dublin Computational Linguistics Research Seminar*. http://www.cs.tcd.ie/research_groups/clg/DCLRS/2001/11/1916155329815.htm

Bach, E. (1968). 'Nouns and Noun Phrases', in Bach and Harms (1968: 90–122).

—— (1979). 'Control in Montague Grammar', *Linguistic Inquiry* 10: 515–32.

—— and Harms, R. (eds.) (1968). *Universals in Linguistic Theory*. New York: Holt, Rinehart & Winston.

Baker, C. L. (1970). 'Notes on the Description of English Questions: The Role of an Abstract Question Morpheme', *Foundations of Language* 6: 197–219.

—— (1995). *English Syntax*, 2nd edn. Cambridge, Mass.: MIT Press.

—— and McCarthy, J. J. (eds.) (1981). *The Logical Problem of Language Acquisition*. Cambridge, Mass.: MIT Press.

Baker, M. (1987). 'Thematic Roles and Syntactic Structure', in L. Haegeman (ed.), *Elements of Grammar*. Dordrecht: Kluwer, 73–137.

—— (1988). *Incorporation: A Theory of Grammatical Function Changing*. Chicago: University of Chicago Press.

Baker, M. (1996). 'On the Structural Positions of Themes and Goals', in J. Rooryck and L. Zaring (eds.), *Phrase Structure and the Lexicon*. Dordrecht: Kluwer, 7–34.

—— (1997). 'Thematic Roles and Syntactic Structure', in L. Haegeman (ed.), *Elements of Grammar*. Dordrecht: Kluwer, 73–137.

—— (2001). *The Atoms of Language*. New York: Basic Books.

Barker, C. (1995). *Possessive Descriptions*. Stanford, Calif.: CSLI.

Barss, A. (1986). 'Chains and Anaphoric Dependence: On Reconstruction and Its Implications'. Doctoral dissertation, Cambridge, Mass.: MIT.

—— and Lasnik, H. (1986). 'A Note on Anaphora and Double Objects', *Linguistic Inquiry* 7: 347–54.

Bates, E., and MacWhinney, B. (1982). 'Functionalist Approaches to Grammar', in E. Wanner and L. R. Gleitman (eds.), *Language Acquisition: The State of the Art*. Cambridge: Cambridge University Press, 173–218.

Beck, S. (1997). 'On the Semantics of Comparative Conditionals', *Linguistics and Philosophy* 20: 229–32.

Belletti, A., and Rizzi, L. (1988). 'Psych-Verbs and Th-Theory', *Natural Language and Linguistic Theory* 6: 291–352.

Benincà, P., and Poletto, C. (2004). 'A Case of DO-Support in Romance', *Natural Language and Linguistic Theory* 22: 51–94.

Bickerton, D. (1981). *Roots of Language*. Ann Arbor, Mich.: Karoma.

Blevins, J. P. (1994). 'Derived Constituent Order in Unbounded Dependency Constructions', *Journal of Linguistics* 30: 349–409.

Bloom, P. (2000). *How Children Learn the Meanings of Words*. Cambridge, Mass.: MIT Press.

Bloomfield, L. (1933). *Language*. London: Allen & Unwin/New York: Holt, Rinehart & Winston.

Boeckx, C., and Grohmann, K. K. (eds.) (2003). *Multiple Wh-Fronting*. Amsterdam: Benjamins.

—— and Hornstein, N. (2003). 'Reply to "Control is Not Movement"', *Linguistic Inquiry* 34: 269–80.

—— (2004). 'Movement Under Control', *Linguistic Inquiry* 35: 431–52.

Booij, G. (2002). 'Constructional Idioms, Morphology, and the Dutch Lexicon', *Journal of Germanic Linguistics* 14: 301–29.

Borer, H. (1984). *Parametric Syntax*. Dordrecht: Foris.

Borsley, R. D. (2003). 'Some Implications of English Comparative Correlatives'. MS, University of Essex.

Boškovic, Ž. (1997). 'Pseudoclefts', *Studia Linguistica* 51: 235–77.

Bouma, G., Malouf, R., and Sag, I. A. (2001). 'Satisfying Constraints on Extraction and Adjunction', *Natural Language and Linguistic Theory* 19: 1–65.

Bowers, J. S. (1981). *The Theory of Grammatical Relations*. Ithaca, NY: Cornell University Press.

Brame, M. (1978). *Base Generated Syntax*. Seattle: Noit Amrofer.

Bratman, M. (1987). *Intention, Plans, and Practical Reason*. Cambridge, Mass.: Harvard University Press.

Bresnan, J. (1969). 'On Instrumental Adverbs and the Concept of Deep Structure', *RLE Quarterly Progress Report* 92 (15 Jan. 1969), 365–75.

—— (1972). 'Theory of Complementation in English of Syntax'. Doctoral dissertation, MIT.

—— (1977). 'Variables in the Theory of Transformations', in P. W. Culicover, T. Wasow, and A. Akmajian (eds.), *Formal Syntax*. New York: Academic Press, 157–96.

—— (1978). 'A Realistic Model of Transformational Grammar', in M. Halle, J. W. Bresnan, and G. Miller (eds.), *Linguistic Theory and Psychological Reality*. Cambridge, Mass.: MIT Press, 1–59.

—— (1982a). *The Mental Representation of Grammatical Relations*. Cambridge, Mass.: MIT Press.

—— (1982b). 'Control and Complementation', in J. Bresnan (ed.), *The Mental Representation of Grammatical Relations*. Cambridge, Mass.: MIT Press, 282–390.

—— (1982c). 'The Passive in Grammatical Theory', in J. Bresnan (ed.), *The Mental Representation of Grammatical Relations*. Cambridge, Mass.: MIT Press, 3–86.

—— (2000). 'Optimal Syntax', in J. Dekkers, F. van der Leeuw, and J. van der Weijer (eds.), *Optimality Theory: Phonology, Syntax and Acquisition*. Oxford: Oxford University Press, 335–85.

—— (2001). *Lexical Functional Syntax*. Oxford: Blackwell.

—— and Grimshaw, J. (1978). 'The Syntax of Free Relatives in English', *Linguistic Inquiry* 19: 331–91.

—— and Kanerva, J. (1989). 'Locative Inversion in Chichewa: A Case Study of Factorization in Grammar', *Linguistic Inquiry* 20: 1–50.

Briscoe, E., Copestake, A., and Boguraev, B. (1990). 'Enjoy the Paper: Lexical Semantics via Lexicology', in *Proceedings of the 13th International Conference on Computational Linguistics* (Helsinki), 42–7.

Brody, M. (1995). *Lexico-Logical Form*. Cambridge, Mass.: MIT Press.

Burzio, L. (1986). *Italian Syntax: A Government-Binding Approach*. Dordrecht: Reidel.

Byrne, R., and Whiten, A. (eds.) (1988). *Machiavellian Intelligence: Social Expertise and the Evolution of Intellect in Monkeys, Apes, and Humans*. New York: Oxford University Press.

Cantrall, W. R. (1974). *Viewpoint, Reflexives, and the Nature of Noun Phrases*. The Hague: Mouton.

Carlson, G. N. (1987). 'Same and Different', *Linguistics and Philosophy* 10: 531–65.

Carrier-Duncan, J. (1985). 'Linking of Thematic Roles in Derivational Word Formation', *Linguistic Inquiry* 16(1): 1–34.

Carter, R. (1976). 'Some Linking Regularities', in B. Levin and C. Tenny (eds.), *On Linking: Papers by Richard Carter*. Cambridge, Mass.: MIT Center for Cognitive Science Lexicon Project, 1–92.

Cattell, R. (1984). *Composite Predicates in English*. New York: Academic Press.

Chierchia, G. (1988). 'Structured Meanings, Thematic Roles, and Control', in G. Chierchia, B. Partee, and R. Turner (eds.), *Properties, Types, and Meanings*, ii: *Semantic Issues*. Dordrecht: Kluwer, 131–66.

—— (1995). *Dynamics of Meaning: Anaphora, Presupposition, and the Theory of Grammar*. Chicago: University of Chicago Press.

Chomsky, C. (1969). *The Acquisition of Syntax in Children from 5 to 10*. Cambridge, Mass.: MIT Press.

Chomsky, N. (1957). *Syntactic Structures*. The Hague: Mouton.

—— (1964a). *Current Issues in Linguistic Theory*. The Hague: Mouton.

—— (1964b). 'The Logical Basis of Linguistic Theory', in H. Lunt (ed.), *Proceedings of the 9th International Congress of Linguists*. The Hague: Mouton, 914–77.

—— (1965). *Aspects of the Theory of Syntax*. Cambridge, Mass.: MIT Press.

—— (1970). 'Remarks on Nominalizations', in R. Jacobs and P. Rosenbaum (eds.), *Readings in English Transformational Grammar*. Waltham, Mass.: Ginn, 184–221. Repr. in Chomsky (1972b).

—— (1971). 'Deep Structure, Surface Structure and Semantic Interpretation', in D. Steinberg and L. Jacobovits (eds.), *Semantics*. London: Cambridge University Press, 183–216. Repr. in Chomsky (1972b).

—— (1972a). 'Some Empirical Issues in the Theory of Transformational Grammar', in S. Peters (ed.), *Goals of Linguistic Theory*. Englewood Cliffs, NJ: Prentice-Hall, 63–130. Repr. in Chomsky (1972b).

—— (1972b). *Studies on Semantics in Generative Grammar*. The Hague: Mouton.

—— (1973). 'Conditions on Transformations', in S. Anderson and P. Kiparsky (eds.), *Festschrift for Morris Halle*. New York: Holt, Rinehart & Winston, 232–86.

—— (1975a). *The Logical Structure of Linguistic Theory*. New York: Plenum.

—— (1975b). 'Questions of Form and Interpretation', *Linguistic Analysis* 1: 75–109.

—— (1975c). *Reflections on Language*. New York: Pantheon.

Chomsky, N. (1976). 'Conditions on Rules of Grammar', *Linguistic Analysis* 2: 303–51.

—— (1977). 'On Wh Movement', in P. W. Culicover, T. Wasow, and A. Akmajian (eds.), *Formal Syntax*. New York: Academic Press, 71–132.

—— (1980). 'On Binding', *Linguistic Inquiry* 11: 1–46.

—— (1981). *Lectures on Government and Binding*. Dordrecht: Foris.

—— (1986a). *Barriers*. Cambridge, Mass.: MIT Press.

—— (1986b). *Knowledge of Language*. New York: Praeger.

—— (1993). 'A Minimalist Program for Linguistic Theory', in K. Hale and S. J. Keyser (eds), *The View from Building 20*. Cambridge, Mass.: MIT Press, 195–227.

—— (1995). *The Minimalist Program*. Cambridge, Mass.: MIT Press.

—— (1999). *Derivation by Phase*. MIT Occasional Papers in Linguistics. Cambridge, Mass.: MITWPL.

—— (2000). 'Minimalist Inquiries', in R. Martin, D. Michaels, and J. Uriagereka (eds.), *Step by Step: Essays on Minimalist Syntax in Honor of Howard Lasnik*. Cambridge, Mass.: MIT Press, 89–156.

—— (2001). 'Beyond Explanatory Adequacy', in *MIT Occasional Papers in Linguistics 20*. Cambridge, Mass.: MIT Dept. of Linguistics.

—— (2002). *On Nature and Language*. Cambridge: Cambridge University Press.

—— (n.d.). 'Language and Mind: Current Thoughts on Ancient Problems (Part II)'. http://fccl.ksu.ru/papers/chomsky2.htm

—— and Lasnik, H. (1977). 'Filters and Control', *Linguistic Inquiry* 8: 425–504.

—— —— (1993). 'Principles and Parameters Theory', in J. Jacobs, A. von Stechow, and T. Vennemann (eds.), *Syntax: An International Handbook of Contemporary Research*. Berlin: de Gruyter.

Chung, S. (1982). 'Unbounded Dependencies in Chamorro Grammar', *Linguistic Inquiry* 13: 39–77.

—— Ladusaw, W., and McClosky, J. (1995). 'Sluicing and Logical Form', *Natural Language Semantics* 3: 239–82.

Cinque, G. (1990). *Types of A-Bar Dependencies*. Cambridge, Mass.: MIT Press.

—— (1996). 'The "Antisymmetric" Programme: Theoretical and Typological Implications', *Journal of Linguistics* 32: 447–64.

—— (1999). *Adverbs and Functional Heads: A Cross-Linguistic Perspective*. Oxford: Oxford University Press.

Citko, B., and Grohmann, K. K. (2001). 'The (Non-) Uniqueness of Multiple Wh-Fronting', in S. Franks, T. Holloway King, and M. Yadroff (eds.), *Formal Approaches to Slavic Linguistics: The Bloomington Meeting, 2000*. Ann Arbor: University of Michigan Press, 117–36.

Clark, H. (1996). *Using Language*. Cambridge: Cambridge University Press.

Collins, C. (1997). *Local Economy*. Cambridge, Mass.: MIT Press.

Cooper, R. (1983). *Quantification and Syntactic Theory*. Dordrecht: Reidel.

Corver, N. (1990). 'The Syntax of Left Branch Extractions'. Doctoral dissertation, Tilburg University.

—— (1992). 'On Deriving Certain Left Branch Extraction Asymmetries: A Case Study in Parametric Syntax', *Proceedings of NELS* 22: 67–84.

Croft, W., and Cruse, D. A. (2004). *Cognitive Linguistics*. Cambridge: Cambridge University Press.

Csuri, P. (1996). 'Generalized Dependencies: Description, Reference, and Anaphora'. Doctoral dissertation, Brandeis University.

Culicover, P. W. (1970). 'One More Can of Beer', *Linguistic Inquiry* 1: 366–9.

—— (1972). 'OM-Sentences', *Foundations of Language* 8: 199–236.

—— (1997). *Principles and Parameters: An Introduction to the Theory of Government and Binding and Its Extensions*. Oxford: Oxford University Press.

—— (1999). *Syntactic Nuts*. Oxford: Oxford University Press.

—— (2004). Review of R. Huddleston and G. Pullum, *Cambridge Grammar of the English Language*, *Language* 80: 127–41.

—— and Jackendoff, R. (1995). '*Something Else* for the Binding Theory', *Linguistic Inquiry* 26: 249–75.

—— —— (1997). 'Syntactic Coordination Despite Semantic Subordination', *Linguistic Inquiry* 28: 195–217.

—— —— (1999). 'The View from the Periphery: The English Comparative Correlative', *Linguistic Inquiry* 30: 543–71.

—— —— (2001). 'Control is Not Movement', *Linguistic Inquiry* 30: 483–511.

—— and Levine, R. D. (2001). 'A Reconsideration of Locative Inversion', *Natural Language and Linguistic Theory* 19: 283–310.

—— and Nowak, A. (2002). 'Markedness, Antisymmetry and the Complexity of Constructions', in P. Pica and J. Rooryk (eds.), *Language Variation Yearbook*, ii. Amsterdam: Benjamins, 5–30.

—— —— (2003). *Dynamical Grammar*. Oxford: Oxford University Press.

—— and Rochemont, M. S. (1983). 'Stress and Focus in English', *Language* 59: 123–65.

—— —— (1990). 'Extraposition and the Complement Principle', *Linguistic Inquiry* 21: 23–48.

—— and Wilkins, W. (1984). *Locality in Linguistic Theory*. New York: Academic Press.

—— —— (1986). 'Control, PRO and the Projection Principle', *Language* 62: 12–153.

Curry, H. B. (1961). 'Some Logical Aspects of Grammatical Structure', in R. Jakobson (ed.), *Structure of Language and its Mathematical Aspects: Proceedings of the 12th Symposium in Applied Mathematics* (American Mathematical Society), 56–68.

Dalrymple, M. (1991). 'Against Reconstruction in Ellipsis', Technical Report SSL-91-114. Stanford, Calif.: Xerox PARC.

—— Shieber, S., and Pereira, F. (1991). 'Ellipsis and Higher Order Unification', *Linguistics and Philosophy* 14: 399–452.

Dayal, V. (2002). 'Single-Pair vs. Multiple-Pair Answers: Wh In-Situ and Scope', *Linguistic Inquiry* 33(3): 512–20.

Deane, P. (1992). *Grammar in Mind and Brain: Explorations in Cognitive Syntax.* New York: Mouton de Gruyter.

Dehé, N., Jackendoff, R., McIntyre, A., and Urban, S. (eds.) (2002). *Verb-Particle Explorations.* Berlin: Mouton de Gruyter.

Den Besten, H. (1986). 'Decidability in the Syntax of Verbs of (Not Necessarily) West-Germanic Languages', *Groninger Arbeiten zur Germanistischen Linguistik* 28: 232–56.

den Dikken, M. (2004). 'Comparative Correlatives Comparatively', *Linguistic Inquiry*, to appear.

—— Meinunger, A., and Wilder, C. (2000). 'Pseudoclefts and Ellipsis', *Studia Linguistica* 54: 41–89.

Dong, Q. P. (1971). 'English Sentences Without Overt Grammatical Subject', in A. M. Zwicky, P. H. Salus, R. I. Binnick, and A. L. Vanek (eds.), *Studies Out in Left Field: Defamatory Essays Presented to James D. McCawley on the Occasion of His 33rd or 34th Birthday.* Edmonton: Linguistic Research (Current Inquiry into Language and Linguistics 4): 3–10.

Dowty, D. (1985). 'On Recent Analyses of the Semantics of Control', *Linguistics and Philosophy* 8: 291–331.

—— (1991). 'Thematic Proto-Roles and Argument Selection', *Language* 67: 547–619.

—— (1996). 'Towards a Minimalist Theory of Syntactic Structure', in H. Bunt and A. van Horck (eds.), *Discontinuous Constituency.* Berlin: Mouton de Gruyter, 11–62.

Emonds, J. (1970). *Root and Structure Preserving Transformations.* Bloomington: IULC.

—— (1976). *A Transformational Approach to English Syntax.* New York: Academic Press.

—— (2003). 'English Indirect Passives', in M. Ukaji, T. Nakao, M. Kajita, and S. Chiba (eds.), *Empirical and Theoretical Investigations into Language: A Festschrift for Masaru Kajita.* Tokyo: Kaitakusha, 19–41.

Enç, M. (1989). 'Pronouns, Licensing and Binding', *Natural Language and Linguistic Theory* 7: 51–92.

Erbach, G., and Krenn, B. (1994). 'Idioms and Support Verb Constructions', in J. Nerbonne, K. Netter, and C. Pollard (eds.), *German Grammar in HPSG.* Stanford, Calif.: CSLI, 365–96.

Ernst, T. (2001). *The Syntax of Adjuncts.* Cambridge: Cambridge University Press.

Erteschik, N. (1973). 'On the Nature of Island Constraints'. Doctoral dissertation, MIT.

Erteschik-Shir, N. (1979). 'Discourse Constraints on Dative Movement', in T. Givon (ed.), *Discourse and Syntax.* New York: Academic Press, 441–67.

—— (1997). *The Dynamics of Focus Structure*. Cambridge: Cambridge University Press.

Evans, G. (1980). 'Pronouns', *Linguistic Inquiry* 11: 337–62.

Evers, A. (1975). 'V-Raising in Dutch and German'. Doctoral dissertation, University of Utrecht.

Farkas, D. (1988). 'On Obligatory Control', *Linguistics and Philosophy* 11(1): 27–58.

Farmer, A. K. (1987). '*They Held Each Other's Breath* and Other Puzzles for the Binding Theory', *Linguistic Inquiry* 8: 157–63.

Farrell, P. (1998). 'Comments on the Paper by Lieber', in S. Lapointe, D. Brentari, and P. Farrell (eds.), *Morphology and its Relation to Syntax and Phonology*. Stanford, Calif.: CSLI, 34–53.

Fauconnier, G. (1985). *Mental Spaces*. Cambridge, Mass.: MIT Press.

Felser, C. (2003). 'Wh-Copying, Phases, and Successive Cyclicity'. MS, University of Essex, Dept. of Language and Linguistics.

Fiengo, R., and May, R. (1994). *Indices and Identity*. Cambridge, Mass.: MIT Press.

Fillmore, C. J. (1963). 'The Position of Embedding Transformations in a Grammar', *Word* 19: 208–31.

—— (1965). *Indirect Object Constructions and the Ordering of Transformations*. The Hague: Mouton.

—— (1968). 'The Case for Case', in E. Bach and R. Harms (eds.), *Universals in Linguistic Theory*. New York: Holt, Rinehart & Winston, 1–88.

—— (1988). 'The Mechanisms of Construction Grammar', *BLS* 14: 35–55.

—— (1992). 'The Grammar of *Home*', LSA Presidential Address, Philadelphia.

—— and Kay, P. (1993). *Construction Grammar Coursebook*. Berkeley, Calif.: Copy Central.

—— —— and O'Connor, M. C. (1988). 'Regularity and Idiomaticity in Grammatical Constructions: The Case of *Let Alone*', *Language* 64(3): 501–39.

Fischer, S. D., and Marshall, B. (1969). *The Examination and Abandonment of the Theory of 'begin' of D. M. Perlmutter as Carried Out by Two of the Inmates of Room Twenty-E-Two-Fifteen, Under the Direction of Divine Providence*. Bloomington: IULC.

Fodor, J. A. (1975). *The Language of Thought*. Cambridge, Mass.: Harvard University Press.

—— and Lepore, E. (1999). 'Impossible Words?', *Linguistic Inquiry* 30: 445–53.

Fodor, J. D. (1998). 'Unambiguous triggers', *Linguistic Inquiry* 29(1): 1–36.

—— (2001). 'Parameters and the Periphery: Reflections on Syntactic Nuts', *Journal of Linguistics* 37: 367–92.

Foley, W., and Van Valin, R., Jr. (1984). *Functional Syntax and Universal Grammar*. Cambridge: Cambridge University Press.

Frank, R., and Kroch, A. (1995). 'Generalized Transformations and the Theory of Grammar', *Studia Linguistica* 49: 103–51.

Freidin, R. (1978). 'Cyclicity and the Theory of Grammar', *Linguistic Inquiry* 9: 519–49.

Freidin, R. (1999). 'Cyclicity and Minimalism', in S. D. Epstein and N. Hornstein (eds.), *Working Minimalism*. Cambridge, Mass.: MIT Press, 95–126.

Gao, Q. (1994). 'Chinese NP Structure', *Linguistics* 32: 475–510.

Gazdar, G., Klein, E., Pullum, G., and Sag, I. A. (1985). *Generalized Phrase Structure Grammar*. Cambridge, Mass.: Harvard University Press.

Gibson, E. (1998). 'Linguistic Complexity: Locality of Syntactic Dependencies', *Cognition* 68: 1–76.

—— and Warren, T. (2004). 'Reading Time Evidence for Intermediate Linguistic Structure in Long-Distance Dependencies', *Syntax* 7(1): 55–78.

Ginzburg, J., and Cooper, R. (2004). 'Clarification, Ellipsis, and the Nature of Contextual Updates in Dialogue', *Linguistics and Philosophy* 27(3): 297–365.

—— and Sag, I. A. (2000). *Interrogative Investigations: The Form, Meaning, and Use of English Interrogatives*. Stanford, Calif.: CSLI.

Godjevac, S. (2000). 'Intonation, Word Order, and Focus Projection in Serbo-Croatian'. Doctoral dissertation, Ohio State University.

Goldberg, A. (1993). 'Making One's Way Through the Data', in A. Alsina (ed.), *Complex Predicates*. Stanford, Calif.: CSLI.

—— (1995). *Constructions: A Construction Grammar Approach to Argument Structure*. Chicago: University of Chicago Press.

——. (to appear). *Constructions at Work: Constructionist Approaches in Context*. New York: Oxford University Press.

—— and Jackendoff, R. (2004). 'The English Resultative as a Family of Constructions', *Language* 80: 532–68.

Golde, K. (1999). 'Binding Theory and Beyond: An Investigation Into the English Pronominal System'. Dissertation, Ohio State University.

Goldsmith, J. (1985). 'A Principled Exception to the Coordinate Structure Constraint', in W. Eilfort, P. Kroeber, and K. Peterson (eds.), *Papers from the 21st Regional Meeting of the Chicago Linguistics Society*, 133–43.

Goodall, G. (1984). 'Parallel Structures in Syntax'. Doctoral dissertation, University of California at San Diego.

Grice, H. (1967/76). 'Logic and Conversation: The William James Lectures, Harvard', in D. Davidson and G. Harman (eds.), *The Logic of Grammar*. Encino, Calif.: Dickenson, 64–75.

—— (1989). *Studies in the Way of Words*. Cambridge, Mass.: Harvard University Press.

Grimshaw, J. (1987). 'Psych Verbs and The Structure of Argument Structure'. MS, Brandeis University.

—— (1990). *Argument Structure*. Cambridge, Mass.: MIT Press.

—— (1997). 'Projections, Heads and Optimality', *Linguistic Inquiry* 28: 373–422.

—— and Mester, A. (1988). 'Light Verbs and Theta-Marking', *Linguistic Inquiry* 19: 205–32.

Grinder, J. (1970). 'Super Equi-NP Deletion', in *Proceedings of the 6th Meeting of the Chicago Linguistic Society*, 297–317.

Gruber, J. (1965). 'Studies in Lexical Relation'. Doctoral dissertation, MIT.

Guéron, J., and May, R. (1984). 'Extraposition and Logical Form', *Linguistic Inquiry* 5: 1–31.

Haegeman, L. (ed.) (1992a). *Theory and Description in Generative Syntax: A Case Study in West Flemish*. Cambridge: Cambridge University Press.

—— (1992b). *Introduction to the Theory of Government and Binding*. Oxford: Blackwell.

Haider, H. (2000). 'Scrambling: What's the State of the Art?', in S. M. Powers and C. Hamann (eds.), *The Acquisition of Scrambling and Cliticization*. Dordrecht: Kluwer, 19–40.

Haik, I. (1987). 'Bound VPs That Need to Be', *Linguistics and Philosophy* 10: 535–65.

Hale, K., and Keyser, S. J. (1991). *On the Syntax of Argument Structure*. Cambridge, Mass.: MIT Center for Cognitive Science.

—— —— (1993). 'On Argument Structure and and the Lexical Expression of Syntactic Relations', in K. Hale and S. J. Keyser (eds.), *The View from Building 20: Essays in Linguistics in Honor of Sylvain Bromberger*. Cambridge, Mass.: MIT Press.

—— —— (1999). 'A Response to Fodor and Lepore, "Impossible Words?" ', *Linguistic Inquiry* 30: 453–66.

—— —— (2002). *Prolegomena to a Theory of Argument Structure*. Cambridge, Mass.: MIT Press.

Hall, B. (1965). 'Subject and Object in Modern English'. Doctoral dissertation, MIT. Published by Garland, 1979.

Hankamer, J. (1974). 'On the Non-Cyclic Nature of WH-Clefting', *CLS* 10: 221–33.

—— (1979). *Deletion in Coordinate Structures*. New York: Garland.

—— (1989). 'Morphological Parsing and the Lexicon', in W. Marslen-Wilson (ed.), *Lexical Representation and Process*. Cambridge, Mass.: MIT Press, 392–408.

—— and Sag, I. A. (1976). 'Deep and Surface Anaphora', *Linguistic Inquiry* 7: 391–426.

Hardt, D. (1992). 'VP Ellipsis and Contextual Interpretation', in *Proceedings of the International Conference on Computational Linguistics (COLING-92)*, Nantes, 303–9.

—— (1999). 'VPE as a Proform: Some Consequences for Binding', in F. Corblin, J.-M. Marandin, and C. Dobrovie-Sorin (eds.), *Empirical Issues in Formal Syntax and Semantics: Selected Papers from the 2nd Paris Colloquium on Syntax and Semantics (CSSP 1997)*. Berne: Lang.

Harman, G. H. (1963). 'Generative Grammars Without Transformational Rules: A Defense of Phrase Structure', *Language* 39: 597–616.

Harris, R. (1993). *The Linguistic Wars*. Oxford: Oxford University Press.

Harris, Z. (1951). *Methods in Structural Linguistics*. Chicago: University of Chicago Press.

Hartmann, K. (2000). *Right Node Raising and Gapping: Interface Conditions on Prosodic Deletion*. Philadelphia: Benjamins.

Hauser, M. (2000). *Wild Minds: What Animals Really Think*. New York: Holt.

—— Chomsky, N., and Fitch, T. (2002). 'The Faculty of Language: What Is It, Who Has It, and How Did It Evolve?', *Science* 298: 1569–79.

Hawkins, J. A. (1994). *A Performance Theory of Order and Constituency*. Cambridge: Cambridge University Press.

—— (2004). *Complexity and Efficiency in Grammars*. Oxford: Oxford University Press.

Heim, I. (1982). 'The Semantics of Definite and Indefinite Noun Phrases'. Doctoral dissertation, University of Massachusetts, Amherst.

—— Lasnik, H., and May, R. (1991). 'Reciprocity and Plurality', *Linguistic Inquiry* 22: 63–101.

Hellan, L. (1988). *Anaphora in Norwegian and the Theory Of Grammar*. Dordrecht: Foris.

Hendriks, P., and de Hoop, H. (2001). 'Optimality Theoretic Semantics', *Linguistics and Philosophy* 24(1): 1–32.

Hestvik, A. (1995). 'Reflexives and Ellipsis', *Natural Language Semantics* 3: 211–37.

Higginbotham, J. (1985). 'On Semantics', *Linguistic Inquiry* 16: 547–94.

Higgins, R. (1973). 'The Pseudocleft Construction in English'. Doctoral dissertation, MIT.

Hornstein, N. (1999). 'Movement and Control', *Linguistic Inquiry* 30: 69–96.

—— (2001). *Move!* Oxford: Blackwell.

—— and Weinberg, A. (1981). 'On Preposition Stranding', *Linguistic Inquiry* 11: 55–91.

Horvath, J. (1997). 'The Status of "Wh-Expletives" and the Partial Wh-Movement Construction of Hungarian', *Natural Language and Linguistic Theory* 15: 509–72.

Huang, C.-T. J. (1982a). 'Move *Wh* in a Language Without *Wh*-Movement', *Linguistic Review* 1: 369–416.

—— (1982b). 'Logical Relations in Chinese and the Theory of Grammar'. Doctoral dissertation, MIT.

Huck, G. J., and Goldsmith, J. A. (1995). *Ideology and Linguistic Theory: Noam Chomsky and the Deep Structure Debates*. London: Routledge.

Huddleston, R. A., and Pullum, G. K. (2002). *The Cambridge Grammar of the English Language*. Cambridge: Cambridge University Press.

Hudson, R. (1984). *Word Grammar*. Oxford: Blackwell.

Hukari, T., and Levine, R. D. (1991). 'On the Disunity of Unbounded Dependency Constructions', *Natural Language and Linguistic Theory* 9: 97–144.

Hust, J., and Brame, M. (1976). 'Jackendoff on Interpretive Semantics (Review of Jackendoff 1972)', *Linguistic Analysis* 2: 243–77.

Jackendoff, R. (1969a). 'An Interpretive Theory of Negation', *Foundations of Language* 4: 218–41.

—— (1969b). *Speculations on Presentences and Determiners*. Bloomington: IULC.

Jackendoff, R. (1969c). 'Some Rules of Semantic Interpretation for English'. Doctoral dissertation, MIT.

—— (1971). 'Gapping and Related Rules', *Linguistic Inquiry* 2: 21–35.

—— (1972). *Semantic Interpretation in Generative Grammar*. Cambridge, Mass.: MIT Press.

—— (1973). 'The Base Rules for Prepositional Phrases', in S. R. Anderson and P. Kiparsky (eds.), *Festschrift for Morris Halle*. New York: Holt, Rinehart & Winston, 345–76.

—— (1974). 'A Deep Structure Projection Rule', *Linguistic Inquiry* 5: 481–506.

—— (1975). 'Morphological and Semantic Regularities in the Lexicon', *Language* 51: 639–71.

—— (1976). 'Towards an Explanatory Semantic Representation', *Linguistic Inquiry* 7: 89–150.

—— (1977). *X-Bar Syntax: A Study of Phrase Structure*. Cambridge, Mass.: MIT Press.

—— (1983). *Semantics and Cognition*. Cambridge, Mass.: MIT Press.

—— (1985). 'Believing and Intending: Two Sides of the Same Coin', *Linguistic Inquiry* 16: 445–60.

—— (1987). *Consciousness and the Computational Mind*. Cambridge, Mass.: MIT Press.

—— (1990a). *Semantic Structures*. Cambridge, Mass.: MIT Press.

—— (1990b). 'On Larson's Treatment of the Double Object Construction', *Linguistic Inquiry* 21: 427–56.

—— (1991a). 'Mme. Tussaud Meets the Binding Theory', *Natural Language and Linguistic Theory* 10: 1–31.

—— (1991b). 'Parts and Boundaries', *Cognition* 41: 9–45.

—— (1995). 'The Conceptual Structure of Intending and Volitional Action', in H. Campos and P. Kempchinsky (eds.), *Evolution and Revolution in Linguistic Theory: Studies in Honor of Carlos P. Otero*. Washington, DC: Georgetown University Press, 198–227.

—— (1996). 'The Proper Treatment of Measuring Out, Telicity, and Perhaps Even Quantification in English', *Natural Language and Linguistic Theory* 14: 305–54.

—— (1997a). *The Architecture of the Language Faculty*. Cambridge, Mass.: MIT Press.

—— (1997b). 'Twistin' the Night Away', *Language* 73: 534–59.

—— (1999). 'The Natural Logic of Rights and Obligations', in R. Jackendoff, P. Bloom, and K. Wynn (eds.), *Language, Logic, and Concepts: Essays in Memory of John Macnamara*. Cambridge, Mass.: MIT Press, 67–95.

—— (2002a). *Foundations of Language*. Oxford: Oxford University Press.

—— (2002b). 'English Particle Constructions, the Lexicon, and the Autonomy of Syntax', in N. Dehé, R. Jackendoff, A. McIntyre, and S. Urban (eds.), *Verb-Particle Explorations*. Berlin: Mouton de Gruyter, 67–94.

Jackendoff, R. (to appear, a). *Language, Culture, Consciousness: Essays on Mental Structure*. Cambridge, Mass.: MIT Press.

—— (to appear, b). 'Construction After Construction: #9 in a Series', Brandeis University.

—— and Culicover, P. W. (2003). 'The Semantic Basis of Control', *Language* 79: 517–56.

—— Maling, J., and Zaenen, A. (1993). '*Home* is Subject to Principle A', *Linguistic Inquiry* 24: 173–7.

Jacobson, P. (1992). 'Antecedent Contained Deletion in a Variable-Free Semantics', in *Proceedings of the 2nd Conference on Semantics and Linguistic Theory*, Columbus, OH.

—— (1994). 'Binding Connectivity in Copular Sentences', in *Proceedings of the 4th Conference on Semantics and Linguistic Theory*. Ithaca, NY: Cornell Working Papers in Linguistics.

Jaeggli, O., and Safir, K. (eds.) (1989). *The Null Subject Parameter*. Dordrecht: Kluwer.

Jespersen, O. (1949). *A Modern English Grammar on Historical Principles*, Part vii: *Syntax*. London: Allen & Unwin.

Johnson, D. E., and Lappin, S. (1999). *Local Constraints vs. Economy*. Stanford, Calif.: CSLI.

—— and Postal, P. M. (1980). *Arc Pair Grammar*. Princeton, NJ: Princeton University Press.

Johnson, K. (2000). 'Gapping Determiners', in K. Schwabe and N. Zhang (eds.), *Ellipsis in Conjunction*. Tübingen: Niemeyer, 95–115.

Joseph, B. D. (1976). 'Raising in Modern Greek: A Copying Process?', *Harvard Studies in Syntax and Semantics* 2: 241–78.

—— (1991). 'Diachronic Perspectives on Control', in R. K. Larson, S. Iatridou, U. Lahiri, and J. Higginbotham (eds.), *Control and Grammar*. Dordrecht: Kluwer, 195–234.

Joshi, A. K. (1987). 'An Introduction to Tree-Adjoining Grammars', in A. Manaster-Ramer (ed.), *Mathematics of Language*. Amsterdam: Benjamins, 87–114.

Jun, J. (2003). 'Syntactic and Semantic Bases of Case Assignment: A Study of Verbal Nouns, Light Verbs, and Dative'. Doctoral dissertation, Brandeis University.

Kadmon, N. (2001). *Formal Pragmatics: Semantics, Pragmatics, Presupposition and Focus*. Oxford: Blackwell.

Kamp, H., and Reyle, U. (1993). *From Discourse to Logic*. Dordrecht: Kluwer.

Karimi, S. (ed.) (2003). *Word Order and Scrambling*. Oxford: Blackwell.

Karttunen, L. (1969). 'Pronouns and Variables', in *CLS 5*. Chicago: CLS, 108–16.

Kathol, A. (2000). *Linear Syntax*. Oxford: Oxford University Press.

Katz, J. J. (1981). *Language and Other Abstract Objects*. Totowa, NJ: Rowman & Littlefield.

—— and Fodor, J. (1963). 'The Structure of a Semantic Theory', *Language* 39: 170–210.

—— and Postal, P. M. (1964). *Toward an Integrated Theory of Linguistic Descriptions*. Cambridge, Mass.: MIT Press.

Kay, P., and Fillmore, C. J. (1999). 'Grammatical Constructions and Linguistic Generalizations: The "What's X Doing Y?" Construction', *Language* 75: 1–33.

Kayne R. S. (1975). *French Syntax*. Cambridge, Mass.: MIT Press.

—— (1981). 'ECP Extensions', *Linguistic Inquiry* 22: 93–133.

—— (1983). 'Connectedness', *Linguistic Inquiry* 24: 223–49.

—— (1984a). *Connectedness and Binary Branching*. Dordrecht: Foris.

—— (1984b). 'Principles of Particle Constructions', in J. Guéron, H.-G. Obenauer, and J.-Y. Pollock (eds.), *Grammatical Representation*. Dordrecht: Foris, 101–40.

—— (1994). *The Antisymmetry of Syntax*. Cambridge, Mass.: MIT Press.

Keenan, E. (1988). 'Complex Anaphors and Bind Alpha', in *CLS 24*. Chicago: CLS.

—— and Comrie, B. (1977). 'Noun Phrase Accessibility and Universal Grammar', *Linguistic Inquiry* 8: 63–99.

Kehler, A. (1993). 'A Discourse Copying Algorithm for Ellipsis and Anaphora Resolution', in *Proceedings of the 6th Conference of the European Chapter of the Association for Computational Linguistics (EACL-93)*, Utrecht, 203–12.

—— (2000). 'Coherence and the Resolution of Ellipsis', *Linguistics and Philosophy* 23: 533–75.

Kennedy, C. (2003). 'Ellipsis and Syntactic Representaiton', in K. Schwabe and S. Winker (eds.), *The Interfaces: Deriving and Interpreting Omitted Structures*. Amsterdam: Benjamins, 29–53.

Kim, J.-S. (1997). 'Syntactic Focus Movement and Ellipsis: A Minimalist Approach'. Doctoral dissertation, University of Connecticut.

Kiparsky, P. (1997). 'Remarks on Denominal Verbs', in A. Alsina, J. Bresnan, and P. Sells (eds.), *Complex Predicates*. Stanford, Calif.: CSLI, 473–99.

Kitagawa, Y. (1991). 'Copying Identity', *Natural Language and Linguistic Theory* 9: 497–536.

Klein, E., and Sag, I. A. (1985). 'Type-Driven Translation', *Linguistics and Philosophy* 8: 163–202.

Klein, W., and Perdue, C. (1997). 'The Basic Variety. Or: Couldn't Natural Language Be Much Simpler?', *Second Language Research* 13(4): 301–47.

Kluender, R. (1992). 'Deriving Island Constraints from Principles of Predication', in H. Goodluck and M. Rochemont (eds.), *Island Contraints: Theory, Acquisition and Processing*. Dordrecht: Kluwer, 223–58.

—— (1998). 'On the Distinction Between Strong and Weak Islands: A Processing Perspective', in P. W. Culicover and L. McNally (eds.), *The Limits of Syntax*. New York: Academic Press, 241–79.

—— and Kutas, M. (1993). 'Bridging the Gap: Evidence from ERPs on the Processing of Unbounded Dependencies', *Journal of Cognitive Neuroscience* 5: 196–214.

Koenig, J.-P., Mauner, G., and Bienvenue, B. (2003). 'Arguments for Adjuncts',
     Cognition 89: 67–103.

Koopman, H. (2000). *The Syntax of Specifiers and Heads*. London: Routledge.

Köpcke, K.-M., and Panther, K.-U. (2002). 'Zur Identifikation Leerer Subjekte in
     Infinitivischen Komplementsätzen: ein Semantisch-Pragmatisches Modell' (On
     the identification of empty subjects in infinitival complement sentences: a se-
     mantic-pragmatic model) *Folia Linguistica* 36(3–4): 191–218.

Koster, J. (1978). *Locality Principles in Syntax*. Dordrecht: Foris.

—— (2000). 'Variable-Free Grammar'. Unpublished paper, University of Gron-
     ingen. http://odur.let.rug.nl/~koster/papers/v-free.pdf

—— and Reuland, E. (eds.) (1991). *Long Distance Anaphora*. Cambridge: Cam-
     bridge University Press.

Kraak, A. (1967). 'Presuppositions and the Analysis of Adverbs'. MS, MIT Dept. of
     Linguistics.

Kroch, A. (1989). 'Amount Quantification, Referentiality, and Long *Wh*-
     Movement'. MS University of Pennsylvania Dept. of Linguistics.

Kuno, S. (1976). 'Gapping: A Functional Analysis', *Linguistic Inquiry* 7: 300–18.

—— (1987). *Functional Syntax: Anaphora, Discourse and Empathy*. Chicago:
     University of Chicago Press.

—— and Takami, K.-I. (1993). *Grammar and Discourse Principles: Functional
     Syntax and GB Theory*. Chicago: University of Chicago Press.

Ladusaw, W., and Dowty, D. (1988). 'Toward a Nongrammatical Account of
     Thematic Roles', in W. Wilkins (ed.), *Thematic Relations*. San Diego, Calif.:
     Academic Press, 62–74.

Lakoff, G. (1965/1970). *Irregularity in Syntax*. New York: Holt, Rinehart &
     Winston.

—— (1968). 'On Instrumental Adverbs and the Concept of Deep Structure', *Foun-
     dations of Language* 4: 4–29.

—— (1970). 'Global Rules', *Language* 46: 627–39.

—— (1971). 'On Generative Semantics', in D. Steinberg and L. Jakobovits (eds.),
     Semantics. Cambridge: Cambridge University Press, 232–96.

—— (1986). 'Frame Semantic Control of the Coordinate Structure Constraint', in
     A. Farley, P. Farley, and K.-E. McCullogh (eds.), *Papers from the Parasession on
     Pragmatics and Grammatical Theory, 22nd Regional Meeting, Chicago Linguis-
     tic Society*.

—— and Ross, J. R. (1967/73). 'Is Deep Structure Necessary?', Bloomington:
     IULC.

Lakoff, R. (1968). *Abstract Syntax and Latin Complementation*. Cambridge,
     Mass.: MIT Press.

Landau, I. (2000). *Elements of Control*. Dordrecht: Kluwer.

—— (2003). 'Movement Out of Control', *Linguistic Inquiry* 34: 471–98.

Langacker, R. (1969). 'On Pronominalization and the Chain of Command', in D. Reibel and S. Schane (eds.), *Modern Studies in English*. Englewood Cliffs, NJ: Prentice-Hall, 160–86.

—— (1987). *Foundations of Cognitive Grammar: Theoretical Prerequisites*. Stanford, Calif.: Stanford University Press.

—— (1991). *Foundations of Cognitive Grammar. Practical Applications*, vol. ii. Stanford, Calif.: Stanford University Press.

Langendoen, D. T., and Postal, P. M. (1984). *The Vastness of Natural Languages*. Oxford: Blackwell.

Lappin, S. (1993). 'The Syntactic Basis of Ellipsis Resolution', in S. Berman and A. Hestvik (eds.), *Proceedings of the Stuttgart Workshop on Ellipsis*. Working papers of the Sonderforschungsbereich 340, Report No. 29-1992, SFB 340, University of Tübingen.

—— (1996). 'The Interpretation of Ellipsis', in S. Lappin (ed.), *Handbook of Contemporary Semantic Theory*. Oxford: Blackwell, 145–75.

—— and Benmamoun, E. (1999). *Fragments: Studies in Ellipses and Gapping*. Oxford: Oxford University Press.

—— Levine, R. D., and Johnson, D. (2000). 'The Structure of Unscientific Revolutions', *Natural Language and Linguistic Theory* 18: 665–71.

Larson, R. (1987). ' "Missing Prepositions" and the Analysis of English Free Relative Clauses', *Linguistic Inquiry* 18: 239–66.

—— (1988). 'On the Double Object Construction', *Linguistic Inquiry* 19: 335–91.

—— (1990). 'Double Objects Revisited: Reply to Jackendoff', *Linguistic Inquiry* 21: 589–632.

—— (1991). '*Promise* and the Theory of Control', *Linguistic Inquiry* 22: 103–39.

—— Iatridou, S., Lahiri, U., and Higginbotham, J. (1992). *Control and Grammar*. Boston: Kluwer.

Lasnik, H. (1976). 'Remarks on Coreference', *Linguistic Analysis* 2: 1–22.

—— (1999a). 'Pseudogapping Puzzles', in S. Lappin and E. Benmamoun (eds.), *Fragments: Studies in Ellipses and Gapping*. Oxford: Oxford University Press, 141–74.

—— (1999b). 'Verbal Morphology', in *Minimalist Analysis*. Oxford: Blackwell, 97–119.

—— (2000). *Syntactic Structures Revisited*. Cambridge, Mass.: MIT Press.

—— (2001). 'A Note on the EPP', *Linguistic Inquiry* 32: 356–62.

—— (2002). 'The Minimalist Program in Syntax', *Trends in Cognitive Science* 6: 432–7.

—— (2003). *Minimalist Investigations in Linguistic Theory*. London: Routledge.

—— and Fiengo, R. (1974). 'Complement Object Deletion', *Linguistic Inquiry* 5: 535–71.

—— and Saito, M. (1991). 'On the Subject of Infinitives', in L. Dobrin, L. Nichols, and R. Rodriguez (eds.), *Papers from the 27th Regional Meeting of the Chicago Linguistic Society*. Repr. in H. Lasnik, *Minimalist Analysis*. Oxford: Blackwell.

Lasnik, H., and Saito, M. (1992). *Move Alpha.* Cambridge, Mass.: MIT Press.

Lawler, J. (1972). *A Problem in Participatory Democracy.* Bloomington: IULC.

Lebeaux, D. (1990). 'The Grammatical Nature of the Acquisition Sequence: Adjoin-a and the Formation of Relative Clauses', in L. Frazier and J. De Villiers (eds.), *Language Processing and Language Acquisition.* Dordrecht: Kluwer, 13–82.

Lees, R. B., and Klima, E. S. (1963). 'Rules for English Pronominalization', *Language* 39: 17–28.

Levelt, W. (1989). *Speaking.* Cambridge, Mass.: MIT Press.

—— (1999). 'Producing Spoken Language: A Blueprint of the Speaker', in C. Brown and P. Hagoort (eds.), *The Neurocognition of Language.* Oxford: Oxford University Press, 83–122.

Levin, B. (1989). 'The Basque Verbal Inventory and Configurationality', in L. Maracz and P. Muysken (eds.), *Configurationality: The Typology of Asymmetries.* Dordrecht: Foris, 39–62.

—— (1993). *English Verb Classes and Alternations.* Cambridge, Mass.: MIT Press.

—— and Rappaport Hovav, M. (1995). *Unaccusativity: At the Syntax–Lexical Semantics Interface.* Cambridge, Mass.: MIT Press.

—— —— (1999). 'Two Structures for Compositionally Derived Events', in *SALT* 9: 199–233.

Levin, L. (1982). 'Sluicing: A Lexical Interpretation Procedure', in J. W. Bresnan (ed.), *The Mental Representation of Grammatical Relations.* Cambridge, Mass.: MIT Press.

Levine, R., and Sag, I. A. (2003a). 'Some Empirical Issues in the Grammar of Extraction', in S. Mueller (ed.), *Proceedings of the HPSG03 Conference.* Stanford, Calif.: CSLI, 236–56.

—— —— (2003b). 'WH-Nonmovement', *Gengo Kenkyu,* 123: 171–220.

Liberman, M., and Prince, A. (1977). 'On Stress and Linguistic Rhythm', *Linguistic Inquiry* 8: 249–336.

Lidz, J., Waxman, S., and Freedman, J. (2003). 'What Infants Know About Syntax But Couldn't Have Learned: Experimental Evidence for Syntactic Structure at 18 Months', *Cognition* 89: B65–73.

Lin, V. (1999). 'Determiner Sharing', *MIT Working Papers in Linguistics* 33: 241–77.

Lobeck, A. (1995). *Ellipsis.* Oxford: Oxford University Press.

Mahajan, A. (1990). 'The A/A′ Distinction and Movement Theory'. Doctoral dissertation, MIT.

Manzini, M. R. (1983a). 'Restructuring and Reanalysis'. Doctoral dissertation, MIT.

—— (1983b). 'On Control and Control Theory', *Linguistic Inquiry* 14: 421–46.

Marantz, A. (1984). *On the Nature of Grammatical Relations.* Cambridge, Mass.: MIT Press.

Marantz, A. (1997). 'No Escape from Syntax: Don't Try Morphological Analysis in the Privacy of Your Own Lexicon', in A. Dimitriadis, L. Siegel, et al. (eds.), *University of Pennsylvania Working Papers in Linguistics, Vol. 4.2: Proceedings of the 21st Annual Penn Linguistics Colloquium*, 201–25.

May, R. (1977). 'The Grammar of Quantification'. Doctoral dissertation, MIT.

—— (1985). *Logical Form*. Cambridge, Mass.: MIT Press.

McCawley, J. D. (1968a). 'Concerning the Base Component of a Transformational Grammar', *Foundations of Language* 4: 243–69.

—— (1968b). 'Lexical Insertion in a Grammar Without Deep Structure', *CLS* 5: 71–80.

—— (1970). 'English as a VSO Language', *Language* 46: 286–99.

—— (1971). 'Where Do Noun Phrases Come from?', in D. Steinberg and L. Jakobovits (eds.), *Semantics*. Cambridge: Cambridge University Press, 217–31.

—— (1975). Review of Noam Chomsky, *Studies on Semantics in Generative Grammar*, *Studies in English Linguistics* 5: 209–311.

—— (1981). 'The Syntax and Semantics of English Relative Clauses', *Lingua* 53: 99–149.

—— (1988a). *The Syntactic Phenomena of English*. Chicago: University of Chicago Press.

—— (1988b). 'The Comparative Conditional Construction in English, German, and Chinese', in *Proceedings of the 14th Annual Meeting of the Berkeley Linguistics Society*. Berkeley, Calif.: BLS, 176–87.

—— (1988c). 'Comments on Noam A. Chomsky, *Language and Problems of Knowledge*', in *University of Chicago Working Papers in Linguistics*, 4.

—— (1993). 'Gapping with Shared Operators', in *Proceedings of the 10th Annual Meeting of the Berkeley Linguistics Society*. Berkeley, Calif.: BLS, 245–53.

McCloskey, J. (1984). 'Raising, Subcategorization and Selection in Modern Irish', *Natural Language and Linguistic Theory* 1: 441–85.

McDaniel, D. (1989). 'Partial and Multiple Wh-Movement', *Natural Language and Linguistic Theory* 13: 709–53.

Merchant, J. (2001). *The Syntax of Silence*. Oxford: Oxford University Press.

—— (2003). 'Subject–Auxiliary Inversion in Comparatives and PF Output Constraints', in K. Schwabe and S. Winker (eds.), *The Interfaces: Deriving and Interpreting Omitted Structures*. Amsterdam: Benjamins, 55–77.

—— (2004). 'Fragments and Ellipsis'. *Linguistics and Philosophy* 27: 661–738.

—— (to appear). 'Variable Island Repair Under Ellipsis', in K. Johnson (ed.), *Topics in Ellipsis*. Cambridge: Cambridge University Press.

Michaelis, L. A. (1994). 'A Case of Constructional Polysemy in Latin', *Studies in Language* 18: 45–70.

—— and Lambrecht, K. (1996). 'The Exclamative Sentence Type', in A. Goldberg (ed.), *Conceptual Structure, Discourse and Language*. Stanford, Calif.: CSLI, 375–89.

Miller, G. A., and Chomsky, N. (1963). 'Finitary Models of Language Users', in R. Luce, R. Bush, and E. Galanter (eds.), *Handbook of Mathematical Psychology*, vol. ii. New York: Wiley, 419–91.

Miyagawa, S. (1989). *Structure and Case Marking in Japanese*. New York: Academic Press.

Miyamoto, E., and Takahashi, S. (2001). 'The Processing of Wh-Phrases and Interrogative Complementizers in Japanese', in N. Akatsuka and S. Strauss (eds.), *Japanese/Korean Linguistics* 10. Stanford, Calif.: CSLI, 62–75.

Mohanan, K. P. (1983). 'Functional and Anaphoric Control', *Linguistic Inquiry* 14: 641–74.

Moltmann, F. (1992). 'Reciprocals and *Same/Different*: Towards a Semantic Analysis', *Linguistics and Philosophy* 15: 411–62.

Montague, R. (1974). *Formal Philosophy*. New Haven, Conn.: Yale University Press.

Müller, G. (1997). 'Partial Wh-Movement and Optimality Theory', *Linguistic Review* 14: 249–305.

Napoli, D. J. (1983). 'Missing Complement Sentences in English: A Base Analysis of Null Complement Anaphora', *Linguistic Analysis* 12: 1–28.

—— (1985). 'Verb Phrase Deletion in English: A Base-Generated Analysis', *Journal of Linguistics* 21: 281–319.

—— and Hoeksema, J. (1993). 'Paratactic and Subordinative *So*', *Journal of Linguistics* 29: 291–314.

Neale, S. (1990). *Descriptions*. Cambridge, Mass.: MIT Press.

Newmeyer, F. (1980). *Linguistic Theory in America*. New York: Academic Press.

—— (1986). *The Politics of Linguistics*. Chicago: University of Chicago Press.

—— (1998). *Language Form and Language Function*. Cambridge, Mass.: MIT Press.

—— (2001). 'Grammatical Functions, Thematic Roles, and Phrase Structure: Their Underlying Disunity', in W. D. Davies and S. Dubinsky (eds.), *Objects and Other Subjects*. Dordrecht: Kluwer Academic, 53–76.

—— (2003). Review article: Chomsky, *On Nature and Language*; Anderson and Lightfoot, *The Language Organ*; Bichakjian, *Language in a Darwinian Perspective*, *Language* 79(3): 583–99.

Nicol, J., Fodor, J. D., and Swinney, D. (1994). 'Using Cross-Modal Lexical Decision Tasks to Investigate Sentence Processing', *Journal of Experimental Psychology: Learning, Memory, and Cognition* 20: 1220–38.

Nikanne, U. (1990). *Zones and Tiers: A Study of Thematic Structure*. Helsinki: Suomalaisen Kirjallisuuden Seura.

Nishigauchi, T. (1984). 'Control and the Thematic Domain', *Language* 60: 215–50.

—— (1990). *Quantification in the Theory of Grammar*. Dordrecht: Kluwer.

Nunberg, G. (1979). 'The Nonuniqueness of Semantic Solutions: Polysemy', *Linguistics and Philosophy* 3: 143–84.

—— (2004). 'Deferred Interpretation', in L. R. Horn and G. Ward (eds.), *The Handbook of Pragmatics*. Malden, Mass.: Blackwell, 344–64.

—— Sag, I. A., and Wasow, T. (1994). 'Idioms', *Language* 70: 491–538.

Oehrle, R. T. (1987). 'Boolean Properties in the Analysis of Gapping', in G. J. Huck and A. E. Ojeda (eds.), *Syntax and Semantics: Discontinuous Constitutency*. San Diego, Calif.: Academic Press, 203–40.

O'Neil, J. (1997). 'Means of Control: Deriving the Properties of PRO in the Minimalist Program'. Doctoral dissertation, Harvard University.

Ostler, N. (1979). 'Case Linking: A Theory of Case and Verb Diathesis Applied to Classical Sanskrit'. Doctoral dissertation, MIT.

Panther, K.-U., and Köpcke, K.-M. (1993). 'A Cognitive Approach to Obligatory Control Phenomena in English and German', *Folia Linguistica* 27 (1–2): 57–105.

Partee, B. (1975). 'Montague Grammar and Transformational Grammar', *Linguistic Inquiry* 6: 203–300.

—— (1989). 'Binding Implicit Variables in Quantified Contexts', *CLS* 25: 342–65.

Perlmutter, D. (1968). 'Deep and Surface Constraints in Syntax'. Doctoral dissertation, MIT.

—— (1970). 'The Two Verbs *Begin*', in R. Jacobs and P. Rosenbaum (eds.), *Readings in English Transformational Grammar*. Waltham, Mass.: Ginn, 107–19.

—— (1971). *Deep and Surface Structure Constraints in Syntax*. New York: Holt, Rinehart & Winston.

—— and Postal, P. M. (1983a). 'Toward a Universal Characterization of Passivization', in D. M. Perlmutter (ed.), *Studies in Relational Grammar*. Chicago: University of Chicago Press, 1–29.

—— —— (1983b). 'Some Proposed Laws of Basic Clause Structure', in D. Perlmutter (ed.), *Studies in Relational Grammar*. Chicago: University of Chicago Press, 81–128.

—— and Ross, J. R. (1970). 'Relative Clauses with Split Antecedents', *Linguistic Inquiry*, 1: 350.

Pesetsky, D. (1982). 'Complementizer-Trace Phenomena and the Nominative Island Condition', *Linguistic Review* 1: 297–343.

—— (1987). 'Wh-in-Situ: Movement and Unselective Binding', in E. J. Reuland and A. G. ter Meulen (eds.), *The Representation of (In)definiteness*. Cambridge, Mass.: MIT Press, 98–129.

—— (1995). *Zero Syntax*. Cambridge, Mass.: MIT Press.

Petkevic, V. (1987). 'A New Dependency Based Specification of Underlying Representations of Sentences', *Theoretical Linguistics* 14: 143–72.

Phillips, C. (2003). 'Linear Order and Constituency', *Linguistic Inquiry* 34: 37–90.

Pickering, M., and Barry, G. (1991). 'Sentence Processing Without Empty Categories', *Language and Cognitive Processes* 6: 229–59.

Pinker, S. (1989). *Learnability and Cognition*. Cambridge, Mass.: MIT Press.

Pinker, S. and Jackendoff, R. (2005). 'The Faculty of Language: What's Special About It?', *Cognition* 95: 201–36.

Pollard, C., and Sag, I. A. (1987). *Information-Based Syntax and Semantics*, vol. i: *Fundamentals*. Stanford, Calif.: CSLI.

—— —— (1992). 'Anaphors in English and the Scope of Binding Theory', *Linguistic Inquiry* 23: 261–304.

—— —— (1994). *Head-Driven Phrase Structure Grammar*. Chicago: University of Chicago Press.

Pollock, J.-Y. (1989). 'Verb Movement, Universal Grammar and the Structure of IP', *Linguistic Inquiry* 20: 365–424.

Pope, E. (1971). 'Answers to Yes–No Questions', *Linguistic Inquiry* 2: 69–82.

Postal, P. M. (1962). 'Some Syntactic Rules of Mohawk'. Doctoral dissertation, Yale University. Published as *Some Syntactic Rules in Mohawk* (New York: Garland, 1979).

—— (1964). 'Limitations of Phrase Structure Description', in J. Katz and J. Fodor (eds.), *Readings in the Philosophy of Language*. Englewood Cliffs, NJ: Prentice-Hall, 137–51.

—— (1969). 'Anaphoric Islands', in R.I. Binnick, A. Davison, G. Green, and J. L. Morgan (eds.), *Papers from the 5th Regional Meeting of the Chicago Linguistic Society*, 205–35.

—— (1970). 'On Coreferential Complement Subject Deletion', *Linguistic Inquiry* 1: 439–500.

—— (1971). *Crossover Phenomena*. New York: Holt, Rinehart & Winston.

—— (1972a). 'The Best Theory', in R. S. Peters (ed.), *Goals of Linguistic Theory*. Englewood Cliffs, NJ: Prentice-Hall, 131–79.

—— (1972b). ' "Pronominal Epithets" and Similar Items', *Foundations of Language* 9: 246–8.

—— (1974). *On Raising*. Cambridge, Mass.: MIT Press.

—— (1993). 'Remarks on Weak Crossover Effects', *Linguistic Inquiry* 24: 539–56.

—— (1997a). 'Islands', in M. Baltin and C. Collins (eds.), *The Handbook of Syntactic Theory*. Oxford: Blackwell.

—— (1997b). 'Strong Crossover Violations and Binding Principles', paper presented at the Eastern States Conference on Linguistics, Yale University.

—— (1997c) 'Extraction'. MS, New York University.

—— (1998). *Three Investigations of Extraction*. Cambridge, Mass.: MIT Press.

—— (2004). *Sceptical Linguistic Essays*. Oxford: Oxford University Press.

—— and Pullum, G. K. (1988). 'Expletive Noun Phrases in Subcategorized Positions', *Linguistic Inquiry* 19: 635–70.

Prince, E. (1998). 'On the Limits of Syntax, with Reference to Left-Dislocation and Topicalization', in P. W. Culicover and L. McNally (eds.), *The Limits of Syntax*. New York: Academic Press, 281–302.

Pullum, G. K. (1996). 'Nostalgic Views from Building 20': review of K. Hale and S. J. Keyser (eds.), *The View from Building 20, Journal of Linguistics* 32: 137–47.

Pallum, G. K. (1997). 'The Morpholexical Nature of *To*-Contraction', *Language* 73: 79–102.

—— and Scholz, B. (2002). 'Empirical Assessment of Stimulus Poverty Arguments', *The Linguistic Review* 19: 8–50.

Pustejovsky, J. (1995). *The Generative Lexicon*. Cambridge, Mass.: MIT Press.

Reinhart, T. (1983). *Anaphora and Semantic Interpretation*. Chicago: University of Chicago Press.

—— and Reuland, E. (1991). 'Anaphors and Logophors: An Argument Structure Perspective', in J. Koster and E. Reuland (eds.), *Long Distance Anaphora*. Cambridge: Cambridge University Press, 283–321.

—— —— (1993). 'Reflexivity', *Linguistic Inquiry* 24: 657–720.

Reuland, E., and Koster, J. (1991). 'Long Distance Anaphora: An Overview', in J. Koster and E. Reuland (eds.), *Long Distance Anaphora*. Cambridge: Cambridge University Press, 1–25.

Riehemann, S. Z., and Bender, E. (1999). 'Absolute Constructions: On the Distribution of Predicative Idioms', in S. Bird, A. Carnie, J. D. Haugen, and P. Norquest (eds.), *WCCFL 18*. Somerville, Mass.: Cascadilla Press, 476–89.

Rizzi, L. (1990). *Relativized Minimality*. Cambridge, Mass.: MIT Press.

—— (1996). 'Residual Verb Second and the Wh-Criterion', in A. Belletti and L. Rizzi (eds.), *Parameters and Functional Heads*. Oxford: Oxford University Press, 63–90.

Roberts, C. (1998). 'Focus, the Flow of Information, and Universal Grammar', in P. W. Culicover and L. McNally (eds.), *The Limits of Syntax*. Academic Press, 109–60.

Rochemont, M. S., and Culicover, P. W. (1990). *English Focus Constructions and The Theory of Grammar*. Cambridge: Cambridge University Press.

—— —— (1997). 'Deriving Dependent Right Adjuncts in English', in D. Beermann, D. LeBlanc, and H. van Riemsdijk (eds.), *Rightward Movement*. Amsterdam: Benjamins, 279–300.

Rosen, S. T. (1989). 'Two Types of Noun Incorporation: A Lexical Analysis', *Language* 65: 294–317.

Rosenbaum, P. (1967). *The Grammar of English Predicate Complement Constructions*. Cambridge, Mass.: MIT Press.

Ross, J. R. (1967). 'Constraints on Variables in Syntax'. Doctoral dissertation, MIT.

—— (1969a). 'Guess Who', in R. I. Binnick, A. Davison, G. M. Green, and J. L. Morgan (eds.), *Proceedings of the 5th Annual Meeting of CLS*, 252–86.

—— (1969b). 'Auxiliaries as Main Verbs', in W. Todd (ed.), *Philosophical Linguistics*. Carbondale, Ill.: Great Expectations Press.

—— (1970). 'On Declarative Sentences', in R. A. Jacobs and P. S. Rosenbaum (eds.), *Readings in English Transformational Grammar*. Waltham, Mass.: Ginn, 222–72.

Rudin, C. (1988). 'On Multiple Questions and Multiple *Wh* Fronting', *Natural Language and Linguistic Theory* 6: 445–501.

Ruwet, N. (1991). 'Raising and Control Revisited', in J. Goldsmith (ed.), *Syntax and Human Experience*. Chicago: University of Chicago Press, 56–81.

Růžička, R. (1983). 'Remarks on Control', *Linguistic Inquiry* 14: 309–24.

—— (1999). *Control in Grammar and Pragmatics*. Amsterdam: Benjamins.

Sadock, J. M. (1991). *Autolexical Syntax: A Theory of Parallel Grammatical Representations*. Chicago: University of Chicago Press.

—— (1999). 'An Optimality-Theoretic Account of Certain Word Order Facts in English'. MS, University of Chicago.

—— (2003). 'Mismatches in Autonomous Modular versus Derivational Grammars', in E. J. Francis and L. A. Michaelis (eds.), *Mismatch: Form–Function Incongruity and the Architecture of Grammar*. Stanford, Calif.: CSLI, 333–55.

Safir, K. (1991). 'Implied Non-Coreference and the Pattern of Anaphora', *Linguistics and Philosophy* 15: 1–52.

Sag, I. A. (1976). 'Deletion and Logical Form'. Doctoral dissertation, MIT.

—— (1997). 'English Relative Clause Constructions', *Journal of Linguistics* 33(2): 431–84.

—— (1998). 'Without a Trace'. MS, Stanford University.

—— and Fodor, J. D. (1994). 'Extraction Without Traces', in R. Aranovich, W. Byrne, S. Preuss, and M. Senturia (eds.), *Proceedings of the 13th Annual Meeting of the West Coast Conference on Formal Linguistics*. Stanford, Calif.: CSLI, 365–84.

—— Gazdar, G., Wasow, T., and Weisler, S. (1985). 'Coordination and How to Distinguish Categories', *Natural Language and Linguistic Theory* 3: 117–71.

—— and Pollard, C. (1991). 'An Integrated Theory of Complement Control', *Language* 67: 63–113.

Samek-Lodovici, V. (2003). 'The Internal Structure of Arguments and Its Role in Complex Predicate Formation', *Natural Language and Linguistic Theory* 21: 835–81.

—— (to appear). 'Prosody–Syntax Interaction in the Expression of Focus', *Natural Language and Linguistic Theory*.

Šaumjan, S. K., and Soboleva, P. (1963). *Applikativnaja Porozdajuščaja Model' i Isčiselnie Transformacij v Russkom Jazyke*. Moscow: Izdatel'stvo Akademii Nauk.

Saxon, L. (1984). 'Disjoint Anaphora and the Binding Theory', in M. Cobler, S. MacKaye, and M. Westcoat (eds.), *Proceedings of the 3rd West Coast Conference on Formal Linguistics*. Stanford, Calif.: Stanford University, Dept of Linguistics, Stanford Linguistics Association, 242–62.

Schachter, P. (1976). 'A Nontransformational Account of Gerundive Nominals in English', *Linguistic Inquiry* 7: 205–41.

Schmerling, S. (1975). 'Asymmetric Conjunction and Rules of Conversation', in P. Cole and J. L. Morgan (eds.), *Speech Acts*. New York: Academic Press, 211–31.

Searle, J. (1983). *Intentionality*. Cambridge: Cambridge University Press.

—— (1995). *The Construction of Social Reality*. New York: Free Press.

Sells, P. (1987). 'Aspects of Logophoricity', *Linguistic Inquiry* 18: 445–79.

Seuren, P. (2004). *Chomsky's Minimalism*. New York: Oxford University Press.

Sgall, P. (1992). 'Underlying Structure of Sentences and its Relations to Semantics', *Wiener Slawistischer Almanach* 30: 349–68.

Shibatani, M. (1976). 'The Grammar of Causative Constructions: A Conspectus', in M. Shibatani (ed.), *The Grammar of Causative Constructions*. New York: Academic Press, 1–40.

Shopen, T. (1971). 'Caught in the Act', in *Papers from the 7th Regional Meeting of the Chicago Linguistics Society*, 254–63.

—— (1972). 'A Generative Theory of Ellipsis'. Doctoral dissertation, UCLA.

Simpson, J. (1983). 'Resultatives', in L. Levin, M. Rappaport, and A. Zaenen (eds.), *Papers in Lexical-Functional Grammar*. Bloomington: IULC, 143–57.

Skarabela, B., Maling, J., and O'Connor, C. (2004). 'The Monolexemic Possessor Construction: Pragmatic Constraints Inside the NP', *LSA Annual Meeting*, Boston.

Spencer, A. (1995). 'Incorporation in Chukchi', *Language* 71: 439–89.

Sperber, D., and Wilson, D. (1995). *Relevance*, 2nd edn. Oxford: Blackwell.

Sportiche, D. (1996). 'Clitic Constructions', in J. Rooryck and L. Zaring (eds.), *Phrase Structure and the Lexicon*. Dordrecht: Kluwer, 213–76.

Stainton, R. J. (1994). 'Using Non-Sentences: An Application of Relevance Theory', *Pragmatics and Cognition* 2: 269–84.

—— (1998). 'Quantifier Phrases, Meaningfulness "in Isolation," and Ellipsis', *Linguistics and Philosophy* 21: 311–40.

Steedman, M. (1996). *Surface Structure and Interpretation*. Cambridge, Mass.: MIT Press.

—— (2000). *The Syntactic Process*. Cambridge, Mass.: MIT Press.

Stillings, J. (1975). 'The Formulation of Gapping in English as Evidence for Variable Types in Syntactic Transformations', *Linguistic Analysis* 1: 247–74.

Stowell, T. (1981). 'Origins of Phrase Structure'. Doctoral dissertation, MIT.

—— (1983). 'Subjects Across Categories', *Linguistic Review* 2: 285–312.

Sweet, H. (1913). *Collected Papers*. Oxford: Clarendon Press.

Swinney, D., and Fodor, J. D. (eds.) (1989). *Journal of Psycholinguistic Research* (special issue on sentence processing).

—— Zurif, E., Prather, P., and Love, T. (1996). 'The Neurological Distribution of Processing Resources Underlying Language Comprehension', *Journal of Cognitive Neuroscience* 8: 174–84.

Tada, H. (1990). 'Scramblings', paper presented at Workshop on Japanese Syntax and Universal Grammar, Ohio State University, Columbus.

Takagi, H. (2001). 'On So-Called "Obligatory Control": A Cognitive Account', *English Linguistics* 18: 57–85.

Talmy, L. (1980) 'Lexicalization Patterns: Semantic Structures in Lexical Forms', in T. Shopen et al. (eds.), *Language Typology and Syntactic Description*, vol. iii.

New York: Cambridge University Press. Revised version in L. Talmy, *Toward a Cognitive Semantics*, vol. ii. Cambridge, Mass.: MIT Press, 21–146 (2000).

Talmy. L.(1985). 'Force-Dynamics in Language and Thought', CLS 21.

—— (1988). 'Force Dynamics in Language and Cognition', *Cognitive Science* 12: 49–100. Revised version in L. Talmy, *Toward a Cognitive Semantics*, vol. i. Cambridge, Mass.: MIT Press, 409–70 (2000).

Tancredi, C. (1992). 'Deletion, De-Accenting, and Presupposition'. Doctoral dissertation, MIT.

Tesar, B. (1995). 'Computational Optimality Theory'. Doctoral dissertation, University of Colorado, Boulder.

Toivonen, I. (2002). 'The Directed Motion Construction in Swedish', *Journal of Linguistics* 38: 313–45.

—— (2003). *Non-Projecting Words: A Case Study of Swedish Particles*. Dordrecht: Kluwer.

Tomasello, M. (1995). 'Language is Not an Instinct': review of S. Pinker, *The Language Instinct, Cognitive Development* 10: 131–56.

—— (2003). *Constructing a Language*. Cambridge, Mass.: Harvard University Press.

Van Hoek, K. (1992). 'Paths Through Conceptual Structure: Constraints on Pronominal Anaphora'. Doctoral dissertation, La Jolla: UC San Diego.

—— (1995). 'Conceptual Reference Points: A Cognitive Grammar Account of Pronominal Anaphora Constraints', *Language* 71: 310–40.

Van Valin, R. D., Jr. (1990). 'Functionalism, Anaphora, and Syntax': review article on Kuno (1987), *Studies in Language* 14: 169–219.

—— (1992). 'Incorporation in Universal Grammar: A Case Study in Theoretical Reductionism': review article on Baker (1988), *Journal of Linguistics* 28: 199–220.

—— (1998). 'The Acquisition of Wh-Questions and the Mechanisms of Language Acquisition', in M. Tomasello (ed.), *The New Psychology of Language: Cognitive and Functional Approaches to Language Structure*. Hillsdale, NJ: Erlbaum, 221–49.

—— and LaPolla, R. J. (1997). *Syntax: Structure, Meaning and Function*. Cambridge: Cambridge University Press.

Wanner, E., and Maratsos, M. (1978). 'An ATN Approach to Comprehension', in M. Halle, J. Bresnan, and G. Miller (eds.), *Linguistic Theory and Psychological Reality*. Cambridge, Mass.: MIT Press, 119–61.

Ward, G. (2004). 'Equatives and Deferred Reference', *Language* 80: 262–89.

Wasow, T. (1972). 'Anaphoric Relations in English'. Doctoral dissertation, MIT.

—— (1977). 'Transformations and the Lexicon', in P. W. Culicover, T. Wasow, and A. Akmajian (eds.), *Formal Syntax*. New York: Academic Press, 327–60.

—— (1997). 'Remarks on Grammatical Weight', *Language Variation and Change* 9: 81–105.

—— (2002). *Postverbal Behavior*. Stanford, Calif.: CSLI.

Watanabe, A. (1992). 'Subjacency and S-Structure Movement of Wh-in-Situ', *Journal of East Asian Linguistics* 1: 255–91.

Webelhuth, G. (1989). 'Syntactic Saturation Phenomena and the Modern Germanic Languages'. Doctoral dissertation, University of Massachusetts, Amherst.

Wells, R. (1947). 'Immediate Constituents', *Language* 23: 81–117. Repr. in M. Joos (ed.), *Readings in Linguistics*, vol. i. Chicago: University of Chicago Press, 186–207.

Wertheimer, M. (1923). 'Untersuchungen Zur Lehre von der Gestalt II' (Laws of organization in perceptual forms), *Psychologische Forschung* 4: 301–50. Translation published in W. Ellis (ed.), *A Source Book of Gestalt Psychology*. London: Routledge & Kegan Paul (1938), 71–88.

Wexler, K., and Culicover, P. W. (1980). *Formal Principles of Language Acquisition*. Cambridge, Mass.: MIT Press.

—— and Hamburger, H. (1973). 'On the Insufficiency of Surface Data for the Learning of Transformations', in J. Hintikka, J. M. Moravcsik, and P. Suppes (eds.), *Approaches to Natural Language*. Dordrecht: Reidel, 167–79.

Wiese, H. (2000). 'Towards an Integrated Model of Semantic and Conceptual Representations'. MS, Humboldt University.

—— and Maling, J. (2004). 'Beer, Schnaps, and Kaffi: Different Grammatical Options for "Restaurant Talk" Coercions in Three Germanic Languages'. MS, Humboldt University and Brandeis University.

Wilder, C. (1995). 'Rightward Movement as Leftward Deletion', in U. Lutz and J. Pafel (eds.), *On Extraction and Extraposition in German*. Amsterdam: Benjamins, 273–310.

Williams, E. (1975). 'Small Clauses in English', in J. Kimball (ed.), *Syntax and Semantics 4*. New York: Academic Press, 249–73.

—— (1977). 'Discourse and Logical Form', *Linguistic Inquiry* 8: 101–40.

—— (1980). 'Predication', *Linguistic Inquiry* 1: 203–38.

—— (1985). 'PRO and the Subject of NP', *Natural Language and Linguistic Theory* 3: 297–315.

—— (1992). 'Adjunct Control', in R. K. Larson, S. Iatridou, U. Lahiri, and J. Higginbotham (eds.), *Control and Grammar*. Boston: Kluwer, 297–322.

—— (1994a). 'Remarks on Lexical Knowledge', in L. Gleitman and B. Landau (eds.), *The Acquisition of the Lexicon*. Cambridge, Mass.: MIT Press, 7–34.

—— (1994b). *Thematic Structure in Syntax*. Cambridge, Mass.: MIT Press.

Winkler, S., and Schwabe, K. (2003). 'Exploring the Interfaces from the Perspective of Omitted Structures', in K. Schwabe and S. Winker (eds.), *The Interfaces: Deriving and Interpreting Omitted Structures*. Amsterdam: Benjamins, 1–26.

Wurmbrand, S. (2001). *Infinitives: Restructuring and Clause Structure*. Berlin: Mouton de Gruyter.

Zaenen, A., Maling, J., and Thráinsson, H. (1990). 'Case and Grammatical Functions: The Icelandic Passive', in J. Maling and A. Zaenen (eds.), *Modern Icelandic Syntax*. New York: Academic Press, 95–136.

Zurif, E., Swinney, D., Prather, P., Solomon, J., and Bushell, C. (1993). 'An On-Line Analysis of Syntactic Processing in Broca's and Wernicke's Aphasia', *Brain and Language* 45: 448–64.

Zwart, C. J.-W. (1994). 'Het Ontstaan van I′ en C″ (The origin of I′ and C′), *Gramma/TTT* 3: 55–70.

—— (1997). *Morphosyntax of Verb Movement: A Minimalist Approach to the Syntax of Dutch*. Dordrecht: Kluwer.

—— (1999). ' "Referentie" en de Typologie van NPs: De Status van PRO' ('Reference' and the typology of NPs: the status of PRO), *TABU* 29: 49–66.

Zwicky, A. (1994). 'Dealing Out Meaning: Fundamentals of Syntactic Constructions', *BLS* 20: 611–25.

Index